Contributors

THOMAS A. BISHOP, JD, Private Practice, New London, Connecticut

EMILY M. BROWN, ACSW, Divorce and Marital Stress Clinic, Inc., Arlington, Virginia

WILLIAM A. DONOHUE, PhD, Department of Communication, Michigan State University, East Lansing, Michigan

HENRY M. ELSON, MA, JD, Private Practice, Berkeley, California

STEPHEN K. ERICKSON, JD, Erickson Mediation Institute, Edina, Minnesota

JAY FOLBERG, JD, Northwestern School of Law, Lewis and Clark College, Portland, Oregon

LYNN GIGY, PhD, Northern California Mediation Services, Corte Madera, California

LINDA K. GIRDNER, PhD, Congressional Fellow, American Anthropological Association, Washington, DC

LOIS GOLD, ACSW, Private Practice, Portland, Oregon

SARAH CHILDS GREBE, MEd, Family Center for Mediation and Counseling, Kensington, Maryland

SHERYL HAUSMAN, PhD, Northern California Mediation Services, Corte Madera, California

JOHN HAYNES, PhD, Haynes Mediation Associates, New York, New York

FLORENCE W. KASLOW, PhD, Florida Couples and Family Institute, West Palm Beach, Florida

JOAN B. KELLY, PhD, Northern California Mediation Services, Corte Madera, California

SALLY DIXON MARUZO, ACSW, Family Division, Superior Court, Hartford, Connecticut

ANN MILNE, ACSW, Private Practice, Madison, Wisconsin

CHRISTOPHER W. MOORE, PhD, CDR Associates, Denver, Colorado

JESSICA PEARSON, PhD, Center for Policy Research, Denver, Colorado

ANTHONY J. SALIUS, MS, Director, Family Division, Superior Court, Hartford, Connecticut

MARY TALL SHATTUCK, PhD, Marin County Probation Department, San Rafael, California

LINDA SILBERMAN, JD, New York University School of Law, New York, New York

KARL A. SLAIKEU, PhD, The Center for Conflict Management, Inc., Austin, Texas

ALISON TAYLOR, MA, Clackamas County Family Court; Private Practice, Hillsboro, Oregon

NANCY THOENNES, PhD, Center for Policy Research, Denver, Colorado

DEBORAH WEIDER-HATFIELD, PhD, Department of Speech Communication, University of Georgia, Athens, Georgia

Preface

One legacy of fault divorce is a tradition of adversarial proceedings. Adversarial divorce casts spouses as opponents rather than as joint decision makers. As opponents in a legal proceeding, spouses are discouraged from face-to-face negotiation and instead turn to separate lawyers to represent them in sorting out the tangible aspects of their marriage. Similarly, they often turn as well to separate mental health professionals to help them sort out the emotional aspects of their marriage. The result is frequently unsatisfactory for families and professionals because divorce is both a legal proceeding and an emotional process, a matter of the heart and the law. Feelings become facts that must be accommodated in the divorce process in order to achieve a satisfactory dissolution. The divorcing family must live with the actual result, which may never be known to the professionals involved in structuring it.

Divorce mediation recognizes the intertwined emotional and legal dimensions of divorce and the importance of spouses themselves making informed decisions about the terms of their divorce. Mediation occurs at the intersection of several professional practices and can be fully understood and realistically assessed only from an interdisciplinary perspective. This book grew out of the need to bring together under one cover a systematic examination of both the theory and practice of divorce mediation by experienced mediators and researchers of different professional training and backgrounds.

The result is a book that we believe is unlike any other. It draws upon a generation of diverse experience with divorce mediation. Psychologists, lawyers, social workers, anthropologists, sociologists, communication experts, and others working in the emerging field of mediation have contributed chapters that together provide a comprehensive picture of what is known about divorce mediation. The reader will learn what divorce mediation is, how it is practiced, and the issues confronting the field.

The 23 chapters in this volume are organized into six parts that flow from a macro overview to more micro applications. Part One places divorce mediation in perspective. Following our introductory chapter, we look at the nature of divorce disputes and then, in Chapter 3, provide an around-the-world anthropological perspective on how people settle disputes. Part Two presents a step-by-step walk through the mediation process, followed by an overlay of the psychological dimensions and the legal dimensions of divorce mediation. Part Three examines the practice of divorce mediation in different professional settings and in various modes. Chapter 7 describes successful mediation in a private mental health clinic. Chapter 8 shows how mediation can be offered within a law firm. The most frequent setting for divorce mediation is the courthouse or its annex; Chapter 9 looks at a statewide, court-connected mediation program, and Chapter 10 presents an insider's view of California's mandatory custody and visitation mediation. Consistent with our interdisciplinary theme, Chapter 11 presents the pros and cons of lawyer and therapist team mediation. This section concludes with the history and current variations of structured mediation as first developed by O. J. Coogler.

Progressing from the general to the specific, Part Four focuses on techniques and strategies. Breaking impasse, the heart of success in mediation, is the first topic of this section. Methods for balancing power are next presented and illustrated. Details about effective communication strategies gleaned from actual divorce mediation transcripts are offered in Chapter 15. Part Five examines legal and ethical issues in divorce mediation, beginning with nagging problems of confidentiality and privilege. Liability concerns are addressed in Chapter 17. Ethical constraints are explicated in Chapters 18 and 19, first from a legal perspective and next from a mental health perspective. The existing standards of practice for divorce mediators and how they came to be are then explained.

The concluding section of this book, Part Six, sets out significant research findings. Important questions about the utility of divorce mediation and its results compared to adversarial proceedings are answered here. Finally, a revealing study is presented of divorce mediation behaviors and how they relate to settlement.

No book can, by itself, transform the reader into a mediator. This book is intended to provide the foundation on which personal training and experience can be stacked to build a mastery of mediation theory and practice. Those with some mediation experience will find here refinements and insights from the collective reflections of seasoned mediators and researchers who provide thoughtful analysis about their work. It is our hope that practitioners and students alike will benefit from the diverse views and ideas brought together in this book.

Acknowledgments

The contributing authors have graciously shared their experience and wisdom to make this book possible. We acknowledge their generosity and their tolerance for the many delays encountered. The book might never have seen the light of day without the word processing skills and patience of Lenair Mulford, as well as the assistance and staff of Lewis and Clark Law School. Our spouses, Diana and Bill, have endured a project in which we invested more of our time and energy than anticipated. We dedicate this book to our marriages.

Contents

DIVORCE MEDIATION

PART ONE

DIVORCE MEDIATION IN PERSPECTIVE

1

The Theory and Practice of Divorce Mediation: An Overview

ANN MILNE
Private Practice, Madison, Wisconsin

JAY FOLBERG
Northwestern School of Law, Lewis and Clark College

The increased acceptance of divorce and its changing pattern has resulted in no-fault divorce and other legal reforms. The professional assistance provided to help divorcing families make decisions is also changing into more collaborative interventions directed toward future needs and relationships rather than past wrongs. Divorce mediation has evolved from the juncture of law, counseling, and social work. In this chapter the editors of the book provide an overview of the emerging theory and practice of divorce mediation. They offer a comprehensive perspective of what mediation is, its conceptual framework, how it is practiced, and critical issues facing the field.

Divorce is now essentially a matter of private choice. With the acceptance of no-fault divorce has come the recognition that the state regulates divorce less and promotes private ordering more (Mnookin, 1985). When a marriage dissolves, legal proceedings become entwined with emotional dynamics, making decisions about divorce a matter of the heart and the law. It is often difficult to determine the "real" issues in divorce disputes (Goldberg, Green, & Sander, 1985, p. 313). Feelings become facts that must be accommodated in the divorce process in order to reach a workable result. Divorce mediation facilitates private ordering and recognizes both the emotional and legal dimensions of marital dissolution (Folberg, 1985b).

Divorce mediation is an alternative to traditional judicial intervention and third-party decision making. A divorce mediator serves as a neutral who assists divorcing couples to develop their own parental, financial, and property agreements and promotes decision making within the family. This chapter introduces the theory and practice of divorce mediation and discusses some of the critical developmental issues facing the field.

THE ORIGINS

Mediation, as a cooperative dispute-resolution process, has a long history in a variety of cultures and social contexts (see Chapter 3). A palaver hut sits in the

3

center of town in Liberian native villages and serves as a gathering place for the discussion and resolution of a variety of interpersonal disputes. Mediation was the principal means of dispute resolution in ancient China and continues to be practiced today through the People's Conciliation Committees, which place considerable importance on self-determination in the mediation of all types of disputes. Observers of Japanese institutions note the relative absence of lawyers in that society. Conciliation services have been used in Japan since prior to World War II to assist individuals in resolving personal disputes (Schimazu, 1982).

Over the centuries, religious institutions have played a prominent part in resolving conflicts. The New Testament chronicles the tradition of mediation when Paul encouraged the Corinthians to appoint people from their own community to resolve disputes, rather than take disputes to court (1 Corinthians 6:1–4). Today, local religious leaders are frequently called upon to serve as mediators, particularly in family disputes.

Various ethnic institutions have evolved to provide for the resolution of disputes and to avoid the imposition of an outside authority. Chinese immigrants to the United States established the Chinese Benevolent Association and use mediation to resolve disputes between members of the community and within the family (Doo, 1973). The United States Jewish community established the Jewish Conciliation Board as its own mediation forum in 1920 (Yaffe, 1972). More recently, the Christian Conciliation Service has established offices to train and provide church mediators for the resolution of personal disputes (Buzzard, 1982). Early Quakers in the United States practiced both mediation and arbitration to resolve marital disagreements (Auerbach, 1983). Each of these groups has provided a means of conflict resolution that maintains a tradition of cultural values, retaining cherished independence and ethnic traditions without turning to outside authorities.

The resolution of family disputes in contemporary United States society has evolved from a geographically centralized, extended family unit, where a patriarchal family leader offered wisdom and precedence, to a nuclear family whose internal structure provides less of a resource for conflict resolution, because of family mobility and urbanization. As a result, family conflicts have increasingly been directed to external sources for resolution (Teitelbaum, 1985).

As the incidence of divorce has grown, society appears to be more accepting of divorce as a common life event. The increase and acceptance of divorce has led to sweeping changes in the substantive law of divorce, the most significant being the adoption of no-fault provisions for divorce. All states now provide some form of no-fault divorce. No-fault divorce shifts from the court to the parties the responsibility for determining whether or not a divorce is warranted. The decision to end a marriage now belongs to the parties rather than to judicial discretion. Other substantive legal changes include legislative provisions for shared parenting and joint custody. Alimony based on fault and entitlement has begun to give way to financial provisions based upon need and ability to pay. Rigid rules of property division are being replaced in many states by considerations of equity and fairness based upon the unique circumstances of the parties.

Despite these substantive legal reforms, we are just now beginning to see changes in the procedural aspects of divorce. Until recently, legal procedures continued to embody traditional adversarial norms. Divorce actions commenced by a lawsuit naming a plaintiff and a defendant and settlement negotiations conducted under the threat of trial reinforced the competitive underpinnings of "winner takes all." In the early 1970s a handful of attorneys took to heart the emerging no-fault divorce philosophy and began offering "non-adversarial legal services" (see Chapter 8). These attorneys risked bar-association sanctions by meeting with both spouses to help settle financial, property, and child-custody issues. The idea of a friendly attorney set the stage for other members of the legal profession to promote the principles of mediation in divorce-related matters.

Mental health services in the area of divorce have also offered new options since the 1970s. Historically, divorce has been viewed by mental health professionals as being outside the domain of psychotherapy. The psychodynamic model, with its focus on an individual's unconscious conflicts and intrapsychic pathology, did not allow couples in conflict to be treated together in a clinical setting. The traditional schools of therapy (psychoanalytic, Adlerian, Jungian, Ericksonian, etc.) do not direct themselves to the psychological and emotional issues of the divorcing family; instead they see divorce as a legal process that begins at the point of separation (Milne, 1986).

Within the past decade, we have begun to see therapists who identify themselves as divorce counselors and specialize in services directed toward the mental health concerns of the divorcing family. Therapeutic interventions now combine an insight approach with the action-oriented focus of the behaviorists. Divorcing spouses attempt to resolve conflicts to effect a satisfactory postdivorce adjustment. Out of this has emerged a body of theory directed toward the emotional–psychological process of divorce (Bohannon, 1970; E. Brown, 1976; Federico, 1979; Kessler, 1975; Weiss, 1975; Wiseman, 1975). This divorce theory has moved the social scientists from a one-dimensional view of divorce as a legal process to a more integrated view of divorce as a multidimensional process involving both legal and psychological matters (Kaslow, 1979–1980). The advent of divorce mediation has furthered these principles. Mental health professionals view mediation as a means of helping the divorcing family with the psychological dissolution of the marriage and to a contractual definition of independent and shared responsibilities (see Chapter 5).

California established court-connected conciliation services in 1939. The initial focus of these services was to provide marriage counseling aimed at reconciliation. Conciliation court personnel were probably the first to offer mediation services, as the focus of conciliation shifted from reconciliation to divorce counseling and custody mediation (D. Brown, 1982). These court-connected mediation services have grown in number, encouraged by judicial support and enabling legislation (see Chapters 9 and 10).

In 1974, O. J. Coogler, an attorney and marriage and family counselor, established the Family Mediation Center in Atlanta, Georgia. Spurred by his own emotionally and financially costly divorce, Coogler helped popularize the idea of divorce mediation, through the publication of his book *Structured Mediation in Divorce Settlement* (1978). Coogler proposed a framework for third-party mediators to assist a couple in contractually resolving issues of finances, property division, support, and child custody, using communication and intervention techniques borrowed from labor mediation and the social sciences. Coogler later established the Family Mediation Association, an organization of individuals interested in the development and advancement of divorce mediation (see Chapter 12).

Other focused organizations, such as the Academy of Family Mediators, have emerged to promote the concept of divorce mediation and provide a network for practitioners. Preexisting national organizations, like the Association of Family and Conciliation Courts, the American Arbitration Association, the Society of Professionals in Dispute Resolution, and the American Bar Association, developed special programs and formed committees to consider appropriate standards of practice for those offering divorce mediation services (see Chapter 20).

THE THEORY

The divorce mediation field has attracted individuals from a variety of disciplines, particularly law and mental health. Because divorce mediation borrows from several disciplines, attempts to define it succinctly and differentiate it from other services have met with limited success. How divorce mediation is defined is largely dependent on what is being mediated, who is doing the mediating, and where the mediation is offered (Folberg, 1982).

Mediators from a clinical background tend to define mediation by emphasizing the resolution of emotional issues. "While the social work mediator helps settle the economic division, he/she also helps the couple place the marriage behind them, deal with the emotional issues that caused the divorce, and look forward to the future" (Haynes, 1978, p. 7). Mediators from a legal background tend to define mediation as a contractual and nontherapeutic process

> in which a lawyer helps family members resolve their disputes in an informative and consensual manner . . . based on sufficient factual data; and that each . . . participant understands the information on which decisions are reached. (American Bar Association, 1984, p. 363)

The setting of mediation may also affect its definition. When mediation is provided within the context of a mental health setting, it tends to be defined in a more clinical fashion. As Brown says in Chapter 7 of this volume, first, it conveys the message that mediation is therapeutic. It also says that the emotions and problems associated with divorce are solvable. More important, it implies an approach that considers the needs and feelings of family members and that respects and protects family relationships.

The difference between divorce therapy and divorce mediation can be elusive. Divorce therapy has been described as a new profession or a subspecialty within the existing profession of marriage and family therapy (D. Brown, 1982; E. Brown, 1976; Framo, 1978; Hunt, 1977). As the literature on divorce mediation grows, we see a distinction emerge between divorce therapy and divorce mediation.

Divorce therapy may be differentiated from divorce mediation in that the former is focused more on stress relief, individual behavior change and increased self understanding, while the latter is focused more on dealing with specific problems, resolving disputes and negotiating differences inherent in the dissolution of the marital state. While successful divorce therapy may facilitate mediation and while successful mediation may be therapeutic, these two processes should be clearly separated. (D. Brown, 1982, pp. 30–31)

Despite the difficulty of distinguishing mediation from therapy, as well as from the practice of law, there is a growing consensus that divorce mediation is evolving into a professional process separate and distinct from its parental roots (Kelly, 1983; Milne, 1984). The first step toward a workable definition of mediation as an identifiable service is agreement on its nature. Mediation is first and foremost a *process* that emphasizes the participants' responsibility for making decisions that affect their lives. It is, thus, a self-empowering process. The process minimally consists of systematically isolating points of agreement and disagreement, developing options, and considering accommodations through the use of a neutral third-party mediator whose role is described as that of a facilitator of communications, a guide toward the definition of issues, and a settlement agent who works toward the definition of issues by assisting the disputants in their own negotiations (Folberg, 1983; Milne, 1982).

Some refer to mediation as a process of "conflict management" rather than "dispute resolution" (Chapter 4). A distinction may be made between the ostensible dispute and the underlying conflict. Resolution of the dispute does not necessarily eliminate the conflict. Even if all elements of the dispute cannot be resolved, the conflict can be reduced to a manageable level. For now, let us accept both dispute resolution and conflict management as complimentary and obtainable goals of mediation.

In 1973, social psychologist Morton Deutsch presented his theories on the nature of human conflict and described the constructive use of a third party in conflict resolution (Deutsch, 1973). Two years later, Jeffrey Rubin and Bert Brown added to Deutsch's conceptual framework of conflict resolution. Their description of how mediation facilitates conflict resolution provides an operational definition of the process (Rubin & Brown, 1975). Mediation is described as a means of reducing irrationality in the parties by preventing personal recriminations by focusing and refocusing on actual issues; by exploring alternative solutions and making it possible for the parties to retreat or make concessions without losing face or respect; by increasing constructive communication between the parties; by reminding the parties of the costs of conflict and the consequences of unresolved disputes and by providing a mediator model of competence, integrity and fairness. (D. Brown, 1982, p. 14)

Negotiation should be distinguished from mediation. Negotiation is typically a sounding out and bartering process, often conducted through representatives. Negotiation is usually conducted in an adversarial and competitive manner and does not normally include a neutral resource person assisting the parties in reaching a settlement.

Mediation is not arbitration. In arbitration a designated third person has the responsibility for making a finding or providing a decision for the parties. The arbitration process is adjudicatory but typically less formal than the traditional court process. In mediation a neutral third party is used, but the parties do not authorize the mediator to make decisions for them.

Mediation is not treatment. No diagnoses are made, and the parties do not analyze past behaviors but reach agreements that provide for the future (Milne, 1982). Unlike traditional forms of therapy, mediation does not focus on obtaining insight into the history of the conflict, nor does it attempt to change personality patterns. Although insights and changes may occur, they are fringe benefits of the mediation process. The goal of mediation is not to restructure relationships or lessen anxiety and stress, as is common in therapy. Again, these may be a net result, but they are not the primary purpose of the mediation process.

Divorce mediation acknowledges that the emotions associated with divorce are an integral part of the resolution process and must be recognized. Mediation provides for an airing of emotional issues even if irrelevant to the court proceedings. Therefore these feelings can be managed in mediation so they are not merely suppressed, only to surface later in the form of postdivorce litigation.

Though different practitioners mediate differently, most mediators would agree it is a finite process that helps to (1) enhance communication, (2) maximize the exploration of alternatives, (3) address the needs of all parties, (4) reach an agreement perceived by the parties as fair, and (5) provide a model for future conflict resolution (Folberg, 1985a).

Divorce mediation can be conceptualized as a multistage process. Building rapport and gaining trust pervade the early stages. A holistic family system approach, rather than a focus on the interests of one party, is a hallmark of each stage. Though writers may divide or categorize the stages differently (compare Chapter 4 with Moore, 1986), the following stages are most frequently listed (Folberg & Taylor, 1984):

1. introduction and orientation
2. fact-finding and disclosure

3. isolation and definition of issues
4. exploration and negotiation of alternatives
5. compromise and accommodation
6. reaching tentative agreement
7. review and processing settlement
8. finalization and implementation

Regardless of the mediator's background, mediation helps educate spouses about each other's needs and provides a personalized approach to dispute resolution, both now and in the future when circumstances change or differences arise. Mediation can help the parties learn to solve problems together, isolate the issues to be decided, and recognize that cooperation can be of mutual advantage. Mediation is bound neither by rules of procedure and substantive law nor by other assumptions that dominate the adversary process. The ultimate authority in mediation belongs to the parties. With the help of the mediator, the parties may consider a comprehensive mix of their needs, interests, and whatever else they deem relevant irrespective of rules of evidence or legal precedent. Unlike the adjudicatory process, the emphasis is not on who is right and who is wrong or who wins and who loses, but on establishing a workable resolution that best meets the needs of the participants (Folberg, 1985b).

Mediation is conducted in private, so the most personal of matters may be freely discussed without concern that the discussion is part of a public record. Participants formulate their own agreement and emotionally invest in its success. They are thus more likely to support the agreement than if the terms were negotiated or ordered by others (Chapter 21).

Mediation reduces hostility by encouraging direct communication between the participants. This facilitates the permanence of a settlement agreement and reduces the likelihood of future conflict. Mediation tends to diffuse hostilities by promoting cooperation through a structured process. In contrast, litigation tends to focus hostilities and harden the disputants' anger into more rigidly polarized positions. The adversarial process, with its dependence upon attorneys who communicate on behalf of their clients, tends to deny the parties the opportunity of taking control of their own situation and increases their dependency on outside authority. Feelings of esteem and competence are important by-products of the mediation process, which also help to provide self-direction and lessen the need for participants to continue the fight between themselves.

Divorce mediation furthers the policy of minimum state intervention. The arguments for minimum state intervention in determinations of child care and custody have been widely discussed (Goldstein, Freud, & Solnit, 1979; Marlow, 1985; Mnookin, 1975). Mediation presumes that parents have the authority and responsibility to determine and do what is best for their children as well as what is best for their entire family constellation, regardless of how it might be rearranged following divorce. Psychological theory, as well as constitutional considerations, argue for parental autonomy and family privacy when there is not direct evidence that the interests of children are jeopardized in the process. Parents, whether married or divorced, should have the opportunity to meet the needs of their children and continue the maintenance of family ties without state interference. Once the state intrudes into the decision-making role, the family is less likely to function cooperatively or independently, and continued state involvement is promoted (Folberg, 1985b).

The arguments for self-determination are less controversial when applied to the appropriateness of divorcing parties privately deciding their future economic relationship. Divorcing parties should be free to contract between themselves and encouraged to do so. The state should use its increasingly precious resources to intervene in economic relationships between adults only when all efforts for private ordering or settlement fail. The legal system cannot easily supervise or enforce the fragile and complex interpersonal and economic relationships among family members that often continue after divorce (Folberg, 1984).

We are seeing divorce mediation grow up and out of the disciplines of law and social sciences into a new and separate field reflective of its roots. Mediation has been extolled as being expeditious, inexpensive, private, procedurally reasonable, and amenable to the airing of grievances. It is said to reduce the alienation of the parties and to lead to the development of agreements that are satisfying to the parties as well as fair and acceptable over time (Thoennes & Pearson, 1984). It is further stated that mediation aids the parties in resuming a workable relationship with one another and enhances the adjustment of children (Pearson, Thoennes, & Hodges, 1984). Proponents of mediation cite reduced costs for the spouses and the taxpayers, as well as reduced postdivorce litigation (Bahr, 1981; Orlando, 1982).

The mediation of divorce disputes appears to be an attractive process because it validates the rights and duties of the individuals who know best on what terms they are willing to settle. Mediation as a less formal process than adjudication or arbitration allows for the ventilation and management of emotions as part of the settlement process. Divorcing individuals can identify the particular needs of their family and arrive at creative solutions which they have participated in formulating.

Mediation will not be a replacement for counseling and therapy, and it will not replace the need for legal information and advice. It can, however, be a useful intervention technique when the situation calls for a structured, express agreement to a conflict.

Mediation, as a conflict-resolution theory, provides a process that, when integrated with a supportive legal system, helps the participants develop a plan of action and a sense of self-satisfaction about working together (Pearson & Thoennes, 1984). It is ideally suited to the resolution of complex conflicts between individuals with a continuing relationship. Mediation minimizes intrusion, emphasizes cooperation, utilizes self-determined criteria for resolution, and provides a model of interaction for the settlement of future disputes.

THE PRACTICE

An understanding of divorce mediation is most complete when viewed in context. This context includes a description of the professional background and training of mediators who are now practicing, an examination of the organizational structure of existing services, and a survey of the various mediation models and approaches used.

Divorce mediators tend to come to the field from other professional backgrounds. According to the Divorce Mediation Research Project survey (Pearson, Ring, & Milne, 1983), nearly 80% of all mediators hold a graduate degree. Social workers comprise 42% of the mediators in the private sector and 72% of the mediation staff in the public sector. Marriage and family therapists, psychologists, and psychiatrists comprise the next largest professional group, accounting for 36% of the mediators in the private sector and 18% in the public sector. Thus mental health professionals taken as a group (social workers, marriage and family therapists, psychologists, and psychiatrists) account for 78% of the mediators in the private sector and 90% of the public sector. Attorney mediators comprise 15.4% of those surveyed in the private sector and only 1% in the public sector. Other professionals drawn to the practice include accountants, clergy, educators, financial planners, and guidance counselors, although in total they account for only 6.5% of the mediators in the private sector and 9% of the mediators in the public sector.

Terms such as private sector/public sector and lawyer/nonlawyer are often used as a means of describing and distinguishing divorce mediation services. These dichotomous labels, although useful for drawing distinctions, tend to add to the territorial competitiveness between the divisions. A description of the settings of practice is a more productive way of viewing the range of organizational entities and approaches to divorce mediation. Divorce mediation services are typically organized in one of three settings—court based, private practitioner, and agency or clinic.

COURT-BASED MEDIATION

Many conciliation courts or court-connected family services now provide mediation along with reconciliation counseling, divorce counseling, and custody and visitation investigations. Some courts completely separate the administration of mediation services from the conduct of custody investigations; others utilize the same office and staff for both functions (McIsaac, 1982). Most court-connected mediation services limit themselves to the issues of custody and visitation. The mediators are, for the most part, mental health practitioners, primarily social workers and some psychologists, who are supervised by a director reporting to the chief judge of the family/domestic court (Comeaux, 1983). A few court-connected services, such as those in Maine and Connecticut, also mediate financial matters or are considering expanding mediation to include support and property issues. The mediation of financial matters in the court setting may also be conducted by a volunteer lawyer, as in

Los Angeles, or by a court-employed commissioner, referee, or master. Many of these individuals also have quasi-judicial powers.

Mediation in the court setting may be initiated through both mandatory and voluntary procedures (Comeaux, 1983). Statutorily mandated mediation, as first established in 1981 by California's Civil Code section 4607(a), has attracted considerable attention, and an increasing number of states, including Kansas and Maine, have adopted similar legislation. In Oregon and Washington, state statutes permit each county the option of mandating custody and visitation mediation. In contrast to mandated mediation, other jurisdictions, such as Florida, Michigan, and New Hampshire, strongly encourage mediation through statute or court rule but do not require it.

Court services are generally funded by local tax revenue. Increasingly, however, these services are being funded by divorce and marriage-license fees and postdivorce modification filing fees earmarked for court services (McIsaac, 1981b). In California, $5 of the marriage license and $15 of the divorce-filing and postdivorce modification fees are designated for the support of court mediation services and provide the total funding for most of these court-based programs.

Many court-connected mediation programs were initiated by family court judges who were motivated by their firsthand observation of the dysfunctional effects of the adversarial/trial process on divorcing families (Pearson et al., 1983). Some of these family court judges were further influenced by increasing workloads and the need to make critical custody and visitation decisions based on information limited by the rules of evidence and their own lack of training in the social sciences (Milne, 1983).

In some jurisdictions family court judges were able to turn to existing conciliation and probation departments and expand services to include custody and visitation mediation. Where no prior services existed, some judges explored the development of mediation programs through legislative means or worked with community agencies in developing a court-connected or court-referred mediation service.

The two most notable features of court-based mediation services are the limitation of the issues being mediated to the parent–child relationship and the department's symbiotic relationship with the court system. Isolation of child custody and visitation issues from the other divorce issues has drawn both support and criticism (Folberg, 1982; Pearson & Thoennes, 1984; Saposnek, 1983). On one hand, separating parent–child issues from financial and property issues may allow children to be treated as distinct issues and lessens the potential for using them as pawns in the negotiation of property and spousal support. On the other hand, the isolation of these issues artificially segments a divorce agreement, when property, finances, and children are indeed related and decisions in one area affect decisions made in other areas.

Critics of court mediation programs focus on the potential abuse of confidentiality and the power of the mediator to influence an agreement between the parties. Some court-based mediators will divulge information gained from the mediation process or will make settlement recommendations to the attorneys and to the judge. Implicit in this is empowering the mediator, as opposed to empowering the parties, to reach an agreement or even to reach an impasse (McIsaac, 1985).

A defense of this practice is that court-based mediators are often working with highly conflictive individuals who perhaps have little likelihood of reaching an agreement through less coercive means (Chapter 9; Duryee, 1985). An aggressive mediation approach, bordering on arbitration, may provide the reality and structure necessary to allow these parties to reach a settlement and preclude further destructive and costly litigation. Court-connected mediation is generally the last opportunity for resolution without a contested court hearing. The service is provided in the shadow of the adversarial process, and tight time limits are imposed by congested court calendars. Public resources, usually provided free to the spouses, are limited. Allowing the mediator to make a custody recommendation conserves resources, eliminates duplication, and saves time. Many couples prefer the mediator to recommend an outcome and request that this be done if impasse is reached (Chapter 10). The context in which these court-connected mediation services are offered makes the service distinct from private services and renders comparisons difficult and not very useful.

THE PRIVATE PRACTITIONER

The private practitioner offers a second type of organizational structure. These private practitioners operate on a fee-for-service basis, establish policy and procedures independent of any supervising body, and rely on referrals from others or on direct client contact. Services provided by these individuals vary according to the issues mediated, mediation model used, and professional orientation of the mediator.

Most common is the mental health mediator working as a sole proprietor and offering divorce mediation in addition to counseling services (see Chapter 7; Pearson et al., 1983). Mental health mediators often use a therapeutic mediation model. This includes a discussion of the marriage and the reasons for the divorce, and an exploration of the potential for reconciliation. Typically the couple are seen together during mediation, although it is not uncommon for parties to be seen individually in the therapeutic model. Mediators who limit their practice to custody and visitation issues tend most often to be therapists and to use this model. Upon resolution of the issues, the mental health mediator typically drafts a summary of the agreed-upon issues for the parties to take to their attorneys as they continue the formal legal process.

A closer look shows that most mental health mediators decided to offer divorce mediation services because of their background in family therapy and their conviction that mediation is a healthy alternative to the adversarial system. A further attraction to mediation for some is the promise of a new and open field and the anticipation of financial gain. A number of these individuals have themselves been divorced and became interested in the need for professional mediation services through their personal divorce experience.

Lawyers who provide divorce mediation services are fewer than mental health mediators. Attorney–mediators view the family as the client and perceive the goal of mediation to be the maximization of the interests of all family members, much as in the dissolution of a business partnership (see Chapters 6 and 8).

Lawyer–mediators appear to fall into two groups. Those in the larger group have been practicing traditional domestic relations law and have become disenchanted with the adversarial process for divorcing clients. A few of these individuals have given up the practice of traditional law and now practice what Elson terms "nonadversarial law" (Chapter 8). Most, however, still maintain their law practice and offer mediation to select couples who seek such services and who appear to be appropriate candidates for mediation. As the market-place for mediation develops, a number of these lawyers intend to continue to shift their law practice more toward mediation. Some in this group are relatively new to law practice and are dedicated to pursuing alternatives to traditional practice because of what they consider to be excesses in the adversarial system. This subgroup tends to see mediation as a way to achieve needed reform in the values of our legal system and the behavioral norms of attorneys (Riskin, 1982).

A second type of lawyer providing mediation services includes those individuals who hold degrees in both the legal and mental health fields. These cross-trained individuals draw upon their legal expertise to assist couples with the legal and financial issues and use their counseling skills to assist with the communication process and surface underlying psychological issues. Most of these lawyers chose to obtain a law degree after practicing as a social worker or therapist.

Many attorney–mediators and those from other than nonclinical backgrounds were originally trained in dispute resolution to use a structured mediation approach. The "structured mediation model" was first developed by O. J. Coogler (Coogler, 1978; see Chapter 12). Over the years this approach has been modified and has many variations. The conceptual focus of Coogler's model is on the legal or topical issues emphasizing finances and property. Practitioners of this model concentrate on providing a description of the mediation process, obtaining the parties' commitment to the process, defining the issues, contracting to resolve these issues, and drafting an agreement. No extensive social and family history is taken, and the events leading to the decision to divorce are discussed only as they relate to the couple's readiness to mediate. When it is apparent that the couple's ability to negotiate these topical issues is hampered by unresolved emotional issues, a referral for counseling is usually deemed appropriate. Upon the completion of the process, the mediator provides the couple with a written agreement or memorandum of understanding that is either reviewed by an advisory attorney or taken by the parties to separate legal counsel for review and processing. Some aspects of Coogler's structured mediation have been grafted on to other models and approaches, resulting in many variations with unifying similarities.

Included in the private practitioner structure are co-mediation arrangements consisting of a lawyer and a therapist who mediate as a team (see Chapter 11). Most of these practitioners continue their respective legal and counseling practices and work together on a part-time basis. Typically the lawyer and therapist together meet with the couple to mediate all the issues in the divorce settlement. Often the emphasis is on separating the emotional issues from the topical issues. The interdisciplinary model bridges the philosophical approaches of the therapeutic and structured mediation models without becoming a duplicate of either. Each team member uses interventions reflective of his or her training background. The lawyer–mediator attends to the legal issues and concerns, and the therapist mediator identifies the emotional and psychological obstacles to settlement and assists the couple to communicate in a cooperative, as opposed to a competitive, fashion (Milne, 1982). At the conclusion of mediation, the lawyer team member drafts the agreement or summary memorandum, which the parties then take to independent legal counsel for review and processing.

AGENCIES AND CLINICS

A third type of divorce mediation practice is provided in an agency or clinic setting. This tends to take the form of a community mental health agency or clinic that offers a range of services and employs a number of individuals and professionals. Within the clinic or agency are individuals who espouse the principles of divorce mediation, probably having participated in mediation training, and who offer mediation as a part of their practice. Agencies may specifically market divorce mediation as one of a number of available services including individual and family counseling, financial planning, and other family services.

Many of these agency employees see themselves as child advocates and as a result are motivated to provide custody and visitation mediation because of their commitment to children and their belief that mediation is a valuable service for divorcing families. Directors of such clinics view the agency as meeting a community need and may see mediation as a possible client- and fee-generating service or as a new basis of fund-raising.

Some community dispute-resolution centers, such as those originally encouraged by the United States Department of Justice or promoted by law enforcement agencies, also provide limited divorce mediation services. These neighborhood dispute-resolution centers were established to provide mediation services as a part of their mandate to offer an alternative to the court for a broad range of disputes, including criminal misdemeanor offenses and landlord–tenant, business–consumer, neighborhood, and family conflicts (Shonholtz, 1984). These agencies are often staffed by trained volunteers and administered by an executive director and board of directors. Most often the services are free or low cost and tend to be short-term in nature. The underlying principle of these neighborhood justice centers and community boards is to tap neighborhood resources to solve neighborhood problems and prevent civil disputes from being resolved by criminal behavior. Divorce mediation has not been a primary service in most of these neighborhood dispute centers.

Because divorce mediation has not developed a distinct discipline or academic tradition of its own and most practitioners approach the field from their previous professional orientation, it is difficult to present a singular picture of divorce mediation. The diversity and absence of established protocols has caused concern about divorce mediation. This concern has resulted in significant activity among many organizations to draft standards of practice and a call for legislative controls. Interdisciplinary conferences, symposia, and institutes have contributed to the conscientious effort to shape the development and practice of divorce mediation.

CRITICAL ISSUES

As the practice of divorce mediation continues to grow, accompanied by the emergence of more conceptual theory and evaluative research, the field will face a number of critical developmental issues. Public policy issues include the selection criteria and determination of appropriate cases for divorce mediation, mandatory versus voluntary services, equality of bargaining power, safeguards against exploitation, accessibility, and affordability. Procedural issues include the compatibility of different models of practice, relationship between the mediator and clients, confidentiality, and interface between mediation and legal procedures. Professional issues include qualifications to practice, training, education, licensure, certification, and legal liability. These policy, procedural, and professional issues will likely be the focus of considerable dialogue and debate, particularly if divorce mediation is defined as a distinct professional field. These critical issues are addressed in the chapters which follow. A few of these issues are highlighted here.

Appropriate Cases

Determining appropriate cases for the use of divorce mediation raises two central questions: For what types of clients is mediation likely to be successful without being exploitative, and what subjects are best suited for mediation? Limited research exists regarding successful users of divorce mediation services. One of the more ambitious mediation research efforts, the Divorce Mediation Research Project (see Chapter 21), included a survey of practitioners' views on the types of clients most appropriate for mediation. Practitioners indicated that mediation is inappropriate for clients when (1) allegations or evidence indicate child abuse or neglect; (2) the parents and/or children have had multiple social agency or psychiatric contacts; (3) considerable post-divorce conflict is accompanied by frequent court appearances; and (4) one or more of the parties has evidenced serious psychological problems or has demonstrated erratic, violent, or severely antisocial modes of behavior (Pearson et al., 1984 or Pearson & Thoennes, 1984).

Kressel, Jaffee, Tuchman, Watson, and Deutsch (1980) examined a small sample of divorcing couples in an attempt to describe the relationship between the spouses and how this affects their ability to mediate. Couples were found to fit into four separate categories: enmeshed, autistic, direct conflict, and disengaged.

Enmeshed couples exhibit extremely high levels of overt conflict and ambivalence about the divorce, engage in prolonged conflict over minutiae, and appear to expand conflict for its own sake. They appear to be what Hugh McIsaac (1981a) has described as "hostility junkies." Autistic couples display a relative absence of overt conflict accompanied by minimal communication and mutual avoidance during the decision-making stages of the divorce. Direct-conflict couples engage in overt conflict and communicate directly with each other, including about the decision to divorce. Disengaged couples demonstrate a low level of ambivalence about the divorce, appear ready to terminate the marital relationship, and display a lack of interest in each other. According to Kressel et al. (1980), direct-conflict and disengaged couples have a greater likelihood of reaching an agreement through mediation than those couples exhibiting enmeshed and autistic relationships.

Critics of mediation cite concerns about mediation being used in cases where parties may be intimidated into settlements that are not in their best interests (Schulman & Woods, 1983). An imbalance of power between the parties is often central to the debate regarding who should and should not mediate (Beer & Stief, 1985). This objection is voiced by feminist groups and others concerned about the financial and parental status of women. Some fear that a more submissive, dependent, nonverbal spouse would not fare well in mediation (Cohen, 1984).

Diversity of power is common in many marriages. Rarely are two spouses evenly matched in skill and background. Rarely are two attorneys equally matched in negotiation or litigation. Pairs of experienced attorneys negotiating the same simulated case reach widely disparate results (Williams, 1983). Different judges in the same jurisdiction do not necessarily consider the same factors in reaching a custody decision and thus might rule differently when faced with similar facts (Kapner & Frumkes, 1978). In considering whether a case is appropriate for mediation, we should ask, "Compared to what?"

It would be ironic and a blink at reality to compare mediation to a romanticized vision of the adversarial model, the shortcomings of which led to the current interest in alternatives. Many marital settlements negotiated outside of mediation are the result of unequal bargaining power due to different levels of experience, sophistication, resources, and risk taking or risk avoidance. Past patterns of dominance, emotional needs, and psychological warfare do not disappear when settlement decisions must be made by the spouses, even when attorneys have done the negotiation. Should the divorce proceed to actual litigation, the same inequalities as in negotiations may influence the outcome in court. There may also be unequal resources to bear the costs of litigation, different expertise in choosing the right attorney, and different luck as to which judge is assigned to make a decision (Folberg & Taylor, 1984).

Mediation can help the spouses evaluate their strengths and weaknesses so they can make reasoned decisions together that seem fair to them. A skilled mediator attends to and balances power (see Chapter 14). The mediator assists the parties in combining their strengths toward the goal of resolving an issue and educates parties to use their strengths for settlement as opposed to dominance. A mediator can confront an imbalance of power by educating the parties regarding the need for full disclosure and informing the parties that joint input into the decision-making process reinforces the longevity of an agreement. Mediation need not mean "giving up the ship" but rather should allow for and encourage the full participation of both parties. Provisions for disclosure of assets and a meaningful opportunity to obtain independent counsel, aid in lessening these concerns.

The types of clients suitable for mediation will, no doubt, continue to be debated and researched. Individuals who are unable to understand the terms of an agreement to mediate, unable to represent themselves satisfactorily, and unable to ascertain their own interests and the interests of their children are probably not good candidates for mediation services. This would include individuals displaying severe psychological disturbances and a history of anti-social behaviors, as well as those couples chronically enmeshed in conflict who, as a result, are unable to work together.

Appropriate Subjects

There is also debate about what are appropriate subjects for mediation. Disputes over legal norms and clashes over principles on which public policy is shaped may not lend themselves to the mediation process. In some cases we need a judicial answer to set precedence and guide future cases (Fiss, 1984). In reality, most divorce disputes are case specific and distinguishable from all other cases. Clients are, generally, less concerned about precedent than they are with an expeditious and workable result.

Even cases of domestic violence and child protection that some believe to be beyond the scope of mediation (Battered Women's Advocates Caucus, 1983) are the subject of experimental mediation programs facilitating agreements on treatment plans and future family interaction. Although controversial, these programs are producing high levels of satisfaction and results acceptable to prosecutors and public officials, as well as the affected parties (Pearson, Thoennes, Mayer, & Golten, 1986; Bethel & Singer, 1982). There is agreement that stopping the violence is a prerequisite to mediation and that ending the violence cannot be conditioned upon any concession or the subject of bargaining (Lemmon, 1985).

Should divorce mediation be limited to child-related conflicts? Does the bifurcation of parenting and financial issues preclude parties from reaching agreements on the full range of divorce-related subjects? If divorce mediation is a good idea whose time has come, its benefits may be needlessly restricted by focusing the mediation process solely on child-custody issues, leaving the resolution of the financial issues to a different process. Financial issues are an implicit and integral part of the decisions about who incurs the daily expenses for the child and who sets aside the time necessary to care for the child. Each parent may be willing, within a given range, to exchange custodial rights and obligations for income or property. Support duties may be tied to custodial prerogatives as one way to enforce economic rights without going to court. As much as we would like to help divorcing spouses concentrate on parenting and separate children's needs from the financial needs of parents, we know that custody and the attendant financial arrangements in the United States represent some trade-offs in the minds of those going through divorce (Folberg, 1984).

Mandatory Mediation

The issue of mandatory mediation versus voluntary mediation is most commonly focused on the mediation of custody and visitation disputes. An increasing number of jurisdictions, following the lead of California, are mandating the mediation of these disputes (see Chapter 10). To the purist, mandatory mediation seems antithetical to the voluntary and cooperative tenets on which mediation is premised. Are we transforming mediation from a noncoercive, voluntary conflict-resolution process into a coercive mandated procedure (Sander, 1983)? If the principles of self-determination are intended to further the policy of minimal state intervention, are we now undermining that philosophy by mandating mediation? It is argued in response that no one is compelled to use mediation; it is only imposed as a precondition for those who cannot resolve their own dispute and choose to ask the court to decide for them. Perhaps this controversy can be addressed by mandating the provision of information about mediation and its benefits. This could be accomplished by requiring that attorneys and court personnel advise clients of the availability of mediation and that courts sponsor informational programs to educate spouses about divorce and the alternative approaches to dispute resolution.

Fairness

Because mediation is conducted in private and is less hemmed in by rules of procedure, substantive law, and precedent, there will be questions about whether the process is fair and if the terms of a mediated agreement are just. Parties might reach agreements that provide for less than the law allows or that are not viewed as being in their individual best interests or the best interests of the children. The concern for a fair and just result has particular applicability to custody and child-support disputes because children are rarely present or independently represented during mediation. The fairness issue calls into question the responsibility of the mediator for the nature and content of the final agreement. It has been suggested that the mediator could address the issue of fairness directly with the parties, could refuse to participate in unconscionable agreements, could refer the parties to legal counsel for an independent review, and could report to the court any objections and nonconcurrence with the agreement (see Chapter 19).

Safeguards against the exploitative use of mediation include encouraging the parties to avail themselves of independent legal advice and clarifying that any party, including the mediator, may withdraw and terminate the process. Judicial review generally occurs for mediated settlement agreements as it would with any other stipulated matter presented to the court. Available court remedies for incomplete disclosure and fraudulent agreements are presumably similar to existing remedies for voiding negotiated settlement agreements.

Mediator Role

The role of the mediator, the model of practice, and the relationship between mediator and clients raise several procedural issues. The clients' perception of the mediator as a therapist or as a lawyer may cause them to expect that the mediator will be able to resolve certain issues normally beyond the scope of mediation. For example, a therapist–mediator may be sought in the hopes of working out a reconciliation, or a lawyer–mediator may be looked to for legal advice or advocacy regarding the merits of a particular offer. It is incumbent on the mediator continuously to clarify the role of the mediator. This becomes more difficult when the mediator does things that are typically identified with lawyers or therapists, such as drafting agreements or meeting with parties individually. Further confusion occurs when the mediator shifts to the role of custody evaluator when custody mediation is unsuccessful, or when the mediator provides counseling during an impasse in the mediation process. Although this is usually done with the best interests of the clients in mind, these activities cause problems regarding confidentiality and trust and often result in a conflict of interest and confusion for all participants. Important questions about confidentiality and privilege in mediation are beginning to be answered (see Chapter 16).

As the public becomes more aware of the availability and benefits of mediation, there is some concern that mediation may become a "quick-stop" divorce service. A couple without conflict may turn to mediation in hope of saving money and avoiding attorneys. Mediation does not eliminate the need for attorneys in divorce. Parties should be encouraged to consult with individual attorneys during the mediation process. In order to protect individual interests, provide perspective, and help insulate a mediated settlement agreement from later attack, all mediated agreements should be reviewed by independent counsel for each party before the agreement is finalized. The mediator, even if an attorney, may not represent or advocate for one or both of the parties. A nonattorney–mediator must be cautious not to promote mediation as a substitute for lawyers (see Chapter 18).

Divorce mediation is a practice merging from the juncture of several helping professions. Because divorce mediation is a new practice that crosses traditional professional boundaries and recognizes divorce as a process within legal and social science contexts, there are likely to be interdisciplinary struggles for turf and assertions of professional dominance through claims of right, experience, or unique expertise. Professional separateness is not necessary for divorce mediation to develop into a distinct practice. Practically, professional conflicts between the disciplines that support mediation are the antithesis of the values underlying mediation and send a dissonant message to the public. A more reasonable approach seems to be that of providing an opportunity for the various disciplines to explore collectively what accounts for good practice and to develop a code of practice that can be supported by all mediators. The development of parameters of practice that cross professional boundaries will assist in the convergence of disciplines and allow divorce mediation to become a profession in its own right (see Chapter 20).

Public and Private Services

Mediation services do not currently exist in some communities; other communities are undecided whether mediation will become an accepted practice. Clients are not flocking to private mediators, and some court mediation programs are having a hard time selling voluntary mediation services to clients and their attorneys. Should comprehensive family mediation services be administered and financially supported by the public sector, making them available to all income levels, or should they be offered only by the private sector on a fee-for-service basis? Should court-employed mediators limit services to custody and visititation or assist with the full resolution of the issues? Is it good policy to require that parties submit disputes to mediation before being allowed their day in court? Does mediation preclude a party's protection by the adversary system in its rules of evidence, use of the compelled discovery process, and support of an advocate? Should mediation services be expanded to include spousal abuse, status offenses, and nonsupport? Who represents society at the bargaining table when these types of conflicts are resolved privately through mediation rather than in a public arena?

Are court-connected mediation programs destined to become a service only for those who cannot afford the fees of private mediators? Are we developing two systems of divorce justice, one coercive system for the poor and one of self-determination and private ordering for the rich? Is it reasonable to conclude that if we provide a publicly financed, judicial dispute-resolution process, we ought to also provide other publicly financed settlement procedures—including mediation (see Sander, 1983)?

Mediator Professionalism

Questions of certification, competency, licensure, and training have yet to be answered. Should professional associations engage in training, accreditation, or certification? Will professional organizations of mediators perform a public-interest role or function as a guild to protect existing practitioners? The need to determine professional qualifications for divorce mediators, the establishment of a code of ethics, and the establishment of some form of regulatory control over the practice have been noted by several authors (Coogler, 1978; Crouch, 1982; Elkin, 1982; Harbinson, 1981; Haynes, 1981; Milne, 1983a; Milne, 1983b; Silberman, 1981, 1982). These concerns center on the need to establish some form of quality control to protect both the consumer and the credibility of a developing profession (Milne, 1983a, 1983b).

The development of a system or structure to sanction the providers of mediation services would provide one means of establishing divorce mediation as distinct from that of legal services and counseling. Depending on the degree of restrictiveness, these sanctions may assure a minimum level of training and experience in the field and allow for referrals to individuals who have met preestablished practice requirements. A system of sanctions may provide some assurance for the public against the fraudulent practice of mediation by unqualified individuals and may promote more uniformity of service (Milne, 1983a, 1983b). To establish a set of qualifications for practice, however, requires a consensus on definitions, minimum qualifications, and standards. At this stage in the developmental process of divorce mediation, such a consensus may not be realistic. Then there is the question of who will provide the certification of proficiency. Should the certifying body be a professional organization providing divorce mediation training, an independent interprofessional board that reflects the multidisciplinary practice of divorce mediation, or a government agency?

The ingredients of successful mediation are not yet clearly defined. Promising clinical research is now taking place (see Chapter 22) but is not yet sufficiently broad-based or longitudinal in nature to establish what is effective and what provides for agreement making that holds up over time. Although progress is being made in research concerning what behaviors and communication strategies work best in mediation (see Chapters 15 and 23), training programs, typically 1–5-day workshops, are limited by the lack of more evidence concerning effective mediation techniques. Academic programs encompassing the legal, psychological, economic, and communication aspects of divorce mediation are still in the formative stages and face institutional barriers. It is unlikely that the practice will flourish and be established as a recognized and distinctive professional service until academic curriculums are implemented and training is institutionalized in an academic setting.

The public is entitled to some degree of protection when considering the selection of divorce mediation services, because the resolution of divorce-related disputes can have long-term implications for families and individuals. The legal liability of divorce mediators has not been well defined or tested, although both opponents and proponents agree the issue is important (see Chapter 17). How best to assure quality without unreasonably restricting choice and needed experimentation is problematic in a field that is still developing. The opportunity now exists, in the youth of divorce mediation, to help shape the practice in a conscientious manner. This can be accomplished in part by developing a professional conscience. The following chapters address many of the issues raised here and provide a base for creating a shared professional conscience.

REFERENCES

American Bar Association. Standards of practice for lawyer mediators in family disputes. *Family Law Quarterly*, 1984, *18(3)*, 363–368.

Auerbach, J. *Justice without law: Resolving disputes without lawyers.* New York: Oxford University Press, 1983.

Bahr, S. Mediation is the answer. *Family Advocate*, 1981, *3(4)*, 32–35.

Battered Women's Advocates Caucus. Resolution on mediation, 14th National Conference on Women and the Law, Washington, DC, April 10, 1983. *Women's Advocate*, 1983, *4(3)*, 3.

Beer, J., & Stief, E. Mediation and feminism. *Conflict Resolution Notes*, 1985, *2(2)*, 27–28.

Bethel, C., & Singer, L. Mediation: A new remedy for cases of domestic violence. *Vermont Law Review*, 1982, *7*, 15–32.

Bohannon, P. (Ed.) *Divorce and after: An analysis of the emotional and social problems of divorce.* New York: Doubleday, 1970.

Brown, D. Divorce and family mediation: History, review, future directions. *Conciliation Courts Review*, 1982, *20(2)*, 1–44.

Brown, E. A model of the divorce process. *Conciliation Courts Review*, 1976, *14(2)*, 1–11.

Buzzard, L. *Alternative dispute resolution: Who's in charge of mediation?* Transcript of program presented by American Bar Association, Young Lawyers' Division and Special Committee on Alternative Means of Dispute Resolution, Chicago, January 1982, 45–51.

California Civil Code § 4607(a) (1981).

Cohen, H. Mediation in divorce: Boon or bane? *Women's Advocate*, 1984, *5(2)*, 1–2.

Comeaux, E. A guide to implementing divorce mediation in the public sector. *Conciliation Courts Review*, 1983, *21(2)*, 1–25.

Coogler, O. J. *Structured mediation in divorce settlement: A handbook for marital mediators.* Lexington, MA: Heath, 1978.

Crouch, R. Mediation and divorce: The dark side is still unexplored. *Family Advocate*, 1982, *4(27)*, 33–35.

Deutsch, M. *The resolution of conflict.* New Haven, CT: Yale University Press, 1973.

Doo, L. Dispute settlement in Chinese–American communities. *American Journal of Comparative Law*, 1973, *21*, 627–663.

Duryee, M. Public-sector mediation: A report from the courts. *Mediation Quarterly*, 1985, *8*, 47–56.

Elkin, M. Divorce mediation: An alternative process for helping families to close the book gently. *Conciliation Courts Review*, 1982, *20(1)*, iii–iv.

Federico, J. The marital termination period of the divorce adjustment process. *Journal of Divorce*, 1979, *3(2)*, 93–106.

Fiss, O. Against settlement. *Yale Law Journal*, 1984, *93*, 1073–1090.

Folberg, J. Divorce mediation—A workable alternative. In J. Davidson, L. Ray, & R. Horowitz (Eds.), *Alternative means of family dispute resolution* (pp. 11–41). Washington, DC: American Bar Association, 1982.

Folberg, J. A mediation overview: History and dimensions of practice. *Mediation Quarterly*, 1983, *1*, 3–13.

Folberg, J. Divorce mediation—The emerging American model. In J. Eekelaer & S. Katz (Eds.), *The resolution of family conflict: Comparative legal perspectives* (pp. 193–210). Toronto: Butterworths, 1984.

Folberg, J. Mediation. In A. Rutkin (Ed.), *Family law and practice* (Vol. 4, pp. 55-1–55-38). New York: Matthew Bender, 1985a.

Folberg, J. Mediation of child custody disputes. *Columbia Journal of Law and Social Problems*, 1985b, *19(4)*, 1–36.

Folberg, J., & Taylor, A. *Mediation—A comprehensive guide to resolving conflicts without litigation.* San Francisco: Jossey-Bass, 1984.

Framo, J. The friendly divorce. *Psychology Today*, 1978, *2*, 77–79, 100–102.

Goldberg, S., Green, E., & Sander, F. *Dispute resolution.* Boston: Little, Brown, 1985.

Goldstein, J., Freud, A., & Solnit, A. *Beyond the best interests of the child.* New York: Free Press, 1979.

Harbinson, K. Family law–attorney mediation of marital disputes and conflict of interest considerations. *North Carolina Law Review*, 1981, *60*, 171–184.

Haynes, J. Divorce mediator: A new role. *Social Work*, 1978, *23(1)*, 5–9.

Haynes, J. *Divorce mediation—A practical guide for therapists and counselors.* New York: Springer, 1981.

Hunt, M., & Hunt, B. *The divorce experience.* New York: McGraw-Hill, 1977.

Kapner, L., & Frumkes, M. The trial of a custody conflict. *Florida Bar Journal*, 1978, *52(3)*, 174–178.

Kaslow, F. Stages of divorce: A psychological perspective. *Villanova Law Review*, 1979–80, *25(4–5)*, 718–751.

Kelly, J. Mediation and psychotherapy: Distinguishing the difference. *Mediation Quarterly*, 1983, *1*, 33–44.

Kessler, S. *The American way of divorce: Prescription for change.* Chicago: Nelson-Hall, 1975.

Kressel, K., Jaffee, N., Tuchman, B., Watson, C., & Deutsch, M. A typology of divorcing couples: Implications for mediation and the divorce process. *Family Process*, 1980, *19*, 101–116.

Lemmon, J. *Family mediation practice.* New York: Free Press, 1985.

McIsaac, H. Conference remarks. Mediation of Child Custody and Visititation Disputes, Vallambrosa Retreat, Menlo Park, CA, September 1981a.

McIsaac, H. Mandatory conciliation custody/visitation matters: California's bold stroke. *Conciliation Courts Review*, 1981b, *19(2)*, 73–77.

McIsaac, H. The family conciliation court of Los Angeles County. In J. Davidson, L. Ray, & R. Horowitz (Eds.), *Alternative means of family dispute resolution* (pp. 131–151). Washington, DC: American Bar Association, 1982.

McIsaac, H. Confidentiality: An exploration of issues. *Mediation Quarterly*, 1985, *8*, 57–66.

Marlow, L. The rule of law in divorce mediation. *Mediation Quarterly*, 1985, *9*, 5–13.

Milne, A. Divorce mediation—An idea whose time has come. *Wisconsin Journal of Family Law*, 1982, *2(2)*, 1–10.

Milne, A. Divorce mediation: The state of the art. *Mediation Quarterly*, 1983a, *1*, 15–31.

Milne, A. Divorce mediation—Shall we sanction the practice? In H. Davidson, L. Ray, & R. Horowitz (Eds.), *Alternative means of family dispute resolution* (pp. 1–8). Washington, DC: American Bar Association, 1983b.

Milne, A. The development of parameters of practice for divorce mediation. *Mediation Quarterly*, 1984, *4*, 49–59.

Milne, A. Divorce mediation: A process of self-definition and self-determination. In N. Jacobson & A. Gurman (Eds.), *Clinical handbook of marital therapy* (pp. 197–216). New York: The Guilford Press, 1986.

Mnookin, R. Child custody adjudication: Judicial functions in the face of indeterminancy. *Law & Contemporary Problems*, 1975, *39(3)*, 226–297.

Mnookin, R. Forward—Children, divorce and the legal system. *Columbia Journal of Law and Social Problems*, 1985, *19(4)*, 1–5.

Moore, C. *The mediation process.* San Francisco: Jossey-Bass, 1986.

Orlando, F. Where and how—Conciliation courts. In H. Davidson, L. Ray, & R. Horowitz (Eds.), *Alternative means of family dispute resolution* (pp. 111–129). Washington, DC: American Bar Association, 1982.

Pearson, J., Ring, M., & Milne, A. A portrait of divorce mediation services in the public and private sector. *Conciliation Courts Review*, 1983, *21(1)*, 1–24.

Pearson, J., & Thoennes, N. A preliminary portrait of client reactions to three court mediation programs. *Mediation Quarterly*, 1984, *3*, 21–40.

Pearson, J., Thoennes, N., & Hodges, W. The effects of divorce mediation and adjudication procedures on children. In J. Pearson & N. Thoennes (Eds.), *Final report of the divorce mediation research project* (pp. 1–31). Denver, CO, 1984.

Pearson, J., Thoennes, N., Mayer, B., & Golten, M. Mediation of child welfare cases. *Family Law Quarterly*, 1986, *20(2)*, 303–322.

Riskin, L. Mediation and lawyers. *Ohio State Law Journal*, 1982, *43*, 29–60.

Rubin, J., & Brown, B. *The social psychology of bargaining and negotiation.* New York: Academic Press, 1975.

Sander, F. Family mediation: Problems and prospects. *Mediation Quarterly*, 1983, *2*, 3–12.

Saposnek, D. *Mediating child custody disputes.* San Francisco: Jossey-Bass, 1983.

Schimazu, I. *Japanese perspectives on the procedural aspects of marriage dissolution.* Paper presented at Fourth World Conference of the International Society of Family Law, Harvard Law School, Cambridge, June 1982.

Schulman, J., & Woods, L. Legal advocacy vs. mediation in family law. *Women's Advocate*, 1983, *4-3*, 3–4.

Shonholtz, R. Neighborhood justice systems: Work structure and guiding principles. *Mediation Quarterly*, 1984, *5*, 3–30.

Silberman, L. Professional responsibility problems of divorce mediation. *Family Law Reporter*, 1981, *7*, 4001–4012.

Teitelbaum, L. Family history and family law. *Wisconsin Law Review*, 1985, *5*, 1135–1181.

Thoennes, N., & Pearson, J. Predicting outcomes in mediation: The influence of people and process. In J. Pearson & N. Thoennes (Eds.), *Final report of the divorce mediation research project* (pp. 1–20). Denver, CO, 1984.

Weiss, R. *Marital separation.* New York: Basic Books, 1975.

Williams, G. *Legal negotiation and settlement.* St. Paul, MN: West, 1983.

Wisemann, R. Crisis theory and the process of divorce. *Social Case Work*, 1975, *56(4)*, 205–212.

Yaffe, J. *So sue me! The story of a community court.* New York: Saturday Review Press, 1972.

2

The Nature of Divorce Disputes

ANN MILNE
Private Practice, Madison, Wisconsin

The successful mediation of disputes is dependent on an understanding of the origin of the conflict and the use of appropriate interventions. The ability to diagnose a dispute effectively is the first step toward its resolution. This chapter provides the mediator with a taxonomy for diagnosing disputes and discusses how the elements of conflict affect the nature of divorce disputes and their resolution.

Susan and John Brown were married at their respective ages of 22 and 24. They had known each other and dated steadily for several years before marrying. They were well suited for each other. They were in love. The Browns have now been married 12 years. They have two children, ages 8 and 10, a house, two cars, and both work outside the home. They're no longer in love.

To see them in court, one wonders how they could ever have cared for each other. Susan and John are fighting over everything—the children, the house, property, finances, even the bills. They've each hired attorneys who have pursued all legal avenues—depositions, interrogatories, multiple appraisals, private investigators, outside consultants, and witnesses—to protect the interests of their clients and to attempt to obtain the best deal. Susan and John have put their marriage on trial.

Each expects to be able to tell his or her story to the judge, to be heard and understood, and to receive a fair settlement. Unbeknownst to the Browns, the rules of evidence do not permit them to tell all, and the judge finds that much of the story is irrelevant to the disposition of the case. The children are torn between taking sides and withdrawing from both parents. The lives of friends and family have been disrupted, and Susan and John have depleted their meager estate in litigation.

The judge's decision does not end the warfare. Each spouse feels resentful of the process as the conflicts continue. The Browns could spend the rest of their lives acting out the hurts, angers, and other emotions that occur before, during, and after divorce.

This scenario is repeated daily in courtrooms across the country. Spouses compete for a limited amount of resources including money, property, and children. Most observers, and even participants, would readily agree that the resolution of these issues alone does not end the conflict of divorce.

This chapter begins with the premise that divorce-related conflict is natural and normal. Conflict can be constructive when it allows for the airing and resolution of a problem and promotes the reconstruction of a stable environment (Deutsch, 1973). Conflict in divorce can be productive when it forces a creative solution that would have been missed without the impetus of a dispute. Conflict in divorce can be functional when it provides needed emotional distance between two hurt individuals. Conflict, however, is destructive when it leads to prolonged tension, pathology, destruction, and war. Conflict in divorce is destructive when it results in chronic hostility, depleted life savings, impaired psychological well-being, and ruptured families.

The constructive resolution of conflict begins when participants and intervenors understand the nature and purpose of conflict. Mediation of disputes is dependent upon an understanding of the origin of the conflict and the use of appropriate interventions. Divorce conflict is the result of psychological barriers, communication failures, substantive differences, and systemic influences. This chapter discusses these elements of conflict and how they affect the nature of divorce disputes (see Chapter 13 for a discussion of the causes of impasse; see Table 2-1 for a taxonomy of divorce disputes).

PSYCHOLOGICAL CONFLICTS

Psychological conflict is produced by a disturbance in one's internal feelings of emotional well-being or self-esteem. A marital relationship establishes one's role in society and often forms the basis of self-definition. As the companionship and intimacy of a marriage ebbs, the "social scaffolding" (Weiss, 1975) on which one's self-definition rests is cracked. This loss of structure and support

Table 2-1. Taxonomy of Divorce Disputes

Psychological conflicts:
 Internal
 Adjustment dissonance
 Decision theory
 Divorce account
Communication conflicts:
 Unresolved prior issues
 Ineffective communication
 Tactical communication
 Structural impediments
Substantive conflicts:
 Positional conflicts
 Incompatible needs and interests
 Limited resources
 Differences in knowledge and expertise
 Value conflicts
Systemic conflicts:
 Family system
 Legal system

can result in emotional upheaval and psychological conflict. Several authors have discussed the psychological process of divorce (Bohannon, 1970; Brown, 1976; Fisher, 1983; Kaslow, 1981; Kessler, 1975). The psychological divorce process is often described as a series of stages that begins at the point of emotional upheaval and concludes with an acceptance and understanding of the divorce. Conflict of a psychological nature may occur at many points along the way.

Internal Conflict

Internal conflicts are disturbances in feelings about oneself. Feelings of confusion, failure, inadequacy, and self-doubt often permeate the early psychological stages of divorce and result in internal conflict. Internal psychological conflict can be a primary influence on the nature and occurrence of other divorce conflicts. These internal conflicts are often acted out under the guise of divorce disputes, where individuals are not only fighting over the immediate issues of children, finances, and property, but also fighting with their internal feelings about the relationship.

The internal psychological process of divorce often begins several years before the physical separation. Disillusionment with the relationship and unmet emotional and physical needs may build over time until a precipitating event, "the last straw," or an accumulation of unfulfilled expectations provides the momentum behind the decision to divorce. Emotional attachments, however, may still exist. Mixed feelings about the marriage and the pending divorce often result in approach–avoidance behaviors where conciliatory gestures are followed by distancing and rejection. The psychological reluctance to let go of the marriage conflicts wtih the cognitive understanding that the marriage is over. These mixed feelings cause spouses to behave erratically and to send mixed messages leading to confusion and eventual conflict. A couple may enter into last-minute counseling to attempt to save the marriage at the same time one of the parties files for divorce. This contradictory behavior causes conflict between the spouses and feelings of exposure and vulnerability. These feelings may result in maneuvers to protect vulnerable areas, including refusing to talk with the other spouse or clearing out the joint checking account.

The loss of emotional attachments and withdrawal of affection can also precipitate internal psychological conflict of a historical nature, such as fears of abandonment dating from one's youth. When these latent internal conflicts are activated, divorcing individuals are responding not only to the immediate loss of a love object but also to earlier fears and rejections. These internal conflicts can escalate the external and more visible conflict and lead to legal disputes and an adversarial relationship.

Internal psychological conflict can be difficult to manage in mediation. The exposure of these issues may only enhance feelings of vulnerability, force a party to deny their existence, and result in further retrenching. A skilled mediator may be able to surface these issues if sufficient trust and rapport has been built. A mediator can stress the normalcy of these conflicts and explore remedies, such as counseling, with the individual.

Adjustment Dissonance

The psychological adjustment to divorce is often described as being similar to a process of grief or mourning. The loss of relationship with one's spouse, friends, neighbors, and other family members precipitates feelings of anger, abandonment, depression, and rejection similar to those experienced with grief (Kübler-Ross, 1969).

Spouses rarely begin the psychological or grief process at the same time or travel through it at the same rate. Some individuals quietly adjust to the inevitability of a divorce long before the other spouse is even aware of the eventuality. The dissonance between each spouse's adjustment may result in conflict, as one spouse is ready to move ahead and turn his or her attention to other issues, while the other spouse is just beginning the grief process. It may be several years before a spouse adjusts to these losses, particularly when the decision to divorce is a unilateral one.

Insensitivity, or a perception of insensitivity, to the other spouse's psychological state and an inability to accommodate to the other's psychological needs will result in a conflict that may spill over to the negotiations about children, money, and property. As one spouse pushes to discuss the division of assets, the other resists reaching a resolution or attempts to extract a penance.

Adjustment dissonance can be effectively addressed in mediation by educating the parties about the psychological process of divorce and helping them identify their respective positions on the adjustment scale. Understanding how this adjustment dissonance creates a conflict between their psychological needs and interests helps focus the conflict. Using a fundamental principle of the mediation process, reframing issues from those of self-interest to mutual gain, the mediator can help the parties acknowledge their shared predicament and search for ways to accommodate to each other's needs.

Decision Theory: Mutual versus Unilateral

The decision to separate, whether mutual or unilateral, has a direct effect on the conflictual state of the relationship. It is the exceptional couple who mutually and simultaneously reach the decision to divorce. In many cases one spouse has made a decision to divorce in isolation from the decision making of the other. This often results in a conflict over whether to divorce. The lack of symmetry between the couple over the decision to separate begins a cycle of conflict. How this difference is resolved will directly influence the potential for conflicts over other matters.

The unilateral decision-making process may take several forms. A spouse who has been "lying in wait," now able to cross the decision-making threshold, must often protect the decision to separate out of fear of being coerced back into the relationship. The emotional armor necessary to protect the decision frequently results in an unwillingness to communicate with the other spouse, to explain the reasons for the separation, and to participate in counseling to help the partner adjust to the divorce. The inability and unwillingness to deal with the other spouse reinforces the lack of understanding between the couple and leads to conflict.

A second example of the unilateral decision-making process is that of the spouse who is unable to openly discuss his or her dissatisfaction with the marriage and is reluctant to initiate a divorce due to feelings of guilt or shame. Instead, this spouse behaves in such a manner as to force the other to begin a divorce action. The spouse who is forced to begin the divorce is angry both about the incidents presented and the "forced-choice" position. The first spouse, eager to compensate for the injustice and to quell feelings of guilt, may relinquish the right to a fair settlement and only later react to the loss of property, finances, and children. This causes an immediate conflict over the forced choice and a subsequent conflict over unrealistic and unacceptable settlements on the substantive issues.

During the initial orientation session, the mediator can talk with the parties about how they reached the decision to divorce and can foreshadow some of the dysfunctional effects of a unilateral decision-making process. Alerting the parties to potential pitfalls helps to avoid an impasse at a later stage in the negotiations.

Accounting for the Divorce

In an effort to understand the marital breakdown, individuals attempt to piece together an explanation that provides an account of the relationship. How individuals account for the divorce influences the amount and type of conflict.

Because the events and transgressions of the marriage are observable, they often become the focus and provide the accounting for the divorce. The account of the divorce as one of fault and blame necessarily sets the stage for defensiveness and continued antagonism. More difficult, but more productive, is an account that focuses on the underlying differences between the spouses and steers clear of the more symptomatic, superficial behaviors. This type of an accounting may include themes of growing in different directions, unfulfilled expectations, or unmet emotional needs rather than a victim–villain scenario. An account that includes a validation of the good intentions of each spouse and avoids blame and finger pointing lessens defensiveness and moves the couple from an antagonistic posture of individual enhancement to a more cooperative posture of shared understanding.

Although most spouses have developed an accounting of the divorce before they reach mediation, the mediator can reinforce and help shape an account that focuses on the less provocative aspects of the marital discord. The use of less stinging vocabulary, such as asking, "What happened to the two of you to bring you to the point of divorce?" as opposed to allowing a recital of who did what, helps the parties to view both the divorce and the mediation process as a shared event.

Psychological factors may be the most potent protagonists in divorce disputes. These factors are personal, private, and predatory. They eat at one's self-esteem and may be resistant to resolution because of their historical nature and the functions they serve in providing needed emotional distance during the uncoupling process. Efforts to extinguish them may be lengthy, as in individual psychotherapy, or unrealistic, as in couples' counseling. Psychological conflicts are not conducive to legal interventions: they are not disputes over facts or the appropriate subjects of legislation. At best, the mediation process may provide an opportunity to assist disputants in diagnosing the nature of psychological conflicts and formulating an agreement about how these issues will be addressed or, more typically, how they can be neutralized, in order to allow for the resolution of the substantive issues. The acknowledgment, labeling, and management of psychological conflicts may provide an opportunity for the constructive resolution of other issues.

COMMUNICATION CONFLICTS

Divorcing spouses are prime candidates for conflicts due to communication barriers. Conflict does not exist without a means of being communicated. Even internal conflicts are messages sent to oneself. Communication conflicts are caused by unresolved prior issues, ineffective communication, tactical communication, and structural impediments to communication.

Unresolved Prior Issues

Divorcing couples may have a number of issues from the marriage that remain unresolved. These conflicts may have been suppressed during the marriage out of fear that the conflict might not be adequately resolved or might lead to additional conflicts. These conflicts may reappear now that the reasons for containing dissatisfactions are less. The repetitive communication of these prior issues hampers the ability of the couple to communicate effectively and resolve other issues.

Once the floodgate is opened, spouses can become immersed in arguing about the past and rectifying old wrongs and lose sight of the immediate issues. A mediator can interrupt this dysfunctional communication by corralling these issues, contrasting them with the other issues on the agenda, and requiring the parties to identify what issues they wish to resolve. Most clients can see that their time in mediation is better spent resolving immediate and future plans rather than rehashing those issues that were not resolvable before.

Ineffective Communication

Ineffective communication, messages not clearly sent or not clearly received, causes conflicts between divorcing parties. A number of factors influence the sending and receiving of messages. The intensity of the relationship can lead to misunderstandings. The reciprocal nature of effective communications is often absent between divorcing spouses. Individuals react to what each assumes the other is feeling or thinking (Heider, 1958). Both parties are unlikely to feel heard and understood when they feel defensive and discounted. Conflict escalates when individuals feel that they are misunderstood and misjudged. This leads to negative reciprocal communications, which are counterproductive to settlement. A party, perceiving he or she has been maligned or rejected, maligns and rejects in return. This negative reciprocal communication escalates until one or both parties typically stop all communications and further overtures to communicate decrease as efforts to communicate are rebuffed.

Injecting a substitute issue into the conflict may act as a shield for psychological conflicts (Walton, 1969). The expression of anger, resentment, and envy is considered by many to be bad manners or symptoms of immaturity. These feelings are often camouflaged through secondary conflicts. The parties give themselves permission to argue about the secondary issue and misrepresent it as the primary issue. A fight about the appropriateness of a boyfriend or girlfriend being present during visitation may camouflage feelings of anger, envy, jealousy, or rejection. The deflection of these feelings onto a secondary issue may avoid a confrontation on the primary issue but typically results in additional conflicts which, when resolved, do not still the battle because of the unaddressed and underlying primary issue.

"Facsimile issues" (Walton, 1969) are related to the primary issue and may serve as face-saving issues or a means of testing the water with the other person. They allow for the exchange of ideas relevant to the topic but may preclude the direct resolution of the issue. A parent's refusal to consider joint custody of the children may be a facsimile issue that avoids communicating concerns about a reduction in financial support for the children.

"Bundling-board" issues (Walton, 1969) serve to keep parties apart and provide emotional distance during the separation and divorce. The bickering prohibits the resolution of the issues; resolution would lead to an increased understanding and thus jeopardize needed emotional detachment. A spouse's refusal to assist with selling the house, even though he or she has no interest in residing there and could use the capital, may reflect a need for continued conflict. Accommodation would draw the parties together at a time when one of them needs to view the other as the enemy.

The ability to listen and accurately decode messages is essential to effective communication. Hampered listening skills are frequently the cause of conflict. Negative perceptions of the other may cloud the communication process and result in attributing unintended meanings to communication. A simple question of "Where were you?" can be heard in a variety of ways depending upon the mindset of the listener. Preoccupation with myriad issues can also hamper the ability to accurately hear and will affect the communication process.

The absence of communication is also a barrier to the resolution of conflict. Just as communication may cause conflict, the lack of it may produce a similar end. The absence of communication precludes the airing of issues.

Divorce counseling may help parties understand the underlying reasons for communication conflict and develop more productive ways of airing disputes and reaching a satisfactory resolution. Divorce mediation may also assist parties in defining communication barriers. The mediation session may offer a safe haven for parties who are unable to discuss the primary conflicts and who resort to secondary issues. The mediator can educate the parties about more effective ways of communicating, can model listening skills, and can extinguish unproductive communication patterns.

Tactical Communication

Divorce negotiations, often adversarial and competitive in nature, are ripe for communication conflicts. Tactical communications are like stage directions. They are not intended to address substance but rather set the stage or define the parameters of future communications. The posturing of the hard bargainer (Fisher & Ury, 1983) is meant to coerce the other party into "talking my language." Extreme positions are taken with the hope of forcing concessions from the other side. This may result in an impasse when the other party retaliates with an equally positioned argument.

Bluffing, the sending of inaccurate messages about one's position, circumstances, or needs, results in communication conflicts. Agreements reached as the result of inaccurate data rarely hold up over time. The exposure of the bluff may lead to new conflict, punitive behavior, or an unwillingness to recognize a party's future requests. Crying wolf one too many times will erode credibility and trust between the parties and may end all communication.

Other tactical communication styles are designed to "seize the high ground" (Walton, 1969). This includes flooding the discussion with issues in an attempt to overwhelm the other side or directing communication away from one issue to another that is more advantageous. The use of highly technical language, assuming an overly informed attitude ("I know the children better than you do"), or referring to venerable resources ("The children's teacher thinks they should stay with me") may be ploys to communicate a more powerful position. Power tactics may result in a settlement but procedurally may result in an alienation of the parties and further conflict.

Structural Impediments

The adversarial structure of the legal process may contribute to communication barriers. The use of a third-party negotiator, such as an attorney, opens the door to miscommunications and misrepresentations. Although the use of a delegated negotiator may take the heat out of the communications, the legal responsibility for advocating a client's position reinforces the competition of the communication process.

Third-party communications allow for miscommunication similar to that old party game where one guest whispers in the ear of the next guest. Messages can come back distorted and misunderstood. Divorcing spouses are more likely to modify views and positions on an issue when they are satisfied they have presented and supported their unique views. The use of a third-party advocate rarely satisfies this need, as spouses are reduced to the role of bystanders. As a result, present conflicts are not resolved and new conflicts arise.

Legal prohibitions of communication, such as restraining orders, orders to limit contact, and orders to vacate the home, not only anger the recipient but limit the ability of the parties to resolve issues. Such orders are necessary when contact has resulted in violence or abuse, but their injudicious or pro forma use can result in structural barriers to communication. As mentioned above, the absence of communication can result in conflict as much as the presence of communication.

Courtroom procedures can also cause impediments to the communication process. Limitations on testimony, such as the rules of evidence that prohibit hearsay, preclude the telling of one's story and often leave parties feeling as though they have not had an opportunity to be heard. The examination and discovery process often limits answers to a yes or no response, rather than a full recital or explanation of the issues. Although these procedures facilitate the orderly conduct of court proceedings, they typically result in additional communication conflicts where parties feel abused by the procedures and pertinent information can not be related.

The often-referred-to "settlement on the courthouse steps" may lead to future conflicts as parties begin to live with agreements hurriedly packaged by their attorneys. Although the substantive issues may be resolved, these procedures may lead to future conflict—if not between the parties themselves, then between the client and the attorney.

Other structural impediments may include the absence of a forum for communication. The parties' refusal to meet obviates direct communication. The lack of court-connected conciliation and mediation services limits the opportunity for clients to communicate on safe ground with the assistance of a professional who can facilitate effective communication. Geographic distance between parties limits direct communication and the ability to resolve conflict. Messages sent through the children are often lost in the translation or inaccurately reported, and lead to misunderstandings and conflict.

Communication conflicts may be more overt than psychological conflicts because of their behavioral aspects. This may also make them more amenable to resolution through mediation. A mediator can call attention to these conflict-producing communication styles. By virtue of agreeing to mediate, the parties have given permission to the mediator to facilitate the communication process and prohibit destructive exchanges.

SUBSTANTIVE CONFLICTS

Substantive conflicts are independent of parties' psychological and communication disputes. Most disputes are initially labeled by their substantive content. They are the "point-at-ables" or tangible issues in the divorce, such as property division, financial provisions, or plans for the children. Substantive conflicts are influenced by parties' on-point positions, incompatible needs and interests, differences in knowledge base and expertise, limited resources, and personal values.

Positional Conflicts

According to Fisher and Ury (1981), people approach conflicts from a negotiating position of either a hard bargainer or a soft negotiator. Both styles involve the taking and giving up of a position relative to the issue in dispute. The taking of positions identifies the dispute and marks the parameters of the conflict.

Divorce disputes typically begin with positional conflicts. One party makes a claim, and the other makes a counterclaim. Each side then proceeds to advocate his or her position in an effort to convince the other of the merits of the claim. Positional conflicts may be resolved by convincing the other side, wearing the other party down, or by turning to a third-party adjudicator. Resolution may also be reached through compromise, often mechanical in nature, such as splitting the pie in half.

Positional negotiations may escalate conflict because of the need to mount evidence for one's position. This tends to solidify positions and may transform the conflict into one of face-saving. Mechanical resolutions that divide property and finances may not take into account parties' underlying needs and interests and often result in both sides feeling dissatisfied with the settlement.

Positional conflicts over substantive issues are not easily resolved. Mediation interventions typically focus on redefining or reframing positional conflicts to the needs and interests that led a party to a particular position. Redefining positions to needs and interests may allow for resolutions that are more acceptable to both parties.

Incompatible Needs and Interests

Redefining positional conflicts to those of needs and interests may lessen the conflict as alternative solutions become more evident. Conflict will still exist, however, when parties' needs and interests remain incompatible. The division of pension and retirement benefits is one example. When income is viewed as marital property, deferred income may be viewed as a marital asset subject to division at the time of divorce. A pension and/or retirement fund may be the largest asset the family holds. A spouse who has worked to provide for a secure retirement through investment in a deferred compensation plan will feel that his or her future security is threatened by the other spouse's claim to a portion of this asset. One spouse's interest in claiming a portion of the marital estate will be in direct conflict with the other spouse's need to provide for retirement.

Incompatible needs and interests where alternatives do not exist can become highly conflictual. These needs and interests are often basic survival issues, such as financial security or an ongoing relationship with one's children, and are not amenable to being put aside or compromised. A parent's interest in maintaining a fulfilling relationship with the children and spending a quantity of time with them may be in conflict with the other parent's desire to make a geographic move to take advantage of a lucrative promotion. Foregoing a career opportunity may sacrifice an individual's professional growth and a higher standard of living. Transporting the children back and forth between residences may interrupt their educational needs and may be too costly for the family.

Incompatible needs and interests may involve interested third parties, including children, grandparents, and new spouses. A decision to split the children's physical living arrangements between the parents may be in direct conflict with the children's desire to remain in one household even though they may be emotionally attached to both parents. Grandparents' desires to maintain a close and involved relationship with the children may be in conflict with a parent's desire to move out of the community and begin a new life. A stepparent's interest in building a new family and having a say in family activities may be in conflict with plans that are made around the children of the first marriage and financial responsibilities that cut into the standard of living of a second marriage.

These incompatible needs and interests often result in an impasse in both legal negotiations and the mediation process, as there appears to be no "good" solution. On the other hand, examining the best alternative to a negotiated agreement (BATNA) may convince the parties that even a less than satisfactory agreement may be better than an adjudicated one (Fisher & Ury, 1981).

Limited Resources

Once positional conflicts have been redefined to address parties' needs and interests, their incompatibility may be less of a conflict than a lack of resources that would satisfy even compatible needs and interests. Limited resources such as money, time, and energy can affect the resolution of substantive issues.

Divorce is a costly proposition. Income that covered the expenses of one household may not stretch over two. The lack of financial resources will become even more conflictual for those families who were living at a subsistence level. The family assets may be tied up in the home. The ability to sell the home in order to divide the property and provide working capital for each spouse may be hampered by a poor real estate market or the inability to find a buyer who can make a cash offer or secure an affordable mortgage. Selling on a land contract or renting the residence may tie up physical assets for an indefinite time and incur future financial obligations such as maintaining the home while it is being rented.

Time also becomes a limited resource in many divorces, as spouses return to work or school and are less available to care for the children and geographic separations may cut into time with children as they travel between households.

Energy, both physical and emotional, also becomes a limited resource for many divorcing families, as they are dealing with the emotional upheaval of divorce and new parenting responsibilities without the support and relief of the other parent.

Substantive conflicts over plans for the children may touch on each of these limited resources of money, time, and energy. Although these problems are not readily resolved, parties probably have more latitude in working out creative solutions than a court would provide. Conflicts can be toned down, if not resolved, when parties recognize that the absence of a resolution is due to external circumstances rather than their own failings.

Differences in Knowledge and Expertise

Substantive disputes over property, money, and children may result from differences in knowledge and expertise. A spouse who has had no experience in paying the bills may have difficulty in establishing a household budget and determining a level of financial support. The value of a professional practice or business may not be understood by a spouse unfamiliar with the practice. The division of a stock portfolio may become a substantive conflict when one party lacks knowledge and expertise in these investment and management areas.

Differences in knowledge and expertise may also result in substantive conflicts over the children. A parent who has not been closely involved in child-rearing and the day-to-day demands of this responsibility may be unrealistic in assessing his or her own abilities.

Knowledge-based disputes may be resolved through an educational process or through third-party expertise, as when an accountant provides a spouse with financial information, a financial counselor assists with the establishment of a realistic budget, or a stockbroker is chosen to administer a stock portfolio.

Differences in knowledge and expertise may also be resolved through learned experience, as when a parent spends an increasing length of time with the children and can better evaluate his or her abilities and enhance parenting skills over time. Information alone, however, will not resolve these types of conflicts when a party is not inclined either by personality or ability to absorb, understand, and apply the information.

Value Conflicts

Substantive conflicts may be rooted in value differences between the couple. Value differences may involve life-style, religion, political persuasion, and child-rearing philosophies. Value differences may permeate the negotiations over substantive issues such as time with the children, entitlement to property, and entitlement to financial support. Value conflicts between spouses with children may be long-lasting, as the parental relationship continues after divorce, whereas value conflicts between childless couples may ultimately be resolved by the termination of the marriage.

Differences over religious activities, such as children attending church or synagogue, may affect substantive conflicts over the time children spend with a parent. Certain religious practices such as fasting, meal preparation, communal activities, dress, and education may also provoke value disputes over substantive issues. The desire of one parent to have children participate in extracurricular activities such as sports and camp may also affect disputes over time with children and over financial provisions.

These types of value conflicts can escalate as they are transformed into disputes over power, control, and autonomy. A parent's desire to expose a child to his or her values may be overlooked, as may creative solutions to these disputes, when these conflicts become focused on a "my way is better than your way" perspective. The transformation of value conflicts to conflicts over power and authority will lead to new conflicts and will eventually result in a tightly wound helix of disputes.

Mediation provides an opportunity for parties to air these substantive disputes; in the legal process disputes may be suppressed, merely to resurface at a later date. The resolution of these issues is a challenge—one the parties can meet better than outsiders.

SYSTEMIC CONFLICTS

Systemic conflicts are attributable to factors outside of what the parties bring to the dispute. Systemic factors may be endemic to the setting of the conflict. Divorce occurs within both family and legal systems. These systems can affect the course of conflict. These systemic conflicts must be recognized before they can be resolved.

Family System

Conflict within the family system may be viewed as a series of concentric rings that begins with the individual's internal conflict and extends to interpersonal conflicts, intrafamily conflicts, and intergroup conflicts (see Figure 2-1). Like a pebble tossed into a pond, the internal dissatisfaction with the relationship initiates subsequent rings of conflict that make divorce a naturally conflictual event. The psychic need to attach to another and to feel accepted is shaken, irrespective of whether one is the divorce initiator or respondent. The potential loss of a love object, even if the love has faded, causes an *internal conflict* that has a potent effect on subsequent activities. How this internal conflict is attended to will set the stage for the resolution of the interpersonal, intrafamily, and intergroup conflicts.

Figure 2-1. Systemic conflicts during divorce.

Internal conflicts may be denied, deflected, or addressed privately, as with prayer, reflection, and meditation. Third parties may be called in to provide a listening ear, friendly advice, or therapy. The restoration of inner balance precipitates the calming of the outer rings of conflict. According to Waller (1970), "The task of settling one's conflicts is at first one of learning to live with one's self and with one's wounds, and only later does positive reconstruction become possible" (p. 106).

Interpersonal conflict results from incompatible activities between the marital partners. Interpersonal conflict may result from incompatible feelings and emotional needs, such as when one partner wants a divorce and the other does not; from incompatible physical needs, such as a cigarette smoker and a nonsmoker; from incompatible preferences, such as a desire to live in the country as opposed to the city; and from incompatible values and beliefs, such as religious ideology or political persuasion.

Interpersonal conflicts may result from the form of the relationship; one party's desire for autonomy and independence may be incompatible with the other's need for intimacy and dependence. An individual's ability to detect a conflict or to tolerate conflict may also be at odds with the partner's.

Interpersonal conflicts may be handled privately by the parties through direct negotiations, or by one party successfully forcing the other to withdraw or move into a compatible position. External interventions may include the use of an objective referent, such as a toss of a coin or the application of an agreed-upon rule, or the introduction of a third party. The third party may assume the role of delegated negotiator, ombudsperson, mediator, or decision maker.

The interpersonal conflict affects and is affected by the internal conflict and the intrafamily and intergroup conflicts. As interpersonal conflicts are resolved, the internal tension may be quelled as a new balance in one's life evolves.

Intrafamily conflict occurs within the extended family system including children, grandparents, aunts, uncles, and so forth. Children may attempt to encourage a reconciliation between two unwilling spouses, causing incompatible activities within the system. Conflict will also occur when family members take sides. Intense disputes may occur over the children or the allocation of material possessions. A resolution between one pair of family members may only cause further conflict among others in the system, as when two parents reach a custodial agreement that is not acceptable to all the children.

Intrafamily conflicts may be addressed by the participants through negotiations within the system or by one or more parties causing other members to withdraw or change positions. External interventions, such as the objective referrent or third party, may be used. Intrafamily conflicts are significantly different from interpersonal conflicts, however, because of the number of people involved and the exponential number of interactions that may occur.

As the concentric circles of conflict extend beyond the family system, they include colleagues and friendship groups. *Intergroup conflict* expands the number of potential disputants and the complexity of the conflict. Yet like the concentric ripples caused by a pebble tossed into a pond, the further removed the conflict circles are from the source of the conflict, the less energy exists. As the consequence of the conflict becomes more distant, the intergroup participants dissolve into interested onlookers.

Mediation may be most effective for interpersonal and intrafamily disputes. The disputants are closely associated with the issues and have a vested interest in outcome. Mediation provides a structure and procedure that help the parties define the issues and work toward the resumption of accord and harmony. Divorce does not end the family. Mediation acknowledges these ongoing family ties and provides a way for the system to reorder itself.

Legal System

The legal system, adversarial by design, sets the stage for competition. Conflict is inherent in competition, as one party attempts to best another. Representing and advocating for one's client, as lawyers are required to do by the canon of ethics, may place the spouses in direct competition and ignore the broader picture of children and extended family. The adversarial system may kindle the spark to fight in those parties who are already feeling wounded by the divorce. Presenting the opportunity to recoup former losses or to vindicate oneself may fan a simmering conflict into a fiery blaze. Left alone, these emotional wounds might have healed themselves as individuals proceed through the normal recovery process.

The attitude of each party's attorney will have a direct impact on the nature and intensity of the conflict and the potential for effective resolution. Lawyers who pride themselves in aggressively representing their clients may be fighting more for their own needs than for those of their client. The attorney who wants to put on a good show for his or her client may introduce conflict where it did not exist before. Approaches such as nit-picking, dive-bombing, and making mountains out of molehills may so alienate the other attorney that the conflict spreads from the divorcing parties to a personal battle between the lawyers. At this point, the attorneys are driving the conflict; the parties may be too intimidated by the professional aura of their attorneys to pull in the reins.

The legal system provides a number of technical vehicles that can escalate a potentially conflictual situation into an openly conflictual one. Legal proceedings may begin by the service of notice on a party in a manner that is embarrassing or intimidating, as when a deputy sheriff arrives at an individual's place of employment. The titlement of the lawsuit as *plaintiff versus defendant*, as opposed to *petitioner* or *copetitioners*, fosters a climate of opposition and conflict. The use of ex parte motions and orders (where a spouse has not received notice that a judicial determination is being sought) may be necessary in the face of potential physical abuse but typically escalates an already conflictual situation.

The information-gathering process of the legal system assumes a lack of full disclosure. Discovery procedures may include extensive interrogatories, and depositions may take on the flavor of a kangaroo court when parties are examined and cross-examined on their finances, business practices, and social activities without the tempering protections of the judicial process.

The use of a temporary hearing at the commencement of the divorce to establish physical, financial, or parental rights forces the parties to take adversarial positions and present their case to the commissioner, referee, or master. A local practice of excluding the parties and having only the attorneys present at these temporary hearings further distances the parties from the resolution and adds to the feeling of being a bystander while others are making determinations about very personal matters. Feelings of anger and impotence as the result of these procedures can be projected onto the other spouse rather than seen as conflicts produced by these systemic procedures.

The negotiation process of the legal system is fraught with potential conflict as lawyers communicate between themselves and use positional bargaining tactics which result in win–lose agreements rather than a mutual accommodation of needs and interests. Third-party communications can result in miscommunication. Spouses feel an estrangement from the process as agreements are reached in which they have not directly participated. As a result, the parties often lack an investment in the success of these agreements.

Although all states now provide for some form of no-fault divorce, grounds are still available in many states. The use of grounds requires substantiation or proof. The offering of proof typically escalates the conflict, as parties exchange accusations and denials. Even states that provide solely a no-fault process for the granting of the divorce may reintroduce fault concepts when issues of custody, visitation, maintenance, and property division are being determined. Although fault may be relevant to a fair legal determination, it nonetheless sets the stage for conflict, as parties gather their ammunition and prepare to defend themselves.

The legal system as a trier of fact is handicapped in being able to resolve the less salient conflicts of feelings and emotions. As a result, true conflict is often left unaddressed while the symptoms of the conflict are debated. Battles over sole custody of the children may only be symptomatic of the deeper conflicts over loss of spouse and family. The legal system struggles with these types of conflict.

Bound by law and case-law precedent, resolutions are reached that do not take into consideration the unique and perhaps idiosyncratic situation of the family. The legal system is required to operate in a sphere of normative decision making, which limits the use of creative problem solving. A bird's nest custodial arrangement, where the parents move in and out of the family home while the children remain stationary, may be an ideal arrangement for a family in the initial stages of separation but would not be encouraged through legislative or case-law provisions.

Legal remedies do not exist for families in conflict who live outside the normative community, cultural, and moral standards of the system. Family members are expected to conform, rather than the system conforming to their needs. The "spare the rod, spoil the child" families may be referred to the local child welfare department where a new conflict system will begin.

Designed to resolve conflict, the legal system is handicapped when presented with disputes of an interpersonal nature such as divorce. Well-intentioned players, such as lawyers, judges, and family members, often become pawns in a system that, as it attempts to promote peace, precipitates pernicious conflict.

Advocating mediation in preference to the present adversarial system is a subject for conflict and debate. The conflict that emerges from dissatisfactions with both the adversarial system and the mediation process may force creative solutions and result in further improvements in our dispute resolution system.

CONCLUSION

Divorce is a conflict medium. Whether or not it produces virulent conflict is determined by the nature of the dispute and the type of resolution procedures available. Dispute-resolution processes range from avoidance to attendance, from cooperative to competitive, from singularly imposed to mutually accommodated. Dispute resolution may occur through personal and direct negotiations, third-party negotiations, arbitration, adjudication, and mediation, to name a few possibilities. Each process has unique applications befitting particular situations. No one process is universal in its ability to resolve all disputes or meet the needs of all disputants. Professor Frank Sander advocates a multidoor approach to dispute resolution (Sander, 1983). The availability of a variety of dispute-resolution processes provides disputants with a choice of how and where they want to resolve their dispute. Clearly couples are entitled to dispute: they ought to be able to choose how they want to resolve those disputes as well.

The diagnosis of conflict is an essential skill for professionals in the dispute-resolution field. This would seem to hold true for judges, lawyers, and mediators. Without an adequate diagnosis and understanding of the conflict, solutions will be reached or imposed which attempt to fix the wrong problem. A doctor can not medicate without an adequate understanding of the problem; a mediator can not mediate without an adequate understanding of the conflict. Understanding the nature of a divorce dispute is the beginning of its resolution.

REFERENCES

Bohannon, P. The six stations of divorce. In P. Bohannon (Ed.), *Divorce and after: An analysis of the emotional and social problems of divorce* (pp. 29–55). New York: Doubleday, 1970.

Brown, E. A model of the divorce process. *Conciliation Courts Review*, 1976, *14*(2), 1–11.

Deutsch, M. *The resolution of conflict.* New Haven, CT: Yale University Press, 1973.

Fisher, B. *Rebuilding—When your relationship ends.* San Luis Obispo, CA: Impact, 1983.

Fisher, R., & Ury, W. *Getting to yes: Negotiating agreement without giving in.* Boston: Houghton, 1981.

Heider, F. *The psychology of interpersonal relations.* Wiley, 1958.

Kaslow, F. W. Divorce and divorce therapy. In A. Gurman & D. Kniskern (Eds.), *Handbook of family therapy* (pp. 662–696). New York: Brunner/Mazel, 1981.

Kessler, S. *The American way of divorce: Prescription for change.* Chicago: Nelson-Hall, 1975.

Kübler-Ross, E. *On death and dying.* New York: Macmillan, 1969.

Sander, F. Keynote address at First American Bar Association Conference on Alternative Means of Family Dispute Resolution, Los Angeles, 1983.

Waller, W. The old love and the new: Divorce and readjustment. In P. Glasser & L. Glasser (Eds.), *Families in crisis* (pp. 95–106). New York: Harper & Row, 1970.

Walton, R. *Interpersonal peacemaking: Confrontations and third party consultation.* Reading, MA: Addison-Wesley, 1969.

Weiss, R. *Marital separation.* New York: Basic Books, 1975.

3

How People Process Disputes

LINDA K. GIRDNER
Congressional Fellow, American Anthropological Association, Washington, D.C.

The anthropological study of a dispute provides an opportunity to understand conflict and its resolution within a broad social context, independent of the specific issues and participants. Various forms of mediation occur in both traditional and industrial societies. Divorce mediation and its significance for society and social order can be better understood when viewed from an anthropological perspective. This chapter provides an around-the-world view of dispute resolution and discusses the impact of divorce mediation on interpersonal issues in our present-day society.

Alternative means of dispute resolution between individuals have not been well developed or understood in United States society. Much can be learned by examining other societies where people have relied primarily on nonjudicial means of settling disputes. Anthropologists have studied the disputing process in communities in Africa, Asia, Latin America, and Europe as well as the United States. Most of the interactions in these communities, and thus most of the disputes, occur between people who know one another and are connected by ties of kinship and marriage, economic cooperation, and shared community identity. Anthropologists generally study the disputing process by living in the community for an extended period of time and learning its norms, values, and social organization. When a dispute arises they are able to examine it in its social context as well as from the perspectives of the disputants.

Anthropologists are interested in discovering the choices people have in seeking justice, the characteristics of different disputing processes, the role of power and norms in dispute settlement, and the social and cultural contexts of conflict and its management. From in-depth studies of particular communities, comparisons can be made about disputing processes, independent of the issues in dispute or particular values of the society.

In this chapter, a few of the theoretical contributions of anthropology will be discussed with reference to their importance to the understanding of divorce mediation. First, various disputing processes are briefly defined. Second, the concept of justice is examined in relation to moral and legal aspects of relationships. Examples from other cultures are used for comparative purposes. Third, the social context and characteristics of mediation in small-scale societies are examined. Finally, issues and questions relative to divorce mediation in the United States are discussed in light of the anthropological perspective.

MODES OF DISPUTE PROCESSING

Conflicts between individuals arise in all societies. A Haitian man is troubled by the neighbor's goat, which keeps trespassing in his garden and eating his crops. In a Lebanese village an argument between two men about a past debt leads to insults and violence. In the hills of Mindanao, in the Philippines, a man is upset and angry that one of his wives has left him for another man. Norms have been broken, and the individuals feel that they have been wronged. Although every society has multiple modes of dispute processing, certain modes may be seen as more appropriate for different types of issues or different sets of disputants.

Norms exist not only in relation to the way disputes originate, but also in the appropriate ways of dealing with them. The first time the goat is in his garden, the Haitian man chases it out but does nothing more. After repeated invasions, he talks to his neighbor, letting him know that he needs to keep better watch over his animal. If the goat continues to enter his garden and eat his crops, he chops its head off and by saying "*m prin mouin; vin prin pao*" ("I have mine; come take yours"), informs his neighbor that he can retrieve the carcass. The man is justified in killing the trespassing goat after attempting to resolve the problem in other ways.

Across cultures there are a limited number of ways in which people deal with disputes. The methods include "lumping it," avoidance, self-help, deflection or displacement, dueling, negotiation, mediation, arbitration, and adjudication (Gulliver, 1979; Nader & Todd, 1978).

"Lumping it" means that the person who feels wronged chooses to do nothing about the situation and essentially acts as if it did not occur. This may be the path chosen by persons who need to maintain an ongoing relationship but who "lack information or access (to law), or who knowingly decide gain is too low, cost too high" (Galanter, 1974, pp. 124–125). If, however, the offending actions continue to occur, the person may decide to take a different course of action.

Avoidance is different than lumping it, since it involves purposely limiting or suspending any interaction with the other person. The mobility of United States society allows use of avoidance as a common means of handling disputes (Felstiner, 1974, 1975). In societies where people spend their lives in the same small community, total avoidance is often not possible.

Self-help is the term used for action taken by one party and imposed upon the other. Self-help may be seen as a viable option to the person who feels at a disadvantage in another disputing process.

Deflection or displacement involves disputes being "transformed and redefined in symbolic and supernatural terms" (Gulliver, 1979, p. 2). The ice hockey game between the Soviet Union and the United States in the 1980 Winter Olympics served as a symbolic arena for the two world powers to engage in conflict without dangerous consequences.

Dueling is an institutionalized contest, in which the disputed issue is decided in favor of the person who wins the duel. Duels with weapons were common in early Euro-American history. In contrast, Eskimo dueling traditionally took the form of song contests.

Negotiation is a process in which two parties, or their representatives, seek a mutually agreeable outcome to their dispute. Negotiation is used by parties to arrive at joint decisions about terms of a new arrangement between them (e.g., bride-price). Negotiation appears to exist in all cultures, although the issues that are negotiated and the values relevant to the situation vary.

Mediation, arbitration, and adjudication are all processes of dispute settlement involving third parties. The distinction between the three lies primarily in the role and power of the third party relative to decision making and the dynamics between the disputants. In mediation, the third party assists the disputants in coming to an agreement but has no authority to impose a decision. Mediation can be seen as "negotiation by brokerage" (Koch, 1979, p. 4). In arbitration, the disputing parties give the third party power to decide the dispute. In adjudication, the third party has the legitimate authority to impose a decision on the disputants whether or not they wish it. The boundaries of these roles and processes are not always distinct. A judge may operate in a mediating capacity in a pretrial hearing, rather than as an adjudicator (Girdner, 1985). Among the Zinacantan in Mexico, the *presidente* has the power to impose sanctions as an adjudicator but works first as a mediator toward an agreement that will reconcile the parties (Collier, 1973).

FORUMS OF JUSTICE

The Justice Motive

Laura Nader, a leading anthropologist and director of the Berkeley Law Project, states that justice first needs to be understood from the point of view of the disputants by examining "what people do when they feel they have been wronged and why, as well as what is done to them in relation to that wrong" (Nader, 1975, p. 153). Further, "what one does about an injustice, or felt injustice . . . is directly related to what forums are available and how they operate" (Nader, 1975, p. 163).

In examining issues of justice in disputes between family members, it is helpful to differentiate between the moral and legal aspects of family relations. The legal aspects relate to the reciprocal rights and duties attributed to persons in specific types of relationships (e.g., husband and wife, parent and child). These rights and duties are enforceable by institutions external to the family, such as courts in United States society, and include, for example, laws relating to spousal maintenance and inheritance.

The moral values "are seated in the sentiments and conscience of the individual and they cannot be induced by coercion, for free will is their very essence" (Pitt-Rivers, 1975, p. 96). The moral aspect involves a notion of giving without the calculation of debt. The source of the moral obligation is in the kinship bond, is based on trust, affect, and sentiment, and may be reinforced by mystical notions. The moral obligation could include respect, love, fidelity, and solidarity.

It is important to bear in mind that the moral and legal aspects are not often differentiated in the course of everyday life. Parents provide economically and emotionally for the well-being of their children. The obligation is both moral and legal. The moral aspect derives from the irreducible bond of kinship between parents and children. The legal aspect relates to the rights and duties each person has within the relationship. A parent should *want* to care for his or her child. The act should be based on love, not an obligation. To perform the act only because it is a duty conforms to the legal responsibility but is morally bereft. Not to perform one's parental or filial obligations is to renege on one's moral and legal obligations. This can involve moral sanctions, which in many societies take the form of religious sanctions, such as being excommunicated or cursed by one's ancestors. It also means that legal sanctions can be brought to bear. Legal sanctions can force the person to perform the duties (or may punish the person for not performing them), but they cannot make the person *want* to perform them. In the United States, the trend is toward increasing legalization of moral norms, for example, the right of aging parents to sue their adult children for support and the right of children to sue their parents for neglect and collect damages based on injuries sustained in childhood accidents.

A sense of injustice is often felt when the moral aspect of the relationship is believed to have been transgressed. Dispute forums differ, however, in the degree to which the moral and legal aspects are addressed. The Kpelle moot in Liberia and the Tururay *tiyawan* in the Philippines are two examples of forums for justice in small-scale societies.

The Kpelle Moot

Members of the Kpelle, a Liberian tribe, have the choice of handling matrimonial disputes in the court or in the community moot. The court is "particularly inept at settling the numerous matrimonial disputes because its harsh tone tends to drive spouses farther apart rather than to reconcile them" (Gibbs, 1963, pp. 2–3). The court is more likely to consider the case in its legal aspects, whereas the moot addresses the moral aspects of the relationship.

The moot, as described in J. R. Gibbs's seminal article "The Kpelle Moot" (1963), is an informal airing of a dispute before an ad hoc group of kinsmen and neighbors. The mediator, a kinsman of the complainant, holds a public office and represents the wider community. After an opening blessing, each disputant has an opportunity to speak. Anyone present can ask questions and comment on the behavior of the disputants. The mediator controls the process and can fine people for speaking out of turn by ordering them to bring rum for the others.

The moot enables parties to air their grievances fully. The procedure is therapeutic as it "re-educates the parties through a type of social learning brought about in a specially structured interpersonal setting" (Gibbs, 1963, p. 6). An important aspect of the moot is the reality testing that the group provides for each party's perceptions of the situation. A man who had ousted his wife after telling her to go have an affair with a suspected lover was told by those present at the moot that he had acted unreasonably. Moot participants pointed out that there was no indication of her infidelity with the other man and that her husband's overly suspicious attitude was not conducive to marital stability.

The success of the moot depends partly on the willingness of the parties to cooperate and their joint desire to mend the breach. Each needs to be able to express grievances fully and to accept and admit his or her contribution to the problem. Although in the moot no one is singled out as being at fault, inappropriate behavior by anyone involved is pointed out. The parties give gifts of apology to symbolize the repair of relationships and the acknowledgment of their wrongs. The moot has no authority to impose decisions. Generally, the process of clarification and understanding leads the disputants and the participants to a consensual outcome.

The Tiruray Tiyawan

The Tiruray are hill people of Mindanao in the Philippines. To understand the way the Tiruray settle disputes, one first must understand certain concepts basic to their belief system.

The Tiruray have a shared body of custom called *Padat*, which means both "paying respect" and "what ought to be done." Respect for others is the moral duty of all Tiruray. When everything is as it should be, then it is good and proper, or *fiyo*. To respect the feelings of other people means not to give them a bad *fedew*, literally a "bad gallbladder." *Fedew* is used metaphorically, and refers to "one's state of mind or rational feelings, one's condition of desiring or intending" (Schlegel, 1970, pp. 32–33).

There are two kinds of bad *fedew*. One is a "painful" feeling, when a person feels sad, grieved, worried, lonely, or envious. The other type is "hurt" feeling, when a person feels wronged in some way and feels angry, hateful, or vengeful. The painful feeling is considered an unavoidable part of life and often can be treated through religious ritual. A hurt feeling is triggered by human actions that could have been avoided if people behaved appropriately or according to *sadat* (custom). The moral obligation for a Tiruray is to avoid causing bad feeling.

The *tiyawan* is a gathering for settling disputes. The *tiyawan* may be "hot" or "good." The hot *tiyawan* addresses bad feelings; the person with bad feeling brings the case as an alternative to revenge killing. The hot *tiyawan* involves strong feelings, and failure to arrive at an agreement could lead to bloodshed. The good *tiyawan* arises out of negotiations over bride-price and therefore does not involve bad feeling or issues of blame or fault. Each party to the negotiations chooses from his kindred a *kefeduwan*. The *kefeduwan* is the moral leader who has skills in settling disputes and expertise in Tiruray custom and law. Leaders must be able to handle both types of *tiyawan* gathering, since a good one can become hot if someone turns a feeling bad in the course of negotiating bride-price.

The leaders do not act as adversaries but "are committed as a group to an ultimate respect for just decisions, decisions that set every *fedew* (feeling) right" (Schlegel, 1970, p. 61). The leaders make authoritative decisions, decide blame, and assess fines, but they have no coercive power to impose their decisions. Decisions must be voluntarily accepted by the parties. It is the duty of the leader to restore the parties to a state of *fiyo* instead of hurt feeling. Thus, the outcome must be emotionally acceptable to all parties. The moral and legal aspects of relationships are synonymous among the Tiruray.

The Tiruray *tiyawan* blurs the boundaries of the different disputing processes of negotiation, mediation, and arbitration. The Tiruray exemplify a culture in which disputes are clearly seen as originating in feelings of being wronged, angry, or hurt by another's behavior. The resolution of the dispute must address not only behavior but also feelings.

The good *tiyawan* does not involve a dispute or hurt feelings, but rather the need to negotiate a new arrangement. Arranging marriage payments is a situation that involves a change in the status and role of the parties, the establishment of right and duty, and the transfer of property. The leaders have extensive knowledge of past bride-price negotiations, which they refer to as guidelines in the negotiations. Thus, among the Tiruray, the *tiyawan* is used both for resolving issues that arise from a sense of injustice and those that arise from the need to make agreements governing new relationships. The Tiruray differentiate clearly between the two. The hot *tiyawan* has to do with past behavior, a notion of damages, and the need to repair the relationship. The good *tiyawan* focuses on the creation of a future relationship and contractual agreements over the transfer of property.

Divorce in the United States

If the Tiruray *tiyawan* met to consider a divorce in the United States, would it be a hot or a good *tiyawan*? If hot, it relates to a sense of being wronged, of felt injustice on the part of one or both parties. If good, it is viewed as a situation involving the need to negotiate terms relating to the change in the relationship, concomitant rights and duties of the parties, and the transfer of economic goods.

In the United States people perceive the courts as a forum of justice but often do not realize that the procedural and legal justice administered by the courts is not the same notion of justice the disputants often wish to have addressed. The courts define the legal aspects of disputes. Divorce-related disputes, particularly chronically relitigated cases, may be rooted in a sense of moral injustice, as would be addressed in a hot *tiyawan*. Taking the case to court does not address this aspect but reduces it to its legal components.

A man who feels he has been a good husband and father, has worked hard, and has provided for his family as he felt he should, finds that his wife wants a divorce. He acknowledges the marital problems but is willing to live with them. When he learns that his wife wants him to move out and that she expects to keep the house and the children, he feels a growing sense of injustice. Why should he move out and lose his home and family when he does not feel he has done anything wrong?

His wife has felt an increasing sense of injustice over the years of the marriage. She has felt stymied in her attempts to develop herself and to be treated as an equal partner. She has often felt taken for granted in her role as wife and mother. She perceives divorce as the only viable option for herself and feels she has earned or is owed certain things as a result of the years she invested in the marriage.

The issues are defined legally as the grounds for divorce, the division of property, spousal maintenance, child support, and custody and visitation. The perceptions of the parties and the parties' feelings of injustice are irrelevant to the judicial determination of the case. Most lawyers treat the nonlegal aspects as troublesome but immaterial, since they are "bargaining in the shadow of the law" (Mnookin & Kornhauser, 1979). When the sense of injustice is not addressed, it can lead to anger, blame, and sometimes revenge. The courts can become a weapon to use against the other spouse rather than a forum for resolving the dispute.

Moral values "cease to be *moral* once sentiments become subjected to jural concepts of right and obligations, and the moral autonomy of the individual to the judgments of the society" (Pitt-Rivers, 1975, p. 96, emphasis in original). In child-support cases, the court determines the amount a parent will pay. The definition of the issue as a legal one negates the moral aspect of the parent's role. In one case I observed, the father had voluntarily increased the amount of child support, and the judge told his attorney, "I can assume they needed it if he paid it. But anyway, the amount of child support is up to me to determine" (Girdner, 1983, p. 342). Fathers, who are usually the parents paying child support, are seen as paying because they have to, which implies that none support their children out of a willingness to do so. If they respond to the coercion by not paying, then greater coercive forces can be brought to bear. The father's sense of injustice often grows as he feels his role reduced to check writer. The courts deal with law and the legal aspect of relationships, not with the moral aspects and the search for moral justice.

In divorce mediation, the parties consider not only the legal aspects, the rights and duties that are defined by law, but also the moral aspects, the personal meaning of their relationship as parents and former spouses. Mediators vary in terms of the degree to which they allow parties to air grievances relating to their marriage and express feelings of blame and injustice. The effect of different strategies in this regard has not yet been fully explored. In any event, it is not uncommon in mediation for one party to need to hear from the other a statement acknowledging his or her self-worth or recognition of his or her efforts in the marriage. A woman may acknowledge to her husband that he did his best to provide for his family, or he may tell her that he always felt she was a good mother. It is as if there are certain magic words, varying from person to person, that when spoken sincerely by a spouse are able to alleviate the other's sense of moral injustice. The moral aspect addressed in this way can serve as a catalyst in the negotiations of the issues.

In mediation spouses can refer to their moral values when making commitments, while recognizing the applicable legal rights. The high rate of compliance attributed to mediated agreements may stem from their basis in the moral autonomy of the individual rather than their legal enforceability.

Access to justice involves the availability of various forums of dispute processing. Forums differ in their treatment of the moral and legal aspects of relationships. The Kpelle moot and the Tiruray *tiyawan* are disputing processes that address moral aspects of relationships. Divorcing couples in the United States who use the traditional adversary system often are seeking a type of moral justice which cannot be found in the courts. Although retributive justice is not condoned in divorce mediation, mediation has the capacity to address the sense of injustice or bad feelings that divorcing parties often feel.

MEDIATION: THE TRIADIC NEGOTIATION

The Role of the Mediator

The cultural notion of the mediator as a neutral, disinterested party or simply a catalyst is not borne out in practice, for the most part, in the United States or in other societies. Mediators have their own interests to protect, which may involve their standing in the community and their prestige and reputation. A mediator cannot be neutral to the extent that he "seeks and encourages an outcome that is tolerable to him in terms of his own ideas and interests" (Gulliver, 1979, pp. 213–214). The mediator "facilitates and to some degree influences, even controls, the exchange of information, the concomitant learning, and the consequent readjustment of perception, preferences, and choices" (Gulliver, 1979, p. 219). Thus, the mediator can be seen as an additional party with preferences, strategies, and interests, whose presence turns the process into a triadic negotiation. The role of this party, however, needs to be differentiated from that of the disputants.

Gulliver (1979, pp. 221–227) defines several roles or strategies of the mediator, which can vary throughout the course of mediation. A mediator can deliberately take on a *passive* role, which sometimes facilitates change in the disputants' interaction. In a *chairperson* role the mediator maintains order and controls the procedural aspects. He or she also restates points of agreement and disagreement. The mediator adopts an *enunciator* role when raising norms and rules that are relevant to the disputed issues. As a *prompter* the mediator works to "clarify information and interpretation and to encourage coordination between the parties" (Gulliver, 1979, p. 224). The mediator attempts to restate the arguments or concerns of each party. In operating as a *leader*, the mediator suggests options and solutions to the issues in dispute or to the packaging of issues.

In some societies there is also a role of the mediator as a *go-between*, such as the *monkalun* among the Ifugao of the Philippines and the *du-wrai* among the Waigali of Afghanistan. The go-between has a high degree of control over the information exchange, which can be a useful strategy if the parties are increasingly unproductive and hostile when together. In divorce mediation the role of go-between may be an appropriate caucus-like strategy for working with enmeshed couples (Girdner, 1985) whose attachment and reactivity make them unsuccessful candidates for mediation using only joint sessions (Kressel, Jaffee, Tuchman, Watson, & Deutsch, 1980).

In nonindustrial societies, mediators are usually older men who are respected members of the community, known for their skill and experience at resolving disputes. They represent the values and norms of the community and are experts in issues of morality and justice. Mediators have a vast and detailed knowledge of past settlements on similar issues, which provide a comparative basis for the extant dispute. They usually have extensive knowledge of the community, of the appropriate way for people to behave toward one another, and of the reputations of the disputants. In fact, the disputants are rarely strangers to the mediator (Merry, 1982, p. 30; Witty, 1980, pp. 46–47).

Although the mediator does not have the power to impose a decision on the parties, social, moral, and/or supernatural constraints can often facilitate acceptance. For example, among the Nuer, cattle herders in East Africa, the institutionalized role of mediator is the "leopard-skin chief," who has the power to curse a disputant who does not accept a fair settlement. In addition, a recalcitrant party is sanctioned by public opinion and the possibility of violence by the other party if the dispute remains unsettled (Merry, 1982, pp. 22–23).

Whether mediators adopt a role of passive participant or directive intervenor like the leopard-skin chief, they operate within the context of the social and moral norms of the community. Mediators influence settlements in those terms and are likely to remonstrate one or both parties for behavior that transgresses commonly held norms. In sum, although mediator roles are diverse, their function is to influence in terms of community norms the process of settling the dispute and the substantive outcome.

The Disputants in Mediation

In nonindustrial societies the disputants in mediation share a community or cultural identity with one another and the mediator, although the mediator usually is of higher social status. Thus the norms and values raised in the mediation setting are those of the parties as well as the larger community (Merry, 1982, p. 40; Witty, 1980, pp. 13–15). The parties are also familiar with local settlement norms from past mediated cases, so they have a sense of the boundaries of fairness and customary practice.

Mediation is "most likely to succeed between disputants whose various residential and kinship ties require them to deal with one another in the future" (Merry, 1982, p. 31). An ongoing past relationship does not guarantee that the disputants will have a future need to interact. If there is no need to relate on an ongoing basis, the parties have less need for a mutually agreeable settlement.

Parties in mediation are willing to voice their personal needs and are able to express their concerns in the language in which they are comfortable. This is in marked contrast to adjudication, in which expression of personal needs is restricted and specialized legal language and rules of speech dominate (Witty, 1980, pp. 12–13).

Mediation is more likely to be successful if disputants are interested more in reaching agreement than in establishing absolute right or wrong. According to Witty (1980, p. 19), "this principle further illustrates the future orientation of mediation; the resolution is less concerned with past events or precedents, and takes the transgression or disputed act as a given." The parties are more interested in seeking harmony in the relationship than victory in the dispute.

Mediation is more likely to succeed when the disputants are concerned with tangible social resources at least as much if not more than tangible resources (Witty, 1980, p. 18). If the dispute involves scarce resources, however, "individuals may rank the resource higher than they rank the relationship, and may be willing to sacrifice the social relationship with their opponents in order to gain access to, or exclusive use of, the resource" (Nader & Todd, 1978, p. 18).

Mediated Agreements

Mediation in many cultures is an informal process but not usually a private one. In many societies, such as the Kpelle, the dispute is mediated before a gathering of relatives, neighbors, and other community members who "as a group attempt to solve the dispute" (Koch, 1979, p. 4). Not only is the outcome consistent with community values, but community members often have an active voice in the settlement process.

For mediation to work effectively, both disputants need to "believe in the relative egalitarian relationships within the context of the dispute" (Witty, 1980, p. 10). Witty (1980, p. 16) explains that differences in status and power are equalized in mediation, through the recognition of the common need to reach a conciliatory resolution. Since community norms may embody status differences (e.g., based on gender or age), however, the outcome will tend to reflect those differences. Merry's cross-cultural study indicates that mediation between disputants of unequal status leads to a settlement that reflects the inequality. The more powerful party is likely to end up with a more favorable agreement, although the "greater the power of the mediator, the more leverage he has to impose a solution that disregards the inequality of the parties" (Merry, 1982, p. 33).

Mediation outcomes usually involve concrete payments, such as the payment of damages or the exchange of goods. Rarely does mediation occur without some notion of damages (Merry, 1982; Schwartz & Miller, 1964). In some instances the tangible object that is given symbolizes the repair of the relationship. The property or money agreed upon in the settlement is usually transferred immediately, decreasing the opportunity for further conflict because of noncompliance (Merry, 1982, pp. 29–30).

DIVORCE MEDIATION IN THE UNITED STATES

What implications does our knowledge of mediation in small-scale societies have for divorce mediation in the United States? It does not exist within the context of a cohesive community with a set of shared values and norms. In other societies, the mediator, disputants, and community members share the same notions of appropriate behavior and fairness. There is great heterogeneity in the United States in this regard, particularly relating to gender roles and child rearing. Whose norms and values are to be reflected in the mediation process and the settlement outcomes?

Members of a profession often share a set of values. Members of the legal community are aware of local settlement norms on divorce-related issues and can use that information in negotiations. Mental health professionals share a knowledge of human development and family functioning, despite differences in training and theoretical orientation. Mediators are drawn from both professions. Since family mediation is an emerging profession, a cohesive set of shared norms and values does not yet exist, although there are certain general values that many mediators appear to share. For example, mediators tend to favor coparenting (Coogler, 1978; Haynes, 1981; McKay, Rogers, Blades, & Gosse, 1984; Saposnek, 1983), believe that fault, guilt, and blame are inappropriate criteria for decision making (Coogler, 1978; Haynes, 1981), and incline toward economic independence of former spouses as a worthy goal (Coogler, 1978; Haynes, 1981).

These values are reflected in recent trends within the legal system as well as in the society. As changes in ideology, these trends were perhaps necessary preconditions for divorce mediation to develop as a social practice. Divorce mediators are not representing traditional values as mediators do in other societies but are reflecting values that have only recently gained cultural ascendancy and then only among certain segments of the population and within certain institutions.

In small-scale societies the community and the mediator exert pressure on the disputants to settle disputes and reestablish harmony. In divorce mediation, mediators also subtly or directly pressure clients toward agreement. One ramification of this is that mediating clients do not have a sense of community standards of fairness as part of the process. They must rely on their individual perceptions and information from the mediator about fairness or from the attorney about local settlement norms, reflecting legal bargaining.

In many societies where mediation is practiced, resolving the dispute amicably is more important than victory or establishing right or wrong. In United States culture, competition, winning, and individual gain are dominant cultural values. Compromise and accommodation are seen as weaknesses and are not positively valued, except in terms of the traditional view of women's role in the family. These value differences may be reflected in the findings of Pearson, Thoennes, and VanderKooi (1982), that women tend to choose mediation over an adversarial process because they like the values it reflects, whereas men choose it because they think they can maximize their own advantages. What are the possible consequences of these differences in motivation?

The cross-cultural literature indicates that mediation between people of unequal power tends to lead to agreements that reflect that inequality (Gulliver, 1963; Merry, 1982). The dimensions of power in divorce mediation relate partly to gender differences in areas of expertise, perceptions, skills, experience, and resources and partly to the bargaining endowments created by law, and the emotional dynamics of divorce (Friedberg & Girdner, 1984). Little is known at this point of the mediator's strategies and effectiveness in balancing power between divorcing couples.

Mediation is a disputing process that exists cross-culturally and has a long tradition in many societies. The trends in divorce mediation are to make the mediator role professional and the process private, in marked contrast to mediation in small-scale societies. This is understandable, however, considering the complexity and heterogeneity of United States society. Recognition of the similarities and differences between divorce mediation in the United States and mediation in small-scale societies can broaden the practitioner's understanding of mediation as a disputing process within its social context and the mediator as an actor within it.

REFERENCES

Collier, J. F. *Law and social change in Zinacantan.* Stanford, CA: Stanford University Press, 1973.

Coogler, O. J. *Structured mediation in divorce settlement: A handbook for marital mediators.* Lexington, MA: Heath, 1978.

Felstiner, W. Influences of social organization on dispute processing. *Law and Society Review,* 1974, *9(1),* 63–94.

Felstiner, W. Avoidance as dispute processing: An elaboration. *Law and Society Review,* 1975, *9(4),* 696–706.

Friedberg, P., & Girdner, L. K. *Sources of power applicable to divorce mediation.* Paper presented at the National Conference on Peacemaking and Conflict Resolution, St. Louis, MO, September 1984.

Galanter, M. Why the "haves" come out ahead: Speculations on the limits of legal changes. *Law and Society Review*, 1974, *9(1)*, 95–160.

Gibbs, J. R., Jr. The Kpelle moot: A therapeutic model for the informal settlement of disputes. *Africa*, 1963, *33(1)*, 1–11.

Girdner, L. K. Contested child custody cases: An examination of custom and family law in an American court. (Doctoral dissertation, American University, 1981). *Dissertation Abstracts International*, 1983, *43*, 08A.

Girdner, L. K. Adjudication and mediation: A comparison of custody decision-making processes involving third parties. *Journal of Divorce*, 1985, *8(4)*, 33–47.

Gulliver, P. H. *Social control in an African society*. Boston: Boston University Press, 1963.

Gulliver, P. H. *Disputes and negotiations: A cross-cultural perspective*. New York: Academic Press, 1979.

Haynes, J. M. *Divorce mediation: A practical guide for therapists and counselors*. New York: Springer, 1981.

Koch, K. F. Introduction. In K. F. Koch (Ed.), *Access to justice vol. IV The anthropological perspective. Patterns of Conflict Management: Essays in the Ethnography of Law* (pp. 1–16). Milan: Giuffre Editore, 1979.

Kressel, K., Jaffee, N., Tuchman, B., Watson, C., & Deutsch, M. The typology of divorcing couples: Implications for mediation and the divorce process. *Family Process*, 1980, *19(2)*, 101–116.

McKay, M., Rogers, P. D., Blades, J., & Gosse, R. *The divorce book*. Oakland, CA: New Harbinger, 1984.

Merry, S. E. The social organization of mediation in nonindustrial societies: Implications for informal community justice in America. In R. Abel (Ed.), *The politics of informal justice: Vol. 2: Comparative studies* (pp. 17–45). New York: Academic Press, 1982.

Mnookin, R. H., & Kornhauser, L. Bargaining in the shadow of the law: The case of divorce. *Yale Law Journal*, 1979, *88(5)*, 950–997.

Nader, L. Forums of justice: A cross-cultural perspective. *Journal of Social Issues*, 1975, *31(3)*, 151–170.

Nader, L., & Todd, H. F., Jr. Introduction. In L. Nader & H. F. Todd, Jr. (Eds.), *The disputing process—Law in ten societies* (pp. 1–40). New York: Columbia University Press, 1978.

Pearson, J., Thoennes, N., & Vanderkooi, L. The decision to mediate: Profiles of individuals who accept and reject the opportunity to mediate contested child custody and visitation issues. *Journal of Divorce*, 1982, *6(1–2)*, 17–35.

Pitt-Rivers, J. The kith and the kin. In J. Goody (Ed.), *The character of kinship* (pp. 89–105). New York: Cambridge University Press, 1975.

Saposnek, D. T. *Mediating child custody disputes*. San Francisco: Jossey-Bass, 1983.

Schlegel, S. A. *Tiruray justice: Traditional Tiruray law and morality*. Berkeley, CA: University of California Press, 1970.

Schwartz, R. D., & Miller, J. D. Legal evolution and society complexity. *American Journal of Sociology*, 1964, *70*, 159–169.

Witty, C. J. *Mediation and society: Conflict management in Lebanon*. New York: Academic Press, 1980.

PART TWO

DIVORCE MEDIATION THEORY AND DIMENSIONS

4

A General Theory of Divorce Mediation

ALISON TAYLOR

Consultant, Clackamas County Family Court; Private Practice, Hillsboro, Oregon

The diversity of divorce mediation may create the impression that it is a practice in search of a theory. In this chapter, the author provides a general theory of mediation as a set of stages. She offers a systematic analysis of the goals, tasks, and skills applicable to each stage, as well as the interrelation of the stages. A conceptual framework is integrated with a step-by-step description of what the mediator must do and how to do it.

DEFINITIONS AND USES

Mediation is a process for conflict resolution or conflict management; an alternative to violence, self-help, or litigation, it is different from the processes of counseling, negotiation, and arbitration. In the mediation process the participants, with the help of an impartial mediator (or team of mediators), systematically identify disputed issues, develop and consider options, and make choices, to reach consensual agreements that will realistically meet the participants' needs and concerns. Mediation is a self-empowering process that emphasizes the participants' responsibility for making decisions that affect their lives (Folberg & Taylor, 1984).

The mediation process can be defined by a description of predictable stages that include a series of techniques for accomplishing necessary tasks (Taylor, 1981). It is a finite process that produces specific outcomes, using the values, norms, and principles of the participants rather than those of the neutral third-party mediator. The goals of mediation are (1) to reduce, resolve, or manage conflicts and (2) to make appropriate decisions. Mediation includes the following objectives:

1. to reduce the anxiety and other negative effects of the conflict by helping the participants reach a consensual resolution

2. to prepare the participants to accept the consequences of their decisions

3. to produce an agreement or plan that the participants can accept and with which they will comply

4. to focus on the specifics of how the participants will reduce and resolve the conflict, rather than what causal factors led to the conflict

The participants' personalities and behaviors (including manipulation, overt anger, withdrawal, and power struggles), which may have created the interactional problem, may be identified and discussed during mediation, but they are not the primary focus. Mediation is concerned more with the present and future than with the past.

Before discussing mediation, it is helpful to examine the fundamental principles of conflict. Conflict, whether between individuals, groups, or nations, has certain basic features and a definable sequence. Conflict can be divided into two categories; intrapersonal and interpersonal. The causes and effects of intrapersonal conflict are most often addressed through counseling rather than the mediation process. The counseling process requires that the counselor establish a rapport with the conflicted person, assess the intrapersonal problems, and apply an intervention strategy that is based on some therapeutic model or psychological principle.

Mediation is primarily concerned with interpersonal conflict, those disputes that arise between individuals or groups of individuals. Although the issues or options that are discussed during mediation may trigger internal conflicts for participants, it is not the job of the mediator to delve into the realm of intrapersonal conflicts unless such conflicts affect the resolution of issues and options.

A comprehensive analysis of conflict has been offered by R. J. Rummel (1976), who describes conflict as "the process of powers meeting and balancing" (p. 238). Rummel views conflict as a continuing spiral, set into motion by change and shaped by the type of power or society in which it is manifested. In this view, conflict is inevitable. Resolving conflicts requires the use of coercive or noncoercive means to balance the power between conflicted parties or entities. Rummel further points out that the wish to eliminate all levels of conflict is a desire for a state of unchanging, static balance, which is not common in the natural world and perhaps not even desirable. Mediators ought to convey this to participants to reduce their feelings of guilt and frustration about being involved in a conflict situation and to legitimize the need for change.

Morton Deutsch's analysis of conflict offers a conceptualization that is useful in understanding the development and application of mediation (1973). He describes manifest conflict as overt or expressed, whereas underlying conflict is implicit, hidden, or denied. Manifest conflict often involves symbolic components of the underlying conflict but is felt or perceived to be "safer" by one or more of the participants. Mediators must sort out which issues are manifest and which are underlying, to develop effective options and outcomes during the mediation process.

Deutsch (1973) also points out that the outcome of conflict is one of three dichotomies: mutual loss (lose–lose); gain for one and loss for the other (lose–win); or mutual gain (win–win). Mediation has a distinct advantage over some other methods of conflict resolution because it promotes a win–win outcome.

It is most helpful to see conflict as a set of divergent aims, methods, or behaviors. The degree of divergency is a determining factor in the severity and duration of the conflict and in the likelihood of successful conflict resolution. Conflict resolution and management are processes designed to realign those divergent aims, methods or behaviors. While conflict resolution creates a state of uniformity or convergency of purpose or means, conflict management merely blunts or realigns the divergence. Conflict management does not require that each participant give up individual perceptions and resolve the dispute by creating identical aims, methods, or processes. It simply requires that both participants create agreements that are aligned and sufficiently coordinated to allow unobstructed progress.

Mediation includes conflict resolution and conflict management. Divorce mediators must assess on a case-by-case basis whether the goal for a particular couple is conflict resolution or conflict management. Conflict management may be an appropriate and adequate goal for divorcing spouses, although conflict resolution might be the ideal condition. Mediators may not be able to help all participants resolve their differences but may be able to help them realign their positions to reduce the harmful effects of a continued conflict. Both conflict management and conflict resolution lead to a balanced, but temporary, state between the participants.

In summary, conflict resolution provides convergence, whereas conflict management produces realignment sufficient to render cooperation and does not require total unity. The most desirable conflict resolution and management methods are noncoercive, and address both manifest and underlying conflicts, to prolong the state of equilibrium.

THE MEDIATION PROCESS

The mediation process can best be described as a set of stages (Moore, 1983; Folberg & Taylor, 1984). These stages are illustrated in Figure 4-1. Each stage in the mediation process has its goals and tasks, as well as methodology and skills. The mediator must often change the dimension of his or her role within any given stage of the mediation process. Progress from session to session may include minor variations from the universal process, because of the unique circumstances of the case. Participants may not be ready emotionally to move from one stage to the other. They may need to return to earlier stages or may reverse the stages because of preexisting conditions, the requirements of the particular jurisdiction in which they reside, or the policies and procedures of the agency or individual serving the parties. Despite tailoring to individual needs, all stages should be addressed, since each is necessary for completion of the mediation process.

Stage 1: Introduction—Creating Structure and Trust

The introductory stage is vital to the establishment of a relationship that will facilitate the rest of the mediation process. Creating a therapeutic relationship

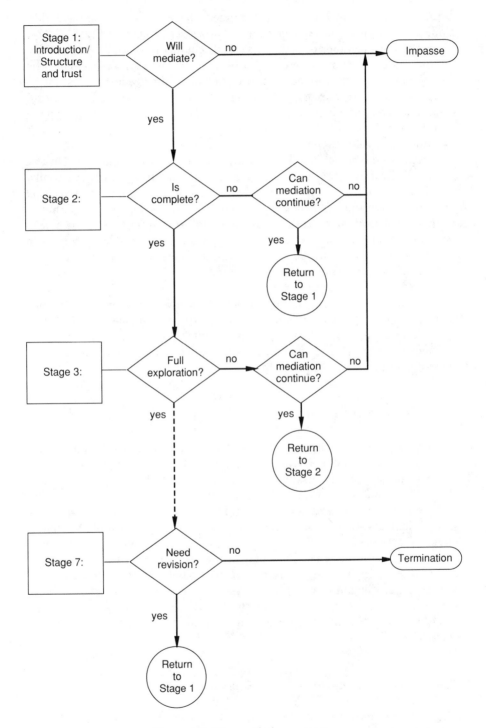

Figure 4-1. The mediation process.

is not a goal of this stage, as it is with counseling. Sufficient confidence and rapport between the mediator and participants, however, is necessary to successful mediation. Because divorce issues and conflict cut across a participant's self-concept as a sexual being, an economic provider, a parent, and a member of a larger community, most of the information the mediator elicits and helps order is very threatening. If the mediator has enough rapport and has gained enough trust, the participants will be better able to bring out and discuss these very personal issues.

This stage is used to gather relevant information about the participants' perceptions of the conflict, their goals and expectations, and the conflict situation. Data that should be gathered includes

1. the participants' motivation to use mediation
2. the immediate background and precipitating event(s) to the conflict
3. the interactional and communication styles of the participants
4. the present emotional state of the participants
5. the arrangements for attorney involvement and/or legal formalization of the agreement
6. the presenting problem or conflict as opposed to the hidden agenda or underlying conflicts
7. immediate safety and security concerns for participants and their dependents

The following sequence helps elicit the needed information and serves as a guide to the mediator for facilitating this first stage.

Sequence	*Data Obtained*
Brief introductions and seating	Nonverbal impression
Preparatory statement by mediator (repeated if one participant is late)	Present emotional state of participants and legal processes
Confirm case data	Immediate past and precipitating events; extra-participant involvement
Review guidelines	Interactional style; emotional state
Handover of communication to participants	Interactional and communication styles; emotional state
Discuss expectations	The presenting problem or conflict versus any hidden agendas and conflicts
Review and sign an agreement to mediate and pay fees	The participants' motivation
Distribute and discuss financial worksheets or handouts	Immediate safety and security concerns
Trade mutual assurances	Needs and willingness to provide concrete help
Homework of additional data, tasks	Abilities to carry through

As can be seen from this chart, the mediator is both acting and presenting, and receiving and evaluating the participants' responses. The participants begin to understand the structure of the mediation process and determine that the mediator is trustworthy and neutral when the mediator limits small talk, ensures a comfortable physical setting for mediation with appropriate spatial arrangements, and reviews the explicit expectations for participants and the mediator in the session. It is important to allow adequate time for each participant to present his or her view of the situation. A definitive verbal signal from the mediator, termed here a *handover* to the participant, indicates a need for that participant to become an active part of the communication patterns.

In this beginning stage, most conversation will flow between the mediator and each participant, forming a V-shaped pattern of communication. To ensure that participants have adequate time to present their sides of the situation, some mediators rely on a protocol that requires that the complainant (the person who brought the issue to mediation) should be the first one to tell the story. Other mediators prefer to start off involving the least active participant, the one with whom they have had less contact, or the one who has been coerced or mandated to the mediation process. By starting with the complainant, the mediator reassures that person that they will be heard. Starting with the least active or lesser known person confirms lack of bias created by prior contact or intimidating style. Allowing the first statement to come from the mandated participant can diffuse the usual mixture of anger and sullen resentment that person often feels.

The mediator's preparatory statement or discussion of the mediation rules or guidelines should make clear to the participants that the mediator will not make substantive decisions but that he or she is responsible for control of the session. In this stage of mediation, such information is conveyed not only by written rules, contracts, and verbal discussion, but also through judicious use of nonverbal indicators of authority and control. This stage is over when the mediator's picture of the nature of the manifest and underlying issues in the case is complete. The participants should now have a clear understanding of mediation and be able to determine if they wish to commit to the process. For most private practitioners, this commitment is in the form of an employment agreement or an agreement to mediate.

Stage 2: Fact-Finding and Isolation of Issues

Before good decisions can be reached, both participants must have equal information and must fully understand which issues are open to being resolved or managed. The mediator helps the participants find out where the conflicts really lie and which areas have yet to be discussed. Divorce requires decisions about the future, including finances, property, plans for the children, support, legal processes, and relationships. The specific content and issues in these areas must be organized and discussed.

Factors that can help the mediator organize and discuss issues can be divided into four categories: (1) the immediacy of the conflictual issue, (2) the duration of the conflictual issue, (3) the intensity of feelings about the conflictual issue, and (4) the expressed and perceived rigidity of positions.

The intrapersonal and interpersonal dimensions of these conflicts must be separated at this point. The task of this stage of mediation is to provide a safe place for the participants to set aside personal defenses and for the underlying issues to surface. Often this requires that the mediator reframe the dispute to explore the underlying interests or fracture the dispute into smaller, manageable pieces that can form the components for later agreements and plans. The participants must raise the issues. The mediator helps raise issues and more clearly define, reframe, and redirect them.

The mediator can assist by using communication skills such as open-ended questions, summary, prioritizing, reflection, and clarification. Table 4-1 lists the types and functions of questions.

Because mediators may be held legally and ethically responsible for the assurance of complete disclosure and discussion, it is advisable for the mediator to use a worksheet to write the participants' starting positions on issues and, in later stages, mutually made decisions. The mediator must take the raw information the participants provide and form this into a constructive, usable concept or coherent set of concerns. This requires that the mediator connect disparate bits of information into a comprehensive package of disputes and agreements. To accomplish this, the mediator must use an associative, rather

Table 4-1. Using Questions in Mediation

Goals	Type of question	Best time to use	Reaction by respondent
Keep a reticent client talking	Open	Beginning of session, when participants are silent	Will usually comply
Establish parameters of situation	Open	During early questioning	Will feel empowered
Pinpoint specific information	Closed	Later fact-finding; during review of agreement	Can stop easy flow of conversation as client waits for next question
Get an acknowledgment	Yes/no	During review of agreement	If sensitive issue, anger and nervousness, or withdrawal
Heighten the negative judgment	Either/or	During negotiations concerning options	A (skewed) answer
Frustrate, embarrass, or discredit	Either/or	As a paradoxical intervention during fact-finding	Anger; silence
Redirect conversation	Open, preceded by directive statement	Middle of interview	May produce startled reaction but will change conversation pattern

than a linear, thought process. For example, if a participant is telling why he must have custody and then seems to switch into a discussion of transportation, the associatively thinking mediator will pursue a line of questioning to help clarify in what way these two things are connected for the participant, rather than just redirecting and dealing only with one subject until it is done. Since the major task at this stage is the reduction of information into definable issues, the mediator must use all the available skills and techniques in order to keep the participants involved (see Folberg & Taylor [1984] for a more complete discussion of verbal and nonverbal skills for mediators).

Forcing the participants to divulge underlying conflicts is anxiety producing for them and hard work for the mediator. The mediator is likely to encounter some level of resistance from one or both of the participants during this stage of the mediation process. Participants may become defensive and resist, stating to the mediator that all the problems and conflicts have been resolved, that they cannot or will not discuss the past, that they have supplied complete information (although they are actually withholding some), and that their attorney will handle the issue. Often this resistance is not expressed openly but surfaces as a specific action or inaction by the participants during the session. Examples of these actions are emotional and verbal withdrawal, verbal battles for dominance, unexpected rescheduling or cancellation of a session, arriving late or inebriated, and refusing or failing to do an assigned task, such as completing a worksheet.

The resistance a mediator sees is only a mirror of the issues that must be resolved or managed during all stages of the mediation process. The mediator should not allow resistant behaviors to evoke an emotional response or take them as a sign of personal failure. As a general rule, such resistance should be discussed openly in private session before returning to the other substantive conflicts. By doing this, mediators directly confront the participant in a way that the other participant has never felt capable of doing. Because it is done at this time, the person may be more receptive to changing, or at least acknowledging, the resistant behaviors. Meanwhile, the other person is able to see an effective model of confrontation that helps rather than makes the situation worse. The outcome is more discussion of understanding issues. If the resistance continues, the mediator should adhere strictly to any previously accepted rules about impasses and termination.

The mediator should try to refocus the discussion, whenever possible, rather than call an impasse. A decision to suspend mediation and declare an impasse may be made at this time, should one or both of the participants remain adamant despite good efforts by the mediator to reduce resistance. Allowing mediation to continue if one participant remains obstructive is an unproductive waste of time and money for both participants, and frustrating for the one who is active and open.

Stage 2 ends when the mediator knows where the disagreements and conflicts lie, what the underlying and manifest conflicts are, and what each participant wants or will not accept under any circumstance. Before moving to the next stage, the mediator should ask, "Is my understanding of the issues complete?" This stage may take several sessions or only part of a session, depending upon the openness of the participants, the amount of personal threat to the self-concept inherent in the underlying conflict, and the skill of the mediator.

In addition to completeness, the mediator must also assess realistic, case-specific goals. Although the goal of mediation is the resolution or management of the manifest conflicts, a case-specific goal may be to bring about a personal awareness of internal, underlying conflicts that impinge on the mediation process. Other appropriate case-specific goals might include cognitive consensus on a certain point and the reduction of certain self-defeating affective or emotional responses.

The goal of a couple disputing custody might be the reduction or cessation of behaviors that continue to disrupt the child's life. The case-specific goal might be to create limits, to stop an overbearing attitude and verbal intimidation, or to create a more equal power structure between the parents during the mediation session, which will carry over into their future parenting of the child. Another case-specific goal might be to reduce the amount of disruption to the child's education through agreeing by conceptual consensus that the parents will not move during a school year or during the remainder of high school.

Such case-specific goals should not be based upon the mediator's value structure. They should be taken from the participants' desires and perceptions that have been communicated to the mediator, often indirectly, during each participant's opening statements and later discussion of the issues. The mediator must know by this time which goals are consistent with each participant's worldview and personality structure. Mediation during this stage can dissolve into rather random questions and answers, unstructured and unguided, unless a knowledgable mediator helps the participants see the areas of agreement and individual priorities.

Stage 3: Creation of Options and Alternatives

Stage 3 asks the basic question, "How can you do what you want to do in the most effective way?" Both participants must be actively involved in finding the answers to this question. After going over the worksheets or notes made during the earlier stages, the mediator needs to review the open issues. Sometimes the answer to the above question rests upon the solution to the most basic or highest priority issue. For example, how to divide property such as a house may depend on the higher priority issue of the custody plan for the children. The "domino effect" created by ordering priorities can be maximized by a skillful mediator who brings the participants to an awareness of which issue is the stumbling block. When a stumbling block is identified, the mediator must focus both participants' attention on creating realistic and workable options for resolving or managing that issue. Mediation skills are the same for all stages: well-timed questions and reflections.

The tasks of Stage 3 are (1) to help the participants articulate the options they know or want and (2) to develop new options that may be more satisfactory. The mediator's role must reflect this duality: the mediator must be a facilitator for the first task and a creator or synthesizer for the second. It is important to keep both in balance, since a mediator who produces too many new options too fast will inhibit the expression of the participants' views. To reduce this task, some mediators find it helpful to list all the options that come to the attention of the participants before brainstorming additional options. Brainstorming, either during the mediation session or as homework, can be a useful tool for accomplishing the first task of this stage. Some mediators use forms to list the most likely options, for visual evaluation by participants. Several cases have found the matrices by Janis and Mann (1977) to be a helpful tool. These matrices help clients evaluate different options on the basis of criteria and the gain or loss for themselves or others if the option were selected. Mediators may want to use their own adaptation of such decision-making forms. To help participants who have become confused by possible options and alternatives, each option can be written onto each form; then the discussion can be limited to each form separately and sequentially.

After a brief review of the open issues, any options that have been mentioned during a participant's opening statements should be listed. The mediator should remind the participants of the criteria that might be used to evaluate options. The following list provides some general criteria for developing and evaluating the effectiveness of options and alternatives that are mentioned by the participants and mediator:

1. needs of the participants and others who will be affected by the decision
2. projections of the past into the future (likely predictions)
3. general economic and social forecasts that may affect an option
4. legal and financial roadblocks and limitations
5. anticipations of new people and new situations
6. predictable changes in any of the above

Mediators may want to suggest criteria and help the participants use them effectively in developing options. Rephrasing these criteria into "what if" scenarios may be helpful to participants in evaluating options. Mediators help participants project themselves into the future by using this technique.

When the participants are emotionally and psychologically ready, a trial period can be used to determine the practicality of a particular option, before a final decision is made. When trial periods are used, both participants are able to experience the consequences of that option. This is particularly effective when one participant has rejected an option because he or she believes that it will not work. The terms of a trial period should be written, including the starting and ending dates, the specific contingencies for continuation, and most important, that implementation of the trial period will not prejudice any future decisions.

Stage 3 of the mediation process is the most creative and active stage for the mediator. The mediator's role during this stage is vastly different from the nondirective, nonauthoritarian role espoused by many counselors and the highly authoritarian role of a traditional attorney acting as advocate for the client. The mediator is a resource person, an expert who suggests new options based on more extensive knowledge of the subject in conflict. The mediator may also offer information regarding the availability or statistical success of certain options. In states where custody laws require a presumption or preference for joint custody, the mediator may want to provide information about various joint custody arrangements and the success and family satisfaction of such options. Options offered by the mediator must be delivered in a manner that participants can comfortably accept or reject. The participants should not be pressured by the mediator to consider any particular option, nor should they be persuaded to use a trial period that they do not see as beneficial.

The mediator often feels a strong need for completion and closure. The mediator who ties self-worth to the selection of a particular option will be an ineffective facilitator. Coercion, favoritism, and bias should not be allowed. A mediator should be aware of the ethical responsibilities of the role when providing new insight and guiding the participants (Folberg & Taylor, 1984).

Mediation proceeds to the next stage when there has been full exploration of all options, without prejudice and judgmental attitudes. Options and alternatives are often conglomerate; they pull together several issues. High-priority issues, such as legal and physical custody, to some extent determine other issues, such as child support or visitation plans; decisions made on priority issues can prefigure other contingent issues. Saying yes to one thing automatically means saying no to something else. It is important for mediators to make participants aware of the connections between issues.

Stage 4: Negotiation and Decision Making

At this point in the mediation process participants select one or more options from those generated earlier. The option selected must be something both participants can live with, even if it is not what either participant originally wanted. Mediators must encourage the participants to take the risky step to decide, to make choices, and to compromise or give in on some of the smaller items. This cooperative effort is more likely to bring about the final outcome that the participants want. If the mediator has helped the participants deal successfully with each case-specific goal, the overall goal of resolution of conflict will be reached.

Having several options that seem workable will not necessarily help the participants make a selection. Often the development of several options during Stage 3 only confuses the participants. Most people can mentally manipulate only a small number of variables. One way the participants can try to get closer to making a decision is by bargaining, a simple form of negotiation. This can take the form of horse-trading or "this for that," simple exchanges of desirable features or options, similar to what a person does in the marketplace or in economic bargaining. The basic messages conveyed during bargaining are, "What is it you want (or don't want) the most?" or "What is it worth to you to have X?"

Most people in mediation, when confronted with a display of options, need to reduce them to a smaller number. Participants in mediation often do not have a preset start position, come-down position, and final limit, as they would if they were involved in traditional negotiation. Indeed, part of the function of the mediator during this stage is to help the participants avoid positional bargaining and use a softer negotiation style, such as the principled negotiations described by Fisher and Ury (1981). Often participants can rule out certain options immediately, based on their perception of what is necessary or what is practical. They are left with some options that cannot be ruled out but that must be negotiated between them.

If one participant cannot get the other to agree to a favored option, mutual agreement may eliminate both persons' preferred option, since they realize that neither will select the other's. This reduction leaves the couple with those options developed during Stage 3. Sometimes this elimination process is not as easy as the sequence implies. The mediator's task is to reframe this bargaining and negotiation into a question to ask each participant, "Which option will best meet everyone's needs?" Mediators should move the participants from a competitive negotiation process to a more cooperative interaction. This is often done by getting cognitive consensus on fundamental principles that are then applied to the particular situation.

During Stage 4 the mediator must reduce his or her involvement and change the communication pattern. Instead of responding primarily to the mediator, the participants must now communicate directly with each other. To accomplish this conversational switch, the mediator can make specific suggestions to the participants to help them evaluate an option. The mediator can clarify the goal and remind the participants of the procedures they can follow to get to that goal. The mediator supplies the technique, but the participants should be doing the conversing and exploration. During this stage of mediation, the mediator's role is an agent of reality, someone who makes the participants doubt the assumptions and firmness of their original positions or perceptions.

Instead of undermining or blocking this "talking-out," the mediator amplifies it through reflection, clarification, and simple questions. The mediator listens and acts as a process observer and monitor who periodically intervenes in the exchange, to question the practicality or advisability of the option and to prevent coercion during negotiations. During this stage, the mediator must be aware of the content being discussed and the process being used by the participants to arrive at a decision. The mediator should help the participants by drawing them back to their fears, hopes, and expectations, which were originally stated shortly after the handover in Stage 1. These can also be brought out by techniques of reflection, summary, and clarification. The mediator starts the interchange between the participants and monitors it so that each person has a chance to talk, can make offers and consider them, and can communicate without undue pressure, coercion, or harassment. Each participant must have the opportunity to understand the other's perspective in evaluating the importance of a certain option. Each must feel that his or her perspective is understood by the other.

To help the participants carry on this principled style of negotiation, as opposed to positional bargaining, the mediator must direct them away from their original opening statements and help the parties develop objective criteria for decisions. Deciding to take the average of two independent appraisals is a principled way of reaching a decision, as compared to arguing over what the price should be. The mediator should point out gains made by the participants in agreeing to a fair standard and procedure and may reiterate the consequence of delay in decision making.

Maintaining some sort of equality in communication during this important negotiation stage is essential, so that a verbose participant does not stifle the expression or preference of a more quiet or passive participant. In this way, decision making is protected from becoming self-defeating or manipulative; decisions are made by an active, cognitive process rather than out of frustration or a need for emotional closure. In order to equalize communication, the mediator may have to be quite controlling and may want to use directive statements such as, "Tell us what you think, Jim," or reflections such as, "Elaine, you've said all along how happy you'd feel if you could find a way out of this problem." Verbally reinforcing the participants is also helpful.

Another method that often works to explain a participant's resistance to a particular option is to highlight the objection and acknowledge the right to have such conflicts. Using this method, the mediator can ask each participant to imagine the worst possible scenario that could happen, should the couple select that particular option. This is then scrutinized with help from the mediator's role as agent of reality. For example, a custody dispute may be stalled after developing three options: sole custody for the father, sole custody for the mother, or joint legal and physical custody. If the mother is violently opposed to the father's sole custody, she should be encouraged to project the negative consequences of this option, since it will allow her to say her underlying fears and give the mediator a chance to question her projections.

Direct confrontation by the mediator is sometimes necessary to activate decisions. The mediator can acknowledge the block to decision making and give his or her view of the resistance to such a decision. Confrontational techniques must be used in such a way that the participant clearly understands them to be directed toward the lack of progress in the mediation process, not toward the people. Guilt and shame should not be used to motivate movement during a session; a realistic assessment of resistances and consequences is a more productive approach. Another method that sometimes works to motivate a decision is arbitrarily withdrawing the power to choose from the resistant participant. The mediator may pretend to deny access to the decision by declaring an impasse or suggesting that the matter must go to arbitration or to the court because the participants cannot decide. Since the mediation process provides far more empowerment for the participants, they will often jump to recover their right to choose for themselves if they fear its loss. Another variation of this method is to normalize the participant's right to block decision making. A paradoxical intervention by the mediator provides the participant with a rationale for the indecision. The mediator could say, "You shouldn't try to make a choice right now. You should wait until you are sure, and continue as you are currently doing until then." The paradox is that suggesting or even demanding that no choice be made yet legitimizes the person's right to be ambivalent and therefore gives him or her reverse permission, as well as a needed sense of control. Most participants will voluntarily move toward a choice when this method is used; they need to feel that control before they give it away by accepting an option they perceive as belonging to the other participant. It is important, however, that mediators use such paradoxical interventions cautiously, only as a last resort.

Throwing the weight and responsibility for a decision back on the participants can temporarily block progress, even if the participants are willing to make a choice. Yet it is important to reconfirm that it is the participants who must not only make, but live with, the choices. A way of softening this often overwhelming responsibility is to remind the participants that they have already determined a process for future conflict resolution, should their current decisions not work. They can and should change their agreements when those decisions are no longer useful, with the exception of certain legal decisions, such as property division, that cannot be changed after the divorce is finalized.

Often participants during Stage 4 will ask the mediator's opinion or advice on which option to select. This is a difficult moment for mediators, who should not tell participants what to do. While mediators cannot make decisions for participants, they can remind participants of the sociological and statistical data about the options. Mediators in this situation have often reminded disputants of community norms or values; however, this must be done in a nonjudgmental manner. The response to such an inquiry can either augment or break down rapport between the mediator and the participants. Mediators should avoid responses such as "I'm sorry I can't advise you on this, you must make your own choice,' which tend to break down rapport and support of the participants. It is far better to say, "Well, I remember you saying earlier that you wanted to [minimize disruption, maintain contact, etc.], and it seems as if this option [could, could not] promote that."

Readiness for decision making is an important and personal thing. Sometimes it requires the reduction of perceptual errors or internal conflicts, sometimes merely an added bit of cognitive information, and sometimes just enough time to create a change in individual development and maturation. Before proceeding with this stage, mediators should assess and evaluate the readiness of each participant to make decisions and should be aware of the alternatives for dealing with participants who are not yet ready. A referral to counseling or other community resource may be needed. Often concurrent services, such as counseling or career development programs, can ease the decision-making process. The question that must be answered affirmatively by the participants is, *Have all choices been made for all issues?* If the answer to that question is no, the mediator may offer to return to an earlier stage of mediation, either to create new options or to make more decisions (see Figure 4-1). Four options are available to the mediator at this point: return to an earlier stage, referral for adjunctive services, declaration of impasse, or termination of the case. It is hoped that mediators will be skilled in reducing resistance so that most mediations move into the next stage and that mediators lacking in skill will not blame the clients for an impasse. By this stage all but the most manipulative or unwilling participants will have invested enough time and energy in the mediation process to motivate them to continue. It is the mediator's responsibility to determine under what conditions that process will continue.

Stage 5: Clarification: Writing a Plan

Most participants will be able to make choices and select options during Stage 4. The function of Stage 5 is to produce a document, a mediated plan, that clearly outlines the participants' intentions and decisions. This document should define the current decisions and anticipated behavior. It should be drawn up in a written form that the participants can easily read and review and should constitute a working document for the participants' purposes. It should be complex enough to cover most probable contingencies. This document can be used by the participants in the next stage of the mediation process. It can be modified in response to the inevitable changes that occur over time.

Usually the mediator organizes, records, and accurately reflects the decisions reached during the mediation sessions. The participants, separately or jointly, may need to use their own words so that the agreement accurately reflects their understanding of the verbal agreement. This should be submitted to the mediator before writing the mediated plan or can be discussed during a session. Using the participants' own wording makes the document more meaningful and relevant. When participants are highly motivated and literate, the mediator may want to supply a model that they can use for the agreement. Allowing participants to write their plan separately will forestall passive-aggressive behaviors and many revisions. Writing their own plan may not, however, be appropriate for participants who want to "wrap it up quickly" as a way of ending their internal tension and conflict. It is also not appropriate to request this type of cooperation and responsibility when one or more of the participants would be overwhelmed because of lack of skills or when the power dynamics between the participants are such that they would compete with each other over whose version is acceptable.

Copies of the proposed mediated plan should be given to the participants to review before the next session. Underlying conflicts that have not been adequately resolved in earlier stages of mediation often surface when the mediated plan is discussed; they are often presented as a manifest conflict over the wording of a section that addresses the underlying conflict. Getting the participant to articulate the specific objection to the wording and at the same time determining the underlying conflict are hard work for the mediator. It requires the use of such skills as reflection, summary, and open-ended questions. Most participants feel relieved at this stage and need verbal reassurance that they have produced an accurate document that reflects their needs. Participants may need to make word changes to feel a sense of ownership of the document. The mediator should be prepared to revise the document immediately upon the parties' review or have the proposed mediated plan retyped and ready for signing within a day or two of the session. Participants as well as mediators often have a strong urge for closure at this point. Mediators, however, must not take on the responsibility for producing the final synthesis. The participants themselves must see that the mediator has no interest in the outcome of mediation beyond a professional duty to facilitate the session.

The signing of the mediated plan or agreement is a symbolic act that carries great meaning for the participants. Mediators may want to mark and enrich this by using some ritual or special behavior. A toast to the hard work and success of the participants in coming to consensual resolution may be appropriate and can start their living the agreement on a positive note. The mediated plan is a symbol of cooperation and closure and should reflect the present and the future. If one of the participants is still involved in the grief–loss process and is mourning the demise of the marital relationship, the mediated plan should be framed positively, but less joyfully; that participant may need referral to a support group.

Stage 6: Legal Review and Processing

The legal process is necessary when the conflicts being mediated must be connected to larger social systems and institutions, as occurs with divorce. Stages 6 and 7 are contingent upon forces external to the mediation process; power, control, and responsibility are no longer entirely in the hands of the participants and the mediator. Legal review or processing serves as a watchdog to the earlier stages by passing the agreements through socially accepted processes that check and sanctify the mediated agreement. This provides the participants with a stronger sense of closure and commitment. It also allows a brief respite form the stressful task of developing options and making choices. It gives participants a chance to gain useful input from others who will critique the agreement's completeness and feasibility.

Divorce mediation cases are subject to two types of legal review: by a private attorney before submission to the court and by a judge with a request that the mediated plan be made a part of the decree of dissolution, so that it can more easily be enforced by the court should either of the participants violate the terms of the mediated agreement. Review by either or both sources can help identify new issues or options that can be handled by further mediation or by more traditional legal processes. In other words, if a participant's attorney advises reconsideration on a specific issue, that issue can be mediated again while leaving the other items as agreed and written. This is preferable, from the participants' standpoint, to litigating the issue, which usually halts any acceptance of other agreements that have been mediated.

Legal review by independent counsel may be conducted at any point during the mediation process. Many private attorneys prefer to see any proposed mediated plan before their clients sign it. Some lawyers prefer that their clients leave all financial issues for attorney-assisted negotiation or litigation but are pleased to have their clients mediate custody issues and schedules. Mediators should make it clear, in any case, that legal review can add to the participants' understanding of the relevant issues and options.

In some states the ethical requirements of the bar association prohibit an attorney from representing both parties to a divorce. Participants in mediation who wish to hire the services of only one attorney may have to decide who will receive such legal representation. Each participant may hire an attorney to review the mediated plan with that participant's best interests in mind, regardless of which attorney appears in court. Mediators of divorce disputes should review with an attorney the state bar ethics and opinions in order to more fully understand legal review options in their state. If the mediator (or a member of the mediation team) is an attorney, the function and role that mediator will take regarding legal review should be clarified in Stage 1 and reconfirmed in the agreement to mediate. The participants should understand clearly whether the attorney–mediator is advising both of them and whether he or she can later represent either of the participants in a related matter.

Review by the court adds dimension to legal review. Submitting the mediated plan to the court for its ratification and approval lends additional support and enforceability of the mediated plan. Mediators should check local state laws and court rules regarding the formal requirements for submission of mediated plans as part of a total marital settlement agreement. Self-help materials are available for those who cannot or will not go to an attorney first.

Legal processing can be defined as the submission of all necessary forms in the proper format and the payment of fees to complete the review and subsequent ratification by the court. Mediators who refer mediation participants to self-help materials must be very cautious. Since it may be considered the unauthorized practice of law to discuss *how* to fill out such self-help forms, mediators are well advised to avoid such charges by limiting discussion to general terms and alternatives. Mediators have a responsibility to help mediation participants understand the alternatives for legal review and legal processing and help them make appropriate decisions. Mediators should translate legal terminology, such as petition, order, and dissolution, to lay language.

Any decisions that participants reach regarding the legal review and processing of their mediated plan should be stated within the mediated plan itself. These need not be commitments but may be intentions, such as, "It is Jim's intention to hire a lawyer to review the mediated plan before its signing." Mediators may want to educate local judges and laywers regarding the dimension and limitation of the mediated plans. Mediators can protect themselves against charges of unauthorized practice of law by clarifying to attorneys and participants the difference between a mediated plan, which is usually not in legal form, and a marital settlement agreement, which conforms to the requirements of the court and which the participants may submit to the court.

Stage 7: Implementation, Review, and Revision

During the final stage of mediation the participants are trying to implement the terms of the mediated plan. As with Stage 6, this stages takes place outside the confines of the mediation session and does not demand the active, continuous involvement of the mediator. Although this stage relies on the participants, the mediator has a dynamic, though indirect, role. The important process of *follow-up* begins, initiated either by the mediator or by the participants, who may need further help.

During the first few weeks and months following the signing of the mediated plan, the participants are trying to actualize what was only conjectured and idealized before. It is a difficult time at best. Although they may intend to follow the agreement as it was written, the participants' abilities to match those intentions may have been suddenly and drastically altered. Unforeseen problems may arise, stemming either from the fluidity of the divorce context or from the introduction of external factors beyond the parties' control. Additionally, some families are in the process of further reconstruction when remarriage, cohabitation, or residence with the participants' parent affects the extended family. Participants who have been receiving additional counseling and therapy services may be making personal growth which directly affects their ability or desire to live by the previously agreed-upon terms. Similarly, unresolved underlying conflicts may threaten the mediated plan during the implementation stage.

Printed materials that educate the participants about common problems and difficulties can be provided when the mediated plan is signed. These can prevent or alleviate some predictable problems. The mediator is the only professional many participants will see about the issues, either because of their limited time, money, or attitudes. When problems occur during implementation, many participants prefer to talk to the mediator rather than starting over with another helping professional.

Routine follow-up initiated by the mediator at specific intervals can put out brushfires of discontent and provide positive reinforcement for the continuation of the mediated plan. Follow-up can take the form of phone calls, letters, or personal contact initiated by the mediator. A participant experiencing some level of discontent with the mediated plan can also initiate follow-up procedures. Follow-up contacts can help the participants clarify the meaning and reality of the mediated plan by adding the perspective of time. Enough time must elapse in the implementation stage to make such follow-up useful. Generally, follow-up should start no sooner than 1 month after the signing of the mediated plan. The next intervals for follow-up could be at 6 months and 1 year after the signing of the agreement. If, however, an earlier or later date is directly related to the issues involved in the mediation, it should be substituted. Follow-up not only gives the participant a chance to ventilate and achieve support, but also can provide mediators with useful information regarding the effectiveness of certain options and techniques during mediation.

A helpful, generic follow-up sheet should ask questions regarding the general trends for the agreement, subsequent legal and nonlegal processes used, evaluation of the helpfulness and satisfaction with mediation, and what needs the participants continue to have. It should use open-ended questions with easily tabulated, multiple-choice answers. This worksheet not only organizes the discussions during the follow-up but also provides data for later statistical evaluation of mediation. Whether such follow-up is initiated by the calendar, the client, or the mediator, the content should be handled with warmth and reassurance. If the problems are multitudinous or complicated, or if the contacts are frequent, the mediation participants should be invited to return for additional mediation services or referred to appropriate community resources.

Things change, children grow, new situations are encountered, structures and institutions switch their procedures, and new alliances are formed. Mediation is unique among conflict resolution processes because it can create a process for future review and revision. Mediators can choose either to include a short *review session* into their schedule of sessions and fee structure or to make it clear that review sessions will be provided only upon request of one or both of the participants with payment of additional fees. The mediator should clarify who will attempt to contact the other participants. Noncooperation or nonattendance according to the terms of the review process outlined in the mediated plan may hold negative consequences, such as invalidation of the entire document or a breach of contract. Including one review session as part of the original mediation fee is probably preferred for family mediation cases because the participants are more likely to use it when they need it.

Unlike the follow-up contact, usually done by phone or individually in private session, a review session is a "mini-version" of the earlier mediation process and usually encompasses the first six stages in one marathon session. Both participants should be present, with the mediator inviting exploration of any current or impending issues, options, and needed choices. When decisions have been made by the participants, the mediator can write them up, have a quick discussion of the wording, and have signed copies of revisions attached to the mediated plan. These amendments should be submitted to the court and made a matter of record if the original mediated plan was so submitted.

In summary, the implementation stage is the time when participants in mediation try to live the terms of the plan. Some level of involvement by the mediator, either through a follow-up evaluation and feedback mechanism or through a review session to make revisions in the original mediated plan, is desirable in divorce mediation. Although a follow-up contact is most often initiated by a mediator, a review session, which usually includes Stages 1 through 6 of the mediation process in a single session, is usually started by the participants because of substantial problems or desired changes.

CONCLUSION

Knowing the stages of mediation can help the mediator plan the pace of sessions. The following is a generic overview of a six-session mediation case. Six sessions seem to be about average for most divorce cases involving money as well as child-related issues. Integrating the stages with the sessions helps define a beginning, a middle, and an end.

First Session: Stage One, Stage Two

If joint:

1. Complete forms as usual for a first interview, meeting briefly with each participant individually to augment rapport and collect data.
2. If participants are ready, sign the Agreement to Mediate/Contract in joint session. If not, show it to them; let them take it home.

If individual:

1. Complete interview guidelines for the one participant; explain letters of invitation and mediation checklist that may be sent.
2. Show the Agreement to Mediate/Counsel; explain that it will be the first thing to be done in the first joint session.
3. Get an idea of areas of agreement, conflict, and general positions, and the flexibility of each.

If finances are involved, consider handing out financial forms. Are clients ready for this as homework? Go over how you want forms filled out.

Second Session: Stage Two, Stage Three

1. If not done already, get signed Agreement to Mediate/Counsel as commitment to mediation process.
2. Select the most immediate (or easiest) issues and do fact-finding, isolate issues, reframe and reflect, and see if options are available, develop them.
3. Determine readiness for decision making: If they are ready, see if agreement is forthcoming.
4. Record any decisions on Mediation Worksheet, or send out as Memorandum of Understanding.

Third Session: Stage Three, Stage Four

Continue as before for each topic or issue listed on the Agreement to Mediate/Counsel.

Fourth Session: Stage Four

1. If one party is very resistant, use individual session to explore concerns, fears.

2. By now, most fact-finding should be complete, and each should be able to negotiate from equal base of information.

3. Make referrals as needed for side issues.

Fifth Session: Stage Five

1. Start summing up progress, giving strokes for hard work; encourage.

2. Act as agent of reality; point out how parties skirt issues and financial needs and what could be done.

3. Start foreshadowing end of series: limited time.

4. Write up draft of Mediated Plan for review next session.

*Sixth Session: Stage Five, Referral for Stage Six, Preparation for
Stage Seven*

1. Review draft of Mediated Plan (if ready), and determine and explain what is left to do (if anything).

2. Explain how other processes work (going to court, attorney negotiation, arbitration) and the likely consequences of each.

3. Determine need/commitment to continue, and for how many more sessions.

4. Confirm terms on a new Agreement to Mediate/Contract if needed; make sure fees for first series are being paid or payment plan is in place. If not needed: Confirm Mediated Plan, notify attorneys, judges, make referrals if needed, and close case.

Divorce, like other conflict and decision-making situations, requires the use of an effective method of conflict resolution. Mediation provides an opportunity to affect not only the manifest conflict but also the underlying conflict. The more the underlying conflicts are resolved or managed, the more likely agreements reached during mediation will endure. Mediation provides a greater exploration of the issues and the options than other methods of conflict resolution.

Mediation is a process that can be categorized into seven stages. Although the sequence of these stages may be reversed or augmented for any particular case, each stage is necessary for both conflict resolution and management. Each stage provides a unique role for the mediator as well as the participants. Using specific skills and techniques, the mediator, by keeping the participants moving through the process, increases their motivation to make decisions and to live with the results of those decisions. This conceptual framework of mediation allows the practitioner to explore the unique dimensions and uses of the mediation process for divorce.

REFERENCES

Deutsch, M. *The resolution of conflict.* New Haven, CT: Yale University Press, 1973.

Fisher, R., & Ury, W. *Getting to yes: Negotiating agreement without giving in.* Boston: Houghton Mifflin, 1981.

Folberg, J., & Taylor, A. *Mediation: A comprehensive guide to resolving conflicts without litigation.* San Francisco: Jossey-Bass, 1984.

Janis, I. L. & Mann, L. Decision making: A psychological analysis of conflict, choice, and commitment. New York: Free Press, 1977.

Moore, C. Training mediators for family dispute resolution. *Mediation Quarterly,* 1983, *2,* 79–89.

Rummel, R. J. *Understanding conflict and war* (Vols. 1 & 2). New York: Wiley, 1976.

Taylor, A. Toward a comprehensive theory of mediation. *Conciliation Courts Review,* 1981, *19(1),* 1–12.

5

The Psychological Dimension of Divorce Mediation

FLORENCE W. KASLOW
*Private Practice, West Palm Beach, Florida,
and Florida Couples and Family Institute*

This chapter explores the psychological dimensions of divorce in a mediation context and describes strategies to move through the psychological issues. The appropriate choice of strategies is contingent upon the mediator ascertaining an accurate reading of the couple's individual and couple identity, tempos, current intrapsychic and interpersonal resources, and stage of development. These variables are graphically presented here.

STAGE THEORIES OF THE DIVORCE PROCESS: A DIACLECTIC MODEL

Stage development concepts have been applied to the process of divorce only in the past two decades by Bohannon (1970), Froiland and Hozman (1977), Kessler (1978), and Kaslow (1981b, 1983). In divorce mediation it is helpful to assess life-cycle dimensions in terms of several interlocking aspects. The "diaclectic" model of the divorce process does this by incorporating theories of human growth and development, marital dissolution, and family systems (Kaslow, 1984).

The terms *eclectic* and *dialectic* were amalgamated in "diaclectic" (Kaslow, 1981a, 1981b) to encompass various interpretations of behavior dynamics and stage theory, including psychodynamic, object-relations, holistic–systems, and humanistic–existential theory. The theory's thrust is toward a dynamic, diaclectic synthesis of what is known of the emotions experienced, actions taken, and tasks to be handled during severing of the marital bonds if reasonably successful resolution is to be achieved (Kaslow, 1979–1980).

Bohannon articulated a six-station process of divorce (1970). His stations do not occur in an invariant sequence, nor do all individuals feel the same anguish at each phase. Each stage must be experienced and its stumbling blocks overcome before a new, satisfying state of well-being can be achieved.

Both individually and societally, the usual first way of dealing with the overwhelming phenomenon of divorce is to try to deny it and hope the crisis will be averted. When the situation continues to deteriorate, the magnitude of the catastrophe permeates one's total being. Once the likelihood of divorce is fully confronted, it can be framed and addressed as a problem to be solved.

Predivorce Period

Bohannon designates the first station the *emotional* divorce (1970). During this phase, which can be brief or prolonged, the couple become aware of their dissatisfaction and disillusionment. One spouse is apt to realize before the other that the quality of the relationship has been declining. This is communicated to the other spouse, who may become alarmed and try to seduce or badger the retreating mate back into a closer union. They may become suspicious about each other's separate activities. One or both may become disgruntled and question the vitality and viability of their marriage. Criticisms about the irksome characteristics of the spouse and the marriage often escalate, and tension mounts in the household. Children, parents, friends, and neighbors may sense that trouble is brewing.

The roots of this disillusionment can run deep when it is partially a crystalization of long-internalized and treasured childhood dreams of perpetual marital bliss. Reality cannot fulfill such unrealistic fantasies; they must be tempered with warmth, humor, and sound judgment to become realizable. Or, coming from an abusive or conflict-fraught family of origin, a person may embark upon marriage seeking nurturance, longing for parenting and narcissistic gratification more than the reciprocity of a healthy adult peer relationship. As this author has noted,

> if either of these scripts constitutes a major part of the foundation of the marriage and the fairy tale quality expectations are clung to during the early years of marriage, disappointment, depression and/or rage are probable consequences when the dependency needs are unmet and the spouse feels deprived and unloved. (Kaslow, 1984, p. 24)

When the deficiency (D) needs are great (Maslow, 1968), the more dependent and/or demanding partner may anticipate that his or her mate will play all roles sequentially or concurrently as the dependent spouse's desires arise— to be a potpourri of parent, best friend, lover, confidante, playmate, protector, and limit setter. Such extreme demands are likely to irritate and deplete the caretaker spouse; in therapy he or she often states correctly, "Nothing I do is enough—my spouse seems like a bottomless pit." The neurotic dependency that initially was appealing and ego-syntonic soon becomes a burdensome fault and ego-dystonic for the dependent spouse. Conversely, the egocentric pomposity and arrogance that the other partner found intriguing and reassuring can become repetitive and boring, as one promise after another is left unfulfilled (Kaslow, 1982a).

In yet another kind of marriage, serious problems are not experienced for many years. Given that at any moment in time one selects exactly the type of person one most needs, the choice may remain a compatible and valued one for a long time. A long-term marriage will falter if the partners change in vastly different and incompatible directions, if one continues to grow while the other stagnates, or if a major catastrophe occurs and they cannot integrate its resolution into the relationship system.

A relationship capable of surviving the inevitable roller coaster of many years of marital togetherness is most likely to be one with a good balance between symmetrical and complementary elements (Pollack, Kaslow, & Harvey, 1982). These relationships are characterized by effective and honest communication as well as mutual trust and respect. Time-tested ways of negotiating disputes, solving problems, and accepting the other's identity as an individual as well as the couple identity, are usually essential for a satisfying and ongoing relationship. This is manifested in having some separate activities and privacy as well as joint activities and enjoyed togetherness. These have been found to be some of the characteristics of healthy couples and families (Kaslow, 1981d, 1982b; Walsh, 1982).

In 1975 Kessler formulated a seven-stage model denoting Stages 1 and 2 as *disillusionment* and *erosion*. Both are inherent in the emotional splitting apart that precedes the decision to seek a divorce. Sometimes during this phase a partner, abhorring the idea of divorce or experiencing mixed emotions about the prospect of divorce raised by his or her mate, seeks therapy. Initially, conjoint marital therapy is probably the treatment of choice. Research reveals that couples who enter therapy at this stage, where the emphasis is on resolving frustrations, ventilating and understanding repressed anger and gripes, improving spousal interactions, and enriching the relationship, are more likely to be able to work through their marital crisis than when one or both enter individual therapy (Whitaker & Miller, 1969). Once some temporary relief is achieved, the couple are freer to identify and evaluate their problems candidly, so that emotions can be clarified and solutions can be implemented. Through this procedure some couples discover that underneath their discouragement, boredom, and/or rage, enough positive regard, affection, and love can be rekindled to offset the extreme negativism. With some bona fide effort and luck, they may be able to rebuild a worthwhile marriage.

Short-term couple group therapy is an alternative intervention approach to single-couple treatment during this phase of decision making. (See Kadis & Markowitz, 1972; Kaslow, 1981c; and Kaslow & Liberman, 1981, for descriptions of this methodology.) Because it is time limited and focused, most participants are able to determine within the 3–4 months of the life span of the group whether they want to continue the marriage for healthy reasons or whether disbanding it is a better choice. Within the group framework they consider the options from many angles and weigh the potential consequences of each possible decision. The group members support, confront, and reflect back to one another—heightening the intensity and impact of the therapy. This author has previously observed,

> patients report that group therapy for couples serves as a vehicle to help them stop clinging to past hurts and battle cries and from making extreme demands on each other, thereby freeing up much bound energy. Consequently they can expand their activities and their resource network for fulfillment and enjoyment, or utilize their energy to competently begin extricating themselves from the marriage. (Kaslow, 1984, p. 29)

Couples who proceed with a divorce following therapy may find mediation to be a welcome means of resolving the remaining contractual issues.

Those couples who identify and resolve the conflicts during Stage 1 (see Table 5-1), either with or without treatment, tend not to move into Stage 2 on the divorce continuum. The forecast for a rejuvenated and satisfying marriage is fairly good at this point. However, resolution of problems and dilemmas eludes many other troubled pairs. Their sense of being imprisoned in the marriage may be much more intense, and one partner may crave escape from a dying relationship. Sometimes a therapist gets triangled into a relationship when one spouse desires to save the marriage and perhaps threatens suicide or an emotional breakdown if the other departs, while the other spouse is determined to seek a divorce. Ultimately it is the couple's choice; yet it is essential that the therapist guide them in exploring the potential implications and outcomes of both decisions and have them consider short-term options like a trial separation as a cooling-off period for more rational deliberations. A skilled clinician can help the couple to understand and accept their role and responsibility for the choice to be made and its long-range consequences. When one spouse decides definitely to separate and pursue a divorce, the therapist's role may shift to enabling the spouse who feels rejected to assert control of shaping his or her future and encouraging the couple to try to make the divorce process a constructive, rather than a destructive, experience. It would be appropriate for the therapist to suggest that the patient(s) consider mediation at this stage, to facilitate a constructive dissolution of the relationship.

Erosion is Kessler's designation for Stage 2 (1975). This second phase of the predivorce period may be a time of despair, when each partner is confronted by the full realization that the marriage is falling apart. It is a time of turbulent emotions and confused thoughts shifting between denial and the pretense that this too will pass and everything will be all right again. One partner may try desperately to convince the about-to-depart spouse that the partner can again be considerate, understanding, attractive, sexy, or whatever else he or she has been accused of lacking. Feelings of fear, bewilderment, inadequacy, and rejection may abound. One partner may plead with relatives, friends, or their clergyperson to shame the errant spouse into remaining.

If they have been in couple therapy, the partners may no longer be interested in participating in conjoint sessions. Instead, individual therapy now might be preferable, to help the partner being left cope with feelings of abandonment, loss, anger, and failure, and to help the departing partner cope with feelings of guilt and remorse for disbanding the marriage and narcissistically wounding the former beloved—or even for feeling relief that their entrapment may soon end. Couples who enter mediation in this phase may find that continuation of therapy, in tandem with but separate from mediation, provides for the continued resolution of these highly emotional issues while bifurcating them from the mediation process.

During Divorce

As can be seen from Table 5-1, the divorce period encompasses Bohannon's second station (legal), third station (economic), and fourth station (coparental divorce and the problems of custody; 1970). For purposes of understanding strategic interventions in therapy and in mediation, it is helpful to consider these intertwined aspects separately. The legal divorce phase begins when the parties undertake action to legally sever their marital bond. Traditionally this is when one or both seek legal counsel and embark on the adversarial process of a litigated divorce. Consistent with the American Bar Association's *Model Code of Professional Responsibility* (1981), each attorney is mandated to represent only his or her client. The attorney has no concern for the other party's interests, since the assumption in law is that these will be similarly represented by opposing legal counsel. Given that the law surrounding divorce historically has cast the judge's role as one of determining which party is innocent and which is guilty, each attorney tries to show his or her client in the best light, seeking to retain or obtain as much as possible for the person he or she is representing. Sometimes the fray becomes quite an angry and destructive free-for-all, resulting in long-term embattlement and embitterment in which relatives and friends take sides, children are victimized by the continuing strife (Kessler & Bostwick, 1977; Wallerstein & Kelly, 1979, 1980), and everyone is left depleted and feeling like a loser.

MEDIATION: A WAY OF ENHANCING SELF-RESPECT

The mid-1970s saw the burgeoning of divorce mediation following publication of Coogler's seminal work (Coogler, 1978) and the expansion of knowledge about the mediation process (Folberg, 1983; Haynes, 1981, 1982; Neville, 1984; and many others). Now couples who want to participate maximally in the critical decisions about custody, visitation, and distribution of assets and who dislike the prospect of litigation can pursue an alternative dispute-resolution pathway.

Basic principles of mediation, such as empowerment, consideration of the best interests of all involved family members, cooperative problem solving, and equitable distribution of assets, are consonant with the theory and practice of marital and family systems therapy. Arriving at a mutually acceptable agreement with the least anguish possible is conducive to resolving the psychic tasks of the divorce process and to facilitating a more rapid and solid personality reintegration and life-style reequilibration. If the parties show a modicum of interest, this is an appropriate time for therapists and other professionals, like clergy, who are concerned about the parties' welfare, to refer them to a well-trained and qualified mediator. If they can cooperatively reach an agreement that flows from consideration of the best interest of all parties concerned, then they can learn during this period to assert their own convictions and exercise their competencies more fully. Increased self-respect evolves as the partners

Table 5-1. Diaclectic Model of Stages in the Divorce Process

Divorce stage	Station[a]	Stage	Feelings	Actions and tasks	Therapeutic interventions	Mediation[b]
Predivorce A time of deliberation and despair	I. Emotional divorce	A	Disillusionment Dissatisfaction Alienation Anxiety Disbelief	Avoiding the issue Sulking and/or crying Confronting partner Quarreling	Marital therapy (one couple) Couples group therapy	
		B	Despair Dread Anguish Ambivalence Shock Emptiness Anger Chaos Inadequacy Low self-esteem Loss	Denial Withdrawal (physical and emotional) Pretending all is okay Attempting to win back affection Asking friends, family, clergy for advice	Marital therapy (one couple) Divorce therapy Couples group therapy	
	II. Legal divorce	C	Depression Detachment Anger Hopelessness Self-pity Helplessness	Bargaining Screaming Threatening Attempting suicide Consulting an attorney or mediator	Family therapy Individual adult therapy Child therapy	Set the stage for mediation Ascertain parties' understanding of the process and its appropriateness for them
During divorce A time of legal involvement	III. Economic divorce	D	Confusion Fury Sadness Loneliness Relief Vindictiveness	Separating physically Filing for legal divorce Considering economic arrangements Considering custody arrangements	Children of divorce group therapy Child therapy Adult therapy	Define the rules of mediation Identify the issues & separate therapeutic issues from mediation issues

Stage		Feelings	Tasks	Therapeutic Intervention	Mediation[b]
IV. Coparental divorce and the problems of custody	E	Concern for children Ambivalence Numbness Uncertainty	Grieving and mourning Telling relatives and friends Reentering work world (unemployed woman) Feeling empowered to make choices	Same as above plus network family therapy	Negotiate & process the issues & choices Reach agreement Analyze & formalize agreement
V. Community divorce	F	Indecisiveness Optimism Resignation Excitement Curiosity Regret Sadness	Finalizing divorce Begin reaching out to new friends Undertaking new activities Stabilizing new life-style and daily routine for children Exploring new interests and possibly taking new job	Adults Individual therapy Singles group therapy Children Child play therapy Childrens' group therapy	
Postdivorce A time of exploration and reequilibration IV. Psychic divorce	G	Acceptance Self-confidence Energetic Self-worth Wholeness Exhilaration Independence Autonomy	Resynthesis of identity Completing psychic divorce Seeking new love object and making a commitment to some permanency Becoming comfortable with new life-style and friends Helping children accept finality of parents' divorce and their continuing relationship with both parents	Parent–child therapy Family therapy Group therapies Childrens' activity group therapy	Return to mediation when changed circumstance require a renegotiation of the agreement

Source: Reprinted from Kaslow (1984) and slightly revised.

[a]These stations are taken from the work of Bohannan (1973).

[b]The process of mediation was not an original element of the diaclectic model (Kaslow, 1984) but has been added here do illustrate the interface between the processes of divorce & mediation.

come to rely on their independent judgments, to negotiate assertively, to compromise effectively, and to take charge of redirecting and refashioning their lives.

Notwithstanding all of the accolades mediation has been accorded, it is not a panacea and is not the marital dissolution pathway of choice for everyone. For example, a party who is mentally retarded, brain damaged, or mentally ill may well need a hard-hitting attorney to forcefully represent that party's interests. If there is an enormous power disparity which means that the weaker partner cannot or will not be assertive, recourse to an attorney may be advisable so that the more passive member does not give in too easily. And if the parties are so enraged that equity is the last principle they are interested in, they may need to battle ferociously and drag out the divorce in order to work through the anger and be able to let go of the relationship and heal psychologically.

A therapist can indicate to patients embarking on divorce that they are apt to feel much more helpless and pessimistic in the adversarial process than in mediation. Adversarial negotiations depend on the attorney, and final authority for all decisions rests with the judge. Anxiety and apprehension color the ambiguity of the tumultuous waiting period until the final decree. The bewilderment, detachment (Kessler, 1975), loneliness, anger, grief, and mourning over all the losses wrought by the breakup of the marriage and family may increase until a state of desperation prevails. The forced distribution of valued possessions, acquired as part of the couple's life together, is a traumatic experience. In Table 5-1 these are interwoven with the delineation of feelings and tasks and Bohannon's Stations 2 and 3.

THE DIACLECTIC MODEL OF DIVORCE AND THE STAGES OF MEDIATION

Kessler has described mediation as a four-stage process of (1) setting the stage, (2) defining the issues, (3) processing the issues, and (4) resolving the issues (1978). We shall use her concise model as the framework within which to analyze the impact of the emotional process of divorce on the stages of mediation.

Setting the Stage

During the introductory session, it is important for the mediator to ascertain what each party's concept of mediation is and what each hopes to accomplish through this process. It is necessary for the mediator to differentiate between mediation and therapy. Sometimes the decision to divorce is not really firm, and the couple are really seeking marital therapy. In this instance, it may be important to refer them for marital therapy so that they have an opportunity to try to improve their marriage before plunging prematurely into the divorce stream.

Other times, one partner is adamant about dissolving the marriage, and the other, frightened and unhappy, is trying desperately to hold it together and seeks mediation as a fantasized lifeline to reconcile the difficulties and rescue the drowning partnership. Others hope the mediator will become their advocate or ally or will be weak and easily deceived, so that they will acquire a decided edge in the bargaining and not be required to negotiate in good faith and under guidelines of full disclosure. Still others are seeking a "fast-lane" divorce—wanting out immediately to ease the pain or to pick up a new, more exciting relationship and life-style. Most want a less expensive passage out of marriage. A clear description of the mediation process and its objectives may deter parties from attempting to manipulate the process, which will result in eventual impasse.

Some clients come to mediation fairly well informed about its basic tenets of empowerment, cooperation, equity, full disclosure, and mediator neutrality. They have selected this strategy because they want to be fair and noncombative and to participate maximally in making decisions that effect their lives and the lives of their significant others. Where there is lack of familiarity with or confusion about this modality, it is incumbent upon the mediator to clearly articulate the nature of the process and communicate what the rules are. This can be accomplished by offering each of the parties a copy of the mediation rules, set up in contract form, and reviewing it during the session. The parties are encouraged to ask questions, make comments, assert their needs and objectives, and speak out as individuals. The mediator's apparent expectation that they can and will think independently facilitates their moves toward greater individuation and autonomy—goals of the psychic divorce.

Engagement in the mediation process helps to reduce the feelings of depression, hopelessness, helplessness, self-pity, anger, and detachment that often accompany the legal and economic phases (see Table 5-1). Innuendos about contemplated self-destructive (not always suicidal) or retaliative behaviors diminish as individuals are empowered to determine what will happen to them and to shift their perceptions and behaviors gradually from the victim's position as a loser to a creator's stance as a winner. Trust is enhanced as the principle of full disclosure of assets is implemented, and a cooperative win is sought through bargaining and negotiating techniques.

Haynes's chart (Table 5-2) encapsulates his view of the essence of divorce mediation. His steps to be taken occur during the second stage of divorce and coincide with Bohannon's second, third, and fourth stations (the legal, economic, and coparental divorces, respectively). The values espoused are almost identical to those of many systems-oriented marital/family/divorce therapists. The requisite skills encompass and go beyond those cited by mental health practitioners. Haynes adds, as do many mediators, such functions as power balancing, conflict management, agreement drafting, and interprofessional communication. Assisting mediation clients in this way is consonant with the thrust of therapy, which in all philosophic schools is toward enabling patients to be more self-determining and self-actualizing. The entire mediation should be conducted within the context of the mediator's ongoing psychodynamic assessment of the following factors:

Table 5-2. Knowledge, Skills, Values, and Aids Used by the Mediator during the Process

Step	Knowledge	Skills	Values	Aids
1. Referral	Divorce adjustment process	Interviewing	Nonjudgmental	Directory of resources
2. Intake/orientation (Issue Identification (State I)**	Mediation process Family therapy theory	Assessment Referral Issue identification Relationship	Empathic to divorce as one choice	Client handbook Financial data forms Temporary agreement
3. Budget development (Issue Identification Stage II)	Family dynamics Dysfunctional behavior Conflict styles Budgeting Debt counseling Conflict management Power relationships	Maintaining task focus Intervening to change patterns of communication "Third ear" listening Family assessment Process control Power balancing	Right of client self-determination Concept of client empowerment Maintaining a sense of balance	Easel and newsprint Other professionals Real estate broker/appraiser Accountant Investment broker Pension expert Business appraiser Life insurance consultant
4. Reconciliation of budget needs (Issue Identification Stage III)	Accounting Tax regulations Job market Body language	Productive use of conflict Separating emotional from economic aspects Engagement Timing Problem definition and solving		
5. Identification of assets (Issue Identification Stage IV)	Investing Pensions Appraising Financial management discovery"	Option development Measuring communication consonance		
6. Identification of parenting goals (Issue Identification Stage V)	Human growth and development theory Age-specific impact of divorce on children	Assisting clients to separate own needs from those of other family members Separating spousal from parenting needs Communicating professional knowledge to parents Family structure assessment	Right of children to access to and from both parents and extended family Accepting that divorce changes a single family into two families for spouses and a single one for the children	Test instruments

7. Clarification of issues	Negotiation theory Game theory State domestic relations law	Conflict management Negotiation management Goal clarification Option development	Equitable distribution of resources and responsibilities	Books Magazines Reprints
8. Rank order of issues	Intervention theories	Defining range of options Rank ordering of priorities Limiting the use of therapeutic skills to only those strategies that assist the mediation process Use of family assessment	Right of mediating couple not to receive therapy	Interim memorandums
9. Identification of options			Right of clients to choose any option developed in mediation Right of clients to change previous agreements	
10. Bargaining	Equity theory	Maintaining clear lines of communication between the couple Clarifying the consequences of chosen solutions Family interaction management Involving the children in the process	Right of the children to participate Respect for and maintenance of family decision-making process	
11. Drafting the Memorandum of Understanding	Format & content of memorandum	Accurate note-keeping Agreement drafting	Maintaining a balance in writing the memorandum and excluding mediator biases	Tape recorder
12. Consultation with attorney(s)	Interface of law and mediation	Interprofessional communication and interaction	Respect for integrity of mediation and the practice of law	

Source: Reprinted from Haynes (1982).

Note. The specific entries are made when they are normally first used in the mediation process. Once introduced they are used throughout mediation. The location in this table indicates either original or primary use of the actual knowledge, skill, value or aid.

[a]The identification of issues and the family assessment are usually carried between sessions. All other activities are normally conducted during sessions with the couple.

- The couple's readiness to mediate
- Level of acceptance that divorce is imminent
- Individual emotional stability and maturity
- Power and control issues
- Amount of eruptive anger in each spouse
- Need to punish each other or retaliate for hurts and rejections
- Ability to formulate their own agreement and enter into a contractual process voluntarily
- Possession of or ability to acquire correct factual information about finances and property (including assets and debts) and children's developmental and affectional needs
- The ability to function rationally while mediating the tangible issues and temporarily encapsulating the emotional wounds

In the first and second mediation sessions, it is crucial that the mediator establish good rapport and a trusting relationship with his or her clients. The couple may find that many of their prior relationships feel shaky and uncertain and that mediation can provide a stabilizing anchor during a turbulent, stormy period. If either partner is seeking an advocate, ally, or guardian angel, the mediator should guard against being triangulated (Bowen, 1978) or getting caught in power battles between or with the partners.

The adversarial process often nullifies the right to be self-determining since it sets up a pattern where lawyers do the negotiating and the bargaining and judges answer the ultimate questions. Psychological factors and the long-range emotional recuperation receive little, if any, consideration. Unlike the adversarial process, mediation embodies the philosophy of self-determination. The agreement to participate in mediation sets the stage for future joint decision making and cooperation. This phase of the mediation process allows for an appraisal of the parties' psychological adjustment. The natural and normal emotional responses to divorce can be acknowledged rather than aggravated or sublimated.

Defining the Issues

Individuals in the divorce process do not mediate in a vacuum. Factors such as level of participation in the decision to divorce, overall psychological well-being, verbal skills, and attachment to the issues in dispute will influence the issues the parties raise in mediation.

Kessler (1978) categorizes the issues as personal, relationship, and topical. Personal issues refer to conflicts related to the individual and specific to him or her. These include overall psychological well-being, nature of ego functioning and its mechanisms of defense, unresolved issues from family of origin, and unsatisfactory accomplishment of maturational goals. Paranoia, lack of self-esteem and trust, or rejection may present themselves as repetitive themes and issues during mediation. A spouse's request for alimony or maintenance may be wrapped around unmet dependency needs and a fear of financial insecurity, emanating from childhood. A parent's insistence upon custody and control of the children may camouflage fears of loss, humiliation, or rejection, or self-imposed, rigid role expectations.

Relationship issues refer to the conflicts surrounding the marital relationship and the decision to divorce. A spouse's grief over the unfulfilled expectations of the marriage, anger toward an abandoning mate, and desires to punish or to assuage guilt typically appear in mediation when individuals are in the early and emotionally laden stages of divorce.

Refusal to provide economic support for the children may spring from anger and jealousy toward a spouse's newfound lover. An unwillingness to allow children to spend significant and meaningful time with the other parent may relate to the anger and competition between the parents over how the decision to separate was made. The underlying refrain is likely to be, "You left me, you must pay for that, you can't have the children, I was willing to keep the marriage going."

Topical issues are the contractual issues that need to be resolved in the divorce agreement: property distribution, financial division, child support, custody, and visitation. Agreements about these salient aspects of the divorce must appear in the final decree. They are often the pared-down personal and relationship issues, reframed and unfettered by psychological and emotional vestiges.

Mediation addresses the topical issues while it acknowledges the existence of the personal and relationship issues. Participants in mediation are assisted in resolving the terms of the divorce by separating the issues in this fashion. Personal and relationship matters can be so labeled, reframed into topical issues, or referred to therapy for resolution.

The careful definition of the issues at this stage in mediation provides structure to the process and allows the parties to identify what the "real" fight is about. The mediator can choose appropriate interventions for the different categories of disputes, leading to a greater chance of resolving each of the issues. Separating psychological disputes from legal issues early can facilitate the culmination of the marriage.

Processing the Issues

Individuals who are hazy about their income, expenses, and financial assets and liabilities can be severely jolted when they realize that soon they will have to live on less income and will have to manage their own financial affairs. Drawing up budgets and financial statements, having assets evaluated, and compiling an inventory of outstanding debts can be a powerful learning experience, which, when accomplished, can heighten a person's self-esteem and sense of competency. Being capable of handling one's own finances augments one's sense of independence and autonomy. These are all critical aspects of progressing toward the psychic divorce and overcoming the awesome fears of being incompetent regarding sophisticated financial concerns and transactions. This financial education can help overcome long-held feelings of inadequacy partially attributable to a spouse's put-downs about stupidity in financial matters. As the couple come to agree on the equitable distribution of assets, they may be incorporating principles of fairness and consideration, thereby enhancing their sorely shattered self-respect and slowly moving from wanting retribution for perceived injustices to gaining a distinct financial advantage.

In many marriages, the most precious asset and joint production is the children. Neither parent may want to relinquish full-time parenting, and therapy and mediation seem to be prejudicial in favor of children's having easy access to both parents and parents' remaining vitally involved in their children's lives. In mediation, as the parents' desires, rights, and responsibilities are emphasized, each parent may be encouraged to recognize the other's strengths as a parent and the children's need to remain connected to both without fear that loving one will be misconstrued as disloyalty to the other. When the children's reactions to the divorce, developmental needs, desires for the future, and changing perspectives are given credence, the written agreement will much more adequately reflect "the best interest of everyone" and will be easier to implement, since everyone's feelings and desires have been taken into consideration (Hetherington, Cox, & Cox, 1977). When children and parents continue to be closely involved with each other in co-custody arrangements, the sense of loss and abandonment is minimized, and the grief and mourning that accompany more drastic separations from the noncustodial parent in traditional postdivorce restructurings of the family are not as intense or prolonged. This maximizes everyone's chances of psychic well-being.

Just as when custody decisions are made in the therapeutic arena, a family systems perspective seems to be the most comprehensive and illuminating one for a divorce mediator. Inevitably, once the decision to part has been made, there is work to be done with the couple concerning how they have been dealing with the children's perceptions and reactions, interpreting what is occurring to them, and helping the children grieve and reintegrate. Both therapist and mediator can interpret the profound impact parents' behavior will have on the children and relate how the nature of the adults' adjustment will correlate with the children's adjustment (Wallerstein & Kelly, 1980). This includes highlighting the children's need to know that both parents continue to love them and will be involved in their lives. Children's "rights" include not having to hear one parent disparage the other. A pledge to refrain from doing so can be written into the child custody and visitation section of the agreement.

When the separating pair are too angry to participate in a conjoint mediation session, they can be asked to sit in separate rooms, and with the couple's permission, the mediator can conduct a short period of shuttle mediation, trying to understand and then defuse the fury and frustration so that conjoint mediation can continue. When this does not seem possible, because one or both are too emotionally disturbed or dysfunctional to proceed or because the interpersonal transaction level is so beset by pain, anguish, and unabated anger that the parties cannot negotiate with each other, they can be referred to therapy to deal with the emotional distress, asking that the partners return to mediation when they think they can focus on the topical issues needing resolution. It is not advisable to serve as therapist and mediator in the same case. Therefore, it is best to separate these functions when the level of dysfunction, pathology, or conflict seem to require in-depth psychotherapy during the mediation process. In these cases, it is often advisable for the antagonists to have individual therapy and, perhaps, for the children to be seen as a sibling system (Bank & Kahn, 1982). When possible, however, family sessions are preferable, so that the children can ask their parents, as well as the therapist, questions, and express their feelings, apprehensions, and hopes. This strengthens the possibility that, within the safety of the therapist's sanctuary, all can take an active part in shaping the two single-parent families as these evolve (Sager et al., 1983).

If the couple's parents are trying to influence their choices, and the couple feel unable to withstand these pressures, separate multigenerational family-of-origin sessions with the respective parents and siblings may be in order. If it becomes apparent that the children need nearly total attention and empathy from the therapist, child therapy may stand out as the treatment of choice, with play therapy or art therapy serving as useful vehicles for enabling young children and teenagers to express their internal conflicts and confusion. As this author has noted earlier,

> these approaches are particularly compelling with young patients who have difficulty verbalizing their turmoil because they provide diagnostic clues and a shared vehicle through which to build a therapeutic alliance and a multifaceted intervention strategy (Kaslow, 1984).

Here again we see a similar philosophic approach in family therapy and in family mediation. The members of the family who attend a session should be determined not by hard and fast rules, but by ascertaining who is making input into the decisions and who will be greatly affected by the outcome.

In order to understand the social forces that have a bearing on the divorcing parents' lives, it is imperative that divorce therapists be conversant with local mores and the divorce laws in their state. Since the type of guidance the parties may be receiving from their mediator is another critical factor, the therapist should be aware of this aspect of the patient's informational system and be able to collaborate with other involved professionals in a team approach. This reinforces the cooperative model the clients are using in working together on their divorce agreement, enhances their learning of effective communication skills, and demonstrates consistency between what is recommended and what is actually done.

Each mediator and therapist, to be ethical, should clarify his or her own pertinent values (Abroms, 1978), indicating a preference for the "best interest of the child" doctrine. The therapist can point out that consideration of the children's emotional needs and future well-being may be more critical and far-reaching than financial considerations. Such a stance coincides with the one the mediator is taking and helps diminish the level of confusion the parties are experiencing when they receive conflictual messages from other domains in their lives.

Some children seem neglected during the divorce process. Their parents may be behaving erratically because their energies are depleted by the physical and financial uncoupling and the tedious effort to arrive at a final agreement. Often one or both parents assume extra job responsibilities to offset mounting economic burdens. They may have little time or energy left to expend on the children and little sympathy for their bewilderment and hurt. Some parents become enraged that the children are not more sensitive to their plight and more nurturing of the parent; they desire a partial role reversal. Other parents become extremely protective and possessive, trying to shield their children from the pain of separation and feelings of desertion and to make them allies against the other parent (Kaslow, 1983). Sometimes such behavior intensifies when one spouse is engaged in litigation and is trying to make a case against the other; all of the negative qualities are emphasized in the battle to prove that the partner is less deserving financially and less fit to be the primary parent. Inherent in mediation is a commitment to promoting the physical and emotional well-being of the children.

During this phase, children's group therapy with other children of divorce has much to commend it. The therapist can foster an environment in which youngsters can express their sadness, explore their feelings, and acquire some understanding about and perhaps mastery of the crises they are experiencing, while they gain support from each other and from an empathic, gentle, authentically caring adult. In these sessions children can enact ways to handle the troublesome situations they are likely to encounter (Kessler & Bostwick, 1977). This intervention approach can also be effective during the postdivorce stage for children who have many personal unresolved issues that they do not want to deal with in the presence of other family members. Sometimes these children need a therapist all to themselves; then individual therapy is the treatment of choice. Parents going through mediation and becoming aware of their own power and strength are more likely to be willing to provide opportunities for their children to deal with pain, express their grief, and move toward self-realization while finding their evolving niche in the family.

While all of this is happening emotionally in the lives of the participants in the divorce drama, in the mediation sessions they are working on issues of child custody and visitation, child support, spousal support, property distribution and the tax consequences of various possible decisions. This requires an ability to search out and pull together budget information, financial statements and tax returns, appraisals of real estate holdings and stock portfolios, and so forth. Usually the mediator requests that the partners do this like a homework assignment, if necessary contacting experts acceptable to both to help them with these tasks. Concurrently, if there are minor children, custody and visitation arrangements will be a major area of discussion. The parents are asked to try to keep the child's needs as the main focal points, balanced with their parenting abilities. Such factors as stability and predictability are highlighted, yet flexibility is also stressed. Periodic reevaluations of primary physical residence (perhaps every 3 years) and visitation plans may be considered, since children's needs change as they enter different developmental phases and parents' circumstances also can change drastically. The mediator can tell the parents it is better to plan ahead for a change in primary residence than to have it occur when the main custodial parent can no longer cope and frantically calls the ex-spouse, saying, "You wanted him, come get him, I give up." It can be suggested, even urged, that couples write a rather specific visitation plan to avoid future confusion, ambiguity, and misunderstanding.

While drawing up a custody and visitation plan, future budgets, and a distribution plan for household and other material possessions, clients use their cognitive abilities to the fullest and remain task centered and goal oriented. This superimposes some structure on their otherwise often chaotic lives and enables them to achieve a sense of mastery and accomplishment as they gather requisite data, brainstorm options and choices available, select those they prefer, and formalize their areas of agreement in a written document. All of this heightens the partners' ability to state their positions and needs, to differentiate needs from wants, to negotiate from knowledge and strength as opposed to ignorance and weakness, to learn more cooperative and constructive ways to bargain and resolve disputes, and to begin to shift from living in the past to being interested in the present and planning for a potentially bright future.

Resolving the Issues

During this final phase of mediation, all of the areas that the parties agreed to negotiate are completed. Generally, the easiest decisions are made first, so that the partners can accept each other's ability to take a stance and to make some concessions, thus enhancing their ability to make real headway in the mediation process. Based on these successes, the couple can proceed into the remaining difficult, highly charged items and make some trade-offs. Usually these issues are inextricably intertwined with holding on to the last vestiges of the relationship, such as a favorite possession purchased on the honeymoon or an anniversary trip or an item one spouse treasures, and withholding it signifies a wish to continue being punitive. Sometimes the toughest decision is custody of children or animals, for dividing them is the final acknowledgment of the severed bonds. This is when the physical letting go has to occur, and both partners have to take full responsibility for their part in negotiating the agreement in good faith and their stake in implementing the spirit and letter of the agreement. This takes maturity, determination, trust of the other's integrity, and a future orientation. Letting go often occurs temporarily before the full psychic divorce, which may take 2 to 4 years to complete after the legal divorce (Kaslow, 1984). Letting go may also hasten the completion of the psychic disengagement.

The type of supportive network one has during the divorce process is a major factor in one's readjustment. Wallerstein and Kelly (1980) found that women with a strong support system of family and friends who offer financial help, housing, and child-care services during the trauma and transition fared much better than their counterparts who lacked this. Bohannon designates the fifth station "community divorce and the problem of loneliness" (1970).

Many patients indicate that their sense of isolation and anomie can become acute and inundating and that they long for community approval to overcome their humiliation and sense of failure. Bach (1974) relates that undergoing a divorce ceremony helps facilitate closure, and he performs a quasi-religious, therapeutic ceremony. Similarly, participants in mediation will sometimes decide that some celebration is called for on the day they cosign their agreement. It is an occasion that symbolizes a judicious handling of a major event. In the admixture of feelings, there is a glimmer of relief at having achieved a degree of finalization. Marking divorce ceremonially helps the partners in their closing of an important chapter of their lives and enhances the flow of the regenerative forces (Kaslow & Schwartz, 1987).

Postdivorce

Following mediation, the animosity and rancor should be markedly reduced, the global hatred of the opposite sex that may have been present should fade more rapidly, and the divorced person should be ready to begin building a new life. The communication skills learned or improved in mediation and the techniques for tuning into another's needs and sentiments should stand the parties in good stead as they attempt to make new friends.

It is standard procedure for some mediators to have their clients return at periodic intervals after the divorce decree has been awarded. Three-month, 6-month, and 1-year follow-up sessions can enable the parties to see how the agreement is being operationalized and to renegotiate any impasses. Another time when this can be particularly important is when one or both are about to be or have recently been remarried and the postdivorce family is again restructured, necessitating another series of modifications and accommodations.

The postdivorce period can be one of exploration (at least for those who have the inclination, time, energy, and money to be adventuresome) of one's internal world and changing external environment. One may try out new activities, resume dormant hobbies, travel, return to school, or change jobs. It can be an exciting time of new challenges. In individual or group therapy one may sense "permission" to sample the pleasures of freedom in the singles' world and begin to evolve the perspective that will channel one's pursuits. Here, too, the divorced parties can learn to synthesize the multicolored collage of a complex life as parent, homemaker, lover, friend, employee, student, coach of homework, and to mobilize their resiliency to use the available opportunities in their new phase of life (Kaslow, 1984).

For some, positive feelings of competence to assess facts and figures and of empowerment to make choices and mistakes may result from the mediation process. For others, the time of pessimism and reactive depression, unremitting anger, and a quest for retaliation continues unabated. Mediation may hold less promise for these individuals and may, in fact, provide a forum only for the exacerbation of the conflict and the harassment of a former spouse. People in this group are apt to denigrate their former spouse, try to turn children and friends against him or her, wallow in self-pity, and perceive the divorce as the most critical and far-reaching event in their life. When this is the case, individual therapy geared to resolving anger and to accepting a role in provoking and sustaining the marital discord may be in order. These ex-spouses must seek to diminish their negativism and sense of helplessness and to release the children from a parental role and from becoming overly enmeshed with the distressed parent to the detriment of the children's ability and freedom to individuate. Unless and until this is accomplished, they cannot join in completing what Bohannon (1970) calls the sixth station, the psychic divorce.

The tentative hypothesis advanced here is that those who enter and complete mediation adjust better and quicker than those who pursue an adversarial divorce. Solid research of this hypothesis is important to identify the kinds of couples most amenable to mediation, which will assist in appropriate referrals, and to relieve court systems of clients who can be better served elsewhere.

SUMMARY AND CONCLUSION

Mediation entails an intricate modern dance that includes legal, economic, and emotional themes. The couple's willingness and ability to confront and negotiate about these themes sets the tempo for their departing pas de deux. It seems crucial that mediators be fully cognizant of the psychodynamics of divorce, its emotional vicissitudes and accompanying anguish, and the stages and content of the mediation process, if they are to be maximally effective in helping couples draw up viable agreements. It is equally imperative that mediators remain detached enough, while being aware of the emotional suffering, to function as mediators and not as therapists. Mediators must be knowledgeable in behavioral dynamics and family law, and be skillful directors capable of guiding the couple to a rational, equitable agreement.

REFERENCES

Abroms, G. The place of values in psychotherapy. *Journal of Marriage and Family Counseling,* 1978, *4(4)*, 3–18.

American Bar Association. *Model code of professional responsibility.* Chicago: National Center for Professional Responsibility, 1981.

Bach, G. R. Creative exits: Fight therapy for divorces. In V. Frank & V. Burtle (Eds.), *Women in therapy: New psychotherapies for a changing society* (pp. 307–325). New York: Brunner/ Mazel, 1974.

Bank, S. P., & Kahn, M. D. *The sibling bond.* New York: Basic Books, 1982.

Bohannon, P. The six stations of divorce. In P. Bohannon (Ed.), *Divorce and after: An analysis of the emotional and social problems of divorce* (pp. 29–55). New York: Doubleday, 1970.

Bowen, M. *Family therapy in clinical practice.* New York: Aronson, 1978.

Coogler, O. J. *Structured mediation in divorce settlement.* Lexington, MA: Heath, 1978.

Folberg, J. A mediation overview: History and dimensions of practice. *Mediation Quarterly*, 1983, *1*, 3–14.

Froiland, D. J., & Hozman, T. L. Counseling for constructive divorce. *Personnel and Guidance Journal*, 1977, *55*, 525–529.

Haynes, J. *Divorce mediation.* New York: Springer, 1981.

Haynes, J. A conceptual model of the process of family mediation: Implications for training. *American Journal of Family Therapy*, 1982, *10(4)*, 5–16.

Hetherington, E. M., Cox, M., & Cox, R. The aftermath of divorce. In J. H. Stevens, Jr., & M. Mathews (Eds.), *Mother–child, father–child relations* (pp. 149–176). Washington, DC: NAEYC, 1977.

Kadis, A. L., & Markowitz, M. Short-term analytic treatment of married couples in a group by a therapist couple. In C. Sager & H. S. Kaplan (Eds.), *Progress in group and family therapy* (pp. 463–482). New York: Brunner/Mazel, 1972.

Kaslow, F. W. Stages of divorce: A psychological perspective. *Villanova Law Review*, 1979–1980, *25(4/5)*, 718–751.

Kaslow, F. W. A diaclectic approach to family therapy and practice: Selectivity and synthesis. *Journal of Marital and Family Therapy*, 1981a, *6(3)*, 435–451.

Kaslow, F. W. Divorce and divorce therapy. In A. A. Gurman & D. P. Kniskern (Eds.), *Handbook of family therapy* (pp. 662–696). New York: Brunner/Mazel, 1981b.

Kaslow, F. W. Group therapy with couples in conflict: Is more better? *Psychotherapy: Theory, Research and Practice.* 1981c, *18(4)*, 516–524.

Kaslow, F. W. Profile of the healthy family. *Interaction*, 1981d, *4*, 1–15.

Kaslow, F. W. Group therapy with couples in conflict. *Australian Journal of Family Therapy*, 1982a, *3(4)*, 197–204.

Kaslow, F. W. Portrait of a healthy couple. *Psychiatric Clinics of North America*, 1982b, *5(3)*, 519–527.

Kaslow, F. W. Stages and techniques of divorce therapy. In P. A. Keller & L. G. Ritt (Eds.), *Innovations in clinical practice: A source book II* (pp. 5–16). Sarasota, FL: Professional Resources Exchange, 1983.

Kaslow, F. W. Divorce: An evolutionary process of change in the family system. *Journal of Divorce*, 1984, *7(3)*, 21–39.

Kaslow, F. W., & Lieberman, E. J. Couples group therapy: Rationale, dynamics and process. In P. Sholevar (Ed.), *Handbook of marriage and marital therapy* (pp. 347–362). New York: SP Medical & Scientific Books, 1981.

Kaslow, F. W., & Schwartz, L. L. (1987). *Dynamics of divorce: A life cycle perspective.* New York: Brunner/Mazel.

Kessler, S. *The American way of divorce: Prescription for change.* Chicago: Nelson Hall, 1975.

Kessler, S. *Creative conflict resolution: Mediation.* Atlanta, GA: National Institute for Professional Training, 1978.

Kessler, S., & Bostwick, S. Beyond divorce: Coping skills for children. *Journal of Clinical Child Psychology*, 1977, *6*, 38–41.

Maslow, A. *Toward a psychology of being.* New York: Van Nostrand Reinhold, 1968.

Neville, W. G. Mediation—For therapists and their spouses. In F. W. Kaslow (Ed.), *Psychotherapy with psychotherapists* (pp. 103–122). New York: Haworth Press, 1984.

Pollack, S., Kaslow, N. J., & Harvey, D. In F. W. Kaslow (Ed.), *The international book of family therapy* (pp. 170–184). New York: Brunner/Mazel, 1982.

Sager, C. J., Brown, H. S., Crohn, H., Engel, T., Rodstein, E., & Walker, L. *Treating the remarried family.* New York: Brunner/Mazel, 1983.

Wallerstein, J. S., & Kelly, J. B. Divorce and children. In J. D. Noshpitz (Ed.), *Handbook of child psychiatry IV* (pp. 339–347). New York: Basic Books, 1979.

Wallerstein, J. S., & Kelly, J. B. *Surviving the breakup: How children and parents cope with divorce.* New York: Basic Books, 1980.

Walsh, F. *Normal family processes.* New York: Guilford Press, 1982.

Whitaker, C. A., & Miller, M. H. A re-evaluation of "psychiatric help" when divorce impends. *American Journal of Psychiatry*, 1969, *126*, 57–64.

6

The Legal Dimension of Divorce Mediation

STEPHEN K. ERICKSON
Erickson Mediation Institute, Edina, Minnesota

Divorce mediation is distinguishable from other applications of mediation because divorce is, by definition, a legal procedure. Understanding the legal dimension of divorce and how traditional adversarial divorce differs from a mediated approach is essential in helping divorcing couples reach a comprehensive marital settlement. The author, an attorney mediator, draws on ten years of divorce mediation experience to offer a detailed comparison between the legal process of divorce and the process of mediation. The questions that must be answered in making decisions about divorce are reframed from an adversarial posture to the problem-solving language of mediation.

Only a very few of the approximately 1.2 million divorces each year in the United States are actually taken to a court for resolution. In fact, if a substantial percentage of divorces were to fully use the court system and trial process, there would be a massive overload and failure of the system. Therefore, negotiated divorce settlements are encouraged, stimulating the growth of divorce mediation.

There are few absolutes or rigid rules for divorce settlements or court rulings if the spouses do not resolve the issues. In most states, the divorce codes continue to be guidelines that merely touch upon the vast discretionary power of divorce courts to make rulings that are "fair and equitable." The disparities in rulings and uncertainties about what a trial judge will do in a particular divorce case have caused a movement towards enactment of mandatory support schedules as well as other attempts to create more uniformity in decisions. Nevertheless, most divorces are negotiated in the shadow of laws that remain vague, vary greatly from state to state, and present vast differences among jurisdictions and individual judges concerning the question of what is fair and equitable.

Except where some public policy is violated, courts routinely enter orders based on divorce settlement agreements, whether reached through adversarial negotiation or mediation. The courts are generally reluctant to meddle in the private ordering of the divorcing couple if they have made adequate provisions for their children and have addressed the other issues that must be resolved in divorces. This chapter examines the legal side of mediation and compares the resolution of divorce issues in the adversarial system to the process of divorce settlement in mediation.

COMPARISON OF ADVERSARIAL AND MEDIATION PROCESSES

The goal of the mediation system is exactly the same as the adversarial system in most cases, that is, to present the court with a settlement agreement. The mediation process parallels the legal process in several other important ways. (Appendix 6-1 compares the mediated divorce to the adversarial divorce, step by step.) The discovery stage of the adversarial process parallels the requirement of full disclosure and other methods used by mediators to ensure the truth of the information relied upon to reach settlement. Both systems make liberal use of experts. All the issues essential to a complete agreement that are normally raised by attorneys must also be raised by mediators. This is why competent divorce mediators must have knowledge of the adversarial divorce process, in order to assist the couple in meeting the requirements for a complete divorce agreement.

If the mediation process in many ways mirrors the legal process and is primarily concerned with the settlement aspect, what makes mediation more desirable than the system of adversarial negotiations used by the vast majority of the divorcing public? If the legal system encourages settlement and divorce attorneys assist the public in the settlement process, why do we need mediators and how is their task different from the lawyers' task? The answers to these two questions are found through an analysis of mediation and adversarial divorce, focusing on the difference in the questions asked by each system and the way in which each defines the issues. Whatever the approach, the divorce process is complete only when the couple has resolved the questions raised by the decision to divorce or separate: "Who will have the children?" "How much money do I get or pay?" "What will happen to the house?" The list often seems endless and depends on the unique circumstances of each couple.

In the adversarial system, the process for answering these questions is ruled by a set of procedures. The attorney is the primary interpreter to the client of what is fair, based upon what might happen in court. Because the rules of the game are adversarial, the attorney responds to the above questions with advice about what can be expected if the case goes to trial. The couple may base decisions on normative predictions instead of on the couple's circumstances and wants. The legal process tells the couple what is fair based on the point spread if the real contest is ever played out, whereas the mediation process asks the couple to define their own law of fairness. It is not unusual in mediation for a couple to decide to do something quite different than what the court might have decided if the case had gone to trial.

Mediation says that what the legislators or courts have said should occur in divorce cases is less important than what the couple thinks is fair. This doctrine of creating one's own law of fairness may result in alimony provisions for a dependent spouse in Texas or Indiana, even though those states have no law requiring such an outcome in a case tried in family court. Mediated agreements have also provided for the payment of child support past the age of majority.

The mediator and the attorney may both produce an agreement, but they differ in the process used. The mediator helps the parties negotiate their settlement, while in the traditional legal process the two attorneys advise and negotiate a settlement on behalf of their clients. Attorney negotiations are based on the assumption that an adversarial, competitive approach to conflict allows the attorney for each spouse to argue and compete for the best result. The attorneys define the most common divorce issues in a way that reflects the basic assumptions inherent in the adversarial court process, in terms of competitive, win–lose outcomes. In contrast, mediators define divorce issues in mutual, cooperative terms that require a different effort to answer the questions.

REDEFINING AND FRAMING DIVORCE ISSUES

How can cooperation be encouraged and a win–win outcome be achieved in mediation when a conflict exists? Mediators define the issues in ways that make it easier for the parties in conflict to find solutions. Skilled mediators have long known that the ability to define the conflict is one of the most important factors in determining the outcome. An example of this principle in another context has frequently been used by Morton Deutsch in his lectures on cooperative conflict-resolution methods.

The Cuban missile crisis in 1961 was first defined as a global conflict that pitted the East against the West, the free world against communism. During the first few days of the conflict, newspapers reported the global implications and cited the possibility of nuclear war between the superpowers. As the days passed, more details of the Cuban missile site were reported in newspapers and other media. By the last few days of the crisis, the papers were beginning to report that intelligence photos showed the missiles lying disassembled on flatbed trucks. The conflict was resolved when both sides began stating that the problem was not a communist war against the free world but the deployment of a relatively small number of disassembled missiles in a remote eastern province of Cuba. The conflict was much easier to deal with when the United States and the Soviet Union stated the issues in narrow, more easily managed terms.

It is often said that the person who defines the problem controls the outcome. Mediators take advantage of this principle by skillfully assisting parties to state the issues of the conflict in mutual terms, which are more manageable than global terms. The underlying strength of divorce mediation is that it has developed a new language and a new way of stating the typical divorce issues. This results in a more manageable and more humane process of reaching settlement.

In my divorce mediation practice, I have found that one of the most powerful techniques to promote cooperative and constructive negotiation is to frame all questions about divorce issues in mutual, future-oriented terms, in contrast to the adversarial system's win–lose, past-oriented approach. This critical difference is most evident when the adversarial model and the mediation model are compared and contrasted using the major divorce issues as focal points. Consider the differences between the way the legal adversarial model frames the basic questions of divorce and the way the mediation process frames those questions.

Parenting

The legal adversarial system asks, "Who will be awarded custody of the minor children?" The result is that the parent who is not awarded custody is then labeled a noncustodial, visiting parent. In many ways, this question is much like the law school professor's example of an inappropriate leading question, the most famous of which is, "When did you stop beating your wife?" Just as the wife-beating question assumes an answer by the way it is asked, the usual custody question assumes that it is necessary to determine two levels of "ownership" of the minor children. This is absurd, because the question of ownership need not even be asked; the focus should be establishing the parenting obligations that must be practiced in the future by the spouses.

Given a choice, few people would wish to be labeled noncustodial, visiting parents. Yet asking the custody question results in a battle to determine who will be designated the custodial parent and therefore have the stamp of approval placed on his or her past behavior. Being labeled a noncustodial parent is like having the mark of Cain branded permanently upon your parenting ability. You are a failure, and if you are not good enough to be the custodial parent, there must be something wrong with you.

Another fault with the adversarial phrasing of the parenting question lies with the term "custody." Not only does custody imply ownership, it designates control. Custody often implies prison or confinement. Use of the word "custody" creates the wrong focus and motivation for dealing with children of divorce.

The adversarial system, in the way it asks the custody question, looks primarily to the past to determine who has been a better parent. Usually the court awards custody based upon past parenting performance. Mental health professionals know that this is unhealthy and that such a system of determining parenting roles leads to a future parenting relationship based on acrimony. It is no wonder then that so many couples who experience custody trials or the adversarial negotiations that lead to a custody determination have difficult visitation problems.

A more appropriate question to ask the divorcing couple is, "What future parenting arrangements can you agree to, so that each of you can continue to be involved, loving parents?" This version of the custody question creates a different focus and a very different outcome. First, the question is mutual, and answering it requires cooperation. Asking "Who shall have custody?" creates a competitive focus and is likely to produce an adversarial or fighting response, but asking the couple to agree to create certain parenting arrangements requires collaborative discussions and mutual planning.

Second, the question is future oriented. Mediation pushes couples to look more to the future because it can be controlled and changed. When the mediator asks a future-oriented, mutual question, couples find it easier to work through the difficult task of being two parents living in different houses.

A further step in redefining the custody questions is the development of new language and new words used by divorce mediators to make the issues more easily resolved in an atmosphere of mutuality. The following words may be substituted for adversarial terminology:

- *parenting* instead of custody
- *access* instead of visitation
- *time-sharing arrangements* instead of visitation schedules
- *shared duties* instead of rights
- *limited parenting duties* instead of noncustodial parent
- *residential parent* instead of custodial parent

Child Support

Developing new ways of stating the issues for divorcing couples is not limited to custody and parenting conflict but applies also to financial and property questions. The adversarial system asks, "What amount of child support will the husband pay to the wife for the support of the children in her custody?" This question sets up a tug of war that creates positional bargaining. The question frames the problem as one of what amount of money should be paid to the wife and, conversely, what amount of money should be expected from the husband. Usually, since the payor is afraid of paying too much and the payee is afraid of not getting enough, both try to protect their own sphere of interest. The husband and wife are again focused on protecting themselves against loss from the attempts of the other to achieve gain.

In the United States mothers are most likely to have custody of minor children, and fathers usually pay child support. Unfortunately, the fathers who are supposed to be paying child support have a dismal track record. Recent studies by the Census Bureau show that less than half of all women who are awarded court-ordered support from their ex-husbands receive the full amount. One common reason for poor payment performance is that the man does not like passing support payments for the children through his ex-wife's checking account. He may not trust his ex-wife and may fail to conceptualize the child-support exchange as being for the benefit of the children, rather than for the benefit of the ex-spouse. As a divorce attorney, I frequently heard husbands suggest generous payment offers to a college trust fund in order to keep the money out of the wife's hands. The manner in which the adversarial system frames the child-support question is a major part of the current disgraceful statistics about support payment compliance.

Divorce mediators try to encourage couples to attack the problem rather than attacking each other, and a different framing of the child-support question helps accomplish this goal. The first, basic question is, "How will both of you share the cost of raising your children?" This question is framed in a mutual manner and leads to a series of questions and issues that must be resolved. As in Deutsch's example of the Cuban missile crisis, where the conflict was more easily managed when the problem was narrowly defined, the traditional child-support issue is more easily solved when a series of narrowly focused questions are asked.

First the mediator and the couple need to know, "What amount of money does each of you need to meet basic monthly expenses?" In most United States family courts, litigants are required to submit some kind of affidavit or evidence of basic monthly expenses. This evidence is usually collected in the attorney's office, by interviewing the client and completing a standard court affidavit budget form. Other information such as verification of income is also required. Since, by the rules of the game, your spouse has become your opponent, the goal of the budgeting affidavit completed in preparation for court is to show as high expenses as possible. It is always better to err on the high side as long as the line items don't get too outrageous, such as $600 a month for food for a single father. If a client persisted in claiming such a high expense item, the attorney might argue that the client has been living in a weekly rental room since separation and must eat all meals at restaurants. Showing such high expenses is part of the strategy to demonstrate that the payee needs high levels of support and the payor, because of the high expenses, has very little left over to give to the custodial parent as support.

In mediation, a couple are told that each partner must complete a budget to determine what amount of money is required to meet basic living expenses. At first glance this may not seem much different from the adversarial process, but the couple are further told that they must mutually agree that both budgets are fair and reasonable. This is accomplished in a joint session, and the mediator tells the couple that in order to determine how they will share the costs of raising the children, they must first know and agree to the amounts that each needs to pay their bills each month. When the couple grasp the logic of the process they are engaged in, they no longer need to inflate budgets. In fact, I have found that when most couples engage in a mutual budget session, examining and discussing separate line items, both partners have a tendency to underestimate their expenses.

Once the budgets are nearly complete and displayed for the couple on flip-chart paper, the next question is, "Do you both agree that these expenses listed are reasonable for each of you?" Rather than trying to convince a judge that inflated expenses are real, the husband and wife use the mediation process to examine and comment on each other's budget in a safe environment (the mediation office), with the goal of reaching agreement about required expense totals before the next step is taken. Skilled mediators know that budget expenses can change and encourage the couple to present new or changed budget information at later sessions.

Just as the adversarial process, when addressing support issues, asks for income data, the mediation process asks, "What amount of income is now being shared by both of you, even though you may be living apart?" Both mediation and litigation require knowledge of the income available to the husband and wife. However, the adversarial process seems to place undue emphasis on one party's income in answering the child-support questions. Many family courts, in an effort to establish some consistency of rulings, have resorted to a rigid application of support tables and guidelines. In the three counties where I most often represented husbands or wives as their attorney, each county court used a different support table. Yet all three tables, as well as other tables in use or suggested for use in other parts of the country, rely primarily on two factors to determine the amount of child support paid by the noncustodial parent: (1) the net income of the noncustodial payor and (2) the number of children. Some tables also take into account whether the custodial parent is earning an income, but no tables that I have examined ever take into account more than three factors. Once the factors are inserted into the table, the amount of support is found as a percentage of net income. (For example, unemployed wife with two children at home requires the noncustodial husband to pay 35% of his net take-home salary per month as child support.)

In mediation, the disclosure and exchange of income information is only one part of the solution. This important variable answers the immediate question of how much money is currently available to the couple for meeting their own needs as well as sharing the costs of the children. In mediation, however, it would not be fair to use rigid support tables. Such tables, applied uniformly to all couples appearing in family court, fail to take into account the fact that one family may be paying $950 a month for a mortgage, while another couple may be paying only $250 a month. The income data, considered with the couple's expense statements, often create the realization that there is not enough money available to support two households. At this point, the family court may conclude the temporary support hearing by welcoming the couple to the real world and entering an arbitrary amount for support, whereas in mediation, couples have just begun to tackle the problem.

The mediator must next ask, "What is the amount of the shortfall?" (the difference between agreed-to necessary expenses for both and the available income earned by each). This is a simple task of subtraction. However, it should be noted that the mediator is asking the couple to calculate not their individual budget shortages, but rather the combined budget shortfall. At this point the couple has not yet decided the support exchange amount and therefore does not know what each will be able to spend each month.

The next question asked of the couple is, "Can the budget expenses be decreased?" Asking the couple to examine this issue at this point gets both of them thinking about ways in which they can jointly attack the problem of not having enough money to pay for the costs of two households. Although it is dangerous to encourage them to strip down what already may be a bare-bones budget, they should be asked to look at eliminating nonessential expenditures in each budget, as well as considering possible future changes. If this part of the process is managed properly by the mediator, the spouses will both try to determine if expenses can be reduced. When both the husband and wife, in the presence of each other, indicate several areas in which they can reduce expense, such agreements become the small building blocks of trust and fairness that need to be constantly encouraged by the skilled mediator.

Continuing the search for mutual solutions, the converse of the above question asks, "Can the combined income now being shared by both of you be increased?" It would not be fair to ask the budget-cutting question without asking this one. This question usually leads to discussion about the future plans for the more dependent spouse. Most often the wife, who may not be employed, has an opportunity to present her thoughts about employment, training, and education. This question is also a good point to begin some preliminary discussions about possible tax planning to create additional income. Whatever the result, the question is framed and timed in such a way that the couple share with each other their plans for becoming financially independent.

In most cases, available income cannot be immediately increased. The focus of the question is to encourage both the husband and wife to see that they share responsibility for the cost of raising the children, rather than to create a frame of mind in which the noncustodial spouse merely owes money to the custodial spouse. In situations where both agree it is impossible for the custodial parent to work, such as the case where there are three children under the age of five in the home and the youngest is still breastfeeding, it is important for the mediator to suggest that some plans be considered for employment in the future. The mediator might also point out that sharing the cost for raising the children can be temporarily answered by showing that one parent will make "in-kind payments" of full-time care. This is seldom more than a temporary solution, and since many couples in mediation choose joint custody with more than every other weekend visitation, the dependent primary custodian has some time to explore contributing to the income pie.

In wrestling with this problem of how to fairly share the costs of raising the children, many couples need to know, "What are the separate, special costs attributable only to the children?" These costs typically include private-school tuition, day-care expenses, orthodontia costs, extracurricular activity fees, special medication costs, and all other costs that can be identified for the children. Some couples find it particularly useful to determine a separate budget that attempts to compute or apportion all costs related to the children. This may mean ferreting out of each of their personal budgets those expenses that are related to the children. This "children's expense budget" is again part of the process of narrowing each issue into separate and more easily managed components. Once the couple know the total amount of the costs related to raising a child, they can better determine how to share that cost. Ultimately, this makes more sense than simply referring to a child-support table and picking a support figure.

The task of deciding a fair way to share the cost of raising the children would be easy if all couples agreed to a fifty–fifty time-sharing parenting arrangement and the husband and wife earned exactly the same salaries. In these circumstances, money spent on the children for food and meals when with each parent would be about equal, and the dollars spent by each parent would be "equal" dollars because of the equal incomes. Most couples do not have equal time-sharing, however, and one parent, usually the husband, earns more than the wife, which means that a dollar spent by the wife for the children represents a larger percentage of her income than a dollar spent by the husband.

Framing the problem in this fashion usually helps the couple see more clearly the possible solutions. Even though most couples in mediation still settle their child-support issues with a monthly transfer payment for child support, they see more clearly the reasons why such a transfer payment is needed. They understand that the spouse with a higher income should pay something to the lower income spouse because the dollars used by each to share the cost of raising the children are not equivalent dollars, and if the lower income spouse has more responsibility for the children, such child-support payments become even more necessary.

In the past year of my mediation practice, several couples have created innovative mechanisms for determining child support. In one case, the task was to develop options for division of a duplex they owned, and their duplex checkbook was lying on the table in front of us. One of them said, "Why don't we go to the bank and open a children's account?" As the three of us talked about the idea, it began to make sense. They had already agreed that a separate budget for the child, age 14 months, amounted to $740 per month for formula, baby-care items, some baby-room furniture, clothing, and all other costs attributable to the child that the couple could think of at the time. Although they had agreed to joint custody, the child would be with the mother about 75% of the time. In addition, the husband's earnings were approximately two and one-half times the income of the wife, who was also employed full-time. They agreed that the husband would contribute $500 per month to the account and the wife would contribute $240. From the child's account, the wife would purchase all items necessary for the care of the child and would be the accountant. In this way, they would begin to have a record of all child-support expenses, which would make it easier for them to make adjustments to the amounts when child-support needs increased or decreased.

While this arrangement may not work for all couples, it has worked for many mediation couples. The record of canceled checks, periodically reviewed by both, will provide detailed information needed to support future modifications.

In summary, the roadmap I have described for helping couples agree on child-support issues is in many ways like the Cuban missile crisis scenario. Couples begin the journey knowing that they are in a crisis and fearing that the worst will happen, that they will be unfairly treated by the courts or their spouse and not have enough money to exist. The problem need not be viewed as the beginning of a global battle but rather can be taken step by step in manageable pieces. Both spouses begin to see that they can continue to coexist only if they begin to attack problems mutually, rather than attacking each other.

Spousal Support

Another aspect of support is perhaps an even more pressing problem for some couples. Many couples arrive at a divorce decision with one person, usually the wife, totally or partially dependent upon the marriage relationship for financial support. The dependency may be both an emotional and a financial dependency, and if the divorcing couple end up in family court, the adversarial system in most states asks, "What amount of alimony or spousal support should the husband pay to the wife and for how long?" State statutes may offer guidelines about considering the financial circumstances of both parties, the length of the marriage relationship, and some background characteristics of each. Many appellate courts and some legislation indicate that spousal maintenance should not be deemed to be a permanent profit-sharing plan of the husband's income and that a wife may take no more than a few years on alimony to rehabilitate herself. But trial court judges are generally given wide discretion in deciding what is fair in each particular case.

Asking the question in this fashion creates a situation where the wife tries to show how bleak her circumstances are and the husband usually presents evidence about his limited income and tries to prove that his wife really is capable of supporting herself, if only she would look for work. This is unhealthy for both spouses, especially if they have children and need to cooperate in the future.

As a mediator, I always reframe the basic question, "How will each of you share responsibility for the more dependent spouse to become independent?" When the alimony issue is framed in this way, the responsibility for solving the problem rests with both spouses. Before this question is asked, however, it is necessary to complete the budgeting process as outlined above in the child-support section. As with the child-support discussion, the spousal support issue also requires a series of narrowly defined issues and questions that the spouses must consider before they can decide how each of them share responsibility for a dependency created during the marriage relationship.

The mediator asks the couple, "Do you both agree that one of you is now dependent upon the marriage relationship for financial support?" Although the dependency may seem so apparent that the question need not be asked, the couple usually engage in a discussion of how they got to the point where one earns all the money and the other stays home and takes primary responsibility for the children. If the wife has no source of income, other than sharing the husband's earnings, she is obviously dependent upon the marriage. Engaging in this type of discussion is important for both spouses to see and understand that, because of choices they both made earlier, they now find themselves in difficult circumstances where one spouse has no employment or very little earning capacity. If the couple can agree and understand how they got to this point, the husband is less likely to blame the wife for her unemployment and her need for his support.

The second narrow question is, "Do you both agree that a goal of the negotiations is to find a plan that allows each of you to become financially independent from the other?" I have never asked this question without hearing from the dependent spouse a response like this, "I would like to be able to stop getting support from him as soon as is humanly possible." Husbands have often expressed relief at hearing their wife say that she wishes to become financially independent. Many men have the perception that women enjoy fat alimony checks by relaxing at home, eating peppermint bonbons and waiting for the children to come home from school. In the eyes of many women, alimony is a sign of continued dependence upon a person with whom they would like to cut ties and who is usually just as eager to be free of those ties. Most dependent spouses would like to become financially self-sufficient, but how and when become fearful questions that seem impossible to answer. As long as the spouses can agree on the above goal, the seeds of a new beginning for each one are in the ground, waiting to grow.

The next question follows from that above but is separate and distinct. The mediator asks the couple to determine, "What plan will make each of you financially independent of the other?" This question should help the couple understand that a successful spousal maintenance plan involves more than one spouse's paying money to the dependent spouse for a period of time. Both partners must discuss and agree on a plan of action that helps the dependent one reach financial self-sufficiency. The adversarial system defines this concept as rehabilitative alimony, a term that conveys the proper goal but seems to further degrade the status of those who often are dependent only because of mutual choices, explicit and implicit, made during the marriage relationship.

The mediation focus should convey the idea that both the husband and wife are responsible for solving the spousal maintenance problem. The adversarial system commonly sees the husband as having primary responsibility for solving this problem by transferring money to the dependent spouse. However, the dependent spouse also has responsibility for contributing to the solution by adopting a plan that will reasonably be expected to create financial self-sufficiency. The discussions of this stage require an examination of educational and retraining possibilities. Possible referrals to work opportunity centers run for displaced homemakers or retraining counseling may be necessary. Although the independent spouse cannot tell the dependent spouse what to do, this question involves both in the process of searching for a solution.

The final question, after completing work on the above issues, is, "What length of time will it take for the dependent spouse to become independent?" The adversarial system tries in several ways to answer this question. In some states, the courts rule that alimony ends immediately upon the dependent spouse's graduation from a course of education or retraining. In other jurisdictions the courts may award alimony for a length of time equal to half the duration of the marriage relationship. Whatever legal guidelines are followed in a particular jurisdiction depend on the political process of the state legislature or upon the rulings of the state courts.

In mediation, deciding the length of time for spousal support is perhaps one of the most difficult of all problems. It raises a whole package of emotions and fears for each spouse. Dependent spouses are very willing to have alimony terminate upon their finding adequate employment but are unable to say exactly when that will be. The paying spouse, usually willing to pay what it takes to eliminate the dependency as soon as possible, wants some certainty and may request definite time limits on the length of the alimony obligation. However, if the spouses have done their homework and if the mediator has been sensitive to the needs of both and has involved them in developing a plan, then an agreement becomes easier.

Property Division

The fourth main area of decision making in most divorces is the division of marital property. As with the issues of parenting and support, the property questions framed by the adversarial process create a tug of war. Couples in the midst of divorce, threatened in their parenting relationships and financial security, also fear loss of their property. When first visiting an attorney about a divorce, a client is told about the law and about what the courts usually do when dividing property. In community property states, the concept of equal division of community property tells the couple that an equal division of all marital property acquired during the marriage is what the state considers fair. Other states have a concept of "equitable division," which gives judges more discretion in dividing property, even though the standard approach taken by most equitable-division courts is an equal division. The division of property is emotionally and legally complex: it means the dividing and distributing of the material things needed for one's continued existence, such as shelter, transportation, investments, pensions, and all other marital assets.

For couples entering the adversarial process, the first questions about their property are often, "What can I get? What are my rights?" In the adversarial system, participants are encouraged to ask, "How can I obtain as much for myself as possible?" This question must be faced in the attorney's office because the ethical rules of the legal profession require the attorney to engage in zealous advocacy on behalf of the client, and the other side is not only asking the same question but also preparing the case to demonstrate that their side is more worthy of prevailing on the claims. This usually means that spouses and their attorneys approach the problem from the attitude, "I can only get the things I need for myself at the expense of the other person." This attitude pits the parties against each other, creating a focus that mediators try to avoid.

In mediation, both parties are seen as worthy, but since the pie is only so big, the question is, "How can the two of you divide your property in such a way that meets both of your needs in the future?" In mediation, the focus is more on the process and less on the outcome. The property issue is perceived less as a tally sheet of items awarded to the client and more as a method of enabling both sides to meet their needs as they have defined them in the mediation discussions.

Trained family mediators ask five separate subquestions:

1. What property are you going to divide?
2. What understanding and knowledge do you need to arrive at an intelligent, fair property division?
3. What is the value of your property assets?
4. What standard of fairness should be applied to the property division process?
5. Given that the above four questions have been answered, what property should each of you have?

These questions are essentially the same steps that attorneys follow in preparing the typical divorce case for trial, except that attorneys usually answer Step 4 by applying the statutory and case law of the particular state where the divorce is occurring. The mediation process, however, takes the couple through these five steps in a different way.

Deciding what property will be divided requires an inventory of all property, both marital and nonmarital. Attorneys and mediators use standard questionnaires and client interviews to assemble this information, but mediators have no need to schedule depositions of the opponent because both sides to the controversy are in the same room and the questions can be asked jointly. Keeping in mind that the process is most important, mediators find that when both parties are in a room completing the work of the inventory, this sharing of information tends to help the less-informed spouse take responsibility for working on further solutions and also lessens some of the fears and suspicions that are inherent between spouses in a dissolving marriage. Mediators, as well as attorneys, ensure that this step is accomplished completely and accurately by asking for documentation such as bank records, investment summaries, pension plan statements, tax returns, and all other documents that might verify the existence of an asset.

The couple needs to assess their ability to discuss a property division. They may need continuing education in the subject. Many spouses in a divorce, both men and women, have very little understanding about the standard options available to them concerning their property assets. Many couples do not have a basic understanding of financial matters; their education is essential to making their own decisions. A good mediator assists the couple in reaching a level of knowledge that ensures good decisions are made. The adversarial system, in contrast, often takes the position that these matters are too complex for most clients to understand, and therefore the attorney is charged with telling the client about what is happening, because only an expert can sort these things out.

The third question, about valuing assets, is an integral step in the divorce process. I often remind couples that it is difficult to bargain and negotiate about your property unless you know the color of the chips you are using. In the adversarial system, this is the area where attorney advocates can display some of their most zealous competitiveness. Even in states where community property laws seem to dictate an equal property division, differences over the value of a family business or house can be exaggerated when the parties realize that, if the law says they must divide everything equally, then one way to get a larger share is to undervalue one party's portion and overvalue the opponent's share. This tactic can, of course, be tried by individuals regardless of the system they are using, but the mediator can encourage the couple to use one neutral appraiser when necessary. Rather than taking each spouse's expert to court for a judge to determine which expert is more credible, the couple in mediation meet jointly with the experts and ask questions, often with the assistance of the mediator, thereby allowing the parties themselves to judge what is credible.

The fourth step, asking the couple to determine the standard of fairness they will use to divide their property, is perhaps the most innovative part of the mediation process. Stated very simply, this means the parties apply whatever fairness principle they deem appropriate to the property division. If parties in conflict agree beforehand on the standard of fairness they will use to judge the outcome of their negotiations, they will arrive at a more fair and certainly more understandable result (Fisher & Ury, 1981). I practice in a state where the most common outcome in litigated divorces is an equal division of marital property. Applying a fifty–fifty division to the marital property division question is applying a standard of fairness. Yet it is not uncommon in my mediation practice for couples to agree upon an unequal division of property, giving the dependent spouse a greater share of the marital assets. Another standard of fairness that may be adopted by couples is that the home should not be sold until the children graduate from high school. Similarly, a spouse might be allowed to continue to operate his or her business as if it were the primary means of supporting the family. The mediator asks the parties to review and choose between several standards of fairness. The goal is to ask the couple to participate in negotiating all aspects of the divorce process, including the "law" to be applied to their circumstances.

The final division of the marital property is much easier to complete when the couple have worked through the first four steps rather than being told by their attorneys or the court what the outcome must be. In mediation, couples have more freedom to use innovative ways of redistributing the property and assets accumulated during their partnership.

CONCLUSION

In this chapter, I have attempted to highlight some of the major similarities and differences between a litigated, adversarial divorce process and a mediated, cooperative divorce process. My presentation has been biased because I believe that mediation principles, when appropriately used by a trained, professional family mediator, always result in a better method of ending the marriage relationship.

I have handled about as many clients as a divorce attorney as I have as a divorce mediator using a structured process. My partner and I have just begun an in-depth analysis of close to 400 couples we have separately mediated through Family Mediation Services since we began in 1977. Less than 30 of those couples reached impasse, the rest being successful in mediation. (Couples at impasse are those who signed an agreement to begin mediation, attended more than three sessions, and were unable to reach complete agreement on all the issues in their divorce process.)

Providing divorce mediation services has been a rewarding professional experience. I have also had many disappointments, particularly with those attorneys who view divorce mediation as a threat to their livelihood. Through it all, I have been sustained by the clients and their excitement upon learning that conflict need not be overwhelming or distasteful but can be a point for a new beginning in their lives.

The next several years will see continuing debate about divorce mediation, and like any new concept, it will continue to have birth pains as well as growth pains. However, one observation does seem safe. Just as the medical profession has experienced dramatic changes in the area of service delivery, pricing, and methods of practice in the past decade, so too can the legal profession expect significant changes in how the public chooses to resolve divorce conflicts.

APPENDIX 6-1: A STEP-BY-STEP COMPARISON

The following steps trace the significant points in divorce and describe the similarities and differences between the adversarial and mediation processes.

Adversarial Process	Mediation Process
Decision to Divorce	
Couples have usually made the decision to divorce before visiting a lawyer, although many individual spouses obtain information about their rights prior to actually making a decision to proceed with the divorce process. In the event one spouse wishes the other to refrain from some type of behavior, a divorce or separate maintenance action must be filed to activate the court's power to force the other spouse to act.	The decision to divorce need not be a firm decision, and the couple may take advantage of the mediation process without filing papers. Voluntary decisions about management of money, separation, and freezing of assets can be obtained without commencing legal action. However, such mediated decisions do not have binding legal effect.

Commencement of Legal Action

Filing of a petition for divorce by service of process upon the opposing spouse is usually completed prior to beginning negotiations about a possible settlement.

Filing of a petition for divorce is usually done after the couple have completed mediation and they and their attorneys are provided with a memorandum of understanding that serves as the basis for the stipulated settlement agreement and divorce decree.

Temporary Hearing

A temporary hearing is seldom scheduled unless court restraint is deemed necessary because one spouse is in physical danger or it appears possible that one spouse will abscond with or significantly deplete marital funds or property. Where uncertainty about support exists, the hearing establishes temporary levels of child and spousal support and determines occupancy and use of homestead and other property during pendency of the proceeding.

Signing an agreement to mediate, where the couple contractually agree to rules and conditions prohibiting depletion of assets, cancellation of insurance policies, and so forth, serves as a substitute for the orders issued at a temporary hearing. The first mediation sessions will cover other temporary or immediate decisions that must be made before the couple begin to work on settlement of long-term issues. The mediator asks the couple if they wish to have their temporary agreements filed with the court by their attorneys, and where trust level is low, some couples will ask their attorneys to prepare a temporary agreement based upon the mediation decisions reached at the initial sessions. Converting temporary mediated agreements into temporary legal orders may be desirable, to take advantage of the spousal support tax deduction.

Discovery

Discovery is accomplished informally or formally through motions to produce, depositions, and interrogatories. Because comprehensive formal discovery is expensive, it is only used in those cases with sufficient assets to justify the expense, although discovery of expert wit-

The mediator supervises and manages discovery. Should one party become uncooperative, the sessions are usually terminated and the couple are returned to their lawyers, who will then proceed with formal, court-supervised discovery. Documentation of assets and identifica-

nesses' opinions and possible testimony is used in contested custody matters. Since fair divorces are based on complete disclosure, the integrity of the discovery process is supervised and managed by the individual attorneys, with resort to the court system for assistance if the other attorney or spouse becomes uncooperative. Under existing rules of ethics, attorneys are generally not required to volunteer information unless and until it is requested by the other side.

tion of property and income are quite similar to the adversarial method. Couples beginning mediation are asked to sign an agreement to mediate that requires them to produce copies of tax returns, pay stubs, business records, and all other documents and records requested either by the mediator or the other spouse. Because the mediator supervises and manages disclosure, he or she must be familiar with the documents needed by the attorneys who are asked to review and approve mediated decisions.

Settlement Documents

The attorneys prepare the settlement document after reaching agreement on all issues in the divorce. The jurisdiction may call it a stipulation for settlement, marital settlement agreement, or marital termination agreement. The language most often has special legal significance and contains legal descriptions and boilerplate language as dictated by local custom.

The mediator prepares a memorandum of the decisions or a mediated plan. The mediation document is not signed by the couple and has no binding legal effect until reviewed and converted to a legal document. Some mediators ask the couple to sign the mediation memorandum after it is reviewed and approved by the attorneys, so that it can be attached as an exhibit to the court papers. The memorandum of understanding is drafted in plain English and usually contains background information about how the decisions were negotiated and reached, providing a basis for evaluating the entire settlement.

Contested Hearings

Contested hearings are the last resort if negotiations fail, and may be used by attorneys to coerce a better settlement. This stage of the adversarial process often presents some internal conflict for the divorce attorney, who understands that settlement may be desirable but is wary of being viewed as soft

Most couples attempting settlement through the mediation process wish to avoid the cost, stress, and delay of acrimonious, contested proceedings. Resort to contested proceedings represents a failure of the mediation process to the extent that the couple have placed themselves in the position of allowing the

or unwilling to do what is necessary to represent fully the interests of his or her client.

court to make decisions for them. Mediation may be partially successful in narrowing issues to be litigated.

Law or Legal Precedent

The law is the foundation of most settlement choices, and the divorce outcome is judged according to what might have happened in court or how the court will rule on a particular factual situation. Where the law does not mandate certain agreements, attorneys will approve such agreements with caution.

The law is seldom discussed because divorce mediation is not viewed as the practice of law. Thus, all legal predictions about the outcome or result in a particular case or issue are referred back to the couple's attorneys. Couples are asked to determine their own law of fairness rather than to speculate on what the litigation outcome might be.*

Time to Complete

In a contested case, the divorce process is long, often in excess of 1 year. In a negotiated settlement, the time to complete depends on how fast the attorneys complete discovery and conclude the negotiations.

In most cases the mediation process is quicker than the adversarial, as mediators generally meet with the couple either weekly or every other week. The total time spent in mediation ranges from 6 to 20 hours and varies with the complexity of the case, the skill of the mediator, and the attitudes of the couple.

Compliance with Decree

In theory, the adversarial system should have a good record of compliance because the court's power of contempt stands behind each order that it issues. However, statistics show high levels of nonpayment of child and spousal support and many contempt proceedings on issues of custody and visitation.

Research has shown high rates of compliance with mediated agreements, compared to compliance with adversarial decrees. Couples are more likely to abide by an order that they helped create, and most couples choose to include an agreement to mediate future disagreements or changes of circumstances.

Qualifications of Professional

Attorneys must have met the requirements for admission to the bar. All attorneys are licensed by the state, and many states require

At present, no state has enacted licensure of mediators. Most professional divorce mediators are either mental health professionals or at-

mandatory continuing education for attorneys. There is no requirement that an attorney have any specialized training in counseling, human behavior, or conflict resolution.

torneys. The Academy of Family Mediators has recommended training requirements for divorce mediators, and special training is required of lawyers who mediate in some Canadian provinces.

Ethics

The attorney has a duty of vigorous advocacy on behalf of a client. An attorney is required to advance the position or cause of the client, regardless of the impact upon the rest of the family. Attorneys must guard against conflicts of interest and are generally prevented from representing divorcing couples.

The mediator has a duty to remain neutral and impartial while managing the discussions. The mediator does not represent either party and has a duty to prevent overreaching. Some critics of mediation claim that the mediation will not work where there are disparities in power and negotiating abilities. Defenders of mediation claim that couples, regardless of their strengths and weaknesses, can be taught effective bargaining skills in mediation.

Cost

The adversarial system is presently under attack from many quarters because of the increasingly high costs of legal services. It is not uncommon to pay fees in excess of $10,000 for representation in a long, contested divorce. Newer attorneys apply pressure by offering low-cost packages for divorce cases where there are no children, no real estate, and no contest.

A mediated settlement is probably less costly than settlement through the adversarial process, although there is no accurate way to compare the costs in a particular case because only one method is used. It is certainly less costly when compared to contested litigation.

Outcome

Since the outcome is the product of a competitive conflict-resolution process, it is viewed as a victory or defeat.

The outcome is a win–win solution that attempts to balance the needs of each spouse, through compromise.

NOTE

*Not all attorney–mediators adhere to this model.—Ed.

REFERENCE

Fisher, R., & Ury, W. *Getting to yes: Negotiating agreement without giving in.* Boston: Houghton
    Mifflin, 1981.

PART THREE

THE PRACTICE OF DIVORCE MEDIATION

7

Divorce Mediation in a Mental Health Setting

EMILY M. BROWN
Divorce and Marital Stress Clinic, Inc., Arlington, Virginia

Mental health professionals have generally embraced the concept of divorce mediation, viewing it as compatible with the goals of therapy and as an antidote to the ills of the adversarial system. The practice of divorce mediation by a mental health professional is likely to differ from that provided by a mediator with a legal or other background. This chapter, written by an early advocate and practitioner of divorce mediation, presents an insider's account of the establishment of mediation within the mental health community, and describes the practice—its similarities and differences to therapy, its strengths and weaknesses, and its relationship to the law.

Although mental health professionals have provided marriage counseling for many years, it is only since the mid-1970s (Brown, 1974) that attention has been directed to the problems of divorce. When it became clear that not all marriages could or should be saved, some therapists began to explore ways to meet the needs of divorcing families (Brown, 1974; Kressel & Deutsch, 1977). Experience in working with these families brought therapists face to face with the shortcomings of the adversarial system (Brown, 1976; Hallett, 1974). Michael Wheeler (1974), an attorney, described the adversary system:

> It not only tolerates perjury, it encourages it. . . . That everyone seems to be in on the sham—the lawyers and the judges—makes the whole system seem corrupt. . . . (p. 8) The concept of fault not only is unrealistic in terms of the real causes of marital breakdown, but it also fails to provide guidance for the solution of the financial and custody problems which often arise. Fault encourages people to look to the courts for personal vindication. Victory is measured in dollars. (p. 17)

And, it might be added, in children.

O. J. Coogler's pioneering work in divorce mediation came about as a direct result of his own experience with the adversary process (1978). As Coogler's work in divorce mediation became known in the late 1970s, the mental health profession was more than ready to embrace it. Therapists had been confronted with increasing numbers of divorcing couples and were more aware of the problems of adversarial divorce. Mediation, which has values compatible with therapy and requires many of the skills of the therapist, was a natural area for development by mental health professionals. Data collected in 1981 (Pearson, Ring, & Milne, 1983) indicates that 80% of the mediators in the private sector are mental health professionals, and in the public sector this figure rises to 90%. Since then, mental health–based mediation services have proliferated at such a rate that it is impossible to get an accurate estimate of their numbers.

In addition to providing mediation services, mental health professionals are heavily involved in the provision of mediation training in a variety of settings that include agencies (the Parkside Center in Illinois, the Divorce and Marital Stress Clinic in Arlington, Virginia), domestic relations courts, universities (University of Illinois at Champaign–Urbana, Catholic University), private training organizations (Haynes), and professional associations (Association of Family and Conciliation Courts, Academy of Family Mediators, and state mediation councils). Considering that before the advent of mediation, therapists rarely had contact with lawyers and knew little and often cared less about the legal aspects of divorce, the promotion and development of mediation in the mental health field is a dramatic and welcome change.

This chapter will describe mediation as it is offered by mental health professionals in the private sector. It will describe mediation's unique qualities, its strengths and weaknesses, and its relationship to law and other professions, and will identify issues of special concern to therapist mediators.

THE ESTABLISHMENT OF MEDIATION IN A MENTAL HEALTH SETTING

What does the provision of mediation in a mental health setting mean? First, it conveys the message that mediation is therapeutic. It also says that the emotions and problems associated with divorce are solvable. More important, it implies an approach that considers the needs and feelings of family members and that respects and protects family relationships. The "eye for an eye" and "winner take all" traditions that so color the public's view of the legal system are not part of the mental health philosophy.

Providers of divorce mediation in the mental health field include the self-employed private practitioner, associates in small group practices, and employees of small counseling services and larger multiservice organizations. The most common settings are private practice and the small marriage-and-divorce center. In these settings counseling and therapy are usually offered as well as mediation.

The Family Service Agency (FSA) in Winston-Salem, North Carolina, was one of the first large mental health organizations to establish a divorce mediation service. The convergence of several factors made the establishment of this service possible. Coogler had recently moved to Winston-Salem and was beginning to offer training in mediation. One of the first trainees, Virginia Stafford, was a social worker on the staff of FSA, a United Way agency. A community-needs assessment completed by the United Way had identified divorcing families as a priority target group, and the United Way issued a mandate for member agencies to develop programs for these individuals. The FSA responded by making Stafford responsible for setting up, administering, and providing mediation services within FSA.

Despite some difficulties with the concept of mediation, the FSA board was generally supportive. The major obstacle was a lack of understanding by the FSA administrators and staff about what mediation is and how to use it. Continual staff education was and continues to be necessary to differentiate mediation from counseling. Even now staff tend to see attorneys rather than mediators as the first choice for high-conflict couples or where there is a large power inequity between the spouses.

The FSA mediation program began in 1979 on a fee-for-service basis. No sliding scale for fees was offered. The mediation service was separate from therapy services, and the mediator did not serve as both therapist and mediator with the same clients. Initially, separate offices were used because it was thought that mediation clients might not come to a counseling facility. A year later, when the offices were merged, it was found that this made no difference.

Factors that were important in making the program work included

1. extensive contact with the bar and attorneys, especially those identified as most amenable to amicable divorce
2. networking and providing information to therapists and other key people in the community on how and when to make a referral
3. the credibility of FSA and Stafford in the community
4. not insignificantly, no client stealing

Typical of the smaller marriage-and-divorce center is the experience of the Divorce and Marital Stress Clinic in Arlington, Virginia. The decision to offer mediation grew out of the Clinic's overall purpose of providing better ways for divorcing families to resolve the problems associated with ending a marriage. Since its inception in 1972, the Clinic has pioneered in offering services to those divorcing. Mediation was another step in the same direction. In contrast to the FSA, Clinic staff were sold on mediation and were eager to promote it when the Clinic's mediation program began in 1979. As with the FSA, the Clinic's mediation clients pay out of pocket a set hourly rate. Therapy and mediation are separate, and the mediator never serves as a therapist with his or her mediation clients.

The Clinic has always nurtured contacts with competent domestic relations attorneys for purposes of referral and professional collaboration (mutual cases, workshops for the public, professional training, etc.). Some of these attorneys were quite interested in mediation and were eager to be involved from the beginning. Couples completing mediation have been referred to these and other attorneys for preparation and review of the separation agreement and for other legal advice. Among the attorneys who were initially skeptical about mediation, one has subsequently achieved prominence as a mediator, and others have added mediation to their practice. Contacts with attorneys are continually being developed.

The biggest difficulty encountered by the Divorce and Marital Stress Clinic has been educating the public about mediation and conveying the idea that mediators in a mental health organization have sufficient expertise to handle matters that have traditionally been handled by lawyers. Obstacles include feminists who insist that women lose in mediation, attorneys who are competing for business, and spouses who want a gladiator to do battle for them. To that end, the Clinic has offered to the public and to referral sources seminars on mediation. The mediators also seek opportunities to speak to community groups. Extensive networking with other professionals, especially with therapists, has been very important in obtaining referrals.

With the recent growth of mediation in the Washington, D.C., area, the job of education has become both easier and more difficult. More mediators are available to educate the public, but as in any new field, some of the new practitioners are untrained, incompetent, or purely opportunistic and therefore provide an inaccurate or negative picture of mediation. For example, some "mediators" describe their role as deciding what the couple should do and convincing them to do it. With others, their obvious lack of credentials has raised questions about the viability of the entire field. Once mediation is established and there is a generally accepted process of certification for mediators, these problems will diminish.

Establishing a solo mediation practice is similar to establishing a mediation practice in a small private organization. Credibility can be more difficult to establish for the solo practitioner, since it is based only on one's own efforts and is not backed by the reputation of an organization. If one is known already for related professional endeavors, such as marriage and divorce counseling, others are likely to view mediation as a logical extension of the practice. Establishing contacts with lawyers and networking with potential referral sources throughout the community are essential. The solo practitioner carries total responsibility for this, as opposed to the mediator in an organization, where others help with networking and public education. In some cases solo practitioners join forces to maximize public education efforts, such as joint sponsorship of a seminar on mediation for the public. Joining forces also provides opportunities for peer supervision.

COMPARISON OF MEDIATION AND THERAPY

It is not surprising that many mental health practitioners are comfortable with the concept of mediation, for similar values underlie both fields. Mental health professionals place a high value on problem solving, prevention of emotional damage, fair play, client responsibility, self-determination, and strong family relationships, particularly between parents and children. Effective parenting is seen as extremely important. Negotiation and cooperation are viewed as desirable ways to resolve differences, especially when the alternative is assignment of fault and blame. These are the same concepts upon which mediation is based.

Saposnek (1983a) highlights the good fit between therapy and mediation in discussing child-custody mediation:

> The mediator must be competent to give valid, current, and helpful information about child development, about children's typical and atypical responses to family conflicts, about family members' needs and feelings, about family dynamics, about the divorce process (emotionally, structurally and legally), and about the likely future outcomes for children and parents of a variety of different post divorce family structures. The mediator should be knowledgeable about individual psychodynamics, interactional dynamics, family systems, and behavior change, and have a broad general knowledge of psychological functioning. Child custody mediators who are not specifically trained in these areas may seriously compromise the benefits of child custody mediation. (p. 37)

The similarity in values between therapy and mediation accounts for the ease with which the mental health profession has adopted mediation. Yet mediation is different from therapy. Both the goals and the process are different.

The goal of therapy, including divorce counseling, is to help the individuals resolve emotional problems so as to become more comfortable and functional in their lives. The goal of mediation is to help the divorcing couple make decisions about the business aspects of their marriage and to develop a workable plan for the future. The process is concluded with the preparation of a written document detailing the couple's agreement.

Learning to "listen with your gut" is a primary part of all mental health training programs. This ability is considered crucial to effective performance. This training enables the mental health mediator to identify the emotional dynamics between the spouses, to assess whether the importance of an issue is based on rational or emotional factors, and to develop some hunches about the underlying emotional basis of the occasional impasse. It is in this area of assessment that mediation and therapy are most similar, although the depth, purpose, and use of the assessment differ. The mediator assesses the process in order to formulate strategies to facilitate decision making; the therapist makes a more extensive assessment to promote insight and change in behavior.

Therapists and mediators are responsible for managing the process of the session, but how they manage the process is different. The therapist pursues emotional issues, focusing attention on them, getting more information, often encouraging or even provoking the expression of feelings. The goal is to resolve problematic feelings and behaviors. The mediator, however, anticipates where emotional problems will occur and begins to formulate strategies designed to limit and diffuse the situation. The mediator may decide to ignore a client's tears to avoid reinforcing them or may simply acknowledge that the situation is painful and redirect the couple to the task. The mediator's careful structuring of the discussion gives spouses an opportunity to talk about what is important to each of them and to develop a set of common principles.

The difference between the therapy process and the mediation process is just as striking as the difference between their goals. Therapy focuses on feelings, searches them out, explores them, even provokes them. Conflict and anger may not be avoided or diffused but may be made central. Looking for nice, neat answers is discouraged. Mediation is almost the opposite. The focus is on gathering information, much of which is quantifiable, and making decisions about the business aspects of the marriage. Feelings that are expressed may be ignored, restricted, or diffused, so that they do not interfere with the primary goal of reaching an agreement. In short, the major focus of therapy is on the process, while that of mediation is on achieving a specific goal.

STRENGTHS AND WEAKNESSES OF THERAPIST–MEDIATORS

While the tasks of mediation are the same whether performed by a lawyer–mediator or a therapist–mediator, the therapist brings valuable skills to the mediation process. The most important of these are counseling and communication skills, knowledge of child development and family dynamics, assessment skills, and experience in dealing with emotionally difficult situations. Professional values play a role as well.

The therapist–mediator's counseling skills are used in mediation to elicit information, provide reassurance and support, reframe issues, and acknowledge the difficult nature of the situation faced by the couple. The ability to listen to the nuances and subtleties of the spoken message, and to note nonverbal messages, provides a better basis for selecting interventions than does the content alone. The communications skills of the therapist help the spouses clarify their messages to one another. Therapists who work with couples develop many techniques, transferable to mediation, for facilitating communication in the midst of strong emotions.

The issues of separation and loss that are so much a part of divorce are familiar to therapists:

> The feelings of sadness, anxiety, guilt, rejection, fear, anger, and sometimes panic often have the power and force of a lifetime of poorly or incompletely resolved experiences with separation and loss. . . . These are the feelings that serve as a backdrop for the emotions that people feel as they contemplate and move through divorce. (Yahm, 1984, pp. 60–61)

Therapists have expert knowledge about families, about child development, and about effective parenting. Because of this knowledge they are able to provide information about the needs of children and are in a position to help parents thoroughly examine their parenting options. Saposnek (1983b) believes that "by viewing custody disputes from a family systems perspective, the mediator is able to understand these contributory elements and utilize interventions to achieve effective resolution" (p. 29).

The ability of the therapist to identify emotional problems is important in the intake process as well as in later stages of mediation. For example, recognition of an alcohol problem will enable the mediator to make some preliminary determinations about whether the couple is suitable for mediation. The therapist–mediator can spot depression and make appropriate referrals for treatment, resuming mediation once the depression has lifted sufficiently. Nontherapists sometimes attribute the symptoms of depression to laziness or other volitional factors and thus are unable to make appropriate interventions or referrals and are unsuccessful at mediation.

In a spouse-abuse situation, the therapist–mediator's professional judgment and experience can help in deciding how and whether the abuse can be forestalled during mediation or whether other measures need to be taken. Some professionals believe that mediation is preferable in abuse situations because it provides an opportunity for the couple to resolve their issues in a new way. The adversarial approach escalates the conflict, encourages scapegoating and victim behaviors, and reinforces just those factors that contribute to abuse in the first place. Therapist–mediators who understand the dynamics of abuse are uniquely qualified to mediate such cases. If the mediator determines that the situation is too volatile for face-to-face negotiation, the referrals made are based on an understanding of the emotional and the practical issues.

Mental health skills may also make it possible to accept couples for mediation that a lawyer–mediator might need to screen out. For example, when a parent is recovering from a psychotic break, mediation is gentler and more specific to the situation in determining parenting arrangements than is an adversarial process. This type of situation requires, however, that the mediator be knowledgeable about mental illness as well as child development, and supportive of the parent's ability to function while ensuring that the child's needs are met. The therapist–mediator has the knowledge to guide the parents in making suitable arrangements for the child. The therapist–mediator is equipped to recognize signs that reconciliation may be a possibility. The mediator's counseling skills permit a sensitive exploration of the situation to determine whether to continue mediation or refer the couple for therapy.

The weaknesses of therapist–mediators tend to fall into two areas: lack of knowledge about financial and legal issues, and confusion of the roles of therapist and mediator. The first is more easily dealt with, provided there is any aptitude for financial matters. A variety of courses in family finances, taxes, and domestic relations are available through universities, continuing-education organizations, and professional associations. The therapist–mediator does not need to become proficient in law or financial planning but does need to know how to use the financial information in mediation sessions, how to interface with the legal system, and when to refer to outside experts.

While most therapist–mediators are aware of the difference between divorce counseling and divorce mediation, a great many are offering mediation without any training in mediation (Musty & Crago, 1984). This blurring of roles has the potential for negative consequences for clients. Musty's experience suggests "that the tendency to blur boundaries can be kept in check only by a mental health professional who has been trained in divorce mediation; . . . [yet] most mental health professionals do not see themselves as needing any additional training in divorce mediation" (p. 75).

Therapists come to mediation with a philosophy of helping families work out their problems. Great value is placed on client self-determination and responsibility and on fair play. The values of the therapist are, for the most part, useful in mediation, particularly in ensuring that children are protected. Occasionally, however, the therapist's values interfere with the mediation process. This is true when the therapist imposes values on the couple, as for example when the mediator believes strongly in the worth of joint custody and persuades or insists that the couple agree upon joint custody. Other issues that often present the same problem for the mediator include alimony, college education for the children, pensions, and various aspects of parenting. These are all areas where attitudes have been changing rapidly in the last few years. New developments that arise in response to inadequacies and abuses of past methods are often viewed at first as panaceas. Joint custody in particular typifies this pattern. The mediator's imposition of values is as likely to result from following the swing of the pendulum as it is from an inability to modify attitudes. The mediator in this situation needs to return to the philosophy of self-determination, which undergirds the mediation process. If the mediator moves too far in the opposite direction and loses control of the process, chaos results. This happens when the mediator applies the concept of self-determination to the process instead of the outcome.

Confusion of values and roles sometimes results in selecting cases on the basis of value judgments, rather than on suitability for mediation. Abuse cases, for example, are often screened out in this manner, despite the fact that the therapist–mediator may be the best qualified person to help the family. Of course, if the mediator has strong personal feelings that make it impossible to be neutral, it is advisable to refer the couple to another mediator. It needs to be clear, however, that it is the mediator's problem and does not necessarily mean the couple is unsuitable for mediation.

Some mediators meet separately with each spouse at one or more points during the mediation process. Usually the purpose is to uncover relevant information that one spouse is reluctant to share in the joint session, or to convey information between spouses. When this works, it can shorten the time required to reach resolution. The danger is that this maneuver will be seen as taking sides with one spouse, with the result that mediation is terminated. Even when separate meetings are effective, the couple loses an opportunity to work through the issue, thus reducing any attendant gains in learning to communicate with each other, and reinforcing avoidance behaviors. Mental health mediators, especially those who are used to seeing family members individually, need to be particularly cautious about using this technique.

Therapist–mediators, especially those with limited experience, seem reluctant to trust the *process* of mediation. For example, they allow too much discussion of a single item, rather than ensure sufficient development of options. To some extent this is a matter of experience, but the professional background also plays a role. The importance of structure is not nearly as clear to therapists as it is to lawyers. Moore (1983) notes that "mediation requires an individual to practice new behaviors and to alter old assumptions about the role of a third party assisting families in disputes. . . . Therapists . . . often feel uncomfortable with short-term, more superficial interventions and settlements" (p. 82).

The mental health mediator's communication skills are particularly useful in delimiting the mediation process to provide a safe environment in which to negotiate an agreement. In the early stages, the mediator builds rapport with both spouses while maintaining a focus, setting limits, and ensuring that each spouse has an opportunity to express his or her concerns. With all but a few couples, there is considerable testing of the limits during this period. It is often necessary for each spouse to tell his or her story before being able to proceed. Therapists are accustomed to handling this type of situation and are usually adept at doing so, although the less-experienced therapist–mediator may be tempted to hear too much of the story and will take longer to get down to business. The mediator who manages the story-telling so that honest emotions (not attacks) are directed toward the spouse, and not toward the mediator, avoids the appearance of taking sides.

The middle stages of mediation focus on collecting and sharing information about the issues and about the needs and preferences of each family member. The therapist's expertise in family dynamics and child development provides a resource for the couple and a guide for the mediator in the planning of sound parenting arrangements. Although it is the parents' responsibility to make decisions about the children, it is the mediator's responsibility to raise questions and issues that will help the parents consider all relevant factors. Often parents are not aware of the broad range of options open to them and gladly accept new information and suggestions. For example, a couple who thought that alternating days was the only fair form of joint custody were relieved to have the mediator suggest several less strenuous methods for sharing daily responsibility for two young children. "Fair" and "equal" are terms that come up frequently in discussions of postdivorce parenting. The mental health mediator is particularly well equipped to reframe the issue in terms pertaining to the needs of each child and the unique contributions of each parent.

Insufficient knowledge or skill regarding financial and property issues can cause problems for therapist–mediators and their clients during this stage of mediation. Such a problem occurred in a dissolving second marriage when the mediator was unaware that the house had been purchased by the husband long before the marriage, that it was titled in his name alone, and that it was not considered marital property in that state. Fortunately, a friend heard the husband grumble, and pursued the issue. When the husband realized the mediator's error, he terminated mediation although originally he had been the prime mover for a nonadversarial settlement. Mediators need to be knowledgeable about domestic relations law and about the services of accountants, appraisers, financial planners, and attorneys. It is essential that mediators recognize the limits of their knowledge and arrange for couples to obtain the needed expertise from appropriate sources.

The final stage of mediation is concerned with negotiating the remaining issues, often the most difficult ones. Facilitating successful negotiations while managing conflict is the major task of this stage. The skills needed are mediation skills and as such are not the province of either law or mental health. Many of these techniques are drawn from the labor mediation field. Mental health skills, however, play a supporting role, as when the mediator who is attuned to emotional signals recognizes a verbal "yes" that really means "no" and realizes that further negotiation is needed.

The communication skills of the therapist are useful throughout mediation. They help in gaining and reinforcing cooperation, clarifying issues, setting limits, and focusing on the positive and the possible. When dealing with a couple who lose control easily, the therapist's ability to control communication is essential to the mediation process and is reassuring to the couple. Because of the strong emotions of divorcing couples, techniques that are most effective combine emotional sensitivity with an active role and a firm hand.

The enmeshed couple (Kressel, Jaffee, Tuchman, Watson, & Deutsch, 1980) is characterized by high levels of communication and conflict, and by ambivalence about the decision to divorce. The couple's behavior is so provocative that the mediator may get angry and be tempted to cut off all discussion, or throw up his or her hands in despair and walk away. Mental health professionals, especially those accustomed to working with couples, are not so easily thrown by this performance. Moreover, their training and experience have provided them with tools for assessing what is underneath the anger. An understanding of the emotional dynamics facilitates choosing an appropriate intervention to diffuse and redirect the discussion. The experienced therapist-mediator will intervene before the situation is out of hand.

Mediators who do not have an understanding of the couple's emotional dynamics or whose general strategy is to take an authoritarian position run into difficulty at this point. Telling a wife to "stop crying and acting like a baby" or "blasting" a difficult husband may help the mediator regain a feeling of control, but this behavior does little to help the couple or the mediation process. Just as unproductive is a passive approach, which allows this type of interaction to continue unchecked. Interventions that shift the focus to the intrapsychic issues, more properly the subject of therapy, are unproductive in mediation. However, the struggle about what each wants, and may or may not get, is an echo of the couple's marital problems. Thus, a limited discussion of what each had wanted emotionally from the other, and the disappointment at not getting it, can be useful. The mediator's skill in selecting and using conflict resolution techniques makes or breaks the case. If the process gets out of hand, the couple will terminate mediation or will continue to use mediation as an arena for unproductive fighting until they get bored or until they succeed in moving to arbitration or litigation.

The therapist's professional training provides an advantage in recognizing and addressing a particular type of impasse that does not respond to the usual conflict-resolution strategies. This type of impasse has more to do with personal feelings of loss and self-esteem than with differences in needs and interests. The eye of the skilled mental health professional can correctly identify the issues, and the impasse is unlocked when the therapist–mediator assists the couple in acknowledging the importance of a particular aspect of the partner's role or of the marriage. This technique, although borrowed from therapy, is appropriate for mediation. It is not a change of focus but a detour that enables the parties to continue in mediation.

Saposnek (1983a) suggests that the mediator keep in mind that

> the most challenging aspect of the entire mediation process is the unpredictability of the outcome until the very end. The mediator never knows from moment to moment in the negotiations whether a couple will suddenly escalate their hostilities to the point of stalemate, or proceed to resolve the issues peacefully. (p. 27)

Once agreement has been reached and the mediator has drafted a summary of the decisions that have been made (the memorandum of understanding), the therapist–mediator needs to ensure that the legal document is drafted by an attorney. The therapist–mediator who attempts drafting the agreement is open to charges of practicing law without a license. The attorney's role is to review the memorandum of agreement, making sure that it is clear and complete and that the couple understand it; to provide legal information and advice to the spouses; and to draft or review the separation agreement. The lawyer provides a useful double check of the mediation process. Some mediation clients will already have attorneys, but most will want referrals. It is helpful if the mediator has contact with several competent domestic relations attorneys and can refer to the most appropriate ones for the particular situation. Recent court rulings hold professionals accountable for the referrals they make, so it is essential to know those to whom you refer.

In some jurisdictions it is possible for the couple to use a single "impartial advisory attorney" to draft the agreement, and many couples prefer to do this. However, some state bar associations have opposed this role for attorneys. When the spouses have had a difficult time in reaching agreement or have been especially contentious, the use of two attorneys provides an added safeguard for the couple and for the agreement.

On occasion, mediators are asked to provide information or are subpoenaed to testify about clients who have been unsuccessful in mediation. Although confidentiality is essential to the mediation process, therapist–mediators do not have the right to claim privileged communication and thus must consider how they will deal with this situation, should it arise. A written contract to mediate, signed by both spouses and specifying that neither spouse will involve the mediator in litigation, discourages but does not totally prevent such occurrences.

VARIATIONS RELATED TO THE SETTING OF MEDIATION

Is there a significant difference in mediation provided by a mental health professional in a private mental health setting as opposed to mediation offered within a court setting or by an attorney? This question can be answered both positively and negatively.

Mediation clients often believe there is a difference. The experience of this writer indicates that clients who choose a therapist–mediator may be different from those who choose a lawyer–mediator. Clients often ask about the discipline of the mediator. Some seem to want the assurance that the mediator has the utmost knowledge of current divorce law and believe a law degree so indicates. Others want to know that the mediator can handle the charged emotions (those of their spouse, if not their own) and prefer someone with a mental health background.

The public image of the legal profession in domestic matters is based on the concept of the lawyer as an expert caretaker who will aggressively pursue the best interests of his or her client. Divorcing couples who find this parental image comforting are more likely to pick an attorney–mediator, as will those who believe the outcome will not be "legal" unless the mediator is an attorney.

Mental health professionals are typically viewed as accepting, caring people who value emotional well-being and who have expertise in working with family problems. Couples whose concerns center on managing the emotional issues are more likely to choose a therapist–mediator.

In addition, mental health mediators receive many referrals from therapists. These clients tend to be more aware of communication problems, though they are not always better at communicating than are other mediation clients. Whatever the perception, the couple's expectations of mediation and their behavior in mediation is colored by their views.

The mediator in the private sector is likely to have clients who have actively chosen mediation. Clients are usually educated, verbal, and middle-class or above and possess some willingness to negotiate. The private practitioner has likely handled fewer cases than the public sector mediator. Private sector mental health mediation differs from public sector mediation in other significant ways. This has more to do with organizational requirements than with theoretical or methodological differences. A recent survey (Pearson et al., 1983) indicates that 81% of public sector mediation services limit mediation to child-related issues. Only 31.5% of private sector organizations limit mediation services to these issues.

Comprehensive mediation, because it addresses the full range of issues, provides more trade-off opportunities, thereby facilitating the bargaining process. When mediation is completed, all the issues are settled, and there is some sense of closure enabling the spouses to move forward as individuals. In single-issue mediation, couples who settle custody matters may still have to use litigation to settle the other issues, thereby negating some of the benefits of mediation. Since the decisions regarding children, money, property, and related matters are worked out piecemeal, they are less likely to fit together into a cohesive plan. On the other hand, success in deciding upon parenting arrangements can increase the willingness of the spouses to settle other matters.

The court is the major source of referral for 81.6% of public mediation services, whereas in the private sector, 9.3% of cases are referred by the courts. This suggests that mediation clients in the public sector are more likely to be contentious than are private sector clients.

Therapist–mediators differ more from attorney–mediators than from public sector mediators. The difference is not organizational in nature, as it is with the court-connected mediators, but derives from a basic difference in approach and orientation to the resolution of personal problems. Simply stated, lawyers believe that getting the facts is essential, and they focus on obtaining hard data. Therapists believe it is important to understand feelings. They explore the emotional dynamics of a situation. The strength of one type of mediator is often the area in which the other has the least training and experience. Attorney–mediators may be less likely to involve children in mediation sessions than are therapist–mediators. They often refer mediation clients for therapy as an adjunct to mediation but may lack expertise in when and how to refer. Lawyers are often clearer than therapists on when to use appraisers and accountants.

Public sector mental health mediators understand the legal system well and can explain it to couples. They have more experience with lawyers and tend to be more comfortable working with them than do private sector mental health mediators. They also have the authority of the court behind them, which provides extra clout with some couples but makes others wary. They are likely to have a large caseload and limited time with the couple, but they are also likely to have more mediation experience than do mediators in the private sector.

Private sector mediators are not bound by the time limitations of the court and can schedule mediation sessions in an optimum manner. Couples are somewhat more likely to reach agreement (Pearson et al., 1983), and the agreement is likely to cover all issues. Therapist–mediators in the private sector usually have therapy clients as well as mediation clients, which helps prevent burnout. Girdner (1986) points out that as mediators gain experience and interact with other mediators, a third orientation is emerging:

> The emphasis on differences between primary training and substantive knowledge of the issues (for example, child development, family law) has led to a divergent conceptualization of mediation. (p. 26) . . . A third orientation is emerging, which seeks to balance these attributes [cognitive and affective dimensions, needs, and rights] and operates as a synthesis of the other two orientations. (p. 27)

ISSUES: ETHICAL AND OTHERWISE

Because mediation fits so well into the mental health professional's value system, the major ethical issues focus on differentiating therapy from mediation.

Is it ethical to function as both therapist and mediator with the same couple? Most mental health professionals think not. All the mediators' codes of ethics that have been drafted to date prohibit mediators from taking dual professional roles with the same clients. Such codes have been or are being developed by the American Bar Association, the Academy of Family Mediators, the Association of Family Conciliation Courts, and various local mediation organizations.

A recent survey (Musty & Crago, 1984) indicates that many mental health professionals provide divorce counseling and divorce mediation to the same clients, a practice the researchers question. Although most of these practitioners had not been trained in mediation, my experience suggests that separation of counseling and mediation is an issue for some trained mediators as well. The separation of therapy from mediation must be addressed in marital therapy cases when the couple reaches the decision to end the marriage. When rapport has been established and the work together has proved productive, either the couple or the therapist may be tempted to consider continuing the relationship in mediation.

For the couple it may seem easier to continue working with a known and trusted professional, particularly if the couple is wary of the legal system. Alternatively, the spouse who did not want the marriage to end may hold the therapist responsible for the breakup. A request by one spouse that the therapist move into the role of mediator may be an attempt to gain an advantage. Sometimes it is the therapist who wants to continue, out of naivete, confusion about roles, or misguided ideas about being helpful. Clarity and limit setting about roles provides a positive model for divorcing couples.

The distinction between mediation and therapy may be further blurred if the mediator attempts to provide therapy during mediation. This does not mean that the mediator should ignore all emotions or refrain from using interventions directed toward the emotions, but that the mediator's goal in using such interventions is in deliberate pursuit of mediation goals, not therapeutic goals. When therapeutic goals do result, they must be the by-product of mediation. Grebe (1986) notes that whether interruption of dysfunctional patterns of behavior carries over permanently is not a consideration in mediation. When therapy is needed during or after mediation, the mediator should refer the couple or individual to a competent therapist. To do anything else is an abuse of the mediator's contract with the couple to provide mediation. It also jeopardizes the couple's ability to return to the mediator should they need help in revising their agreement.

The use of health insurance reimbursement for mediation is another issue. Although mediation can be therapeutic, it is not therapy, but rather an alternative to litigation. Asking insurance companies to pay for a non-mental health service is unethical. Moreover, it provides insurance companies with ready ammunition to undermine reimbursement of legitimate mental health services.

In the absence of a credentialing process for mediators, it becomes the responsibility of each mediator to promote competence in the field. This is done by being knowledgeable about domestic relations law, mediation techniques, and the emotional process of divorce. Continuing education, peer and professional supervision, and regular contacts with lawyers and mediators need to be part of each therapist–mediator's practice.

INCENTIVES FOR THE MENTAL HEALTH MEDIATOR

There are rewards for the mental health practitioner who develops mediation skills. These skills are transferable to a variety of situations, including therapy. Interacting with other disciplines is exciting and challenging. A practice including both therapy and mediation provides professional variety. Broadening one's own sense of competence is satisfying. Mediation also provides an opportunity to be creative. Because mediation is a new field, there is room for innovation. It is rewarding to participate in a process appropriate to reaching closure in a relationship as important as marriage.

At the same time, mediation is probably most important for those couples with moderate to considerable emotional conflict. While low-conflict couples are able to resolve the issues of separation and divorce with or without skilled help, other divorcing couples are not. Therapist–mediators are ideally equipped to help these couples reach agreement by virtue of the therapists' understanding of family dynamics, their communication skills, and their tradition of helping families resolve problems constructively. In a society where litigation is increasingly used to resolve disagreements, it is encouraging that mediation is flourishing. The mental health profession's unique contribution to mediation is especially important in these times.

REFERENCES

Brown, E. (Ed.) *Task force report: Divorce and divorce reform*. Minneapolis, MN: National Council on Family Relations, 1974.

Brown, E. Divorce counseling. In D. H. Olson (Ed.), *Treating relationships* (pp. 399–429). Lake Mills, IA: Graphic, 1976.

Coogler, O. J. *Structured mediation in divorce settlement: A handbook for marital mediators*. Lexington, MA: Heath, 1978.

Girdner, L. Family mediation: Toward a synthesis. *Mediation Quarterly*, 1986, *13*, 21–29.

Grebe, S. A comparison of the tasks and definitions of family mediation and those of strategic family therapy. *Mediation Quarterly*, 1986, *13*, 53–59.

Hallett, K. *A guide for single parents*. Millbrae, CA: Celestial Arts, 1974.

Kressel, K., & Deutsch, M. Divorce therapy: An in-depth survey of therapists' views. *Family Process*, 1977, *16*, 413–443.

Kressel, K., Jaffee, N., Tuchman, B., Watson, C., & Deutsch, M. A typology of divorcing couples: Implications for mediation and the divorce process. *Family Press*, 1980, *19*, 101–116.

Moore, C. Training mediators for family dispute resolution. *Mediation Quarterly*, 1983, *2*, 79–89.

Musty, T., & Crago, M. Divorce counseling and divorce mediation: A survey of mental health professionals' views. *Mediation Quarterly*, 1984, *6*, 73–85.

Pearson, J., Ring, M., & Milne, A. A portrait of divorce mediation services in the public and private sectors. *Conciliation Courts Review*, 1983, *21(1)*, 1–34.

Saposnek, D. *Mediating child custody disputes*. San Francisco: Jossey-Bass, 1983a.

Saposnek, D. Strategies in child custody mediation: A family systems approach. *Mediation Quarterly*, 1983b, *2*, 29–54.

Wheeler, M. *No-fault divorce*. Boston: Beacon Press, 1974.

Yahm, H. Divorce mediation: A psychoanalytic perspective. *Mediation Quarterly*, 1984, *6*, 59–63.

8

Divorce Mediation in a Law Office Setting

HENRY M. ELSON
Private Practice, Berkeley, California

In 1972, shortly after no-fault divorce was implemented in California, the author pioneered "nonadversarial" divorce services within his general law practice. Here he explains in detail the mediation service he offers and how it has evolved, the techniques he employs, and the nature of his clientele. He also provides an analysis of the results. A sample letter of agreement and excerpts of letters to clients are included as appendices to this chapter.

INSPIRATION AND CONCEPTION

In 1970 I had been practicing law for about 17 years. I was in a three-person partnership that was engaged in the general practice of law in Berkeley, California. Each of the partners leaned towards an emphasis in one or two areas of the law. My clients and the community were coming to associate me with an interest, if not a specialization, in family law. My representation of clients involved in divorce and related family law problems continued to increase in numbers of clients and the complexity and difficulty of the cases. My experience in this field led me to become dissatisfied with the manner in which divorce cases were processed in the adversary system, primarily because of what I perceived to be the incongruity of practicing family law in the adversary system. Many lawyers who felt the same way, consciously or unconsciously, simply eliminated divorce cases from their caseload, usually with a sigh of relief, or continued the practice with a heavy heart. To the extent that one can enjoy practicing family law I did, or at least found it more interesting and challenging than other fields, so when no-fault divorce became the law in California with the passage of the Family Law Act of 1970, I decided to try to practice family law outside of the adversary system. I was fortunate to be able to take a sabbatical in 1971, and far from the law office and the courtroom, I designed a preliminary and tentative approach to family law cases, which became the basis for that part of my practice I refer to as nonadversary family law.

On July 2, 1971, in a letter postmarked Corsica, France, I wrote to my law partners, explaining why I planned to stop practicing family law in the adversary system. The following quotation from that letter states what I felt at that time.

> I have concluded that it is possible to formalize a family law practice in a non-adversary context which would be beneficial to individual clients, socially useful, professionally valid, as well as personally acceptable to me. . . . Basically I am convinced that the adversary procedure, with its apparent alternatives of victory or defeat, is inconsistent with the needs of parties whose marriage is in trouble or being dissolved, particularly when there are minor children. At that juncture, the involved persons need understanding of each other in all their relationships and of the reasons for their problems. Such awareness could avoid the need for a dissolution of the marriage or it could contribute immeasurably to an intelligent resolution of the problems if a dissolution is inevitable. Unfortunately, lawyers, judges, and others involved in the application of the adversary process to family law cases often interfere with the possibility of an intelligent resolution and create conditions which only complicate and worsen existing situations, which are complicated and bad enough. The present system of handling family law disputes leads to unacceptable delays, expense and frustration when the matter is "contested." The result only too often is the aggravation of existing problems and the creation of new ones. Of course, there are many examples of satisfactory results under the present procedure. Reasonable litigants, often in concert with good lawyers and/ or good judges, will avoid the pitfalls. However, the system does not encourage good results. It is essentially oriented towards a contest—which generates a desire to win or a fear of loss. No matter how benign, skillful and wise the attorneys and/ or judges, the atmosphere created and fostered by the adversary process is contrary to the real needs of the parties under the circumstances: knowledge about themselves; why they have the problems; how to resolve the problems; how to avoid similar problems. California has made substantial modifications in substantive law which as we know makes the termination of marriage much easier and eliminates some of the most abrasive aspects of previous legislation and common law precedent. I think that the bar should also adjust to the realities. . . . Lawyers can offer an alternative to clients, an alternative that will permit the client who has marital problems an opportunity to get good legal advice without the necessity of declaring war on his spouse.

In the same letter I proposed a model for what I then called a nonadversary law practice. When I returned to my practice, I simply told my partners, the bar, and my clients that I was no longer available as a conventional advocate lawyer in family law cases, but would be willing to practice family law on my terms in an effort to assist clients to work out their own agreements. It was my intention to continue the general practice of law with nonadversary family law as an additional way of serving my clients. I have continued to do so since 1972, and these cases now constitute a substantial part of my practice.

IS IT LEGAL? THE ADVERSE LEGAL INTERESTS QUESTION

After researching the existing California cases and statutes, I was satisfied that I was on safe and ethical grounds even though I was consulting with clients who clearly had adverse legal interests. Under California law, it is legally permissible for a lawyer to work with clients who have adverse legal interests if they acknowledge in writing that this was explained to them. The attorney must be satisfied that the clients really understand what they are doing—in short, their consent must be informed consent. This legal principle was not discussed in a case dealing with family law until the decision in *Klemm v. Superior Court* (1977). In that decision the appellate court confirmed my belief that attorneys may, under carefully protected procedures, consult with both parties to a divorce. The court urged caution and reminded lawyers of the potential danger in this work.

I never had any personal difficulty accepting the role of a "nonadversary" attorney. Many lawyers find it hard to accept. I simply view myself as a neutral, nonadvocate attorney performing a legal counseling role in very much the way attorneys deal with clients forming a business association or prepare wills for a married couple who have separate property and children from previous marriages. Lawyers in our system are so overidentified with the advocate role that the idea of serving as counselor, adviser, and mediator has to be accepted once again as a valid, ethical alternative.

SOURCE OF CLIENTS

With the exception of a small sentence describing the mediation process after my listing in the Yellow Pages for a few years (since discontinued, probably because of a vestigial feeling that advertising is unethical), my promotional work was by word of mouth among clients, attorneys, psychotherapists, other professionals, and friends. There were occasional talks before interested groups and university classes. From time to time, there have been newspaper and magazine articles that referred to the mediation process and, occasionally, to me personally. There are now frequent conferences, meetings, training seminars, law review articles, and substantial amounts of media coverage. This publicity has generated some clients, although the major sources continue to be other attorneys, therapists, and former clients. Clients who come in as a result of newspaper and magazine articles often present difficult cases. I think many of these clients have rather unrealistic expectations. They include a disproportionate number of people looking for a deus ex machina way out of difficult marriages.

I believe that I get some referrals from lawyers who may not necessarily like the mediation system. But, because they knew me as an attorney with experience in the adversary system and therefore do not consider me just a "reformer type," they have confidence that I have the legal skills necessary to protect their clients. It is likely that I get some referrals from mental health professionals because I have a degree and a license as a marriage, family, and child counselor, which gives them some confidence that I will be sensitive to the interpersonal issues.

It is my intention to maintain the general practice milieu, although I now do very little adversary law. I continue to be available for clients who require legal services across the broad spectrum of legal matters. Of course, the needs of the client and my own self-protection require that I refer many cases to colleagues who are specialists. It is important to keep in touch with colleagues in the bar and bench so I can be part of what is happening in the legal community. Also, I do not want to become isolated and characterized as a lawyer with an exotic specialty. My hope is that I can serve as a model for other lawyers who wish to add mediation to the other legal services they offer their clients.

A NONEXCLUSIVE ALTERNATIVE FOR A LIMITED NUMBER OF CLIENTS

Although it has been refined over more than a decade of practice, I still see divorce mediation essentially as a nonexclusive alternative to the adversary process. The emotional pain that almost always accompanies divorce makes it difficult for clients to work together in the business of undoing their relationship. It quickly becomes apparent that mediation is no panacea. It is not a substitute for the adversary process; it is simply another way of proceeding for those clients who prefer, for any number of reasons, not to use the adversary system to resolve their family law problems. It never occurred to me to characterize the product as an amicable divorce. Personally I don't even think "amicable" is a good way to describe a successful marriage. If an adjective is necessary to describe divorces obtained in mediation, I prefer to use the word "cooperative."

Intuitively, I knew that only a limited number of clients could function well in this system. My experience confirms this. It is not easy to decide which clients are good subjects for mediation. Certainly if either or both clients are feeling very hurt, disappointed, or angry, the couple are not good candidates, nor are clients with substantial differences in intelligence, competence, or self-esteem. The presence of children is a positive indicator.

Most of my clients are not in great conflict over child custody. Agreement about the children often seems to be a lubricant that makes the mediation process function more smoothly. The presence of children is evidence that the entire marriage is not obliterated by the judgment of dissolution. It often supplies the motivation for cooperation where otherwise it would not be possible. Joint custody is a very important part of the life-style of many of my clients and frequently an important issue in the negotiations. Most of my clients seem to have been involved with one or more counselors or therapists before they see me. If not, I often make referrals, usually, but not always, regarding the child-custody issue. I have infrequently seen the children of my clients, both with and without their parents.

Self-aware clients capable of flexibility are obviously easier to work with in mediation than rigid or otherwise psychologically defensive parties. Cases with multiple issues permitting trade-offs work far better than those in which someone is going to have to give up something without any equivalent return.

For similar reasons, affluent clients are more successful than their less economically fortunate counterparts. The sine qua non, however, is a certain minimum of trust and respect. I say "minimum" because there is always going to be some exaggeration, or "puffing," and some hostility. Without the minimum of trust and respect, this process becomes quite burdensome and usually will not work. With it, it can work remarkably well, if at least some of the other positive variables are also present.

Clients who are still experiencing their "emotional divorce" are difficult mediation subjects compared to those who come in after a prolonged separation. It is helpful to meet once or twice with clients who are experiencing the acute pain of recent separation, just to arrange a temporary agreement and let them return when they have somewhat recovered. Although it is true that clients who have been separated for a long time are easier to deal with, there are exceptions. I have had several experiences with clients who seem stuck in protracted separations and cannot seem to end the marriage. They may well remain in the process of terminating their legal marriage for years.

All of my clients, whether their special characteristics make them good or bad risks, are carefully, clearly, and repeatedly advised that the lawyer–mediator cannot protect them in the same way as the lawyer–advocate. Mediation clients may choose not to pay the price for that protection, but they should know they are giving up something. Here, as everywhere else, there is no free lunch.

NEUTRALITY OF THE MEDIATOR

The neutrality of the mediator is critical. I emphasize this from the first telephone contact with the prospective client by requiring a call back from the other spouse before meeting. It probably is not always necessary, but it dramatizes the point. I believe the clients appreciate this, and it sets the tone for the future. Almost all of my conferences are with both clients. Exceptions are only with everyone's consent. Occasionally separate meetings are helpful if the clients are very hostile to each other or there is an impasse. Rules about disclosures should be made in advance if separate meetings are held. The clients should be reminded that the mediator will not represent either party in a subsequent adversary proceeding if the mediation does not continue. A surprising number of clients do not seem to realize this, and I am not really sure if more do not have unrealistic fantasies. These can be dispelled by making this point quite clear at the outset.

The mediator's neutrality is more than a moral and legal requirement. The success of mediation depends on the cooperation of clients who have adverse interests. All clients, even those who choose to try mediation, have the capacity to confront each other adversarily as well as the capacity to cooperate. The neutrality of the mediator catalyzes the cooperative spirit of the clients into a mutual process of direct negotiation assisted by the mediator, who supplies legal information and counseling skills. The neutrality of the mediator is thus both a model for the clients and an operative force in the process.

There is no such thing as absolute neutrality. To mitigate the negative consequences of this inevitable problem requires constant attention. General reference to the possibility of biases and prejudices is desirable, and a willingness to acknowledge and confront specific instances is helpful. Because my clients are almost always parties of opposite sex, my presence as a man creates a gender imbalance which is unavoidable in the single-mediator model. A former client who left the mediation process before its completion later told me that she felt outnumbered, powerless, and threatened by the presence of two men. This will always be a problem, but talking about it can be helpful. In a recent first interview a woman client reported that she was angry at the way I referred to her husband's rigorous work schedule compared to hers. She perceived this as a biased value judgment diminishing her worth. We discussed it and, by dealing with it, improved the atmosphere, even though the irritation was not eliminated.

Related to this is my understanding that some women's organizations are less than enthusiastic about the mediation process. The ameliorative mood generated in the mediation process must appear inconsistent with the view of those whose major concern is correcting the inequities of a sexist society. Those who are devoted to remedying the unfairness usually operate from an understandable desire to prevail, which conflicts with the basic thrust of the mediation model. Presumably, "pro-fathers' rights" groups will have similar objections. Unfortunately, it frequently happens that there can be two virtuous movements that, ironically, are somewhat opposed to each other.

TRAINING AND EDUCATION

After a year or so of doing this work, I decided to get a degree in counseling, and I entered a graduate program, received an MA, and eventually became licensed as a marriage, family, and child counselor in 1978. I have a separate counseling practice, which I conduct in a different office setting. (I am just now beginning to offer my services as a counselor–therapist to clients interested in divorce mediation. Because it will be necessary to refer those clients to attorneys for drafting of legal documents and court papers, it will offer an opportunity for collaboration not available in the single lawyer–mediation model. I expect the counselor–mediator model to permit me to deal in more depth with interpersonal and other psychological issues.) My special training as a counselor permits me additional insights and flexibility, which I find invaluable. I do not, however, think that every lawyer who does mediation need obtain graduate education and clinical training. (It does not hurt, of course.) Some minimum education in interpersonal dynamics and human development is necessary. This is true for lawyers in the adversary process but more so for lawyer–mediators. Some lawyers have a propensity for this kind of work, because of personality and inclination, and others do not. I doubt if many who do not will stay in mediation work.

There are many classes and training sessions available for those who want to practice divorce mediation. These opportunities to learn techniques that facilitate the mediation process are useful and important. Nonlawyers who do divorce mediation should be familiar with basic family case law and statutes as well as court procedure. Lawyers who are involved in mediating custody matters should learn about child development, and all divorce mediators should have a grounding in psychology and human development. The many legal and tax problems that are present in all but the simplest divorce case makes me doubt that lawyers can be kept entirely out of the process without serious risk to the clients at some point. The same is true for mediating any but the simplest custody case; resort to child therapists is almost always a requirement for the caring and careful practitioner.

Many young lawyers talk to me about getting into mediation work. On one hand, it is encouraging to see so many bright young people interested in alternatives to the adversary process. On the other hand, I am convinced that it is not desirable to go from law school into mediating cases without some rigorous apprenticeship in dealing with conflict resolution. I realize that the age-old problem for the young practitioner is present in this new field: "How do I get experience if I am too inexperienced to practice?" Internships, supervision, and consultation may be partial answers.

THE FIRST CONFERENCE AND THE LETTER OF AGREEMENT

My major goal in the first meeting is to be sure the clients understand the nature of the mediation process. This is legally required. I call it my "Miranda warning." These caveats are presented to the clients, with other material, in a contract letter that is sent to them after the first session. I generally do not proceed beyond the first session without a signed agreement. A copy of the most recent version of my letter of agreement is in Appendix 8-1. The letter of agreement serves a number of purposes.

Warnings

I remind the clients of the adverse legal interests point and make it clear once again that mediation is a process that is congenial only to a limited number of clients and that does not provide the same protection as the more conventional advocacy model. By securing their signatures to this letter of agreement, I protect myself and make sure the clients know what they are doing, to the extent it is possible. If some immediate and significant legal action must be taken before the letter contract can be prepared and read, I will sometimes get signatures on a brief interim agreement. It may seem that I am overprotective to insist on all these warnings and caveats, but at this stage in the development of the mediation process, I think it is worth the risk of appearing overcareful while the public and the legal community get used to a new idea.

Confidentiality

The understanding as to confidentiality is described and the relevant California Evidence Code is set forth.

Checklist

The agreement contains a general checklist of legal issues that must be dealt with before the work is completed.

Interim Agreements

Five very general agreements entered into in this basic document relate to privacy, maintenance of the economic status quo, reference to income taxes, modification of interim agreements, and the fee arrangement.

I seek the parties' agreement to respect the privacy of the other. Discussing the privacy issue may open up the question of other romantic relationships and their effect on the parties' feeling toward each other and implications for the minor children.

The agreements about maintaining the status quo (no transfers of property, incurring of debts, etc., without consent and notice) are very important. Many clients come in when they are quite angry and hurt. No real progress can be made in that mood. Sometimes minimal agreements can be reached that will permit the parties to separate and survive economically while they heal sufficiently to return at some later time and deal more comprehensively with their legal and personal problems. There is some danger that some clients will, by using these interim agreements, try to avoid unpleasant confrontations. Whether the lawyer–mediator should be active in needling them into activity can be a difficult question. I have had a number of couples who have played out the ultimate legal dissolution of their marriage over a period of many years. In some cases this is not a problem, but in others it may be regressive for one or both parties. It is a problem that should be discussed. Also, it is important to structure these temporary arrangements carefully to avoid as much as possible any prejudice that may result from arrangements that could be precedents for future long-range agreements or judgments. This part of the agreement is somewhat like a temporary court order after an "order to show cause" hearing.

The income tax understanding has the parties acknowledge that this is an area that cannot be determined in a final way at the inception of mediation, and constitutes an agreement to cooperate, which is probably more morally than legally binding. A provision permits modification of all interim agreements, which prevents the parties from being locked into an unsatisfactory arrangement.

Particular Facts

Finally, the letter agreements can contain a reference to the specific facts of the particular case, pointing out special problems and indicating tentative agreements beyond the general understandings. In effect this can become the first in a series of letters summarizing what was accomplished at the mediation conferences.

OTHER IMPORTANT MATTERS TO BE DISCUSSED WITH CLIENTS

Independent Legal Advice

The importance of separate and independent legal consultation is emphasized, and each spouse is encouraged to engage a lawyer, particularly at the early stage of negotiation. Essentially the clients are negotiating an agreement with the assistance of the lawyer–mediator. Clients negotiate more effectively when they know what their rights are during the negotiations. To wait until the negotiation is completed and then have an independent lawyer review the final agreement may guarantee that the agreement correctly states the terms of the agreement; however, it can pose a serious problem if the negotation is reopened because the reviewing lawyer raises new points for the first time. I encourage clients to check out difficult points with independent counsel *during* the negotiation process, as they arise. This can be expensive, and many clients choose not to do so. Realistically, lawyer–mediators are protecting themselves, as well as their clients, when they encourage independent legal consultation. It appears that fewer clients obtain independent legal advice than I would have predicted.

As time goes by and I do more of this type of work, I find my relationship with my clients' independent attorneys varies with different cases. Generally my contacts with other lawyers are cordial and cooperative. I have not been able to keep track of these contacts as they are too numerous and many clients see lawyers without informing me or the other party.

Confidentiality

I promise not to reveal what the clients say to me or to each other without mutual written consent; the clients promise not to ask me to make such revelations. I believe this is an enforceable agreement. I tell the clients that I am not sure if each of them has a right to the other's silence about the subject matter of the sessions, but I ask them as a matter of honor to agree not to reveal such information irrespective of the law's requirements. Only once have I been subpoenaed (to a deposition), and rather than spend the money to resist, the other party did not object to my testifying. In that case there had been only one session with the clients, and no agreement had been signed.

Court Papers and Appearances

It is my practice to prepare the court papers for the clients; however, I do not appear as attorney of record. The clients appear in their own names. Often I am requested to get the papers on file at the very beginning just as we commence negotiations. In this way the 6-month period in California between the approximate time of commencement of the proceeding and the final judgment can begin to run. The parties agree on who is to be petitioner and respondent. If they cannot agree, a coin is flipped. If the parties cannot complete the matter in the mediation system, the pleadings I have prepared can be converted to use in the adversary system, with no prejudice.

It is not my practice to go to court. On rare occasions I have had to go to clarify a problem that arose. I encourage both the clients to go, although only the petitioner must be there. I think the clients who go to court prefer going together. Their conjoint appearance in court is consistent with the mutuality of the process and affords a ritual that I believe is desirable. I prepare a script for the moving party, which is read to the court. Having such a document reduces the anxiety for the average client.

It is now possible in California to present the uncontested dissolution to the court by affidavit (declaration), requiring no personal appearance. Many of my clients are choosing this alternative. It is simple and less stressful, but it has some disadvantages. First, you cannot be sure when you will get back papers you mail to the court with no hearing date. Second, it separates the clients from the transaction, which makes the clients feel less involved and responsible. There is some question in my mind about the danger of allowing marriages to dissolve too easily. Bad marriages should, of course, be dissolvable, but the parties should have to be responsible for what they do. The mediation system encourages direct participation by the clients themselves in contrast to the adversary system in which it is so easy to abandon responsibility by relying on one's attorney. The nonappearance system, in my judgment, is a step backwards in that respect. I am aware of the pro forma nature of the appearance in the uncontested dissolution, but at least it requires some participation. With dissolution by affidavit, there need be none.

Use of Other Experts

One of the leading motivations for clients who seek mediations services is the desire to avoid the heavy costs of divorce litigation today. I have been trying with some success to develop relationships with accountants, appraisers, and actuaries who will serve as neutrals. Some clients can reach their own decisions even as to complex assets by simply getting horseback opinions and being willing to rely on these informal assessments. The lawyer–mediator must make it clear in writing to these clients that they have the right to more precise evaluations. A group of neutral professional appraisers (accountants, actuaries, and real estate and personal property evaluators) appears to be developing, just as neutral lawyer–mediators have come on the scene. It is also interesting that in the San Francisco Bay area there are now in active practice a substantial number of experienced psychotherapists who will prepare only neutral evaluations in child-custody cases.

Fees

I charge by the hour and bill monthly. I ask for no retainer. I recommend that each party pay one half of the bill. If there are community cash resources, I suggest that my fee come from those funds. If one party pays all of the fee, I often suggest that that client get a credit when the community property is divided. These are general rules. There are exceptions. I have had a few problems in collecting fees from disappointed clients, and some others are rather slow in payment. Generally I am paid regularly. The same resistance to fees is experienced as in my nonmediation cases.

USEFUL TECHNIQUES

A few props are very helpful, if not necessary. A blackboard, easel pad, or similar device for purposes of in-session illustration is useful. Desks or other writing surfaces that each client can use should be available. It is preferable not to have a big desk separating the attorney from the clients. A copy machine should be available so the clients and the lawyer can have the same material before them.

During the sessions, the mediator's role-playing the part of an independent adversary attorney for each party is an essential part of the process. From time to time each client is addressed by the lawyer–mediator as if he or she were that party's lawyer and the other party were not present. This is a simple and dramatic way to bring reality to the clients.

Most important is the use of postsession letters that summarize what happened at the last meeting. The legal and psychological implications of alternative courses of conduct are indicated. Copies of statutory or case material that are relevant often accompany the letter. Appendix 8-1 has three excerpts illustrating the use of postsession letters to clients. Writing the letters is time-consuming and expensive; therefore, I get the clients' permission before doing it so there are no surprises in the monthly billing. In any case, if I do not use the postsession letter, I try to dictate a memorandum to the file after each session, as the give and take of the sessions often makes note taking ragged at best.

ATTITUDES FOR EFFECTIVE MEDIATION

There are a number of observations that come to mind as I review the last 12 years. Choosing divorce mediation is clearly not a way to avoid stress, either for the clients or the mediator. Obviously, there is substantial emotional pressure in almost all family law matters. Although there are many positive aspects to the mediation process, it is extremely difficult for most people to sit in the same room and try to cooperate with a person who is perceived to have hurt and disappointed you and who probably perceives you that way. It is also a difficult process for the attorney–mediator, who is participating in the commendable but somewhat quixotic task of assisting both parties to cooperate when they are, according to some psychologists, experiencing the third most stressful situation (after death and separation) that people ever face. The neutral lawyer has the dubious distinction of probably, at some level, disappointing both clients, each of whom secretly or unconsciously expect to be supported against the other party. The positive factors outweigh the negative ones for me, but this process is not an easy one.

The mediator should try to be aware of his or her own feelings and should respond to his or her internal messages. If something does not feel right, it should be brought out in the session or at least in correspondence. Avoidance, rationalization, denial, and other similar defenses have no place in the mediator's repertoire of responses. The mediator usually should comment on obvious incongruences and indirect nonverbal communication such as eye-rolling, groans, head dropping, sighs, and tears. Of course, good judgment has to be exercised, and there may be times when it is best not to say anything, but only after a conscious choice is made. Consciousness is virtue in these situations.

The mediator should not discourage conflict; rather, mediation should supply a safe place for the clients to ventilate and express themselves. This opportunity is usually not provided in the adversary system, which often allows only the lawyers to express themselves, particularly in these days of no-fault divorce. Of course, there are certain minimum standards of civility without which the process cannot operate.

Clients should not be permitted or forced to make irreversible decisions on significant issues in sessions. There is too much emotional pressure "to get an agreement and get out" or a fear of being labeled "a bad guy." The clients should have the right to consider their tentative decisions outside the session before they are even morally bound. As usual, there are exceptions, and only experience will tell the mediator when it is right to strike while the iron is hot.

Inequality of bargaining power or negotiation skills is a serious problem. Many of the critics of mediation are understandably concerned about how often this inequality is gender based. If the mediator sees this disparity as causing unfairness, it has to be mentioned, and some assistance in the negotiation has to be given to the "weaker" client. However, both parties must first acknowledge the problem. The situation is complex; the mediator must also be on the lookout for the passively aggressive client as well as the obviously aggressive one.

Clients in great stress should be discouraged from making irreversible decisions. Temporary arrangements that preserve the status quo are, however, extremely useful, with the caveat that the mediator should avoid prejudice to long-range legal positions.

ADVANTAGES OF DIVORCE MEDIATION

Most of my clients are educated, relatively comfortable economically, middle or upper-middle and professional class, and white. Essentially this is the same population from which my premediation and nonmediation clients have come. Advantages that these clients can derive from divorce mediation include:

- a feeling of autonomy and self-control
- a period of moratorium with protection of rights
- an opportunity, if they want it, to ventilate in a safe place
- a place to consider alternatives
- an opportunity, if they want it, to preserve appropriate aspects of relating with a former spouse
- an opportunity to reduce trauma for children (and an opportunity to model constructive conflict resolution for them)
- relative economy, and for some, avoidance of financial disaster

STATISTICAL ANALYSIS

Almost 13 years have elapsed since I began to offer divorce mediation as part of my general practice. When I began in 1972, the divorce mediation model was virtually unknown. I am now carrying a caseload that takes a substantial portion of my time.

In this period I have seen more than 300 couples who have consulted me specifically for mediation services. I have examined 262 of these files and present the following statistical insights.

Nearly one half of these cases, 129, resulted in a mediated resolution. In 105 cases, or just about 40%, there were one or two consultations, but the parties did not continue with me to an agreement. I do not know how many of these cases reconciled, simply stayed separated, went into the adversary process, or were resolved by some other nonadversary process. In 28 cases, or something over 10%, there was substantial consultation with me, but the process did not continue, and the parties completed their divorce in the adversary system.

The 262 cases included two groups: an earlier group of 168, and a later group of 94. Of the earlier group, 52% of the cases were completed, 40% were treated as consultations, and 8% had to be finished in the adversary system. The later group of 94 cases show 45%, 40%, and 15%, respectively, in these categories.

I also calculated the time involved in 98 of the cases that ended in mediated agreements. The average number of hours per case for all of the 98 is just about 21 hours. Included in the 98 cases are three subgroups of 29, 17, and 52 cases each. The 29-case group is from an early sample, and it averaged 16.33 hours per case. The 17-case group was later and averaged 21.01 hours. The 52-case group was most recent, and it averaged 23.54 hours. Another breakdown of the time looks like Table 8-1.

The average time in mediation for the cases that eventually required completion in the adversary system was 13 hours.

These statistics confirm that a substantial number of clients are interested in trying to resolve their family law cases by using a nonadversary model. About one half of those clients who consulted me were able to pursue the process to completion. At first I thought of those cases who did not complete the process with me as failures. Upon reflection and discussion with colleagues, I have revised that opinion.

Many of the one- or two-session consultations were the first contact with the legal system for these clients. Of course, I do not know where they went or what they did next, so it is hard to judge the effect of the consultation on them. My feeling is that in most cases it was helpful for both spouses together to get a legal overview from a neutral attorney–mediator.

I carefully considered the 28 cases that ultimately required adversary lawyers in a court setting to resolve the conflicts that brought them to me. Several of those clients spoke or wrote to me after their cases were completed, and it was obvious that they derived substantial benefit from the mediation process. For many, the mediation supplied a moratorium and a safe forum

Table 8-1. Number of Hours Needed to Complete Mediation through Executed Agreement and Court Judgment

Hours	First Group	Second Group	Third Group
5–10	6	6	9
11–15	10	4	5
16–20	5	2	17
21–30	5	1	6
31–40	2	2	4
41–50	1	1	7
51–60		1	2
Over 60			2
Total cases	29	17	52

when the clients were in acute distress. In others of this group of cases, substantial agreement was reached in my office, but separate lawyers were necessary to reassure one or both of the clients, who did not completely trust the mediation process to protect them.

There are some trends that can be inferred from these figures and the information gleaned from this observation of my practice. There has been an increase in the time necessary to complete the average case of clients who are interested in mediation, from 16.33 hours to 23.54 hours. My present caseload has a number of active cases that are in the 30–50 hour range, and some may require even more time. These increases can be attributed to the fact that the mediation process now attracts more complex, more difficult, and higher-value asset cases than previously. The earlier clients were often a self-selected sample, less contentious and more committed to a nonadversarial resolution. Now I find a larger number of couples who come to me both to avoid the increasing expense of the adversary process and to choose what they hope will be a less stressful experience.

Another apparent trend is a larger number of one- or two-session consultations that do not develop into finally mediated transactions. I think there is a growing number of clients who consult me to get an overview from a nonadversary perspective before deciding how to proceed. In a similar vein, there are now many preliminary telephone consultations that do not develop into office visits. Admittedly I do a rigorous screening in telephone interviews, which seems to filter out clients who are not really interested in mediation, at least with me.

CONCLUSION

Because the emotional and economic costs of conventional adversarial resolutions of family law disputes are not acceptable to many clients and professionals, alternatives have been developed for those who wish to try a different method. My experience supports the conclusion that the divorce mediation model described in this chapter is, for some, a workable alternative.

APPENDIX 8-1: SAMPLE LETTER OF AGREEMENT

Dear _____ and _____ :

This will confirm that we met on ___, and I promised you a summary of the substance of our meeting and the letter agreement I use in nonadversary family law consultations.

First, in regard to the matter of legal representation, it is important to recall that I advised each of you that you have adverse legal interests in regard to the matters about which you consulted me. This means that a particular resolution of any of the outstanding issues between you, such as spousal support, property division, or even the date of separation, may be relatively advantageous or detrimental. Thus, often when married people separate they retain their own attorneys to negotiate the best result for themselves in these matters. When you both consult one attorney, the law requires that you be advised carefully that you have such adverse legal interests, that they are substantial, that you acknowledge that this has been explained to you, that you understand the implications of this advice, and that you are willing to receive this type of legal service, at least for the present.

Let me add, without detracting from the significance of the above admonition, that at any time either of you wishes to consult an attorney of your own choice you should do so, and I urge you to do so. It is not necessary to inform me or the other party that you are doing so. This can occur at the same time you are continuing to consult with me. In short, there is no limitation on your right to be independently advised even while participating in this process. It is my opinion that consultations with independent lawyers are most helpful when they are made at this time so you can have some idea from your own attorney what your position would be if you had your family law case handled in the adversary system.

You should also be informed that in my opinion this nonadversary process is not always appropriate for every individual. Some people who are separating and possibly ending a long and complex relationship simply cannot deal with one another in a manner that permits a cooperatively achieved result. Some other couples who require a clean break find this process makes it difficult to achieve that result as it could exacerbate old feelings of anger, dependency, control, or guilt. Also, this process does not permit you to be protected in the same way that you might expect from the adversary process. It is impossible for a neutral lawyer functioning as a mediator to represent either of you as would a more conventional lawyer–advocate. Although I believe you will be receiving excellent legal services from me, it simply is not the kind of representation usually associated with lawyers at this time. This all must be viewed in the context of an area of law that is constantly changing and often difficult to predict. To proceed in this mode in effect means that you may give up the opportunity to prevail on some issues in order to secure a workable, mutual arrangement through your own direct negotiation.

I also consider that I have a confidential relationship with both of you. In no event will I reveal to others any of your communications to me, or to each other in my presence, without the consent of both of you. By signing this letter you each agree not to ask me to make such disclosures without your joint consent. By this reference you are informed that Section 1152.5 of the California Evidence Code provides in part as follows, and you both agree that it shall apply to the mediation process you are entering:

> (a) Subject to the conditions and exceptions provided in this section, when persons agree to conduct and participate in a mediation for the purpose of compromising, settling or resolving a dispute:
> (1) evidence of anything said or of any admission made in the course of the

mediation is not admissible in evidence, and disclosure of any such evidence shall not be compelled, in any civil action in which, pursuant to law, testimony can be compelled to be given.

(2) unless the document otherwise provides, no document prepared for the purpose of, or in the course of, or pursuant to, the mediation, or a copy thereof, is admissible in evidence, and disclosure of any such document shall not be compelled, in any civil action in which, pursuant to law, testimony can be compelled to be given.

(b) Subdivision (a) does not limit the admissibility of evidence if all persons who conducted or otherwise participated in the mediation consent to its disclosure."

This agreement is an example of a document that is not subject to the restrictions of Evidence Code Section 1152.5.

If for any reason we are unable to complete this transaction and you secure the representation of your own attorneys, I will not, of course, be the attorney for either of you.

One final point about this process. It requires a substantial amount of mutual trust if it is going to work. For instance, unless you direct me to check into the representations of each of you as to relevant facts and valuations, it is my practice to use that information you give me as the basis for the negotiation and agreement. As you can see, this requires that each of you be confident that the other person is trustworthy and believable in regard to the facts presented to me. We can, of course, agree on the use of experts such as appraisers, actuaries and accountants to assist us in reaching valuations.

If, after carefully considering the above caveats and warnings, you want to continue working with me, please sign the extra copy of this letter sent to each of you and return it to me so I may have a record of your consent for my files.

The following are the issues that typically must be resolved if you go ahead with a dissolution of your marriage or a formal separation agreement:

1. effect of any premarital agreement
2. child custody/visitation
3. child support
   a. to whom
   b. amount
   c. duration
   d. Agnos minimum support legislation
   e. court schedules
4. spousal support
   a. to whom
   b. amount
   c. duration
   d. court schedules
5. property/debt division
   a. identification of separate/community property/debts
   b. valuation of community property
   c. division of property/debts

    d. retirement—social security

    e. effect of separation

    f. effect on existing deeds of trust

6. education, training, and professional licenses

7. life insurance/disability insurance

8. health insurance/expenses

9. income tax (It may be important that your tax adviser play a significant role in these negotiations, as I do not consider myself an expert in this area.)

    a. liability for pre-1987 taxes

    b. 1987 taxes

    c. consequences of property division, including the consequences of transferring tax-deferred income

    d. consequences of support payments, particularly in light of recent federal tax law changes

    e. future income tax on sales of transferred assets

    f. implications of separation, particularly as it affects taxability of support payments

Although we didn't necessarily discuss all of these points at our recent meeting, it is my practice to urge my clients to agree to the following when they are consulting with me. By signing this letter you will be bound by the following agreements as well as the above understanding regarding confidentiality.

1. Each of you will respect the privacy of the other.

2. There will be no transfers of community property, without mutual consent, pending our negotiations, nor will there be any debts incurred for which the other is responsible without mutual consent. Transfers of separate property acquired during or before the marriage shall not be made without informing the other of the proposed transfer in sufficient time for the non-transferring party to take appropriate protective measures. This can be explained further upon request.

3. It is acknowledged that there may be income tax implications in some of the interim agreements between you, and that you will attempt to cooperate in this regard to minimize the net tax consequences of your actions.

4. All interim agreements are subject to modification after consultation, upon reasonable notice to the other party.

5. My fees are $___ an hour plus any costs incurred. My practice is to bill both clients monthly for the entire amount. You may, of course, decide between you how the fee is paid, but each of you is responsible to see that my bill is paid. Enclosed is a memorandum detailing my fee policy.

In regard to your particular situation, let me mention some of the specifics to which our attention has been directed.

[A discussion of the particular circumstances follows.]

                                     Best regards,

                                     Henry M. Elson

Excerpts from Letters to Clients

The following is my response to a client's concern that I was not being objective.

> Let me review where we are. It was in November of last year that A made a proposal for division of assets in a letter dated 11/4/83. B responded in two parts; in a letter dated 1/31/84 and a second letter dated 2/25/84. At that time, during the negotiations B wrote to me with concern about my objectivity. We dealt with that in telephone conversations and I hope he feels comfortable about that issue now. It frequently is a problem in these matters to keep the confidence of both parties when so many emotional factors impinge on the legal–financial issues. I am pleased that B was willing to express his feelings as he did and I expect each of you to continue letting me know when you feel something on my part is causing you concern. I will try to do the same.

The following is a portion of a letter I wrote during protracted negotiations, reminding the parties of the confidentiality issue and the right to independent counsel and telling them that I had done no independent investigation of valuation. When the mediation extends over a long period, I will often repeat important caveats in corespondence and in person.

> You each must be reminded that, by agreement, the communications from you to each other and to me remain confidential. This makes it easier to be candid in the negotiations without fear of possibly being disadvantaged by that openness if an agreement cannot be reached. While I am reminding you of mutual understandings, please remember that you each have an absolute right to and should consult an independent attorney to make sure you understand your legal position. No matter how hard I try to "role play" what your separate attorneys might advise about your "legal rights," it is simply not the same as a separate consultation. Finally, in this regard I remind you that I have not done any independent investigation to determine the value of any of the assets, i.e., the residence, retirement, etc. I may allude to this again when I discuss the "variables."

The following is a portion of a letter referring to the issue of spousal support. The parties changed their minds after this letter and agreed to have the court keep jurisdiction.

> We discussed the spousal support issue during our November 10th session. Since that meeting B called and informed me that you both agreed to waive your respective rights to spousal support. I believe you both understand that such waiver at this time means that at no future time would either of you have a legal right to support from the other party.
>
> I believe we all agreed that if B's income projections are correct you would each have about the same annual income—$48,000+. I have asked you about the meaning of that figure and my recollection is that it was a pre-income tax figure. What this could mean in terms of available cash for each of you is not clear to me. I think it appropriate to make a projection of the cash available to each of you based on B's figures. The amount of depreciation available would certainly affect the post income tax cash availability as would other factors possibly. You each are entitled to more detail about the income figures.

It was generally expected that you each would be self supporting at about the same income level based on the allocation of properties and debts. I don't know of any income potential for A other than from her properties. B has income from literary property. Obviously either of you is free to earn money from other investments or jobs, or writing. It would appear that neither of you would have a present need for support assistance from the other party at this time.

It is my opinion that if either of you requested it, the court would retain jurisdiction ($1.00 per year) to award future support if the requesting party was unable for reasons beyond that person's control to continue to be self supporting. To waive that option is giving up a valuable right. Obviously it can be done legally if you both agree. Whether it is wise is another question. If I were A's lawyer I would be very careful to remind her that B has been the source of most of the expertise that led to the accumulation of your very ample community property. It could be argued, morally, that he has done his share and now you should release each other from future obligations. No one could say that B was being outrageous to take that position. However, there is no retirement plan for either of you and it is not clear whether either of you is covered by social security (I suggest that be checked out with the local Social Security office).

If the proposal B made for division of property and debts is accepted by A, she will be relying on his wisdom and fairness and also cutting off all ties for legal support if the economics don't work out for her. If I were B's lawyer I would argue that you both have exactly equal estates and approximately equal incomes and there is no basis for an award of spousal support when the parties are independent. Frankly, as I said above, it is my opinion that a court would not refuse to protect both of you against the future with a retention of jurisdiction. I can supply you with copies of the relevant cases which make this point about lengthy marriages and the retention of jurisdiction to award spousal support.

REFERENCES

California Evidence Code, Section 1152.5.
Klemm v. Superior Court, 75 Cal. App. 3d 893 (1977).

9

Mediation of Child-Custody and Visitation Disputes in a Court Setting

ANTHONY J. SALIUS
SALLY DIXON MARUZO
Family Division, Superior Court, Hartford, Connecticut

The Family Division of the Connecticut Superior Court offers a statewide service of custody mediation. The Connecticut divorce mediation service, initiated in 1977, is comprehensive but not mandatory. It incorporates many innovations, including the use of gender-mixed mediator teams and the occasional resolution of family finances. The history, philosophy, operation, and experience of the Connecticut Superior Court mediation service is described here and evaluated. This chapter provides detail and analysis helpful for understanding application of the family mediation process in a court-connected setting. The insights offered by the program's founding director and an experienced staff mediator will prove worthwhile for anyone interested in the dynamics of mediation.

Contested child-custody and visitation cases continue to be the most complex and difficult matters encountered by judges in the family relations divisions of courts. Decisions in these cases have far-reaching and lasting effects on the interests and welfare of children and parents.

The determination of child-custody issues has become a matter of growing judicial, professional, and public concern (King, 1979). As a result of the upsurge in family litigation during the last decade (National Center for Health Statistics, 1985), the courts are overwhelmed by the increasing demands made upon their resources. The delay between the initiation of litigation and final resolution has risen rapidly, straining judicial capacity.

Also during this period all jurisdictions have adopted no-fault divorce legislation (Survey of American Family Law, 1985), and courts have responded to this societal change by altering their approach to resolution of the pseudo-legal issues involving children that often accompany marital breakdown (Ricci, 1980; Wallerstein & Kelly, 1979). Judges have retreated from the narrow application of specific standards (e.g., guilt or maternal preference) and instead have embraced more general standards such as "the best interest of the child" or "the least detrimental alternative" (Goldstein, Freud, & Solnit, 1979).

The custody dispute is often clouded by issues related to personal, marital, and family dysfunction, and decision making is further complicated by the changing roles of men and women, as well as dramatic changes in family structure and child-rearing patterns. The growing number of custody conflicts and their traumatic effects on the family have demonstrated that the judicial process has done little to effectively resolve family dissension or to help the family adapt to a reorganized structure following divorce (Milne, 1978).

These problems have resulted in a growing recognition within the legal and mental health communities that the adversary system is neither appropriate nor helpful for many couples seeking judicial solutions to custody and visitation disputes (Wheeler, 1974). The major basis for such dissatisfaction is that the adversary system often escalates conflict between couples (Bohannon, 1970; Coogler, 1977) while exacerbating the emotional trauma already associated with separation and divorce (Irving, 1981).

It was because of this concern that the Family Division of the Connecticut Superior Court developed in 1977 a custody mediation service as an adjunct to the traditional case study or evaluation procedure utilized in most custody and visitation disputes. The assumptions that underlie the custody mediation service, the mediation strategies and techniques employed, program procedures and goals, and an evaluation of program results for a 4-year period will be discussed in the following sections.

SCOPE AND CONCEPT

During recent years, judges across the nation have turned with growing frequency to the use of reports and evaluations prepared by court-appointed mental health professionals as an aid in the adjudication of custody and visitation issues. It is generally agreed that the use of the evaluative report has benefited the court by providing information that would be difficult, if not impossible, to gather through other means (Milne, 1978).

Custody evaluations in most jurisdictions, including Connecticut, have undergone an evolutionary process during the past decade. The initial role of the Family Division in the custody investigation was similar to that of a probation investigator, with heavy emphasis on cause, fault, and extensive historical compilation. Changes in societal values subsequently brought about the concept of no-fault divorce and best interests of the child, and "investigations" became "case studies." Court-connected social service professionals with specialized training and skills now place increased emphasis on the identification of parenting abilities and examination of the primary parent–child relationships rather than discussion of unrelated and extraneous behavior (Annual Reports of Family Division, 1975–1981). With this perspective, the court-appointed family relations counselor provides a more meaningful description of the family circumstances to the court, and the value of the report in the decision-making process has been enhanced.

The value of case study reports and clinical evaluations in the litigation of child-oriented issues has been demonstrated and will continue to be an effective aid in appropriate cases in the future. However, a pronounced limitation of the traditional adversarial approach is that courts and supportive services have assumed responsibility for decision making in these situations, without any meaningful attempt to evaluate the ability of the parents to make such decisions. Further, issues relative to children in divorce proceedings are more emotional than legal, and the adversary system does not provide a true or lasting resolution of these issues (Hodges, 1986). This concept is eloquently expressed in the June 1981 report of the New Jersey Supreme Court Committee on Matrimonial Litigation. Chaired by Justice Morris Pashman, the committee observed,

> No area of matrimonial litigation better lends itself to fashioning ways to create a cooperative and conciliatory environment for the benefit of parents and children. Court administrators and personnel throughout the country have questioned whether the courtroom is the best forum for the resolution of child custody issues, and whether the traditional adversarial system is the most appropriate means for presenting the issues. . . . The use of professionals trained to assist family members to resolve their problems is, in the Committee's opinion, an idea whose time has come. (p. 40–41)

The Custody Mediation Service developed by the Family Division of the Connecticut Superior Court was the product of the collective experience of family relations counselors in working with families going through the process of separation and divorce. This experience produced the following observations and assumptions, which formed the basis of the mediation program in Connecticut:

1. Most persons are responsible parents and are capable of mutually determining the postdivorce parenting arrangement that best meets the needs of the children. The goal of mediation is to provide people with a choice and leave the responsibility for making decisions where it belongs—with the family.

2. Self-determination and active involvement in the decision-making process is effective in promoting positive and lasting results for parents and children. Parents who invest time and energy developing a plan for their children are less likely to undermine it than in those situations where the decision has been made for the parents.

3. The stress and anxiety associated with the separation and divorce experience, particularly for children, can be reduced. Participation in the mediation process assists parents in affirming their affection and concern for their children, reducing the fears and anxieties of the children concerning the "loss" of one parent.

4. Mediation perceives conflict as natural and normal and views disputes concerning parenting as more emotional than legal, requiring a system for conflict resolution that can deal more effectively with those relationship issues.

5. Mediation emphasizes that divorce is not the end of the family and that continuing to be parents together in a reorganized family is possible for most couples.

6. The neutral, confidential, and nontherapeutic nature of the mediation sessions encourage participation by parents who might not otherwise involve themselves in the process of discussing issues related to the interests of their children.

7. Mediation can involve in the conflict resolution process other persons significant to the family situation. Third parties such as stepparents and grandparents often act to prolong the conflict. Mediation is able to involve them in a constructive manner, either to neutralize their obstruction or gain their cooperation in development of the postdivorce parenting arrangement.

8. Divorcing parents and their children are helped to construct a new and reorganized basis for their postdivorce relationships with one another. A major objective is that parents can utilize the negotiation skills learned in mediation to resolve future conflicts without returning to the court.

The Connecticut mediation program was developed as an adjunct to existing judicial procedures and is not intended to replace or disrupt those procedures. Neither is it intended that mediation become another procedure that must be exhausted prior to adjudication of the case. This would only serve to increase the costs and delays that already plague the dissolution process and would arbitrarily preclude the individual application of judicial alternatives, which may be more appropriate to disposition of a particular case.

The mediation program, as developed by the Family Division, is an alternative dispute-resolution mechanism available to the court in appropriate situations to provide skilled assistance to families attempting to resolve child-oriented issues through a rational, problem-solving process. The goal of court referral to the mediation service is to provide families with the opportunity to resolve disputes in a nonadversarial forum, thereby avoiding protracted litigation with its resultant costs and trauma for the couple and their children.

THE MEDIATION MODEL

The techniques and procedures employed by the Family Division in the mediation process were developed as part of a pilot program conducted in the New London Judicial District in 1977 with the cooperation of the bench and bar in that area. Communications were also established with two other judicial systems involved in the development of court-connected mediation programs: the Family Counseling Service of the Conciliation Court in Los Angeles, California, and the Domestic Relations Division of the Family Court in Minneapolis, Minnesota. Exchange of information and experience with these programs has made significant contributions to the evolution of the Connecticut program.

Use of the mediation model of intervention was not an entirely new concept to the Family Division in 1977. During the preceding years, a number of family relations counselors throughout the state successfully utilized a mediation approach in working with families who experienced postjudgment visitation problems and who sought assistance directly from the agency without filing formal actions in the court. The technique was found to be particularly effective in the resolution of these visitation disputes. Experience indicates that the majority of visitation conflicts are a product of communication problems and understanding between the parents rather than the behavior or attitude of the children. An educational session was conducted by the division in 1976 to improve staff skills and techniques in this area.

The success of the pilot program in New London led to establishment of a statewide mediation service in early 1978. The concept was subsequently incorporated into the Superior Court Rules of Practice in October 1978. Section 481 A of the Connecticut Practice Book (1984) was amended to authorize family relations counselors to conduct "investigations or mediation conferences in domestic relations matters as may be directed by the court." Concurrently, section 481 A was expanded to provide that family relations counselors, "under the direction of the court, or upon agreement of the parties as provided in General Statute section 46-41, attempt the reconciliation and adjustment of differences between the parties to dissolution of marriage and legal separation proceedings, particularly where there are minor children involved."

The concept of mediation in family cases was recognized by the state legislature in 1981 when section 46b-56 of the General Statutes was amended. The amendment also addressed the issue of joint custody and provided that "the court may also order both parties to submit to conciliation when only one parent seeks joint custody."

COURT REFERRAL

Pursuant to the Connecticut General Statutes and Rules of Practice, the court may refer matters to the Family Division for mediation of disputed issues. Normally referrals are limited to contested custody and/or visitation matters but have also included disputes concerning occupancy of the family residence and other related issues. Issues involving family finances and disposition of property are considered inappropriate for mediation by the Family Division unless requested by the parties and their attorneys. There are two referral options available to the court.

Referral for Mediation

Referral, for mediation authorizes the division to conduct mediation conferences in an attempt to assist families in resolving their conflicts. If the sessions are helpful to the parties in constructing their own postseparation child-care arrangement, a report outlining the agreement of the parties is forwarded to the attorneys and the court. Following an opportunity for each parent to reiew and discuss the agreement with his or her attorney, the agreement may be submitted to the court for review. If the agreement is approved by the court, it will be entered as an enforceable order of the court.

Where mediation has not assisted families in reaching an agreement, counselors prepare a report to the court and attorneys advising only that the parties participated in mediation and that the issues, some or all, remain in dispute. This report includes no personal or social information concerning family members or the marital situation.

Referral for Mediation Followed by Case Study Report

Should the couples be unable to resolve their differences in mediation, the matter is referred to a family relations counselor (other than the counselors who were involved in the mediation sessions with the family) for the purpose of conducting a case study of the family situation and filing a formal evaluative report with the court, including recommendations for disposition. This counselor undertakes the evaluation independently, with no knowledge of what transpired in the mediation process. All information related to mediation is confidential, and any notes or summaries made by the mediation counselors are placed in a separate file.

SCREENING OF REFERRALS

A family relations supervisor or counselor is in attendance at most court sessions and assists the court in identification of cases for mediation counseling or other appropriate services, discussing options with the attorneys and, wherever possible, with the parties. Since the inception of the mediation program in 1978, it has been demonstrated that certain situations can readily be identified as inappropriate for mediation:

1. cases involving children who have been or are alleged to be physically or emotionally abused or neglected
2. situations in which one or more of the adults have experienced serious emotional problems or have demonstrated erratic, violent, or severely antisocial patterns of behavior
3. families having multiple and continuing social agency or therapeutic involvement for the adults or children

Referrals include both pre- and postdissolution disputes, involving initial petitions, contempt actions, and modifications. Conflicts concerning child-care arrangements between unmarried couples as well as issues concerning grand-parent visitation are also referred.

PROGRAM PROCEDURES

Mediation conferences with the family are normally limited to from one to three 2-hour sessions with a team of two mediators. The initial session is scheduled as soon as possible following referral, optimally within 2 weeks. The objective is to complete the mediation process within 45 days of referral. Conferences are conducted during late afternoon or evening hours wherever possible to minimize disruption of employment and child-care schedules. Brief personal and demographic data for the purpose of research and program evaluation is collected from clients at the time of referral, if the participants are present in court or at the office locations prior to the scheduled mediation session. Practice has shown that extensive collection of historical information is not beneficial at this phase of the process. A booklet explaining the procedures, goals, and purposes of the mediation program is provided to both parents at the time of referral. The booklet was developed by the Family Division with the assistance of attorneys in family law practice and is available at no cost to the parties.

Family Division mediators seldom discuss the issues with the attorneys prior to the mediation session. Attorneys are not involved at any time in the actual mediation sessions, as dispute resolution must be accomplished by the parties themselves. However, the couple are encouraged to contact their attorneys during the process, to discuss the issues and options being dealt with in the sessions.

A conference with the attorneys may be conducted in certain cases where the mediators feel such contact would be necessary and helpful in achieving specific objectives. Mediators report that discussions with attorneys are conducted in 11% of the cases completed. In no event do the mediators confer individually with either attorney. Of course, any agreement will be reviewed by the parties with their attorney before being submitted to the court.

The mediators rarely interview the parties separately, as it is felt that this procedure tends to increase each party's adversarial attitude at a time when promoting mutual cooperation and trust is essential. The individual interview frequently arouses client suspicion that the mediator has been prejudiced by hearing the unchallenged perceptions of the other party. Judicious use of separate caucuses with the litigants may, however, be conducted as a strategy for resolving impasse during the mediation process and is employed in a small number of cases.

A meeting for the children with the mediators may be scheduled if the parents and mediators feel their participation might be helpful. In most cases, the children are seen alone by the mediators but, at the discretion of the mediators, may be included in the mediation session with the parents. The involvement of children in the mediation process will be discussed in a following section. Significant other persons (grandparents, stepparents, etc.) may, in the discretion of the mediators, be included in the mediation session or interviewed separately. On one hand, involvement of third parties in the mediation process can neutralize their obstruction or gain their cooperation and understanding. On the other hand, it is frequently found that the involvement of third parties with the primary family unit can prolong conflicts.

The program model generally includes no more than three sessions, each 2-hours long. The mediators do exercise flexibility, extending individual sessions beyond 2 hours or scheduling additional sessions if it is felt this would be helpful to the parties in resolving their conflicts or in achieving a better understanding of their situation. Such exceptions, however, continue to be extraordinary rather than the rule.

Where the mediation process has been helpful to the parties in resolving some or all of the issues, subsequent sessions may be scheduled to review and assess the long-term suitability of the child-care arrangement and to discuss new and changing needs. In other cases, a provision specifying that the parties will return to mediation should future conflicts arise is incorporated into the actual agreement. In the majority of cases, however, a review session is not specifically established, and the family is advised that they are free to return to the service should future conflicts arise. Access to subsequent mediation is available without the necessity of filing motions with the court.

Couples are asked to sign agreements only if both parties are unrepresented by counsel. Although called an agreement, the document setting forth the terms of their accord is treated as an understanding subject to further reflection and discussion with attorneys. Copies of the agreement are provided to both parties and to their attorneys. Clients are advised that their agreement is not binding on the court and that a judge at the time of hearing may not approve all or parts of the plan. However, it is made clear that this is a rare occurrence.

MEDIATION TECHNIQUES

The mediation conference is a structured, goal-directed process based on rational problem-solving techniques rather than the nondirective model utilized in many group or family counseling programs. The parties are investing considerable time and energy in the mediation sessions rather than concentrating on other conflict-resolution alternatives, and it is reasonable for them to expect a discernible result. This result may be either an agreement resolving the conflicts or an understanding that all options and concerns have been explored and that no resolution could be achieved at that time. The goal-directed approach, though nonrigid, is formalized to the extent of establishing rules of conduct, expectations, goals, and the formalization of areas of agreement.

The process is not a therapeutic one, directed toward treatment goals and objectives. It is a cooperative dispute-resolution process which relies on honest and open communication, reinforcement of positive bonds and shared goals, and the avoidance of blame. The goal is to reorient the parties toward each other not by imposing rules on them, but by helping them to achieve a new and shared perception of their relationship, a perception that will direct their attention toward one another (Fuller, 1971).

The mediation process has been described in various ways in social psychology and labor relations literature. Kessler (1978) divides the process into four steps: setting the stage, defining the issues, processing the issues, and resolving the issues. Kressel (1971) observed that mediation falls into three phases. In the early stages, "reflexive" strategies prevail; then "contextual" strategies predominate; toward the end of the process, "directive" strategies are more common.

The role of the mediator has also been the subject of a variety of definitions. Deutsch (1973) proposes that the role is to (1) help the conflicting parties identify and confront the issues in conflict; (2) help remove blocks and distortions in the communications process so that mutual understanding may develop; (3) help establish such norms for rational interaction as mutual respect, open communication, and the use of persuasion rather than coercion, and the desirability of reaching a mutually satisfying agreement; (4) help determine what kinds of solutions are possible and make suggestions about possible solutions; (5) help provide favorable circumstances and conditions for confronting the issues; (6) help make a workable agreement acceptable to the parties in conflict; and (7) help make the negotiations and the final agreement seem prestigeful and attractive to the interested parties.

Mediation within a court setting, more than private sector mediation, involves the management of conflict and client resistance. Therefore the single most important tool of the mediator is structure. The relationships between divorced and divorcing couples tend to be volatile, and the ability of mediators to establish a structure for conflict negotiation and to adhere to the process is critical to a positive outcome.

Court and governmental administrators too often tend to evaluate mediation programs on the basis of agreements reached, failing to recognize or measure the positive effects of mediation on family functioning, even where immediate resolution is not achieved. Faced with evaluation from this perspective, the temptation for court mediators is to engage in a premature search for solutions. The key to effective conflict management is the way the mediator defines and frames the issues in dispute and sets an agenda for examination of those issues. However, it is precisely these intermediate steps that mediators tend to overlook in the push for agreement.

Clients referred by the court are normally anxious to ventilate their anger and frustration, attack the other parent, and defend their own positions, with little attention to the needs of the children. The task of the mediator is to slow the parties down and gain control of the process, avoiding the early impasse created by premature bargaining between two polarized positions. Effective mediation requires a focus on an intermediate step between the client's statement of the problem and the search for solutions. This involves the mediator's taking an active role in defining and framing the issues and establishing the agenda for further discussion, even before the information-gathering phase. The conscious and thoughtful ordering of the issues is an important opportunity to create positive movement and momentum in the mediation process.

The experience of family relations counselors in Connecticut during the past 4 years indicates that each family brings into mediation its unique needs, conflicts, and personality. Consequently, mediator styles vary in particular cases to best meet individual needs or circumstances. However, in general, the similarities in mediators and the mediation process far exceed the differences.

STAGES OF THE MEDIATION PROCESS

Initial Phase: Setting the Scene

Couples entering the court mediation program in Connecticut have generally been found to be pessimistic about the prospect of amicably resolving disputed issues. They question their ability to succeed based on failures of communication in the marital relationship and their perception of their roles as contestants in the adversarial process. Mutual trust and commitment to the task of resolution is absent. Clients frequently attempt to enlist the mediators as their allies. Feelings of anxiety, anger, and hurt result in a need to prove that they are right and their spouse wrong. It is common for people to perceive the mediators as evaluators, and communications are initially directed to the mediators rather than to the other spouse. Mediators must continually demonstrate to the parties that neutrality will not be compromised and that the responsibility for decision making is that of the parents.

The goal of the initial stage of mediation is to set the tone for the process. The goals and purposes of the mediation process are explained, and the role of the mediator is defined. The couple are informed that everything discussed is confidential and no information will be shared with the court. Parents are assured that there is no obligation to reach an understanding and that there are other alternatives for resolution of the issues. These alternatives are not discussed in detail, however, unless the parties are unable to resolve their conflicts. Experience has demonstrated that discussion of the adversarial nature of such alternatives at this stage has a limiting effect on the level of meaningful participation in the mediation process.

The mediators attempt to reinforce the confidence of the parties as competent problem-solvers and capable, responsible parents able to make their own decision regarding their children. Parents are advised that the goal is to construct a way that both can continue to be parents in a reorganized family, not to award custody to one parent and make a visitor of the other.

An important element of the initial session is discussion of the role of attorneys. Parties are informed that their attorneys will not be present to provide advice and representation in the mediation session. However, the couple are encouraged to consult with their attorneys between sessions and are free to review with the attorneys the information and options being dealt with in sessions. Parties who are represented are assured that they will not be asked to sign an agreement until they have had an opportunity to review any resolution with the attorneys. A period of 2 weeks is allowed for this purpose.

The focus of mediation on the future is discussed. It is explained that the process can do nothing to rectify or compensate for past actions, hurts, or unfairness and the intent is to restructure family relationships in terms of a plan for future parenting. Although the past will be discussed, parties are advised that the mediator will act to minimize those discussions. The process will direct the focus away from relationship issues that could not be resolved during the marriage and toward those parenting issues that must be resolved prior to the divorce.

The time frame for the process (three 2-hour sessions within 45 days) is made clear. It has been found that couples share information and negotiate more effectively within time limits and that the most productive work is accomplished as the various deadlines are approached.

Parties are encouraged to express their feelings, needs, and concerns and are assured that both will be provided the opportunity to express themselves fully. The fact that the issues to be discussed are often sensitive and provocative and that interruptions will occur is acknowledged. Parties are asked to not interrupt the other or talk at the same time and are told that the mediator will act to enforce this ground rule.

Couples are informed of the important role that significant other persons often play in the mediation process. The roles of children, stepparents, grandparents, and others are discussed, and the rules for their potential inclusion in the process are outlined. A consensus of the couple for the process of involvement or noninvolvement of others should be reached, subject to that need arising in subsequent discussions.

Although couples may have been ordered into mediation by the court, this is interpreted as only requiring that the purposes, objectives, and procedures of mediation are explained and discussed. Participation in the process must be voluntary, and the parties, not the mediator, must "own" the process. Couples are advised that they are free to terminate the mediation at any time, without prejudice.

Once the mediator is clear that the mediation process is fully understood by the parties, they are asked to make a commitment to continue. If a party is reluctant to proceed and further explanation and clarification fails to gain a commitment, the mediation is terminated with a report forwarded to the court and attorneys, stating only that both parties attended and were unable to resolve their dispute. Since the inception of the Connecticut program, no client has opted out of the process at this juncture.

Defining the Issues

At the second mediation phase, the parties have an understanding of the mediation process, and the mediator has a general idea of each client's readiness to work toward resolution. The mediator must be firmly in control of the process, and parties are usually communicating with the mediator rather than with each other. In order to pursue an understanding of the issues involved and the parties' ability to proceed, the mediator invites the parties to share their perceptions of the issues. This can begin with a review of the court history, if applicable. Included will be the length of the marriage or relationship, the length of the separation, and the date of the divorce, if applicable. The existence of any court orders or agreements is explored to the extent of determining if the orders were entered by private negotiations, attorney-assisted negotiations, mediation, or trial. It is important to discuss the feelings of the parties toward the process of reaching prior orders or arrangements and the workability of those arrangements.

Mediators at this stage permit the individuals to air their grievances within reasonable limits, although the focus may be on the adult interpersonal relationships rather than on the children. This ventilation may lead to bickering between the couple, and the mediators intervene in situations where one person either monopolizes conversation or interrupts frequently.

It is important that communications between the parties and mediators be balanced, ensuring that each is allowed equal time. Lengthy statements by the parties, beyond a minute or two, should not be permitted; experience indicates that the other party rarely hears anything beyond the initial statement, usually an attacking statement or an attempt to justify a position, as he or she begins to formulate a response or counter to the initial statement and is not listening to the other party. Lengthy statements are often overwhelming and result in increasing levels of anger and conflict. As a means of interruption the mediator should attempt to clarify the statements made and allow the other party to share his or her perceptions. Most statements are of an attacking nature at this point and are stated in a provocative manner. Mediators should attempt to reframe statements in a more positive, neutral way, with a focus on parenting and children's needs.

The ventilation process should be relatively brief and should elicit only sufficient information to achieve a general agreement or understanding of the issues to be resolved. It must be understood that identification of the issues is not final and that enhancement of the issues in dispute and discussion of alternatives will occur later in the process.

The ventilation period provides mediators with an opportunity to assess the clients' capacity to mediate and the relative bargaining power of the parties. Some people may be unable to participate meaningfully, because of severe emotional stress or psychological problems, and in these situations, it would be best to abandon the process at this early juncture and explore with the parties other alternatives for resolution.

As previously mentioned, couples are normally anxious to begin the bargaining process as a continuation of the ventilation phase without the prerequisites of defining and reframing the issues, establishing an agenda for discussion, and developing the necessary informational foundations. An effective strategy for slowing the process down is addressing the issues of whether both parties desire the divorce. Nonmutuality of the decision to divorce is often a significant factor precluding an individual's readiness to negotiate. Addressing this issue early in the process can avoid subsequent stalling tactics or sabotaging of the process by a spouse attempting to keep the relationship intact.

It is important at this juncture that the parties provide information and share perceptions about the child or children. Habits, personality, needs, and problems should be discussed for each of the children. This discussion heightens the awareness of the parties that each child is an individual and that the unique qualities of each must be respected and addressed in construction of the parenting plan. As there is normally great commonality in parents' description of their children, this process can assist in establishing meaningful and effective levels of communication. If there is little commonality, the need for further information, either from children or an expert outside of mediation, is indicated. It is also vital that mediators provide information concerning the developmental needs of children. Discussion of the parenting patterns of the parties in terms of the past and/or current distribution or sharing of child-care responsibilities and involvement in activities can also be helpful to the mediation process. This exchange helps parents to focus on the children's needs and reinforces the joint responsibilities of parenthood.

The mediators assist clients in sharing their hurt, frustration, and anger, as such unspoken feelings or hidden agendas may ultimately preclude resolution or undermine agreements. Clients normally begin to experience the mediation process as a safe forum in which to discuss feelings and concerns. Communications should begin to shift at this point from between the couple and the mediators to between the spouses.

During the first part of this phase the role of the mediators is relatively nondirective. The mediators begin to restate and clarify certain salient feelings expressed by the parties, to demonstrate the mediators' understanding of the problems and emotions involved as well as to increase the perception of the parties regarding each other's feelings and interests. The empathetic listening by the mediators legitimizes those feelings that may pave the way for future resolution of the issues, and the process of helping the parties to define the issues can begin. The mediators should avoid, as far as possible, the use of the confining and often provocative terms "custody" and "visitation," which to many people entering the mediation process connote power and loss of power and which limit the bargaining process. It is useful to permit the couple to develop their own language, substituting terms such as "physical residence," "being with mother (father)," "at father's (mother's) home," and other more specific language. Although it may be necessary to incorporate the statutory terms in the final agreement, this can be accomplished at that point by using the definition of the parties for those terms. During this phase, the mediators assist the couple to move from the abstract levels of feelings and emotions to the task of identifying and defining the issues. Clients should begin to experience the success of give and take and improved ability to communicate meaningfully in a controlled forum.

The role of the mediator becomes increasingly more directive, assisting the parties in focusing on the children and identifying the issues. Mediators control and balance communications between the parties and point out unproductive behavior. Issues that cannot be resolved in mediation are eliminated.

This stage closes once basic accord concerning the needs of and goals for the children is achieved, even if only on a hypothetical level, and there is general agreement on the issues to be resolved. The hard work of having the parties confront the areas of conflict between them can begin.

Processing the Issues

Mediators begin by emphasizing the areas where couples agree or share common goals and concerns. Parents are encouraged to listen to one another: they may be in basic agreement with each other but unaware of this, because they are not attentive to what the other is saying. Clients are helped to reach agreement on relatively minor issues in an effort to increase their confidence in their ability to resolve conflicts. Mediators build on these minor areas of agreement to move the parties toward working on the larger areas of dispute.

The mediator's understanding of the complexity of the communication process and ability to know when and how to respond to what is being communicated are critical to the mediation process. Most clients enter mediation with fixed attitudes toward their spouse and their family situation as well as their own goals for mediation. These attitudes operate on different levels of client consciousness and manifest themselves in both verbal and nonverbal communication. Mediators must be sensitive to this and must be attentive to the process as well as the content of the information transmitted, to avoid overlooking information that may be critical to the problem-solving process.

For example, clients may take quite rigid positions regarding the children, despite substantial evidence that the position would result in an impractical or unworkable arrangement. Impasse can result unless the client is assisted in exploring and articulating needs, fears, and motivations beyond those verbalized. The rigid position may in fact be a reaction to a perception of the other party's rejection or a fear of losing influence. Assisting parties to verbalize such previously unspoken fears and perceived vulnerabilities may prove instrumental to resolution.

Another instance where uncommunicated feelings may be operative in prolonging impasse is in regard to the financial ramification of potential resolutions. Parents may fear that they would appear insensitive to the needs of the children were they to initiate discussion of finances. Without mediator intervention designed to bring such issues into the open, cooperative behavior would be blocked and a stalemate reached. The importance of assisting clients to verbalize these unspoken issues is not for the purpose of helping clients work through the issues. Mediation is not therapy. Rather, the purpose derives from an appreciation of the power that such issues, when unspoken, may have in preventing resolution. A basic requisite for promoting cooperative behavior in mediation is the client's belief that the critical issues and dynamics of the family relationships are known and understood by the mediators.

Clients also communicate information about their attitudes and feelings by nonverbal means. Posture, level of eye contact, smiles, frowns, glances at the clock, and other forms of nonverbal cues are all forms of communication, and mediators must be aware that these communications often serve as more accurate indicators of client feelings than the actual statements made. While it is neither necessary nor appropriate to respond to every expression of this kind of communication, there are times when the mediator should decide to comment. The prolonged silence of a client during discussion by the other spouse of a particularly sensitive issue or traumatic incident may be an appropriate point for intervention. The mediator might invite the silent client's response by asking what the client was experiencing while listening to the other spouse.

Two important mediator tasks in the bargaining process are identifying mediator interventions that promote cooperative behavior and trust and providing information regarding possible alternatives for resolution. Construction of a postdivorce parenting plan must be a conscious choice from viable alternatives, not mechanical application of established formulas. In this regard, mediators perform an important educational function, informing parents of the range of possible plans. Self-determination requires a foundation of information, and failure to assist parents in exploring alternatives may lead to development of a plan that is like the one their friends, neighbors, or relatives have. Experienced mediators continually work with various plans and have identified potential troublesome arrangements and conflict-producing areas. Mediators have also identified techniques that make plans easier to live with and more adaptable. This knowledge is most helpful when shared with the parents.

Mediators initiate the actual bargaining process by encouraging the parties to offer plans that they feel would best accomplish these goals. It is stressed that divorce is not the end of the family but a restructuring in which both parents will continue parental roles and responsibilities. The focus is on the future rather than the past. Alternatives are examined and discussed, assessing how each alternative meets certain of the needs of the parents and children, with the mediators emphasizing areas of agreement or commonality in the proposals. The mediators help the couple separate extraneous information and avoid unproductive attitudes and conduct. Attempts are made to avoid the problem of the parties fixating on a particular position or plan by continual presentation and discussion of other alternatives. This is the most critical point in the mediation process. If the mediators are unable to maintain the concentration of the parties on the task, the mediation can quickly reach insurmountable impasse.

The goals of this third phase are to identify and narrow the alternatives that appear workable and to determine the extent to which they offer acceptable components to either party. It is at this time that unacceptable or unconscionable plans are eliminated by open and frank discussion of the realities of the proposal. Should the mediators be unable to redirect the parties from arrangements that would not appear to protect the interests of the children or adults, the mediation process could be terminated at this point without a feeling of failure on the part of the parties and without the mediators being forced into the position of openly rejecting a plan already agreed to by the parties.

Once a range of viable alternatives has been established, discussion becomes focused on sifting the issues involved in those alternatives, expanding areas of agreement, and reducing areas of conflict. It is at this point that impasse may occur. In many situations, the impasse can be resolved and meaningful negotiations continued through the mediators' stressing of the benefits of cooperative resolution versus burdens of surrendering the power of decision making to external authority, or by restatement of the shared goals of the parties for their children as well as any areas of agreement. On occasion, couples may appear to be at impasse but in reality are on the verge of reaching agreement. They are either unable to articulate the solution or are reluctant to make the final compromise for fear of losing face. In these situations clients need the mediators' assistance in the form of verbalizing potential solutions and offering hypothetical solutions.

Some impasse situations may appear insurmountable. Mediators must encourage the parties not to give up the bargaining process but to continue working toward resolution. In this regard, mediators must be aware of the variety of techniques (Metzner & Reasbeck, 1982) that can be employed to resolve the impasse, and be innovative in determining the interventions that would have the best chance of success in the particular situation. Eight possible impasse-breaking strategies are described here.

1. When parents become locked into arguments concerning the merits of their respective positions, the mediator should redefine the problem and stress that there are more than two possible solutions. It is often helpful to identify the various areas of child-rearing responsibilities such as physical residence, discipline, education, religious training, medical care, recreational activities, cultural activities, and financial support. Working through these various areas often leads to construction of postdissolution child-care arrangements. Parents are often able to deal more successfully with the component parts of long-term parental responsibilities than with broader, conceptual plans for future child care.

2. The length of time for the individual sessions can be extended beyond the 2-hour guidelines. This allows more time for parties to thoroughly ventilate their feelings to each other. On occasion, this emotionally draining experience helps to reduce the rigidity of positions and open the door for compromise and problem solving.

3. Mediators can suggest ending the session and scheduling a further session soon for continuation of discussion. Sometimes the opportunity for the parties to reflect on the issues or discuss their position with friends, relatives, or their attorneys may help to break the stalemate. Further, the mere fact of allowing a fresh start on another day may be conducive to resolution.

4. An unusual, but sometimes effective, technique is recessing the session for a short time. The break may serve to lessen the tension, and in other cases, leaving the parties alone for a short period can encourage them to renew their commitment to work together toward resolution.

5. Mediators can make use of humor either in suggesting absurd alternatives which neither party could accept or by describing the deadlock in amusing terms. This type of intervention, if properly employed, can relieve the tension and lead to renewed efforts toward compromise.

6. Although the children may be seen by the mediator for a number of reasons, in the case of a deadlock the information obtained from the children often provides new direction and options in the parental negotiating process. In Connecticut, meetings are scheduled for the children when the parent and mediators feel that their participation would be helpful. Children are normally interviewed separately from the parents, and the information obtained is, within the discretion of the mediators, introduced in the mediation session. Of course, children are not asked to make a choice and are informed that any decision will be made by adults, whether the decision is that of the parents or the court. In a few cases, depending on the age and maturity of the children, the nature of the parental conflict, and the quality of the relationship between the parents, children are included in the mediation session with the parents. When children are participants, the mediators must establish and exercise control of the discussions.

7. Other significant parties can be either interviewed separately or, with the agreement of the disputants, invited to participate in the mediation session. It is not uncommon that grandparents, stepparents, and other persons may be the cause of an impasse, and their influence must be identified and neutralized. Further, the influence of third parties may be a positive one, and they can prove to be allies in breaking the deadlock.

8. Continuation of scheduled mediation sessions to a later date to allow parties to experiment with trial solutions is often useful in getting past an impasse. An arrangement that a parent cannot agree to for the long term may be acceptable for a brief trial period. The process provides parents with a safe atmosphere in which various alternatives can be attempted, and sessions can be scheduled to discuss the results of the homework assignment. This often provides parties with experience and information about how a proposed solution would work in practice.

This phase of the mediation process ends with the identification of areas of agreement and a range of alternatives that appear, at least in principle, workable and realistic to the parties.

Resolving the Issues

The goal of the fourth and final phase is to assist clients in verbalizing their commitment to specific agreements. Mediators must help parties feel that they individually, as well as the family unit collectively, have something to gain from amicable resolution. Instances of cooperative behavior are reinforced, and the progress the parties have made to that point is continually emphasized. Mediators must be alert to the tendency of clients at this stage of critical decision making to revert into the more comfortable, nonproductive communications of the past rather than to make necessary compromises.

During the course of discussions a shift of emphasis may occur and one party may offer a plan that represents something of a shift from an original position. The mediator must be alert to these statements, as they may be used as a starting point for final resolution. It is effective for the mediators to frequently reframe the statements of the parties, demonstrating how each party is trying to compromise for the common interest and shared goals in the best interest of the children.

The mediation team formally notes areas of agreement as they are reached and removes these items from discussion so that the parties can experience the dwindling number of issues. The discussion is moved from one area to the next, not allowing conflict in one area to prevent agreement in others. Mediators must ensure that areas of agreement are real and not the product of overt or covert pressure, as this would be counterproductive to the long-term stability of any eventual agreement. If mediators sense that a party is uncomfortable or uncertain with any aspect of agreement, decision on that particular item should be postponed for further consideration.

If the process has been conducted professionally, with open, frank, and informed discussion rather than with coercion and superficial examination of potential alternatives, the parties, regardless of outcome, will come away from the experience with an increased confidence in their ability to communicate and make decisions as parents. While mediation cannot erase past hurts and scars, it can increase the level of trust between the adults and help to focus their attention on the needs of the children in their reorganized family.

MEDIATION OUTCOMES

Agreements

It is the responsibility of the mediation team to write the agreement of the parties and to provide copies to the parties and their attorneys. It should be reiterated that the parties will have an opportunity to review and discuss the agreement with their attorneys and that the agreement, once approved by the court, becomes an enforceable order of the court. The agreement forwarded to the court is intended to be a legally enforceable document and, as such, states the terms of the custody and visitation plan. It may also be useful to assist the parties in preparation of a second, less formal agreement outlining guidelines for future parenting, including certain assurances, if any, made by the parties to one another about their respective roles and cooperation between them.

A provision specifying a future date for the parties' return to mediation may be incorporated in those situations where the agreement was established as a temporary plan to be reviewed and clarified after a specific interval. Also, an agreement may be incorporated to return to mediation in the event of future conflict, prior to either party's initiating formal legal action. In every situation the parties are advised that they are free to return to the service at any time to resolve new problems and conflicts. This access is available without having to file new motions with the court.

The court and attorneys are provided only the terms of an agreement, and no information concerning settlement negotiations or social and personal information should be transmitted by the mediators. If some, but not all, of the issues have been resolved, a report is provided outlining the areas of agreement and the issues remaining in dispute.

If an agreement is achieved, both parties in all cases are encouraged to be present to explain to their children the terms of the agreement. It is explained that this reaffirms the concern and affection of both parents for the children and reduces the anxiety levels of the children. Where appropriate, the mediators will arrange an additional session for the parents and the children for this purpose. Such joint sessions often serve to increase the level of commitment of the parties to the agreement.

The parties are advised that child-care arrangements must be viewed as flexible and that they are free, subject to mutual agreement, to modify any provision to better meet changing needs and circumstances which may not have been contemplated. It is emphasized that most arrangements will logically require change over the course of time with the increasing age and changing needs and schedules of children, remarriage, change of residence or employment, and so forth. The parties are encouraged to make the needed adjustments between themselves in a cooperative and compromising atmosphere.

No Agreement

Where mediation sessions have not assisted the parties in resolving their conflicts, the mediation should terminate with the mediators reinforcing the positive efforts of the parties and dispelling any sense of failure. Mediation is hard work, and parents participating in the process demonstrate commitment and concern for the well-being of their children. If no substantial progress toward resolution is made by the close of the second session, the mediation process should terminate with the mediators using that session or a third to commend the parties' efforts and to attempt to achieve accord on an alternative method of resolving the dispute. This may include agreements to attend family or individual therapy sessions, obtaining counseling, seeking specialized services for such problems as drug or alcohol abuse, arranging for psychiatric or psychological evaluations for family members, or a broad range of other actions designed to provide family members with more information and, possibly, a new set of alternatives.

As previously discussed, in Connecticut the majority of cases are referred for mediation to be followed by mandatory case study or evaluation if no agreement is achieved. A small number of cases are referred for mediation services only. In either event, when no agreement results, the mediators prepare a report for the attorneys and the court stating only that both parties participated in mediation and were unable to resolve the issues. No personal or social information is included. In appropriate cases the parties are advised that the matter will be referred to another family relations counselor for case study and evaluation. No information from the mediation sessions will be provided to the counselor conducting the evaluation, and the mediatior's file will be sealed.

CO-MEDIATION TEAMS

A unique aspect of the Connecticut court-connected mediation program is the use of male–female mediation teams in all cases. No empirical evidence has yet been developed as to whether the mediation team is more or less effective than a sole mediator, and the model remains a matter of personal choice. There is no question that the costs of conducting mediation are increased with the use of two mediators. However, these costs remain significantly less than the costs associated with court trial or an evaluation. The use of a team of mediators makes an important statement to the participants concerning the level of judicial recognition of the complexity of the issues involved and the investment the court has made in attempting to assist families in making their own decision.

The mediation team concept was established at the inception of the Connecticut program and has been continued, as mediators feel that the model provides a number of important benefits.

1. Co-mediation permits maximum flexibility in responding to the complex issues involved, and the interaction provides for a greater range of task-oriented interventions.

2. Clients can benefit from observing the communication and interaction of the mediators. The mediators are able to share their confusion or doubts and to seek clarifications. Clients can experience this mediator interaction as encouragement to share their own concerns without fear of rejection or deprecation. The level of cooperation and effective interaction between mediators can be a model for the disputants.

3. The mediators' communication with one another outside of the session provides an excellent opportunity to compare impressions and discuss possible intervention strategies for the forthcoming session.

4. The sex balancing provides clients the opportunity to be understood, validated, or challenged by persons of both sexes, minimizing sexual stereotyping and triangling. The use of one counselor may create, in particular situations, an imbalance where one party feels outnumbered and disadvantaged. This imbalance may exacerbate existing power struggles so common in couples involved in dissolution proceedings. Co-mediators can equalize the relationships involved and provide an atmosphere of objectivity and neutrality.

5. Balance can be provided in terms of maintaining neutrality, equalizing bargaining power, and sharing responsibility for control of communications. It

is possible for one mediator to be confrontive or supportive, with the co-mediator intervening or responding from the other point of view.

6. The model has been extremely effective in providing continuing training for experienced counselors and particularly helpful for the training and development of new counselors, who are provided an opportunity to observe and interact with an experienced mediator.

PROGRAM DATA

During the past 5 years over 9,000 couples have been referred by the court for mediation of custody and visitation disputes. This total represents 71% of those cases where custody or visitation issues were formally contested. Approximately 55% of the referrals involve postdivorce disputes. The program was successful in assisting families to resolve conflicts regarding their children in 64% of the cases referred.

Of the 9,000 referrals, 56% involved child-custody issues, 41% dealt with visitation conflicts, and 3% related to financial matters or exclusive occupancy of the family residence. The agreement rate has been consistent regardless of the nature of the dispute referred.

Mediation has not been successful in assisting the parties to resolve their disputes in 32% of the cases referred. In 10% of these cases a report is forwarded to the court and attorneys, advising that the issues remain in dispute. Pursuant to the court referral, the remaining 90% of these cases are subsequently referred for case study and evaluation by a third counselor. Preliminary research conducted by follow-up questionnaire and review of court records indicates that in 95% of the matters referred for study following unsuccessful mediation, the parties entered into agreements resolving the child-care issues and the disputes have not required court litigation. Therefore, preliminary examination indicates that few of the disputes referred to the mediation–case study procedure required resort to formal litigation for resolution.

PROGRAM EVALUATION

Connecticut is one of three court jurisdictions selected as part of a multiyear study of the effectiveness of court-connected programs offering mediation services to divorced or divorcing couples. The study, initiated on October 1, 1980, is sponsored by the Children's Bureau of the United States Department of Health and Human Services and administered by the Association of Family and Conciliation Courts. The Divorce Mediation Research Project, now in the final stage of data evaluation, is a comprehensive and multi-faceted study of public-sector mediation. Some of the major components of the study are examination of the characteristics of disputes and disputants, structure and format of mediation services, impact of mediation and adversarial forms of dispute resolution, impact on children and families, user satisfaction, and the durability of mediation agreements. A more in-depth analysis of this study can be found in Chapter 21; there is an unambiguous finding that mediation is associated with a high degree of user satisfaction (Pearson & Thoennes, 1984). Regardless of outcome, mediation participants clearly would recommend the process to others. This is consistent with the earlier response to agency follow-up questionnaires which found that two thirds of the participants would encourage others to mediate.

NEW DIRECTIONS

The counselors of the Family Division have mediated thousands of custody and visitation disputes since the program was established on a statewide basis in 1978. Observation of mediation sessions and the mediators' own analysis of their role and experience indicates that the mediation strategies and techniques employed are numerous and vary from passive to highly directive interventions. Court mediators are often not conscious of the actions they have taken that helped bring about a resolution, and many of the interventions appear to be spontaneous.

The fact that nearly two thirds of couples are able to construct a postdivorce parenting agreement in mediation appears to indicate that the mediator's sensitivity and intuitive grasp of individual situations and circumstances are significant to the process. While mediators find that sharing mediation strategies and alternatives for resolution is extremely useful and broadens the range of potential interventions, allegiance to a rigidly structured and patterned format tends to limit the mediator's ability to generate creative and individualized strategies for resolution.

Experience indicates that the initial training of mediators, including program concept and philosophy, stages of mediation, strategies for promoting cooperative behaviors, and impasse-avoiding techniques, is vital prior to entering into actual mediation. Following formal training it is most effective for new staff members to work as co-mediators with experienced staff members for a period of time. With increasing experience mediators begin to feel more comfortable in the process and to develop individual styles and new strategies.

Development of the Connecticut court-connected program, which involves over 50 counselors located in twelve regions of the state, has not been without problems. The observation of many experienced staff members is that mediators are often successful in assisting resolution of disputed custody and visitation issues simply because mediation provides a safe and secure setting for parents to discuss their feelings and concerns. Too often mediation becomes a mechanical process where the focus is negotiation of an agreement from preconceived alternatives, and the value of exposing, clarifying, and communicating thoughts and feelings is lost. Frequently, inadequate time is devoted to strengthening the commitment of parents to the agreement and to focusing on the cooperative decision-making aspects of parental responsibility.

Where the focus of mediation is bargaining among alternatives, to the exclusion of exploring of feelings and concerns, the probabilities of lower levels of participant satisfaction, of negative participant perception of the process, and of failure to construct a durable parenting plan are significantly increased.

It is felt that this mechanical approach to mediation is the product of the heavy volume of cases, expectations by judges and attorneys of expeditious resolution, inadequate ongoing education programs, and the limited sharing of information and experiences between mediators due to geographical separation.

In response, the Family Division has recently initiated a series of educational sessions for mediators, which will be conducted periodically on an ongoing basis. The program involves not only information concerning the concept, structure, and goals of mediation but, also in small-group workshop sessions, specific skills-building exercises and an opportunity for informal sharing between mediators. The training will emphasize the dual goals of mediation: (1) to provide an opportunity for open discussion of feelings and concerns, which can lead to increased levels of awareness and understanding; and (2) to assist parties in examining a full range of alternatives defining their parental rights and responsibilities in the reorganized family. Specific training will initially be focused on three aspects of the role of the mediator.

1. An important component of the mediation process is education. In the majority of cases it is vital that the mediators provide information on the developmental needs of children and ideas (alternative plans) concerning childcare and parenting arrangements consistent with the needs and resources of the parents.

2. Creating a comfortable and relaxed atmosphere for the discussion of feelings and providing a full opportunity for the parents to express their individual viewpoints and concerns are important to the process. Feelings and thoughts should be brought into the open, and the parties should feel that the mediators understand the problems.

3. The degree of informed commitment by the parties to the agreement is essential for the long-term durability of the plan. Discussion of the various components of an agreement, once achieved, can do much to reaffirm the understanding previously reached and improve the potential of the process as a model for the resolution of future conflicts. A part of this postagreement discussion can include a plan for explaining the agreement to the children. This can help to increase the level of commitment of the parties to the arrangements.

The formal training program will include seminars and workshops presented by mental health professionals and by staff of the Family Division. The mediation program is presented to new staff members as an alternative to nonadversary process that does not usurp the autonomy of the family unit and recognizes the right of the family to maintain control over family decision making. Following program orientation, mediators are educated to the age-appropriate needs of children whose parents are divorcing as well as to the responses of children to parental separation. Mediators are also trained to identify the realistic alternatives applicable to a wide range of differing family situations.

Mediation techniques training focuses upon facilitation mechanisms which enable the process to progress through each stage successfully. Techniques to ensure a smooth transition from one stage to the next and strategies that reinforce the commitment made in the final stages of mediation are also presented. Role-playing is an effective tool in techniques training. A prospective mediator is provided the opportunity to observe and discuss both actual and filmed mediation sessions, before participating as a mediation team member, and less experienced mediators work with a more skilled colleague.

In addition to formal introductory training, ongoing professional dialogue has been identified as an important aspect of mediator education. Presentations by mediators from different settings and by consultants from academic disciplines acquaint experienced staff with alternative mediation models and innovative mediator strategies.

The purposes, goals, and objectives of some mediators may be expanded through the process of internal evaluation and redefinition. This can lead to longer mediation processes, through the scheduling of additional sessions. However, as the average mediation currently involves 1.5 sessions, such expansion, to be practical, should not exceed the three-session, 6-hour guideline. The result will be a strengthening of the process as a resource for divorced and divorcing couples.

CONCLUSION

The mediation program was developed to provide the court with an alternative designed to promote a constructive process for the resolution of conflict. It is intended to supplement existing procedures and not to create additional steps that must be exhausted prior to litigation.

The goal of mediation is to permit a maximum degree of self-determination and involvement in the decision-making process. This action-oriented involvement helps parties deal more effectively with the crisis of marital breakdown, discourages passivity and dependence on the court and attorneys, and enhances self-esteem. The process provides an opportunity for people to traverse the marriage dissolution process with the dignity that flows from the ability to rationally determine the course of one's future through personal strength and intelligence rather than relying on external authority (Elkin, 1982). When mediation focuses on the parental role, separates it from the spousal role, and focuses on the future rather than on past conflicts and failures, the resolutions achieved are likely to be more responsive to the needs and resources of the family and more durable.

The establishment of custody mediation services within the judicial structure appears to be entirely compatible with the purposes and function of the court. Mediation allows minimal intervention by the court into private marital and family relationships, by allowing individual self-determination. This is achieved without infringing or delaying people's rights to full access to the court.

Mediation is not offered as a panacea for all of the problems associated with marital breakdown. Many cases are not amenable to the process and may present problems and conflicts that preclude mediation as a problem-solving alternative. However, in the majority of cases both parents are responsible adults and are capable of making their own decisions with respect to their children. Wherever this is possible, the court will have made a significant contribution to the restoration of equilibrium in the family and increased the potential of successful adjustment in the reorganized family, by referral to mediation.

APPENDIX 9-1: THE MEDIATION PROGRAM—PARENTS MAKING THEIR OWN DECISIONS ABOUT THEIR CHILDREN FOLLOWING SEPARATION AND DIVORCE

STATE OF CONNECTICUT
SUPERIOR COURT
FAMILY DIVISION

Dear Parent:

The court has referred you to the Family Services Office of the court for mediation of conflicts regarding child custody or visitation.

This pamphlet is designed to help you understand the mediation process including the goals and purposes of the meetings to be scheduled for you. It was prepared by the staff of the Family Division which includes counselors with years of experience working with couples going through the process of separation and divorce.

Where children are involved, divorce or separation is not the end of your family; it is a reorganization. Much will be gained by your working together as parents to help your children become caring, responsible adults.

The task of all parents, whether or not their marriage continues, is a responsible one. If you have a good relationship with your children and they feel the love and acceptance of both parents, they will thrive and grow.

FREDERICK A. FREEDMAN
Chief Administrative Judge
FAMILY DIVISION OF THE SUPERIOR COURT

What is Mediation?

Mediation is a way of settling your disagreements about the care of your children following separation and divorce without a courtroom battle. The process directly involves both parents in searching for a resolution of the problems which families normally experience during separation and divorce. Through mediation the rights and responsibilities of each parent are identified. The goal is to reorganize the family, not to "award" custody to one parent and make a "visitor" of the other.

With the assistance of trained counselors, parents meet together in an informal setting to decide on a parenting plan for the future which best meets their individual needs and the needs of their children. The counselors are neutral and objective; their role is to help parents work cooperatively in resolving their disputes so they can carry on with the task of parenting their children.

The mediation meetings are normally limited to from one to three sessions usually scheduled within thirty days of the date the court referred the family to mediation. A meeting may be scheduled just for the children if the parents and mediators feel that their participation would be helpful.

Parents are encouraged to discuss their own desires and plans as well as the present and future needs of their children in an open and positive way. The focus is on the future rather than the past.

Mediation meetings are confidential and no information from the sessions will be revealed by the mediators to any other person including the judge or the attorneys.

Why is Mediation Helpful?

The mediation program was developed to provide people with a choice, leaving the responsibility for making decisions where it belongs—with the family. While every family may not resolve all of the disputes regarding the future care of the children, most have found mediation useful in reaching acceptable agreements defining their ongoing relationships and responsibilities to each other as well as to the children.

There are many reasons why people have found mediation helpful and beneficial:

1. Conflict is natural and normal and issues concerning parenting are emotional and personal rather than legal issues. Mediation is a method of conflict resolution which can deal effectively with complex human relationships.

2. Mediation emphasizes that divorce is not the end of the family and a way of continuing to be parents together in a reorganized family is possible for most couples.

3. The stress and anxiety associated with separation and divorce, particularly for children, can be reduced. Participation in mediation assists parents in affirming their affection and concern for the children and can reduce the normal fears and anxieties of children concerning the "loss" of one parent.

4. Self-determination and direct involvement in the decision-making process is effective in promoting positive and lasting results for the parents and children. Parents who invest time and energy putting together a plan for their children are more likely to adhere to the plan and less likely to undermine it than those parents whose decision has been made for them.

5. Mediation directs the focus away from the issues which could not be resolved during the marriage and toward the issues which must be resolved prior to the divorce.

6. Many attorneys have found that mediation of custody and visitation disputes improves the ability of couples to work successfully through their attorneys to negotiate a settlement of the financial and property issues accompanying separation and divorce.

7. Research indicates that the successful adjustment of children following separation and divorce is directly related to the level of cooperation between parents and the continued involvement of both parents in the lives of their children. Mediation encourages participants to see themselves and each other as capable parents with a continuing responsibility to plan together for the future of their children.

What Happens after Mediation?

The mediation process normally concludes after one to three sessions with the parents reaching a full or partial agreement.

Following completion of mediation a report prepared by the mediators is forwarded to the attorneys and the court. This report contains no personal information concerning family members or the marital situation and includes only an outline of the agreements reached by the parties. Following an opportunity for each parent to review and discuss the agreement with their attorneys, the agreement may be submitted to the court for review. If the agreement is approved by the court, it will be entered as an enforceable order of the court.

In the event that parents are unable to reach an agreement, the attorneys are notified that the issues remain in dispute. The fact that some parents are unable to reach an agreement is not viewed as a "failure". Mediation is hard work, and parents completing the process demonstrate commitment and concern for the well-being of their children.

Most postdivorce child-care arrangements will require periodic revision and adjustments due to changes in the situations and life-styles of the parents and the changing needs of the children as they mature. It is hoped that parents will continue to work together to resolve any new disputes and to modify the original agreement where necessary to meet the changing needs of their family.

However, parents are welcomed to contact the Family Division at any time for assistance in mediating future conflicts or disputes.

NOTE

Prepared by the Family Division of the Connecticut Superior Court.

REFERENCES

Annual Reports of Family Division, 1982–1983, Judicial Department, State of Connecticut, 1983, p. 15.
Bohannon, P. The six stations of divorce. In P. Bohannon (Ed.), *Divorce and after: An analysis of the emotional and social problems of divorce.* New York: Doubleday, 1970.
Connecticut General Statutes §46b-56 (1981).
Connecticut practice book §§481 A (1984).
Connecticut Rules of Practice §§481 A (1984).
Coogler, J. Changing the lawyer's role in matrimonial practice. *Conciliation Courts Review,* 1977, *15,* 1–8.
Deutsch, M. *The resolution of conflict.* New Haven, CT: Yale University Press, 1973.
Elkin, M. Divorce mediation: An alternative process for hleping families to close the book gently. *Conciliation Courts Review,* 1982, *20(1),* iii–vi.
Fuller, L. Mediation—its forms and functions. *Southern California Law Review,* 1971, *44,* 305–339.
Goldstein, J., Freud, A., & Solnit, A. *Beyond the best interests of the child.* New York: Free Press, 1979.
Hodges, W. *Interventions for children of divorce.* New York: Wiley, 1986.
Irving, H. *Final research report of the conciliation project, family court of Toronto* (Demonstration Project No. 4555-1-65). Toronto: Welfare Grants Directorate, Department of National Health and Welfare and the Ontario Ministry of the Attorney General, 1981.
Kessler, S. *Creative conflict resolution: Mediation.* Atlanta, GA: National Institute for Professional Training, 1978.
King, D. Child custody—a legal problem. *California State Bar Journal,* 1979, *54(3),* 156–161.
Kressel, K. *Labor mediation: An exploratory survey.* Albany, NY: Association of Labor Mediation Agencies, 1971.
Metzner, D., & Reasbeck, S. Getting past the impasse. *Newsletter, California Chapter of AFCC,* 1982, 2–3.
Milne, A. Custody of children in a divorce process: A family self-determination model. *Conciliation Courts Review,* 1978, *16,* 2–12.
National Center for Health Statistics. *Monthly Vital Statistics Report,* 1985, *32,* 1–2.
Pearson, J., & Thoennes, N. A preliminary portrait of client reactions to three court mediation programs. *Mediation Quarterly,* 1984, *3,* 21–40.
Ricci, I. *Mom's house, Dad's house: Making shared custody work.* New York: Macmillan, 1980.
Supreme Court Committee on Matrimonial Litigation (Phase Two—Final Report), June 10, 1981.
Survey of American family law. *Family Law Reporter,* 1985, *11,* 3015.
Wallerstein, J. S., & Kelly J. Divorce and children. In J. D. Noshpitz (Ed.), *Handbook of child psychiatry IV.* new York: Basic Books, 1979.
Wheeler, M. *No-fault divorce.* Boston: Beacon Press. 1974.

10

Mandatory Mediation

MARY TALL SHATTUCK
Marin County Probation Department, San Rafael, California

California first mandated mediation of all contested custody and visitation cases in 1980. Court-connected mediation of disputes in which the parents are required to participate necessarily differs from mediation in which the parties choose to make decisions with the help of a mediator. In this chapter the author draws on her experience mediating in two different mandated California court programs, as well as in private practice, to describe the process of mandated mediation and how it differs from voluntary mediation. The characteristics of those who use the court service are presented along with outcome data. A brief, structured process of mandatory mediation focusing on the needs of children and effectively utilizing the authoritarian setting of the court is prescribed.

Most models of family mediation that are presently being developed and articulated have emerged from settings outside the courts. These mediation models, based on voluntary participation of the disputing parties, are seen as alternatives to traditional legal processes and are usually quite separate from judicial proceedings. In some sense these mediation models have been held up as standards or ideals against which to measure what takes place in the mandatory mediation services within the courts. As a consequence, court mediation services have been misunderstood and misjudged (sometimes quite harshly) for their seeming departures from the basic principles and procedures of these models. In fact, mandated mediation within the court system is emerging as a very different form of mediation from that which is private and voluntary. The current models, values, and expectations of private mediation are inappropriate to describe what is and should be going on in the court setting.

There are several factors that contribute to the uniqueness of mandatory mediation. It is applied only to issues of custody and visitation; considerations of the often interwoven aspects of property and finances are excluded by statute from the mediation discussions. Participation in the mediation process is required; failure to meet the requirement can result in the application of legal sanctions. Parties can neither avoid dealing with the conflict nor gain direct access to an evidentiary trial. And finally, the mediator functions as an active advocate for the child and may, after interviewing the child, represent that child's point of view in the mediation session with the disputing parents. In mandatory mediation a skilled, court-appointed mediator meets with disputing parents in order to facilitate their development of an agreement about how they will coparent their child after their relationship has ended.

This chapter describes in general terms the clientele of mandatory court mediation as distinguished from the clients of voluntary private mediation, and in specific terms my mediation practice in two different courts. There is a brief description of the process of mediation, as actually carried out. Some of the essential elements of a successful model for mediation within the legal-authoritarian framework are presented, along with outcome data.

RATIONALE

Inherent in the nature of the custody and visitation issue is a high potential for conflict. Even generally cooperative couples seldom discuss solutions with each other or the children, frequently disagree on what is wanted, and, in a shifting sea of legislative and judicial opinion, suffer from a lack of definitive, expert advice. This ambiguity can generate intolerable tension, fear, and distrust between the parents. Added to the general pain and confusion of a divorce, it can lead all too quickly into an escalating series of claims and counterclaims, covert and overt struggles, and repeated incidents on both sides that justify and hence perpetuate the actions of each parent. Ultimately the conflict itself, rather than the issues under dispute, becomes the problem. In consequence, parents can become locked into a series of repeated disputes, increasing frustration, and multiple legal actions prior to meeting with a mediator.

Each parent enters the court process wanting the judge to find him or her right and the other wrong, seeking redress for the wrongs done by the other, and feeling that the judge will put him or her back in control of the family. But the technology of the adversarial legal system is inappropriate for resolving most disputes over children. The adversarial process is often distressing for the children. Following court decisions, parents are more hostile to each other and, not being committed to the solution, often continue to fight and even to return to court repeatedly (Hetherington, Cox, & Cox, 1979). The California Mandatory Mediation statutes were written to break into the escalating conflict cycle and to shield the children from the traumatizing consequences of repeated parental disagreement.

Section 4600.5 of the California Civil Code (1981) provides that,

> where it appears on the face of the Petition or other application for an order or modification of an order for the custody or visitation of a child or children that either or both such issues are contested, . . . the matter shall be set for mediation of the contested issues prior to or concurrent with the setting of the matter for hearing. The purpose of such mediation proceedings shall be to reduce acrimony which may exist between the parties and to develop an agreement assuring the child or children's close and continuing contact with both parents after the marriage is dissolved. The mediator shall use his or her best efforts to effect a settlement of the custody or visitation dispute.

It further states that

> the mediator shall have the authority to exclude counsel from participation in the mediation proceedings . . . [and] shall have the duty to assess the needs and interests of the child or children involved in the controversy and shall be entitled to interview the child or children when the mediator deems such interviews appropriate or necessary. (California Civil Code, 1981, section 4607a)

CLIENTELE

In mandatory mediation there is little prior information about the parents, and there is often great intensity of feeling. The parents' last attempt to talk may have ended in violence. Frequently there have been threats like, "You'll never see your child again!" The filed petitions themselves are statements of how right the undersigned parent is, and how wrongly the other has behaved. "I have had complete care of Sally since she was born. He never even changed a diaper!" "When Jimmy was 2½, I found her screaming and shaking him. She's a potential child abuser!" "Suzy cries and pleads with me not to send her on the visits. And everybody agrees that I shouldn't force her to go." These, and other statements like them, are commonly written into court documents served by one parent on the other. Parents are angry, frustrated, furious, defensive, and often frightened of meeting with each other. As a father told me recently in objecting to the mandated meeting, "I don't want to sit in the same room with her. All she'll do is tell me how awful I am to the kids. Why should I have to listen to that?"

Custody issues are evocative of intense feelings for both mandatory mediation and private mediation clients. In the face of the shattering of a relationship, the parents' contact with the child assumes great importance. Parents often feel humiliated by the failure of their spousal role and desperately seek a compensatory affirmation through their role as parent. Anger is hot. Struggles over power and control, unresolved during the marriage, undermine the effort to coparent. Milne (1978) has pointed out the very influential role that unresolved marital separation issues play in continuing custody conflicts.

The clientele of mandatory mediation experience all these problems, along with the loss of choice about whether to engage in finding solutions. A young mother came in to my office in a state of rage and fear. She had split from a destructive, heavy drug-using, brutal relationship when her child was two and had gone on to make a stable and healthy life for herself and her child. Now, years later, the child's father had filed a petition requesting his visitation rights, and this mother was being forced to face him and, through him, her own painful past.

By California law, mediation is mandated for all parents within the jurisdiction of the Superior Court who are involved in a dispute over custody or visitation as evidenced by a filing of a dissolution petition, an order to show cause, or an order to show cause in re contempt. Where voluntary mediation tends to attract people from higher educational, socioeconomic, and income levels (Pearson, Thoennes, & VanderKooi, 1982), mandatory mediation clients are representative of the broad spectrum of the local community. Clients may have been married, or simply have had a child together. In some rare cases, mediators are asked to help forge coparenting agreements over the offspring of a brief encounter. Children who are the focus of a dispute range from the not-yet-born to those near emancipation. However, the majority of children fall within a more narrow age range (Pearson & Thoennes, 1984), and courts encourage parents to follow any reasonable preferences expressed by children over 14.

The marital relationship may have included domestic violence or serious substance abuse. Some state courts are ruling out mediation for families where abuse is alleged, or where there are multiple social agency contacts, serious psychiatric psychopathology, or long-standing and bitter conflict resulting in numerous court appearances. An early study of mediation outcome categorized divorcing couples as having enmeshed, autistic, direct, or disengaged patterns of decision making. Kressel et al. stated that "the enmeshed and autistic patterns appeared the most difficult for mediators to deal with" (Kressel, Jaffee, Tuchman, Watson, & Deutsch, 1980). California mandates that mediation be tried with all couples experiencing custody disputes. As a result, court mediators work with a very broad range of clients, including many who are traditionally thought to be "unmediatable."

Parents bring to the mediation disputes over where their child will live, with whom, and when. They argue over access, particularly over the age at which a child may spend the night with the noncustodial parent, and over sharing holidays. Many disputes concern safety; Pearson and Thoennes (1984) found that 40% to 50% of the parents were concerned about the child's well-being when with the other parent. Substantial allegations regarding past or potential sexual abuse of children have risen markedly in the past year (from two a year to two a month, in my own caseload). Joint legal custody, with its demand for cooperative decision making, is another commonly disputed issue and generates further disagreements as parents attempt to carry out their coparenting agreement.

Clients can be divided into three distinct groups in regard to when and why they come to mandatory mediation. Many are newly separated and need to work out their first custody and visitation agreement. The second group have objectively difficult issues to resolve, best typified by the problems posed when one parent moves far away. Changes in family composition require modification of the custody agreement. Underlying many of these filings is the systemic disruption resulting from a remarriage or from the birth of a half-sibling. The third group is composed of frequently-disputing families with long-term problems. They are not numerous but appear so, by virtue of reappearing so many times in a mediator's caseload.

The clients of mandatory mediation come because this is the last resource available to them to resolve their own dispute. They are unable to communicate, at least about their children. Often one parent absolutely refuses to meet with the other. Restraining orders preventing the parents from meeting outside an officially sanctioned setting are frequently in effect. Symptoms of distress in children result in withholding of contact between child and parent; one parent in a mediation may have gone months with sporadic or no contact with a child. There may be marked differences in the perceived power of one of the parents. The stronger parent may use the court as a threat; the weaker parent may use the court as a means of rebalancing the power. Some parents face objectively difficult issues, such as where the child is to reside during the school year, when the geographical distance is great and the nonresident parent will lose a significant amount of contact as a result of the decision. A few parents come to mediation for advice on joint-custody plans or to have an experienced person approve their agreement. These cases are treasured by the counselors who work in the court setting, for they are reminders of what coparenting can be!

PROCESS

Although the issues and philosophy of mandatory mediation are governed by statute, each county's superior court judges have been granted broad latitude in implementation. In this way, each court can develop a process that is best tailored to its unique mixture of judges, attorneys, clientele, and community resources. This flexibility has resulted in the development of many innovative refinements designed to facilitate mediation. According to McIsaac (1981), the resultant variation is both desirable and intentional. The legislature encourages variation with the ultimate aim of determining what processes of mandatory mediation are most helpful for which clientele and in what types of disputes. Courts are encouraged to keep records of processes and outcomes.

Some general features are common to the practice of mandatory mediation in all California courts. First, the overt conflict is clearly defined, with the issues and individual positions in the dispute written out in formalized papers filed with the court. Second, referral to a court mediator is required. Parents may (and are usually encouraged to) choose private mediation; if so, they see the court mediator only if the private mediation fails to resolve the issues under petition. The mediator meets with the disputing parents, and possibly with the attorneys, children, stepparents, or other involved people, to develop as much cooperation and agreement as possible. The court will not pass a final judgment before an attempt at resolution through mediation. Only those issues not resolved through the mediation process will be tried in front of a judge. Third, the agreements reached in mediation can take many forms, ranging from a partial resolution of some issues, through one or more time-limited trial agreements, to a complete agreement resolving all issues in dispute. Fourth, the mediation may be deferred if both parties agree that further data needs to be gathered prior to the mediation. And fifth, the mandatory mediation sessions are free to the parents, being funded out of marriage and divorce-filing fees.

The average time available for mediation with each family is very brief, usually between 3 and 9 hours (one to three sessions).

There are process differences, determined by the policy of the court officers or probation department, and stylistic differences, functions of the individual mediator and particular family system. The court policies differ in whether mediation is scheduled and concluded before the date set for the hearing or is held on the morning of the hearing, with the attorneys waiting in the hall and the court trial before the judge only temporarily in abeyance. In some courts the mediator may recommend a solution to the parties and attorneys when an issue remains unresolved. In other courts a recommendation is made to the parents and court, subject to the provisions specified in *McLaughlin v. Superior Court* (1983). In most courts no recommendations are made. The case returns to trial for disposition or to a settlement conference with a judge. A formal custody investigation is often ordered at this point.

Where mediation is conducted on the day of the hearing, the parents wait, apprehensive and often angry, while their attorneys talk in private with the mediator. Then the parents go to the mediator's office, together if possible, separately if necessary, to talk. This first session, even when carried on in polite tones, is intensely charged with emotion. The parents are primed to dispute, ready to attack and defend in front of the judge. The mediation is conducted in a crisis atmosphere, with all the tension and the openness to change that such a state provides.

When the policy is to hold all mediation sessions before the trial date, the mediator contacts both parties and arranges an appointment. Attorneys rarely attend; other family members, including children, often are invited. The parents themselves define the issues to be mediated. Several courts are experimenting with premediation orientations. Solano County, for example, provides guidesheets for parents to read and consider. Marin County invites parents to a 2-hour orientation group, to help them focus on cooperative solution finding and on the needs of their child, prior to dealing with the disputed issues. The atmosphere is less charged with tension. The emotions present are primarily those attached to facing the disputed issues and to dealing with one's ex-partner.

Fred and Sally are an example of a mandatory mediation referral. Fred, distressed over Sally's control over his contact with their child, asked his attorney to file a contempt petition claiming that Sally was not permitting him his rightful visitation. Upon receipt of these papers, Sally hired an attorney. She countered by filing a claim that their child was not safe with Fred, as he was such a dangerous driver that he had neither license nor insurance. Fred stormed up to Sally's home, demanding that his child come out and vehemently denying that he was an unsafe driver. Mother and child were frightened by his behavior. The police were called in to remove Fred, and the court issued temporary restraining orders to keep the parents apart. Tempers grew hotter.

Meanwhile, the paperwork proceeded through the court system and arrived on the mediator's desk within 2 weeks of filing the pleadings. The mediator sent appointment letters requesting attendance at the orientation meeting and the first mediation session, and included a note inviting the child (age 10). Fred and Sally went to the same orientation group. They sat across from each other in a hostile silence, in the company of 10 other tense parents. They listened to a discussion on mediation and on the needs of postdivorce children for contact with both parents. As the speaker talked about conflict-escalating tactics, Fred and Sally looked thoughtfully at one another. The tension between them lessened. When the family came together for their mediation session the following week, the child greeted her father affectionately and sat between her parents. The mediator used this opening to quickly establish that both parents had enjoyed a close and positive relationship with their child ever since the divorce 5 years ago. Sally readily affirmed the quality of Fred's parenting.

The dispute was over the safety of the child when with her father. Sally was frightened for the life of the child; she gave as the cause a recent collision in which Fred had totaled his car in a head-on crash while their child was in the car. The child spoke a little about the crash, expressing her fears without blaming her father. She then left the room. The mediator spoke with the parents, exploring the basis of Sally's fears and Fred's denials. Fred produced a valid driver's license and proof of insurance, and Sally apologized about her misunderstanding that Fred's lost license had been literally lost, not revoked. The parents began to laugh a little over this. The parents went on to discuss their concerns about driving while drinking and agreed not to do so or to allow their respective mates to drive after drinking. The mediator then focused the parents on the difficult issue of Fred's accident record. Once the facts were listed for all to look at, everyone, even Fred, was surprised. Fred had been involved in a serious car accident on an average of every 3 months for the past several years. He was not found to be at fault but was carrying several scars and disabilities from the accidents. That session ended upon a discussion of accident proneness. The parents were asked to consider ways Fred could be with the child without the necessity of driving while with her.

In a second session, the parents worked out a short-term solution (Fred's girlfriend and Sally shared the transporting of the child for Fred's visitation weekends), and a long-term solution (resolving Fred's accident-proneness through a combination of goal-directed counseling and specialized driver training). They bargained over the time limits to the short-term solutions and the proofs of "cure" and arrived at a satisfactory agreement. Fred and Sally helped the mediator to draft the agreement and went home to put it into effect. The mediator filed the agreement with the court and mailed copies to the parents' attorneys.

PRESCRIPTION FOR A MODEL

To be effective within the framework imposed by the nonvoluntary, brief, structured process of mandatory mediation, the mediator must bring to the disputing couple a perspective that will enable them to see their solution to the conflict. The mediator must be able, from the beginning, to reach beyond the polarization by which the couple have become locked into opposing and adversarial positions. By being clear and confident that a solution exists and that the parties can find that solution if they can gain sufficient perspective, willingness, and information, the mediator opens the mediation with the search for a synthesis that will build cooperation while resolving the conflict. The mediator has available many resources, which can be gathered into the following five elements of an effective model for mandatory mediation: (1) the effective use of power to empower the parents, (2) a focus on the child of the dispute, (3) strategic counseling interventions, (4) education of the family in dealing with divorce and in conflict resolution, and (5) use of the authoritarian setting provided by the presence of laws and court. Used in correct proportion, these elements enable the mediator to guide parents rapidly to a stable resolution. Too much of any one may well yield an agreement, but it will be the mediator's agreement, not the parents'. They will not be committed to adhering to it, and they will not be able to revise it on their own as needed. Too little use of these elements may mean that parents who could have come to a satisfactory coparenting agreement continue instead to battle over their child. These five elements are summarized in Table 10-1.

Effective Use of Power

The mediator is empowered by law to require that parents attend the mediation and to return the case for judgment if the issues are not resolved. The mediator must exercise power, to ensure the safety of the participants and keep the sessions focused on the issues. And paradoxically, the mediator employs this power to empower the parents to make their own decisions. The empowerment of both parents is a key element in successful mediation. This transfer of power from mediator to clients takes place gradually, as the mediator sees that they are working toward a solution. Only if the parents refuse this power is the case returned to the judge. A simple way to explain this to parents is to tell them that in mediation, they hold all the decision-making authority. They can make any agreement that suits their family, as long as they both agree to it. (There are certain rare exceptions, such as a mother willing to allow a father unsupervised visits with a child whom he has seriously abused, where a mediator refuses to countersign an agreement and refers the case back to court.) If the parents fail to develop an agreement, a custody investigator and a judge will make recommendations and decisions for the family, and neither parent will retain the authority for their family. For example, parents who fought bitterly over whether their vegetarian children should have vitamin supplements and/or milk in their diet rapidly agreed to compromise when the mediator pointed out that the judge who they hoped would make the decision for them had been a lifelong meat-eater and was unlikely to order the children not to be fed beef. Keeping the authority within the binuclear family may be

Table 10-1. The Five Basic Elements of Mandatory Mediation

Element	Purpose	Results of overuse	Results of underuse
Effective use of power	Ensures safety and maintains focus by transferring responsibility and power to parents	Parents do not feel in control, do not assume responsibility for making agreement work; result reflects mediator's needs	Mediation is unfocused; issues are not resolved; couple's power games predominate; violence may erupt
Focus on child	Highlights impact of dispute on child; provides accurate data about child's capacities	Child experiences the pain of the conflict too much	Result may seem fair to parents but be destructive to child
Strategic counseling interventions	Mandates *minimal* intervention; deals only with issues under dispute; uses reframing and redefining of issues, fencing off, paradox	Mediation bogs down in venting feelings, and factual content becomes lost in welter of emotions	Solutions are incomplete or biased by partial understandings and poor communication
Parental education	Provides data about impact of divorce on children and teaches skills of conflict resolution; separates parent issues from spousal and financial issues	Parents may be overwhelmed by the knowledge, and not value their own solutions	Result may not suit needs of child or of separation between parents; parents may not be empowered to revise their agreements as needed
Court setting	Defines a clear structure, with the alternative an expensive and difficult trial	Parents may feel unduly pressured to make an unsatisfactory agreement	Parents may fail to come to agreement in a situation where a flexible resolution is possible

difficult, but in most cases agreements will be closer to that family's values and practices than judicial decisions could be.

Along with power goes responsibility, and a similar paradox applies: the mediator assumes responsibility for leading parents to take responsibility for the development of a workable solution to their conflict. In mandatory mediation, far more than in voluntary mediation, parents expect the mediator to make a recommendation that agrees with the position of each. They look to the mediator for agreement with their views of each other, for sympathy with the awful way they have been treated, and for judgments based on the difficulties of the divorce (Walters, 1984). Reorientation of the parents is a critical ingredient in leading them to assume responsibility for a satisfactory outcome.

If the mediator retains too much power for too long, parents do not feel in control of the process and fail to take responsibility for making the solutions work. Clients do not participate, with the result that the real issues do not surface and the family's creative problem-solving potential is not brought to bear on the issues. Solutions are reflective of the mediator's and court's biases instead of the family's needs and strengths. Agreements may be signed one day, but the parents are calling back the next with reports of disaster.

If the mediator exercises too little power or transfers authority to the parents too soon, the session remains unfocused, and the clients' own power games become the controlling feature of the session. One tenders an insult, the other stalks out in a huff, and both turn to the mediator, saying, "See, we told you it wouldn't work." In more seriously pathological couples, one client may verbally abuse or cause excessive emotional pain to the other. The conflict may even escalate to the point of physical violence.

Focus on the Child

Mandatory mediation deals exclusively with disputes over children and, unlike private divorce mediation, ignores issues of property division and family support. Further, although issues left from the marriage are a major contributing factor to custody disputes, they too are eliminated as rapidly as possible. The mediator's role is to move the parents toward solutions, and solutions are to be found in the present and future, not in the family's past. Parents do talk about their marriage and divorce; they talk with heat and rage. The mediator listens and redirects them toward the present. At the point where the parents are remaining focused on their child's needs and on their needs as parents now, the mediator can sit back. The conflict is not over yet, but the parents can carry on the search for a satisfactory resolution.

The key in shifting focus lies in involving the child. This can be done directly, by bringing the child into the mediation session and facilitating family interaction so that the parents can have a safe and immediate experience of coparenting. Often it is safer for the mediator to include the child indirectly, encouraging the parents to share perceptions, swap stories, and show photographs of their child. Sometimes the mediator can only include the child symbolically, by telling the parents stories about other children of divorced and fighting parents or having them tug apart the "tear bear" (a Velcro teddy bear designed to tear in half when pulled on by both parents). Whatever means are used, it is important to focus both parents on the reality of the child. Parents often engage in symbolic disputes over their child, whereby one parent seeks to resurrect the former spousal relationship or to punish the ex-spouse by depriving him or her of the child. Discussion of who the child is and what the child needs in order to grow into a healthy adult helps parents become willing to find solutions to the difficulties inherent in coparenting.

Involving the child serves two purposes: it highlights for the parents the impact on the child of their continued conflict, and it provides accurate data on the child's needs and tolerance for any particular agreement that the parents are considering. A 7-month-old baby was fretful despite her tired-looking mother's efforts to comfort her. When Mom reached the point of utter frazzle, Dad gently reached out for the baby and began to rock and soothe her. Mom got a much-needed break. Yet when Mom left the room, the baby immediately began to cry. The parents went on to develop an agreement by which Dad gave Mom a regular break from baby care, by visiting in her house while Mom remained nearby. Both the parents' and the child's needs, once made apparent, could be met by a satisfactory agreement. Adolescents need to be involved in the mediation more directly, so that they own and are committed to keeping any agreements made. Parents usually recognize this and ask to have their older children participate in discussions.

If the focus is too much on the child, he or she may be put into the center of the conflict, resulting in an increase in the child's pain and expressed symptoms. In most families who come for mandatory mediation, this has already happened, and involving the child simply uncovers what is going on so that the parents can see it and deal with it. But where family values are such that the child has been shielded from the conflict, these values need to be respected by the mediator. It is possible to give children too much power by involving them too much. This can lead to a role reversal, in which the child determines what kind of contact he or she will have with each of his or her parents, and how often. The child may be confirmed in an immature and judgmental view of one or both parents or not be encouraged to respect both parents. Ultimately, it is the parents who need to be empowered by the mediation process, not the child.

Too little focus on the child can result in an agreement that may suit the parents' needs very well but be destructive for the child. Unless they are encouraged to consider their child's needs carefully, parents can, in the spirit of cooperation, agree to a fair and equal sharing that has the child changing home, friends, and school every 3 months, in order to be with parents who reside in different states. In their desire to end the conflict, some parents may agree to withdraw from the child's life forever, unless they are reminded of the loss the child will feel. Finally, failing to focus on the child may result in the parents just continuing their fight. Becoming aware of the destructive impact of that continued conflict on their child is one of the most compelling reasons for parents to face the anxiety and pain involved in finding ways to coparent.

Strategic Counseling Interventions

The mandate for custody mediation should also be a mandate for minimal intervention. Throughout the period that children in a divorced family are minors, the court retains the right to reconsider decisions regarding custody and access. Courts can intervene in divorced families in ways that would require established criminal acts before involvement with intact families. All that is needed is the filing of a petition by one of the parents. In order to avoid the iatrogenic effects of unnecessary intervention and to respect the sociocultural diversity of the clientele and the personal integrity of the family system, it is important that the court mediator be committed to a philosophy of minimal intervention.

To carry out this commitment, the mediator deals only with the issues under dispute. It is important not to disrupt major areas of agreement already reached by the parents; the mediator should avoid reviewing and questioning these agreements, or even insisting on making them explicit. What has been billed as a custody dispute may, upon closer examination, not require major review of the child's living arrangements. It may be simply a question of where the child is to attend school or what is to become of the family home, or frustration over unilateral decisions by the other parent. What the pleadings describe as a major visitation problem may be more specifically a failure to communicate and clarify problems with pickup and drop-off, fear of losing the child when the ex-partner remarries, or concern over a child's symptomatic stress reactions.

The mediator immediately clarifies the problem areas and issues with the parents and, when needed, utilizes brief and strategic interventions. These are directed at identifying the nature of the dispute over the child and very quickly helping the parents generate options and employ problem-solving techniques to arrive at a practical solution well suited to the parents' needs. The most effective interventions to use during mediation are those derived from strategic family therapy. Reframing and redefining both the problem and the parents' past actions helps many parents see each other in a more tolerable light. Building fences around hotly disputed but irrelevant issues by requesting the parents' agreement not to discuss them enables many parents to proceed to deal with the current issues with dispatch. Paradoxical interventions, such as asking a violently explosive father why he lets his ex-spouse control him by making him mad whenever she wants (resulting in his making a magnificent and successful effort to control his rage) or requesting quarreling parents to continue their argument for the next hour so the mediator can step out for lunch (resulting in astonished silence), are very fruitful when not overused. Behaving in unexpected ways often breaks an impasse; agreeing heartily when a parent claims the courts are not fair to fathers, and going on at length that starvation in Ethiopia is not fair, napalming babies is not fair, drunk drivers killing children on the way to school are not fair, income taxes are not fair, and so forth, often defuses the victim's frustration and enables him to focus on how to meet his particular child's needs. The interventions may be as creative as they are unorthodox, as long as they are specifically aimed at dissolving or working around the impasse and releasing the family's own potential for self-determination.

When counseling interventions are overused, the mediation bogs down in venting feelings, recounting the past marital woes, and rehashing separation issues. The factual content becomes lost amid a welter of emotions. Clients may feel listened to, and counselor-trained mediators may feel a sense of satisfaction, but the issues that brought the family to mediation do not get resolved. In a few situations, it may be more important to build cooperation and trust between the parents and refer the factual issues back to a judge for decision. For example, a family with a very disturbed child was engaged in a custody dispute; each parent demanded custody in order to rescue the child from the problems being caused by the other parent. The mediator concentrated on having the parents develop a clear picture of their child's problems, understand that these were not caused by the other parent, and work out some cooperative solutions to the child's difficulties, regardless of where the child resided. The parents then went before the judge and obtained a decision about the actual issue of custody. If the emotions fueling the family conflict cannot be sufficiently defused, then the issues cannot be seen and solved. While an overemphasis on counseling tactics may result in affirmation of the weaknesses of the family or the identified patient, an underemphasis may lead to an incorrect solution, based on a partial understanding of the nature of the problem or an angry parent's inability to communicate the real issues.

Parental Education

From the opening of the first session, the mediator functions as an educator, teaching parents the skills of conflict resolution and communicating to them needed data on the divorce process and on the special needs of the children of divorce. The mediator may not know what the solution to the parents' conflict is but does know where that solution is to be found. Much of the mediation will be spent on the reorientation of the parents; in Marin County, this is formalized into a 2-hour group meeting which parents attend prior to mediating their issues. In other counties orientation is done less formally, but nonetheless firmly, in the early stages of the sessions. Parents are told, shown, encouraged, led, and otherwise educated in the steps necessary to find resolution. Parents learn to separate spousal issues from coparenting issues, distinguish between their needs as ex-partners and the child's need for continuing contact with both parents, and learn to divorce each other as spouses while remaining joined in parenting.

Because parents often misinterpret a child's symptomatic behavior as being caused by the other parent, the mediator provides information and access to resources for learning about the impact of divorce and postdivorce conflict on children. Parents learn to distinguish between normal transition-time behavior and danger signs. They get help in supporting their children through the divorce period and advice on parenting issues. The education offered during the mediation is brief and problem focused, designed to give parents a map with which to look over their family territory and locate solutions to their conflicts. Parents needing more information are referred to community resources.

There are some traps for the mediator who provides too much education during the session. The parents may feel overwhelmed by the mediator's knowledge and undervalue their own awareness of their unique family needs. Any agreement resulting under these conditions will not be owned by the parties and may not even be relevant to them. A common example is the elegant agreement spelling out precise dates and hours of visitation for a family of grown-up "flower children" who do not even own a watch. Another trap results in the mediator's becoming enmired in the family dynamics, as one parent agrees with the mediator's data and the other disagrees, and they proceed to fight over the mediator's perception of them.

At the other extreme, failing to provide needed education for the parents often results in an agreement that is not suited to the needs of the child or the process of separation between the parents. Parties can continue their cycle of blame, with no map to offer a different understanding of the events. Opportunities for the real growth of the family are passed by.

Court Setting

If volitional divorce mediation is conducted in the shadow of the law, mandatory mediation is conducted in the direct presence of the law. The alternatives to a negotiated agreement are clear and immediate: if the parents do not deal with each other, they will be dealt with by a judge. As Walters (1984) has said, "The power of the court to intrude into and affect the lives of the conflicted parents becomes a reality to them when mediation takes place within the atmosphere of the court" (p. 5). The mandate and the setting pressure people to reach for new strategies of dealing with conflict and with each other. Because the mediator is not the source of the pressure, he or she can be sympathetic and supportive in helping parents search for their own resolutions.

The mediation is informed and guided by law. Mnookin and Kornhauser (1979) describe divorce law as a framework within which a divorcing couple can order their postdissolution rights and responsibilities. Custody mediation is governed by a statutory standard that calls for close and continuing contact between the child and both his parents. There are, in California, legal provisions for visits with grandparents and former stepparents. Joint legal custody, with its emphasis on shared decision making, is routinely ordered by the court (except for extreme situations) in California. These statutes provide the family with a framework within which their individual solutions may be found. The mother who enters mediation seeking to cut the child off from his father is immediately reoriented to finding ways to ensure the child's safety when with his father. The father who wants the right to determine where his child goes to school learns that instead he must seek a consensus with his ex-spouse about the child's schooling, and so he is ready to shift to a discussion based on the child's educational needs.

There is a second aspect to working in a court setting that may facilitate mediation. The procedure is clearly laid out in the local court rules. Families in the midst of divorce are often confused and disoriented. To be told that they will deal with their child-related disputes by meeting with a mediator at the courthouse for a maximum of three sessions, and that if any issues remain unresolved, they will meet with a judge, helps the family to organize itself. This beginning organization can be tapped by the mediator in mobilizing the family's capacity to pull together a coparenting structure from the scattered pieces of their lives.

Finally, because of working for the court, the mediator has some control over the timing of the process. According to Waldron (1984), "it may be that timing is important, and that mediation attempts should be coordinated with the parents' progress in moving through the emotional phases of processing the divorce" (p. 18). When parents need time to rebuild shattered trust, they can often make a series of temporary agreements that gradually increase the degree of coparenting. If additional information about a child's special needs must be available before the parents can develop a satisfactory agreement, the mediator can request a delay. The timing of the negotiation is one of the critical variables influencing outcome. The court mediator's access to the court and the docket provides more control over this factor than private mediators can generally exert.

The authoritarian nature of the setting has the potential for abuse. Parents may be unduly pressured to make an agreement that is in line with prevailing statues but that fails to protect their child. Mediators are required to report serious allegations of abuse or neglect to Child Protective Services and do not finalize an agreement until the situation has been investigated and cleared. But some parents, faced with a limited time and statutes calling for coparenting, fail to bring up their concerns over the child's safety. In addition, an overly rigid application of the procedures and structure may mean that parents have to conclude the mediation too rapidly, at the wrong stage of their divorce, or else face an even more destructive adversarial trial.

A LOOK AT OUTCOMES OF MANDATORY MEDIATION

The primary purpose of mandatory mediation is to assist parents in developing an agreement that resolves the issues under dispute. Its effectiveness can be seen in the following data. These results are the outcomes of mediation for my caseloads during employment as a court mediator in two California courts, the San Francisco Superior Court and the Marin County Superior Court. The first sample consists of 41 families referred for mediation between October 1981 and February 1982. The customary procedure of the San Francisco court was to undertake the mediation on the day of the scheduled court hearing. If needed, the mediation was to make temporary recommendations for settlement directly to the parties and their attorneys. The second sample reports on 41 families receiving mediation between April and December 1984. The months were chosen because of the availability of consistent statistics, but I have no reason to think that they are not reflective of my ongoing caseload referrals.

The families in both courts were from diverse socioeconomic and ethnic backgrounds, reflecting the diversity of each of the counties. While the majority of the families in both examples were from middle- and lower-economic levels, the sample includes upper-income and professional parents. As a very wealthy parent put it, "After all, I pay a large amount of taxes; I ought to get some direct benefit from them!" This diversity is consistent with the findings of

Pearson and Thoennes (1984), that the demographic variables of mediation clientele are consistent with those of the area from which they come. In the San Francisco sample, 29% of the parents showed marked evidence of serious psychopathology (such as poor reality contact, paranoid ideation, severe depression, and ego decompensation). In 32% of the families there had been domestic violence, with most of the incidents occurring at the time of separation or during the current conflict. In evaluating these, only gross behavioral symptomology was considered. Many more families showed stress responses that suggested the presence of a more disguised pathology. There are no comparable figures for the Marin clientele, only a note that the most seriously decompensating person from the San Francisco sample later showed up in the Marin office following a change of venue.

In the San Francisco sample, 17 (41%) were recently separated couples and 24 (58%) had settled divorce issues but were continuing to dispute over the children. In one case the conflicts had continued for 18 years. In Marin, 24 (35%) of the referred families had recently separated, and 52 (68%) were postagreement disputes. I am assigned a higher-than-average proportion of repeated-conflict families, and so there are more postdivorce dispute cases in my samples. Comparable figures for Los Angeles are listed by Pearson and Thoennes (1984) as 63% new separations and 40% postdivorce disputes.

Under the San Francisco procedures, 26 (63%) couples from my caseload settled their disputes through the mediation process. Of these, 23 completed their agreement in mediation, and 3 agreed to utilize private counseling to settle remaining issues. Another six accepted a recommendation for counseling and resolved their dispute there. Nine of the families were unable to agree through mediation or private counseling. Of these, six accepted the mediator's temporary recommendation, and three went on for a formal custody investigation, psychiatric evaluation, and judicial decision.

Of the Marin County families referred by the court for mediation following the filing of a petition, 19 (27%) reached agreement following a brief phone contact or through the assistance of private resources. Often a dispute would settle when the parents, at the mediator's suggestion, met for coffee and discussion. This is consistent with Kelly's observation (1984) that many basically cooperative parents had not talked about the children prior to separating. Ten of the families' cases were closed by other means, such as a referral for investigation by Child Protective Services or moving out of the county. I completed the dispute-resolution process with 41 families in the indicated time period. Of these, 31 (76%) reached agreement on the issues; these agreements were written, signed, and filed with the court, and the case closed as having been completed. Only one family requested private mediation, and sent in the resultant agreement for filing. Another five developed an agreement with the assistance of the judge at a settlement conference. Three families requested a custody investigation and reached a compromise based on the investigator's recommendations, with the help of the judge at a second settlement conference. One went on to a trial, and custody was decided by the judge. In a more recent and much larger sample (147 families), which consists of my full-time caseload from January 1986 through June 1987, 71% of all cases closing did so with full agreement on custody and visitation issues. Only 2% were resolved through a custody trial. The remainder settled either through brief hearings, or during the process of a formal investigation, or by withdrawing from the court.

Pearson and Thoennes (1984) report that in Los Angeles, 41% of the families reached complete agreement, 19% developed either a temporary or visitation agreement, and 40% were referred to the Custody Division for investigation. The agreement outcome for voluntary custody mediation was 58% during mediation, increasing to 82.5% following the mediation (Pearson, Thoennes, & VanderKooi, 1982).

CONCLUSION

As these outcome statistics demonstrate, court-mandated mediation is an effective process of dispute resolution when used with skill and care. It is a distinctive process, drawing upon the principles and techniques of voluntary and non-court-related mediation, but differing in significant ways. Mandatory mediation is applied in California only to disputes over the custody of and access to children following a parental separation. Participation of the parents is required by law, and the mediator actively advocates a resolution that benefits the children involved.

The purpose of mandatory mediation is to break into the escalating cycle of conflict that so often perpetuates custody disputes and to shield children from the traumatizing consequences of repeated parental conflict over their care. Parents are assisted in meeting, in communicating in a focused and nondestructive manner, and in developing a cooperative agreement that they can tailor to the specific needs of their family and to which they can adhere. These parents fall into three categories: parents newly separated and still disoriented about the changes in their lives; parents with objectively difficult issues to resolve; and frequently disputing parents with long-term problems. Within each group are many clients who have been traditionally considered "unmediatable." Court-mandated mediation offers the structure needed to help many of these families resolve their disputes and develop workable agreements, rather than resort to adversarial court trials.

Court mediators engage in a careful balancing of many factors in guiding a hotly disputing family toward success in mediation. They utilize their power as a mediator to empower the parents to develop their own resolutions. They keep the focus of the mediation on the child, and on the particular needs and strengths of each child under dispute. Following a mandate for minimal intervention, they employ strategic counseling tactics to release parental impasses and free people to move toward finding solutions. They provide families with education regarding the process of divorce and in conflict-resolution skills. They use the authoritarian nature of a courthouse setting and the law to engage parents in facing and dealing with the disputed issues. Where there is too much use of any of these factors, the parents may agree, but the agreement will be more reflective of the mediator's ideas than those of the parents and is not likely to last. Where there is too little application of these factors, parents may continue their destructive conflict instead of moving toward cooperative parenting of their child.

REFERENCES

California Civil Code §§4600.6, 4607a (1981).

Hetherington, E. M., Cox, M., & Cox, R. *The family: Setting priorities.* New York: McGraw-Hill, 1979.

Kelly, J. Workshop on visitation schedules, 1984. Marin County Probation Department, San Rafael, California.

Kressel, K., Jaffee, N., Tuchman, B., Watson, C., & Deutsch, M. An exploratory study of patterns of divorce: Their impact on settlement negotiations, the role of a mediator and post-divorce adjustment. *Family Process*, 1980, *19(2)*, 101–116.

McIsaac, H. Conference remarks. Mediation of Child Custody and Visitation Disputes, Vallambrosa Retreat, Menlo Park, CA, September 1981.

McLaughlin v. Superior Court, 140 Cal. App. 3d 473 (1983).

Milne, A. Custody of children in a divorce process: A family self-determination model. *Conciliation Courts Review*, 1978, *16*, 2–12.

Mnookin, R., & Kornhauser, L. Bargaining in the shadow of the law: The case of divorce. *Yale Law Journal*, 1979, *88*, 950–997.

Pearson, J., & Thoennes, N. A preliminary portrait of client reactions to three court mediation programs. *Mediation Quarterly*, 1984, *3*, 21–40.

Pearson, J., Thoennes, N., & VanderKooi, L. The decision to mediate: Profiles of individuals who accept and reject the opportunity to mediate contested child custody and visitation issues. *Journal of Divorce*, 1982, *6(1)*, 17–35.

Waldron, J. A therapeutic mediation model for child custody dispute resolution. *Mediation Quarterly*, 1984, *3*, 5–20.

Walters, M. *A study of client satisfaction in child custody and visitation mediation.* Unpublished master's thesis, San Francisco State University, 1984.

11

Lawyer and Therapist Team Mediation

LOIS GOLD
Private Practice, Portland, Oregon

Mediation conducted by a lawyer and a therapist working as a team offers advantages not available when either a lawyer or a therapist practices alone. Team mediation is used to address a number of issues—including gender bias, neutrality, power balancing, and the interface of legal and emotional issues— that are germane to the mediation process. The limitations of cost and logistics notwithstanding, the team model, as presented by this author, who has practiced both as a sole mental health mediator and as a member of an interdisciplinary team, provides a unique synthesis of skills and expertise.

If we accept divorce as a problem of restructuring rather than dissolving the family unit (Ahrons, 1980), the interdisciplinary mediation team can assist the divorcing family to restructure itself legally, economically, and psychologically. The lawyer and therapist mediation team provides a famework of change for the divorcing family that neither traditional legal intervention nor counseling can independently provide.

In conventional practice, the lawyer and therapist respond to their clients quite differently. Legal intervention focuses on individual advocacy. The lawyer is concerned with championing the cause of the client and may be compelled to ignore the family unit in favor of the individual, given the ethical and professional considerations that encourage adversarial as opposed to conciliatory posturing.

Clinical intervention focuses on the transition of the family unit by attending to the emotional alliances and reducing the intensity of the divorce so that the parenting function can be maintained. The clinician may not be aware of the legal ramifications of these decisions for the individual adults. The attorney–therapist team mediation model has the potential to offer a "full service" divorce and to respond to the interrelated psychological and legal problems of dissolution more comprehensively than a single mediator. Interdisciplinary co-mediation played a significant role as one of the earlier models of mediation. Many practitioners seemed to have abandoned this approach as they became more experienced. There has been no research evaluating co-mediation in divorce or comparing it to other models. At best we have clinical experience and impressions. The chapter describes the interdisciplinary mediation model, discusses theory and practice, and suggests guidelines for using this approach.

LAWYER AND THERAPIST ROLES IN CO-MEDIATION

The most common structure for co-mediation in divorce is the gender-balanced lawyer–therapist team, which functions either collaboratively or conjointly. In the collaborative approach (Wiseman & Fiske, 1980), either the attorney- or therapist–mediator meets with a couple to discuss the issues relevant to his or her area of expertise and refers the couple to the other mediator as indicated. In this model, the attorney and the therapist are consultants to each other and meet with the couple sequentially, not jointly.

The second model, and the focus of this chapter, is the conjoint mediation team. In this approach a gender-balanced attorney–therapist team together meet with the couple and respond to both the legal and the emotional content. Although most of the sessions involve both the attorney and therapist, separate meetings may be arranged around specific issues in which the role of one mediator would be so minimal as to make joint sessions cumbersome or unnecessarily expensive. For example, when detailed evaluation of retirement benefits or business partnerships is involved, or when time must be spent on the development of workable parenting agreements, it can be more effective to meet with one member of the team. Typically the team meets with a couple for three to six 90-minute sessions, spanning a period of 1 to 6 months. If the couple have not separated, interim financial and parenting arrangements are established. The parties agree to view these arrangements as temporary, even though this could establish precedent if litigation were to take place later. The attorney team member may draft the temporary separation agreement or memorandum and refer the parties to legal counsel to formalize the agreement. Alternatively, the couple may decide an informal agreement is sufficient. When a couple are not separated, it is generally premature to deal with details beyond temporary financial and living arrangements. This seems to be the limit of what most people can absorb at the time of initial separation. The next appointment is usually not scheduled for 1 to 2 months.

In the conjoint team model, the roles of the attorney and therapist are defined as mediators, neutral facilitators, problem solvers, and resource people. Neither team member is functioning in a traditional role, and this must be made clear to the clients. The team members' training and expertise represent resources available to the couple. Although the lawyer is not defining his or her role in traditional terms and may have the clients sign waivers to that effect, there is controversy about the constraints and liabilities on attorney–mediators, and bar ethics opinions about this vary (Silberman, 1981).

The focus of the therapist is to improve communication, identify the underlying issues, and deal with emotional conflict that interferes with negotiations. The therapist can also function as a resource person by providing information about the children's needs, the emotional dynamics of divorce, and the restructuring of the marital relationship into an effective parenting unit.

The lawyer provides information about statutes, case law, and local judicial tradition. Legal standards can be used to establish parameters within which bargaining can take place. It is assumed there are rights to private ordering (Mnookin & Kornhauser, 1979). The lawyer serves to remind the couple that they are bargaining "in the shadow of the law" and that, if negotiations fail, legal rules would be invoked. The extent to which parties choose to use legal standards is negotiable. Having an attorney as part of the team may make the parties more aware of the legal standards, although the lawyer does not represent either party and each is advised to seek independent legal counsel.

The lawyer–mediator reviews the list of issues to be addressed, the range of resolution that might be imposed in a court setting, and the options available for a negotiated settlement. Both parties can rely on the lawyer's expertise and experience knowing that full disclosure and review of all the issues and options will lead to a more informed and a more satisfactory set of client choices.

Both team members actively engage in the bargaining and negotiation process, but bring different skills to the table. The lawyer is trained to *give* information, and the therapist is trained to *elicit* information. The attorney helps identify the "what" of the options, and the therapist the "why." The attorney makes sure the parties understand their rights, the facts, and the options. The therapist probes for fuller exploration of needs and clarifies motivation so the parties can make informed decisions.

It is important that the parties reach decisions that are based on a realistic assessment of needs, goals, and available resources. Often negotiations begin before the parties have achieved a level of objectivity about the other person or a sense of their own independence. When feelings of guilt, anger, or fear remain strong and the parties are emotionally attached, it is difficult not to use the economic settlement for emotional ends. The question of what is fair is highly subjective and influenced by the circumstances of the marital break-down. Many decisions about the ending of the marital relationship do not "feel" fair, especially for the nonconsenting partner or when a third party is involved. A person may feel he or she has already lost what was valued and may not be inclined to view an equal distribution of assets as fair. If the emotional issues are not resolved and the parties do not come to understand their part in the failure of the relationship, the demand will be to organize the settlement to correct past injustices, rather than to assess future needs and goals. A party who feels victimized often attempts to align the mediator. In these instances, the therapist may explore the compensatory demands and clarify the feelings involved. The attorney, on the other hand, serves to remind the parties of the separation of legal and emotional issues, reinforces the boundaries within which rational decisions need to be made and can prevent the therapist from being co-opted into alignment by the party with strong, emotionally laden perceptions of entitlement.

Three variables seem to influence the functioning of the team and the level of activity of each team member: (1) the stage of the emotional disengagement and acceptance of the decision to divorce (Federico, 1979; Kessler, 1975); (2) the stage of the mediation process (Haynes, 1981); and (3) the complexity of the assets.

The therapist tends to be most active in the initial sessions in terms of creating a context for cooperation and a positive emotional climate, particularly when there is anger, mistrust, or nonmutuality about the decision to divorce. Addressing these issues directly is often necessary for the parties to be able to move beyond them. A brief marital history is elicited and feelings about the divorce decision and the possibility of reconciliation are explored.

Most couples approach mediation with a mixture of anxiety and hope and with the experience of failure in communicating and resolving issues. Many divorcing couples are in an interdependent survival relationship, each controlling what the other needs. Mediation is hard work. The stress is greater in face-to-face contact. Historical issues and patterns emerge, often making the parties feel stuck and mistrustful. Some couples discontinue mediation because they cannot tolerate the pain and frustration of dealing with each other, even though the substantive disagreements may be narrow. These negative patterns, when they exist, must be reversed for the couple to feel that they are making progress. A skillful therapist, particularly in the beginning of mediation, can reduce defensiveness, diffuse tension, and help keep the process emotionally manageable, especially when a couple's readiness to mediate is questionable.

The attorney, in the initial sessions, tends to focus on the factual circumstances. The attorney outlines the legal parameters and begins to establish a data base by asking questions and eliciting financial and legal information. Although this is a more structured approach, the attorney is not indifferent to the couple's emotional concerns. Support, validation, and rapport are equally important. The attorney's more systematic interventions help a couple organize their thinking and remind them of the external standards that must be considered in making decisions. Implicit in the interdisciplinary approach is the message that emotional expression may be allowed, but decisions must be within legal guidelines and must be based on equity, not emotional compensation.

The fact-finding and negotiation phases of mediation are relatively businesslike in tone compared to the emotional intensity of the previous sessions. The therapist may be inactive as the attorney discusses the more technical aspects of the division of assets. Even when not actively participating, however, the therapist has a valuable symbolic presence, providing gender and power balance and a safety net when negotiations are fragile.

As settlement offers are formulated, the attorney reviews the details and drafts a memorandum or proposed agreement. The attorney is responsible for raising other issues that should be addressed, such as insurance, provision for children's education, medical costs, extraordinary expenses, and tax consequences. It is important to note that a judge has a wide range of discretion to divide property, establish support, and impose visitation schedules and limitations. It is unlikely that cases with identical facts would result in identical resolutions if heard by different judges. Therefore, an attorney can only relate the range of options and potential resolutions. In mediation, this should be an incentive for the parties to create their own terms for settlement.

The therapist reviews plans for the children and guidelines for handling the continuing parental relationship, forecasts changing circumstances, and suggests procedures for resolving future conflicts. The therapist may help the parties prepare for closure by asking each person for feedback about the process and for his or her view of the final agreement.

It is the attorney–mediator's responsibility to see that the legal issues and ramifications are understood by the parties. At the conclusion of mediation, the attorney–mediator drafts a memorandum setting forth the parties' agreement, which they will take to independent legal counsel for review and incorporation into the final decree. The proposed agreement may be modified in mediation following the parties' consultation with their attorneys, or modifications may be made outside mediation. The agreement belongs to the couple. If the parties do not return to mediation after consultation with their attorneys, the mediation agreement will be formalized when the final decree is submitted to the court. In practice, many couples do not proceed immediately with the divorce, and minor modification of the agreement may be made by the parties' attorneys in the months following the conclusion of mediation.

THE PROCESS OF CO-MEDIATION

The real potency of mediation may lie in the experience of a constructive, corrective process. The process as a whole has an integrity and healing power that is greater than the benefits derived in any given session.

Many clients report feeling more positive about each other, able to communicate better, more resolved about the decision to divorce, and able to handle their conflicts less destructively. These issues are not the focus of mediation and are rarely addressed directly in any systematic or consistent manner. They are a function of a constructive process and are generally considered secondary benefits or subgoals of mediation.

Although there are considerable differences among practitioners regarding the relative emphasis on content versus process and settlement versus relational issues, the team approach is characterized by the inherent and intended balance of the process/substance focus. Interdisciplinary mediation is based on a view of divorce mediation that recognizes the interplay of the emotional resolution of divorce with the settlement tasks of divorce. Although the goal of mediation is to reach agreements regarding financial distribution, support arrangements, and the parenting of children, it is in this process that new learning takes place. The method creates the new experience that for many couples may be the first significant exposure to constructually resolving conflict.

The inherent structure of co-mediation changes and probably enhances the process of mediation. The modeling of collaboration, the symbolism of the gender balance, as well as the increase in technical resources, has the potential to indirectly augment the secondary therapeutic benefits. For instance, the mediators model alternatives to dysfunctional communication or act as role models for individuals whose sense of identity or competence has been shaken, and this has an impact on the parties' perceptions and attitudes. Because psychological change is not the primary function of mediation, there has been little attention in the literature to investigating the impact of the process on the individuals or the postdivorce family, or to investigating how to augment the psychological benefits. Mediation is a multilevel experience that affects clients on more levels than the mediator can be aware of at any given time. Most practitioners make process interventions when this interferes with the settlement tasks. What is not sufficiently understood is how to capitalize on the positive aspects of the process to promote psychological growth and adjustment without changing the goals & focus of mediation. The single mediator has limited resources to focus on other than the settlement tasks. Co-mediators, like co-therapists, change the process and have greater symbolic and indirect impact psychologically.

Three dimensions of the team process may have an impact different from that of the single-mediator model: (1) empowerment or teaching new skills, (2) "seeding" behavioral and cognitive change, and (3) enhancing the psychological adaptation to the divorce.

The process of mediation gives the parties the opportunity to develop new skills. The mediator can interrupt and redirect dysfunctional patterns. Substantive discussions about support, child custody, and so forth are the vehicles to teach and model new communication patterns and provide a positive experience in resolving conflict. For example, a couple involved in a power struggle that stems from the need to be right may be arguing about time-sharing plans and who can better assess the children's needs. A mediator can simply focus on consent and help negotiate a reasonable plan (bypassing the power issue), or can ask if what they are doing is constructive. If they agree it is not, the mediator can work with the couple to develop new ways to share control, accept differences, and be solution-oriented instead of power-oriented. Two mediators have more resources to teach new skills without losing sight of the settlement goals.

A second dimension of the mediation process can be called the "seeding" function of the process. This refers to introducing an idea that is not part of the client's typical range of cognitive or behavioral responses. Seeding can be accomplished directly, through reframing a statement, or indirectly, through the use of paradox or metaphor. It forces clients to think of themselves and their problems in new ways. These ideas then become the cornerstone for change. For example, the mediator might say, "I wonder what your children will think about you and the way you handled the divorce when they are grown." Or, "You are like people fighting over who started the fire while the house is burning down all around you." This kind of intervention usually stems from intuitive thinking. It is difficult for a single intervenor to step back and get that kind of perspective when concentrating on factual information and analysis, but the mediation team has the resources to have an observing and an interactive member at any given time.

A third dimension is the psychological change that occurs as a function of the negotiating. The process of negotiating helps the parties through the stages of emotional disengagement. The concrete act of separating possessions or discussing child-sharing arrangements has parallel meaning on a deeply emotional level. As each detail is negotiated, compromised, or conceded, a simultaneous, perhaps unconscious, emotional shift occurs about the approaching reality of divorce (Gold, 1982). Discussion of entitlement or fairness can bring out feelings that increase understanding of the reasons for the marital breakdown and help a couple feel more resolved about the decision to divorce. A cooperative process in which painful feelings can be aired is healing and allows a couple to make peace with one another. The division of roles between the two mediators allows one mediator to attend to and acknowledge these underlying feelings while the other can refocus on the settlement tasks. Couples probably receive more emotional support with two mediators.

THE ADVANTAGES OF THE TEAM MEDIATION MODEL

The most obvious advantage of interdisciplinary mediation is the expertise of both professionals. Each has broad training and experience that a single mediator would not possess unless cross-trained. The team approach affords a fuller exploration of the legal and psychological issues and allows the team to confront unforeseen complexities and questions that otherwise might require referral to a lawyer or a therapist. The therapeutic benefits are likely to be greater because of the presence of the clinically trained mediator. The need to table issues or interrupt negotiations in order to obtain information about a point of law can be minimized because of the presence of the lawyer. The parties may have fewer nagging doubts about the settlement because the legal questions and the emotional aspects are aired in tandem.

It is important, however, that each mediator's role be defined and differentiated so that the clients do not have unrealistic expectations based on the traditional view of each profession. Even with this clarity, the expectation of traditional role performance may carry over. The team approach may be attractive to couples who have different agendas regarding reconciliation or divorce. The person wanting to move forward with the divorce may see the attorney as an ally. The person hopeful of a reconciliation may see the process as an opportunity to review the marital breakdown and may appeal to the therapist for help.

Screening for reconciliation is an important task in any model of mediation. The team approach may be beneficial when a couple have a high degree of ambivalence about a divorce. The therapist's skills in raising questions about the viability of the marriage and exploring the decision to divorce may open new doors for the relationship. The role of the therapist at this juncture is to surface and explore the issues sufficiently for the couple to make a decision about continuing mediation, seeking marriage counseling, or talking more on their own. Should the couple decide to seek marital counseling, a referral is made. The therapist is advised against changing the contract to become the couple's therapist, according to the Model Standards of Practice (1985). The team approach may also heighten ambivalence about the decision to divorce, particularly for couples who separate without having consulted a marriage counselor. Each professional traditionally represents a different choice regarding a troubled marriage, and the presence of both a lawyer and a therapist serves as a visible reminder of those choices. The professional background of the mediator may influence the process more in team mediation than in individual mediation, where there is no functional division of labor.

The team approach provides an important male–female balance and a secondary modeling function. The mediators' autonomous and cooperative behavior provides an example of how a couple can communicate constructively and work together. The gender balance provides an opportunity to be understood, validated, or challenged by persons of both sexes, thereby minimizing sexual stereotypes and triangulation. If the mediators are divorced, they can share their successful divorce resolution as an intervention technique. The mediator, as a survivor of a divorce, seems to impart a sense of hope to the client facing the challenge of being alone.

Although there are no data about the influence of the sex of the mediator on the outcome or process of mediation, the gender-balanced team seems to reduce potential problems. The team mediator can capitalize on gender identification, whereas a single mediator needs to guard against it. Marital rupture often creates a deep sense of vulnerability toward people of the opposite sex. Some clients may feel threatened by a mediator of the opposite sex or may fear the mediator will be more sympathetic to the spouse. The single mediator is more likely to be perceived as biased because of the increased caution and mistrust toward members of the opposite sex that seems to occur during a divorce. This anxiety can be eased because the client sees the same-sex mediator as someone who can identify with the client's situation and be sympathetic, if not an ally. Confrontations, therefore, may be more effective because of common gender. A client may be more willing to hear from the same-sex mediator because he or she feels less threatened and less concerned about mediator bias. Rigid positions can sometimes be deflated by acknowledging and identifying with a client's feelings in a way that a person of the opposite sex cannot convey. Humor or discussion that capitalizes on sexual identity ("man to man" or "woman to woman" jokes) can also be used with greater liberty. Generally the team can use gender-linked rapport as a strategy in ways that would be risky for a single mediator.

Negotiation about spousal support can be eased by the male–female balance of the team. The duration and amount of spousal support is often a highly charged conflict that raises many issues relating to changing values about men's and women's roles in our culture. Beliefs and positions concerning what is owed or what is fair can run deep. The same-sex mediator's support and careful reframing of the issues for each person seems to increase understanding and ease positional bargaining at a more effective level than when one mediator has to interpret and support two people in such a value-laden conflict. It may be easy to achieve a settlement figure for spousal support, but if the myths and realities that surround this issue are not fully explored, they can tear at the fabric of the agreement.

The conjoint team also minimizes the influence of personal and professional biases. Team consultation provides checks and balances to personal reactions and an opportunity to explore different professional views about settlement terms. Given the lack of definitive guidelines in divorce settlements, clients are probably better protected with the input of two people helping them evaluate what is fair. The biases or countertransference reactions of a mediator can be countered by the other mediator, either during a session or in postsession consultation. There is a built-in peer review.

Maintaining a sense of balance and impartiality is extremely important. A mediator who is perceived as biased loses credibility and effectiveness. A single mediator is vulnerable to real and perceived biases because of the emotional reactivity of the clients, the changing values of fairness, and the wide range of discretion in the legal process. The team approach helps to guard against bias and maintain impartiality and balance.

Another advantage of the team approach is the management of client projections and complaints. Some individuals in a divorce crisis will be acutely vigilant toward the mediator and will project emotional needs onto the mediator or misinterpret the mediator's responses. Trust, power, fairness, and dependency are sensitive issues. They represent areas in which emotional wounds may have been suffered as a result of the marital breakdown. To the extent that a person is working through these issues, he or she will be sensitive to that behavior in the mediator. With the team, when a client projects a grievance, the co-mediator can provide another perspective and help process the issue without being personally caught up in it. The single mediator runs a greater risk of becoming defensive or becoming involved in a power struggle with the complaining client.

In a case in which an 18-year marriage was terminating, the wife was frightened, resisted having to stand on her own, and expressed continual dissatisfaction with the male attorney–mediator for not being more helpful. She was being asked by the team to try to develop some of her own goals, but she seemed to want the attorney–mediator to tell her what to do. Her desire to be taken care of was being transferred from the husband to the male mediator. The attorney–mediator was confused about what was really being asked of him and responded by being more supportive and giving more information while trying to maintain balance and neutrality. Even with the therapist's interventions to try to sort out the issues, the woman decided that she wanted the protection and security of her own attorney and, to the husband's consternation, terminated mediation.

Another aspect of the team relates to the symmetry of four people. This can minimize triangulation, help maintain impartiality, equalize bargaining power, and divide the labor. One facilitator can be more actively confrontive or supportive because the cofacilitator is capable of responding on the other side of the issue, thus reducing the potential for the process to be perceived as biased. Confronting unreasonableness can also be more effective when both mediators respond. It is more difficult to dismiss confrontation by two people. Greater risks can be taken with innovative strategies because there is a backup system in the co-mediator.

In addition, the mediators have collegial support, the opportunity to check perceptions, and the benefit of cross-disciplinary expertise and learning.

Unequal power relations between the participants are among the major difficulties facing any mediator. Power inequities can be the result of differences in knowledge, verbal abilities, emotional vulnerability or leveraging bargaining chips. If the power relationship cannot be equalized, the couple may not be appropriate for mediation. Two facilitators have more resources within the mediation process to equalize bargaining relationships and thus have less need to use outside referral.

The lawyer and therapist working as a team may deter legal or psychological manipulation because of the implicit or assumed monitoring of the process by both professions. A person is less likely to take advantage of another when knowledgeable authorities are so close at hand. This can provide a feeling of safety for a person who is at an emotional disadvantage because of a historic interaction pattern, at a legal disadvantage because of a gain by the other, or at a financial disadvantage because of a lack of information or skill.

When the spouses have different levels of skill regarding financial matters or knowledge of the family assets, this power imbalance can be made explicit, and one mediator can define his or her role as that of a consultant to the less informed party in order to make bargaining more equitable. The "consulting" mediator can help the less informed spouse ask the right questions, make sure he or she understands what is being discussed, and ensure that the spouse is not being intimidated. It is important that the less informed spouse be protected in mediation. Sometimes it may be necessary for the less knowledgeable person to consult more regularly with his or her attorney or an independent financial advisor.

The dominant–accommodating spousal system is another pattern with inherent bargaining inequities. The submissive spouse's quiet manner can be mistaken for agreement or comprehension. That person's concerns and feelings may, in fact, have to be carefully and painstakingly elicited. A single mediator will need to focus on the substantive issues and may not sufficiently attend to the needs of the quiet, unassertive spouse. In a team approach, with the therapist assisting the process, the submissive person can be drawn out and encouraged to be more assertive. In addition, the mediator of the same gender as the unassertive spouse is often a good role model for businesslike, assertive behavior.

When fear of the spouse or guilt underlies a bargaining stance, the therapist can help the person understand this and feel safe enough to raise issues in his or her own behalf. The attorney's job is to make certain the parties comprehend their rights and options; the therapist must attempt to bring an understanding of the reasons underlying the choices. If, for an emotional reason, a person chooses to give up entitlement, it is important that this be an informed choice.

The use of the team as a training vehicle has been largely unexplored (Folberg & Taylor, 1984). The interdisciplinary mediation team may be the best training vehicle for exposing beginning mediators to the full range of psychological and legal issues in divorce. Whether it is the intent of a practitioner to mediate the full range of issues or limit practice to either the financial or parenting aspects, it is important to understand both. Team mediation can serve as an internship providing formal or informal experience for two beginning mediators, or for a senior mediator to supervise or train a beginning practitioner.

Although it is not the responsibility of clients to pay for the training of mediators, advantages are likely even with a beginning team, because of the protection offered by the fuller exploration of the issues. When the team model is used in training or supervision, the fee can be reduced or a sliding scale may be used.

DISADVANTAGES OF THE TEAM MEDIATION MODEL

An evaluation of team mediation must consider the economic implications. Team mediation costs more per hour than employing a single mediator unless each team mediator proportionally reduces his or her hourly fee. In practice it appears that the total number of hours to reach an agreement using the team mediation model may be sufficiently less than with a single mediator, so that the overall expense is similar. The costs of team mediation may even be less when the reduced attorney time outside mediation is considered. From 1979 to 1982 the average team mediation case from the Family Mediation Center in Portland was concluded in 5 hours, plus an additional 1 to 2 hours of drafting time, for an average cost of $500.00, compared to $440.69 as reported in a survey conducted by the Divorce Mediation Research Project (Pearson, Ring, & Milne, 1983). If mediation is seen only as a way to save money, a higher hourly fee to compensate the team may be difficult to justify. The principal advantage of the team is not economy. It is a better service, not a cheaper one (Folberg, 1983).

Establishing and structuring the service may be problematic for the mediation team. There are ethical constraints on attorneys working with nonattorneys. Structuring a practice, establishing a fee schedule, and determining method of payment all require careful consideration. Legal ethics prohibit attorneys from forming partnerships, splitting fees, or practicing under a trade name with nonattorneys. Most clinicians do not have such ethical constraints. The most acceptable method for payment of fees is for each mediator to serve as an independent contractor, billing separately for the hours worked.

Logistics can also be a problem with the team approach. Scheduling or changing an appointment is easier with three people than with four. Many attorneys and therapists who mediate together do not share offices. Deciding whose office to use for a case or session can be an issue for the mediators. It is important for clients to meet in the same office each time. The familiarity of the surroundings can ease some of the anxiety for the clients but causes additional travel time for the person whose regular office is not used. Reserving regular blocks of time each week for mediation may simplify scheduling for the mediators but create a hardship for clients, as they must accommodate a more limited appointment schedule.

The other challenge for the team is to develop a working relationship. Attorneys and therapists are trained to think differently, to view their roles with a client differently, to analyze the process differently, and to respond to different aspects of a situation. Even if both team members have similar training in mediation, each is likely to draw on familiar strengths as he or she develops a new set of mediation skills. The attorney–mediator may offer advice and give suggestions too readily, depriving clients of opportunities to think for themselves. The therapist–mediator may explore emotional issues too readily, losing sight of the objectives of mediation.

Team mediation provides opportunities for considerable learning, but not without effort and additional time commitments to develop the team relationship and to consult before and after sessions. The mediators must have rapport and feel they can work well with each other. The team must learn how to share authority, territory, and control. They must work together enough to be comfortable with each other's style and develop shared perceptions of procedures, interventions, and strategies. They must be able to collaborate and avoid competition. Early in practice, each will probably defer questions to the other according to their respective spheres of expertise. The longer a team works together, the more likely role boundaries are to blur, as each member learns more about the other's area. The attorney becomes more comfortable discussing emotional and parenting issues, and the therapist becomes more comfortable with financial issues. Even within this merging of functions, each retains the responsibility and authority for the issues related to his or her primary professional identity.

ASSESSING TEAM REFERRALS

To date, no clear-cut rules guide the use of the team mediation model over the single-mediator model. General guidelines might follow a medical or managerial model for the use of teams; more complex cases require greater resources or specialized expertise. The complexity of a case—a primary reason for a team referral—should be considered in both economic and emotional terms. The team is rarely used when custody is the only issue presented for mediation.

The following six considerations, derived from clinical experience, can be used to evaluate the potential complexities of a case. Couples with these profiles seem most likely to benefit from the team approach.

1. *High levels of conflict or manipulation.* The team approach can be useful to help couples who are enmeshed or who display negative intimacy patterns stay focused and separate their marital dynamics from the settlement tasks. The level of limit setting and behavioral management necessary with this type of couple can often be more effectively managed by two mediators than by one.

2. *Power imbalance.* The team can help balance power where inequities exist because of different levels of financial knowledge, negotiation and communication skills, or dominant–accommodating marital systems. One mediator can support the less powerful spouse.

3. *Complex assets.* Marital dissolutions involving businesses, real eastate

holdings, professional corporations, partnerships, and pensions can involve strong feelings, disparate beliefs about entitlement, and different levels of knowledge about the assets. The resources of the team can address the technical financial details while also assisting the less knowledgeable spouse.

4. *Informational consultation.* Couples who want basic legal information about the divorce process and information about children's needs and restructuring family relationships can benefit from the specialized expertise of an interdisciplinary team. These tend to be lower conflict couples who may not have decided to divorce yet need information and wish to avoid adversarial conflict.

5. *Nonmutuality regarding decision to separate.* Some couples may not be separated and are at different levels of emotional readiness to negotiate, despite the need to resolve certain issues. One party may have grudgingly agreed to attend mediation. The issues are likely to be emotionally charged. Because the needs of these couples are so disparate, they are often turned away from mediation as unready. With the team, each person can be emotionally supported; both can feel that they have someone in their corner. Feeling understood and supported may increase a person's ability to negotiate when the separation or divorce decision is strongly opposed.

6. *Adversary posturing.* The breakdown in trust and communication when there has been litigation is difficult to reverse. The commitment to mediation may not be based on good will, but may be an effort to avoid a potentially worse outcome in court. These couples must learn to problem solve, develop a minimum level of trust around the issues that require cooperation, and understand the legal implications of changing existing orders and bargaining positions.

Another consideration for using the team relates to beginning mediators. Working in teams provides an excellent opportunity for learning from each other and serves to better protect the client. In deciding whether to use the team approach, all the options need to be presented and discussed.

A telephone interview or an initial half-hour consultation can be used to evaluate whether the team is appropriate. The following information is useful in making that determination:

1. The length of separation and mutuality of decision to divorce
2. level of deterioration in communication and trust
3. whether the parties have seen a therapist, together or separately
4. ages of children and whether there is a dispute about them
5. whether there is a business, partnership, or professional corporation, or extensive real estate holdings
6. whether attorneys been retained and whether there are legal orders in effect or motions pending.

Generally, the team is most appropriate for couples with poor communication, a volatile situation, and complex assets. Child-related conflicts and cases with simple assets can be handled by the therapist–mediator. An emotionally disengaged couple (sometimes measured by length of separation), ready to do the business of dissolving the marriage, may be most comfortable seeing just the attorney–mediator. Couples who have been in therapy and are more resolved about divorce and thus more objective about settlement may also prefer the attorney–mediator.

All couples using the Family Mediation Center in Portland from 1979 through 1982 were seen by teams. From 1982 through 1983 the couples were given the options referred to earlier, and the fees for each mediator were reduced in team mediation. In 1984 we did very little team mediation because of economic considerations for both the clients and the mediators and because our experience allowed us to be comfortable mediating alone for most situations. An experienced mediator will be more comfortable mediating alone than a beginning practitioner. A second mediator can always be called in after mediation has begun, but the beginning practitioner should err on the side of the team approach.

Experience in the private sector has shown that clients who choose to mediate their divorce settlement—that is, property as well as custody—tend to screen themselves. Most are self-referred. They are usually looking for an amicable outcome, wish to preserve a decent relationship, and want to avoid the adversary system. Many are distrustful of lawyers and are not represented by legal counsel. They are often more highly motivated toward resolution than clients referred by attorneys. Eighty-five percent of our clients reach agreements. Severe conflict over custody is low. There is often agreement in principle about the best interests of the children but a lack of knowledge about options and arrangements. Many choose joint custody.

Despite the high degree of motivation and the desire to work with mediators rather than lawyers, couples in the private sector are not necessarily convinced of the benefit of mediation and often have major disagreements about entitlement and serious communication problems. Some couples simply want a neutral place to divorce. These individuals have usually accepted the divorce and are in agreement about some of the issues, but want the informational and educational resources of the team.

Sometimes a couple negotiating only custody with a single mediator may subsequently choose to mediate the financial issues. At that point they can continue with the therapist, the team, or the attorney, depending on the complexity of the financial issues involved and their own emotional volatility. A second team member coming into the process in the middle, however, presents some potential problems because rapport, credibility, and a relationship have already been established with the first mediator, and it will take time for the couple to feel comfortable with the new mediator. The second mediator may be viewed primarily as a consultant, may not be as effective, and may not develop as strong a relationship with the couple as the initial mediator.

One couple seen collaboratively at the Family Mediation Center in Portland had been separated for 4 months. The father was living in the family home with temporary custody of two preschool daughters. He resisted allowing the mother access and had gained custody through a restraining order when the mother decided not to reconcile after a temporary 4-week separation. The father felt the mother had significant parental inadequacies, and the mother was in a rage at the limited access to her daughters. Their interaction was characterized by accusations, threats, manipulation, and angry outbursts. The mother had a volatile temper, and the father knew how to rile her. She would threaten to terminate mediation and would leave the room in hysterics at least once during each session. The investment in this behavior pattern was so high that it was very difficult to keep the couple problem-focused and behaving rationally for an extended period. It was questionable whether this couple were even appropriate for mediation.

A lawyer–mediator joined the process after the third session, because a $25,000 bank note was due. The note required both signatures to refinance, and each was using this note for leverage. The tenor of the session changed remarkably with the lawyer's presence. With his questions and with the authority he represented, the lawyer created a structure that forced the couple into a more rational mode of operation. He could more directly thwart manipulative, infantile responses because he represented the boundaries of what is acceptable or unacceptable under the law. Dynamically, this couple acted like rivalrous children. They were simply more than a single parent could handle!

In general, this type of couple is a poor mediation risk. In the typology of divorcing couples developed by Kressel, Jaffee, Tuchman, Watson, and Deutsch (1980), the enmeshed couple is described as having the poorest outcome in mediation because strong forces of attachment run counter to the mediator's goal of resolution. A team might be able to deal with this kind of couple more successfully than a single mediator even when the only issue is custody. The attorney provides structure by imposing legal rules, which establish limits that force the couple to respond more rationally. It is also easier for two mediators to manage volatile couples. If need be, the team can take a time-out during joint meetings, and each team member can talk with one client when things become too tense.

Experimenting with the team approach will provide additional information about its use. Dividing the issues between the team members may be efficient and cost-effective, but it does change the dynamics and potency of the process, reducing the benefits of gender balance and emotional support for the clients and the mediators. Therefore, the importance of these less tangible aspects needs to be weighed against the advantages of separating the team.

CONCLUSION

Interdisciplinary team mediation holds much promise for many divorcing couples and may provide an effective training vehicle for mediators. Research is needed to isolate the significant variables in the team approach and to compare outcomes with those for other approaches. The symbolic aspects of the team, the dynamics of a gender-balanced process, and the power of the context are theoretical concepts derived from clinical experience but unsubstantiated by research. Their value has not been measured in any systematic analysis.

The interdisciplinary team presents a unique synthesis of skills by providing a level of expertise that is rarely available with a single mediator. The goals of team mediation generally go beyond simply reaching an equitable financial settlement. They include the quality of the coparental relationship, the parent–child relationship, and the restructured family formation. The team also emphasizes the educational use of mediation. The negotiation process can be used to teach communication and problem-solving skills and to facilitate post-divorce adjustment. These subgoals are not unique to the team but should be considered basic to the team approach.

There are currently no models for service that integrate the multiple needs of the divorcing family. Perhaps as our social concept of divorce incorporates more models for a constructive divorce process and a healthy postdivorce family, team mediation will be seen as a service that can meet the comprehensive needs of the divorcing family. The team approach, like the full-service bank, has the expertise and resources to expand the definition of mediation and to offer a broad range of services to the divorcing family, beyond the model described in this chapter.

REFERENCES

Ahrons, C. Redefining the divorcing family: A conceptual framework for post divorce family reorganization. *Social Work*, 1980, *25(6)*, 437, 441.

Federico, J. The marital termination period of the divorce adjustment process. *Journal of Divorce*, 1979, *3*, 93–106.

Folberg, J. Divorce mediation, promises and pitfalls. *Advocate*, 1983, *3*, 4–7.

Folberg, J., & Taylor, A. *Mediation: A comprehensive guide to resolving conflicts without litigation*. San Francisco: Jossey-Bass, 1984.

Gold, L. The psychological context of the interdisciplinary co-mediation team model in marital dissolution. *Conciliation Courts Review*, 1982, *20*, 45–58.

Haynes, J. M. *Divorce mediation*. New York: Springer, 1981.

Kessler, S. *The American way of divorce: Prescription for change*. Chicago: Nelson-Hall, 1975.

Kressel, K., Jaffee, N., Tuchman, B., Watson, C., & Deutsch, M. A typology of divorcing couples: Implications for mediation and the divorce process. *Family Process*, 1980, *19*, 101–116.

Milne, A., Model standards of practice for family and divorce mediation. *Mediation Quarterly*, 1985, *8*, 73–81.

Mnookin, R., & Kornhauser, L. Bargaining in the shadow of the law: The case of divorce. *Yale Law Journal*, 1979, *88*, 960–977.

Pearson, J., Ring, M., & Milne, A. A portrait of divorce mediation in the public and private sector. *Conciliation Court Review* 1983, *21(1)*, 1–24.

Silberman, L. Professional responsibility: Problems of divorce mediation. *Family Law Reporter*, 1981, *7*, 4001–4012.

Wiseman, J. M., & Fiske, J. A. A lawyer–therapist team as mediator in marital crises. *Social Work*, 1980, *25(6)*, 442–445.

12

Structured Mediation and Its Variants: What Makes It Unique

SARAH CHILDS GREBE
Family Center for Mediation and Counseling, Kensington, Maryland

A comprehensive book on divorce mediation would not be complete without a chapter on O. J. Coogler and the structured mediation model. The author, a friend and colleague of Coogler's, offers a concise description of structured mediation and its more popular variants in use today. The rules of structured mediation were developed to assist the typically naive negotiators in divorce to settle divorce issues. Although the rules and practice of structured mediation have engendered comment and criticism, this chapter aptly describes how the rules establish the conditions for cooperative conflict resolution and financial and emotional independence—goals that continue to guide the divorce mediation field today.

In the preface of his book *Structured Mediation in Divorce Settlement: A Handbook for Marital Mediators* (1978), O. J. Coogler refers to his divorce experience and how he decided to handle the aftermath. He states:

> I am indebted to my former wife and the two attorneys who represented us in our divorce for making me aware of the critical need for a more rational, more civilized way of arranging a parting of the ways. Her life, my life and our children's lives were unnecessarily embittered by that experience. In my frustration and anger, I kept thinking of something Mahatma Gandhi wrote over half a century ago:
>
> > "I have learnt through bitter experience that one supreme lesson, to conserve my anger, and as heat conserved is transmuted into energy, even so our anger can be transmuted into a power which can move the world."
>
> This system of structured mediation is, therefore, my anger transmuted into what I hope is a power to move toward a more humane world for those who find themselves following in my footsteps. (p. v.)

O. J. Coogler was born in 1915 and raised in Jonesboro, Georgia. He received a bachelor of science in psychology from the University of Georgia in 1934. Coogler received his law degree from Emory University in 1937 while serving in the Georgia State Legislature. He was appointed honorary consul to Mexico (1946–1956) and later served as legal counsel to the Consulate of Germany (1955–1960) and ran several successful businesses before turning to the practice of family therapy. Coogler was certified by the Western Institute of Group and Family Therapy and was accepted as a clinical member of the American Association for Marriage and Family Therapy. In addition he trained in Transactional Analysis and was certified as an instructor by the International Transactional Analysis Association. His work with the conflict styles of Transactional Analysis led him to become interested in conflict resolution and to consult with Morton Deutsch, author of *The Resolution of Conflict: Constructive and Destructive Processes* (1973). Deutsch & others later conducted a study of Coogler's structured mediation model (Kressel, Jaffee, Tuchman, Watson, & Deutsch, 1980).

O. J. Coogler was divorced from his second wife in 1970. This experience left him questioning the traditional adversarial approach to divorce. As a result, he was motivated to pull together his accumulated knowledge and experience to develop a marital dispute-resolution process called structured mediation.

However, Coogler first investigated arbitration as an alternative to the traditional adversarial system for resolving separation and divorce disputes. He felt that a set of rules governing the resolution process would provide the structure necessary in this emotion-laden situation. He began compiling definitions and guidelines taken from states that had the most advanced divorce laws and from the Uniform Marriage and Divorce Act. This information served as a blueprint for the development of equitable procedures for the arbitration of divorce and separation disputes.

At the same time, Coogler became a member of the board of directors of The Bridge, a house for runaways, located in Atlanta. The Bridge was an experimental institutional setting using mediation to provide a neutral ground, on which to resolve disputes between runaway teenagers and their parents.

Struck with the success of this sytem, which allowed parties to resolve their own disputes, Coogler began to design a mediation procedure, instead of an arbitration one, for use in separation and divorce settlements. The rules developed for arbitration were retained as part of a backup system, and a corresponding set of rules was developed for use with mediation.

During this period, Coogler also became aware of a change in social policy resulting in no-fault divorce. In conjunction with this, he saw a need to redefine the divorce experience from one of dissolving the family to one of restructuring it. He sought to return control of decisions to the family, hoping that this would pave the way for parents and former spouses to cooperate with each other long after the date on the separation agreement.

Coogler sought to provide a system of private ordering (Mnookin & Kornhauser, 1979) that respects the abilities and insights of the disputants to resolve their own differences. His goal was to design a system that would not duplicate lawyer negotiations, which he believed mimic judicial determination (Coogler, 1977). The foundation for Coogler's structured mediation model (Coogler et al., 1979) lies in the theoretical work of both Caplow (1968) and Deutsch (1973) and the principles of Transactional Analysis (Berne, 1964). Caplow discusses the formation of coalitions in triads, Deutsch describes the constructive and destructive conflict-resolution processes, and Transactional Analysis provides techniques for dealing with the different conflict styles.

Since the development of structured mediation in the early 1970s, several studies have borne out Coogler's beliefs. Couples are satisfied with the outcome of mediation (Kelly, 1987; Parker, 1980; Pearson & Thoennes, 1982; Pearson & Thoennes, 1984), they have a sense of control over their lives (Kressel et al., 1980), and they honor the agreements reached in mediation (Pearson & Thoennes, 1982, Saposnek et al., 1984).

The structured mediation model is distinguished from other mediation approaches by a set of rules that comprise the Agreement to Mediate (Coogler, 1977, Coogler 1978, Coogler, 1982; Grebe, 1987). The rules set forth the settlement areas to be addressed and the order in which they will be addressed. The advisory attorney and the emphasis on developing a history of agreement making through the use of an initial temporary agreement are also unique to the structured mediation model. What follows is an in-depth description of structured mediation and how it works.

THE RULES OF STRUCTURED MEDIATION

Structured mediation has as its central feature a set of rules designed to establish the parameters within which a couple mediate their disputes (Coogler, 1978; Coogler et al., 1979; Grebe, 1987). The rules provide instructions for predivorce settlements, separation agreements, postdivorce modifications, arbitration of an impasse, and court enforcement of temporary agreements. These rules also delineate the four main settlement areas in separation and divorce and provide the necessary framework for the mediation process. The structured mediation rules are a compilation of law from states with more advanced thinking and from the Uniform Marriage and Divorce Act. The rules were revised by Grebe (1982) for the Family Mediation Association in 1982, for the National Center for Mediation Education in 1984 (Grebe et al., 1985), and have been revised again (Grebe, 1987).

A separating couple, coming for help in resolving their dispute, are asked by the mediator to engage in a rational process of cooperative negotiation and decision making at a time when they are feeling emotionally overwhelmed by their situation. Most couples are seeking a structure that will resolve their problems for them. The conflicts involved in the dissolution of a marriage are associated with underlying feelings that interfere with resolution. The individuals are looking for someone to administer "justice" because they feel morally wronged (Girdner, Chapter 3, this volume). Without help, the couple can rarely focus on the long-range impact that these decisions will have on their restructured family (Grebe, 1984). The mediation rules provide a structure for sorting out feelings from issues but allow a couple to retain the responsibility for the resolution of the conflict.

Coogler maintained that the structure provided by attorneys and the adversarial system allows clients to avoid active participation and thus avoid personal responsibility. As a result, couples expect easy solutions. By agreeing to use the mediation rules, a couple choose a clear, detailed structure and frame of reference within which to proceed. The rules call for the couple's active participation as well as an assumption of personal responsibility (Coogler, 1978; Grebe, 1986c).

The rules also outline the role of the mediator (Coogler, 1982), making it clear from the outset that the mediator is neither judge nor lawyer. The mediator does not sit in judgment between the parties, evaluate the couple, or explore all the underlying emotional aspects of the conflict. At the same time, the mediator is more than a scribe, as he or she also keeps the couple on track, assigns tasks (e.g., compiling budgets, collecting financial information), and facilitates the flow of communication and the exchange of information.

Furthermore the structured mediation rules are designed to provide an orderly procedure (Vanderkooi & Pearson, 1983). Issues are mediated in a specific progression: custody, property, and support. Sessions are scheduled on a weekly basis, and failure to proceed with mediation after 10 days' notice (with limited exceptions) results in a forefeiture of the deposit fee.

In addition, the specific guidelines contained in the rules for support, custody, and property division are designed as a rational frame of reference within which to reach settlement. For example, the premise underlying spousal maintenance is that of "achieving the highest degree of financial independence of the former husband and wife at the earliest possible time" (Coogler, 1978, p. 16). Plus, the rules provide a mechanism for dealing with custody disputes that are in reality conflicts over finances. If custody is strongly contested, the parties are required to resolve all financial matters before child custody is settled. Property that was acquired previous to the marriage is not considered marital property. This rule conforms with most state law. The rules specify, however, that if this property was improved or manipulated in some way for gain during the marriage, it is then considered marital property (Coogler, 1978).

The rules are designed to encourage completion of and commitment to the process. For instance, a deposit for 10 hours of mediation is required before the first session starts. In accord with this requirement, Deutsch (1973) indicates that there are three fundamental ways to guarantee that an exchange of information vital to the mediation process will be reciprocated:

1. setting up arrangements that make for simultaneous giving and receiving
2. using third parties (i.e., mediators)
3. using "hostages" or "deposits," which enable each person to commit to the exchange and to be convinced that the other person is also committed

Relating to this, one would expect that in instances where one party pays for the costs of mediation and the other does not, that the commitment of the nonpaying spouse would be less than that of the paying spouse, unless some other understanding regarding payment has been reached. The typical procedure when one spouse canot pay directly is to make payment from a joint asset or to deduct payment from his or her share of the marital assets.

The rules of structured mediation not only are explicit and unbiased but also contain some specific items that distinguish the structured mediation model from other approaches. For example, caucuses between the mediator and one spouse are prohibited. Since the issue of trust is fundamental to the success of mediation (Deutsch, 1973), Coogler maintained that individual meetings or phone calls were more counterproductive than helpful. This absence of an opportunity to sway the mediator protects the integrity of the mediation process and the role of the mediator.

By ensuring confidentiality, the rules are also designed to prevent one party from using the mediation process to obtain information for use in litigation. The parties agree not to call the mediator to testify in court nor to adversarily introduce in court information obtained during settlement negotiations. This rule is based on Federal Rule of evidence 408, which according to Jokipii (1984) has been adopted by all 50 states, either by directly enacting the Federal rule, by enacting their own statute or by adopting the principle through case law. This rule speaks both to trust between the parties and to the protection of the mediator. Furthermore, it encourages adherence to the rule requiring full financial disclosure, by protecting such disclosure (Grebe, in press-a).

Participants begin the structured mediation process on an equal footing, as each understands what is expected of them and of the other party. The rules are clear, unambiguous, and consistent, making it easier for a couple, as naive negotiators, to bargain effectively and fairly with each other. The couple agree to the rules of the game and understand what those rules are before they begin the process. Surprises are eliminated or lessened, and the uncertainty that can fuel the emotional fire of the situation is avoided or considerably decreased.

Theoretical support for a framework of mediation rules comes primarily from the work of Morton Deutsch. In *The Resolution of Conflict* (1973), Deutsch writes; "It is evident that conflict can be limited and controlled by institutional forms, . . . social roles, . . . rules for conducting negotiations, . . . and specific procedures" (p. 377). When mediation is viewed as an institutional form, the role of the mediator as intervenor becomes legitimized. Structured mediation is a means of limiting conflict through the use of rules for the negotiations and by specific procedures to encourage open communication.

Deutsch states that one of the most important functions of the third-party intervenor or mediator is to assist inexperienced or "naive" negotiators by establishing norms for rational interaction. The parties to the conflict are "helped to fight fairly under rules that prevent them from hitting below the belt or yelling foul when a fair but intense exchange is taking place" (Bach & Wyden, 1969, cited in Deutsch, 1973, p. 384). Rubin and Brown (1975) postulate that norms that govern the bargaining process heighten the staying power or endurance of the bargaining relationship. Each rule is a "contractual norm, a commonly understood and agreed upon prescription for acceptable behavior, which . . . specifies the rules to be observed as well as the sanctions that may be applied for their violation" (Thibaut & Francheux, 1965, cited in Rubin & Brown, 1975, p. 13).

With most separating and divorcing couples, neither spouse is likely to have used constructive negotiation skills during marital disputes. Most people have no experience with fighting fairly. They need coaching, and as in any game, they can benefit from a clearly defined set of rules that prevent surprises or misunderstandings about procedure. According to Deutsch (1973), "Fair rules of procedure are valuable in any kind of discussion, but are vital in conflicts. The essence of fair rules is that they are unbiased" (p. 385).

For the rules to be of value, they must be adhered to. Inexperienced mediators are often concerned with how to assure this adherence. This is accomplished partly by the mediator's being knowledgeable about the rules and the purposes they serve in facilitating settlement, and partly by the form of the rules themselves. Deutsch (1973, pp. 379–380) outlines eight conditions that encourage the adherence to a set of rules. These are listed below with comments describing the relevant process in structured mediation.

1. *The rules are known.* Each party receives and reviews a copy of the structured mediation rules during the orientation session.

2. *The rules are clear, unambiguous, and consistent.* The structured mediation rules are read and explained and continually referred to. There are no ruels that preclude other rules. (The rules have recently been revised to provide a more logical order and to eliminate stuffy language [Grebe, 1987].)

3. *The rules are not perceived to be biased against one's own interests.* In structured mediation one's own interests are not defined as rights under the law, but as one's survival needs and as receiving equal treatment. For example, no one is presumed to be a better parent because of gender, and no one receives a larger or smaller portion of assets because of past earning ability. This is known as the "norm of equity" (J. S. Adams, 1965, cited in Rubin & Brown, 1975, p. 13). The norm of equity exists when one party perceives that the ratio of his or her outcome to input is equal to that of the other party. This norm may act to stabilize the bargaining relationship by specifying the rule by which parties allocate or divide their resources (Rubin & Brown, 1975).

4. *The other adheres to the rules.* The structured mediation rules provide a set of procedures for dealing with a violation of the rules; for example, if marital assets are sold before an agreement is reached, the injured party may seek restitution. In addition, the rule on confidentiality is designed to restrict misuse of the mediation process by a person not truly committed to mediation.

5. *Violations are quickly known by significant others.* This refers to the ability of the mediator or the spouse to detect a violation. In theory, a violation may never be discovered; however, most of the rules are rules of procedure and process, and violations would be self-evident. Violations of confidentiality and full financial disclosure seem to cause most concern among professionals. Familiarity with tax returns, financial statements, and knowledge of human behavior will keep violations to a minimum.

6. *There is significant social approval for adherence and significant social*

disapproval for violation. At present the burden of social approval and disapproval rests with the mediator. If the mediator is fairly strict in applying the rules, the parties to the dispute are more likely to stay within the guidelines. If the mediator allows a lot of discussion and negotiation about the rules, the necessary tasks of mediation will suffer, and the effectiveness of the mediator as social conscience will be undermined. As mediation has become more widely known and accepted as a means for resolving marital disputes, social approval for adherence to the process has broadened in scope.

7. *Adherence to the rules has been rewarding in the past.* As the couple progress through mediation and a history of cooperation is built, the significance of the rules will be reinforced.

8. *One would like to be able to employ the rules in the future.* One rule of structured mediation is that spouses agree to mediate future disputes. If the reason they used mediation in the first place was to avoid the adversarial system, they are more likely to want to mediate in the future as well. If one spouse knowingly violates a rule, he or she is lessening the chance that the other spouse will choose to mediate in the future. The other spouse is less likely to cooperate with someone who has not honored the initial contract and commitment to the rules.

In summary, the structured mediation rules are designed to provide a structure for the couple that facilitates their decision making and provides a frame of reference for those decisions. The roles of the participants are clearly defined, issues and situations are clearly outlined, and procedures are provided for an orderly resolution. In contracting to mediate, the couple agree to adopt these rules and to engage in cooperative behavior.

FOUR SETTLEMENT AREAS IN MEDIATION

Mediation of separation and divorce, regardless of the approach used, deals principally with four main issues or settlement areas: division of marital property, child support, spousal maintenance, and custody. In some settings, such as court-connected mediation services, child custody may be the only issue addressed (Coogler, 1981a; Coogler, 1982; Pearson et al., 1983).

Regardless of which settlement areas will be discussed in mediation, all are interrelated in scope and interconnected in the ultimate resolution. Property decisions may affect income. Living arrangements of the children and the expenses incurred will have an effect on child support. A mediator who is restricted to dealing with just one issue may feel that mediation is incomplete because the settlement of one issue may not be considered in the determination of the other issues in another setting. However, attempting to deal with all the issues together may prolong mediation and lessen the likelihood of settlement, particularly when each area is large and complex. Couples tend to confuse the issues, tying them together in ways that lock them, either inadvertently or purposefully, into one solution (Grebe, 1986b). The couple may then feel overwhelmed by the seeming magnitude of their task. When people feel overwhelmed and frustrated, they tend to become defensive and combative, contrary to what is desirable in mediation.

The literature on this subject reflects the differences in attitude about whether it is more effective to deal with issues one at a time or to deal with them as a package. Coogler's approach in structured mediation (1978) is to address the issues one at a time, in a specific order. Deutsch (1973) holds that the more manageable the size of the issue, the easier it is to resolve. Folberg & Taylor (1984) say that the mediator translates gigantic concerns into smaller items that can be decided one at a time. Rubin and Brown's review of the research (1975) implies that what they term the logrolling approach is most effective. Moore (1986) agrees that logrolling is effective, but he defines it as trading components of differing importance. Rubin and Brown define logrolling as creating a package deal and note that once the number of items to be dealt with increases beyond five, separating them out may be more effective. This apparent disagreement may just be semantics. Property division, custody, spousal maintenance, and child support are settlement *areas*. Each may have a number of internal *issues* to be resolved that can be taken together.

In structured mediation, Coogler postulates both the need for a final package deal and the need, during mediation, to separate the settlement areas of marital property, child support, spousal maintenance, and custody into distinct units. These units are further separated into more manageable subunits or issues. For example, a couple may deal easily with fitting work schedules together with living arrangements for their children, but find resolving the larger issue of custody both threatening and difficult. The actual size of the subunit depends on the couple. They are active participants in defining whether an issue is large or small (Deutsch, 1973).

Coogler held that allowing the couple to resolve small pieces of the controversy helps the couple maintain their commitment to the process and provides for continued success. The self-esteem of a spouse who may have felt less powerful in the relationship is enhanced through successful completion of manageable tasks. A more confident spouse cannot dominate the other by complicating the issues. By addressing the settlement areas one at a time, the mediator can prevent the subterfuge that may occur when one or both spouses has a hidden agenda. The Martins are an example. They came in for mediation, each wanting sole custody of their three children. They declared they would not budge on this issue, thereby immediately issuing a challenge to the mediator's ability to work with them. Upon exploration, it became clear to the mediator that Mr. Martin thought he could avoid paying child support if he had custody of the children, and that Mrs. Martin felt she would automatically receive the house if she had custody. If maintained, these initial positions would automatically result in the parties ending in impasse on this issue. The format of structured mediation forced the couple to deal with each settlement area separately and allowed them to resolve the dispute to their satisfaction.

The goals of most divorcing couples are financial and emotional independence. By structuring the order of the settlement areas, the mediation process encourages and supports the couple in achieving this independence.

The order in which these areas are addressed in the structured mediation format is in the sequence of custody, division of property, and support. This is diagrammed in Figure 12-1. Only if custody is hotly contested will it be taken out of this order and dealt with at the end of mediation. When this occurs, it has important ramifications for the mediation process that will be discussed later in this section.

"Custody" generally refers to providing the child's primary place of residence and to being responsible for decisions regarding the child's upbringing (Figure 12-1). Decisions about religious instruction, educational needs, and health care may be readily resolved in mediation. Most parents, however, do not initially view custody in such a manner. The Arthurs are a typical example. Mrs. Arthur said she wanted sole custody. Mr. Arthur said he wanted joint custody. Neither had a clear picture in mind when they used those terms. Mrs. Arthur explained that she was a teacher in the school where their daughter was enrolled. She could easily take her to and from school. Her husband's job was in the next city, and Mrs. Arthur concluded that transportation for their daughter would be difficult for him. Mr. Arthur countered by saying he could change his schedule in order to be more available and stated that he would like to be with his daughter half of the time.

Mr. and Mrs. Arthur were operating under misconceptions about the meaning of custody and the effects of their proposals on their personal lives. Mr. Arthur wanted joint custody and assumed it meant his daughter had to live with him half of the time. Further discussion revealed that what he really wanted was continued participation in his daughter's life, including input into major decisions about her welfare. Mrs. Arthur assumed that since she had previously provided the major portion of the care of their daughter, this should continue. When Mrs. Arthur explored this further, she found that she would actually prefer something other than total responsibility for their child. She concluded she would welcome Mr. Arthur's increased participation in their child's life, that he was not a bad father, and that it would help her if he had their daughter more often. Reflectively, they agreed that they had shared the major parenting decisions during their marriage and wanted to continue doing so. Mr. and Mrs. Arthur agreed that their daughter would spend approximately 70% of the time with her mother and 30% with her father. They called the arrangement joint custody.

When custody is in severe dispute, it will be mediated as the last settlement area. When resolution of custody is postponed in this way, structured mediation requires that the couple fill out two budgets rather than one. Each spouse fills out one budget as though the arrangement he or she wants will be the final one and a second budget as though the other spouse's proposed arrangement will ultimately prevail. If one party has a hidden agenda, such as avoiding support by having sole custody or automatically retaining the marital home by having primary residence, he or she is forced to decide if such deception in the mediation is worth the amount of work involved in both preparing two separate budgets. Often this motivates the couple to come up with a speedier resolution to the custody issue. Following the preparation of the two budgets,

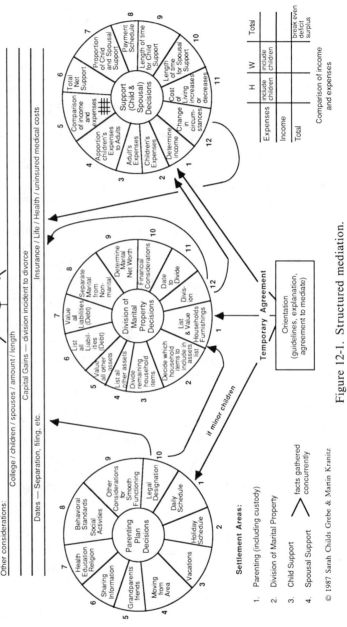

Figure 12-1. Structured mediation.

234

the couple must discuss and agree upon expenses and determine support in both circumstances. This method allows for the separation of issues so the couple can focus on the best solution for each area. The situation where one spouse is talking about apples when the other is discussing oranges is avoided. In practice, this process is rarely necessary, as resolution of custody as the first area is facilitated by the structured mediation format.

During the orientation session (Figure 12-1), the couple are given a packet of forms to assist them in fully disclosing information about their property, income, and expenses (Grebe et al., 1985). Once the custody issue is settled, or postponed if contested, the mediator moves the couple on to a discussion of the property division (Figure 12-1). The financial disclosure forms provide for a listing of all property, including assets and liabilities. The couple must determine what is marital property and agree on a value before it can be divided. Should a parent providing primary residency for the children wish to remain in the house, the couple need to evaluate this, given their overall financial situation.

Additionally, the couple need to determine which assets are liquid and which are income producing. A spouse receiving a larger share of the liquid assets may, for example, be able to reinvest the assets to provide for future income. The couple might decide that the spouse with the lower salary will receive a larger portion of the income-producing assets. As a result of the negotiations on property, the couple may find that the need for support is lessened or possibly eliminated. For this reason, it is important to mediate property issues before support.

In structured mediation, all financial arrangements, both for property and support, are based on need and ability to pay. An accurate accounting of all income and expenses is crucial to the settlement of support. The spouses' combined expenses must be within the limits of their combined income (Figure 12-1). If there is a deficit, budgets must be trimmed (the usual case) or additional income generated. Once these combined expenses and incomes are adjusted, the couple separate them back out to determine support. This particular settlement area offers a great deal of opportunity for the mediator to provide reality testing.

A case in point are the Collinses. Mr. Collins had a low-middle-income job. Mrs. Collins wanted to continue running a seasonal business that required long hours for not much return. This was made particularly difficult because there were two young children. The Collinses tried every way possible to come up with an arrangement that would allow Mrs. Collins to keep her business and that would cover child care costs, plus all their other expenses. They were unable to project an accurate and guaranteed income for Mrs. Collins. After exploring all the options, Mrs. Collins realized she could not justify this type of employment. She was able to obtain a permanent position where her income was nearly equal to that of Mr. Collins. The additional and stable income enabled them to cover their expenditures, including a buy-out of the marital home at a later date and the payments on a new car.

Whether helping a couple resolve a dispute regarding buying a car as part of their settlement or regarding establishing a workable time-sharing arrangement for the children, the mediator must be able to guide the couple through the issues to maximize the benefits to all members of the restructured family. The procedure called for in structured mediation enables the mediator to do that by providing for a logical progression through the four settlement areas. The issues are addressed one by one and in a specific order. This avoids sidetracking and confusion and takes into account the impact each area has on the next.

Once the couple have reached an agreement, the mediator prepares a memorandum of agreement (Figure 12-1). The structured mediation model then calls for the use of an advisory attorney who reviews the terms of the agreement with the couple and drafts the final separation agreement.

THE ADVISORY ATTORNEY

The role of the advisory attorney is an integral part of the structured mediation model (Coogler, 1977, 1978, Grebe, 1987). The advisory attorney is included in the model to complement the nonadversarial nature of mediation (Marlow, 1985). Mediation clients need an attorney who provides legal knowledge rather than advocacy. Coogler saw these aspects of the legal profession as both separate and separable (1978).

At the conclusion of mediation, the couple, the advisory attorney, and the mediator meet together, usually in the mediator's office. The mediator does not employ or pay the attorney. All fees for the advisory attorney are handled directly between the attorney and the couple.

The advisory attorney serves two functions in structured mediation: (1) as a resource person for the mediator and (2) as legal counsel to the couple after they have reached agreement on all relevant issues. He or she does not *represent* either client. The advisory attorney answers any questions, including those about legal rights, and drafts the separation agreement for the couple's signatures.

The memorandum of agreement forms the basis for the discussion with the attorney. Some attorneys prefer the memorandum to be called a memo of understanding, noting that the word "agreement" implies a contract. A mediator cannot draft a contract. The memorandum is basically a list of the agreements that the couple wish to include in their final separation agreement.

Two main criticisms have been noted regarding the use of the advisory attorney. The primary objection to the use of the advisory attorney is that couples are not advised of their legal rights before entering mediation and consequently cannot make a fully informed decision to mediate. Structured mediation allows couples to enter the process because of what mediation offers them rather than because of what it is replacing. Potential mediation clients come to mediation because they do not want to use the adversary system and they do not want to go to separate attorneys. For them, the issue of rights is secondary. Critics of this process believe that both parties need to know what they are entitled to under the law. Structured mediation holds that the law serves as a guide when a couple cannot agree, not as an absolute limit. A couple seeking a method that allows for self-determination and avoids someone imposing judgment on them are not concerned with what they are entitled to but rather what they consider, fair, and equitable and what is feasible.

Couples may, of course, contract to arrangements different from state law. In Maryland, for example, the law provides that the primary residential parent may have the use of the marital home for up to 3 years. A client being advised of his or her rights in this instance could be told that he or she would not be awarded the house for longer than that by a judge. The couple can, in fact, agree to any length of time they want, regardless of what the law would impose in court if they were unable to reach agreement.

Another objection to the advisory attorney is that he or she is not brought into the process until the couple have substantially reached agreement. Critics of this process state that this is too late. They are concerned that mediation clients will decide on one thing without knowing they can get something else and that the couple will have expended so much energy in reaching the agreement that they will be unwilling to reevaluate their agreement even when they find out they could have gotten something better. Couples in structured mediation accept the underlying premises of the process, that both spouses should receive what they need to live on and that no one should be taken advantage of. No one gets less because they are accused by their spouse of misconduct, or because they didn't earn as much as the other spouse during the marriage, or because of any other limiting provision that might be in the law.

This does not mean that couples feel their agreements are set in stone. Couples are repeatedly advised that what they are striving for is agreement in principle on the issues. They are told that the advisory attorney may show them a different way to accomplish the same thing or indicate that the consequences of their decisions are such that they may want to consider doing something else. Since mediation involves the development and exploration of all relevant options, the couple are aware that what they decide is not the only way to resolve the issue. They know that the lawyer may point out legal implications or tax consequences and that this advice may require them to reevaluate ways to implement their agreements.

The Howards exemplify such a situation. In 1983 they worked out detailed budgets for each of their new housholds and made a thorough accounting of their salaries and other income. Mrs. Howard found that her income was $350 less than her expenses each month. Mr. Howard found he had a surplus of about $400 each month. They had been informed by the mediator that alimony is taxable to the recipient and deductible for the payor. In addition, they knew that child support is neither taxable nor deductible. The advisory attorney told them, because of their different tax brackets it would be to their advantage, under then prevailing tax rulings, to have the support unallocated (a provision no longer available); Mr. Howard could pay $625 per month, which would net Mrs. Howard more after taxes than they originally agreed but would not cost Mr. Howard any more because of the increased deduction. The Howards readily agreed to this change and asked the attorney to incorporate it into their agreement.

A third objection to using an advisory attorney is that this role violates the conflict-of-interest provisions of the *Model Code of Professional Responsibility* (American Bar Association [ABA], 1980) for attorneys. Coogler's (1978) reading of the code led him to conclude that people with this reservation are citing the provision (DR5-105A) in which an attorney must represent one party as an advocate. He agreed that in such situations the lawyer may not give advice to the opposing party. Coogler noted, however, that there are other provisions (DR5-105C, EC5-14, EC5-15, and EC5-16) in the code that outline conditions under which an attorney may be employed by multiple clients. Specifically, these provisions allow for the representation of multiple clients if this can be done adequately and if each client understands the possible effects of such representation and consents to it (code provision, DR5-105C). In addition, a lawyer may undertake or continue representation of multiple clients once he or she is certain that professional judgment will not be impaired or professional loyalty divided. The representation of multiple clients should not involve litigation. If litigation is necessary, the lawyer would have to withdraw from employment. Each client should also have the opportunity to obtain other counsel if so desired (code provisions EC5-14, EC5-15, EC5-16).

The role of the advisory attorney as defined by the structured mediation rules falls within these conditions. An impartial, advisory attorney is not an advocate for either party. He or she is mandated by the rules to give fair, equal, and impartial advice to both parties. The parties are no longer in dispute when the advisory attorney enters the process. What they have is the product of a cooperative interaction; they are in agreement. Their goal with the advisory attorney is to learn if what they have decided is feasible and, if so, the best means of implementation. If a dispute should occur at this point, the couple return to mediation and the advisory attorney withdraws until the dispute is resolved. The impartial advisory attorney must also withdraw should the couple decide not to continue with mediation and seek instead to resolve their dispute through the adversary system.

The specific objections addressed here are those leveled at the role of the advisory attorney, not those directed at the process of mediation itself. The objections to mediation typically focus on the unauthorized practice of law and are not unique to structured mediation (Coogler, 1982).

It is significant that the previously noted objections generally come from lawyers and not from mediation clients. Most clients prefer the opportunity for both to be present when conferring with the advisory attorney. They also like the cost savings. They are no longer interested in learning, for example, that she gave up more than she had to or that he could have gotten more than he did. They have specifically refuted that win–lose competitive stance. The couple made their decisions in mediation because they thought these were fair and workable. To arrive at something different from what the law provides does not make it either inadvisable or illegal.

ACHIEVING A HISTORY OF AGREEMENT

Mediators are often asked how long mediation takes. Coogler (1978) maintained that four 2-hour sessions are sufficient for most cases. Many professionals express surprise at the brevity and doubt that one could effectively deal with all the issues in such a short period of time. Therapists are accustomed to dealing with the emotional aspects of separation and divorce and know that there is not a quick resolution to those issues. Brown (1976a), among others, has indicated that most people begin to resolve these issues over a period of at least 2 years. Lawyers find themselves having to deal with unresolved and escalating emotions, without the needed psychological training. Their experience is that working toward a settlement with angry, feuding spouses can take considerably longer than 4 weeks.

Some practitioners of mediation have adopted a traditional view of negotiation and state that the mediating couple must go through a set of stages similar to those identified in labor negotiations. There is a prenegotiation stage where the parties decide whether they will bargain formally or not. The parameters of the negotiations are determined, and the issues are defined. Preliminary demands and proposals occur, and final agreements are reached as the parties make concessions here and stand firm there. Once all is decided, negotiations are closed down. It is characteristic of this type of negotiation that there are no real boundaries between issues; anything may be discussed before the issues are narrowed down. This approach can be bewildering because of the nature of the dispute between separating and divorcing spouses, the emotionality of the situation, the potential complexity of the issues, and the naïveté of the couple as negotiators. Couples in conflict need some immediate sense of accomplishment in mediation in order to stay engaged in the process.

Separating couples may need help in seeing the value of mutually decided solutions in mediation (Deutsch, 1973). Few people will try something new and make it work unless they understand its value. They need to understand that the mediator does not make agreements for them or stand in judgment. An explanation of the concept of a win–win solution in contrast to a win–lose one can help spouses decide to work together.

The procedures in structured mediation help a couple arrive at their common goal. Once the couple have agreed on something, however small, the mediator has a tool to encourage them to continue finding points of agreement. Coogler (1978) based his structured mediation model on providing couples with a history of agreement within the mediation sessions. This helps to eliminate protracted negotiations and allows clients to quickly arrive at a workable solution.

This history of agreement making can be initiated in the first session with the temporary agreement as shown in Figure 12-1. In Structured Mediation, the temporary agreement provides stability by establishing the status quo, that is, documenting the conditions and agreements under which the couple are operating and allowing the couple a quick method of achieving security for the duration of mediation. The temporary agreement provides a sense of accomplishment and commitment to the process. The Rogers are an example. They had just separated;

Mrs. Rogers moved out, leaving Mr. Rogers in the house. The children were staying with Mr. Rogers, who wanted to ensure that he could meet expenses while negotiating a permanent agreement. Mrs. Rogers had agreed to pay support, and this was entered onto their temporary agreement form. The Rogerses did not get stuck in negotiating specifics because they knew this was not a permanent arrangement. The temporary agreement allowed them to proceed with mediation, since their immediate needs were taken care of, and gave them an immediate sense of accomplishment. The temporary agreement does not need to lock a couple into a certain way of resolving a situation, as later Mr. Rogers agreed that Mrs. Rogers would pay for certain expenses directly rather than transferring money to Mr. Rogers as support.

Another area where couples are aided in achieving resolution is through instruction in proper communication techniques (Grebe, 1986a, 1986c). For example, couples are shown how to present proposals constructively; permission to block unproductive interchanges is sought by the mediator and utilized if such exchanges take place. The following case description shows how such instruction was used.

The Richards could not get through a session without throwing barbs at each other. If allowed, they would sidetrack onto any past transgression, real or imaginary. It was difficult for the mediator to block these interchanges and move the parties back on task. However, if this was not accomplished, there would be no movement toward resolution. The Richards presented a challenge to the mediation process and to the mediator. Each had come in with certain issues that they considered nonnegotiable. The patterns of communication were fixed and destructive, and the Richards usually lost sight of their objectives and the mediation process. The mediator had to move them off these positions and prevent their combative interaction. Each time they were blocked from continuing this destructive pattern, they made progress and would even thank the mediator for preventing further escalation. They had to be constantly reminded of their progress and shown that, in contrast to their marital history, they could cooperate in mediation. They finally arrived at a workable and fair settlement.

An effective strategy with this couple was to remind them that they were working together for the best interests of their children. This meant that they needed to work cooperatively. Since they worked best on issues concerning the children, this served to put them on task and remind them of previous positive interactions. Many couples come into mediation having lost sight of cooperation in their marriage. The mediator's job is easier if the couple can recall past cooperative efforts. The couple's agreement to come to an orientation session is a positive first step and can be referred to in encouraging further cooperation.

Couples often feel lost and confused when faced with all the areas to be resolved in separation. The mediator reduces the couple's sense of being overwhelmed by taking the issues to be decided and breaking them down into smaller pieces. The Smiths, for example, were unable to agree on custody or even discuss it calmly. Neither could say what they wanted without getting upset and verbally attacking the other. The mediator had them stop and asked them to think about which holidays they wanted to spend with the children.

They did this readily. From there, they decided on summer vacations and progressed to a weekly schedule. That father was to have the children Wednesday through Sunday, twice a month, and once overnight during the weeks they were living with the mother. They were told they had just worked out approximately a 60%–40% time-sharing arrangement for their children. They were surprised that they had fought so little during this discussion. They then talked about how they wanted to handle religion. They had always agreed on this area in the past and saw no reason to have difficulty with it now. When questioned about medical care, they agreed they would discuss any treatment their children needed. They responded to questions about education in a similar fashion. The mediator informed them that they had just concluded a custody agreement. They were astonished. They had been so concerned about what the custody label implied they had not been able to focus on the issue. When the area of custody was separated into its component parts, the Smiths were able to work together on it. The fear level and the need to lash out in self-defense were reduced. The Smiths agreed to joint custody.

The Smiths illustrate that a more effective bargaining situation results from appealing to an individual's rational, rather than emotional, side. The Smiths were encouraged to look at the facts of their situation—job schedules, school locations, summer vacations, and camp. This approach led to a logical and workable time-sharing arrangement. It kept them from becoming fixated on who is the better parent or what their custody arrangement might say about them to other people.

These three families, the Rogerses, the Richards, and the Smiths, provide examples of how to shorten the mediation process by building on the successful resolution of issues. When Coogler (1978) developed structured mediation, he believed that this element was as important as all the others (i.e., definitions, format, and advisory attorney). He felt couples need a speedy resolution to their dispute in order to reduce the escalation of hostilities between them. The temporary agreement, the instruction in productive communication styles, the fostering of rationality, and breaking the dispute into manageable pieces are all ways to accomplish this goal.

VARIATIONS ON A THEME

In this section, the structure, rules, advisory attorney, and format of structured mediation will be reexamined in light of changes practitioners have made in those aspects that make Structured Mediation a unique model.

Rule Changes

The rules of structured mediation are subject to considerable experimentation among mediators who claim to practice the structured model. Some practitioners eliminate certain provisions, such as arbitration or the advisory attorney, or reword the existing rules to eliminate the legal jargon. Others have either expanded or condensed the rules.

Expanding, rewriting, or eliminating certain rules does not mean a person is not practicing structured mediation. Not every rule has equal importance (Grebe, 1987). However, there are certain rules that, if eliminated, clearly reduce the effectiveness of having rules. An example is the need for a definition of the four settlement areas and the provision for full financial disclosure, including the preparation of budgets and financial statements. In contrast, the mediator's written concurrence or nonconcurrence to an agreement is an example of a rule that is useful but not essential.

Many mediators find themselves reinserting certain provisions after they encounter a case where that rule would have been useful. One mediator, thinking it superfluous, eliminated the rule that prohibits a party from liquidating or transferring more than 10% of the assets during mediation without notifying the other spouse 10 days before the proposed transfer, regardless of whether it involved marital assets. This mediator then encountered a case where property in dispute was transferred by a spouse claiming it as his sole property. Because the rule was not in use, the spouse transferring the property felt justified in his action and the other spouse felt she had no recourse. The mediator was able to help the couple work this out, but it was a difficult situation and might have been prevented. One function of the rules is to alert people to actions that they might think acceptable but which could be counterproductive. In the case just cited, the spouse transferring the assets thought there was no question the property was his and not the marital estate's. Had the rule been in use, he would have known in advance that such a transfer could be problematic.

Contracts

Contracting for services is not unique to structured mediation. Many service providers contract with their clients or patients. Rarely, however, is the contract as detailed and formal as the one used in structured mediation.

There are good reasons to contract with mediation clients. A contract requires a commitment to the process, sets fees, and defines each participant's role. It is an effective means of determining if both parties intend to cooperate (Grebe, 1984). The contract introduces the couple to the general concept of agreement making and the idea that they can legally contract for something other than what the law provides. The temporary agreement is a further use of a contract. Ultimately, the couple will sign their final separation agreement, which is also a contract.

A mediator can practice without a contract and still practice structured mediation, but there are risks involved. One such risk is that unless the parties agree not to, they can more easily call the mediator to testify if their dispute goes into litigation (Jokipii, 1984).

Temporary Custody and Separation Agreements

Mediation can be, and often is, practiced without a temporary agreement. As discussed above, the temporary agreement provides a sense of security and an immediate sense of accomplishment for spouses beginning mediation. Mediators need to be aware that it has been suggested that the use of a temporary agreement by nonlawyer mediators constitutes the unauthorized practice of law. This concern may be lessened if a standard form is used, as is the case in structured mediation. Mediators may also want to obtain expert opinion on tax matters, such as whether a written temporary support agreement is sufficient to establish payment of alimony for tax purposes.

Part of a Professional Team

Working with other professionals is an important consideration in any type of mediation. Recognizing the need for experts other than the advisory attorney, knowing how to work with them (Grebe, in press, a) deciding when to call them in, (Kaslow & Steinberg, 1982) and determining when to refer couples to other professionals (Grebe, in press, b) is more a matter of judgment and experience than a specific and unique aspect of structured mediation.

If a couple are dealing with several therapeutic issues that are blocking the mediation process, it may be advisable to refer them for thereapy (Grebe, in press, a; Kaslow & Steinberg, 1982). It is not advisable, even if the mediator is a therapist, to provide both therapy and mediation to the same couple as this blurs the boundaries of the processes and leads to confusion over the goals. Similarly, if the couple need legal advice and the mediator is a lawyer, it is not advisable for the lawyer to confuse roles by acting as both lawyer and mediator.

The couple may also consult real estate agents, actuaries, estate appraisers, certified public accountants, financial advisers, and others. These experts meet with the parties jointly either in the mediator's office or at the expert's office. The meetings are joint so that one party does not receive information in advance of the other nor furnish or elicit information to his or her advantage.

Co-Mediation

A number of people have described co-mediation or team mediation models (Wiseman & Fiske, 1980; Gold, 1984; Kranitz, 1985). The structured mediation rules provide the co-mediation be conducted by a male–female team. The rationale is that couples requesting two mediators want such a balance. Coogler (1979c) additionally hoped that co-mediators would work in lawyer–therapist teams, though this pairing is not specified in the rules. The goal of this pairing is for lawyers and therapists to share skills and knowledge and for each to appreciate the other's area of expertise and profession. This goal is different from that of others (Gold, 1984; Wiseman & Fiske, 1980) who propose that the co-mediator who is also a therapist handle the emotional aspects of the situation and that the co-mediator who is also a lawyer handle the legal aspects.

Coogler (1977, 1978, 1979a) and others (Girdner, 1986; Grebe, 1986a; Maida, 1986) maintain that the skills, techniques, and knowledge drawn from other professions are useful in mediation. However, the practice of mediation is not merely the amalgamation of these two (or more) professions. In fact, there are distinct differences between the practice of therapy in its various forms (Grebe, in press; Kelly, 1983; Milne, 1985) and mediation, and between the practice of law and mediation (Coogler, 1977, 1978; Marlow, 1985).

The structured mediation model can be practiced with or without co-mediation. There are certain considerations for persons practicing co-mediation to keep in mind. Co-mediation by same-sex mediators is a violation of the structured mediation rules. My sense is that this violation is not particularly important. More important are the negative implications of sex-role stereotyping inherent in the requirement of opposite-sex co-mediator teams. Opposite-sex mediators set up a potential advocacy situation when one party identifies with the mediator of the same sex. This identification is desirable in certain types of therapy but may not be useful in mediation. The goal of mediation is for the couple to take responsibility for their own decisions, including differences of opinion. A spouse may need support for voicing an independent opinion over the short term, but a long-term alignment with one of the mediators is counterproductive. Co-mediation by same-sex mediators may be overwhelming to the lone sex, and opposite-sex teams may foster advocacy. Co-mediators need to be aware of the implications of each type of team (Kranitz, 1985).

Arbitration

The structured mediation rules call for arbitration should the couple reach impasse on a particular issue. Impasse is defined as the couple's inability or unwillingness to resolve an issue within a prescribed amount of time. The couple agree to use the Family Mediation Association's Arbitration Rules. These rules outline the scope of and procedures for arbitration, for choosing an arbitrator (who must be other than the mediator), and initiating the process. The rules for arbitration follow the definitions and guiding principles already agreed to under the mediation rules. Couples could agree to incorporate the same definitions and principles or submit them as evidence while using a different arbitration procedure such as the services provided by the American Arbitration Association (AAA). Because the AAA does not use definitions or established principles for the four settlement areas, the incorporation of the structured mediation definitions already in use by the couple could facilitate the procedure.

Arbitration, in fact, is rarely used, (Meroney, 1979; Grebe, in press, a) and couples initially may be resistant to having to agree to it. They often do not understand the process. An agreement to arbitrate limits the scope of arbitration to the single issue at impasse, whereas it is within a judge's discretion to render a decision on all issues and wipe out any cooperative decisions the couple may have reached and want to keep in effect. Arbitration allows the couple to feel confident that they have time to present all the facts, unrestricted by a crowded court calendar. Nevertheless, some mediators have removed the arbitration rule because they cannot justify including any adversarial procedure in mediation. The removal of the arbitration rule may be more a result of the mediator's inability to accurately describe the process than an objection to its appropriateness. Without the provision to arbitrate impasses, couples have no other choice but to obtain attorneys and possibly go to court. Thus, removal of the arbitration rule weakens the nonadversarial nature of mediation rather than strengthening it.

Transactional Analysis

When Coogler developed the structured mediation model, he drew on his background as a practitioner of Transactional Analysis (TA). TA is the theory of relationships developed by Eric Berne, MD, author of *Games People Play* (1964) (also described in TA primers). TA is based on a psychological approach to interactions, rather than the sociological perspective of investigators such as Morton Deutsch (1973) and Rubin and Brown (1975). In TA terms, the Adult ego state is the mediator, the part of us that works with the facts of the situation to reach a decision by using a rational problem-solving orientation. The Parent ego state can be either supportive or critical as our parents were when we were children, and the Child ego state can be free of the internal parent or reactive to it. Coogler used the principles of TA as a theoretical springboard for a rational, problem-solving approach to mediation and as a source of communication techniques for dealing with the major conflict styles encountered in mediation couples (Coogler, 1979a).

Structured mediation is designed to encourage and foster the use of the Adult ego state (Coogler et al., 1979). Couples are required to gather facts and base their decisions on those facts. The mediator is appealing to a disputant's Adult and does not need to play the nurturing Parent to a disputant's fearful Child. Couples are blocked from finding fault (the critical Parent) or from trying to please or undermine the other person (the adapted Child). They are assumed to be adults capable of operating in a rational, responsible manner.

A mediator can practice structured mediation without being a practitioner of Transactional Analysis. The Transactional Analysis definition of conflict styles and methods of intervention are effective and time-saving tools in mediation, but they are neither necessary nor sufficient components of structured mediation. Probably just as crucial is knowledge of the divorce process (Brown 1976b; Kessler, 1975) and how this impacts divorce mediation (Grebe, 1985).

CONCLUSION

Perhaps the spirit of what Coogler wanted to accomplish in structured mediation is best captured in these lines taken from his poem "Fair Share" (Coogler,
1981b).

> It's O.K. if the Mediator
> Talks about bargaining
> About dividing
> About giving and taking—
> But I don't know how
> To bargain about you.
> About me.
> Or about the children—
> But we can take the broken pieces
> And mend and shape them—
> Not as they were—
> But in a new way—
> Not into pieces for use
> As bargaining chips—
> But into parts that we can share
> With each other
> With our children
> As we begin our separate paths.

Structured mediation resulted from a very personal experience of conflict:
O. J. Coogler's own divorce. He took this unhappy and dissatisfying experience and developed a procedure for resolving conflict that has had far-
reaching ramifications.

Compared to other approaches, the structured mediation model has certain features that are unique: the structure and format of the sessions, the rules
that define the settlement areas and the participants' roles, the use of an
advisory attorney, the provision for arbitration, and the use of the contract to
mediate. The structured mediation rules enable even the most inexperienced
couple to negotiate on an equal footing and to restructure their lives at a time
of family crisis. The structure guides the couple through mediation in a timely
and efficient manner without sacrificing accuracy and accountability.

The structured mediation model has been in use for over 14 years, longer
than any other approach developed for use with separating and divorcing couples. Before his death, Coogler (1979b) had modified his model to meet the needs
of the divorcing poor as well. Although it has generated criticism of certain of its
features (e.g., the advisory attorney provisions), resulting in changes by some
mediators, Structured Mediation continues to be practiced around the country.
According to an important study, more mediators in both the private and public
sector have received Coogler-based training than any other single model (Pearson, Ring, & Milne, 1983). Clearly, structured mediation has had a most significant influence in the development of divorce mediation.

REFERENCES

American Bar Association. *Model code of professional responsibility*. Chicago: Author, 1980.

Berne, E. *Games people play*. New York: Grove Press, 1964.

Brown, E. Divorce counseling. In D. H. L. Olson (Ed.), *Treating relationships* (pp. 399–429). Lake Mills, IA: Graphic Press, 1976a.

Brown, E. A model of the divorce process. *Conciliation Courts Review*, 1976b, *14*(2), 1–11.

Caplow, T. *Two against one*. Englewood Cliffs, NJ: Prentice-Hall, 1968.

Coogler, O. J. Changing the lawyer's role in matrimonial practice. *Conciliation Courts Review*, 1977, *15*(1), 1–8.

Coogler, O. J. *Structured mediation in divorce settlement: A handbook for marital mediators*. Lexington, MA: D. C. Heath, 1978.

Coogler, O. J. *Basic techniques in marital mediation*. Unpublished paper, 1979a.

Coogler, O. J. Divorce mediation for "low income" families: A proposed model. *Conciliation Courts Review*, 1979b, *17*(1), 21–26.

Coogler, O. J. Structured mediation, 100 hour course. Falls Church, VA, 1979c.

Coogler, O. J. Estimating caseload and personnel requirements in court related conciliation programs. *Conciliation Courts Review*, 1981a, *19*(1), 53–63.

Coogler, O. J. *Fair share*. Unpublished poem, 1981b.

Coogler, O. J. Mediation of divorce settlements: Basic notions. *Fairshare*, 1982, *2*(7), 8–10.

Coogler, O. J., Weber, R. E., & McKenry, P. C. Divorce mediation: A means of facilitating divorce and adjustment. *The Family Coordinator*, 1979, *28*, 255–259.

Deutsch, M. *The resolution of conflict: Constructive and destructive processes*. New Haven, CT: Yale University Press, 1973.

Folberg, J., & Taylor, A. *Mediation: A comprehensive guide to resolving conflicts without litigation*. San Francisco: Jossey-Bass, 1984.

Girdner, L. K. Family mediation: Toward a synthesis. *Mediation Quarterly*, 1986, no. 13, pp. 21–29.

Girdner, L. K. How people settle divorce disputes. Chapter 3, this volume.

Gold, L. Interdisciplinary team mediation. *Mediation Quarterly*, 1984, no. 6, pp. 27–46.

Grebe, S. C. Revised marital mediation rules for structured mediation. In Family Mediation Association training materials, 1982.

Grebe, S. C. Checklist for mediation referral. In *Updating your domestic practice*, p. 10. Charleston, SC: Lowcountry Mediation Network, 1984.

Grebe, S. C. Mediation at different stages of the divorce process. In S. C. Grebe (Ed.), *Divorce and family mediation* pp. 34–47. Rockville, MD: Aspen Publications, 1985.

Grebe, S. C. A comparison of the tasks and definitions of family mediation and those of strategic family therapy. *Mediation Quarterly*, 1986a, no. 13, pp. 53–60.

Grebe, S. C. Issues of separation and loss in custody mediation. *Conciliation Courts Review*, 1986b, *24*(2), 85–90.

Grebe, S. C. Mediation in separation and divorce. *Jorunal of Counseling and Development*, 1986c, *64*, 379–382.

Grebe, S. C. The rules of structured mediation. *Conciliation Courts Review*, 1987, *25*(1), 37–51.

Grebe, S. C. Ethical issues in conflict resolution: Divorce mediation. *Negotiation Journal*, in press, a.

Grebe, S. C. Family mediation training programs: Establishing standards. *Mediation Quarterly*, no. 17, in press, b.

Grebe, S. C., Kranitz, M., & Crockett, C. *Starting your own mediation practice: A workbook*. Annapolis, MD: Casamar Enterprises, 1985.

Jokipii, K. *Adoption of the federal rules of evidence by the 50 states: Confidentiality*. Unpublished project. Family Mediation Association, 1984.

Kaslow, F. W., & Steinberg, J. L. Ethical divorce therapy and divorce proceedings: A psychological perspective. In L. L'Abate (Ed.), *Values, ethics, legalities and the family therapist* (pp. 61–73). Rockville, MD: Aspen Publications, 1982.

Kelly, J. Mediation and psychotherapy: Distinguishing the differences. *Mediation Quarterly*, 1983, no. 1, pp. 33–44.

Kelly, J. *Comparisons of mediated and adversarial divorce: Client satisfaction.* Paper presented at Academy of Family Mediators' 4th annual conference, New York City, 1987.

Kessler, S. *The American way of divorce: Prescriptions for change.* Chicago: Nelson-Hall, 1975.

Kranitz, M. Co-mediation: Pros and cons. In S. C. Grebe (Ed.), *Divorce and family mediation* (pp. 71–79). Rockville, MD: Aspen Publications, 1985.

Kressel, K., Jaffee, N., Tuchman, B., Watson, C., & Deutsch, M. A typology of divorcing couples: Implications for mediation and the divorce process. *Family Process*, 1980, *19(2)*, 101–116.

Maida, P. R. Components of Bowen's family theory and divorce mediation. *Mediation Quarterly*, 1986, no. 12, pp. 51–63.

Marital mediation rules (1st rev. ed.). (Available from the Family Mediation Association, c/o William Neville, 10 Cogswood Rd., Asheville, NC 28804, and from S. C. Grebe, 3514 Plyers Mill Rd., Suite 100, Kensington, MD 20895.) 1982.

Marlow, L. Divorce mediation: Therapists in their own world. *The American Journal of Family Therapy*, 1985, *13(3)*, 3–10.

Meroney, A. E. Mediation and arbitration of separation and divorce agreements. *Wake Forest Law Review*, 1979, *15(4)*, 467–505.

Milne, A. L. Mediation or therapy: Which is it? In S. C. Grebe (Ed.), *Divorce and Family Mediation* (pp. 1–15). Rockville, MD: Aspen Publications, 1985.

Mnookin, R., & Kornhauser, L. Bargaining in the shadow of the law. *Yale Law Journal*, 1979, *88(5)*, 950–997.

Moore, C. W. *The mediation process: Practical strategies for resolving conflict.* San Francisco: Jossey-Bass, 1986.

National Center for Mediation Education, 2083 West Street, Suite 3C, Annapolis, MD 21401.

Parker, A. *A comparison of divorce mediation versus lawyer adversary processes and the relationship to marital separation factors.* Unpublished doctoral dissertation, Heed University, Hollywood, FL 1980.

Pearson, J., Ring, M. L., & Milne, A. A portrait of divorce mediation services in the public and private sector. *Conciliation Courts Review*, 1983, *21(1)*, 1–24.

Pearson, J., & Thoennes, N. The mediation and adjudication of divorce disputes: Some costs and benefits. *Family Advocate*, 1982, *4(3)*, 26–32.

Pearson, J., & Thoennes, N. A preliminary portrait of client reactions to three court mediation programs. *Mediation Quarterly*, 1984, no. 3, pp. 21–40.

Rubin, J., & Brown, B. *The social psychology of bargaining and negotiation.* New York: Academic Press, 1975.

Saposnek, D. T., Hamburg, J., Delano, C. D., & Michaelsen, H. How has mandatory mediation fared?: Research findings of the first year's followup. *Conciliation Courts Review*, 1984, *22(2)*, 7–18.

Transactional Analysis primers. Available from Transactional Publishers, 1772 Vallejo Street, San Francisco, CA 94123.

Vanderkooi, L., & Pearson, J. Mediating divorce disputes: Mediator behaviors, styles and roles. *Family Relations*, 1983, *32*, 557–566.

Wiseman, J. M., & Fiske, J. A. A lawyer–therapist team as mediator in a marital crisis. *Social Work*, 1980, *25*, 442–445.

PART FOUR

DIVORCE MEDIATION TECHNIQUES AND STRATEGIES

13

Techniques to Break Impasse

CHRISTOPHER W. MOORE
CDR Associates, Denver, Colorado

The proficiency of a mediator may be measured by the ability to help disputing individuals avoid or overcome impasse. Previous writings on this topic have described various categories of conflict, mediation interventions, and stages in the negotiation process most susceptible to impasse. This author integrates these perspectives into a useful analysis of the psychological, procedural, and substantive forms of impasse. The author's vast experience in mediation and in training mediators is evident as the reader learns useful techniques to break an impasse.

People who divorce request the assistance of a mediator because they have been unable to negotiate a settlement of issues that divide them. The couple have reached an impasse—a psychological, procedural, or substantive block—that prevents them from moving toward an agreement. A mediator, an impartial and neutral third party whose task is to improve the negotiation process, is sought to break the impasse that binds the couple in conflict and to help them reach agreement. Some authors on mediation have argued that assisting parties to avoid or overcome impasse is *the* most important function of the mediator (Fisher, 1978; Wall, 1981).

This chapter examines some of the causes of impasse, identifies the times in divorce and custody negotiation when impasse is more likely to occur, and describes interventions or techniques commonly used by mediators to overcome impasse and promote agreement. Although mediation is widely practiced in numerous conflicts—family disputes, labor management negotiations, landlord–tenant differences, environmental altercations—little has been written in any of the above arenas about the interventions or strategies initiated by mediators to overcome impasse. What has been written tends to follow two paths of analysis: (1) a description of generic categories of conflict—people problems, procedural problems, and substantive problems—and the interventions or techniques to be initiated by a mediator to overcome them (Fisher, 1978; Maggiolo, 1971); or (2) a linear approach that describes stages in the negotiation process and indicates when a deadlock is most likely to occur (Gulliver, 1979; Kessler, 1978; Pruitt, 1981; Zartman, 1982). These two approaches need to be integrated.

CAUSES OF CONFLICT AND IMPASSE

In examining the causes of impasse it is important to understand first what is producing the conflict itself. While the source of impasse may be closely related to the cause of the conflict, there is not necessarily a direct correlation. For example, a couple's conflict may be over a substantive issue, the amount and kind of visitation that they find acceptable in their new relationship. The cause of the couple's impasse in negotiations, however, may be a lack of awareness of problem-solving or negotiation procedures. The cause of the conflict is substantive; the cause of the impasse is procedural.

Conflicts (or impasses) often have complex causality. Often a variety of interventions or moves will be initiated by a mediator to respond to the diverse causes of the dispute or impasse.

While the variables causing impasse are all intertwined in actual disputes, it is helpful for the sake of analysis to separate various causal factors of both conflicts in general and impasses in particular. In observing numerous disputes there are five major variables that influence the dynamics and potential deadlock of a conflict: (1) relationship factors, (2) data problems, (3) competing or incompatible interests, (4) the structure of the relationship, and (5) diverse values. Each of these can cause impasse. These causes and their components are detailed in Figure 13-1. (Moore, 1986).

Relationship Conflict

Relationship factors refer to a specific set of emotions and behaviors that promote or detract from the positive regard or interaction between two or more people. Four variables tend to produce or influence the development of relationship conflict: strong negative emotions, misperceptions or stereotypes, poor communication, and repetitive negative behavior.

EMOTIONS

Emotions or feelings are complex physiological and psychological reactions based on a person's encounter with the world. Strong negative emotions, such as those encountered by a couple in conflict, may be caused by the immediate interaction between husband and wife in the process of negotiating over perceived or actual incompatible interests, or may be the result of restimulation (Jackins, 1978), the surfacing of feelings that remind a person of past interpersonal relations or events not necessarily directly related to the present situation. This distinction between emotions with basis in the present and restimulated feelings from the past is a valuable concept for mediators. On one hand, the conditions that cause immediate emotions can often be handled by direct intervention of the mediator in the negotiating process. By restructuring the communication or behavior patterns of either spouse, the mediator may be able to limit or eliminate the cause of the immediate negative feelings.

Possible   Data   Interventions

Reach agreement on what data
    are important
Agree on process to collect data
Develop common criteria to assess data
Use third-party experts to gain outside
    opinion or break deadlocks

**Possible   Interest-Based
Interventions**

Focus on interests, not positions
Look for objective criteria
Develop integrative solutions that
    address needs of all parties
Search for ways to expand options
    or resources
Develop trade offs to satisfy interests
    of different strengths

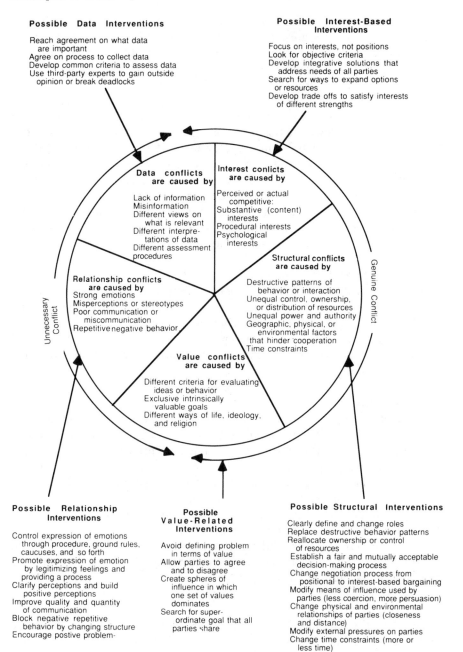

**Data   conflicts
are caused by**

Lack of information
Misinformation
Different views on
    what is relevant
Different interpre-
    tations of data
Different assessment
procedures

**Interest conflicts
are caused by**

Perceived or actual
    competitive:
Substantive (content)
    interests
Procedural interests
Psychological
interests

**Structural conflicts
are caused by**

Destructive patterns of
    behavior or interaction
Unequal control, ownership,
    or distribution of resources
Unequal power and authority
Geographic, physical, or
    environmental factors
    that hinder cooperation
Time constraints

**Relationship conflicts
are caused by**
Strong emotions
Misperceptions or stereotypes
Poor communication or
    miscommunication
Repetitive negative behavior

**Value   conflicts
are caused by**

Different criteria for evaluating
    ideas or behavior
Exclusive intrinsically
    valuable goals
Different ways of life, ideology,
    and religion

*Unnecessary
Conflict*

Genuine Conflict

**Possible   Relationship
Interventions**

Control expression of emotions
    through procedure, ground rules,
    caucuses, and so forth
Promote expression of emotion
    by legitimizing feelings and
    providing a process
Clarify perceptions and build
    positive perceptions
Improve quality and quantity
    of communication
Block negative repetitive
    behavior by changing structure
Encourage postive problem-

**Possible
Value-Related
Interventions**

Avoid defining problem
    in terms of value
Allow parties to agree
    and to disagree
Create spheres of
    influence in which
    one set of values
    dominates
Search for super-
    ordinate goal that all
    parties share

Possible Structural   Interventions

Clearly define and change roles
Replace destructive behavior patterns
Reallocate ownership or control
    of resources
Establish a fair and mutually acceptable
    decision-making process
Change negotiation process from
    positional to interest-based bargaining
Modify means of influence used by
    parties (less coercion, more persuasion)
Change physical and environmental
    relationships of parties (closeness
    and distance)
Modify external pressures on parties
Change time constraints (more or
    less time)

Figure 13-1. Sphere of conflict.

Restimulated feelings, on the other hand, may be harder to handle and overcome because they are the result of past interaction. For a disputant to deal with restimulated feelings, he or she must be able to distinguish the current situation and the emotions it produces from past events that originally initiated the negative feelings. One example of restimulated emotions is what Ricci (1980) refers to as "negative intimacy." When a couple divorce, there is often an accumulation of negative interactions that produce a reservoir of bad feelings. Couples draw upon this sink of emotions to bind them into a negative rather than positive relationship. Negotiations and emotions become tainted by past interactions even when no negative behavior is currently being expressed.

While strong emotions rarely cause a conflict, because they are generally expressions of underlying issues, they do tend to influence the dynamics of a dispute. Handling intense emotions, and especially the degree of expression of feelings, is a crucial area of mediator intervention.

MISPERCEPTIONS AND STEREOTYPES

Misperceptions and stereotypes are the inaccurate images that disputants have of each other. Misperception and stereotypes may be related to the personality, motivation, predicted or expected behavior, or goals of another party. For negotiators to move toward an acceptable settlement, misperceptions and stereotypes must be identified, checked for accuracy, revised, or have their impact minimized.

COMMUNICATIONS

Communication problems are some of the major causes of relationship conflict. By communications we mean verbal or nonverbal signals that are sent and received by disputing parties. Communication problems are the result of inaccurate or inappropriate messages that are sent from one person to another, or problems in listening to or interpreting the messages that are received. Because verbal messages are the major medium by which parties convey messages about what they want and expect from each other, poor verbal communications cause unnecessary conflicts where the parties' interests are in fact the same. For this reason, the intervenor may make a significant effort to improve the quality and, if necessary, the quantity of communication, as a means of managing unnecessary conflict.

REPETITIVE NEGATIVE BEHAVIOR

Some conflict in relationships is caused by specific repetitive behavior, by one or both parties, that hinders productive negotiations. Conflicting negative behaviors are often related to conflict style (Frost & Wilmot, 1978). One party will often start an interaction cycle with a behavior that the other party dislikes. The behavior initiates an escalatory spiral of patterned behavior that is reciprocated by the other person. Managing repetitive negative behavior is crucial if parties are to de-escalate their conflict and reach agreement.

Data Conflict

Data conflict arises from differences in the information used by parties to make a decision. Data conflicts are caused by lack of information, misinformation, diverse views as to what data is relevant, conflicting interpretation of the same data, or differing procedures to assess information. Before a husband and wife can reach an agreement on any substantive question, they must have a common view of relevant data or information and have coordinated their means of assessing its accuracy.

Interest Conflict

Interests are needs or benefits that a party expects to be met or satisfied at the termination of a dispute. Most divorce or custody suits are characterized by a combination of compatible and incompatible interests. The goal of each spouse in negotiations is to maximize the satisfaction of his or her interests, but not to the extent that the other receives so little that they are induced to pursue other means of dispute resolution (i.e., litigation). The effective negotiator attempts to build on compatible interests and to minimize the negative impacts of competing interests. Interest-based conflicts usually occur over a combination of three different categories of interests: substantive benefits, procedural dynamics, and psychological needs.

SUBSTANTIVE BENEFITS OR INTERESTS

Divorcing couples with children must usually reach an agreement on five substantive issues: (1) distribution of marital property, (2) spousal support, (3) child custody, (4) visitation, and (5) child support. Both partners expect to receive at the conclusion of the negotiation some tangible resource—legal rights, money, time with the child, and so forth—by which they can measure the success of the negotiation. Substantive conflicts occur because of perceived or actual incompatibility of substantive needs.

PROCEDURAL INTERESTS

Each party to a negotiation has preferences as to the process or way the decisions about the divorce will be handled. Criteria often used to measure or assess procedural interests or satisfaction include fairness to all the parties, lack of coercion in reaching an agreement, and opportunity to participate in the decision-making process.

PSYCHOLOGICAL INTERESTS

Couples also negotiate over psychological issues and expect interests to be met in this area too. Spouses do not want to be psychologically degraded or debased in the negotiation process. They want to be respected as parents and want to believe that the other spouse is negotiating in good faith. If these needs are not met, agreement and psychological settlement may not be possible. Mediation is not another form of therapy, but the mediation intervention may involve moves to assist the parties to negotiate psychological closure.

Structural Conflict

Structural conflict refers to disputes that develop because of the way a relationship is organized and the patterns of interdependence (independence–dependence) that emerge. Structural conflict is often related to power—its sources, its forms, and the issues over which it is exercised.

Structural variables that influence the dynamics of conflict in a couple include (Galtung, 1975):

• *exploitation*: the degree to which the resources are asymmetrically distributed for the amount of work or energy (the spouses contribute).
• *penetration*: how far the stronger party has been able to penetrate the consciousness of the weaker and create an underdog form of consciousness.
• *fragmentation*: whether the weaker party is structurally separated from people or institutions that would support or empower him or her.
• *marginalization*: the degree to which decision-making power has been concentrated in the hands of one spouse and removed from the other so that the decisions are made unilaterally and without consensus.

Value Conflict

Value conflicts arise over the beliefs and criteria that husbands and wives use for evaluating behavior or differences in intrinsically valuable goals, such as ideologies or religion. Value disputes are extremely difficult to resolve where there is no consensus on appropriate behavior or ultimate goals.

Parents may differ as to how they value each other's sexual behavior or orientation, how much they tell the children about the causes of the divorce, or what an "equal" settlement means. They may also differ about how to achieve intrinsically valuable goals such as economic security or parental relationships with the children. One may define economic security as living luxuriously while the other values comfort but not opulence. One parent may believe that a young child should always stay with his or her mother, while the other wants equal time "because we are both parents."

Values relating to life-style, politics, and religion may also cause conflict. Can the child live with a father who has a gay lover? What kind of religious education should the child have if the father is Jewish and the mother a fundamentalist Christian?

Unnecessary and Genuine Conflict

In reviewing the sphere of conflict in Figure 13-1, we can conclude that disputes (and impasses) have multiple causes. Some disputes, however, are *genuine* or *realistic* in that the objective conditions (interests, structure, or values) for disagreement exist. Other conflicts are *unrealistic*, and in fact *unnecessary*, because the conflict is fueled by strong feeling, misperceptions, poor communications, repetitive negative behavior, lack of information, or misinformation rather than conflicting objective conditions (Coser, 1956). The division of the causes of conflict into unnecessary and genuine is a key concept for disputants and mediators. The goal in productive conflict management is to eliminate the unnecessary relationship and data causes of conflict, so that the parties can focus on genuine issues in contention—interests, structure, and values.

STAGES OF NEGOTIATION AND MEDIATION AND THE OCCURRENCE OF IMPASSE

A variety of researchers and practitioners have postulated theories of negotiations in which disputants progress through a series of identifiable stages and perform specific tasks (Douglas, 1962; Gulliver, 1979). Several researchers have developed stage theories specific to family disputes (Coogler, 1978; Haynes, 1981; Kessler, 1978; Milne, 1981). I prefer a 10-stage theory of negotiation that was developed through previous research into a variety of types of disputes (Moore, 1986). These 10 stages of negotiation are detailed in Table 13-1, as are the specific tasks to be accomplished by the parties in each stage. The stages include (1) searching for an approach and arena; (2) conciliation; (3) determining a negotiation strategy; (4) defining dispute parameters; (5) defining issues and establishing an agenda; (6) identifying interests; (7) generating settlement alternatives; (8) assessing options; (9) final bargaining; and (10) implementing, monitoring, and formalizing the settlement.

The stages of mediation, with a few exceptions, follow the stages of negotiation. The job of the mediator is to assist the parties to move through the stages and accomplish the required tasks. Impasse can occur at a variety of locations along the stages of negotiation and may be caused by multiple factors. It has been noted that impasse is most likely to occur when the parties are making the transition from one stage or task to another (Gulliver, 1979).

In the next section, we will explore each of the five major causes or influences on the dynamics of conflict (relationship, data, interests, structure, and values), describe where they are most likely to occur in the stages of negotiation, and detail some of the mediator moves that may be initiated to respond to the particular type of impasse.

Table 13-1. Stages of Negotiation

Stages	Features
1. Searching for an approach and arena	Assessing various approaches for conflict resolution Selecting an approach Coordinating parties' approaches
2. Conciliation	Preparing psychologically for negotiations Handling strong emotions Checking perceptions and minimizing effects of stereotypes Building trust Clarifying communications
3. Determining negotiation strategy	Identifying interests or needs Identifying issues to be discussed Establishing issue priority Exploring settlement options Designing a general strategy to satisfy interests Preparing an opening strategy
4. Defining dispute parameters	Agreeing on issues that are negotiable Exploring maximal options for the satisfaction of interests
5. Defining issues and establishing an agenda	Identifying issues of importance to each party Ordering issues into a mutually acceptable agenda Selecting first item and beginning to negotiate
6. Identifying interests	Educating parties about interests and needs by position presentation or interest-based negotiations Identification of common and competing interests
7. Generating settlement alternatives	Developing settlement alternatives by position–counterposition process, brainstorming, integrative proposal development, etc.
8. Assessing options	Singly or jointly assessing which options satisfy interests Determining acceptable and unacceptable gains or losses Identifying a bargaining range
9. Final bargaining	Proposing final terms of settlement Converging of parties to an agreement Creating agreements in principle and then making them operational Making minor adjustments in the settlement
10. Implementing, monitoring, and formalizing the settlement	Identifying procedural steps to implement and monitor the settlement Designing a procedure to formalize agreement and encourage commitment to the terms of the settlement

Handling Relationship Problems

It is fair to say that every negotiation over marital issues will have some emotional content. There are, however, specific times in the negotiation process when the presence or expression of strong emotions will be more likely to cause an impasse. The stages in negotiation where these strong feelings most often occur include searching for an approach and arena, where the presence or expression of strong feelings may block the parties from individually or jointly considering a coordinated procedure; conciliation, where the parties are psychologically preparing for negotiations; defining the dispute parameters, where the parties try to convince each other of the general boundaries of issues to be discussed and may test each other's emotional limits; defining issues and establishing an agenda, where the parties identify specific topics and order them for discussion; identifying interests, where the parties attempt to convince each other of specific needs; and final bargaining, where the parties initiate trade-offs, make concessions, or form integrated solutions to their mutual problems and where they attempt to reach psychological settlement.

Yelling or tears are usually not hard to recognize as possible preconditions for emotional deadlock. Emotional impasse, however, may also be expressed in more subtle terms, such as nonverbal withdrawal, failure to talk, constant recycling of the same message, or rhetorical argument. The mediator, upon observing any of the above behaviors, must decide if the parties' feelings are causing impasse. If this is the case, the mediator can initiate moves that respond to the disputant's emotions.

RESPONSES TO EMOTIONAL CAUSES OF IMPASSE

There are three general mediator interventions or responses to current or restimulated emotions when they appear to be influencing the dynamics of the conflict: allow expression of emotions, escalate their expression to promote venting or tension release, or limit their expression.

The mediator may consider the expression of feelings to be productive and may choose not to intervene (1) when the parties are expressing strong feelings about *issues* that divide them but are not degrading the *person* who holds an opposing view (Fisher & Ury, 1981); (2) when the expression of an emotion is serving an educational function in that it explains how intensely a party feels about an issue; or (3) when the expression of the feelings appears to be helpful for cathartic release of tension for one spouse and does not seem to have a detrimental effect on the other. Under the above conditions, the mediator may choose not to intervene and may allow the feelings to be directly expressed.

ESCALATING THE EXPRESSION OF FEELINGS

Numerous researchers and practitioners have stressed the importance of venting emotions as a physiological prerequisite for productive negotiations or problem solving (Bach & Goldberg, 1974; Douglas, 1962; Gordon, 1970; Jackins, 1978). On occasion, the mediator may want to encourage the expression of feelings as a means of moving the parties toward settlement. The principle questions that a mediator should ask when considering a strategy that will escalate the expression of emotions are How can the venting best occur? Does it need to be heard by the other party? What form should it take to have the best effect for the person expressing the feelings and the person hearing them?

To be effective, venting should meet the three criteria for productive release listed above. If the mediator decides that the expression of feelings should be encouraged, he or she should decide if the expression is best achieved through a private caucus (Moore, 1987) between one party and the mediator, where venting can occur out of the presence of the other party, or whether the venting should happen in joint session.

Emotional venting in caucus can be induced or encouraged by the mediator's requesting the party to talk about feelings, actively listening of the disputant (Gordon, 1970), or asking questions about the party's emotions. A caucus focused on feelings must allow adequate time for a disputant to get into feelings, process them, and come out the other side, to be effective. If the mediator does not allow adequate time for processing, the disputant may return to the joint session in more emotional distress than before the caucus was initiated.

Under many circumstances, strong emotions may block the initiation of any productive negotiation. Timing of the emotional stages of divorce and the timing of negotiations clearly has an effect on the ultimate outcome of the dispute and ability of the parties to settle (Pearson, 1981). This often occurs when a couple attempt to begin negotiations too soon after the decision to divorce and one or more of the spouses has not come to terms with the decision to separate. Handling the intense feelings of this enmeshed state (Kressel, 1980) may require a more extended period of time than is available in negotiations. The mediator, under these conditions, may suggest delaying negotiations for a period of time—several weeks to several months—while a couple work through the feelings on their own or with the assistance of a therapist.

DE-ESCALATING THE EXPRESSION OF FEELINGS

In some marital conflicts, the expression of emotions does not lead to productive conflict resolution. This is especially the case in spousal relations where violence has been present. If one party has low impulse control, a history of violence, or difficulty in focusing on the issues, insists on degrading his or her spouse, or appears to want to do psychological damage to his or her partner, then venting in joint session is not appropriate (Berkowitz. 1973; Hokanson, 1970; Straus, 1977). Encouragement of verbal expressions of emotions in these disputes can easily escalate, either in the negotiation session or in later spousal interaction, into physical violence (Straus, 1977). If a mediator suspects, through observation or statements by either spouse, that a display of emotions will lead to dangerous conflict escalation, the major task becomes how to limit the expression of feelings. Several approaches to accomplish this end are having the parties negotiate, or the mediator suggest, an acceptable set of behavioral guidelines that regulate interaction and detail how the parties will be allowed to express their feelings (Bach & Goldberg, 1974); breaking into caucus as soon as strong emotions are expressed; and under extreme circumstances, separating the parties for a significant portion or all of the negotiation sessions and carrying out the bargaining via shuttle diplomacy using the mediator as messenger (Moore, 1983).

MISPERCEPTIONS AND STEREOTYPES

Misperceptions and stereotypes are most common in the early stages of negotiations when the parties are attempting to test and break down negative images of each other and to build trust in the good-faith bargaining of the other party. Misperceptions also occur in midnegotiations when one party initiates activities that restimulate past hurts or other emotions in the other and that shift the parties into stereotyped or patterned negative behavior.

A mediator's recognition of impasse caused by misperception or stereotype is usually triggered by the observation of a discrepancy between the mediator's perception of the issues or parties and the perception of one or more of the disputants. Before assuming that the mediator's perception is correct and that the disputants are misperceiving the situation, the intervenor usually conducts intensive data gathering to verify or disprove his or her hypothesis. If the intervenor believes the parties are operating from a basis of misperception or stereotype, he or she has several options for intervention.

First, the intervenor may establish a situation where the parties can question and check out their perceptions about the other. This can be done by requesting that the spouses talk about their perceptions of each other or certain issues and explaining the accuracy or inaccuracy of the perception.

Second, the mediator can describe the stereotyping dynamic and explain how it affects negotiations. By educating the parties about a dynamic that is common to many conflicts, the intervenor can indirectly or directly suggest that the parties evaluate their own dispute in a new light (Burton, 1969).

Third, the mediator can directly or indirectly challenge the misperception of one or more of the parties and raise doubts about their perceptions. Often the introduction of the view of another party whom a disputant trusts (the mediator) causes enough cognitive dissonance in the mind of the disputant to shift his or her view of the opponent (Rubin & Brown, 1975). The mediator can point out how an opponent's behavior is not consistent with the perception or stereotype held by the other party. This mediator move, however, is riskier than focusing the parties on the topic of perception and allowing them to check out views on their own. Direct challenges of a party's perceptions are most often initiated in caucus, where the mediator's challenge is less likely to be perceived as an alliance with an opponent.

Finally, the mediator may encourage a party to initiate moves that will tend to break stereotypes or modify perceptions held by another party. Often the mediator suggests these moves in caucus. A spouse may express appreciation of the other's parenting abilities, so as to decrease the tendency of the parties to see the dispute as a pure conflict (Kreisburg, 1973); accept a negotiation procedure proposed by the other party; grant small concessions to indicate that cooperation and trust is possible (Fisher, 1978); or initiate symbolic acts (hanging up the other spouse's coat, providing for his or her creature comforts, offering to do some extra work of data collection, etc.) that jar the perceptions of the other party and encourage him or her to revise negative stereotypes.

COMMUNICATIONS CONFLICT

Communication problems are probably the most familiar cause of impasse to mediators. For this reason we will not to into detail on the intervention moves used to enhance communication. However, a brief review of these activities might be helpful.

Communication consists of a combination of signals, verbal or nonverbal, that are encoded in the form of a message. Communications problems in negotiations are usually caused by poor framing and sending of coded messages by the receiver or poor decoding of the message by the receiver. The role of the mediator in enhancing communications between the parties is to improve the way that messages, either verbal or nonverbal, are sent and received.

Improving the way that parties send messages to each other can be accomplished by many types of intervenor moves. The mediator may work with a party prior to meeting jointly with the other spouse to clarify what the party wants to say, balance the content message and the emotions that the party wishes to convey, determine the best way (syntax and means of transmission) to deliver the message so that it is understood by the listener, or determine when the message should be sent. The mediator can work with a party to develop a complete strategy so as to minimize communication problems.

In joint session, the mediator may use a variety of techniques to enhance communications. Among the most common are paraphrasing, summarization, expansion of an idea, ordering ideas into a logical thought sequence, grouping common items, fractionating or breaking issues into smaller parts, generalizing, and reframing (Watzlawick, 1978) the problems so that it is seen in a different way.

Mediators also work with parties to improve their listening abilities. They do this by assisting parties to restate the substantive portion of messages and encouraging parties to actively listen for the emotional portion of the communications (Gordon, 1970) as means to assure the accurate understanding of communications. If a spouse cannot hear what the other spouse has to say, the mediator may also function as a translator. Research seems to indicate that if the same message is delivered by an opponent and a mediator, the message is more likely to be positively received and accepted when delivered by the neutral intervenor (Rubin & Brown, 1975).

Nonverbal communications are integrally related to conflict escalation. A large portion of our meanings and messages are conveyed by nonverbal communications—body language, spatial distance, physical setup of the negotiation site, or physical objects displayed by disputants. The mediator, by varying the parties' utilization of nonverbal communication, may enhance the success of negotiations. Several interventions that modify the nonverbal communications of parties include varying the seating arrangement to a side-by-side setup to induce more cooperative problem-solving behavior, using a wall chart and markers to record ideas and to focus the negotiations off the people and onto the problem (Doyle & Straus, 1976), and arranging the chairs so that the parties have principle eye contact with the mediator and not with each other (Carnevale, Pruitt, Seilheimer, 1981).

An extreme method of managing nonverbal or unproductive verbal communication between the parties is the caucus. The caucus is a separate, private meeting initiated either by the disputants or the mediator as a means of controlling the communication flow between the parties. By separating disputants and meeting with them individually, the mediator can eliminate the exchange of negative nonverbal and verbal messages and assure that only communications that move the negotiations toward settlement are exchanged.

REPETITIVE NEGATIVE BEHAVIOR
Repetitive negative behavior involves repeated actions that trigger escalatory responses from the other party. Often this behavior is patterned interaction that has developed over the duration of the relationship and is subconscious on the part of both parties. Repetitive negative behavior is most likely to result in impasse during the first five stages of negotiation and in the final bargaining stage (see Table 13-1). Mediator interventions to handle repetitive negative behavior may be divided into two levels: direct and indirect interventions.

Direct interventions are mediator moves that overtly identify what is happening and then modify the structure. Often, when the mediator overtly identifies and labels behavior, it makes it more difficult for the parties to repeat since everyone will recognize what is happening and no one wants to be held responsible for a damaging action.

Indirect moves require the mediator to recognize patterns and cycles of repetitive behavior and then to structure the negotiation session so that there is no opportunity for them to occur. For example, a couple who had been divorced for several years came to a mediator for help in renegotiating a visitation schedule. Each time the wife tried to talk directly to the husband, he would interrupt. She would call him on the interruption, he would escalate the dispute by attacking her character, and she would reciprocate. After this happened three times, the co-mediators requested that all communication between the spouses be directed to the mediators and not toward each other. The couple were not allowed to talk to each other. The mediators could then translate and reframe the parties' messages to make them more substantively and emotionally acceptable. This change in the structure of communication broke the pattern of repetitive negative behavior.

Data Conflict

Data conflicts are differences that arise over information used by the parties to make a decision. Data conflicts occur at several stages in the negotiation process. In the early stages—defining dispute parameters, identifying issues and establishing an agenda, and identifying interests—the most common data problems are lack of information, misinformation, and discrepancies in data the parties believe are relevant to deciding the issues. Data, it should be noticed, can refer to concrete substantive information (such as the amount of money needed to feed and clothe two children), procedural information (such as the sequence of filing papers with the court), or psychological data (such as information on a child's increased bedwetting).

Mediator interventions to handle data conflict in the early stages of negotiation are primarily oriented toward assisting the parties to agree on the information needed for problem solving and helping them collect additional data to fill in gaps. Procedures for handling data conflict include: identification of missing data and any discrepancy in the information held by the parties, discussion of how additional data can be obtained and/or how a deadlock can be broken when two sets of conflicting data exist, discussion of objective standards by which data will be accepted or rejected (Fisher & Ury, 1981), and individual or joint research by the parties on the data needed by the next session. Some examples of procedures that parties can use to collect data include joint or individual survey of prices of children's clothing at several agreed-upon stores, as a means of preparing a clothing budget; arranging for appraisal of the house by an independent and mutually acceptable individual or agency; visits to a certified public accountant to obtain information on the tax consequences for the distribution of commonly held capital; or reading books such as *Joint Custody and Co-Parenting* (Galper, 1980), *Mom's House, Dad's House* (Ricci, 1980), or *Divided Children* (Wheeler, 1980) to generate more data on parenting options.

Subsequent data problems in negotiations occur during the assessment and implementation stages. In the negotiation stages of assessing the options and implementing, monitoring, and formalizing the agreement, the parties are engaged in individual and joint evaluation of potential settlement options. Information and objective criteria used to evaluate the acceptability of the settlement must be adequate and acceptable in order to make decisions. Occasionally the parties may need to collect additional information, consult attorneys to determine if the terms of the settlement are legally reasonable, work on establishing acceptable objective criteria for decision making, or obtain information on how an agreement such as they have developed can be implemented.

The primary task of the mediator in these stages is to assist the parties in identifying the additional information needed and to aid them in developing appropriate data collection procedures. Occasionally parties cannot agree on a piece of data. A "data mediator," an independent and mutually acceptable third party who is not the mediator and who is a substantive expert in the area of question, may be consulted to break the deadlock. These third parties often perform an arbiter role in dispute settlement. Assessors, stockbrokers, investment counselors, jewelers, and so forth, can all perform this role.

Another alternative for breaking data deadlocks is to create a procedural solution to a substantive problem. For example, if a couple differ over the evaluation of a piece of art and both have experts that are giving them diverging opinions, the couple may agree to go to a third party for another assessment and then take the middle figure among the three as their basis of assessment.

Interest Conflicts

Conflicts of interest are often the major causes of marital disputes. Interests are specific needs, benefits, or conditions that a party must have met if a settlement is to be considered satisfactory. Interests may refer to the content or substantive outcomes of negotiations (money, time, or other forms of compensation), procedural preferences for the way that negotiations are carried out, or psychological needs (safety, respect, trust, etc.). In most conflicts, the interests are not all mutually exclusive because the satisfaction of one spouse's needs is not always dependent on the denial of the other's needs. This is especially true in marital disputes where couples often have crosscutting and common interests, such as the well-being of their children, as well as competing needs.

SUBSTANTIVE INTEREST CONFLICT

Substantive interest conflicts often result when the parties fail to identify their substantive interests accurately, do not generate enough acceptable substantive solutions, or encounter problems in selecting preferred settlement outcomes (Fisher, 1978). These problems often occur in the identifying interests, generating settlement alternatives, and assessing options stages of negotiation.

Clearly defining interests is a process that is often overlooked by parties. There is a strong tendency to identify a substantive need and then leap to a single preferred solution or position, merely to have it addressed quickly. Parties often lock themselves into a sole solution without clearly defining their needs and determining if other settlement options might be just as acceptable.

Mediators assist spouses in identifying their interests by decoding position statements. Some of the communications skills described above are useful in attaining these ends. Reframing is an especially common technique. For example, the parents' need for legal custody may be reframed into desire for interaction with the child, to be involved in making decisions about the child's life, to influence the child's values, or for vacation time with the child. Once specific interests are defined, the mediator can assist the couple to find integrative solutions that meet both spouses' needs and that are not mutually exclusive.

The second period when substantive interests may conflict is in the process of alternative generation. In this stage, parties must develop mutually acceptable settlement options. Spouses often have trouble visualizing mutually acceptable settlements, and the mediator may have to prod their thinking. Often reading books, such as the three already mentioned, may be helpful for parents in generating options. Other procedures include brainstorming, developing visions of what the couple's new independent relationship would look like in the best of all possible worlds, or discussing parenting options with other divorced parents.

Once substantive options are available, the mediator may help the parties select acceptable alternatives. Usually the mediator refers the couple back to their interests and asks them to assess options according to how well they meet previously identified needs. Assessment is much easier if the interests have been written down and can be cross-referenced to various settlement options.

PROCEDURAL INTEREST CONFLICT

Conflicts are often caused by the process used for the negotiations. Each party has an interest in the way that the dispute will be settled. Parties may be unaware that a process is needed, be using the wrong process, or be ineffectively using the right process. Two of the major tasks of the mediator are to educate the parties in how to negotiate and to assist them to develop a satisfactory procedure to resolve their differences. This includes familiarizing the couple with the various stages of negotiations and the tasks they need to accomplish within each stage, and encouraging them to use effective negotiation strategies. Often, the major reason that couples turn to mediators is their failure to develop an effective negotiation process on their own.

Positional bargaining as a negotiation process is often one of the major procedural obstacles to reaching acceptable resolution of a dispute (Fisher and Ury, 1981; Moore, 1983). Positional bargaining assumes that the resource being negotiated is limited and that a win for one spouse will mean a loss for the other. Interests are couched in maximal terms and formulated into hard positions that are presented to the opposing party. The assumption in positional bargaining is that both sides will give in incrementally until an acceptable settlement range is reached. This range is composed of settlement options, any one of which is preferable to not reaching agreement or to pursuing another means (i.e., litigation) to terminate the conflict. The problem with positional bargaining is that it often produces compromise settlements based on the division of resources or of child custody that are not the best solution for anyone.

For example, in positional bargaining, both parents might start with the demand that each have sole legal custody of the child. They adopt this position because it assures them of having the time they want with the child. Assuming that this is an unacceptable option for each parent and that each is also unsure that they could win this award through litigation, they agree to split the time with the child as a compromise. Each parent starts demanding 6 days with the child and offering to the other parent the remaining day. This option is also mutually unacceptable. Gradually each parent makes concessions of more days until they reach a point of agreement—4 days for one parent and 3 days for the other.

Interest-based bargaining, in contrast to positional bargaining, aims to create a solution that maximizes the satisfaction of all parties' interests. How might an agreement on the child-custody case described above have been handled if the parents or the mediator had initiated interest-based bargaining? When the parents started negotiating and each demanded total legal custody, the mediator would have shifted the parties off their positions and focused them on their interests. The mediator might have done this by reframing the problem from the issue of legal custody to the issue of how each parent could maintain an acceptable and nurturing relationship with the child. The mediator would then ask each parent what they wanted in their relationship with the child. One parent might mention an opportunity to read bedtime stories, while the other might say camping trips with the child. The father might request evening meals, while the mother might want time for sports activities. After the interests are identified, the parents and the mediator jointly put together a plan that integrates the parents' needs, maximizes the opportunity for relationship with the child, and minimizes time conflicts between each of the spouses. While the actual time distribution in this case might not look substantially different than that of the agreement reached through positional bargaining, the substantive, procedural, and psychological satisfaction would probably be much greater due to the interest-based bargaining process. One parent might prefer to have more dinners with the child, while the other might be able to take longer vacations which would not impinge on the relationship of the child with the nonvacationing parent.

Interest-based bargaining attempts to focus the parties on the needs of each party, the interests held in common and non-competing ones that allow for trade-offs, and then search for an integrative solution that mutually satisfies these needs (Walton & McKersie, 1965). Positional bargaining focuses on individual needs, generates an individual solution, and then tries to convince or force the other party to accept the proposed settlement. In positional bargaining it is easy to get caught up in defending a position and forget the interest the position was initially designed to meet. It is also easy to forget that negotiation requires mutual satisfaction of interests and that for the other side to settle, he or she must have some substantive, procedural, and psychological needs met.

PSYCHOLOGICAL INTEREST CONFLICT

Parties also have psychological interests or needs that they would like to have met in a negotiated settlement. Psychological interests include not only a need for positive feelings such as respect, caring, or safety, but also a termination of negative feelings that may bind the couple into the dynamics of negative intimacy.

Mediators assist parties to satisfy their psychological needs by making spouses aware that this type of interest exists and by providing procedures that enable them to attain desired ends. Mediators may assist spouses to make statements that meet each other's psychological needs and make settlement more acceptable, request time-out to enable a party to reconcile his or her feelings with the substantive settlement, or assist in a total restructuring of the relationship so that psychological interests become less important. On this last point, Ricci (1980) maintains that one of the most difficult transitions for spouses and parents to make is the shift from an intimate relationship to that of a businesslike one. Intimate relationships involve high personal disclosure, are informal, and are characterized by implicit expectations. As long as a person remains in an intimate relationship with an ex-spouse, he or she will not make the psychological transition to independence and autonomy. Psychological closure in a divorce requires this transition. Mediators assist spouses to become aware of the need for a new structure for the relationship and to shift their intimate interests to businesslike ones—formality, high personal privacy, low self-disclosure, explicit expectations, and written agreements.

Structural Conflict

Structural conflict is caused by the way that a spousal or parenting relationship is organized and the patterns of interdependence that emerge. Some of the variables that affect the structure of a relationship include resources to be distributed between the couple, time, patterns of spousal involvement with each other and the children, physical space, and power relationships.

Power relationships affect the dynamics of impasse and a mediator can, to a certain extent, prevent negative impacts caused by imbalance and balances of power. Power is the capability of one party to affect the other's rewards or the outcome of a dispute. The range of outcomes in marital disputes may be either positive or negative, depending upon the spouses' exercise of power.

The outcome of a conflict depends upon the exercise by a disputant of various means of influence which either close off or open the way to different settlement options. There are a variety of means of influence that may be used by spouses in relationship disputes: rewards, coercion, claims to authority, association with powerful allies (i.e., attorneys), and expertise and information (French & Raven, 1960).

Power is not a characteristic of a person but rather an attribute of a relationship. In other words, one spouse's power is directly related to the power of the other spouse. Power relations are either symmetrical or asymmetrical. A symmetrical power relationship exists when each spouse controls a range of outcomes for the other that are relatively equal. Symmetrical power is characterized by similar capabilities to affect the outcome for the other. An asymmetrical power relationship occurs when one spouse has a greater capacity to control the outcomes for the other. This type of relationship often results in unilateral attempts to change the conflict outcome (Bagozzi & Dholakia, 1977).

PARTIES WITH SYMMETRICAL POWER RELATIONS

Social–psychological experiments and practical experience indicate that when negotiators have equal or symmetrical power, they behave in a more cooperative manner, function more effectively, and behave in a less exploitive or manipulative manner than when they are in an asymmetrical power relationship (Rubin & Brown, 1975). Furthermore, the smaller the amount of power, particularly coercive power, that is exercised in the negotiations, the more effectively the parties seem to function.

The most common problem of disputants with symmetrical power is perceptual difficulties regarding symmetry and negative effects of the past exercise of coercive power. Perception of spouses' symmetry is usually dependent upon being able to measure or project the potential outcome of a dispute if one or both spouses decide to exercise power. For example, if the couple are in a contest over a piece of property and both have unlimited funds, equally qualified attorneys, and case law to back up their argument, their perception of each other's power may be relatively easy to determine. This is because the variables by which power is measured—capital, personnel, case law—are the same.

When spouses have different quantities or types of power, an assessment problem often develops. This often results in a breakdown of negotiations. Spouses may return to negotiations only after they have exercised and tested their power and developed a more accurate assessment of the power of the other party. For example, many spouses attempt to negotiate issues in dispute, fail, hire lawyers, and take the case to court. A large number of these cases settle on the courthouse steps. The act of testing the strength and will of an opponent may be an important step in developing an accurate perception of the other disputant's power. Power often has to be tested before the actual degree of influence can be verified. Unfortunately, this testing, which involves the exercise of power, may have a negative impact on the couple's ability to cooperate and negotiate. Even in symmetrical relations, exercise of power may lead to an irreversible breakdown of negotiations.

Mediators in disputes where spouses have symmetrical power relationships but where the equality is hard to determine because of different power bases or measures, generally attempt to change the parties' perceptions of each other's power without encouraging them to resort to coercion. Perception can be changed by increasing the perception of spouses that their opposite has *more* potential power in relation to themselves than was originally calculated, or by convincing spouses that they have *less* power in relationship to their opposite than they originally expected. Changing perspectives about power, especially where the parties have symmetrical relationships, is generally an exercise in developing an accurate assessment mechanism. Mediators usually encourage a party to list his or her sources or bases of power and then identify the costs and benefits of exercising it. The same procedure is then followed for the other spouse. A cross-reference of costs and outcomes usually moves the spouses toward a mutual recognition of symmetrical power relations.

PARTIES WITH ASYMMETRICAL POWER RELATIONS

While symmetrical power relations between spouses seem to be the optimum relationship for effective bargaining, this type of relationship is not the norm for a large number of family disputes. Parties differ in the type of their power basis in relation to one another and in the amount of influence they can exercise. Mediators in disputes where parties have asymmetrical power relationships are faced with two kinds of common problems: (1) perceptual problems, where the spouses do not have equal power, but the weaker party, by bluffing or through a misperception by the stronger, has made the other believe that they do have a symmetrical relationship; and (2) extreme asymmetrical relationships, where one party is in a much weaker position in relation to another. Mediators work with both weaker and stronger parties to minimize the negative effects of asymmetrical power relationships on the negotiation process.

Negotiators who claim to have more power and influence that they actually have run a risk of being called upon to carry out actions that they are either incapable of completing or that are undesirable means to achieve a desired end. When a mediator encounters a situation where one spouse is bluffing about his or her power and the other is being drawn into the illusion, the mediator, usually in private, attempts to educate the bluffer about the potential costs of being either found out or called upon to carry out the bluff.

On one hand discovery that one has been the victim of a deception often leads to a deterioration of the couple's relationship and may, if the victim of the bluff is the stronger party, lead to retaliation. On the other hand, if a bluff regarding power held by a weaker party is believed by a stronger one, and the stronger party decides to resist the demand, the weaker party may be forced to follow through on a course of action that will lead to the bluff's demise. In an effort to respond to this situation, the mediator generally raises questions with the weaker spouse regarding the potential cost of bluffing. If the intervenor is successful in convincing the spouse that the costs of bluffing are too high, the mediator and that spouse jointly search for a way to back away from the bluff or minimize the importance of power dynamics in the context of the negotiations. Backing off from a bluff or minimizing the effects of bluff can often be achieved by ceasing threatening statements or false promises and blurring the explicitness of statements describing the consequences of disagreement. A shift to a general description of outcomes rather than explicit coercive moves leaves all parties more maneuvering room to cope with an impasse. The mediator and the bluffing spouse work jointly to minimize the impact of an ill-timed or inappropriate bluff.

In power situations where spouses appear to have an asymmetrical relationship and where their basis of power is very different, the mediator may attempt to blur or obscure the asymetry of the disputants' power. Mediators pursue this strategy as a way of creating doubt about the actual power of the parties. This move is often referred to as keeping the parties off balance. If a spouse cannot determine absolutely that he or she has more power than the other, he or she generally does not feel free to manipulate or exploit the other without restraint. The mediator may destabilize the accuracy of the power assessment of the parties in order to promote cooperation based on doubt.

A second mediator strategy, where the parties do not have a symmetrical relationship and the difference in power is not too great, is to stress the costs to a spouse in pursuing a manipulative or competitive win–lose outcome. Although the stronger spouse may ultimately win, the costs of exercising power may be extremely high and the duration of the contest may be prolonged. In asymmetrical situations where the spouses' powers are close to equal, the mediator may urge the parties to treat the relationship as a symmetrical one in order to maximize benefits and lower costs.

By far the most difficult problem faced by mediators regarding disputants' power relationships is an asymmetrical situation where the discrepancy between the means of influence is extremely great. The mediator, because of his or her commitment to neutrality and impartiality, is ethically barred from being a direct advocate for the weaker spouse. Yet the intervenor is also ethically obligated to assist the couple to reach a fair and acceptable agreement that will hold over time.

Wall (1981) argues that the mediator's job is to manage the power relationship of the disputants. In asymmetrical power relationships the mediator attempts to balance the power between the dominant and weaker party. The mediator initiates moves to assist the weaker party to mobilize the power he or she currently possesses. The mediator does not, however, directly act as an organizer to develop new power for the weaker disputant unless the mediator has gained approval of the stronger party for such activity. To act as a secret advocate risks the mediator's impartiality and, therefore, effectiveness.

Empowering moves may include aiding the weaker party to obtain, organize, and analyze data and identify and mobilize his or her means of influence; assisting and educating the party to plan an effective negotiation strategy; aiding in the development of financial support so that the spouse can continue to participate in negotiations; and encouraging the party to make realistic concessions. Surprisingly enough, stronger spouses often welcome a mediator's involvement. Mediators may assist weaker parties who are unorganized and unable to negotiate to prepare to engage in a productive exchange.

Value Conflicts

A value is an enduring belief that specific behaviors or goals for existence are personally or socially preferable. Values usually imply a comparison in that one set of values is preferred over another. Researchers have identified two levels of values, operational and terminal. Operational values are general day-to-day guidelines, such as truth, honesty, respect, and so forth, while terminal values are often systems such as religious beliefs, views on parenting, lifelong goals, or political values (Rokeach, 1968). Because both levels of values tie into a person's self-concept, it may appear that negotiating over values is an impossible task. Although value-based conflicts are difficult, they are not impossible to handle. Mediators can be of great assistance to parties in resolving this type of dispute.

Value conflicts are most prominent in the following stages of negotiation: searching for an approach and arena, defining dispute parameters, defining issues and forming an agenda, and identifying interests (Table 13-1). The following five procedures are often used by mediators to handle value-based disputes: (1) avoiding value-based issues, (2) agreeing to disagree, (3) translating a value dispute into an interest conflict, (4) searching for superordinate goals, and (5) creating in a party cognitive dissonance between one set of values and another.

AVOIDANCE
Endless bickering about values often results in a deterioration of the couple's relationship and a decline in the spouses' abilities to negotiate. Personal values rarely change in the brief time during which a couple are negotiating a divorce. For this reason, many mediators assertively guide parties away from value-laden issues and focus them on behavioral issues that are more easily resolved. Avoidance of value disputes is often the best way to handle them.

AGREEING TO DISAGREE
On occasion, a couple may not accept avoidance of value-laden issues. They may want to discuss and confront them head-on. Mediators often stress that

the couple may have to agree to disagree about value-based issues. For example, a couple who were divorcing had different religious values. One was a fundamentalist Christian and the other an agnostic. The individuals involved had very different expectations about how they wished the other to live and believe. The mediator convinced them that while the spouses were in the couple relationship, parallel values were important. However, since they were divorcing and would no longer be engaged in intimate interaction, common religious beliefs would not be as important as in the previous relationship. Now they should be able to live their lives as each of them wished. The spouses were encouraged not to force their values on each other and to agree that they could disagree as to what beliefs were right or correct. Agreeing to disagree relieved the burden on each spouse to convert the other and enabled the couple to terminate their conflict. The mediator in this case could point out the importance of allowing individuals in dispute to have their own beliefs, thus encouraging their disagreement.

TRANSLATING A VALUE DISPUTE INTO AN INTEREST CONFLICT
Some value disputes, especially those involving terminal values, many not be resolved in the manners described above. This is especially the case where the parties must continue to interact as parents, and still hold opposing beliefs. Individual beliefs, however, may sometimes be operationalized so that the behavior of the parties (or their children) is deemed to be mutually acceptable.

The process that best illustrates this procedure is reframing a value dispute into an interest conflict. For example, a husband and wife are negotiating over visitation. The husband has an alcohol problem that the wife absolutely abhors. Her father had been an alcoholic, and she hates people who drink. She refuses to allow the child to visit his father. From all appearances this is a nonnegotiable, value-based conflict. With more exploration, however, the mediator discovers that the strong values are expressions of particular interests held by the wife regarding the care and psychological state of the child. She wants the child to be safe and feels she cannot count on this if the father has been drinking. She does not want the child to be a passenger in a car driven by the father when he is under the influence of alcohol, and she does not want the child exposed to the ex-husband when he is intoxicated. The mediator queries the mother as to whether she would agree to visitation if her interests about safety and psychological well-being of the child could be met. She agrees. The parties then begin a joint search for a solution that meets the father's needs for visitation and the mother's needs for safety and psychological well-being of the child. They settle on a 6-month schedule of visitation in which the father can see the child for several hours each week under the supervision of a local hospital program. In this dispute, a difference of values has been translated into an interest conflict.

SEARCHING FOR SUPERORDINATE GOALS OR VALUES
The search for superordinate goals has long been known to be a way to minimize value conflicts (Sherif & Sherif, 1953). In this procedure the mediator

assesses the parties' beliefs and searches to find a superordinate goal or value that bridges either their operational or terminal values.

For example, a couple were fighting over the religious upbringing of their children. One parent wanted one kind of religious training, and the other wanted another. From all appearances the values of the parents seemed to be irreconcilable. The mediator did not attempt to have the parties argue on the basis of their particular religious beliefs but instead asked how each other's religious values would translate into value-based behavior as displayed by the children. The couple talked about general values they would like their children to have—charity, cheerfulness, forgiveness, honesty, compassion—and then discussed how these values were or were not manifest in their children's lives. The couple proceeded to talk about ways, aside from religion, that they could promote these values and behaviors in their offspring. The particular kind of religious training became less important once overarching values had been identified by the couple.

CREATING COGNITIVE DISSONANCE

The fifth, and final, means of handling value conflict is to create cognitive dissonance between one value and another within an individual. Cognitive dissonance as a means of dispute resolution is based on balance theory (Heider, 1958; Newcomb, 1953). Balance theory postulates that people like to maintain internal consistency between their attitudes, perceptions, and beliefs about important events or issues and will attempt to modify these beliefs if there is incongruity between two or more important values. Incongruity in an individual's own beliefs or values is catalyzed by the mediator when he or she contrasts one set of a disputant's values against another. This produces strain on the individual's belief system and promotes efforts to reattain congruity.

In the search for a superordinate goal, the mediator looks for bridging beliefs or principles that would unify the two disputants. In the cognitive-dissonance approach, the mediator searches for a superordinate value held by an individual and contrasts it with a lower value that is causing the conflict. In a case example, Phillip and Rita have decided to separate after an extremely painful break-up of their marriage. Rita has been involved with another man, and this provided the trigger event for the separation. Phillip is "morally opposed" to Rita's "sleeping around" with other men while their young daughter Sheila is living with Rita. He has stated his values very strongly: "I don't want you to see other men while Sheila is with you." His statement provoked a very angry response from Rita. The mediator switched the topic away from the particular moral value in question and encouraged the parties to discuss their principles of fairness. What did a fair settlement mean to them? Both stressed the fairness meant reasonableness, equal treatment for both partners, taking into consideration the needs of those involved, and so forth. The mediator asked Phillip if he intended to date other women some time in the future. Phillip answered that he did. The mediator then asked Phillip if it was out of the question that he might wish to sleep with them. He answered that it was not. The mediator posed a hypothetical question to Phillip, "If you developed a strong relationship with another woman, would you want to live with her prior to marriage?" Phillip answered, "Possibly." The mediator asked Phillip if he would want his child to know about, and have a friendship with, this new woman who was an important person in Phillip's life. Phillip answered in the affirmative. The mediator then asked Phillip if his desire to live with the woman and his desire to have his daughter know her would mean that the daughter might realize that they were sleeping together. Phillip said, "Yes." The mediator asked Phillip if he thought that this knowledge might be detrimental to Sheila. He responded that if it was an ongoing, loving relationship, it probably would not. The mediator asked Phillip whether he thought that he should be allowed to make this decision to expose his daughter to such information. Phillip adamantly stated that he did. The mediator returned to the principle of fairness and asked whether this right should apply to Rita's decision about whom she had relationships with and how she presented her friends to their daughter. Phillip, after considering the previous discussion of fairness, reluctantly agreed and backed off his hard-line, value-based position. He stated that he merely wanted to assure that Sheila was not presented with information that she could not handle. Rita agreed that this was an important principle that they could build an agreement around. The couple proceeded to work out the details about how they would relate to others after the divorce and how they would present and explain their relationships to Sheila. In this case the mediator was succesful in generating cognitive dissonance between the higher values of love, desire for a meaningful relationship, and fairness, and Phillip's lower operational value regarding sexual behavior in relationships.

CONCLUSION

This chapter reviewed some of the causes of conflict and impasse, analyzed the times when impasse is most likely to occur in a negotiation process, and described a variety of interventions or techniques that may be initiated by a mediator to break impasse. We have explored relationship-based disputes in which strong emotions, misperceptions, stereotypes, poor communication, and repetitive negative behaviors have blocked the ability of the couple to agree. We have also examined data disputes where lack of information, misinformation, differing assessment procedures, and differing viewpoints of what data are relevant tended to produce unnecessary conflict between the disputants. Our analysis indicates that mediators should first handle relationship and data disputes, which may be unnecessarily provoking conflict, before dealing with interests, values, and the structure of the relationship, which may be causing genuine conflict.

Interest disputes in a divorce may be over substantive content, such as child custody, visitation rights and responsibilities, child support, spousal support, and property division. Interest conflicts may also be due to differing opinions or desires about negotiation procedures. Concern about a procedure that allows each spouse to be heard and to voice his or her views about principles of fairness, and a desire for a lack of coercion in reaching agreement may be important procedural aspects of the negotiations. Of particular concern in procedural disputes is the tendency of couples to initiate positional bargaining as opposed to interest-based bargaining. We have observed that one of the major tasks of a mediator is to assist parties to make the transition from positional bargaining to interest-based bargaining.

Finally, interest disputes may be caused by differing psychological needs. In order to achieve a psychological settlement, the mediator must assist the parties to break out of negative intimacy and move toward a more businesslike relationship.

Structural conflicts are often caused by an imbalance of the power relationship within a couple. We have reviewed different kinds of intervention techniques that mediators can use depending on whether the power relationship between the parties is symmetrical or asymmetrical.

Value disputes are perhaps one of the most difficult kinds of conflict to resolve. In this chapter we have reviewed five different mediation techniques to handle value disputes: (1) avoiding, (2) agreeing to disagree, (3) reframing a value dispute into an interest conflict, (4) searching for superordinate goals or values held by the parties, and (5) creating internal cognitive dissonance between a set of lower operational values and a higher terminal value in a single party. It is hoped that this review of intervenor techniques may be of assistance in improving skills and in promoting additional dialogue about procedures to overcome impasse and break deadlocks.

REFERENCES

Bach, G., & Goldberg, H. *Creative aggression: The art of assertive living.* New York: Doubleday, 1974.

Bagozzi, R., & Dholakia, R. *Mediational mechanisms in interorganizational conflict.* In D. Druckman (Ed.), *Negotiations: Social psychological perspectives* (pp. 367–387). Beverly Hills, CA: Sage, 1977.

Berkowitz, L. The case for bottling up rage. *Psychology Today*, 1973, 7(2), 24–31.

Burton, J. *Communication and conflict.* New York: Oxford University Press, 1969.

Carnevale, P., Pruitt, D., & Seilheimer, S. Looking and competing: Accountability and visual access in integrative bargaining. *Journal of Personality and Social Psychology*, 1981, 40(1), 111–120.

Coogler, O. J. *Structured mediation in divorce settlement: A handbook for marital mediators.* Lexington, MA: D. C. Heath, 1978.

Coser, L. *Functions of social conflict.* New York: Columbia University Press, 1956.

Douglas, A. *Industrial peacemaking.* New York: Columbia University Press, 1962.

Doyle, M., & Straus, D. *How to make meetings work.* Chicago: Playboy Press, 1976.

Fisher, R. *International mediation: A working guide.* New York: International Peace Academy, 1978.

Fisher, R., & Ury, W. *Getting to yes: Negotiating agreement without giving in.* Boston: Houghton Mifflin, 1981.

French, J., & Raven, B. The basis of social power. In D. Cartwright & A. Zander (Eds.), *Group dynamics* (pp. 259–269). New York: Harper & Row, 1960.

Frost, J., & Wilmot, W. *Interpersonal conflict.* Dubuque, IA: Brown, 1978.

Galper, M. *Joint custody and co-parenting.* Philadelphia: Running Press, 1980.

Galtung, J. Is peaceful research possible? On the methodology of peaceful research. In *Peace-research-education-action.* Copenhagen: Christian Ejlers, 1975.

Gordon, T. *Parent effectiveness training.* new York: Wyden, 1970.

Gulliver, P. H. *Disputes and negotiations.* New York: Academic Press, 1979.

Haynes, J. *Divorce mediation.* New York: Springer, 1981.

Heider, F. *The psychology of interpersonal relations.* New York: Wiley, 1958.

Hokanson, J. Psychophysiological evaluations of the catharsis hypothesis. In J. Hokanson & E. Megarge (Eds.), *Dynamics of aggression* (pp. 74–86). New York: Harper & Row, 1970.

Jackins, H. *The human side of human beings.* Seattle, WA: Rational Island Press, 1978.

Kessler, S. *Creative conflict resolution: Mediation.* Atlanta, GA: National Institute for Professional Training, 1978.

Kreisburg, L. *The sociology of social conflict.* Englewood Cliffs, NJ: Prentice-Hall, 1973.

Kressel, K. A typology of divorcing couples: Implications for mediation in the divorce process. *Family Process,* 1980, *19(2),* 101–116.

Maggiolo, W. *Techniques of mediation in labor disputes.* Dobbs Ferry, NY: Oceana, 1971.

Milne, A. *Family self determination: An alternative to the adversarial system in custody disputes.* Fort Lauderdale, FL: Association of Family and Conciliation Courts Conference Materials, 1981.

Moore, C. *The mediation process: Practical strategies for resolving conflict.* San Francisco: Jossey-Bass, 1986.

Moore, C. The caucus: Private meetings that promote settlement. *Mediation Quarterly,* 1987, no. 16, pp. 87–101.

Newcomb, T. M. An approach to the study of communicative acts. *Psychological Review,* 1953, *60,* 393–404.

Pearson, J. *Child custody mediation project—Progress report no. 5.* Denver, CO: Divorce Mediation Research Project, 1981.

Pruitt, D. *Negotiation behavior.* New York: Academic Press, 1981.

Ricci, I. *Mom's house. Dad's house.* New York: Macmillan, 1980.

Rokeach, M. *Beliefs, attitudes and values.* San Francisco: Jossey-Bass, 1968.

Rubin, J., & Brown, B. *Social psychology of bargaining and negotiation.* New York: Academic Press, 1975.

Sherif, M., & Sherif, C. *Groups in harmony and tension.* New York: Harper & Row, 1953.

Straus, M. A sociological perspective on the prevention and treatment of wifebeatings. In M. Roy (Ed.), *Battered women* (pp. 194–239). New York: Van Nostrand Reinhold, 1977.

Wall, J. Mediation: An analysis, review, and proposed research. *Journal of Conflict Resolution,* 1981, *25(1),* 157–180.

Walton, R., & McKersie, R. *A behavioral theory of labor negotiations.* New York: McGraw-Hill, 1965.

Watzlawick, P. *The language of change.* New York: Basic Books, 1978.

Wheeler, M. *Divided children.* New York: Penguin, 1980.

Zartman, W., & Berman, M. *The practical negotiator.* New Haven, CT: Yale University Press, 1982.

14

Power Balancing

JOHN HAYNES

Haynes Mediation Associates, New York, New York

Among the most difficult and critical challenges in the practice of mediation are the recognition of power relationships between the parties and what to do about them. The author of this chapter, one of the founders of professional divorce mediation, analyzes power relationships in marriage. Methods for identifying power imbalances and developing strategies for balancing them are developed and illustrated by application to cases the author has mediated.

First let us define what we mean by power. The most common theory holds that power is the ability to control resources, or the access to resources, that another wants or needs. A more general definition sees power as social influence, defined as a change in one person that has its origin in another person or group (Raven & Kruglanski, 1970), or as Deutsch (1973) defines it, "the degree that [an actor] can satisfy the purposes (goals, desires, wants) that he is attempting to fulfill in that situation" (p. 84).

Power is a relational concept (Deutsch, 1973). We do not have or exercise power in a vacuum: rather, we enjoy it in relation to other people (Bell, 1975). Power is a property of the social relation rather than of the actor or person exercising the power, supporting the view that the power we have is in relation to other people (Emerson, 1962). In this concept, Robinson Crusoe would have had no power until Friday joined him. At that point each had power in relation to the other.

Bell (1975) suggests that "power implies the existence of a valued object" or resource, which can be "increased or diminished by one actor with respect to another," is "valued by the respondent," and is "in relatively short supply" while also being "divisible" (pp. 82–83). Interpersonal relationships are a mix of physical objects of value, such as money and property, and emotional objects of value, such as love, care, and respect. Most students of power tend to look at either the physical or the emotional side of the issue. In divorce, the mediator constantly monitors both aspects.

In this chapter I define power as control of or access to emotional, economic, and physical resources desired by the other person(s). I use the terms "power" and "influence" interchangeably, believing that power is derived from an ability to influence the actions of others.

In our families we have power in relation to our spouses, our children, and our parents. In addition, we might experience power in relation to other members of the extended family, such as brothers, sisters, aunts, and uncles. For the purpose of this discussion I limit the analysis of power to spousal and parental relationships.

POWER TRANSFER

If power is relational, then it is clear that an individual can have power in relation to one person and not another. Someone can have power in one area but not another. So when looking at power in family relationships, it is important to recognize that the power a member has in one role is not automatically transferred to another role. The husband may hold a powerful position (role) in his business and exercise power in that role frequently and easily. However, it would be a mistake to automatically assume that he is able to transfer that same power to his husband or father role. It is equally important to recognize the different roles one has as a spouse and a parent. A father may exercise a great deal of power over his wife in his spouse role but be successfully prevented from exercising power over her and his children in his parent role. We often see families whose structure requires that all issues relating to the children go through the mother, while the husband sits by.

In an early case I handled for John and Jean Jones, I discovered that the husband was a financial vice president of a large firm. At first I was somewhat intimidated by John's expertise and apparent power. However, in looking at the family organization I discovered that he had never written a check or handled any financial matters within the family. In addition, he had not filed income tax returns for the past 5 years and appeared to be totally incompetent in family financial matters while being highly competent in managing the finances of his corporation.

Here was a man who was powerful in one set of relationships—his work—and apparently unpowerful in another set of relationships—his family. This was further borne out when I learned that both children were engaged in serious delinquent behavior, and he had no idea how to deal with them or with his wife, Jean, who, having admitted to affairs with at least three other men, now wanted a divorce. Inside his family, the vice president–husband was unpowerful and unable to translate or transfer his career power from the job to the family.

Obviously, it is possible to transfer power between relationships, and the Jones case is an extreme example of inability to transfer power. However, the Joneses remind us that power does not reside with one partner *all of the time.* Even in cases where successful businessmen also dominate their wives, I have often found they have great difficulty in expressing their own needs in the emotional and relational areas.

Frank and Brenda demonstrated this. Frank earned over $200,000 a year and was a highly efficient decision maker. At one level he exercised this power in his family and appeared to dominate them on most matters. However, in making a specific proposal to Brenda regarding support he could hardly bring himself to articulate his proposal. He finally got the proposal out after stammering and hiding behind his hands. "That's very hard for you, Frank," I commented. "Yes," he responded, "I am so afraid of Brenda. I am so afraid she will turn the children against me if I don't do everything exactly as she says." Brenda sat incredulous, unable to believe that this man who had dominated her life throughout the marriage was really afraid of her. Brenda had power in the relationship. However, her failure to recognize and use this power left her feeling powerless. In order for power to be exercised, the person owning the power must be aware of it and use it consciously.

I make this distinction because it is important for the mediator to be able to distinguish between real power that one owns and asserts consciously, and power that one spouse has been given by the other and is often unaware of. When it appears that one spouse has and wields power without understanding that he or she has that power, it is useful for the mediator either to identify it or to develop a strategy to permit the power balance to surface so that both partners can understand it. In Brenda's case, once she understood that she had power in relation to Frank, she could be helped to exercise that power in her legitimate self-interest, thus facilitating the negotiations.

These two examples demonstrate that men and women do not easily transfer power from one set of relationships to another. An understanding of the rigid boundaries between different areas in which a family member is permitted to exercise power is helpful to the mediator. He or she needs to work constantly to make these boundaries less rigid, enabling transfer of power between areas and between spouses, and maintaining an overall *balance* of power between the parties.

POWER BALANCE

If one spouse has observable power (i.e., control of money), and the power balance appears to be heavily weighted in favor of that spouse, it is worth looking to see what compensation the other spouse enjoys to make it worthwhile to accede to this loss of power. For example, one partner may control the actual expenditures of the family income, writing all of the checks and paying all the bills. The other spouse loses power as a result of this but also gains some benefits, either by not being responsible for financial management or by reserving the right to criticize the financial judgments of the partner controlling the exchequer.

Usually, as the mediator identifies the compensations, he or she will begin to identify both spouses' real power. The loss of power experienced by one spouse in the marriage is usually compensated by some real benefits to that spouse in another area. In a typical "macho" marriage, the loss of identity by the wife in becoming subordinate to the husband paradoxically gives her power in the relationship. The subordinate condition is a desirable resource to the husband because he needs her in that subordinate position in order to maintain his macho sense of himself. If the wife can threaten the stability of that resource by threatening to decrease her subordination and therefore the value of the relationship to him, she, in turn, exercises power in an apparently powerless situation. The collective benefits of the relationship are measured by both spouses. "When a person decides to yield control of his resources . . . he expects to gain the greater power of combined resources. The decision is between acting independently with more freedom or collectively with more power" (Coleman, 1973, p. 3).

Power balancing is important because, as Rubin and Brown (1975) reported in their study of the role of power in negotiations,

> Equality of initial power or resources among coalition members is likely to result in an approximately equal division of outcomes, whereas differential power or resources is likely to result in an unequal distribution—with members possessing greater power or resources generally demanding a larger share of the outcomes. (p. 79)

This is further supported by Deutsch (1973) who reports in his studies that the more equal the power of the actors, the more likely they were to cooperate in arriving at optimal solutions resulting in more equal outcomes.

Most men have more power in their marriages in the area of finances and decision making, and most women have more power in their marriages over relationships and the children. Thus in a typical adversarial divorce, the husband wields his power through the support and asset distribution while the wife wields hers through the children. This would suggest that any legislative changes in divorce laws should not be piecemeal, but should carefully maintain the balance of power between spouses. A change in the support law ending lifelong alimony was disadvantageous to women, forcing the mother to play her power—control of the children—with greater emphasis and determination in order to achieve a fairer economic outcome. This is not good for the children. Simply enacting presumptive joint-custody bills without balancing the loss of power to the mother by increasing her rights to the asset distribution or support payments is equally bad.

These descriptions of power in families are too gross; they do not tell us of the specific power balances in different areas of the relationship that exist in every family. I have never met a family in which the power resided entirely with one partner or the other. Each had power, and each utilized power in the negotiations. My interest is in analyzing how each person accrues and uses the power and how the distribution of power impacts the negotiations between them. The mediator needs to determine the various power attributes that each partner has and discover where that power lies and whether it is sufficiently imbalanced to adversely effect the negotiations. When the power balance interferes with the couple's ability to negotiate a fair agreement, I believe the mediator has a responsibility to act to correct that imbalance. If after working with the couple the mediator finds that the imbalance is too great, he or she should terminate the mediation.

POWER SOURCES

French and Raven (1959) identify five areas of social influence (which I believe is the same as power) as informational influence, referent influence, legitimate influence, expertise influence, and coercive-reward influence.

Informational Influence

Informational influence might also be called persuasion. One party persuades the other to change a position, by sharing additional information about the matter. The wife might persuade the husband to agree to a higher level of support when she provides specific medical bills showing high medical costs. The husband may persuade the wife to drop her case for a cost-of-living increase tied to a specific indicator by providing information that he had not enjoyed cost-of-living increases in his salary and was unlikely to do so in the future.

Informational power is balanced between the couple by the mediation process. In the early stages the couple are assigned the tasks of collecting and developing the data. This data is then brought back to the mediation and shared. If the mediator sees a gap in the information, he or she assigns further tasks until all of the relevant data is developed by the couple. Even where the information is held primarily by one party, the process of sharing the information, under the guidance of the mediator, diminishes one person's control of that information and thereby tends to balance the power between the couple. When the information is exchanged in the process, the spouses begin to change positions and experience a reduction of conflict because the information becomes independent of the person gathering or holding it (Raven & Kruglanski, 1970, p. 73).

Referent Influence

In divorce mediation referent influence or power refers to the desire of the parties to maintain a joint identification or reference group. The children often act as a major referent force in the negotiations. One spouse may be able to convince the other to move on an issue "in the best interests of the children." That family's standards of fairness may be invoked by one spouse to achieve change in the other. The mediator is a major referent influence since both parties want his or her approval that the proposals are fair and equitable. Thus the mediator can utilize his or her referent power to directly or covertly achieve a change in the position of one or both spouses when their positions are, in the mediator's view, unfair. For example, the husband may propose no mainte- nance support and only a small level of child support and hold to that position. The mediator at some point comments, "Well, the problem with your proposal is that it probably will not get past Mary's attorney, who will insist on a more normative level of support." The husband listens and, because he respects the mediator's expert influence and wants to stay in mediation and work with the mediator, begins to modify his position.

Legitimate Influence

An influence is legitimate when it stems from traditional concepts of rights that a given role carries with it. An elected official has legitimate influence because he or she was elected. In more traditional families, the husband enjoys legiti- mate influence in the sense that society believes the man is the head of the household. If the couple believe that it is right and proper for one or the other to make the decisions on a given subject, then that partner will accrue consider- able legitimate influence in that area of the marriage. This is often typified by the husband's making all the financial decisions ("He always handled the money") and the wife's making all of the decisions affecting the children ("She always took care of the kids' needs"). Breaking legitimate power relationships when their maintenance would result in an unfair or "illegitimate" outcome is difficult, since it involves changing cultural patterns of behavior that are ingrained in the couple.

A paradoxical aspect of legitimate power relates to the power of the powerless. A powerless spouse can legitimately call on the powerful spouse for help, and many concessions are made by the powerful partner to the powerless one under this principle. For example, a father who does not know how to handle the children will receive help from the wife in developing his future parenting role. Or the husband who has maintained the house will make concessions to the wife on fixing up the house because she is powerless and can legitimately demand help from him in this area. The power of the powerless is demonstrated in a typical scene on the highway where a man stops to help a woman change a tire because of an implicit understanding between them as she stood helpless by the car. She could expect her powerlessness to pay off in the form of assistance.

Expert Influence

The expert power of one spouse increases to the extent that the other spouse acknowledges the superior knowledge and/or ability (Raven & Kruglanski, 1970). In normal negotiations the more expert of the two parties uses this expertise to gain an advantage over the other. For example, the husband may offer to pay the support as alimony. The wife, not knowing that she would be liable for taxes on this amount, accepts his promise that, "This will meet your needs." She relied on him during the course of the marriage to make these kind of decisions and may tend to do so in the divorce. His expertise in this area makes him powerful. In mediation, the mediator retains the crucial expert power by explaining each point, assuring that each spouse fully understands the data and the available options, clarifying with both partners all of the choices and options, and explaining the consequences of each option to both partners. By sharing all of the expertise, the mediator tends to balance the power of each partner and limit the use of expertise for personal advantage. This can be seen in the way the mediator uses outside experts for the mutual benefit of both parties rather than to increase the power of either.

Coercive and Reward Influence

Coercion and reward are linked because they are often different sides of the same coin. A useful distinction between coercion or threat and reward or promise is that a promise is a pledge to do something *for* you, but a threat is a pledge to do something *to* you (Searle, 1969, pp. 55–56). A partner who is able to reward ("If you agree to this proposal by tomorrow, I will give you the better of the two cars") is usually also capable of using coercion ("If you don't agree to this proposal by tomorrow, I will take the Jaguar and you will get the VW").

Reward and coercion are closely related because the promise or threat that characterizes the coercion is usually accompanied by a promise of reward if the threatener's terms are met. A threat that is not accompanied by a promise has less persuasiveness or credibility (Schelling, 1960). Therefore, it is helpful for the mediator to ask a threatening spouse what he or she will do positively if the threat is successful. In this way, the mediator reframes the threat into a promise, which has a better chance of meeting mutual needs.

Using the case of the Jaguar and the VW mentioned above, the mediator might help the husband reframe the threat, "I'll take the Jaguar and you will get the VW," into "If you can't agree to this proposal by tomorrow, I will take the Jaguar and you will get the VW, which I will have overhauled and checked out for you so that it is thoroughly roadworthy."

While coercion and reward are usually thought of in terms of concrete items such as money or autos, in families they are often exercised through emotional items such as love, attention, or affection. Punishment is usually used against a partner who has chosen to divorce by the partner who is reluctant to divorce. In this instance it is a power counterplay, because the rejected partner is trying to counter the sense of powerlessness he or she feels in relation to the other spouse, because he or she had little or no part in the decision to divorce. The reward aspect of this appears when one partner is very anxious to get out of the relationship and is willing to give the other partner everything, rewarding him or her in order to end the relationship quickly. The mediator can be very helpful in mitigating the sense of powerlessness the rejected partner feels and in legitimating the right of the anxious partner to leave the relationship. If the mitigation or legitimation strategies are successful, then the need of one spouse to either punish or reward the other is diminished.

Often couples threaten each other without fully understanding that the way they are saying something actually comes across as a threat. In these situations the mediator can use his or her expert influence to rephrase a threat or promise into a sanction-free influence statement that replaces a "threat or promise with a prediction in the form of advice, encouragement, or warning" (Bell, 1975, p. 25). For example, the mediator may say to a wife who is threatening to do something unless the husband agrees to give her the sports car, "If you insist, you can probably get the Jaguar rather than the VW bus; but if you get it, you won't be able to carpool because there won't be room for many kids in the Jaguar."

The process of mediation diminishes the power of one spouse to reward or punish the other. The mediator uses the budget forms and the budgeting process to help the couple determine exactly how much is available for the two new families that emerge from the decision to divorce. By displaying for both parties the exact economic data and by requiring a sharing of this data, the mediator diminishes the ability of the spouse in control of the economic resources to reward the other spouse "if he or she is good," because the sharing helps both partners know what is available. If the wife knows what the real income is, how it is allocated, and what her fair share is, then the husband can't promise to reward her by giving her a fair share of what she already knows she is entitled to.

The power of punishment is different. Here the mediator protects a partner who is threatened with punishment; the mediator either makes a direct statement that such a threat is inappropriate or reframes the threat into a constructive statement. Many people make threats out of weakness rather than strength. The mediator should attempt to understand the underlying fear that prompts the threat and deal with that fear, so as to remove the need for the person to make threats.

The mediator also analyzes the reasons the couple have chosen mediation and uses the threatener's fear to minimize his or her use of threats. Finally, the mediator challenges threats, calling the threatener's bluff to demonstrate to the other spouse that the threats are not necessarily real. In one case the wife was afraid of the husband's constant threats to leave mediation and take her to court. This fear weakened her firmness in the negotiations. At one point, the husband stormed to the door, threatening for the 10th time to leave. The wife rose from her chair to call him back, and I waved for her to be quiet. She sat back down, and the husband stood with his hand on the doorknob, waiting to be placated. I carefully ignored him and continued a low-voiced conversation with the wife. The husband stood by the door for what seemed an uncomfortable period, until he finally raised his voice to complain of being ignored. I promised him he would not be ignored if he came and sat down. When he was again seated, the wife understood that her worst fear had not materialized and that his bluff could be called. From that point on she was more able to assert her position, safe in the knowledge that he really would not walk out.

POWER ASSESSMENT

Each of these areas of influence will be enjoyed by each of the parties at some point and in some areas during the course of the mediation. The task of the mediator is to limit the power of one partner when that power tends to overwhelm the other, and to empower the less powerful partner so that he or she may deal more effectively with the spouse. How is this done? One way is for the mediator to make an assessment of the couple to determine which areas will require power balancing interventions. A lot of information about this issue will emerge during the budget sessions and the asset-identification process. As the mediator sees that one partner has a preponderance of power in one or a number of areas, the mediator makes a power inventory for each of the spouses. The inventory indicates areas of balance power, areas where the husband is powerful, and areas where the wife is powerful. The mediator analyzes areas in which the husband and wife are powerless, not as a result of the other having a preponderance of power but where ignorance, training, or values and beliefs have effectively disempowered either spouse.

Using the relative power relationship assessment form (Table 14-1), the mediator assigns a rating scale from 1 to 10 for each item and rates the spouses individually, assigning either a power factor under the + column or a powerless factor under the −. When the couple share relatively equal power, the mediator compares the relative areas of power and powerlessness and determines whether power in one area can compensate for powerlessness in another.

Table 14-1. Relative Power Relationship Assessment Form

	Money		Assets		Employment[a]		Children		Skills[b]		Rejection	
	H	W	H	W	H	W	H	W	H	W	H	W
	+ −	+ −	+ −	+ −	+ −	+ −	+ −	+ −	+ −	+ −	+ −	+ −
Information												
Referent												
Expertise												
Legitimate												
Reward												
Coercion												

Note. The power of rejection is determined by which partner initiated the divorce and the extent to which the other partner agreed or opposed the decision (Haynes, 1980).

[a]Determine the employment possibilities and income trajectories for each spouse and indicate the extent to which the non–wage earner or lower wage earner of the past is likely to be able to earn sufficient to become economically independent.

[b]"Skills" relates to problem-solving and negotiating skills.

When it is feasible, the mediator notes strategies that enhance the judicious use of power held by one of the parties, to offset the lack of power in another area. When no compensatory power is available, the mediator develops strategies to limit the overuse of the power held by one spouse to the detriment of the other, while developing strategies specifically to empower the less powerful client so as to achieve a balance of power in the negotiations.

For example, the husband may have legitimate power in a traditional family as head of the house. The wife, while recognizing this, will have compensating expert power in the raising of children. In the discussion of the children's access to their father and his access to them, the mediator would encourage the couple to use their respective powers to maintain a balance between them. If the wife was not exerting her expert power, the mediator would raise issues that enhance her expertise and force her to exhibit this power, thus balancing with the husband's legitimate power.

We have discussed power in terms of the five modes of social influence defined by French and Raven and suggested ways in which the mediator can use this knowledge to increase his or her effectiveness to the couple. However, we have been using the framework developed by French and Raven to describe social power. More important in divorce is the ability to identify, measure, and balance interpersonal power. The specific power balance between the husband and wife has an impact on the negotiations. The balance between the couple is based on the application of social power and the ability of others in society to affect them. However, the particular interpersonal relationships that are idiosyncratic to each family and the product of the dynamics of that unit also influence the power balance. In our focus on the specific interpersonal power plays that exist between specific couples in specific marriages, we shall identify the types of strategies used in these power plays and identify concepts of power as they apply to married couples.

In any power analysis the mediator analyzes a series of interactions, making a note of each interaction and determining a *pattern* of power relationships before making a decision as to the actual power balance. A single power attempt, even if successful, will not indicate a systematic power imbalance. Only after a series of interactions, where one spouse repeatedly makes and succeeds at a power attempt, does the mediator note that one party has greater power than the other.

ACCOMMODATION

Certain patterns of accommodation are particularly indicative of a power imbalance and require attention of the mediator. Accommodation indicates one of three factors: discomfort with power, fear of the other, and avoidance of conflict.

We are raised to disdain power. In most families, power attempts by children are thwarted by parents and often result in punishment. Consequently, in adulthood we have trouble asserting ourselves and prefer to accommodate rather than confront a power attempt by another person.

If one partner is accommodating out of fear, then he or she could negotiate away rights and end up with an unfair agreement. At times a wife confides to the mediator, "I'm afraid to push too far or he'll leave me without anything." This may indicate the presence of spouse abuse, in which case the mediator surfaces and deals with the abuse before continuing the mediation. If the abuse is pervasive, the mediator weighs whether mediation is appropriate. I have a firm rule that I will not mediate couples who are still living together if I learn that abuse is involved. I am prepared to mediate if the abuser leaves the marital home and agrees not to visit there except under specific conditions established by the abused. If I believe there is any reasonable chance of the abuse recurring during the mediation, then I refer the abused partner to an attorney with a recommendation that he or she obtain court protection while the divorce is being negotiated.

The most common style of accommodation is to avoid conflict. In the training I do, most people indicate that, when they are faced with conflict, the strategy of first choice is to run. If one partner always accommodates to the other spouse, the mediator can provoke the couple into fighting within the safe environment of the office, to surface the real conflict between the couple.

When Bob and Sue came to see me, they had been living apart for 6 months. They owned two apartments within three blocks of each other. Their son, Chris, spent one half of the time with his father and the other half with his mother. This arrangement worked well because the son maintained his peer relationships while spending time with both parents. They were both professionals earning similar incomes. Sue dealt with issues crisply and often with irony. Bob tended to talk and talk in circumlocutions, often requiring mediator intervention to bring him back on track. Sue waited patiently, and sometimes not so patiently, while Bob ran through his routine. Bob's long-windedness also meant that he carefully avoided conflict by never focusing on a specific disagreement.

Sue lived in the better of the two apartments. It had been the marital home, and they had lavished a lot of care on it. Her apartment also had a lower mortgage than Bob's apartment. So Sue's home was worth about $25,000 more and had another $10,000 less on the mortgage with $35,000 more equity than Bob's apartment. The couple agreed on joint custody and shared parenting of Chris. Each would pay Chris's expenses while he lived with that parent. Bob agreed to pay for all of the son's clothing, medical, and extracurricular expenses as well as his future college expenses. We bogged down, however, on the distribution of assets. Bob proposed an equal distribution of the assets. Sue wanted an equal distribution of all the assets after each took one apartment. In effect, she was asking for an additional $35,000, or about 65% of the assets.

Bob made offer after offer that gave her more than 50% of the assets, but not 65%. Each proposal was met with a firm rejection. Finally, he proposed that they each take their apartments and when, at some future date, Sue sold her apartment, she would reimburse him for the difference without interest or penalty to her. I thought this was generous and would meet Sue's needs. Sue countered, "I tell you what, when I sell the apartment, I will give the money to Chris." Bob swallowed and began another lengthy digression clearly avoiding the issue Sue had provoked. I let him talk for a minute or so and then casually observed, "Gee, I don't see any smoke coming out of your ears, Bob." He stopped in the middle of a sentence. "What do you mean?" he asked me. "Well, I would have expected most men to get very angry at Sue's proposal. But, I'm sorry, I interrupted you." I apologized. Bob continued for a few more minutes, Sue responded, and suddenly Bob exploded, expressing his anger at what Sue was doing and the discounting he felt when she rejected the last offer. When Bob finished, Sue angrily revealed that he had decided to separate over a year ago and told her when the two of them were on a trip to Europe. She was very bitter at this point and talked about being left high and dry in Germany.

As they talked, it became clear that Sue wanted retribution for the way Bob told her of the end of the marriage. Bob wanted Sue's approval of the divorce and kept pushing her to give it. I permitted the discussion to continue until I heard them going around the same issues for a second time. At that point I leaned forward and said, "Bob, you cannot have Sue's approval of the divorce or the way you told her or of the person you are living with now. You must respect her right to be angry and bitter at the divorce and the way you told her." Turning to Sue I said, "And Sue, you can't get monetary retribution for the things that have happened to you. What you need for your own dignity is a fair settlement that enables you to move on with your own life."

Sue nodded, and Bob peered at her through his heavy lenses, seeking some message that she would let go while trying to formulate an appropriate response for himself. Slowly they each talked of the way the marriage ended and their respective parts in the ending. At the close of the session, Sue came up with a proposal to settle the apartments issue that was satisfactory to both of them, and Bob was able to stop asking for her approval of the divorce.

In this case the mediator intervened to prevent conflict avoidance and forced the underlying conflict between Sue and Bob into the open. Once it was in the open, they could each talk about their feelings and let go of the emotional aspect of the economic issue. The mediator provoked the conflict as a strategy for getting it resolved.

A similar approach can be used in cases where a client accommodates because of discomfort with power or fear of the other. In the former, the mediator seeks to challenge the client's refusal to exercise his or her power. In the latter, the mediator provokes by raising issues that one spouse fears, to demonstrate that the other will not leave the mediation if the issue is raised. It is not unusual for the wife to say that she does not want to talk about a cost-of-living adjustment in the support agreement because she is afraid that, "He will just blow his top and walk out." The mediator raises the issue and demonstrates that the husband will not walk out over the issue and, in fact, will talk about it. It might be said that in cases where one spouse does a lot of accommodating, the mediator acts as that person's courage in dealing with the issue.

PATTERNS OF RELATIONSHIP AND POWER PLAYS

All couples have, by the time they come to divorce, established a number of ways of relating that fall into discernible patterns. A mediator can, by observing a series of interactions, begin to identify the nature of the patterns. The patterns of the relationship fall into two categories, each indicating that one partner has more power than the other in this regard. The first is the ability of each spouse to know what the other's "buttons" are. The second is to be able to accurately predict the other's behavior when those buttons are pushed. Many people know the right buttons to push, but when this knowledge is coupled with the ability to accurately predict the other's response and to know when and how to use this weapon, then the spouse with these skills is devastatingly powerful.

The mediator has three basic strategies in dealing with this power imbalance, and I will list them in ascending order of difficulty, in the sense that the most difficult takes more and longer mediator interventions.

Identifying with the Person under Attack

John is fond of putting Mary down regarding her lack of schooling. Whenever the negotiations get difficult, he resorts to an attack on her education, which brings tears from Mary, diverting attention from the key issue under discussion. When the mediator observes that this happens a number of times and a pattern develops, he or she finally intervenes after John makes a particular jab at Mary's education. Leaning towards Mary, the mediator says, "That must hurt a lot when John says that to you, Mary." Mary holds back the tears, probably in surprise, and says, "Yes, it does." The mediator then encourages her to describe to John exactly how and why it hurts.

While this is going on, the mediator maintains good eye contact with John and carefully avoids any judgmental statement about John's behavior, focusing instead on the impact of that behavior on Mary. The mediator then says to John, "It probably surprised you to know how much that hurt Mary. If it's OK with you, John, I'll intervene and stop you if you inadvertently do it again." John agrees and gives the mediator permission to disarm him of this weapon. John is relieved because the mediator has not chastised him or put him down. Rather, he or she has promised to help him avoid doing what has been demonstrated as destructive.

Forbidding an Issue

In the previous strategy the mediator wins the right to forbid a specific interplay. But there are also times when the mediator needs to be able to forbid entire issues from interfering with the mediation. I often use this technique when one spouse tries to bring a third party into the discussions. For example, the husband might say, "Well, my father says I should be crazy not to get at least three quarters of the house." When the husband has a girlfriend, the wife may keep raising it as a weapon: "I don't want her around when the kids are with you." She drops the girlfriend's name into the conversation at crucial moments, causing the husband to get flustered and defensive.

In the first example, the mediator joins one party (this time the husband using his father) and says, "It seems to me unfair that you should be held accountable to your father in the negotiations. After all, you are an adult, married, with children. I think it would be useful if we left your father out of these negotiations so that he does not interfere with your right to conduct your own affairs." The mediator joins the adult husband against his father and gains agreement to preclude the father from the negotiations.

In the example where the wife uses the girlfriend to agitate the husband, the mediator joins the wife and says, "It's outrageous how Jane keeps slipping into these negotiations. She doesn't belong here. She's not a party to these negotiations, and I think we ought to keep her out of this room. She just does not belong here." The wife, who has been using the girlfriend, is caught in a paradox, because while she has been using the girlfriend, she also agrees that the girlfriend does not belong in the room. The husband agrees to the exclusion because he knows that his girlfriend is often used as a weapon against him. The mediator gains the agreement of the couple to forbid certain issues or strategies after he or she has explained to the couple exactly what is happening and how it impacts their negotiations, and it is clear that the couple understand the benefits of the prohibition.

Control of Communications

At times the mediator takes charge of the method of communication, when the couple's pattern is controlled by one partner and the other is unaware of this behavior. Spouses who are very good at predicting the response of the other can often control the outcome as well as the process of communications. In those instances the mediator intervenes to take charge of the way the couple communicate and reorganizes it to disempower the overly powerful spouse and empower the powerless spouse.

When Marge and Jim first came to my office, it appeared that Marge dominated the marriage. She was a large person, full of anger. She had difficulty in talking about anything without sounding angry. Jim was small, quiet, and withdrawn, appearing to be the long-suffering husband of a shrewish wife. As the mediation proceeded, however, it became obvious that Marge's only strength was her voice. Jim controlled the income, paying all the bills (and running up enormous debts), giving Marge $80 a week for the food. Marge was powerless in the key decision making. Jim exercised the power in the family by predicting exactly how Marge would respond in each situation and using that prediction to carefully escalate her response until she lost control and gave up on the argument. How did he do it? Whenever Marge spoke, Jim's eyes would glaze over, and he virtually disappeared behind an imaginary copy of the morning newspaper. Marge would state a position, and Jim simply disappeared. When Marge stated her position, she would look for a response and, getting none, repeat her story with a few choice additional adjectives and a few extra decibels. Still not receiving a response, she would begin the story again, even louder and more rudely, until she lost total control. At that point Jim looked at the mediator, shrugged his shoulders and said, "How can you deal with a crazy person like that?" She could yell and scream, and Jim merely disappeared behind his imaginary newspaper, put on his long-suffering husband look, and refused to respond to any of her points. The more he refused to listen to her point of view, the angrier she became, and becoming even more irrational, she retaliated by escalating her demands, to deal with the old feeling of helplessness that swept over her.

In this case I took complete charge of the communication flow between them. I asked Marge to state her position and as she responded I noted Jim's anticipated disappearing behavior. When she had finished, I interrupted her before she could ask Jim what he thought. I took responsibility for doing that. Turning to Jim I asked him, "What do you think about that, Jim?" "Think about what?" answered a startled Jim. And before Marge could jump in to tell him once more, I held my hand out to silence her and said, "No, wait, Marge, give Jim a chance to respond. He has a point of view also," and turning to Jim again I said, "What you think is also important and I would like to hear it, too." In an earlier article I wrote that this was a case of Jim's withdrawing as a form of conflict avoidance (Haynes, 1980). Upon further reflection and work with other couples, however, I am now more certain that this behavior was a power play on Jim's part and that he was aware of what he was doing. I held Marge in abeyance until Jim replied to the content of her message. As a counterploy, Jim then tried responding to my question by saying that he had not understood or completely heard what Marge had said. In each instance, Marge was ready to tell him in no uncertain terms. However, holding my hand out to stop her, I restated her position, minus the unnecessary adjectives and extra decibels. This forced Jim to respond to the content of the message and deprived him of the ability to goad Marge to a point of irrationality.

By carefully structuring the communication pattern of the couple, I was able to establish a context in which they could focus on the content of their respective messages. By removing Jim's button-pushing and response-predicting tactics I disempowered him and empowered Marge by helping her maintain control of herself and the situation. Thus the mediator adjusts the power imbalance sufficiently to permit the negotiations to proceed fairly and smoothly.

CONFLICT MANAGEMENT

Problem Definition

Power is derived from the ability to define a problem. Once the problem is defined, the couple can proceed to solve that problem. When one person continually defines the problems, that person usually defines them in ways where the solution must accrue to his or her benefit. The solutions to any given problem are limited and may not solve the problems as defined by the other party. For example, when the issue of the marital home comes up for discussion, the wife who has child custody may say, "If you really loved the kids, then you would give me the house." If the problem of what to do with the house is defined in that way, then the husband is faced with two choices: love the kids and give her the house, or not love the kids and not give her the house. Obviously there are more options to the house issue than those two. But as long as the problem is defined in that way, his options are limited. If the mediator intervenes and rephrases the problem definition in a statement that does not favor either spouse, the wife may feel that the mediator is on the husband's side. In addition, if the mediator does the husband's work in the process, the husband is not empowered, and the couple's method of negotiating will remain unchanged.

Therefore the mediator needs a more circuitous route to redefining the problem statement; a route that will end with the husband making the redefinition. This is accomplished by clarifying for the husband his options. At the point the wife makes the statement, "If you really loved the kids, then you would give me the house," and the husband does not act to redefine the statement, the mediator focuses on the couple's parenting. This is what I call retracking the discussion. The mediator casually asks the couple how they spent last weekend. He or she then focuses on the time the father spent with the children. As the father relates this experience, assuming it was a good one, the mediator encourages him to talk about the events, his feelings, and his relationship with the children. When this is firmly established, the mediator apologizes to the couple for wandering off the subject and reminds them of the house issue. Turning to the wife, the mediator says, "Now, Mary, what were your feelings about the house?" At this point, Mary has difficulty restating the problem as before because John has just demonstrated that he does love the children and that they have a good relationship with him. If she does reiterate her position that the measure of his love for the children is his willingness to give her the house, John is more able to challenge that problem definition, because he has just articulated his love for the children in more normal terms.

It is essential that, in the final analysis, the mediator maintain the right to define the problem that the couple must solve. When the mediator has control of the problem definition, he or she can phrase the problems in ways that permit the widest range of options that do not favor one side or the other.

Conflict Labels

Another aspect of conflict management is the labeling of the conflict that emerges from the problem definition. Often when problems are labeled as conflicts, it is a way of not dealing with the problem. In families that do not like conflict, the accusation of being conflictual will be enough to force a partner to withdraw from a particular problem definition. For example, the husband may respond each time the issue of the pension is raised, "There you go, fighting again. You seem determined to have a battle on this item." The wife, not wanting to be accused of starting a fight, backs off the issue. If this is permitted during the life of the mediation, the agreement would be reached without the pension ever being discussed. The mediator breaks this pattern of avoidance by taking responsibility for the dispute. "I know you both find this item very difficult, but it is one we must discuss" is a typical intervention. Thus the mediator relieves the wife of responsibility for raising it and reminds the husband that neither he, the wife, or the mediator can avoid discussing the pension, because it must be included in the separation agreement.

A threat is often used to try to label the conflict as nonnegotiable. In such a case the wife may respond to a cohabitation clause with the threat, "If you raise that again, I'm leaving." The mediator ignores this threat and if, when the husband repeats the position, the wife stands to leave, makes no attempt to stop her. If she is committed to mediation, she either will not leave or, if she does leave, will return shortly; and if she is not committed to mediation, her ultimatum may simply be a means to bring the process to an end. In one case a wife made this threat, and the husband dropped the matter. The following week he raised it again, and she again threatened to leave. I pointed out that all issues had to be discussed. "You don't have to agree, but you at least have to discuss," I explained to her. She ignored me and when the husband said he wanted to talk about it, she stood up, collected her bag and notes and swept towards the door. As she put her hand on the doorknob, I said "You can't leave just yet." "Why not?" she asked. "Because you have not paid me your share of my fee for this session," I responded. She hesitated for a moment and fumbled in her bag, slowly edging her way back to her chair. Finally she sat down and slowly engaged in the discussion about the issue. At the end of the discussion, the cohabitation clause was dropped because in their case, they agreed, it was an essentially unenforceable clause. However, the matter *was* discussed, and the wife was unable to make the threat to leave the talks stick. She had many other items on the agenda that she needed to talk about, so she could not afford to halt the process.

Many men like to claim that a conflict is imaginary and the result of insufficient data. John says, "That's no problem, dear, we just need more data. Here, let me put this into my calculator." He then proceeds to function under the "garbage in, garbage out" theory and often discovers that the new way of calculating the data improves his position. Or, as the new data are sought, the conflict is diffused and often avoided. When one partner uses this strategy, the mediator begins to take responsibility for the lack of clarity and the need to have the data carefully explained by the husband. The mediator says, "Help me understand what you mean by that." As the husband explains it to the mediator, the wife also learns about it and is able to participate as an equal in the subsequent discussions.

A variation of this game is when the wife says, "We don't really disagree, we both want to do what's best for the children." If the husband agrees that they really do not disagree, the mediator asks for a clearer explanation. As the partners explain their positions, the true nature of the disagreement often surfaces, and the conflict is identified and can be dealt with in the open.

Ritualized Relationships

Some couples have interesting rituals that need to be changed if the negotiations are to proceed. At times the husband will say, "I don't know too much about the finances, she always handled the money." At first blush, it appears that he is unpowerful regarding the money. At the end of the first session, the wife writes the check for the mediator, and she brings in the completed budget sheets while the husband has only sketchy points. "She has always handled the money," he notes, explaining his lack of work. As the budget discussion proceeds, the mediator discovers that while the wife handles all the money and the husband takes responsibility for it, the husband retains the right to criticize any and every expenditure she makes. The mediator breaks these rituals through assignments and specific instructions that each are to produce the information independently of the other. Slowly the mediator empowers the husband to learn how to handle the money and disempowers him of his right to criticize all of his wife's expenditures.

The Power of Passivity

Power resides implicitly in a person's dependency (Emerson, 1962). One spouse is powerful only to the extent that the other dependent spouse permits and only for as long as the passive spouse is dependent. The passive person has an extremely powerful, paradoxical way to maintain power. The passive person's standard response to each situation is, "I don't know." Given that response, the partner then makes all the decisions, often trying to determine what the passive partner really wants. Passivity is very difficult to work with in mediation because the normal response is to try to do things *for* passive people rather than *with* them. They try the patience of the mediator and, of course, never accept responsibility for anything that happens. Deeply ingrained passivity is particularly dangerous in mediation because, if not dealt with, passivity forces the mediator to deal primarily with the nonpassive partner, raising the possibility that the mediator and one spouse will shape the agreement, with the passive partner having no allegiance to it.

The passive person also disclaims responsibility for the outcome. A passive husband might resort to tears each time a decision must be made. As the tears dry, he looks helpless and says, "You do what's fair. I can't do it." During the marriage, this behavior has usually been rewarded by the wife doing what she believes he thinks is fair, in an effort to please him. Unless an alternative strategy is developed to deal with passivity, the mediator will be seduced into an alliance with the passive spouse or become that spouse's advocate. There is always the possibility that the passive spouse will receive an unfair deal, if not protecting his or her interests. Two mediation strategies that work against passivity are provocation and reframing.

The mediator uses provocation to try to reduce the dependency factor of the passive spouse. This can at times be accomplished by simply refusing to acknowledge the person's passivity. I will just not accept that one spouse has no opinion on any subject or no preferences to express. I refuse to behave as if that spouse has no ideas to share, no alternatives to offer. I proceed as if he or she is a rational, normal person with opinions, ideas, and preferences. I constantly defer to the passive spouse, seeking an opinion, asking questions, and breaking the patterns established in the marriage. I provoke by asking the passive wife, "What will you do after the divorce to add to the support income to meet your needs?" "I don't know," comes the response. "Starve?" I ask. That last comment provokes a response, often tears, and opens the way for a discussion of needs.

Reframing is accomplished by paying attention to the passive person's dependency and providing information that reduces the dependency (which may mean disempowering the passivity) by empowering the spouse to identify future independent needs and make decisions around them. The balance between the two is fine, and the mediator is careful to empower at each stage of disempowerment. Since passivity is part of a family system requiring the cooperation of both partners, removal of one spouse's passivity is sometimes compensated by new passivity in the active spouse.

Another aspect of passivity is "learned helplessness" (Seligman, 1975), which is usually expressed in terms of a person's inability to accomplish life's tasks. "Oh, I couldn't do that" and "I would never know how to" are common expressions of this mode of behavior. The learned helplessness had a function within the marriage, but it is highly dysfunctional in the divorce. The mediator approaches the problem by deciding that it does not exist and refusing to relate to the helpless person in the way they are accustomed to being treated. I make specific assignments to a person I have identified as helpless. I keep the assignment simple and my instructions clear. For example, I might say to a wife, "I want you to find out the value of Jack's pension plan." Now, this is a highly technical task requiring the aid of an expert. However, I translate it into a simple task. I tell her, "Jack's pension plan will pay $500 a month when he retires at age 65. Now, since you have decided to divide everything equally, you should get the equivalent of one half of that. I want you to go to your local bank and to your insurance company and ask them what it will cost to purchase an annuity that pays you $250 a month when you reach 65." A typical response is, "Oh, I don't know who to talk to at the bank." I respond, "OK, where do you bank?"

"At Chemical Bank."

"Good, go there tomorrow morning and ask to see the manager and then ask him this question."

"I'm not sure I understand the question."

"I thought you might not, so I am writing it out for you."

The same dialogue is repeated for the call to the insurance company. The tasks are relatively simple, and accomplishing them is empowering for the helpless spouse. These spouses are surprised at their competence, and because the mediator is not part of the family system, the assignments have a higher chance of being carried out. The husband, who in the past has encouraged the helplessness, now wants his wife to be independent and is less likely to sabotage her efforts at competency. However, just in case he does, I add a firm instruction to Jack. "Jack, I don't want you involved in this at all. It is important that Mary do this herself so that she can collect and *believe* the information. Mary, if you have a problem, don't talk to Jack about it, rather wait until the next session and we will work it out together."

This is an example of the way in which the mediator, though not a therapist, accomplishes therapeutic interventions while being clear to the clients that she or he is not doing therapy. The mediator deals with the problem in a way that ignores or limits behavior that interferes with efficient problem solving. An assumption of competency is made and articulated, and when the couple fall back on old ways, the mediator predicts this behavior and blocks it through additional instructions to the spouses. The result is that, treated with maturity, people tend to respond more competently. When capability is missing, the mediator spends time increasing the person's ability rather than dealing with the underlying dynamics that cause the helplessness.

REFERENCES

Bell, D. *Power, influence and authority*. New York: Oxford University Press, 1975.

Coleman. Loss of power. *American Sociological Review*, 1973, *38*, 1–16.

Deutsch, M. *The resolution of conflict. Constructive and destructive processes*. New Haven, CT: Yale University Press, 1973.

Emerson, R. Power-dependence relations. *American Sociological Review*, 1962, *27*, 31–41.

French, J., & Raven, B. The bases of social power. In D. Cartwright (Ed.), *Studies in social power*. Ann Arbor, MI: University of Michigan Press, 1959.

Haynes, J. Managing conflict: The role of the mediator. *Conciliation Courts Review*, 1980, *18(2)*.

Haynes, J. Divorce Mediation; A Practical Guide for Therapists and Counselors. New York: Springer, 1981.

Raven, B., & Kruglanski, A. Conflict and power. In P. Swingle (Ed.), *The structure of conflict*. New York: Academic Press, 1970.

Rubin, J., & Brown, B. *The social psychology of bargaining*. New York: Academic Press, 1975.

Schelling, T. *The strategy of conflict*. New York: Oxford University Press, 1960.

Searle, J. *Speech acts*. Boston: Cambridge University Press, 1969.

Seligman, M. *Helplessness: On depression, development and death*. San Francisco: Freeman, 1975.

15

Communication Strategies

WILLIAM A. DONOHUE
Michigan State University

DEBORAH WEIDER-HATFIELD
University of Georgia

Effective communication is the bedrock of the mediation process. This chapter concentrates on the communication process through an analysis of twenty divorce mediation transcripts. The authors highlight the complexity of the communication process and the numerous decisions that the mediator must make when deciding when and how to intervene. The use of the communication strategies presented in this chapter can help the mediator make effective communication interventions to enhance the parties' ability to reach an agreement.

Consider the following husband–wife interaction during a divorce mediation session.

> *Wife:* You are playing dirty with me and I'm not playing dirty with you. I'm being honest. I'm laying it on the line.
> *Husband:* That's a lot of crap, Gwen. You're not playing dirty? Where were you when I asked for us to really work on the relationship? Out with—
> *Wife:* John, that is water under the bridge.
> *Husband:* I think you need to remember something here. It was you who made the decision to leave the relationship. It was you that was looking for an out, and that really needs to be considered when we talk about custody.

Would you have interrupted this sequence in any particular location to provide some sort of intervention? Or should the mediator continue to observe the conflict? If an interruption is appropriate, should it be positioned after one particular party or the other, and what kind of language should be used to frame the interruption? If you have mediation experience, you will recognize that these are only a few of the communication decisions that mediators are forced to make very quickly.

This chapter presents a set of guidelines for making competent communication decisions in mediation. These guidelines are validated by exploring the ways in which the mediators and the disputants organized their communication patterns in 20 actual divorce mediation transcripts. The chapter concludes with a brief example of how the decision guidelines can be applied to specific mediation sessions.

THE COMMUNICATION PROBLEM IN MEDIATION

Defining Competence

Before we address the specific problem of competent communication in mediation, it might be useful to identify generally what is meant by communication competence. While Cooley and Roach (1984) report that there is considerable controversy surrounding the concept of communication competence, there does seem to be general support for their definition of competence as "the knowledge of appropriate communication patterns in a given situation and the ability to use the knowledge" (p. 25). That is, the competent communicator knows how certain gestures, words, and phrases are likely to be interpreted in a specific situation and has the ability to use this knowledge to influence the ongoing definition of the situation.

This definition has four important implications for the mediator. First, knowing how certain symbols are routinely interpreted is culturally determined. If the mediator and the disputants are from different cultures that use very different modes of communication, accurate interpretation is quite difficult. For example, Donohue (in 1985) found that yelling at one's opponent carries distinct cultural interpretations. For some, yelling means intensified threat, and for others it means that the disputant is sincere but not threatening. The interpretation problem is generally solved when the mediator can spend some time prior to mediation in talk with the disputants to learn their interpretative schemes.

The second implication of this definition is that interpretations are situationally specific. For example, when the mediator is working in a divorce dispute, it is helpful to understand how people respond emotionally to issues surrounding divorce. Emotional responses are likely to mean something different in an environmental or labor–management dispute than they might in a divorce dispute. As a result, accurate interpretation is enhanced by using a working knowledge of the specific situation within which the dispute is taking place.

The third implication of our communication competence definition is that the mediator needs ready access to a variety of communication tactics that will move the disputants closer to agreement. More specifically, the mediator's role communicatively is to intervene to create a collaborative context that enables the disputants to make accurate interpretations of one another's messages. Without accurate interpretation, the disputants will have difficulty negotiating their differences. The data are quite clear (e.g., Pruitt, 1981) that accurate information exchange is a prerequisite to creating integrative solutions to disputes.

The fourth implication of this definition is that competence not only depends upon having a working knowledge of communication tactics but also is a function of the timing of a particular intervention. The group communication literature has developed a strong consensus about the role of timing in leadership development. Fisher's review (1983) of the group research suggests that timing is often more important than the content of a statement. Group members will evaluate a leader's contribution in relation to their own current activities. If the contribution facilitates the interaction, the leader's influence grows. For this reason, Fisher explains that group members who have good ideas may not emerge as influential because their contributions were ill-timed.

This definition of communicative competence in mediation may give the impression that the intervention process simply goes by the numbers. All the mediator needs to do is make the proper interpretation, know something about the subject matter, and choose from a select group of tactics at the appropriate moment, to complete a successful intervention. Mediation is never that simple because each interpretation and each intervention must be carefully constructed for the specific context as it unfolds over time. Any practitioner can attest to the difficulty of merging these variables to perform competently. The mediator needs some general guidelines for deciding which kind of intervention at which moment is best suited for which kind of mediation situation. To accomplish this goal, it will be useful to identify the situational parameters that are likely to affect intervention choice.

Situational Parameters

As summarized in Donohue, Diez, and Weider-Hatfield (1984), there appear to be four primary situational parameters that are most likely to affect intervention choice. The first situational parameter, and arguably the most influential in mediation, is *goals of the disputants*. Rubin (1983) argues convincingly that each party's predisposition to settle heavily influences intervention choice. The optimal mediation context appears to be one in which each disputant is very eager to reach an agreement, and each has a high level of aspiration (Pruitt & Lewis, 1975). They are more likely to work hard toward agreement. If goals are very discrepant, that is, one party wants to dissolve the current relationship while the other seeks to sustain the relationship in its current form, then the dispute will be difficult to resolve. Making an early assessment of individual goals and motivation to negotiate provides more direction for selecting intervention tactics.

The second situational parameter that structures interventions deals with the *procedures, rules, and regulations* under which mediation develops. Some mediations occur in a context of confidentiality, while others do not. Also, mediators vary in the extent to which they impose rules on how disputants will participate in the process. In some areas there are several legal constraints on the manner in which disputants can participate. An awareness of these constraints and how they are likely to affect the goals of the participants will enhance intervention decision making. For example, in some states divorce mediation is mandatory, and the proceedings are not confidential. This can dramatically alter the incentive to negotiate, which will again influence intervention choice.

The third situational parameter of interest to mediators is *subject matter*. Some subjects are likely to evoke more intense emotional responses than others. Disputed child custody is likely to stimulate more complex emotions than a tenant–landlord dispute. Some subjects require more expertise on the mediator's part so that the dispute can be better understood and alternative solutions can be generated.

Finally, the *relational history* of the disputants and the *role relationships* that emerge through mediation are likely to structure intervention choices. If the disputants have a very complementary role relationship, with a history of one person dominating the other, the mediator may need to select an intervention that will empower the weaker party. If the disputants have a very symmetrical role relationship, with both competing for control, the mediator may have difficulty gaining access to the interaction. Since roles are negotiated through interaction, the mediator must create a set of role relationships that will provide maximum flexibility in selecting interventions.

These are the situational parameters that are most likely to structure intervention choice. The task now remains to identify the range of choices that, when used within these parameters, will facilitate dispute resolution.

INTERVENTION STRATEGIES

Many different types of intervention strategies have been proposed by a variety of researchers and practitioners (e.g., Moore, 1986; Pruitt, 1981). A desirable objective is to organize these interventions into a usable set of categories that can translate easily into the practice of mediation. Another desirable objective is to provide some direction concerning how the situational parameters discussed above are likely to affect intervention choice.

Given these two main objectives, a communicatively competent mediator pursues three primary strategies:

1. gaining control of the interaction through structuring
2. increasing each disputant's involvement in the process, to encourage collaboration
3. promoting consistency, to develop the mediator's trustworthiness

Within each of these three general strategies, it is possible to identify which tactics are more directive and which less directive in accomplishing their goals. The more directive tactics are used when the mediator seeks a specific response from one or both of the disputants. The less directive tactics are not used with the intention of eliciting an immediate specific response but can have the same effect as the directive tactics over the long term. The tactics listed below under each heading are not intended to be comprehensive; rather, they are a sample of those that appear capable of accomplishing the general objective. Many of the tactics listed are derived from the list of mediator compliance-gaining strategies developed by McLaughlin and Cody (1980).

Gaining Control through Structuring

The objective of this first general strategy is to empower the mediator to direct the course of the mediation, as opposed to either one of the disputants. If the mediator permits the disputants to control the interaction from the beginning, they are likely to regress to prior dysfunctional communication patterns. Clearly, if the disputants could negotiate productively themselves, they would not need the mediator.

Wall's review of mediation (1981) suggests that control can be achieved by imposing structure on the process. Organization presents the appearance of progress, provides clarity to the situation, and serves to orient the disputants away from unproductive communication exchanges. Relative to the situational parameters outlined above, Pruitt and Lewis (1975) contend that structure is most useful when conflict intensity is great and when the topic is likely to promote emotional outbursts that lead to impasse. Controls on such contributions can make the information contained in them more useful to the decision-making process. The more directive tactics that provide such structure include:

1. Lay down rules related to the topic or process of interaction, for example, "we won't be talking about old grievances here; we'll be focusing on the future."

2. Structure and enforce the agenda or the order in which topics are discussed, for example, "First, I would like to explain mediation to you."

3. Create deadlines for reaching agreements.

The less directive tactics for providing structure would include:

1. Increase formality by using more businesslike language and encouraging disputants to do the same.

2. Restructure colloquial language to remove conflict-producing elements; for example, the mediator restates, "He's got some woman living with him" as "So there's a third party involved."

3. Review the purpose of the mediation, to avoid irrelevant arguments.

Increasing Involvement to Encourage Collaboration

Research in mediation shows that a large pool of information is necessary to explore alternatives so that integrative agreements can be created (e.g., Pruitt, 1981). Interventions aimed at creating and evaluating this information can be quite useful. Clearly, the more diverse kinds of information that emerge, the greater the potential for collaboration. A lack of information can quickly lead to impasse, as potential solutions do not become apparent.

Involvement is probably most critical when the motivation to negotiate is low, or when the rules, such as confidentiality, may be a force discouraging involvement. In addition, when the topic is sensitive and the potential for emotional outbursts is great, individuals are less likely to process accurately the information presented by the other. In these instances the information needs to be restructured so both parties can participate in the decision making more productively. The following more directive tactics are intended to manage the information resource.

1. Request proposals for solutions from the disputants.

2. Create alternative proposals: "What if Mrs. Smith were to have the children on alternate weekends?"

3. Negatively compare one person's position with the other: "Mr. Smith, Mrs. Smith has shown some flexibility here; can't you do the same?"

4. Request evaluations of proposals from each of the parties.

The less directive tactics for increasing involvement include:

1. Reinforce points of agreement between the disputants.

2. Explain the benefits of compliance: "The children may feel more secure knowing that you two can work together on matters that affect them."

3. Reframe a particular proposal or idea in terms that identify advantages to both parties.

4. Request clarification and/or information.

Promoting Consistency to Develop Trustworthiness

Research related to communicator credibility has clearly found that communicators who are perceived to be incompetent and untrustworthy will have difficulty gaining compliance from the audience. The difficulty is created because the audience is more likely to misinterpret or reinterpret negatively the speaker's intentions. If the mediator does not gain control or increase involvement, it is likely that the mediator will not be perceived as competent. If the mediator is inconsistent in distributing structuring or involvement tactics, the mediator's trustworthiness may be compromised. Thus *how* the mediator imposes the interventions will contribute a great deal to his or her ability to be understood accurately and gain compliance. As Pearson (1982) indicates, perceptions of fairness contribute significantly to the disputant's judgment of a successful mediation.

Trustworthiness judgments are more likely to be made when the disputants are heavily monitoring the mediator's behavior. Such monitoring is likely to occur when conflict intensity is great and each party is watching to see whether the mediator is going to take sides. Thus, near the interaction, before the mediator has established control and conflict intensity has been relaxed a bit, the mediator must monitor the consistency with which the interventions are made. The following more directive tactics are intended to accomplish mediator trustworthiness.

    1. Allocate floor time fairly so one person is not doing all the talking.

    2. Inquire about disputants' perceptions of the fairness of the process.

    3. Invoke negative consequences of noncompliance equally: "What we would like to avoid here is a painful and costly court battle."

The following tactics promote some less directive means of accomplishing trustworthiness.

    1. Maintain consistent levels of formality so the disputants are not confused by mediators who are sometimes too friendly and sometimes too businesslike.

    2. Use the same level of deference toward each disputant: for example, addressing both parties by either Mr. or Ms., or by first names if appropriate.

    3. Reinforce concessions equally: "I see that as a real step forward in working something out here."

Validating Communication Intervention

Perhaps the best way to validate this approach to studying communication strategies in mediation is to determine whether the three general strategies actually function as predicted. Do successful mediators work more to gain control, increase involvement, and promote consistency than do unsuccessful mediators? After this question is answered, it will be possible to research the specific tactics, some of which are cited above, that contribute more or less to these three general strategies.

Various quantitative and qualitative features of the language that mediators and disputants use to negotiate the issues can be used for validation. The quantitative features that provide insights into how control, involvement, and consistency are being used include the number of utterances made by each party, the number of words per utterance, the frequency with which participants interrupt one another, and the extent to which participants speak directly to one another.

The qualitative feature used to validate communication interventions is language intensity, defined as a quality of language that indicates the degree to which a speaker's attitude toward X deviates from neutrality. X may be a person, place, idea, or object. (See Bradac, Bowers, & Courtright, 1979, for a summary of language-intensity research.) Language intensity can be used to estimate the level of conflict intensity and detect the manner in which the mediator is managing this situational parameter. The specific forms of language intensity and the specific quantitative coding procedures used in this study are described in the methods section.

Regarding these two language features, the following questions should reveal the extent to which successful and unsuccessful mediators differ in their use of control, involvement, and consistency strategies. With respect to *control*, three questions are relevant.

1. Will successful mediators (those fostering an agreement) talk more than unsuccessful mediators as a means of sustaining control?

2. Will successful mediators prevent a disputant from talking over them more than unsuccessful mediators?

3. Are successful mediators more capable of controlling the level of language intensity than unsuccessful mediators?

Regarding the *involvement* strategy, two questions may be addressed.

1. Will successful mediators use shorter utterances than unsuccessful mediators as a means of providing the disputants with opportunities to present their views?

2. Will the disputing parties talk more to each other than to the mediator in the successfully mediated disputes?

Finally, with respect to the *consistency* strategies, the following research questions will be tested.

1. Will the successful mediators interrupt disputing parties on a more equal basis than unsuccessful mediators?

2. Will successful mediators manage the level of language intensity more equally between disputants than unsuccessful mediators?

METHODS

Twenty pre- and postdivorce custody–visitation disputes (10 in which agreement was reached and 10 in which agreement was not reached) were transcribed following the rules of transcription presented by Schenkein (1978). The audio tapes were part of the approximately 80 collected by the Divorce Mediation Research Project of the Association of Family and Conciliation Courts. The 20 sessions used in the present study came from the various branches of the Los Angeles Conciliation Court. There was one female mediator for each group of 10. The format of the mediation service at this court, the sources of user satisfaction, and the user evaluations of mediation outcomes are discussed in Pearson and Thoennes (1984). Any personal names in the transcripts were blacked out to ensure the anonymity of the disputants and the mediator.

The quantitative features of the transcript were coded in the following ways: who spoke each utterance; how many words comprised each utterance; who was the prior speaker; how many husband–wife interactions occurred; was anyone being talked over by the speaker of the utterance; and functional and nonfunctional interruptions, which are utterances in which the speaker successfully or unsuccessfully gained the floor long enough to communicate a complete thought unit. Given the straightforward nature of the coding procedure, only one coder was used, and no reliability checks were done.

Language intensity was coded by identifying the extent to which each utterance contained instances of

1. *obscurity* or uncommonly used words that are used for rhetorical or stylistic effect; for example, "salacious" is more intense than "lustful."

2. *qualifying adjectives or adverbs* or words that modify other words, lending to them a more extreme meaning than if the modified word stood alone, for example, "an *obviously* falacious argument."

3. *profanity* or language that approaches or crosses the bounds of good taste, or is obscene or vulgar, for example, "You piss me off, shit for brains."

4. *metaphor* that involves transferring one meaning of a concept from one context to another through comparison, for example, "The couple was stuck in the sand trap of jealousy."

5. *sex metaphors* denoting the practice of sexual acts or events but also referring to a broader context, for example, "The salesman felt like a whore for the company."

6. *death metaphors* or associations with death, decomposition, or the afterlife, for example, "You killed our marriage."

Whenever a given utterance contained any one or more of these intensity markers, it was coded accordingly. Each utterance was scored according to its level of language intensity. The coding reliability for this qualitative variable was .82 using Guetzkow's formula (1950).

RESULTS

A total of 9,075 utterances were coded, 6,184 utterances in the "agreement reached" (AR) sessions and 2,891 in the "no agreement reached" (NAR) sessions. Each of the control, involvement, and consistency questions, asked above, are addressed in that order.

Control

In response to the first control question, do successful mediators talk more than unsuccessful mediators, Table 15–1 reveals that mediators in the AR condition made 34.9% of the total utterances, while mediators in the NAR

Table 15-1. Utterance Frequencies and Proportions

	Total utterances	Mediator	Husband	Wife
Agreement reached	6,184	2,160 (34.9%)	1,990 (32.2%)	2,034 (32.9%)
No agreement reached	2,891	1,049 (36.3%)	950 (32.9%)	892 (30.9%)

Note. $\chi^2 = 3.84$, $df = 2$, $p > .10$.

conditions made 36.3% of the total utterances. The overall chi-square showed no significant differences among the proportions of utterances spoken by interactants across both conditions. In fact, the fairly equal distribution of utterances across all three parties suggests that the mediators are not using mere quantity of words to either gain or relinquish control in the interaction.

In relation to talk-over frequency, Table 15–2 reveals that mediators are less successful when they allow one party to control the allocation of floor time. Table 15–2 shows a fairly equal distribution of mediator talk-overs across the AR and NAR conditions (12.7% and 12.4%). In the NAR condition, husbands talk over mediators significantly more than wives. Thus, disproportionately relinquishing control to one party or the other may weaken the mediator's ability to move in a productive direction.

Table 15–3 indicates that language intensity was very significantly related to successful and unsuccessful mediation. The data reveal nearly twice as much language intensity in the NAR sessions as in the AR sessions. This result remained consistent for the mediator, the husband, and the wife. Apparently in the NAR condition the mediator was less capable of controlling the kind of metaphors, qualifiers, and other forms of language intensity used by the disputants. The overwhelming significance of these results suggest that the language for formulating an agreement is an important resource for developing a collaborative context.

Table 15-2. Talk-Over of Mediators, Frequencies and Proportions

	Total utterances (husband and wife)	Total talk-overs of mediator	Husband talk-overs of mediator	Wife talk-overs of mediator
Agreement reached	4,024	512 (12.7%)	256 (50.0%)	256 (50.0%)
No agreement reached	1,842	228 (12.4%)	143 (62.7%)	85 (37.3%)

Note. $\chi^2 = 19.27$, $df = 1$, $p < .01$.

Table 15-3. Language Intensity Means per Utterance

	Overall intensity[a]	Mediator intensity[b]	Husband intensity[c]	Wife intensity[d]
Agreement reached	.2071	.2579	.2051	.1751
No agreement reached	.3483	.3759	.3211	.3450

[a]$F = 72.44$, $df = 1/1905$, $p < .001$. [b]$F = 7.81$, $df = 1/568$, $p < .005$. [c]$F = 29.88$, $df = 1/680$, $p < .001$. [d]$F = 55.20$, $df = 1/652$, $p < .001$.

Involvement

Table 15-4 indicates that both mediators and husbands and wives together used significantly shorter utterances in the AR condition. This finding suggests that mediators selecting shorter interventions provide greater opportunities for increasing the information coming from the disputing parties. Also, this finding may be a function of mediators using more verbal reinforcers when the participants are speaking. Using such phrases as "Yes, I see what you mean" or "Uh huh" indicates active listening which encourages the participants to provide more information.

With respect to the second involvement question, whether successful disputants talk more to each other than to the mediator, the data are less clear. An examination of the percentages of talk between disputing parties in both conditions shows that disputants did not speak directly to one another more often in the AR condition. Of the total number of utterances made by the disputants in each condition, disputants in the AR condition made 29.8% of their comments directly to each other to the exclusion of the mediator, while disputants in the NAR condition made 30.6% of their comments directly to each other to the exclusion of the mediator.

Consistency

Table 15–5 addresses the first consistency question, regarding the equality with which the mediator functionally and nonfunctionally interrupts the disputing parties. It is clear that in the AR condition the mediator interrupted both

Table 15-4. Mean Utterance Length for Mediator and Disputants

	Mediator[a]	Husband	Wife	Husband and wife[b]
Agreement reached	16.62	13.50	12.81	13.14
No agreement reached	23.56	16.93	15.87	16.52

[a]$t = 5.03$, $df = 3027$, $p > .001$, [b]$F = 8.71$, $df = 3/5862$, $p > .001$.

Table 15-5. Interruption by Mediator, Frequencies and Proportions

	Mediator interrupting husband	Mediator interrupting wife
Functional		
Agreement reached	210 (50%)	211 (50%)
No agreement reached	124 (62%)	79 (38%)
Nonfunctional		
Agreement reached	40 (53%)	36 (47%)
No agreement reached	17 (74%)	6 (26%)

Note. $\chi^2 = 6.91$, $df = 1$, $p > .01$ for functional interruptions. $\chi^2 = 3.34$, $df = 1$, $p > .06$ for nonfunctional interruptions.

parties nearly equally, while in the NAR condition the mediator interrupted the husband significantly more frequently than the wife.

These data are difficult to explain conceptually; the differential interruption could be a function of the husband's needing more structuring than the wife because of the husband's use of conflict-producing statements. In such an instance these data may indicate that there was a greater differential in willingness to negotiate, which the mediator may have been powerless to alter. Nevertheless, this large discrepancy in interruption frequency may serve as a warning sign to the mediator that agreement obstruction might be taking place in the mediation.

Finally, regarding the consistency question about distribution of language intensity, Table 15-3 provides some rather interesting results. In both conditions, the mediator's language intensity was greater than either of the disputants. However, in the AR condition, the disputants use significantly less intensity than the mediator, while in the NAR condition, the disputants use about the same level as the mediator. One way of interpreting these data is to suggest that the disputants may have trusted the mediator sufficiently to allow him or her sufficient latitude in using expressive language, while at the same time controlling their level of intensity.

A further analysis of these data revealed that the mediator's use of qualifying adjectives and adverbs contributed most to nonsuccess. When the mediator did a great deal of modification and qualification, it may have confused the disputants or signaled that the mediator felt he or she could not be trusted if speaking in a more straightforward manner.

The following conclusions are based upon results from the analyses of the data obtained from 20 custody or visitation dispute sessions. Mediators who successfully fostered an agreement between disputants

1. were better able to control the allocation of floor time among the disputants and the disputants' level of language intensity
2. used shorter utterances in communicating with disputants in an attempt to increase disputants' involvement and increase the information base
3. were significantly more consistent in interrupting disputants and in the kinds of language intensity selected by the mediator

DISCUSSION

The data provide some convincing evidence that more successsful mediators are more in control of the interaction, use more interventions intended to involve participants in finding the information necessary for agreement, and are more watchful of distributing these interventions fairly and consistently between disputants. Research related to the specific content of the interventions is continuing and will eventually point out ways for determining which specific interventions at which specific points in time will lead to greater success in dispute resolution. For the present, the data presented in this chapter provide a general confirmation of the mediation model described above.

An examination of these results reveals some interesting insights into the kinds of mediator interventions used in these 20 custody–visitation sessions. Although mediators successfully fostered an agreement, one is struck by the amount of talk occurring in the AR condition versus the NAR condition. Getting to an agreement clearly took more talk time. At the same time, mediators who successfully fostered an agreement used significantly fewer words per utterance than mediators who did not reach agreement. This suggests that efforts to gain control through monopolizing the floor are not conducive to fostering agreement, even though high expenditures of energy are needed to develop a communicative context that is conducive to agreement making. The more appropriate approach appears to center on involving the disputants in the negotiation, thereby increasing the information pool so more alternatives can be created.

Another insight provided by the data is that maintaining control of the interaction is a significant predictor of success. When the mediator loses control by allowing disputants to differentially talk over him or her or differentially interrupts the disputants, the mediator is less capable of providing the structure that is needed to reduce conflict intensity.

The results of the language-intensity variable confirm this interpretation. When the mediator is unable to provide a proper decision-making structure, the disputants and the mediator significantly increase their level of language intensity. Since language use and context are defined by one another, it appears that the increased language intensity signals greater conflict intensity to all parties in the dispute. When the mediator more carefully monitors the disputants' level of language intensity, the parties can signal a more cooperative approach to one another.

A final implication of these data is related to the gender differences that are a very obvious feature of the results in the NAR condition. Wives are interrupted and talk over the mediator significantly less than their husbands when no agreement is reached. The husband's domination, or the mediator's inability to control the husband, appears to sabotage agreement making. Yet when no agreement is reached, the wife uses significantly greater language intensity than the husband. The picture of the wife's involvement that emerges from these data is that she may be responding to this domination by using more intense language when she does secure a chance to speak. This increased intensity may also serve to intensify conflict, which may then trigger more attempts at husband domination, and a vicious cycle results. Controlling the disputants more consistently may salvage the mediation and prevent it from becoming a conflict escalator.

A COMMUNICATION INTERVENTION EXAMPLE

The following interaction occurred between a couple (who were actually actors portraying a divorcing couple trying to resolve the custody of the son, Mark) and an actual mediator. This is a continuation of the interaction at the beginning of this chapter. The mediation is in its initial, information-gathering stage. (Immediately following this transcript, an analysis of the process focuses on each of the three intervention forms identified above and on the specific language tactics within each of these intervention strategies. You may benefit from performing your analysis prior to reading ours.)

1. *Husband:* You're making it sound—

2. *Wife:* You are playing dirty with me and I'm not playing dirty with you. I'm being honest. I'm laying it on the line.

3. *Husband:* That's a lot of crap, Gwen. You're not playing dirty. . . . Where were you when I asked for us to really work on the relationship? Out with—

4. *Wife:* John, that is water under the bridge.

5. *Mediator:* Now you're both hurting very much from this, I see.

6. *Husband:* She has no idea, no idea whatsoever.

7. *Mediator:* I suspect that Gwen does and Gwen also hurts and perhaps neither of you quite understand how much the other one hurts in this process. And that's a new key in one sense because that really is part of the process, and that each of us will have some of those feelings as we go along. I'm trying to understand how this all fits in with what you want to do, which is to negotiate your separate agreement. And it seems to me that we had agreed that we would focus this week on the issue of Mark and the parenting questions. If I understand it, you both have very strong feelings about Mark and about the parenting. Hm, why don't you share some of those with me at this point?

8. *Husband:* When you said strong feelings, that's an understatement, [mediator's name]. This is the one issue that I feel extremely strong about, and I'm really going to struggle to get custody of Mark.

9. *Mediator:* Um hm.

10. *Husband:* I think one thing needs to be remembered here. It is Gwen who made the decision to leave the relationship. It's Gwen that's looking to get out of the relationship, and that really needs to be considered when we talk about custody.

11. *Mediator:* OK, we're not, however, going to look at the past in terms

of fault or responsibility. We're only going to look at the future in terms of what's best for Mark, right?

12. *Wife:* It's true, I know I have initiated. I really, I don't think you can ignore, however, that the two of us have been thinking along these lines for a long time. I was the one who had the ability to make a first move—

13. *Husband:* First of all, I hardly feel that your leaving the relationship needs to be classified as an ability. I'm not looking for leaving the relationship—

14. *Mediator:* Let me cut you off right here because it doesn't seem to me to be very productive to talk about who left the relationship as what's going to happen to Mark. How are you going to parent Mark?

15. *Wife:* Right. That's exactly how I feel. I don't think it is important who made the decision to move. My concern is that Mark remain where he's been comfortable all along. And he's used to having me be there and—

16. *Mediator:* John, exactly what is your proposal in terms of Mark?

17. *Husband:* Well, Gwen is looking to go back to school . . .

Reading through this interaction provides some very interesting examples of the intervention forms described in this paper. Perhaps the best way to identify these interventions is to provide some general descriptions of the interaction, and then move through each of the three dimensions of our communication model to see how they function.

Interaction Features

The first feature that is apparent from reading this transcript is the intensity of the language used. For example, in her first utterance, the wife talks about playing dirty, which is a fairly confrontive metaphor. The husband responds with some profanity, and the wife retorts in utterance 4 with another disconfirming metaphor. This high level of language intensity ought to communicate to the mediator that some intervention probably should be introduced after this exchange, to refocus the discussion on a key issue. The mediator intervenes in 5 with an involvement strategy to help clarify feelings and perhaps reduce some of the language intensity. However, the language intensity persists in 6 with a qualifier ("no idea *whatsoever*"), and again the mediator must intervene.

In fact, comparing the wife and husband on language intensity, it is clear that the husband is using much more intense language than the wife. Actually, nearly every mediator intervention follows immediately after the husband's comments and is generally aimed at controlling some of this intense language. For example, in utterance 8 the husband says, "I feel *extremely* strong," and in 13 the husband days, "I *hardly* feel . . . ," both of which are intense qualifiers and very confrontive toward the wife. In contrast, the wife's intensity is less confrontive and is generally aimed at supporting the mediator; for example, in response to the mediator's structuring comment 14, the wife says, "That's *exactly* how I feel . . . ," which is an intense qualifier supporting the mediator.

This level of language intensity would indicate that the interaction is probably in a phase where the general level of conflict intensity is high. This is likely to be at the initial stages of interaction, before the mediator has gained control and is capable of moving the couple away from unproductive communication patterns. Another indication of the level of conflict intensity is the interruption pattern. The wife interrupts the husband in 2 and again in 4, by disconfirming the husband's prior response. Combined with the intense language in these utterances, it is easy to see that an intervention was probably appropriate at this point.

Another interruption sequence begins in 13 when the husband disconfirms the wife's comments and again uses intense language to do so. The mediator cuts off this sequence before it can escalate into a destructive exchange similar to the exchange at the beginning of the transcript. Actually, just looking at who is communicating to whom in this transcript provides another indication of conflict intensity. After the first exchange, the mediator does not permit the couple to talk directly to one another. The first exchange probably revealed that the mediator had not yet changed nonproductive communication patterns, and that more cooperative language needed to be used before such an exchange would be permitted.

Gaining Control through Structuring

To reduce some of this conflict intensity, focus on the custody issue, and generally gain control of the interaction, the mediator relies heavily on controlling intervention tactics. For example, in 7 the mediator begins with an involvement tactic that is intended to help clarify feelings and identify points of agreement to reduce conflict intensity. In the second half of the statement the mediator urges the couple to structure the agenda and focus on a parenting plan for Mark, their son. The husband sticks to this agenda in 8 but then diverts in 10. The mediator tries to close down this diversion in 11 by laying down the rules, which is another structuring tactic. Neither the husband nor the wife complies with the mediator's request, and in 14 the mediator is again forced to lay down the rules.

Clearly, in this first stage of interaction, the mediator is using some very directive controlling tactics to keep the interaction on the issue of custody. The mediator is also using several less directive tactics. For example, in 7 the language of the mediator is clearly more formal and businesslike than the disputants. He uses phrases such as "I suspect that" and "perhaps," which are more formal. He also introduces words that are less conflict-oriented, such as "parenting" as opposed to "custody." Increasing formality and restructuring colloquial language are attempts to retrain the disputants to use a language that will provide the basic framework for reaching an agreement, as opposed to continued conflict escalation.

Increasing Involvement to Encourage Collaboration

These intervention tactics are a very important feature of this mediation, particularly at this early phase of interaction. The mediator's first intervention, in fact, is a less directive tactic aimed at reinforcing points of agreement to encourage each person to explore and come to grips with their own emotional states. Such an understanding is an important mission in early mediation phases because misunderstood emotional states can decrease an individual's motivation to negotiate and reach an agreement. The mediator's second intervention is an attempt to clarify emotions, and some success with this attempt is seen in the husband's response 8.

Despite the mediator's best efforts, the husband changes the topic from understanding emotional states to placing blame on the wife for leaving the relationship (utterance 10 and continuing). This forces the mediator in 11 to intervene with a control tactic that tries to refocus the discussion on the son, Mark. In 12, the wife reverts back to the "who left the relationship first" issue, with the husband escalating conflict in 13 by continuing with this topic.

The next utterance for the mediator is critical here because it is clear that the couple is focusing on an issue that is not productive for constructing a parenting plan for their son. The real decision for the mediator here is whether to get the topic back on Mark with a control tactic or to continue with an involvement strategy that helps the couple clarify some of their emotional concerns. It seems clear from the interaction that the couple are not going to talk about a parenting plan until some of the emotional issues are addressed.

In 14 the mediator might have used an involvement tactic that pulled out and confronted these emotions a bit more. The mediator does produce an involvement tactic in 16 by asking the husband for a specific parenting proposal. However, this proposal will not be built upon the husband's understanding of his own emotional biases in this matter. Of course, this is a very difficult decision to make, and since each mediator has an individual style for dealing with this issue, there is probably no one right approach here. What is important is that the mediator made the decision to intervene, probably at the right moment.

One final observation about involvement interventions is that in 9 the mediator simply says, "Um hm." This indicates to the husband that the mediator is listening, and is a verbal reminder that the mediator would like to hear more. Verbal listening cues can be very helpful in increasing a disputant's involvement in the interaction; they increase the information resource for agreement making.

Promoting Consistency to Develop Trustworthiness

Consistency evolves into a large problem for the mediator in this transcript. As we have noted above, nearly all of the mediator's interventions have been control tactics and interruptions following the husband and not the wife. We have made the case that the mediator needed to make such interventions because the husband was addressing unproductive topics and trying to sabotage the interaction. Unfortunately, one of the effects of such a general intervention strategy is that the husband may perceive over time that the mediator is siding with the wife. This may intensify the conflict, particularly when the wife perceives this effect as well and tries to increase solidarity with the mediator. Some evidence of this effect is in 15 when the wife gives the mediator unqualified support for scolding the husband.

The dilemma for the mediator is to decide how to control one party and not appear to take sides at the same time. The mediator could have moved in this direction by distributing control equally for the same crime. For example, when the wife digresses away from the mediator's topic of parenting the son in 12, the mediator says nothing about this infraction. Instead, the mediator waits until the husband comments, to intervene with a direct control tactic.

Another approach, which the mediator selects in this interaction, is to move in a more positive direction for the husband by introducing a control strategy. The mediator skillfully accomplishes this goal by interrupting the wife (for the first time in this transcript) and asking the husband for a specific parenting proposal. This produces a more compliant response from the husband with low levels of language intensity and gives the appearance that the mediation is making some progress.

CONCLUSION

The overwhelming impression to be gained from a communications analysis is that choosing effective communication interventions is difficult. The mediator in the transcript is very experienced, yet even he was struggling at some points to select the appropriate intervention at the appropriate moment. When people are in a state of conflict, communication is more difficult, since disputants mistrust one another's intentions. The approach to mediation suggested here contends that increased structure is the first step toward sorting out the disputants' communication, with involvement and consistency needed to reach an agreement.

This approach raises several key issues that ought to be addressed. The first issue is whether a less directive counseling model or a more directive negotiation model would be most effective in facilitating agreements. We argue that the more directive negotiation model is needed, particularly when conflict is verbally intense and the mediator's control of the interaction is threatened. The data in this chapter demonstrate rather clearly that control is a prerequisite for agreement making. This position does not advocate ignoring the emotional foundations of the disputant's concerns. On the contrary, exposing the emotional bases is critical to success. The negotiation model advocates working these discussions into the structure of the mediation.

The second issue posed by this chapter is whether or not communication training ought to be included in the professional development of mediators.

While this chapter makes it obvious that being able to manipulate key communication variables is a prerequisite for success, very few mediation curricula include any formal communication training. Hopefully, as the research in communication intensifies, more professionals will consider communication instruction as vital to mediation success as to psychology, social work, counseling, and other behavioral science disciplines.

The final issue raised by this chapter is the value of conducting research in mediation as a means of improving the ability of mediators to facilitate agreements. The research presented here demonstrates the value of looking closely at the form and timing of specific interventions. Several communication scholars are currently looking even more closely at other features of mediation interaction, to learn about other communication variables that may affect mediation outcome. For example, are couples who are more deferent to mediators more likely to reach an agreement? How do successful mediators manage interpersonal distance throughout the course of the interaction? Our hope is that the research reported in this chapter will encourage others to share transcripts, ideas, and other resources to increase our understanding of the mediation process.

REFERENCES

Bradac, J. L., Bowers, J. W., & Courtright, J. A. Three language variables in communication research: Intensity, immediacy, and diversity. *Human Communication Research*, 1979, *3*, 257–269.

Cooley, R. E., & Roach, D. A. A conceptual framework. In R. N. Bostrom (Ed.), *Competence in communication: A multidisciplinary approach* (pp. 11–32). Beverly Hills, CA: Sage, 1984.

Donohue, W. A. Ethnicity and mediation. In W. B. Gudykunst, L. P. Stewart, & S. Ting-Toomey (Eds.), *Communication, culture, and organizational processes* (pp. 134–154). Beverly Hills, CA: Sage, 1985.

Donohue, W. A., Diez, M. E., & Weider-Hatfield, D. Skills for successful bargainers: A valence theory of competent mediation. In R. N. Bostrom (Ed.), *Competence in communication: A multidisciplinary approach* (pp. 219–258). Beverly Hills, CA: Sage, 1984.

Fisher, R. J. Third party consultation as a method of intergroup conflict resolution: A review of studies. *Journal of Conflict Resolution*, 1983, *27*, 301–334.

Guetzkow, H. Unitizing and categorizing problems in coding qualitative data. *Journal of Clinical Psychology*, 1950, *6*, 47–58.

McLaughlin, M. L., & Cody, M. J. Situational influences on the selection of strategies to resist compliance-gaining attempts. *Human Communication Research*, 1980, *7*, 14–36.

Moore, C. W. *The mediation processes.* San Francisco: Jossey-Bass, 1986.

Pearson, J. An evaluation of alternatives to court adjudication. *Justice System Journal*, 1982, *73*, 420–444.

Pearson, J., & Thoennes, N. A preliminary portrait of client reactions to three court mediation programs. *Mediation Quarterly*, 1984, *3*, 21–40.

Pruitt, D. G. *Negotiation behavior.* New York: Academic Press, 1981.

Pruitt, D. G., & Lewis, S. A. A development of integrative solutions in bilateral negotiation. *Journal of Personality and Social Psychology*, 1975, *31*, 621–633.

Rubin, J. Z. *Dynamics of third party intervention.* New York: Praeger, 1983.

Schenkein, J. *The organization of conversational interaction.* New York: Academic Press, 1978.

Wall, J. A., Jr. Mediation: An analysis, review, and proposed research. *Journal of Conflict Resolution*, 1981, *25*, 157–180.

PART FIVE

LEGAL AND ETHICAL ISSUES IN DIVORCE MEDIATION

16

Confidentiality and Privilege in Divorce Mediation

JAY FOLBERG
Northwestern School of Law, Lewis and Clark College

As divorce mediation matures and more cases are completed, with or without agreements, a second generation of issues is emerging regarding confidentiality and privilege. What are the professional and legal restrictions when a mediator is subpoenaed for depositions or courtroom questioning about what was said in mediation? Does the recognized need for confidentiality in mediation override the responsibility to report child abuse? Can mediators look to contractual agreements or existing statutory protections to assure complete privacy in mediation? Are new laws or other safeguards needed? These and other questions regarding confidentiality and privilege are addressed in this chapter.

Effective mediation requires spouses to share information and candidly explore new options to meet their underlying interests. Candor and brainstorming can be inhibited by fear that revealed information and discarded options might haunt future proceedings or be at risk of public disclosure. Assurances of confidentiality and privilege promote openness and foster an atmosphere of trust necessary for successful mediation.

The mediator cannot compel spouses to provide information they choose not to reveal in the mediation process. The parties must trust the mediator and the mediator's neutrality before disclosures will be made voluntarily (McIsaac, 1985). This essential perception of neutrality and trust can be compromised if it is thought the mediator might talk about the couple to others or can be compelled to adversely testify as to what was said in mediation. Spouses may also be wary about being candid if they feel the other party can compel them to repeat in court what they confided in mediation. The willingness to be frank with one another in joint sessions is a necessary complement to their willingness to trust the mediator. There must, therefore, be a dual consideration of the need to protect communications with the mediator and between spouses themselves during mediation ("Protecting Confidentiality," 1984).

Divorce mediation is too recent a recognized practice to have developed well-defined legal rules. There are few published cases directly on mediation confidentiality or privilege, and legislation protective of mediation is relatively new. Much of the analysis of confidentiality and privilege in divorce mediation must proceed by analogy and extrapolation from other professional privileges and confidentiality protections. We can, for example, look to rules of evidence devised to promote settlement by protecting offers of settlement in commercial and labor disputes and draw analogies from the law recognizing the confidentiality required for legal advice and therapeutic services.

The literature on privacy in divorce mediation has generally failed to distinguish between confidentiality and privilege. Confidentiality is a broad concept relating to privacy, the breach of which may be the basis of ethics complaints or lawsuits against mediators for damages. Privileges are more narrow applications of confidentiality in the context of what objections can successfully be made in court to stop confidential communications from being received in evidence or whether a mediator can be compelled to state in court or in discovery what was heard in confidence. Confidentiality and privilege will be separately discussed.

CONFIDENTIALITY

Confidentiality is the reasonable expectation that information, documents, and opinions that are exchanged in a professional setting will not be shared with others. Information given in confidence should not be disclosed without client permission or a court order. An expectation of confidentiality may exist because of the private nature of the family dispute being mediated, an express or implied contract of confidentiality, professional ethics and standards, or the wording of a statute.

Marital relations are generally regarded as the most private of matters (*Griswold v. Connecticut*, 1965). The recognized public interest in marriage and divorce is best served by encouraging the private resolution of marital conflicts. The spouses' desire for privacy in discussing their marital life is so great that even the possibility of disclosure of information to third parties may seriously inhibit open discussion and candor. The very private nature of marital mediation implies a contract of privacy. Most mediators using a written employment agreement with divorcing couples include a provision that the mediation will be afforded confidentiality from any voluntary exposure on the part of the mediator. Many mediators have a professional background that traditionally requires that they not discuss or reveal what is said by clients unless legally compelled to do so.

Drawing a parallel from counseling and therapy, courts would probably allow a private action against a mediator who voluntarily reveals confidences shared in divorce mediation. A possible cause of action might exist for breach of contract or for tortious conduct (Deuel, 1983). The contract action may be based on an implied or expressed agreement. Actions in tort seek to compensate a person for damage caused by a breach of some noncontractual duty owed to that person (Keeton, 1984).

When a professional confidence has been breached, some courts have considered a tort action for invasion of privacy through publicity given to private life. The elements of this action and the defenses available limit its applicability in most situations where a confidence might be breached in the context of divorce mediation. There must be a reasonable expectation of confidentiality and a public revelation that would generally be considered offensive. The matter disclosed must not be of legitimate concern to the public. In states where the tort of breach of privacy is recognized, a mediator might defend by showing that the private information was not circulated to the public (lack of publication); the matter disclosed would not be considered offensive to a reasonable person; or the public may have a legitimate interest in knowing the information ("Breach of Confidence," 1982). Disclosure to family or friends of the mediator might not qualify as a publication. The information, such as the client's identity, may be considered inoffensive by most people's standards, thus not protecting the overly sensitive client. If a mediation client is an official or a celebrity, the public interest factor might disallow an action under this particular tort.

Another form of tort remedy that courts have considered against therapists for breach of confidentiality is based on a statutory cause of action. In order for this action to be brought, there must be a statute that prohibits the breach of confidence complained of, a plaintiff within the class of persons protected, and a defendant who is a member of the class of defendants to which the statute applies ("Breach of Confidence," 1982). Some statutes provide for civil damages so a direct action can be brought when a breach of confidence occurs (Oregon Revised Statutes, 1977). Statutes that might provide a basis for an implied action include licensing statutes that mandate those who are licensed to uphold client confidentiality but do not give remedies, or similar statutes pronouncing that mediation sesions are confidential and privileged. These statutes will be discussed later.

At least one court has given recovery on the basis of a specific action in tort for the breach of a "fiduciary duty" of confidentiality. The breach occurred when a psychiatrist informed a client's wife of some information shared in confidence. The court found a duty not to disclose, which sprang from a relationship of trust and confidence between a client and psychiatrist and was in part based on an implied covenant not to disclose confidential information. The court noted that the value in a tort action, as opposed to one in contract, was that a greater spectrum of damages would be available (*MacDonald v. Clinger*, 1982).

Another possible cause of action in tort would be based on malpractice. The concurring opinion in *MacDonald* believed that the psychiatrist's sharing of intimate details with the client's wife was a wrongful and unjustifiable violation of his duty of care.

Some courts have allowed a contract action based on breach of implied elements of the contractual agreement for professional services. An implied obligation not to disclose confidential information can be found in the conduct of the parties, common expectations and practices, and understandings of the parties at the time of contracting ("Breach of Confidence," 1982). Courts have typically looked to professional codes of ethics, and public policy for the grounds of implied elements. In *Martino v. Family Service Agency of Adams County* (1983) a court acknowledged an implied contract for a duty of loyalty to the client, a counseling social worker's duty to withdraw if a conflict of interest arose, and a duty to avoid revealing to others confidential information obtained during counseling. An action for violation of the implied contract was allowed to stand, for the revelation of confidential information, but the court refused to acknowledge an action in tort for malpractice against the social worker.

Exceptions to Confidentiality

Statutes that mandate confidentiality often contain exceptions that may require or allow the divulgence of information without liability, most notably to report abuse. Case law has also established some exceptions where absolute confidentiality cannot be maintained, particularly when danger to others is present (*Tarasoff v. Board of Regents*, 1976). Information may be disclosed without client consent in these six most common instances: (1) reporting child abuse; (2) medical emergencies; (3) the client poses a clear and immediate danger to others; (4) providing information to persons conducting research, evaluation, peer review, and audits; (5) sharing information within an agency and between professionals, as long as only what is needed for professional services is revealed; and (6) a client sues the provider of services. Although each of these exceptions to confidentiality may provide a good defense to complaints that confidentiality was breached, it is a better practice to seek the client's consent for all types of disclosures.

Reporting child abuse is the most noted exception to complete confidentiality in mediation. All states have enacted some type of child abuse reporting law; most of these mandate reporting by designated groups of professionals. The trend has been to expand the reporting group from physicians and nurses to others who may have occasion in their work to discover cases of child abuse. This expanded reporting group includes social workers, teachers, principals, psychologists, chiropractors, public officials, law enforcement personnel, attorneys, clergy, and dentists (Katz, Howe, & McGrath, 1975). Divorce mediation was not prominent as a distinct professional practice in the early 1960s when these laws were generally enacted (Children's Bureau, 1963), so mediators are not separately enumerated as a professional group required to report.

The mediator's "profession of origin" may require reporting even though the mediator is wearing a different professional hat while mediating. The reporting requirements for each profession may vary even in the same state. In Oregon, for example, attorneys, psychiatrists, psychologists, and clergy need not report child abuse if their suspicion is based solely on confidential communications with adults; they must have direct contact with the child or a nonconfidential source of suspicion before reporting is required. Social workers, physicians, and others in Oregon, however, must report any suspicion of child abuse (Oregon Revised Statutes, 1975).

Those states that have legislated confidentiality for mediation sessions have not clarified whether the laws requiring report of abuse override mediation confidentiality. Generally, the reporting statutes and the public policy of protecting children would take precedence over the confidentiality provisions of mediation statutes, just as reporting is required of other professionals whose work is otherwise given legislated confidentiality. Most reporting statutes make it a crime not to report abuse (Braun, 1975). Professional status is generally no defense to a crime, if not specifically exempted in the criminal statute. The typical child abuse reporting statute provides that evidentiary privileges otherwise available to bar testimony on the basis of privileged communications are not applicable in child abuse proceedings.

Those who report child abuse are generally immune from liability, even if child abuse is not established. Most statutes expressly grant immunity from civil and criminal liability to anyone reporting in good faith who has reasonable grounds for reporting (Oregon Revised Statutes, 1975). This should allow a defense to any suit for invasion of privacy, betraying confidences, breach of contract, or malpractice arising from reporting abuse.

Abuse reporting laws vary from state to state and are not necessarily limited to child abuse. Separate statutes may require reporting of elderly abuse, spousal abuse, abuse to patients of nursing homes, and animal abuse. The mediator should become familiar with the reporting laws of the state and inform clients of any notable exceptions to confidentiality.

PRIVILEGES

Even if we assume that a mediator is bound not to discuss with others what is revealed in divorce mediation, that does not mean that a court would prohibit a party from testifying about comments and revelations made in the mediation process, or would not compel testimonial disclosure by the mediator. Privileges protecting clients from testimony about what was said in confidence outside of court may exist by virtue of statutes or court rulings. In recognizing a privilege to block relevant evidence from being presented, the court gives up the value of that evidence in deciding a contested issue in exchange for society's interest in promoting certain confidential relationships or proceedings.

Statutory and Common-Law Privileges for Professional Services

Lawyers, physicians, psychologists, social workers, nurses, the clergy, and certain other professionals may have the benefit in their work of confidential privileges protected by statute. For example, a physician–patient privilege was created by statute in New York in 1828 (New York Civil Practice Law, 1920), and most states have since passed similar legislation. The coverage of these statutes varies from state to state. (See "Privileged Communications," 1971, which collects and analyzes state statutes creating a privilege for mental health professionals.)

Although professional privileges are generally a matter of statutory creation, some courts have been willing, as a matter of public policy, to recognize an evidentiary privilege in the absence of a statute. The test most commonly used by the courts to determine whether information communicated in a helping relationship should be barred from courtroom exposure is a four-part inquiry developed by Dean Wigmore (1935).

> 1. The communication must have been imparted in the confidence that it would not be disclosed to others.
> 2. The preservation of secrecy must be essential to the success of the relationship.
> 3. The relationship must be one that society wishes to foster and protect.
> 4. Any injury to the relationship caused by disclosure must outweigh the expected benefit to be derived from compelling disclosure.

Courts, in other than mediation cases, faced with a request for a privilege not covered by a protective statute, have most often held that the benefits of compelling disclosure were greater than the injury to the professional relationship, and the privilege has been denied (Delgado, 1973; Green, 1986, pp. 31–32). However, cases asserting a privilege for mediators have fared better. In all published court decisions known to have weighed the injury to the mediation process against the benefit from compelling disclosure (as suggested by Wigmore), the courts have ruled to protect the confidentiality of mediation from courtroom disclosures.

The United States Ninth Circuit Court of Appeals was presented an unfair labor practice case where the mediator's testimony was crucial to determine which side was telling the truth about what went on in the mediation sessions. The appellate court affirmed a trial court order refusing to require the federal mediator to testify. The court adapted Wigmore's test by weighing the harm to the cause of truth versus injury to the public interest in mediation and ruled in favor of upholding the confidentiality of mediation (*National Labor Relations Board v. Macaluso*, 1980). The court confirmed that mediation participants "must feel free to talk without any fear that the conciliator may subsequently make disclosures as a witness in some other proceeding, to the possible disadvantage of a party to the conference" (p. 55). The court concluded; "The complete exclusion of mediator testimony is necessary to the preservation of an effective system of labor mediation, and . . . labor mediation is essential to continued industrial stability, a public interest sufficiently great to outweigh the interest in obtaining every person's evidence" (p. 56). (For a similar state court holding, see *Sonenstahl v. L.E.L.S. Inc.*, 1985.) A similar rationale can be stated about the public interest in promoting consensual resolution of divorce disputes.

In *Adler v. Adams* (1979), the United States District Court for the Western District of Washington issued an order to protect from disclosure the testimony and notes of private mediators who had earlier helped resolve an environmental dispute. The court held that "requiring a mediator to make such disclosure would severely inhibit the proper performance of his or her duties, and thereby undercut the effectiveness of the mediation process. There is a substantial public interest in fostering effective mediation techniques in settlement of disputes" (p. 3). The court did, however, require the mediators to produce documents that the participants had presented at those mediation sessions open to the public or that sources not party to the mediation had furnished to the mediator.

In the British Columbia trial court case of *Sinclair v. Roy* (1985), Judge Huddard wrote her reasons for setting aside a subpoena compelling the testimony of a divorce mediator. Although the mediator was a family court counselor whose work with the divorcing spouses was covered by the confidentiality provisions of the British Columbia Family Relations Act, Judge Huddard ruled that the statutory protection was not exhaustive of the privilege applicable to custody mediation and rested her decision on public policy considerations. The wife seeking the testimony of the mediator argued that the mediator could be required to testify on "objective facts" she observed regarding the wife, without violating the confidentiality of privileged communications during mediation. Judge Huddard refused to pierce the blanket of mediation confidentiality even for the limited "purpose of determining whether specific words or conduct constitute objective facts" (p. 25). The opinion noted that "mediation is a profession encouraged by the policy of the federal government" (p. 21) and "that the government is promoting the use of mediation as an alternative to litigation in the resolution of family disputes" (p. 21). The judge emphasized that confidentiality in mediation was necessary for its success, whether offered in a private or court setting.

Several other court orders quashing subpoenas seeking the tesimony of mediators are reported by the American Bar Association Special Committee on Dispute Resolution in its publication *Confidentiality in Mediation: A Practitioner's Guide* (1985). These orders were issued without a statement of reasons. They nonetheless illustrate the support that trial courts, when presented with a proper motion, are likely to give privileges protecting mediation confidentiality.

Limits on Professional Privilege

A testimonial privilege protects the confiding party against court disclosure of what was said, only if the statements were necessary for the rendition of the professional service that the privilege protects. If one definition of mediation as a nontherapeutic process is accepted, for example, the privilege protecting the confidentiality of therapeutic services would never attach. Likewise, if an attorney does not purport to be practicing law while offering divorce mediation services, the attorney does not come within the statutory privilege protecting the attorney–client relationship. (See, for example, *Myles and Reiser Co. v. Loew's, Inc.*, 1948) Nor does the attorney–client privilege apply in a court proceeding between people who had earlier been jointly represented by the same attorney. This rule would appear to doom application of the attorney–client privilege in most divorce cases involving a lawyer–mediator.

It should also be noted that the privilege against courtoom disclosure belongs to the client and not to the professional provider. The client may waive the privilege. In other words, if the client of a lawyer or therapist chooses to have the information made available in a court proceeding—or, most accurately, does not object to testimony about the information—the lawyer or therapist cannot invoke the privilege. Likewise, a mediation privilege belongs to the spouses, not the mediator. A waiver of the privilege by both spouses would normally be required if a privilege was found to exist (*Sinclair v. Roy*, 1985).

The presence of an adverse party when statements are made also defeats most traditional privileges. In divorce mediation, even if it were characterized as a legal, therapeutic, or other privileged relationship, the presence of an adverse party who may be on the other side of a court proceeding would effectively void the privilege. Statements made in the presence of an adverse party are generally not privileged; the adverse party may repeat what he or she hears from the opponent. If the adverse party is able to testify about what was stated, there is no policy served by preventing others present from testifying about what was said. Again we must distinguish between privacy from general public disclosure by the mediator, which is to be expected, and a privilege against court testimony, which is defeated by the presence of an adverse party. (Cleary et al., 1984).

If the otherwise privileged communication is knowingly made in the presence of people not party or necessary to the session, then the information cannot be privileged (Cleary et al., 1984). A televised mediation, for example, could not be considered confidential, and any information disclosed would not be privileged. Similarly, the information presented at public sessions in the environmental mediation case of *Adler v. Adams* (1979) was not privileged, even though the information provided in private sessions with the mediators was protected. There must be a reasonable expectation of confidentiality before a privilege exists.

Because privileges are in derogation of the common-law policy making all evidence available to the court, privileges are narrowly construed to limit their protection. Statutory privileges exempting testimony in civil cases are held not applicable in criminal cases. Even if a statute provides protection against testimony in civil and criminal cases, it may not be applied in cases of homicide. Child and spousal abuse reporting statutes will usually override privilege statutes, unless the privilege statute makes clear that the mediator need not report abuse. If a mediator is sued by a client, the client's privilege would be waived if the confidential information is relevant to the lawsuit. Thus, no privilege can truly be considered absolute (Wilson, 1978).

Settlement Privilege

Another basis for keeping statements made during mediation out of the courts is that offers of settlement and settlement discussions are generally inadmissible. Evidence of proposed compromises is considered unreliable and excluded as irrelevant, even though the common-law rule may have been to the contrary (Cleary et al., 1984; Wigmore, 1935). Modern rules of evidence also bar the use in evidence of statements and conduct that are part of compromise negotiations. The exclusion of this evidence is now based more on a public policy of encouraging settlement than on technical considerations of legal relevancy.

Federal Rule of Evidence 408 codifies the policy of encouraging candid settlement discussions by specifically excluding evidence of settlement discussions and conduct, at least for purposes of proving the validity and value of claims ("Protecting Confidentiality," 1984). Although divorce cases are not heard in federal courts, the substance of Federal Rule of Evidence 408 appears in some form in the evidence code of every state (*Report of the Committee on Confidentiality*, 1985).

It follows that if mediation is deemed a type of settlement negotiation between the parties, statements made to facilitate the mediated settlement should be protected from evidentiary use. A recent Colorado statute defines mediation as settlement negotiations and expressly declares that

> no admission, representation, or statement made in mediation not otherwise discoverable or obtainable shall be admissible as evidence or subject to discovery. In addition, a mediator shall not be subject to process requiring the disclosure of any matter discussed during mediation proceedings (Colorado Revised Statutes, 1983).

Similar statutes should help correct the uncertainty existing in some jurisdictions about whether mediation fits the compromise negotiation provisions of their evidentiary rules. It has been proposed that Federal Rule of Evidence 408 be expanded to explicitly include mediation in the sweep of compromise negotiations. The rules may need amendment in this regard because they were drafted before the current widespread interest in mediation and other alternative procedures (*Report of the Committee on Confidentiality*, 1985).

Even in the absence of new legislation or rules, the existing public policy of promoting private settlement of disputes, especially family disputes, should be persuasive to a court considering the issue of admissibility of testimony revealing what was said during mediation. The court would have to weigh in each case the benefit to justice, obtaining testimony, against the injury to the process of mediation, fear of disclosure (Waltz & Huston, 1979). This weighing process is nicely illustrated in the Canadian case of *Sinclair v. Roy* (1985), previously discussed. The opinion in that case points out another possible limitation of settlement negotiation confidentiality. "While words and conduct constituting admissions made in furtherance of settlement are inadmissible, it is suggested that objective facts which may be obtained during negotiations may be proved by direct evidence (p. 18). The decision in *Sinclair* properly rejected this technical distinction and cloaked all aspects of the mediation process from admissibility in evidence.

The policy excluding evidence from compromise negotiations, including mediation, is generally qualified to allow use of evidence discoverable by other means than what was revealed during the negotiations. In other words, the policy is to prevent a participant from immunizing otherwise available evidence by presenting it during mediation. If, for example, evidence of hidden assets already existed, it does not become inadmissible because it is additionally blurted out during custody mediation. There are also questions whether statements made in mediation are protected against disclosure in a subsequent criminal prosecution (McGinness & Cinquegrama, 1982), in an administrative hearing, or in litigation between other parties (Freedman & Prigoff, 1986, p. 40). If a settlement agreement is reached and submitted to a court for approval, then it would be open to public access and inspection to the same extent as other judicial records and case files in that jurisdiction (*Bank of America*, 1986).

The principal limitation of the protection provided by the evidentiary rule relating to settlement discussion is that the rule was created to bar evidence *in court*, not out of court. If a mediator is subpoenaed for a discovery deposition in preparation for litigation, it is not clear that a rule designed to prohibit disclosure of settlement offers in court would stop inquiry during an out-of-court deposition. Federal Rule of Civil Procedure 26(b), which has served as a model for many state rules, allows discovery of information reasonably calculated to lead to admissible evidence. So even though a confidence shared in mediation may not be admissible in court because the mediation is considered an effort to settle, that same confidential information may be compelled in civil discovery because it may lead to other admissible evidence (Rodgers & Salem, 1987, p. 95). For example, a confession in mediation of a desire not to have custody may lead an opposing spouse to discover an underlying impediment to full-time parenting. This is why proposals have been made to change the discovery rules to protect communications in mediation from discovery before trial (Report of the Committee on Confidentiality, 1985). The Colorado statute, set forth above, defines mediation as a settlement negotiation and specifically exempts communication in mediation from discovery (Colorado Revised Statutes, 1983).

Privilege by Contract

Most private mediators require their clients to sign an agreement providing that the mediation sessions will be confidential and that the mediator will not be called to testify about what is said or to give any professional opinion related to the case in court. A court would not necessarily be bound to honor this private contract in its search for truth, though it may be persuaded by public policy considerations to do so. Oregon considered, but did not pass, a proposed statute that would require courts to enforce privileges contained in written mediation contracts (Oregon House Bill 3192, 1987).

At least one appellate opinion, *Simrin v. Simrin* (1965), has held enforceable an express agreement that communications made during marriage counseling would be privileged and that neither spouse would call the counselor at a divorce trial, even though there was no direct statutory protection. The wife argued that to hold her to her bargain with her husband and the counselor, a rabbi, would sanction a contract to suppress evidence contrary to public policy promoting the admissibility of evidence relevant to child custody. The California Court of Appeals recognized that "for the unwary spouse who speaks freely, repudiation [of the confidentiality agreement] would prove a trap; for the wily, a vehicle for making self-serving declarations" (p. 95). The court, in excluding the rabbi from testifying, compared the public policy favoring marriage counseling to the evidentiary policy protecting "statements that are made in offers of compromise and to avoid or settle litigation, which are not admissible evidence" (p. 95).

A court could also hold that a signatory to the contract to mediate in confidence was equitably estopped from calling the mediator to testify or that it will not compel the mediator, a nonlitigant, to breach a contract. One former spouse could sue the other for breach of the mediation contract in a separate proceeding if damages could be proved. Perhaps the principal value of such a contract provision for confidentiality is the moral constraint it places on each party to honor their commitment and recognize the importance of confidentiality, even if mediation does not result in a complete settlement. One of the dangers in relying on contracts to preserve confidentiality is that a contract only binds the contracting parties; it would not preclude a noncontracting party, such as a child, from trying to obtain and use evidence from mediation.

Mediation Statutes and Court Rules

Traditional professional privileges, as discussed above, do not assure an evidentiary privilege for the confidentiality of divorce mediation, and court decisions do not guarantee mediation confidentiality. Many existing statutory privileges for other professionals are contained in licensing legislation ("Privileged Communications," 1971). However, until mediation becomes a distinct and licensed profession, licensing-related statutory privileges will not exist parallel to those for other professions dependent on trust.

One notable exception is a 1985 Massachusetts law that legislates a comprehensive privilege for mediation conducted by those who qualify within the statutory definition of mediator. All communications "made in the course of and relating to the subject matter of any mediation" is confidential and not subject to disclosure in any judicial or administrative proceeding, as are also the mediator's files, memoranda, and other work product. The statute then defines mediator.

> For the purposes of this section a "mediator" shall mean a person not a party to a dispute who enters into a written agreement with the parties to assist them in

resolving their disputes and has completed at least thirty hours of training in mediation and who either has four years of professional experience as a mediator or is accountable to a dispute resolution organization which has been in existence for at least three years or one who has been appointed to mediate by a judicial or governmental body. (Massachusetts General Laws, 1985.)

This Massachusetts statute has been criticized for, among other reasons, applying only to mediation conducted by a mediator fitting qualifications set forth in the legislation and acting pursuant to a written agreement with the parties (Green, 1986, p. 30). Legislation can protect mediation confidentiality and create a privilege specifically designed to shield mediation evidence, apart from licensure or any other effort to qualify who can conduct the mediation. This type of legislation may be part of a statute sanctioning or compelling mediation, or it may be contained in an evidence or procedure code. The focus of such legislation is the mediation process or setting, and not the qualifications of the mediator. The Colorado legislation deeming mediation to be privileged as a settlement negotiation fits this category and was discussed above.

Oregon has a confidentiality provision as part of its statute authorizing court-connected custody and visitation mediation. The provision broadly provides that,

All communications, verbal or written, made in mediation proceedings shall be confidential. A party or any other individual engaged in mediation proceedings shall not be examined in any civil or criminal action as to such communications and such communications shall not be used in any civil or criminal action without the consent of the parties to the mediation. Exceptions to the testimonial privilege otherwise applicable under ORS 40.225 to 40.295. [lawyer–client, physician–patient, and other statutory privileges] do not apply to communications made confidential under this subsection. (Oregon Revised Statutes, 1983)

Similarly, Florida's mediation statute says that "all verbal or written communication in mediation or conciliation proceedings shall be confidential and inadmissible as evidence in any subsequent legal proceedings, unless both parties agree otherwise" (Florida Statutes, 1982). It is not clear if the Oregon and Florida statutory-based evidentiary exclusion would extend to mediation other than court-connected custody and visitation cases.

The 1981 New York law on community dispute-resolution centers provides,

All memoranda, work products, or case files of a mediator are confidential and not subject to disclosure in any judicial or administrative proceeding. Any communication relating to the subject matter of the resolution made during the resolution process by any participant, mediator, or any other person present at the dispute resolution shall be a confidential communication. (New York Judiciary Law, 1981).

The Supreme Court of New York, a trial-level state court, has relied on this statute in two cases to quash subpoenas for information revealed in mediation. In the first case (*People v. Snyder*, 1985), which involved a murder, the judge refused to allow the district attorney to obtain information revealed in a mediation prior to the fatal shooting. The judge acknowledged the legislative intent to protect the confidentiality of the community dispute-resolution proceedings. In the second case the confidentiality provisions of the New York Community Dispute Resolution Law were upheld even though the assault took place in the mediation room (*People v. Sicard*, 1986).

The Michigan domestic relations mediation statute is most explicit in protecting communications between the spouses as well as those from a spouse to a mediator.

> A communication between a domestic relations mediator and a party to a domestic relations mediation is confidential. The secrecy of the communication shall be preserved inviolate as a privileged communication. The communication shall not be admitted in evidence in any proceeding. The same protection shall be given to communications between the parties in the presence of the mediator. (Michigan Statutes Annotated, 1982)

In order to encase the mediation proceedings with complete confidentiality, none of the participants should be allowed to testify as to what was said. If the statutory wording does not cover the spouses as well as the mediator, a potential leak may exist because legislation creating evidentiary privileges is strictly interpreted. Additionally, legislation protective of mediation would not prevent a spouse from providing by extrinsic evidence what was revealed during mediation. In other words, once the cat is out of the bag, it becomes fair game outside of mediation. Spouses should be made aware that information revealed during mediation cannot be absolutely protected ("Protecting Confidentiality," 1984).

California recently enacted a provision to its evidence code, effective January 1, 1986, that shields "evidence of anything said or of any admission made in the course of the mediation" from introduction in evidence or from being compelled in any civil action. The new enactment provides the same protection for any "document prepared for the purpose of, or in the course of, or pursuant to, the mediation." This sweeping language appears to apply to the mediation of any divorce or other dispute outside of court-required custody mediation. In other words, all private and community mediation can be protected by this new statute. The statute requires that the "persons who agree to conduct and participate in the mediation execute an agreement in writing that sets out the text of subdivisions (a) and (b) [of this statute] and states that the persons agree that this section shall apply to the mediation" (California Evidence Code, 1985).

Other states, such as Washington, have a general statute protecting a "public officer" from courtroom examination of a "communication made to him in official confidence" (Washington Revised Code, 1974). It has been reasoned that this statute would be applicable to court-connected divorce mediation, even if established by local court rule in the absence of a state statute specifically authorizing divorce mediation (Pottmeyer, 1983).

In Maine, where divorce mediation is statutorily mandated in the courts, evidence from mediation is prohibited by an amendment to the rules of evidence: "Evidence of conduct or statements by any party or mediator at a court-sponsored domestic relations mediation is not admissible for any purpose" (Maine Rules of Evidence, 1984). Mediators in Maine, unlike California, have no authority to report or make a recommendation to the court. It is felt by those offering mediation in Maine that this limitation enhances impartiality and trust (Clark & Orbeton, 1986). A recommendation to the court would appear inconsistent with the evidentiary exclusion rule.

The United States Department of Justice Community Relations Service (CRS), which mediates public interest conflicts and community disputes, has federal statutory protection of confidentiality in its mediation sessions.

> The activities of all officers and employees of the Service in providing conciliation assistance shall be conducted in confidence and without publicity, and the Service shall hold confidential any information acquired in the regular performance of its duties upon the understanding that it would be so held. (United States Code, 1964)

Although the CRS does no divorce mediation and the statute is not applicable to domestic relations cases, it is encouraging that this statutory protection has been upheld in the federal courts (*City of Port Arthur, Texas v. United States,* 1980).

Courts generally have the power to control the procedures necessary to carry out their functions and by which they make decisions, including evidentiary decisions. Several local trial court jurisdictions have developed court rules for the mediation of domestic relations cases and minor civil disputes (Comeaux, 1983). These local court rules may furnish details necessary to implement state legislation on mediation or remedy the absence of applicable legislation.

The local mediation rules may also clarify the confidentiality of court-inspired mediation programs. The local rules of the state circuit court in Portland, Oregon, for example, established mandatory custody mediation before statewide mediation legislation existed. The court's rule provided a more comprehensive mediation privilege than that allowed for other existing statutory privileges and become the model for the later state statute.

It is possible that local court rules may conflict with state statutes regarding confidentiality in mediation. The local rule, as in Portland, may indicate that the trial judges will afford greater confidentiality to communications in divorce mediation than required by state statutes. This local exercise of discretion based on the policy of encouraging mediation in family matters is not likely to be overruled by appellate court decision. The Supreme Court of Arizona upheld a local conciliation court policy that refused to make information obtained through court-connected family counseling available to the trial court, even if disclosure was jointly authorized by the counseling participants. There was no statute making the information privileged. The Arizona Supreme Court recognized the inherent power of the local court to refuse disclosure if deemed necessary to fulfill its functions (*Fenton v. Howard,* 1978).

A local court rule that provides less protection for confidentiality than that given by a state statute could be more easily challenged. The state mediation statute may, however, expressly allow a local rule option on confidentiality, provided the local option does not violate other statutes or constitutional prohibitions. (See the discussion below of *McLaughlin v. Superior Court.*)

Opinion Testimony and Recommendations

A topic related to confidentiality and privilege is opinion testimony by the mediator, regarding recommendations for resolution of the dispute. If the mediation does not result in a settlement agreement, may the mediator be allowed or compelled to offer a recommendation to a court regarding how the family dispute should be resolved? The mediator may be in a unique position to recommend an imposed outcome because of likely expertise in the subject of dispute, combined with inside knowledge of facts and feelings revealed during mediation. This dilemma is most apparent in child-custody mediation but may also arise in other divorce conflicts, such as the disputed value of property and the amount and duration of support payments.

There is concern that the trust and candor required in mediation are unlikely to exist if the participants know the mediator may be formulating an opinion or recommendation that will be communicated to a judge. The recommendation of the mediator, particularly in a child-custody and visitation case, might be given such great weight that the mediator, in effect, would be switching roles from decision facilitator to decision maker. The potential for confusion and suspicion created by this crossover role may taint the validity, effectiveness, and integrity of the mediation process (see *Report of the Advisory Panel . . .* , 1987).

The participants may, in some circumstances, agree or contract for the mediator to decide the matter if they are unable to do so or to testify as to a recommendation. Using the informal, consensual process of mediation, with no evidentiary or procedural rules, as the basis for an imposed decision does, however, create a considerable risk that the more clever or sophisticated participant may distort or manipulate the mediation in order to influence the mediator's opinion.

A combined process of mediation followed by arbitration, all performed by one person, has been used with some success in labor conflicts. This "med–arb" approach may work best when the participants are of relatively equal bargaining experience and the efficiency of a combined procedure outweighs the inhibiting or strategic effect of the mediator's anticipated role change. Some have argued for use of the mediator switchover role, from mediator to court custody expert, particularly when it becomes necessary to decide temporary child custody after all else has failed. This has been labeled "open" mediation and characterized as providing the opportunity for the mediator to offer an opinion to the court (Duryee, 1987).

The California statute that mandates mediation in all contested child-custody cases allows the mediator to make recommendations to the court if such a procedure is consistent with local court rules (California Civil Code, 1980). This statutory policy represents a compromise between those counties, most notably Los Angeles, where the court absolutely prohibits its mediators from crossing over to serve as custody investigators, and other California counties, like San Franscisco and San Mateo, where the mediator is asked by the court to recommend a temporary custody order if the parties cannot agree (McIsaac, 1981). The California state statute also makes all mandated custody mediations private and confidential (California Civil Code, 1980). Some California jurisdictions interpreted these provisions to allow the mediator to recommend a custody arrangement to the court but to bar either side from questioning the mediator on the reasons behind the recommendation.

When this policy was challenged by a parent in San Mateo County, the California Supreme Court stayed the proceeding and asked the First District Court of Appeals to rule on the practice. The appellate court ruled that the San Mateo policy was unconstitutional. The mediator can, apparently, testify about a custody recommendation without contravening the provision for confidentiality, but if the mediator cannot be questioned or cross-examined on his or her recommendation, this is in violation of constitutional guarantees of a fair trial and a right to cross-examine adverse witnesses. The court-connected mediator can make a custody recommendation to the court only if subject to cross-examination (*McLaughlin v. Superior Court*, 1983).

It is only fair that a mediator not be allowed to recommend a custody decision to the court without the test of cross-examination. The mediator-investigator, in the absence of cross-examination, may base the recommendation on bias, ignorance, or disprovable facts. The court's opinion in *McLaughlin* appears, however, to miss the central issue of mediation confidentiality. The real question is not cross-examination but whether the mediator should be allowed to testify under any conditions. If the mediator is allowed to testify, confidentiality is effectively lost.

The *McLaughlin* case, as well as accepted evidentiary rules and notions of due process, requires that if the mediator is to make a custody recommendation, the mediator can be examined by the adversely affected party regarding the reasons for the recommendation. If the mediator is questioned, the party doing the questioning could be held to have waived his or her objections to the revelations made by the mediator in court. The other party, for whom the recommendation was favorable, would hardly be expected to object. In other words, the adversely affected party would be compelled to cross-examine the mediator and thus open the door to all the facts revealed during the mediation.

In the more recent California case of *Rosson v. Rosson* (1986), the appellate court upheld the practice of allowing the mediator to testify about what occurred in mandated custody mediation. The parents entered into a routine stipulation that "the mediator could testify as to her recommendation and why she was making the recommendation" (p. 257). The court made clear that even in the absence of such a stipulation, the mediator could testify, provided there was a written local court rule allowing the mediator to make a custody recommendation to the court. The explicit protection of California Civil Code section 4607(c) (1980) declaring that "mediation proceedings shall be held in private and shall be confidential . . ." proved to be elusive because the statute makes all communications revealed in mediation "official information." The appellate decision in Rosson acknowledged that pursuant to section 4067(c) there is a privilege not to have disclosed information received by the court mediator. The court held, however, that "the privilege belongs to the court, not the parties, and . . . the court may choose to waive the privilege" (p. 253).

Work-Product Doctrine

In the *McLaughlin* and *Rosson* cases, the mediator was a court employee expected by the terms of employment to testify in court should mediation not produce agreement. Mediators, private or publicly employed, may be subpoenaed to testify about their opinions regarding the appropriate outcome of a case they unsuccessfully mediated. Apart from the considerations of confidentiality previously discussed, there is also an objection that may be asserted, at least by private mediators, based on the work-product doctrine.

The work-product doctrine was initially formulated to protect attorneys from discovery of their opinions or thoughts regarding a case being prepared for trial and has since been expanded to apply to other professionals (Saltzburg, 1980). The doctrine protects the mental impressions, ideas, theories, and strategies of a professional. The facts underlying those impressions and the specific information gathered in mediation are not protected by the work-product doctrine, although they may be shielded by other doctrines of privacy and confidentiality discussed above. (See *Hickman v. Taylor*, 1947.) The work-product privilege, unlike most of the privacy protections previously discussed, belongs to the professional provider and can be waived only by that person. Opinions are the principal product of many professionals and therefore receive substantial legal protection. (See *United States v. Pfiger, Inc.*, 1977.)

CAUCUSING

Separate caucusing is a powerful technique for breaking an impasse and reaching agreement (Moore, 1986). The purpose of such caucusing is to allow each spouse to reveal to the mediator information he or she would not want to disclose to the other, to explore private feelings about the issues, and to allow the mediator to discuss matters that would be uncomfortable or risky if stated when the spouses were together. Separate meetings allow the mediator to interpret the concerns and perspective of each side to the other. Private meetings individually with each spouse also facilitate mediation between highly conflicted or volatile spouses. This might be similar to shuttle diplomacy between warring nations.

Caucusing in divorce cases is fraught with confidentiality questions (Engram & Markowitz, 1985). It is difficult for the mediator to maintain the appearance of absolute impartiality when it is known that the mediator is party to information about the dispute that is not shared by each side. This information may be quantitative data relevant to the divorce dispute or subjective opinions regarding one side's bargaining or settlement position. A mediation participant who does not share the "secret" information may perceive partiality or a liaison between the mediator and the other side. When the mediator caucuses separately with each spouse, the spouse who shares private information may worry about the mediator disclosing it to the opposing side. If the information appears to have been revealed or used adversely to a disputant's position, the feeling that confidentiality was betrayed may totally frustrate the mediation.

Some mediators caucus with each spouse only if it is agreed that information revealed during the caucus will be shared at the next joint meeting. This approach can also create problems of confidentiality because it is sometimes hard to enforce the mutuality of revelations if during a caucus one of the spouses discloses information but insists on keeping it confidential or disagrees with the ways in which the mediator represents the caucus discussion to the other side. The spouse not present during the caucus may naturally be suspicious and continue to doubt whether all known information from the caucus has been revealed.

Separate meetings with each spouse may raise questions of who can waive confidentiality protections. In court one spouse may seek the mediator's testimony about what that spouse discussed with the mediator in private. That spouse may want to corroborate what was said elsewhere or have the court hear what the mediator stated in private. Can the absent spouse prevent the mediator from testifying when the spouse who was present wants the testimony in evidence? Judge Huddard in the Canadian case of *Sinclair v. Roy* (1985) held that the privilege required the waiver of both spouses, even regarding evidence from private meetings with the spouse that sought to introduce the evidence. The law in the United States on this issue is not clear.

The mediator may be authorized by parents, court rules, or legislation to interview the child privately (Folberg, 1985). Again, the question is raised whether the confidences of the child will be protected from revelation to the parents and to the child's appointed representative. Some experienced mediators who have written about their private interviews with children ask the children for permission to reveal to their parents what was said in the separate session, but honor any request to not reveal the information (Bienenfeld, 1983). Other authorities make it a practice to let the child know that the purpose of the interview is to later share with the parents the child's feelings and concerns (Saposnek, 1983).

CONCLUSION

As divorce mediation matures and moves from theory to practice, questions about confidentiality and privilege will increase. Lawyers have the power to subpoena mediators for depositions and for courtroom testimony. They are, apparently, using this power with increased frequency (America Bar Association Special Committee, 1985, "Introduction"). Court rulings and legislation provide some protection for the privacy of mediation from courtroom exposure. The protection is imperfect. Although at least one noted authority cautions that new blanket mediation privilege statutes may be counterproductive to increased acceptance of private dispute resolution (Green, 1986, p. 2), legislation carefully composed specifically to shield divorce mediation from the uncertainty of evidentiary use would further promote the candor needed for successful mediation.

Mediators can help prevent confrontations over issues of confidentiality and privilege by creating a clear expectation of confidentiality at the outset of mediation. Clients should be asked to sign an employment agreement that states that communications occurring in the mediation process shall remain confidential and not subject to use in court. Both spouses should agree not to call the mediator to testify and not to testify about what is said or done in mediation.

If a mediator is subpoenaed, a friendly request to the issuing attorney is often sufficient to void the subpoena. Many attorneys do not understand the nature of divorce mediation, the importance of confidentiality to the process, the policy arguments favoring a privilege for mediation, and the statutory protection that may exist. A subpoena may represent the opportunity to educate an attorney, particularly if your mutual client has been pleased with your mediation services. Suggest this book to the attorney.

If you are not successful in educating the attorney who initiated the subpoena, then you may have to educate the judge. Although the procedure may differ among jurisdictions, courts can order that a subpoena be voided or service of it be quashed. This will usually require the filing of a written motion requesting an order of the court and submitting documents, most commonly a memorandum of points and authorities and an affidavit. The mediator would be well advised to obtain a lawyer to prepare these documents and present them to the court. If in doubt, the court will schedule a hearing so that arguments can be heard on the matter, and the court can ask questions in aid of a decision. Judges are becoming increasingly aware of mediation and generally encourage any process that would peacefully help resolve conflicts out of court. The judge must weigh the need to consider all relevant evidence versus the public interest in promoting settlement of divorce disputes. Most judges, when properly asked to honor the confidentiality of divorce mediation, have seen the wisdom in protecting it.

REFERENCES

Adler v. Adams, No. 675-73C2 (W. D. Wash. 1979)

American Bar Association Special Committee on Dispute Resolution. *Confidentiality in mediation: A practitioner's guide.* Chicago: American Bar Association, 1985.

Bank of America National Trust and Savings Association v. Hotel Rittenhouse Associates, 800 F. 2d. 339 (3rd Cir. 1986).

Bienenfeld, F. *Child custody mediation: Techniques for counselors, attorneys, and parents.* Palo Alto, CA: Science & Behavior Books, 1983.

Braun, R. Controlling child abuse: Reporting laws. *Case and Comment*, 1975, 10–16.

Breach of confidence: An emerging tort. Comment in *Columbia Law Review*, 1982, *82*, 1426–1468.

California Civil Code §§ 4607(c), (e) (West Supp. 1986).

California Evidence Code § 1040 (West Supp. 1986).

California Evidence Code § 1152.5 (West Supp. 1986).

Children's Bureau. *Prinicples and suggested language for legislation and reporting of the physically abused child.* Washington, DC: United States Department of Health, Education, and Welfare, 1963.

City of Port Arthur v. United States, No. 80-0648, U.S. Dist. Ct., D.C., November 12, 1980.

Clark, L., & Orbeton, J. Mandatory mediation of divorce: Maine's experience. *Judicature*, 1986, *69(5)*, 310–312.

Cleary, E. W., et al. (Eds.). *McCormick's handbook of the law of evidence.* St. Paul, MN: West, 1984.

Colorado Revised Statutes, § 13-22-307 (Supp.) (1983).

Comeaux, E. A guide to implementing divorce mediation in the public sector. *Conciliation Courts Review*, 1983, *21(2)*, 1–25.

Delgado, R. Underprivileged communications: Extension of he psychotherapist–patient privilege to patients of psychiatric social workers. *California Law Review*, 1973, *61*, 1050–1071.

Deuel, P. *Confidentiality in individual, marriage and family counseling.* Unpublished paper, Lewis and Clark Family Law Seminar, Portland, OR, 1983.

Duryee, M. *Open mediation: A systematic view.* Paper presented at conference of Association of Family and Conciliation Courts, Las Vegas, Nevada, December 1987.

Engram, P., & Markowitz, J. Ethical issues in mediation: Divorce and labor compared. *Mediation Quarterly*, 1985, *8*, 19–32.

Fenton v. Howard, 118 Ariz. 2d 119 (1978).

Florida Statutes § 61.21(3) (1982).

Folberg, J. Mediation of child custody disputes. *Columbia Journal of Law and Social Problems*, 1985, *19(3)*, 1–36.

Freedman, L., & Prigoff, M. Confidentiality in mediation: The need for protection. *Ohio State Journal on Dispute Resolution*, 1986, *2*(1), 37–45.

Green, E. D. A heretical view of the mediation privilege. *Ohio State Journal on Dispute Resolution*, 1986, *2(1)*, 1–26.

Griswold v. Connecticut, 381 U.S. 479 (1965).

Hickman v. Taylor, 329 U.S. 496 (1947).

Katz, S., Howe, R., & McGrath, M. Child neglect laws in America. *Family Law Quarterly*, 1975, *9(1)*, 1–372.

Keeton, W. P. (Ed.). *Prosser and Keeton on the law of torts* (5th ed.). St. Paul, MN: West, 1984.

MacDonald v. Clinger, 446 N.Y. S. 2d 801 (1982).

Maine Rules of Evidence 408 (1984).

Martino v. Family Service Agency of Adams County, 112 Ill. App. 3d 593 (1983).

Massachusetts General Laws, ch. 233, §23B (1985).

McGinness, P., & Cinquegrama, R. Legal issues arising in mediation: The Boston Municipal Court mediation program. *Massachusetts Law Review*, 1982, *67(3)*, 123–136.

McIsaac, H. Mandatory conciliation custody/visitation matters: California's bold stroke. *Conciliation Courts Review*, 1981, *19(2)*, 73–81.

McIsaac, H. Confidentiality: An exploration of issues. *Mediation Quarterly*, 1985, *8*, 57–66.

McLaughlin v. Superior Court, 189 Cal. Rptr. 479 (1983).

Michigan Statutes Annotated § 25.176(13)(3) (1982).

Moore, C. *The mediation process: Practical strategies for resolving conflict.* San Francisco: Jossey-Bass, 1986.

Myles and Reiser Co. v. Loew's, Inc., 81 N.Y. S. 2d 861 (1948).

National Labor Relations Board v. Macaluso, Inc., 618 F. 2d 51 (9th Cir. 1980).

New York Civil Practice Law §§ 352, 354 (1920).

New York Judiciary Law Art. 21-A, § 849(b)(6) (1981).

Oregon Legislative Assembly, House Bill 3192, 1987 Regular Session.

Oregon Revised Statutes, §§ 418.740-775 (1975).

Oregon Revised Statutes, § 179.507 (1977).

Oregon Revised Statutes, §§ 107.600, 107.785(2) (1983).

People v. Sicard (N.Y. App. Div. 1986). Reported in L. Freedman, *Dispute resolution*, American Bar Association Special Committee on Dispute Resolution, *Quarterly Information Update*, 1986, *19*, 14.

People v. Snyder, 492 N.Y.S. 2d 890 (1985).

Pottmeyer, T. The confidentiality of child custody mediation. *Washington State Bar News*, 1983, 12-17.

Privileged communciations: A case-by-case approach. Comment in *Maine Law Review*, 1971, *23*, 443-462.

Protecting confidentiality in mediation. Comment in *Harvard Law Review*, 1984, *98*, 441-459.

Report of the Advisory Panel on the Child Oriented Divorce Act of 1987 (California).

Report of the committee on confidentiality in alternative dispute resolution. New York: Center for Public Resources, 1985.

Rodgers, N., & Salem, R. *A student's guide to mediation and the law.* New York: Matthew Bender, 1987.

Rosson v. Rosson, 224 Ca. Rptr. 250 (1986).

Saltzburg, S. Privileges and professionals: Lawyers and psychologists. *Virginia Law Review*, 1980, *66*, 597-651.

Saposnek, D. *Mediating child custody disputes.* San Francisco: Jossey-Bass, 1983.

Simrin v. Simrin, 43 Cal. Rptr. 376 (1965).

Sinclair v. Roy, 47 Reports of Family Law 15 (British Columbia, 1985).

Sonenstahl v. L.E.L.S. Inc., 372 N.W. 2d 1 (Minn. App. 1985).

Tarasoff v. Board of Regents, 131 Cal. Rptr. 14 (1976).

United States Code 42 § 2000g-2(b) (1964).

United States v. Pfiger, Inc., 560 F. 2d 326 (8th Cir. 1977).

Waltz, R., & Huston, J. The rules of evidence in settlement. *Litigation*, 1979, *5(1)*, 1-22.

Washington Revised Code § 5.60.060(5) (1974).

Wigmore, S. A. *A student's textbook of the law of evidence.* Brooklyn, NY: Foundation Press, 1935.

Wilson, S. *Confidentiality in social work: Issues and principles.* New York: Free Press, 1978.

17

Liability of Divorce Mediators

JAY FOLBERG
Northwestern School of Law, Lewis and Clark College

As mediation takes its place among professional services, mediators can right-fully expect to be held to high standards of care and professional integrity. Divorce mediators face potential liability for damages based on claims of malpractice, breach of contract, and fiduciary duties. This chapter explores the legal theories and the elements necessary for recovery against mediators. The defenses available to mediators and the role of malpractice insurance are also discussed.

Legal liability for claims of damages has been of continuing concern to divorce mediators. Lawyers have long warned of the liability exposure faced by mediators and the need for defensive practices (Crouch, 1982). Given the emotionally charged context of divorce mediation, it is not suprising to read predictions that disgruntled clients may initiate lawsuits against mediators (Chaykin, 1984).

There have, however, been few claims against mediators and no reported cases in which a mediator has been successfully sued for damages regarding mediation services. The absence of major lawsuits against mediators is in sharp contrast to the soaring claims made against many other providers of professional services. This chapter first suggests some distinctions that may help to explain this contrast and then examines the legal theories of liability most applicable to divorce mediation and the elements necessary for recovery of damages.

DISTINCTIONS AND LEGAL THEORIES

The favorable difference in claims experience for divorce mediators and other related professionals like lawyers, doctors, and therapists is probably attributable to at least five distinctions. First, divorce mediation as a professional practice is relatively new. Second, by definition the parties must concur on the process and the terms of a mediated outcome. Third, a marital settlement agreement requires judicial approval before being incorporated into a divorce decree. Fourth, the largest volume of divorce mediation occurs under the auspices of court-connected programs, which enjoy some degree of immunity. Fifth, existing legal theories on which a claim is likely to be based and damages measured do not squarely fit the wide variations of divorce mediation practices and the multiple settings in which they are offered.

Private divorce mediation is not yet so common a practice as to generate the large volume of cases that would produce some lawsuits as a matter of statistical probability. Evidence casting doubt about the reasonableness of a particular mediation result or the integrity of the mediator is not likely to come to light until some time after the mediation is concluded. The revelation of mediator impropriety and the development of a large enough number of cases to produce some small percentage of troublesome results or litigious clients may be but a function of time. There is also, as of yet, no established standard to which mediation services can be compared for purposes of easily establishing liability.

Mediation produces a consensual result that reflects the participants' joint determination of what is fair and appropriate. The parties both concur in the resolution process to be followed in mediation and formulate the substantive terms of a settlement. They work with the mediator and exercise responsibility rather than depending on the mediator to produce a favorable result. Because the spouses create the outcome and feel like they "own" the process, they are unlikely to be dissatisfied later or to hold the mediator responsible for the result. One consistent result of the research on divorce mediation is that participants are generally satisfied with mediation regardless of the substantive outcome (see Part 6). Lawsuits and claims against providers of a service are usually the result of dissatisfaction with the process (Folberg & Taylor, 1984).

Marital dissolution and divorce disputes are unique in requiring a court order to end the relationship and approve the terms of a settlement. Courts have the opportunity to review every marital settlement agreement before incorporating it in a divorce decree. Busy court dockets may make detailed judicial review more of a pretense than a reality (Folberg, 1985), but even the fiction of court review serves as some check against overreaching and slows down the process. Knowing that a judge may question the agreed terms tends to prevent outrageous results and avoid impetuous decisions. This judicial "filter" may also help insulate the process from later liability claims that must be heard by another judge.

Although private divorce mediation services are becoming more common, the greatest volume of cases involve custody issues mediated in court-connected programs similar to the Connecticut program described in Chapter 9. Most of the mediators in these court-connected programs are court personnel accountable to the court. Some courts contract with agencies or with individuals to provide mediation services. Court-connected mediators practice under the shadow of judicial immunity from liability. Conducting settlement conferences is an accepted judicial function for which judicial immunity is generally allowed (Peragine v. Mairmone, 1980). It can be argued that mediators who work for the court or who are referred cases from the court replace the judge in this function and should be protected by judicial immunity (Chaykin, 1986, p. 83). Although the immunity of judges is no longer absolute, they can be sued only for a very narrow range of harmful conduct in the process of performing their official duties (*Pulliam v. Allen*, 1984). Additionally, government employees also have some protection against liability within the scope of their official duties (Keeton, 1984, p. 1056). It is, therefore, improbable that a court-employed or court-appointed divorce mediator could be successfully sued except for an intentional wrong.

The legal theories by which mediators not employed or appointed by a court might be held liable for claims have been developed in other contexts. Each imposes requirements that might not be met or would not be appropriate in all the variations of settings in which mediators practice. The imposition of legal liability for divorce mediation is ultimately a question of balancing the public policies favoring the consensual resolution of private disputes versus the policy of holding professionals accountable and providing redress for wrongs ("The Sultans of Swap," 1986).

The potential liability of a divorce mediator to participants may arise from a number of different legal theories. A mediator could conceivably be sued for fraud, false advertising, breach of contract, invasion of privacy, defamation, outrageous conduct, breach of fiduciary duty, and professional negligence or malpractice. One event or set of facts may lead to liability, or at least a lawsuit, on several different legal theories or causes of action (Rodgers & Salem, 1987, Chap. 8). The three that are most likely to be the basis of a legal claim against a mediator are breach of contract, negligence, and breach of fiduciary duty. These three causes of action, as potentially applicable to divorce mediators, are discussed below.

CONTRACT LIABILITY

A mediator must be cautious, in offering and contracting for the provision of mediation services, not to make any implied or expressed promises about the results. If a mediator indicates in the offer or contract for services that mediation will be cheaper, better, or faster than other alternatives such as litigation or arbitration, the mediator may be liable if the promise is not kept. There can be no assurance that mediation will be better than the alternatives in any specific case, and such assurances or representation should be avoided. There is currently a tendency to oversell mediation, which could easily result in disappointed participants and in antagonistic attorneys and other professionals prepared to assist in taming the practice of divorce mediation through lawsuits.

The agreement to mediate should clearly state that no promises as to the outcome or the success of the process are expressed or implied and that the spouses understand that they might be able to seek more for themselves in an adversarial proceeding than they are likely to obtain through mediation. Any implied or expressed promise that mediation will be better or produce a more favorable result could subject the mediator to liability for breach of that contractual promise. (See *Boecher v. Borth*, 1976; Keeton, 1984).

Some contractual obligations are difficult to avoid when providing mediation and may be implied as an imposed standard of practice. For example, a mediator, or the agency for which the mediator works, may, in effect, enter into a contract with the participants that the mediation will be private and confidential, unless agreed to the contrary. The participants may sue if the contract, expressed or implied, is breached. In a reported Illinois case, a client of an agency social worker sued the social worker and the agency for revealing confidences to others in violation of an implied contract for confidentiality, allowing a conflict of interest to develop (the social worker fell in love with and had intimate relations with plaintiff's husband) and incompetently performing counseling services. The suit was allowed to proceed only on the claim of breach of contract because of the revelation of information given in confidence (*Martino v. Family Service Agency*, 1983). As discussed in Chapter 16, no guarantee of absolute confidentiality can be made for mediation sessions. The mediator is, however, contractually and ethically bound to keep confidences unless the participants give permission otherwise or the mediator is compelled by court order or demand of law.

The revelation of confidential information, whether made to a general audience or only in response to specific inquiries, may be the basis of a lawsuit ("Breach of Confidence," 1982). In the New York case of *Doe v. Roe* (1977) a psychiatrist and her psychologist husband published a book containing verbatim accounts of a former patient's thoughts and intimate fantasies. Although the patient's name was not mentioned in the book, the biographical detail provided would allow colleagues and friends to identify her. The court allowed her suit for breach of confidence. In another case a psychiatrist was held to have committed a breach of confidence when he disclosed details of his former patient's therapy, which included electric shock, when asked about it by another doctor. The inquiring doctor was acting in behalf of parents concerned about their daughter's plan to marry the psychiatrist's former patient (*Berry v. Moench*, 1958).

Although the above cases do not involve mediation and may seem unique, rather than risk an implied contract based on false expectations or promising more than can always be delivered, the mediator should use a written contract to limit liability. The contract for employment of the mediator may incorporate mediation guidelines or rules. The contract, or the contract and rules together, should outline the process to be used in the mediation, the role of the mediator, the risks and limitations of mediation, the need for outside review and independent legal advice, the obligations of the participants, the basis for determination of any fees or costs, and the obligation of participants for payment. A separate and clear release should be signed by the parties if their sessions will be taped or used as part of a study, for research, or for any publication.

NEGLIGENCE LIABILITY

Mediator liability based upon allegations of professional negligence, or malpractice, is the most likely liability claim that will be encountered by a mediator. Malpractice claims generally arise under the law of torts and require proof on four elements: (1) a duty owed to the participants by the mediator, (2) a breach of the duty by failure to comply with acceptable standards of practice, (3) damages measurable in money, and (4) a causal relationship between the failure to exercise an acceptable standard of practice and the alleged damages. Proof of all four elements is necessary. Adequate proof may be difficult in a claim against a mediator.

Duty and Breach

The mediator's duty arises out of the agreement, expressed or implied, to provide competent mediation services. In other words, it is reasonably expected that any professional service will be performed competently. Competency is usually measured by compliance with existing professional standards of care for the type of service offered and sometimes for the locality in which it is rendered. The first problem for the claimant in a malpractice case against a divorce mediator would be to produce proof of what is an acceptable standard of care in the practice of mediation.

The standard of care for most professional services is generally defined as "the knowledge, skill and care ordinarily possessed and employed by members of the profession in good standing" (Keeton, 1984, p. 187). Although this definition of responsibility can be applied to providers of mediation, its application may be difficult. The development of mediator standards as explained in Chapter 20 have gone far in establishing expectations and guidelines for divorce mediation. There are, however, no templates by which to measure mediation services and no mechanism for isolating the knowledge, skill, and care required to practice in good standing. The training requirements and skills needed for effective mediation are still being formulated. There are few academic programs in mediation and no standard curriculum.

Divorce mediators may be trained as lawyers, therapists, or financial advisors or have no prior professional background. Should mediators from different professions of origin be held to identical duties and sets of skills, or is the expectation different for each? No doubt if a lawyer–mediator integrated joint legal advice or information into the practice of mediation, he or she could be held responsible if the advice or information is wrong. But what if the lawyer–mediator gives no legal advice when it is known that the spouses are proceeding on incorrect legal assumptions? Is the lawyer–mediator responsible for the error? Would a therapist–mediator be held to the same standard as a lawyer–mediator in this situation? Is the mediator relieved of liability if the parties were urged to consult independent legal counsel? These questions have no tested answer.

Henry Elson in Chapter 8 describes his practice as a lawyer–mediator quite differently than the therapist–mediator described by Emily Brown in Chapter 7. Each is a well-respected and successful mediator. Would they be held to identical standards and duties? Do the interdisciplinary co-mediators suggested by Lois Gold in Chapter 11 share legal liability for one another? Ironically, the high level of client satisfaction with divorce mediation and the uncertainties of establishing liability have resulted in few, if any, legal answers. Litigated cases of claimed mediator liability may eventually provide some answers as well as mark the establishment of divorce mediation as a recognized and defined profession (Folberg & Taylor, 1984).

The claimant's burden of establishing an appropriate measure of competency would be made easier if the mediator is a member of a professional organization, such as the Academy of Family Mediators, which promulgates standards of practice. Similarly, if the mediator subscribes to written standards or standards were prescribed for the mediator by the terms of the mediator's licensure, certification, employment, or referral, then proof of the applicable standard and the consequent duty owed would be facilitated.

As a general rule, proof of the applicable standard of care, as well as its breach, is presented through expert testimony. Because of the newly emerging nature of mediation as a discrete practice, qualified experts may be hard to find, and differences of opinion are to be expected. Differences of opinion are not necessarily inconsistent with the exercise of due care in complying with established professional standards. Testimony that the expert would have practiced differently than the mediator defendant is immaterial on the question of breach of a professional duty. The expert can only testify that the conduct of the mediator defendant did or did not comply with accepted standards of practice and skill as exercised by reasonable divorce mediators practicing in the same locality. This is the approach taken in legal malpractice cases and should serve by analogy in cases of mediator malpractice ("Standard of Care," 1968).

If the mediator purports to have specialized knowledge or experience in the subject area of the mediated conflict, then the mediator may be held to a higher standard of care relating to that subject ("Specialization," 1978). In other words, a mediator's self-designation as having special expertise in the law relating to family disputes or in the phases of child development, such that a divorcing couple might reasonably rely on the mediator's expertise and advice in making their joint decisions, could give rise to a claim that the mediator had a duty to provide correct information on which a decision could be based. If the mediator advertises that mediation is a substitute for legal representation in divorce, the mediator subjects the clients to unreasonable risks and may also subject himself or herself to the standard of knowledge and care of an attorney, regardless of the mediator's training. The divorce mediator must be cautious when providing information or advice and should urge the spouses to obtain independent counsel and input, particularly on any subject beyond the mediator's expertise. In our increasingly complex world a mediator may be held negligent for failure to encourage the participants, from the outset of mediation, to consult with experts or obtain specialized information when relevant or necessary to formulate alternatives and choices for resolution of family conflicts. The same challenge of specialization and expertise is currently facing lawyers, therapists, and professionals of all types (see McCabe, 1986).

Physicians and other health care providers have been held to the duty of informing their patients about the risks in the service provided. Though this duty to inform of risk was originally limited to medical procedures and advice, it has since been expanded to require attorneys to reveal the risks of a trial as compared to its alternatives and would logically require any professional offering a service to reveal the risks involved. The standards discussed in other chapters of this book, as well as many bar association ethics rulings, would clearly require a mediator to advise the participants of the risks of proceeding with mediation rather than the other conflict-resolution procedures available. There is no reason to think that mediators would not be held to such a duty and that liability might not follow from its breach.

A mediator who drafts a settlement agreement for the participants could be held to a duty that the draft be an accurage reflection of the stipulations made during mediation and that it be drawn skillfully enough to effectuate the participants' intended purpose. Drafting settlement agreements can be risky business. Again, the mediator would be wise to make it clear that it is the responsibility of the participants to have any proposed agreement reviewed by independent counsel before being finalized. In any event, no agreement should be offered to the participants for their signature without the opportunity for the participants to read and consider it at their leisure outside of the mediation setting. Any agreement drafted by a mediator who is not an attorney should not purport to be in legal form and should be labeled a "memorandum on points of agreement" or a "mediated plan," rather than designated as a final settlement agreement.

Damages and Causation

Even if a disgruntled mediation participant could establish that a mediator had a duty of care which was breached and that the mediator therefore committed professional malpractice or negligence, there are still two additional interrelated requirements. The intertwined elements of damages and causation require proof of damage measurable in dollars and proof that this damage would not have occurred but for the negligence or malpractice of the mediator. These necessary elements may be particularly difficult to prove in a case involving divorce mediation.

The damages cannot be mere conjecture or speculation. It is the claimant's burden to establish the injury sustained and the value of that injury or loss in terms of dollars. What the claimant might have obtained by resolution of the dispute in some manner other than mediation or what economic consequence may have flowed from any alleged negligence of the mediator is, more likely than not, a matter of speculation and conjecture. Any damages sustained because of the mediator's conduct or misfeasance may be more of an emotional loss and annoyance than a loss measurable in dollars.

The necessary element that would probably be most difficult to prove in a negligence action against a divorce mediator is causation. The claimant must establish that any damages or loss sustained would not have occurred but for the negligence or malfeasance of the mediator. Proving what would have happened in the absence of mediation could be difficult. For example, it would be hard to establish precisely what would have resulted from litigation as an alternative to mediation, and equally challenging to prove that the claimant would have been better off negotiating a marital settlement agreement outside of mediation. If the mediator is careful not to guarantee any specific or more favorable result than could be obtained by alternatives to mediation, it will be difficult to prove that any alleged damages were caused by the mediator's action. Even a claim of unequal bargaining power and overreaching, unchecked by the mediator during the mediation, would not be proof that the same unequal power would not have resulted in a similar or worse outcome in litigation or in adversarial negotiations.

If, on one hand, the claimed damages are sustained after independent review of the agreement or after the mediator has urged such a review, it would be even harder to fix the causative blame on the mediator. On the other hand, a mediator who allows the parties to finalize an agreement without an admonition of the importance of independent review and counsel may have trouble escaping a claim that poor advice during mediation or the allowance of overreaching or unfair bargaining during mediation was not the cause of provable damages.

One of the more likely claims to arise is that, if the mediation is unsuccessful in resolving the dispute, the time passed in mediation may preclude pursuing meaningful alternatives because of the expiration of a statute of limitations, a change in the facts, or an accumulation of more damages because of the passage of time. Again, if the mediator has advised the participants of the risks, urged them to consult with others during and after the mediation, and had the participants sign a contract acknowledging the factors, it would be difficult to prove that any damages were caused by the mediator. This preventive and precautionary safeguard by the mediator would also make it more clear that the participants in mediation assume the risks incurred, so that they will not be heard to complain later.

The only reported case in which a mediator was sued for malpractice illustrates several of the problems in proving damages and causation. In the case of *Lange v. Marshall* (1981), a Missouri court of appeals had occasion to consider the liability of an attorney, Marshall, who undertook the mediation of a divorce settlement for two of his friends who had been married 25 years. After signing the settlement agreement, which was pending before a judge for approval, Mrs. Lange had second thoughts about the settlement terms and hired an independent lawyer who eventually obtained a more favorable divorce settlement for her. Mrs. Lange sued Marshall, claiming he was negligent in not inquiring further as to the financial worth of her former husband, in failing to help her negotiate a better settlement, in not advising her that she could get more if she litigated the matter, and in not fully and fairly disclosing her rights as to marital property, custody, and maintenance. The case went to a jury, which returned a verdict against Marshall in the amount of $74,000.

On Marshall's appeal of the jury verdict, he argued that he was acting as a mediator rather than an attorney. The court of appeals assumed, for purposes of its opinion, that Marshall was acting as a mediator and he owed a duty to the participants that was breached by his failure to do one or more of the things about which Mrs. Lange complained. The court held, however, that Mrs. Lange did not meet her burden as a claimant in establishing that Marshall's alleged negligence actually caused the economic damages that she claimed to have suffered in the way of lost support payments, fees for accountants and private investigators, lost taxes, medical costs, and other expenses, as well as legal fees—all incurred after she obtained her own lawyer and engaged in the lengthy adversarial proceedings eventually leading to a more favorable settlement. The court pointed out that there was no evidence that these expenses would not have been incurred anyway or that her former husband would have agreed to a different settlement had Marshall done the things he was charged with not doing. If anything, the court found the evidence to the contrary. The court noted that Mrs. Lange engaged in 10 months of heated preparation for litigation with Mr. Lange, following her repudiation of the mediated settlement, and that she could not prove that the expenses she incurred would not have happened "but for" the alleged negligence of Marshall.

> [Mr. Lange] testified that he intended to be fair with the plaintiff but that her idea of fairness, and her attorney's idea of fairness, did not comport with his. . . . It is the rankest conjecture and speculation to conclude that Ralph Lange's willingness to settle the marital affairs without litigation on the basis of the original [mediated] settlement established his willingness to settle without litigation at a higher figure acceptable to plaintiff. . . . The parties agreed that defendant was not representing plaintiff as an advocate but in a mediation position. (p. 239)

More recent judicial decisions involving claims by dissatisfied clients against their divorce lawyers illustrate the difficulty of proving causation and damages resulting from alleged malpractice. In the case of *Mariscotti v. Turnari* (1984), the wife alleged that her divorce lawyer's incorrect valuation of her husband's stock holdings weakened her bargaining position. The Pennsylvania Superior Court held that the wife's argument of what might have resulted in divorce negotiation if the stock was valued differently was "pure speculation" and could not support her malpractice claim. Similarly, the Indiana Court of Appeals ruled that a wife's suit against her attorney for negligence in not obtaining a more favorable property distribution called for mere speculation on the issue of causation (*Fiddler v. Hobbs*, 1985). The wife claimed that, but for the attorney's negligence in not putting on additional evidence, she would have done better. The court held that "there is not a scintilla of evidence that but for [the attorney's] acts the distribution of marital assets would have been other than what the trial court determined" (p. 1294). The jury is not allowed to speculate on causation or damages.

Causation and damages can be proved with reasonable certainty in some instances of legal malpractice and perhaps in divorce mediation. The most noted area in which causation can be proved is where a divorce lawyer fails to inform a client of an asset in which an interest could have been claimed but was not, because of misinformation. The attorney is expected to exercise informed judgment with regard to client's rights (*Smith v. Lewis*, 1975). The damages that result from misinforming or not informing a client can be most easily measured in cases involving pensions and taxes or other interests capable of mathematical calculation. If spouses reasonably looked to a mediator for information about their rights or about what should go into the "marital pot" for division between them, then the mediator could be liable for misinformation. Although most mediators specifically decline to offer any judgment about rights and interests, some do give information on which the spouses could claim reliance, particularly if they are not encouraged to seek independent legal advice. However, the result (causation) and the measurable effect (damages) may not be as clear in mediation as in adversarial proceedings.

Liability to Third Parties

One frequently voiced concern about divorce mediation is that children, grandparents, and new partners are usually not present in the mediation sessions even though they may have an interest in the outcome. The question may arise, whether anyone other than the spouses can assert claims against divorce mediators.

Generally, malpractice cases require the existence of a direct professional relationship before a duty is created, the breach of which may be actionable. This rule, dating back for attorneys to at least 1879, holds that no duty is owed to those in which there is no "privity" of relationship with the professional (*National Savings Bank v. Ward*, 1879). It has been held, for example, that children of a marriage may not pursue a negligence claim against the attorney who represented their mother in the divorce and failed to see that they were named as beneficiaries of their father's life insurance, as required by the divorce decree (*Pelham v. Griesheimer*, 1981). The court in the *Pelham* case also discussed and dismissed the possibility that the children may have been third-party beneficiaries to the contract for services between their mother and the attorney. Some mediators state that their role is to protect or promote the best interests of the children by serving as an advocate for the children (Saposnek, 1983). If this protection is considered part of the contract for mediation services, a duty that could be the basis of a claim may then flow in favor of the children.

Another potential liability faced by mediators arises when the mediator obtains information of actual danger to a third party and fails to give notice to help protect the third party. The responsibility to avert known harm to third parties overrides the duty of confidentiality. In the much published case of *Tarasoff v. Regents of the University of California* (1976), a psychotherapist was held negligent for failing to warn a female student that his patient had threatened to murder her. At least one legal commentator believes that liability for breach of the duty to protect third parties from danger is a threat to the practice of mediation. (In the wake . . . , 1985). The *Tarasoff* decision is not, however, as far reaching as some assume and is limited by the requirements that the mediator "(1) know or should have known that such harm will occur and (2) have some special relationship with the party that disclosed the information so that there is a certain degree of control over that party, or (3) have some special relationship with the potential victim of the threatened behavior" (Chaykin, 1986, p. 75).

Defenses to Claims of Negligence

There are two types of legal defenses. A direct defense denies the existence of a necessary element of the plaintiff's cause of action and is the flip side of the above discussion of what is required to prove negligence. For example, the mediator may defend by showing there was no duty owed to the plaintiff, no breach of that duty, no causation, or no measurable damages. An affirmative defense goes beyond a direct denial and attempts to establish some other recognized reason why the mediator should not be liable for the claim. These affirmative defenses include contributory negligence, assumption of risk, ratification, estoppel, public policy, and the statute of limitations.

Because the spouses assume an active role and make their own decisions in divorce mediation, the affirmative defenses that they negligently contributed to the outcome, that they assumed the risks of mediation, that they ratified the outcome, or that they are, in fairness, estopped from later complaining about the outcome may be persuasive to a judge or jury. In a similar context, an appellate court in Georgia held that a client could not obtain damages for his attorney's alleged negligence in drafting a child-support agreement where the client, who was well educated, read and approved its contents, and the language of the agreement was clear and unambiguous (*Berman v. Rubin*, 1976).

A public policy defense would ask the court to consider the value of divorce mediation and the harm that would come to it if mediators were required to assume monetary liability for later dissatisfaction with the result. This question of how to allocate the risk of mediation may arise earlier, in defining what is the duty of care owed by the mediator, and is sometimes expressed in terms of "proximate cause." It is a way of effectuating desired public policy by limiting the application of negligence liability (Keeton, 1984). This public policy consideration is more likely to be applied to court-connected and publicly funded mediation programs than to private sector mediation for a fee.

The applicable limit of time in which a suit for negligence or breach of contract can be brought is determined by state statute and judicial interpretation. Most states have a statute imposing a relatively short period of 1 or 2 years in which a negligence action must be brought and a longer period of up to 6 years for breach of contract. The time when the statute begins to run also depends on state law and varies from when the event complained of occurred to when the plaintiff discovers the facts indicating damages, or reasonably could have discovered them. Many states have enacted separate limitation periods applicable only to medical malpractice or legal malpractice (e.g., California Civil Procedure Code, 1977). No specific time limitation has been enacted for mediation malpractice, probably because it has not been a problem needing legislative attention.

A few states have enacted statutes to protect mediators in circumstances from claims of liability (see Colorado Revised Statutes § 13-22-306(2), 1985; Oklahoma Statutes Annotated, title 12, § 1805(E), 1987). It is now being debated whether more widespread legislation providing mediator immunity from liability claims should be encouraged. Those who argue against legislation protecting mediators fear that "the costs of granting immunity will be borne by individual victims of mediators' incompetence" and that "the high standard of the profession may decline" (Chaykin, 1986, pp. 53, 83). The argument for complete mediator immunity laws centers on the need to promote the use of mediation and the mediator's role as a trusted intermediary in actively facilitating dispute settlements (Stulberg, 1986). It does appear contradictory to urge that mediation be considered a professional practice while arguing for immunity against claims of professional negligence. U.S. liability theory holds professionals to high standards intended to promote care and cautiousness.

FIDUCIARY DUTY

The law of fiduciaries may provide some guidance in determining the legal rights and duties in mediation. The legal doctrine regarding fiduciaries is flexible and does not depend on predefined standards, as in negligence law, nor is a contract required. In his law review article, Arthur Chaykin (1984) argues that the mediator's special relationship with the spouses establishes an affirmative duty upon the mediator to insulate the settlement process by being even-handed, unbiased, trustworthy, and diligent.

The mediator's fiduciary duties are seen as more procedural than substantive. For example, the duty to ensure informed decisions by the spouses requires the mediator to structure the process and initiate questions to help uncover critical facts on which reasoned decisions can be based. If either spouse is injured by the withholding of information and complains about the fairness of the resulting agreement, the mediator would have the burden of showing the *process* was fair and reasonably structured to uncover withheld facts. The parties, in other words, have a right to rely upon and trust that the mediator guided them through a fair process.

The concept of fiduciary duties is not complex to understand, but applying the doctrine to divorce mediation may be difficult. It must be decided, first, that a fiduciary relationship exists and, second, what responsibilities flow from the relationship. Mediators do not act for or represent the parties in mediation and thus may be in a role similar to that of a judge rather than a fiduciary. However, a judge's power is checked by the adversary process and well-established procedural rules. In mediation, the parties are often urged to rely less on the adversarial checks and more on trust, as guided by the mediator. The rules of mediation are flexible and not well refined. The spouses, therefore, must trust the mediator and the fairness of the process that the mediator directs. Both parties are vulnerable to any abuse or failure of the mediator to fulfill the trust expected.

The threshold issue in determining if a fiduciary relationship exists is whether there was justifiable trust. What is justifiable will depend on a number of variables, including the setting, the relative sophistication of the parties, the availability and use of independent advice, and the power relationship of the parties (Chaykin, 1984). These important variables make the application of the law of fiduciaries flexible and somewhat unpredictable.

Once the fiduciary relationship is found to exist, the next question is whether the trust implied in the relationship was breached. For example, spouses justifiably trust their mediator to be evenhanded and unbiased. This evenhanded treatment and absence of partisanship are the very qualities that makes the mediator valuable at a time of conflict between the parties. If the mediator develops a bias or favors one spouse, then the trust has been breached and the value of the mediator has been compromised or, worse, becomes a liability to one spouse. "Under such circumstances, a court should find that the mediator has breached his fiduciary duty of evenhandedness" (Chaykin, 1984, p. 749).

A NEW THEORY OF MEDIATOR LIABILITY

A 1986 issue of the *Harvard Law Review* contains a student note suggesting that existing models of considering mediator liability are not flexible enough for realistic application to the great varieties of mediation practice and that they go "too far in imposing liability on mediators for defects in the contraction process they oversee" ("The Sultans of Swap," 1986, p. 1886). Although recognizing the legitimate fears created because of the expanding roles of mediators in resolving conflict, the author of the note is concerned that "the antidotes they propose would in many cases undermine the mediator's constructive role in resolving disputes" (p. 1886).

It is proposed that the mediator's duty to ensure a fair and open procedure be separated from the question of monetary liability for the breach of that duty. If the mediator's duty regarding the process were breached, the injured party could seek to rescind the resulting agreement and seek restitution from the other spouse, if appropriate. The right of the aggrieved party to set aside the mediated agreement resulting from a flawed process would be separate from any right to collect damages from the mediator. This proposal is little different from existing principles of contract law that allow contracts resulting from duress, misrepresentation, or undue influence to be set aside. Contracts that are generally unconscionable can also be voided under existing law (Dalton, 1985). However, the unconscionable procedure must, under present law, result in substantive unfairness before the contract can be set aside. Under the proposed change, mediated agreements resulting from procedural flaws could be successfully challenged based on the mediator's breach of procedural duty, regardless of the eventual contractual terms.

Separating the mediator's duty from his or her potential liability is intended to safeguard the integrity of the mediation process and the parties' trust in it. The mediator's duty consists of three parts: (1) the duty of impartiality, (2) the duty of noncoerciveness, and (3) the duty of thoroughness. If a mediator breaches one of these duties, the settlement could be voided by judicial decree. In order to obtain damages against the mediator the disgruntled spouse would also have to show measurable harm and causation, as in a legal action based on negligence. It is doubtful that many disappointed spouses would invest the time and energy to move to set aside a mediated agreement if they did not suffer provable harm and causation. All of the defenses previously discussed would then be available to the mediator if sued for damages, including public policy arguments encouraging mediation services.

INSURANCE

The above discussion of potential divorce mediator liability may make the risk appear greater than is warranted by the limited number of actual claims for liability that have been asserted against mediators. The potential for claims does, however, exist. It would be naive to believe that the early euphoria for divorce mediation, the high expectations created by media coverage, and the inflated claims of some mediators will not give way to criticism and disappointment in some cases. As divorce mediation becomes a more recognized professional practice with a better established set of standards, it will probably attract more of the malpractice litigation zeal that has both plagued and improved other professional practices.

The expense of even a successful defense against malpractice claims may be an economically crippling blow to mediators or agencies with which they are associated. Careful and thoughtful mediation techniques, as urged throughout this book, as well as a preventive practice orientation, can minimize the risks for mediators. There can, of course, be no guarantee against error and no assurance that a claim could not be asserted even in the absence of error.

Mediators would be wise to protect themselves with some form of liability or malpractice insurance. Some of the insurance companies and programs that insure the mediator's profession of origin against malpractice claims will cover a claim arising from the practice of divorce mediation. However, some insurance policies may not cover a nontraditional practice or may preclude coverage by reasoning that a lawyer, therapist, nurse, or other insured professional is not practicing within the professional range of services for which the insurance was contracted (see Jacob, 1988). Some insurance companies have indicated a willingness to issue an inexpensive rider to their existing malpractice insurance policies, to cover specifically the risks of mediation. Other companies have indicated, in response to inquiries, that their existing policies, at least for attorneys and therapists, would cover mediation claims. It would be a good practice to check any individual policy and confirm coverage with the insurance carrier.

Liability insurance is now available to mediators through membership in some mediation organizations and professional associations, including the Association of Family and Conciliation Courts, the Academy of Family Mediators, and the Society of Professionals in Dispute Resolution. The cost of this insurance is quite modest because of the low claim experience to date. Mediators are urged to contact these organizations to obtain more information about the insurance that they make available to their membership.

There are at least two different types of professional liability insurance: occurrence and claims-made policies. Occurrence policies provide coverage as of the date of the alleged negligent occurrence. For example, if a mediator provided negligent services in 1987 and was covered at that time with an occurrence policy, the liability protection would be effective whether or not the mediator continued to carry malpractice insurance or had insurance when the claim was eventually asserted years later. Under claims-made insurance, which has become more common, the mediator is protected only during the time the coverage is current. So if a claim is asserted in 1989 for alleged negligence in 1987, there would be no coverage unless the policy was paid and current in 1989. Similarly, if the mediator was not insured in 1987 but was covered by a claims-made policy in 1989 when the claim was asserted, there should be insurance protection (McCabe, 1986). It is also important to determine that the insurance covers the costs of defending the claim as well as any liability that may be established. As with any other insurance, the deductible amount, if any, for which you are responsible should be understood and realistic.

CONCLUSION

This chapter has presented a catalog of legal theories and defenses to consider in assessing the liability of divorce mediators for claims that might be made by disappointed clients. This is a topic ripe for discussion and debate because legal liability is a matter of real concern to mediators, and few clear answers are now provided by court decisions or legislation. Some readers may be alarmed at the attention devoted here to liability exposure, when so few claims have actually been asserted. Discussing legal theories that might be used against mediators before actual cases have been filed in courts may be seen as stirring up the pot and exposing an emerging profession to additional risk, in effect making the problem bigger than life.

Understanding the potential liability and the policies underlying it may help conscientious mediators avoid claims of malpractice and, more important, protect the integrity of the mediation process. The realization that divorce mediators do owe a duty of care, contractual fulfillment, and trust to those served, and even to third parties, can strengthen mediation practice. Although we would certainly prefer not to be personally exposed to claims, public confidence in divorce mediation will be enhanced if we can be held to answerable standards of care and legal liability, as is expected of other recognized professional services.

The absence of licensing or other significant regulation for divorce mediation creates an additional need for remedies to correct insensitivity, carelessness, and abuse. The entire field of mediation practice might benefit in the long run from carefully considered claims and public recognition that poor mediation need not be tolerated and that legal recourse is available. It is a tribute to the inherent virtue of mediation that so few claims have developed and that satisfaction among those who have participated in the process appears so great.

REFERENCES

Berman v. Rubin, 138 Ga. App. 849 (1976).

Berry v. Moench, 8 Utah 2d 191 (1958).

Boecher v. Borth, 377 N. Y. S. 2d 781 (1976).

Breach of confidence: An emerging tort. Comment in *Harvard Law Review*, 1982, *82*, 1426–1468.

California Civil Procedure Code § 340.6 (1977).

Chaykin, A. Mediator liability: A new role for fiduciary duties? *Cincinnati Law Review*, 1984, *53*, 731–764.

Chaykin, A. The liabilities and immunities of mediators: A hostile environment for model legislation. *Ohio State Journal on Dispute Resolution*, 1986, *2*, 47–83. Colorado Revised Statutes, § 13-22-306(2), 1985.

Crouch, R. Divorce mediation, and legal ethics. *Family Law Quarterly*, 1982, *16(3)*, 219–250.

Dalton, C. An essay in the deconstruction of contract doctrine. *Yale Law Journal*, 1985, *94*, 999–1114.

Doe v. Roe, 400 N. Y. S. 2d 668 (1977).

Fiddler v. Hobbs, No. 3-384A(79) (Ind. Ct. App. 1985). Reported in *Family Law Reporter*, 1985, *11*, 1294.

Folberg, J. Mediation of child custody disputes. *Columbia Journal of Law and Social Problems*, 1985, *19(4)*, 1–36.

Folberg, J. & Taylor, A. *Mediation: A comprehensive guide to resolving conflicts without litigation*. San Francisco: Jossey-Bass, 1984.

In the wake of Tarasoff; Mediation and the duty to disclose. Comment in *Catholic University Law Review*, 1985, *35*, 209–243.

Jacob, L. Letter to the editor. *Mediation News* (Academy of Family Mediators), January–February 1988, *7(1)*, 1.

Keeton, W. P. (Ed.). *Prosser and Keeton on the law of torts* (5th ed.) St. Paul, MN: West, 1984.

Lange v. Marshall, 622 S. W. 2d 237 (Mo. 1981).

Mariscotti v. Turnari, (Pa. Super. Ct. 1984). Reported in *Family Law Reporter*, 1985, *1*, 1112.

Martino v. Family Service Agency of Adams County, 112 Ill. App. 3d 593 (1983).

McCabe, J. Lawyer liability: When the practitioner becomes the target. *Trial*, 1986, *22(7)*, 45–50.

National Savings Bank v. Ward, 100 U. S. 195 (1879).

Oklahoma Statutes Annotated, title 12, § 1805(E), 1985.

Pelham v. Griesheimer, 93 Ill. App. 3d 751 (1981).

Peragine v. Mairmone, 504 F. Supp. 136(S. D. N. Y. 1980).

Pulliam v. Allen, 104 S. Ct. 1970 (1984).

Rodgers, N. & Salem, R. *A student's guide to mediation and the law.* New York: Mathew Bender, 1987.

Saposnek, D. *Mediating child custody disputes.* San Francisco: Jossey-Bass, 1983.

Smith v. Lewis, 118 Cal. Rptr. 621 (1975).

Specialization: The resulting standard of care and duty to consult. Comment in *Baylor Law Review*, 1978, *30*, 729–738.

Standard of care in legal malpractice. Note in *Indiana Law Journal*, 1968, *43*, 771–790.

Stulberg, J. Mediator immunity. *Ohio State Journal on Dispute Resolution*, 1986, *2*, 85–91.

The sultans of swap: Defining the duties and liabilities of American mediators. Note in *Harvard Law Review*, 1986, *99*, 1876–1895.

Tarasoff v. Regents of the University of California, 131 Cal. Rptr. 14 (1976).

18

Ethical Constraints: A Legal Perspective

LINDA SILBERMAN
New York University School of Law

Divorce mediation casts lawyers and mental health professionals in new roles for which the ethical rules of their profession of origin do not fit well. A lawyer who mediates does not necessarily turn in his or her bar card when offering mediation services; lawyer–mediators must be concerned with ethical restraints imposed by bar associations. This chapter surveys existing ethical rules and analyzes their applicability to divorce mediation by examining published bar opinions and case rulings. The author, an eminent law professor, suggests that rethinking is in order and more flexible ethical rules are needed.

No discussion of ethical constraints in divorce mediation can begin without allusion to the conventional model of divorce to which mediation is an alternative. That conventional model is one of an arm's-length, adversarial proceeding, with lawyers as the central figures. Mental health professionals figure in this model only to the extent that they may be called upon to pick up the human pieces. Even the marital partners are likely to assume a role secondary to the adverse lawyers. Actual litigation is exceptional and settlement is the norm, but it is a negotiated truce between warring parties represented by professional champions.

In contrast, mediation places the marital partners in the center of things: its goal is a process of compromise with the active, direct participation of the divorcing couple. The primary professional role in mediation shifts from adversarial representation to that of facilitating this process of compromise. This shift in role may cast some doubt as to who should be the preeminent professionals. Although lawyers remain the key figures in some mediation models, others have placed lawyers and mental health professionals in an active partnership. Whatever the model, it seems clear that the lawyer's role changes shape in the context of divorce mediation. There is no doubt that ethical rules must be molded and adapted to the new dispute-resolution alternative. Moreover, the set of ethical concerns that arise in private mediation depend to some extent on whether the mediation model is the solo lawyer, the solo mental health professional, co-mediation by a lawyer and other professional, or the lawyer as the "advisory attorney" or other participant at a mediation center (Silberman, 1982).

The response by state and local bar associations to potential ethical problems has been limited to a rather formalized and technical application of the Code of Professional Responsibility to mediation. Most of the ethics opinions cited in this chapter are those of state bar committees, interpreting their respective state Codes of Professional Responsibility—which are generally adopted from the American Bar Association (ABA) *Model Code of Professional Responsibility* (1969). The Code consists of Canons, Ethical Considerations, and Disciplinary Rules. The nine canons are statements of "axiomatic norms," expressed in general terms. The ethical considerations are "aspirational in character" and constitute a body of principles upon which the lawyer relies for guidance. The disciplinary rules are mandatory in character, and disciplinary action can be taken for violation of such a rule.

The ABA on August 2, 1983, adopted the *Model Rules of Professional Conduct* to replace the *Code of Professional Responsibility*. These Model Rules are being considered for adoption in numerous states and relevant new Model Rules are noted at various sections in this chapter. Nonetheless, it is the earlier *Model Code of Professional Responsibility* (ABA, 1969) on which the bar opinions discussed here are based.

Even the most progressive opinions have been hampered because the ABA Code (1969) was adopted to fit the conventional model of divorce and in many cases has little application to mediation models (Riskin, 1984; Silberman, 1982). This is not to say that there are not serious ethical issues implicated by divorce mediation, but to some degree they are a brand all their own (Coogler, 1977; Crouch, 1982a, 1982b). In surveying the ethical constraints invoked by bar associations to limit divorce mediation efforts, this chapter identifies some of the ethical problems raised by divorce mediation and suggests ways to resolve them.

THE CONFLICT-OF-INTEREST DILEMMA

The major ethical constraint affecting attorneys who provide mediation services arises from the prohibition of Canon 5 of the *Model Code of Professional Responsibility*, which prevents a lawyer from representing conflicting or potentially differing interests. Canon 5 states: "A Lawyer Should Exercise Independent Professional Judgment on Behalf of a Client" (ABA, 1969). Ethical Consideration (EC) 5-1 reads: "The professional judgment of a lawyer should be exercised, within the bounds of law, solely for the benefit of his client and free of compromising influences and loyalties." Even in traditional adversarial contexts, Canon 5 has produced limited exceptions, and dual representation has been permitted in matters not involving litigation, where the lawyer has "explain[ed] fully to each client the implications of the common representation . . . and the clients . . . consent" (ABA, Ethical Consideration 5-15). Despite these exceptions, representation of both spouses in a matrimonial action has traditionally been viewed by most bar associations as so inherently prejudicial that dual representation is usually prohibited (Bedford, 1963).

With the advent of no-fault divorce, however, several bar committees have departed from this classic prohibitive stance. For example, the Ohio State Bar Ethics Committee (1975) ruled that although dual representation would not adequately protect the parties' rights, a single lawyer could draft a separation agreement so long as (1) the lawyer represented one of the parties and the second party was fully aware that he or she was not being represented and was given full opportunity to get independent counsel, and (2) both parties gave written consent to the arrangement—which consent was contained in or attached to the separation agreement. The Arizona State Bar Ethics Committee (1976) went a step further and approved of dual representation in divorce cases when there are few assets and no children, and the divorce is uncontested. Although emphasizing that dual representation in divorce cases would still be the exception rather than the rule, the Arizona Committee took a significant step in giving couples an option to traditional adversarial divorce.

A Virginia ethics opinion (Virginia State Bar Association, 1977) permitted an attorney to give nonpartisan advice to a husband and wife concerning the transfer of property and to draft the property settlement for both parties. The circumstances indicated that the husband and wife had reached a decision to divorce, apparently without animosity, and had determined how they desired to divide their property. Because the relationship was not one in which the attorney "was obligated to argue for one party that which he was obligated to defend for another," the attorney was permitted to advise the parties on tax consequences and to represent one of the parties in securing a no-fault divorce. Additionally, an important California court ruling, *Klemm v. Superior Court of Fresno County* (Cal. App., 1977), approved dual representation in limited circumstances. Responding to a separating couple's writ of mandamus to compel the court to permit them to be jointly represented in their contested dissolution proceeding, the court stated:

> Attorneys who undertake to represent parties with divergent interests owe the highest duty to each to make sure that there is full disclosure of all facts and circumstances that are necessary to enable the parties to make a fully informed choice regarding the subject matter of litigation, including the areas of potential conflict and the possibility and desirability of seeking independent legal advice (75 Cal. App. 3d at 901, 142 Cal. Rptr. at 514).

Of course, the divorce mediation context poses a somewhat different problem, since the mediator does not purport to represent either of the parties. Indeed, a New York State Bar opinion (1972) prohibiting dual representation in the traditional matrimonial action referred to EC 5-20, which permits lawyers to mediate in matters involving former or present clients. EC 5-20 provides:

> A lawyer is often asked to serve as an impartial arbitrator or mediator in matters which involve present or former clients. He may serve in either capacity if he first discloses such present or former relationships. After a lawyer has undertaken to act as an impartial arbitrator or mediator, he should not thereafter represent in the dispute any of the parties involved (ABA, 1969).

The New York State Bar opinion concluded that, "A lawyer approached by husband and wife in a matrimonial matter and asked to represent both may, however, properly undertake to serve as a mediator or arbitrator." Similarly, an opinion of the West Virginia Ethics Committee (1977), which pronounced it improper for a lawyer to represent both husband and wife at any stage of a marital problem, even with full disclosure and informed consent of both partners, observed that a lawyer could serve as a mediator or arbitrator between a husband and wife.

In one of the first ethics opinions directly on the subject, the Boston Bar Ethics Committee (1978) considered the actions of a lawyer who proposed to serve as a mediator to a married couple contemplating divorce and to draft a separtion agreement and related documents setting forth agreed-upon terms arrived at in mediation. As mediator, the lawyer agreed to refrain from representing either of the parties in any proceeding between them. Although stating that it did not "enthusiastically endorse" mediation, the Boston Bar approved the mediation service so long as the attorney did not represent either party and the parties were advised of the possible conflict and of the various alternatives open to them (e.g., appearing *pro se* or obtaining separate representation). The Boston Bar opinion pointed to some of the drawbacks of an attorney serving as a mediator: unequal bargaining power where commitments are made without the benefit of the advice and assistance of counsel, concern by the clients about the mediator's possible bias in giving advice, and the reopening of negotiations if independent lawyers are later consulted. Nonetheless, the Ethics Committee chose to permit a lawyer to render mediation services for clients who wished to experiment, since the committee found that the usual alternatives (resort to the adversarial process and *pro se* divorce) had their own disadvantages.

Traditional Responses

Not all bar committees have accepted the line drawn between traditional lawyering and mediation. Disciplinary Rule (DR) 5-105, which requires a lawyer to decline employment if the interests of another client may impair the independent professional judgment of the lawyer, states that it is improper for a lawyer to engage in representation if the lawyer's "independent professional judgement . . . will be or is likely to be adversely affected" (ABA, 1969) or if representation is likely to involve representation of interests that will adversely affect the lawyer's judgment or loyalty to a client. Relying on DR 5-105, several bar committees advised that lawyers would be acting unethically if they served as divorce mediators. A Washington State Bar Committee in 1980 (Washington State Bar Association, 1980) prohibited a lawyer from offering a mediation service to resolve property, custody, and support issues because he or she could not adequately represent the interests of each party in compliance with DR 5-105 (c), (ABA, 1969) which provides that a lawyer can properly represent multiple clients only if it is obvious that he can adequately represent the interest of each and if each consents to the representation on the exercise of the lawyer's independent professional judgment on behalf of each. Interestingly, a later opinion by the Washington Committee appeared to reverse that ruling so long as the mediator did not represent either party and would forego representation of either if the mediation broke down (Washington State Bar Association, 1983).

The New Hampshire Ethics Committee (March 16, 1982) also rejected a lawyer's proposal to provide mediation for a husband and wife who were former clients, prior to either party filing for divorce. In this context, the Committee ruled that mediation was not an adequate safeguard against a potential violation of DR 5-105. In addition, the Committee expressed doubt that the mediator could invoke the attorney–client privilege to prevent disclosure of confidences divulged in mediation and, to that extent, suggested that divorce mediation might also conflict with Canon 4, which requires a lawyer to preserve the confidences of a client. Given the particular background of this inquiry, where the attorney had previously represented both clients, the New Hampshire Committee ruled that the lawyer should not undertake divorce mediation and should thus avoid even the appearance of professional impropriety, as dictated by Canon 9. Despite its negative decision on this mediation inquiry, the New Hampshire Committee indicated that other mediation plans for divorce might contain adequate safeguards. In addition to advising that the mediator should clearly delineate the "mediating" as contrasted with the "advocating" role, the Committee added that "judicial recognition of mediators as quasi judicial officers would greatly aid the Canon 4 problem." Moreover, the acknowledgment that divorce mediation might be appropriate in some circumstances was to some degree a reversal of the committee's earlier position because a prior draft opinion by the New Hampshire Ethics Committee (April 21, 1981) had revealed a more generally negative view of mediation. One of the premises underlying the New Hampshire Committee's decision seems misplaced. There is no reason to assume that absolute confidentiality is a value that need be maintained at all costs, particularly when the process is no longer the traditionally adversarial one. However, concern about a lawyer's ability to maintain impartiality in the divorce context is less easily dismissed. The Wisconsin State Bar Commitee (January 1980) refused to permit a lawyer to offer a mediation service, in which he proposed to educate the parties as to their legal rights, mediate disputes arising in the negotiations, draft a separation agreement for the parties, and process the divorce through the courts. The Wisconsin Committee found that the lawyer's responsibilities under the proposed arrangement went beyond those contemplated by EC 5-20. And although the step of representing the parties in a divorce litigation seems outside the scope of a mediative role, the Wisconsin Committee did not limit its concern to whether or not the lawyer processed the divorce. The Committee thought that even the task of educating the parties about their legal rights was suspect because the lawyer would be perceived in the role of advice giving, and any "advice" would necessarily be contrary to the interests of one of the parties. Moreover, the Committee speculated that mediated agreements might not endure and that future litigation would result: "Neither the public's interest or the parties' is best served by the creation of future litigation."

A role akin to that of mediator, but slightly different—that of an advisory attorney—was also hampered by Canon 5 restrictions, in the view of the Maryland State Bar Association (August 20, 1980), which had been asked to rule on the propriety of a lawyer's participation as an impartial advisory attorney in a family mediation center. The advisory attorney concept has its roots in the structured mediation design developed by O. J. Coogler (Coogler, 1978). Although Coogler's model was characterized by a body of specialized rules, the concept of the "impartial advisory attorney" has had a more generalized application. Usually the mediation is undertaken by a mental health or other nonlawyer professional. At some point in the mediation, as legal issues are raised, a single advisory attorney is brought in to address the legal questions; later, the advisory attorney will finalize the tentative agreement and draft the formal settlement agreement. Advisory attorneys are often part of the mediation center's staff or may be lawyers in the community who have agreed to participate as advisory attorneys in a mediation program. In the Coogler model, the advisory attorney is selected from a panel of impartial advisory attorneys provided by the center (see Chapter 12 by Grebe, this volume). In the model posed to the Maryland Ethics Committee, the lawyer was not the mediator (that role fell to others at the center) but was available to advise the parties on the legal issues and to draw up the proposed settlement. In this capacity, too, the Maryland Bar detected Canon 5 difficulties for the lawyer. It referred to an earlier Maryland opinion expressing the view that it was virtually impossible, given the wide range of potential disputes in a marital separation, for an attorney representing both husband and wife to come within the scope of DR 5-105 (c). In the present context, the Maryland Bar Committee observed that the parties' consent to mediation did not eliminate the conflicting interests upon which the lawyer would be required to offer an independent professional judgment. Indeed, the Maryland Bar suggested that at least one object of the clients' concern might be whether they made intelligent and proper compromises during the mediation.

The Maryland opinion also indicated that the responsibility placed on the lawyer to draw up the settlement for the parties and the mediator was troublesome. It said:

> If the preparation of a Property Settlement Agreement in mediation can be equated to filling in blanks on forms, then the services of an attorney are probably not necessary. If the preparation of such an Agreement requires the independent judgment of an attorney—to choose what language best expresses the intent of the parties, to allocate the burdens of performance and the risks of non-performance, and to advise whether the Agreement as a whole promotes the best interests of both clients and not just some interests of one client and some interests of the other—then such preparation is likely to place the attorney in a position where he senses a conflict of interest. In any case, where such a conflict exists, the attorney

must comply with the requirements of DR 5-105 (c) (Maryland State Bar Association, August 20, 1980) pp. 8–9.

Ethics opinions restricting lawyers from serving as mediators or advisory attorneys appear to be rooted in an assumption that a lawyer cannot step out of the traditional role of legal advisor, whose obligation is to pursue the best interest of the client, and that the public will perceive the lawyer only in that posture. Broader acceptance of alternative lawyering roles may provide a different perspective on the conflict-of-interest dilemma (Riskin, 1984). Additionally, experimentation with mediation models has introduced traditional lawyering into the mediation process, with each of the parties seeking counsel from his or her own lawyer (Lande, 1984). In such models, there is less reason for the parties in mediation to look to the lawyer–mediator to protect their rights, since each can always consult his or her own counsel.

Progressive Approaches

Later opinions—including two important ones from New York and Connecticut—have endorsed different conceptions of lawyering, and rejected the view that Canon 5 poses a barrier to lawyers serving as divorce mediators (Connecticut State Bar Association, 1982; New York City Bar Association, February 27, 1981). The inquiry to the Committee on Professional and Judicial Ethics of the New York City Bar Association involved a mediation program undertaken by a nonprofit mental health facility, in which mental health professionals consulted with divorcing couples to work out various aspects of their separation or divorce, including economic and custody issues. In determining whether a lawyer could become part of the mediating team, give impartial legal advice to the parties, and draft an agreement for the parties once terms had been generally approved by the parties, the New York Committee addressed the question of a lawyer's nonadversarial role in dispute resolution. The Committee acknowledged competing policies reflected in the *Model Code of Professional Responsibility* and prior ethics rulings: that conflicts inherent in a matrimonial proceeding preclude a lawyer from "representing" both parties but that a lawyer may serve as an "impartial arbitrator or mediator." Resolving this tension is difficult, observed the Committee, because the Code does not explain what activities constitute mediation and what responsibilities a lawyer has when acting as a mediator. Like the New Hampshire and Wisconsin Committees, the New York panel recognized that parties might rely on the professional judgment of the lawyer to identify and explain the significance of legal issues and their impact on the individual's interests, even when the lawyer–mediator disclaims a representative role. However, the Committee also indicated that in some situations a lawyer's professional judgment would not be called upon, and he or she could perform in such a way that he or she did not represent either party.

The New York Committee attempted to differentiate mediation and representation and to find a way to clarify these roles for potential clients. The Committee focused on two themes. First, responsibility is placed on the lawyer to assess the appropriateness of mediation in a particular case and to decline to mediate where separate independent representation is deemed necessary. Second, the lawyer–mediator is charged with the task of differentiating the mediation role from the representation role for the clients. Thus, the thrust of the New York opinion approved a mediating function for a lawyer if the case is an appropriate one for mediation and the clients truly understand the limitations of a lawyer–mediator's role. As to the first requirement, the New York Committee cautioned the lawyer to make an independent judgment as to whether mediation is appropriate and suggested that where there are issues of such complexity or difficulty that the parties cannot prudently reach a solution without the advice of separate and independent legal counsel, the lawyer should not act as mediator. Since the parties may consult independent lawyers in addition to their participation in mediation, and indeed the benefits of such independent representation are stressed later in the ethics opinion itself, the Committee's standard is not particularly helpful. At the same time, however, the Committee is probably correct in directing the lawyer–mediator to evaluate both legal and emotional issues that could impede the mediation process.

As to the second requirement imposed by the New York Committee—the obligation to differentiate the representation role from the mediating one for the couple—the lawyer's duty is twofold. First, the lawyer must *communicate* with the couple to define the nature of the mediating role, to advise the parties not to look to the lawyer to protect interests or keep confidences, and to explain to them the risks of proceeding without separate counsel. Indeed, the lawyer may proceed to mediate only if satisfied that the parties understand the risks and the significance of the fact that the lawyer represents neither party. Second, the lawyer must also *act* in accordance with a nonrepresentational role, and the Committee enunciated a number of guidelines that should be followed to assure consistency with a mediative and not representative role. Legal advice should be impartial and given in the presence of both parties; the lawyer should not represent the parties in later proceedings and should advise the parties to seek independent counsel before they sign any agreement drafted by the lawyer–mediator. As the Committee itself noted, lawyer participation in the mediation process is conditioned on informed consent by the parties, and the guidelines are directed to achieve that end.

The New York City opinion obviously influenced the Connecticut Bar Committee on Professional Ethics (1982), which was also asked to advise on the validity of an interdisciplinary mediation model in which mediation commenced with sessions by a mental health professional, with a mediating attorney called in at the appropriate time to provide legal information, describe options, and draft an agreement between the parties. Noting that

> the adversary approach to divorce proceedings in the United States has contributed so much acrimony to divorce and such extensive post-divorce misunderstand-

ing and contention that other approaches should be encouraged in appropriate cases if there is reasonable likelihood they can more satisfactorily accomplish the task of marital dissolution

the Connecticut Committee approved the lawyer–mediator's role so long as certain precautions were taken. Full disclosure must be made to both parties at the inception of the mediation, concerning its limitations and risks; the unavailability of the attorney–client privilege must be stressed; the parties must be made aware that each may seek independent legal advice at any time; and the mediating attorney may not represent either party in a suit for divorce between the parties in any later proceeding.

The Connecticut Bar panel, which modified an earlier more restrictive draft (1982b), also appeared to have been influenced by a recent New York Court of Appeals case, *Levine v. Levine* (1982), upholding a separation agreement drafted by a single attorney representing both spouses. Although *Levine* did not involve a mediation or a lawyer serving as mediator, it recognized that parties may sometimes opt for lawyers to assume a role other than a strict adversarial one. In *Levine*, the husband and wife had entered into a separation agreement prepared by a single attorney. In fact, the parties had previously agreed to the essential terms of the agreement and had asked the lawyer to prepare the agreement for them. Although advised to seek independent counsel, the wife failed to do so. Later, the wife tried to have the agreement set aside, claiming that the agreement was inequitable and unconscionable because she had not been independently represented by counsel and had been unduly influenced by her husband. The trial court rejected the wife's application, finding that the agreement was fair and that the attorney had remained neutral throughout his involvement with the parties. That decision was reversed by the appellate division, which held that the joint representation evinced a sufficient degree of overreaching to require the agreement to be set aside. The Court of Appeals, in overturning that decision and upholding the separation agreement, stressed the parties' "absolute right" to be represented by the same attorney, provided there was full disclosure. It pointed to an express acknowledgment by the wife in the separation agreement that through this representation she was entering into a better agreement than if she had consulted with independent counsel who tried to bargain on her behalf. And in its acceptance of the trial court's finding that the attorney who had drafted the agreement for the parties remained neutral, the New York Court of Appeals seemed to put a judicial stamp of approval on alternative lawyering roles. In that sense the *Levine* case may have important reverberations for mediation, as evidenced by its citation in the Connecticut ethics opinion.

DEFINING THE MEDIATOR'S ROLE

The precise role of the lawyer–mediator or advisory attorney and the scope of duties remains unclear even in those jurisdictions that have approved mediation.

In 1983 the Oregon State Bar permitted mediation by an interdisciplinary team but, unlike the New York City and Connecticut opinions, characterized the lawyer–mediator as representing both the husband and the wife. The Committee ruled that such joint representation would be permitted if the lawyer–mediator obtained the fully informed consent of both parties. Additionally, the opinion distinguished the role of mediator from that of counsel for co-petitioners and cautioned the lawyer–mediator to "limit his or her services to providing informational assistance to the parties in a neutral fashion." Specifically, the lawyer–mediator is instructed to explain his or her limited role as a "representative" of both parties and advise the parties to have their respective attorneys review any agreement that results from the mediation process.

The differing characterizations of the mediator, as "representing both parties" or "representing neither party," may be only a semantic one or may suggest important assumptions about the role that the mediator may undertake and the tasks he or she may assume. Notwithstanding its view of the lawyer–mediator as the representative of both parties, the Oregon opinion established guidelines almost identical to those required by the Boston, New York City, and Connecticut opinions, which had conceptualized the mediator's function as representing *neither* of the parties.* Thus, under either conception, the mediator seems to be permitted to give legal advice and draft the separation agreement but not to file the necessary papers or process the divorce following the mediation. Shaping the identity and appropriate tasks of the mediator is the critical issue facing ethics committees, rather than deciding which labels attach to the role.

The Model Rules Approach

The "characterization" difficulties of lawyers acting as mediators may be further compounded by the 1983 ABA *Model Rules of Professional Conduct.* Most states, as previously noted, continue to follow, with slight variations, the earlier *Model Code*, but adoptions of the new *Model Rules* will gradually occur. The ABA's new approach adopted a specific rule, Rule 2.2, entitled "Intermediary," which prescribes the circumstances in which a lawyer may ethically act as an intermediary when the lawyer represents all parties. As discussed earlier, the notion of common representation carries with it a vision of a lawyer advancing the self-conceived interests of the client or clients, rather than the neutral orientation of a lawyer who acts as a mediator or impartial advisory attorney (Riskin, 1984). By combining classic dual representation and mediation in a single rule, the *Model Rules* fail to recognize or endorse the

---

Editors' Note. The Oregon Supreme Court subsequently approved a new DR 5-106, proposed by the Oregon state bar, which expressly authorizes a lawyer to act as "a mediator for multiple parties in any matter." The revised language omits any reference to representation but requires the parties' informed consent to the mediator's role. This role is described by the General Counsel's office of the Oregon state bar as representing neither party (Isaacs, 1986).

variety of alternative dispute resolution opportunities embraced in the concept of mediation and thus never indicate any possible clear shift in the lawyer's role. Rule 2.2 does set forth requirements for the lawyer acting as intermediary. Part (a) provides that (1) the lawyer must disclose to each client the implications of the common representation, including the advantages and risks involved, and must obtain each client's consent to the common representation; (2) the lawyer must reasonably believe that the matter can be resolved on terms compatible with the clients' best interests, that each client can make informed decisions in the matter, and that there is little risk of prejudice to the interest of any client if the contemplated resolution is unsuccessful; and (3) the lawyer can act impartially and without improper effect on other responsibilities the lawyer has to any of the clients. Rule 2.2(b) also requires the lawyer acting as intermediary to explain fully to each client the decisions to be made and the considerations relevant to making them. Rule 2.2(c) mandates that a lawyer shall withdraw from an intermediary role if any client so requests, if the conditions under part (a) cannot be met, or if in light of subsequent events the lawyer should reasonably know that a mutually advantageous resolution cannot be achieved.

The comment to Rule 2.2 states that a lawyer acts as an intermediary in seeking to establish or adjust a relationship between clients on an amicable and mutually advantageous basis. Its list of examples includes "mediating a dispute between clients," but the other examples—helping to organize a business in which two or more clients are entrepreneurs, working out the financial reorganization of an enterprise in which two or more clients have an interest—are closer to a practice of common representation. Moreover, in describing situations where the risk of failure is so great that intermediation is plainly impossible, the commentary points to "clients between whom litigation is imminent or who contemplate contentious negotiations" and "where the relationship between the parties has already assumed definite antagonism" (ABA, 1983). These characterizations easily fit potential divorce mediations, and thus the failure to specifically address the subject is distressing. Curiously, commentary in earlier drafts of the *Model Rules* specifically stated that "under some circumstances a lawyer may act as an intermediary between spouses in arranging the terms of an uncontested separation or divorce settlement," but that language was deleted in the final draft (ABA Commission on Evaluation of Professional Standards, 1980, p. 94). In light of the continuing proliferation of mediation programs and conflicting state ethics committee rulings on the subject, a direct and specific response on the subject of divorce mediation should have been forthcoming from the framers of the new code of professional responsibility.

Limits on the Lawyer–Mediator

One troubling aspect of the representation–mediation dichotomy is the possibility that the relevant tasks will be defined in light of the formulation of the lawyer's role that is adopted. Indeed, quite apart from whether the lawyer is seen as representing neither or all of the parties, the ethics opinions have offered varying views of the permissible tasks of the lawyer in a mediation setting.

The general consensus seems to be that the lawyer–mediator or advisory attorney can give impartial legal advice and draw up the separation agreement for the parties but cannot represent them in subsequent proceedings. Indeed, a 1982 Connecticut ethics opinion reversed a prior ruling that a lawyer who acts as a mediator may not draft the agreement for the parties or advise clients with respect to the consequences of such an agreement (Connecticut State Bar Association, 1982).

Other committees, however, have found mediators crossing the "representation" line when they engage in lawyerlike tasks. In 1985, the Massachusetts State Bar Committee on Professional Ethics (June 27, 1985) found that a lawyer–mediator did not represent the parties when he explained "legal consequences of various courses of action" but did represent the parties when he chose to "undertake functions traditionally rooted in the adversary process, such as the drafting of separation agreements for both parties." The Committee concluded that those tasks should therefore not be undertaken unless the standards of DR 5-105(c) could be satisfied. Another limited view of the role of a mediating attorney was offered by the Vermont Bar Ethics Committee (1980), which, in approving co-mediation by an attorney and clinical social worker, advised the mediator to refrain from giving *any* legal advice, leaving that to the parties' respective attorneys. The Committee said that the lawyer would be permitted to "direct attention" to the problems which need to be solved prior to entering a separation agreement, and could work with the parties to reach an agreement on difficult issues but that the final drafting of all agreements should be done by the parties' attorneys.

A 1984 ruling of the Kansas Bar Association Committee on Professional Ethics (1984) adopted a much more expansive role for the mediating attorney in its approach to the Canon 5 conflict of interest problem. Referring to the New York City Bar opinion, the Kansas ruling echoed guidelines that the lawyer performing mediation should follow: advise the parties of the nonrepresentative role of the lawyer, explain the risks of proceeding without separate counsel, provide impartial legal advice and give such advice only in the presence of both parties, and inform the parties of the advantages of seeking independent legal counsel before executing any agreement. In terms of the tasks permissible for the mediator, however, the Kansas Bar permitted the lawyer not only to draft the agreement reached by the parties but also to present the agreement reached by the parties to the court for approval in any uncontested hearing. Only where the agreement was contested or disavowed by one of the parties was the lawyer restricted from representing the parties in subsequent divorce litigation.

As noted earlier, most of the ethics opinions on mediation have heretofore drawn a sharp line between the mediation and any subsequent litigation, prohibiting the lawyer–mediator from processing even a pro forma uncontested divorce—presumably to avoid any perception that the lawyer–mediator was representing the parties and to give the parties every opportunity to raise questions about the divorce or the agreement. Indeed, EC 5-20 specifically states that "after a lawyer has undertaken to act as an impartial arbitrator or mediator, he should not thereafter represent in the dispute any of the parties involved" (ABA, 1969). However, the Kansas approach may in fact be a more realistic and pragmatic one, since the uncontested divorce is almost ministerial following the execution of the agreement. The alternative for the parties, when independent representation is required for the divorce proceeding, is to appear *pro se* or to obtain separate independent counsel merely to process the papers. The real advantage of independent counsel is at the earlier stage, *before* the parties execute an agreement. Thus the Kansas opinion stresses the importance of seeking independent legal counsel before executing any agreement drafted by the lawyer–mediator but does not impose the formality of separate representation for the filing of the divorce.

PROBLEMS OF UNAUTHORIZED PRACTICE

A number of constraints have been raised by bar committees regarding non-lawyer–mediators as well. Although bar committees do not set ethical standards for nonlawyers, all states have laws that prohibit nonlawyers from engaging in the unauthorized practice of the law and that are enforceable through misdemeanor or contempt charges (Fisher & Lachman, 1972). It should also be noted that lawyers who mediate or work with nonlawyers may themselves violate Canon 3, which does regulate lawyers and prohibits them from assisting in the unauthorized practice of law.

Most state bar associations have a standing committee on the unauthorized practice of law. These committees have responsibility for investigating and bringing to the court's attention instances of the unauthorized practice of law by nonlawyers. Several unauthorized practice committees have indicated that they believe that some of the tasks that nonlawyer–mediators undertake border on such unauthorized practice. It does, of course, seem obvious that there has been and will continue to be a role for mental health and counseling professionals in the divorcing process. Many couples seek professional counseling, sometimes in an effort to cope more effectively with the break-up. But these efforts of mental health professionals differ from those in divorce mediation, which contemplate the mediator assisting a couple in reaching an effective agreement, including a settlement of economic and custodial issues. It is difficult for lawyers to imagine that a mental health professional can effectively help the couple reach agreement without some understanding of and advice on the legal issues involved.

Whether a nonlawyer–mediator should appropriately perform those tasks is a separate question. The policy behind the unauthorized practice prohibition is protection of the public; there is concern, on one hand, that no matter how well a nonlawyer knows his or her specialty, the legal issues involved require legal experience. On the other hand, many of the legal issues that arise in divorce and separation are relatively straightforward, and one can imagine a well-trained group of mediators (in the manner of paraprofessionals) acquiring the necessary expertise. The use of paralegals for the performance of simple legal tasks has been sanctioned by the Bar. EC 3-6 approves delegation to lay persons "if the lawyer maintains a direct relationship with his client, supervises the delegated work, and has complete professional responsibility for the work product" (ABA, 1969). Training criteria for paraprofessionals have been suggested by the Bar (ABA Special Committee on Legal Assistants, 1971). In this context, the criticism that the "unauthorized practice" prohibition operates primarily for the benefit of lawyers rather than the public, by securing for lawyers a monopoly of certain social tasks, gains more force.

The primary issue in any unauthorized practice investigation is whether the nonlawyer has engaged in activities properly constituting the "practice of law." Little guidance emerges from case law decisions that restate tautologies and characterize as improper what is "commonly understood to be the practice of law" (*State Bar Association v. Connecticut Bank and Trust*, 145 Conn. at 236, 140 A. 2d at 871, 1958) and "those acts, whether performed in court or in a law office, which lawyers have customarily carried on from day to day through the centuries" (*State Bar of Arizona v. Arizona Lamp Title and Trust Co.*, 90 Ariz. at 87, 366 P. 2d at 9, 1961).

As noted earlier, divorce mediation is inextricably tied to legal issues. At minimum, a mediator would be shaping an agreement "in the shadow of the law" (Mnookin & Kornhauser, 1979) and would eventually need to draw up an outline or memorandum of understanding. Whether the parties later draw up a formal agreement themselves or consult independent counsel, the propriety of the mediator's action and advice would still be in issue. Mental health professionals conducting mediation are likely to argue that any legal advice given or legal instruments prepared in mediation are only incidental to their profession and that therefore they fall outside the unauthorized-practice prohibition.

Analogues and Rulings

The case law and ethics opinion on unauthorized practice are not particularly illuminating for the divorce mediation context. In an early 1962 opinion, the Los Angeles County Bar cautioned that a family counseling organization might be engaged in the unauthorized practice of law if its counselors advised clients about the laws relating to marriage and divorce. It therefore ruled that an attorney could not accept employment with the family counseling service, because the attorney may be aiding the agency in the unlawful practice of law. Similarly, a proposed association of an attorney with a firm of aviation consultants to offer services to owners and prospective owners of public airports was said to involve the lawyer in aiding the unauthorized practice of law (California State Bar Association, 1969). And an attorney's participation in a firm offering financial-planning services including tax and pension advice to its clients was held unethical (Los Angeles County Bar Association, 1978). More recently, the

New York State Bar Association (1983) ruled that it would be an unauthorized-practice violation for a lawyer to form a professional association with an accountant to provide clients with tax-related and accounting services.

The unauthorized-practice issue surfaced in analogous fashion a decade ago with the proliferation of lay divorce kits and divorce kit firms. The need of divorcing couples for low-cost legal assistance prompted two approaches to lay divorce assistance. The first offered for sale a prepared kit containing forms, explanatory data for using the forms, and information concerning the relevant divorce law. The second approach provided not only forms but also personal services, including interviews and aid in completing documents and forms. The attacks on this type of lay legal assistance as unauthorized practice have not produced uniform results ("Lay Divorce Firms," 1973; "The Unauthorized Practice of Law," 1976). In several states the publication of divorce kits itself is considered to constitute the unauthorized practice of law (*Alaska Bar Association v. Foster*, 1973; *Florida Bar v. Stupeca*, 1974), but in other states, so long as the publication does not establish a personal relationship of attorney and client, no unauthorized practice has been found (*Oregon Bar v. Gilchrist*, 1975; *New York County Lawyer's Association v. Darcy*, 1967). However, generally where lay counselors provide interviews, explanations, advice, and other assistance to divorcing couples, the action has been held to be the unauthorized practice of law (*Minnesota State Bar Association v. Divorce Reform, Inc.*, 1975; *State Bar v. Brandon*, 1972). In the wake of these developments numerous suggestions have been made that lay divorce options should be preserved and that such activities are consistent with a specific legislative purpose expressed in various no-fault divorce laws ("Lay Divorce Firms," 1973).

The question of mental health professional mediation presents a stronger case for relaxation of the unauthorized-practice restriction than does assistance with divorce kits and completion of forms. Lay divorce kits and those who assist in completing them provide no specialized service that draws upon lay individuals' talents and expertise; presumably the interest in this type of assistance is only an economic one in that routine tasks performed by nonlawyers are less expensive than if undertaken by lawyers. Mediation, offered by skilled mental health professionals, is an alternative service and process; the imparting of legal information is only an incidental component of the larger task of helping the couple resolve their own differences on the issues surrounding the marriage dissolution. Yet the critical factor in the lay divorce kit cases related to the concern that erroneous or incomplete advice might be given to clients. In approving mediation with a lawyer as mediator, the Boston bar (1978) echoed the concern that the legal issues in divorce mediation should be within the lawyer's province: "If the parties are to be advised as to the legal aspects by a person not engaging in the improper practice of law, that advice must be given by an attorney."

The resolution of the unauthorized practice issue may, to some extent, turn on the structure of the mediation and how the nonlawyer refracts the legal issues that arise in mediation. Co-mediation by lawyers and nonlawyers or use of an advisory attorney model may alleviate some of these concerns. Moreover, since most models of mediation now contemplate that each of the spouses will seek independent counsel during the mediation, the mediator's function looks less and less like the practice of law.

Bar Committee Responses

The New York City and Connecticut State Bar Ethics Committees' opinions regarding the propriety of attorneys working with nonlawyer–mediators were premised on the assumption that the nonlawyers could mediate without practicing law. The New York City Committee (1981), in approving a mediation program undertaken by a nonprofit mental health organization, held that it was beyond the committee's jurisdiction to determine whether the activities of mental health professionals undertaking divorce mediation constituted the unauthorized practice of law. But it assumed for the purposes of its opinion that it was "possible for laymen to perform certain divorce mediation activities without exercising professional legal judgments and without engaging in the unauthorized practice of law." The Connecticut opinion (1982) was even more specific in dealing with an interdisciplinary model of mediation. It instructed the attorney to "be certain that the nonlawyer professionals are not engaged in the unauthorized practice of law while performing their part of the mediation team effort" and suggested that the mediating attorney be called in early during the mediation if the legal rights or options of the parties became relevant considerations at an early stage in the process. Moreover, it stressed that a mental health professional could not give legal advice to the parties at any time.

Other states have taken a more jaundiced view of nonlawyers who undertake mediation. One example comes from Rhode Island, where the Bar Association Committee on the Unauthorized Practice of Law (1981) issued a letter to a psychotherapist conducting divorce mediation, stating that the committee had found the therapist to be "advertising and/or engaging in the unauthorized practice of law in contravention of the General Laws of the State of Rhode Island."

Although other lay divorce mediators have been confronted with unauthorized practice charges, there have been few formal opinions on the matter. The North Carolina State Bar Unauthorized Practice of Law Committee (1980) did rule that a nonprofit organization conducting a divorce mediation service, which required participating couples to sign an agreement by which they agreed to abide by the rules of the organization and to submit unresolved disputes to binding arbitration, was engaging in the unauthorized practice of law. The preparation of the contract itself as well as warnings to the couple about its implications were held to be tasks that could be undertaken only by an attorney. However, in a later North Carolina Ethics Committee ruling (1981a), a lawyer was permitted to participate as an advisory attorney for couples in mediation. The affiliation with a lay marriage counselor was said not to raise an ethical problem for the attorney unless the counselor was involved in the unauthorized practice of law or attempted to influence the lawyer's exercise of independent professional judgment.

In the context of the advisory attorney model, the Maryland State Bar Association (1980) noted that it was possible for a mediator or family mediation center to engage in the unauthorized practice of law by "applying general legal principles to the specific problems" of clients. Though leaving the resolution of that question to the Attorney General, the opinion also stated that "a trained mediator should, of course, be aware of what constitutes the practice of law and carefully avoid overstepping his bounds in his eagerness to conduct a successful mediation, even if pressed by a client." The Maryland opinion found it beyond the scope of committee jurisdiction to determine whether mediators' interpreting and applying a body of "private law" imposed by the mediation rules constituted the practice of law. But the Maryland Bar added that impartial advisory attorneys in such a system could violate DR 3-101(A) by aiding nonlawyers in unauthorized practice. The Bar cautioned lawyers against serving as an impartial advisory attorney if the center or mediator was engaging in the unauthorized practice of law, noting that a lawyer would not necessarily be precluded from serving as a panel attorney if the unauthorized practice was not systematic but only detectable on a case-by-case basis.

Most typically, it is attempts to offer legal services by nonattorneys at mediation centers that have prompted bar committee censure. A divorce resource center in New York, which provided its clients with mental health professionals and financial counselors, along with a lawyer referral service, proposed to prepare net worth affidavits, which are required under New York law. The center's pamphlet stressed that the center "would guide its clients every step of the way with legal help." The Nassau County Committee on Professional Ethics (1984) held that the preparation of any such affidavit by the center would be the unauthorized practice of law in violation of New York law. The Committee also cautioned the center about the legal guidance it was prepared to offer. It emphasized that any such advice or guidance by nonlawyers must be carefully limited so as not to amount to advice of a legal nature. The Committee also admonished lawyers who affiliated themselves with the center that they would violate DR 3-101(A), which prohibits lawyers from aiding nonlawyers in the unauthorized practice of law.

Is Mediation the Practice of Law?

In a sense, it would be ironic if the Canon 3 restrictions, prohibiting lawyers from assisting in the unauthorized practice of law, should impede efforts by lawyers to join with nonlawyers to undertake divorce mediation as co-mediators, as advisory attorneys, or as part of an interdisciplinary mediation center. The very presence of attorneys in these models is designed to overcome potential unauthorized practice by lay mediators. Presumably, if the lawyer undertakes to provide the legal services in mediation and the mental health and other professionals offer their expertise, Canon 3 should be reasonably interpreted to permit these alliances. Nonetheless, several of the Canon 3 Ethical Considerations and specific Disciplinary Rules have been the focus of bar committee rulings prohibiting or limiting such interdisciplinary efforts.

EC 3-8 states that "since a lawyer should not aid or encourage a layman to practice law, he should not practice law in association with a layman or otherwise share legal fees with a layman" (ABA, 1969). Limited exceptions to the prohibition against sharing legal fees with laymen are permissible under this ethical consideration if the exceptions do not aid or encourage laymen to practice law. Of course, if as a mediator the lawyer is not practicing law at all, he or she would not run afoul of this prohibition. This argument relies on the fact that a mediating lawyer does not wear the lawyer's hat while mediating. This view was adopted by the Vermont Bar's Committee on Professional Responsibility (1980) in responding to an attorney who wanted to join a clinical social worker in offering mediation services. The Committee ruled that "the activities of an attorney mediator who carefully restricts his role to that of mediator will not constitute the practice of law." But the Vermont Bar restricted the activities of the attorney–mediator, who must "refrain from giving any legal advice" and must leave the "final drafting of all agreements" to the parties' attorneys. A 1984 Kansas Bar Committee opined that it did believe that mediation "can be the practice of law," but it concluded that nonetheless an attorney could join a social worker and psychologist in mediation, if the attorney gave the legal advice and explained that he or she was solely responsible for legal services, and if the attorney and nonattorney billed separately for their time.

However, other carefully structured mediation practice arrangements have met with resistance from bar committees. A 1983 opinion of the Tennessee Board of Professional Responsibility prohibited a nonpracticing lawyer from joining with a nonlawyer to offer mediation services to the public. Although the mediators advised that they did not provide legal advice, that they encouraged the parties to seek independent legal counsel, and that they submitted the terms of the settlement to independent counsel for drafting, the Committee ruled that divorce mediation "constitutes the practice of law" and the association was therefore improper. The Ohio Bar (1982) expanded upon the view that divorce mediation was the practice of law, and as such made it improper for a lawyer to enter into an affiliation with a lay person to provide mediation services. Observing that the end product of the mediation would be a "memorandum of understanding," the Ohio Bar expressed its opinion that the memorandum of understanding was the same as a separation agreement.

Unholy Alliances

Other specific restrictions on lawyers prohibit the splitting of fees with nonlawyers and the formation of partnerships with nonlawyers. DR 3-102 provides that "a lawyer or firm shall not share legal fees with a nonlawyer" (ABA, 1969), and DR 3-103 states that "a lawyer may not form a partnership with a nonlawyer if any of the activities of the partnership constitute the practice of law."

Thus, even when some type of lawyer–nonlawyer interaction in mediation is deemed permissible, the particular structure of the program may raise independent ethical issues.

For example, a 1983 Oregon State Bar ruling considered the proposal of four attorneys and four counselors to form a divorce mediation service under the name "Family Mediation Center." Although indicating that interdisciplinary co-mediation was permissible, the Bar found that the intended structure of the center was a partnership of lawyers and nonlawyers and thus was expressly prohibited by DR 3-102, if any of the activities included the practice of law. Noting that in acting as a mediator a lawyer was indeed practicing law, the Bar found the intended business arrangement unethical. It suggested that the lawyers could become shareholders in a professional corporation, provided nonlawyers were not shareholders. As to billing, the Bar ruled the arrangement to separately bill for their services would not comply with DR 3-102 and DR 3-103 if the professionals were simply rearranging but continuing their partnership. However, it found no ethical problem if lawyers and nonlawyers, as independent contractors, provided their respective services to family mediation clients and then billed separately. Likewise, the Kansas Bar (1984), in approving a co-mediation plan by lawyers and mental health professionals, cautioned that the proposal to form a closed corporation with the participants as equal shareholders posed a possible DR 3-103 violation and advised that the corporation should be made up solely of attorneys, who then could employ lay specialists.

The Vermont Bar (1980) avoided the DR 3-103 problem by assuming that "the activities of an attorney mediator who carefully restricts his role to that of mediator will not constitute the practice of law, and that the attorneys will not advertise in such a way as to lead the public to believe legal services are offered by the corporation." Thus, it found the participants "free . . . to form any legal entity permitted by the Vermont Statutes."

These various approaches to circumvent DR 3-103 all appear technical and formalistic. The apparent concern in the mediation context is that the public might be confused as to who has responsibility for the consequences of legal advice that is given and agreements that are reached. Thus, if the tasks of the interdisciplinary mediation service are specifically designated and clients separately billed for services, the formal structure of the business entity should be irrelevant. Nonetheless, similar inflexible restrictions reappear in Rule 5.4 of the new *Model Rules of Professional Conduct* (ABA, 1983), entitled Professional Independence of a Lawyer, which contains the traditional limitations on fee sharing and partnership arrangements.

ADVISORY ATTORNEY AND LAWYER REFERRAL RESTRICTIONS

A further difficulty confronts mediation centers that employ lawyers or make lawyer referrals. The prohibition against associating with laymen extends to a lawyer employed by a lay agency. DR 2-103(D), intended to ensure that lay organizations do not control or exploit the professional services of lawyers, places restrictions on a lawyer's ability to service an organization's clients, except in the legal aid context or when the lawyer is employed by a nonprofit organization to provide services for its members under certain conditions. A general qualification of DR 2-103(D) is that in any such affiliation there must be "no interference with the exercise of independent professional judgment in behalf of the client" (ABA, 1969). This concern that a lawyer's advice not be filtered through lay intermediaries was more specifically enunciated in a prior ABA Canon, (old Canon 35) which in part stated:

> The professional services of a lawyer should not be controlled or exploited by any lay agency, personal or corporate, which intervenes between client and lawyer. A lawyer's responsibilities and qualifications are individual. He should avoid all relations which direct the performance of his duties by or in the interest of such intermediary. A lawyer's relation to his client should be personal, and the responsibility should be direct to the client. Charitable societies rendering aid to the indigents are not deemed such intermediaries.

Interpreting that Canon, the Committee on Legal Ethics of the Los Angeles County Bar Association (1962) ruled that it was improper for a lawyer to accept employment by a marriage counseling service for the purpose of giving professional advice directly or through counselors to the clients of the organization. Likewise, a number of opinions have held that an attorney cannot accept employment with an accounting firm for the purpose of rendering legal services to its clients. Specifically, the *Model Code of Professional Responsibility*, DR 2-103, forbids lawyers to solicit employment or request or permit a person or organization to recommend or promote the use of a lawyer's services. This prohibition is waived, however, if the organization falls within one of the exceptions designated in DR 2-103(D). DR 2-103(D) (4), adopted in response to the Supreme Court decisions in *United Mine Workers v. Illinois State Bar Association* (1967), *Brotherhood of Railroad Trainmen v. Virginia* (1964), and *NAACP v. Button* (1963), permits bona fide organizations to recommend legal services to their members or beneficiaries if certain conditions are met. Those conditions state that the organization cannot derive profit from the rendition of legal services and that the lawyer must not have initiated or promoted the organization for the primary purpose of gaining personal financial benefit. Also, the organization must not operate for the purpose of procuring legal work or benefit for the lawyer as a private practitioner outside of the organization's program; the member or beneficiary must be the lawyer's client, not the organization's; and the member or beneficiary must be free to bring in an independent lawyer when and if he or she chooses. Finally, the organization must file an annual report with the appropriate disciplinary authority explaining the legal service plan.

As noted above, DR 2-103(D) (4) was a response to Supreme Court cases that held that organizations like unions and the National Association for the Advancement of Colored People (NAACP) must be permitted to provide or recommend legal representation for their members or beneficiaries. Those decisions are based on First Amendment expression and association rights of the members. Indeed, in some state versions of the professional code of responsibility, referrals under DR 2-103(D) (4) are authorized only from not-for-profit organizations that furnish, without charge, legal services as a form of political or associational expression.

Although DR 2-103(D), like much of the entire *Model Code of Professional Responsibility*, appears ill designed to address divorce mediation models, several bar committtees have found the provision relevant and attempted to determine whether the mediation program in question meets its requirement. For example, the Virginia State Bar Committee on Legal Ethics (1979) concluded that the attorney's participation as an advisory attorney in a mediation program was acceptable, so long as the attorney's participation "remained within the confines of DR 2-103, which prohibits solicitation of employment." Some later correspondence within the Committee raises some doubt as to whether a mediation center could meet any of the referral exceptions to DR 2-103(D) (Letter to Virginia State Bar Association, 1980).

The New York City Bar (1981), in considering a model in which attorneys participated in the mediation program of a nonprofit mental health organization, also invoked DR 2-103(D) (4). The committee viewed the principal issue as whether the divorce mediation program involved an organization that "recommends, furnishes or pays for legal services to its members or beneficiaries. Conceding that couples to whom mediation was offered were not "members" of the program, the committee concluded that nevertheless they came within the scope of "beneficiaries" under the rule, because the divorce mediation program offered professional guidance to couples seeking divorce. Additionally, the committee noted that certain conditions listed in DR 2-103(D) (4) were drafted with an eye to prepaid legal insurance plans and that divorce mediation programs might not be able to meet such conditions. Because it did not consider DR 2-103(D) (4) to be limited to prepaid insurance plans, the committee held that "failure to meet conditions peculiar to such plans is not fatal to the program, provided the other conditions are met." The committee then summarized the rules under which nonprofit divorce mediation programs utilizing lawyers must operate: the organization must derive no profit from the legal services; a lawyer must not promote the program for the primary purpose of providing financial benefit to the lawyer, and the purpose of the program must not be one of financial benefit for lawyers; the individual seeking guidance, and not the program, must be recognized as the object of the lawyer's concern; and the lawyer must not be aware of any violation of law by the mediation program or of any failure by the organization to file a report with respect to its legal service plan. The committee viewed the condition of allowing beneficiaries to select counsel other than that furnished by the program as inapplicable to the divorce mediation situation.

A more recent ruling by the same New York City Bar Committee (1982) reiterated that compliance with DR 2-103 was necessary for approval of any divorce mediation plan. The proposal envisioned a central organization that would refer a variety of services, such as financial mediation, therapy, and legal counsel. Because the cross-referrals appeared intended on a for-profit basis, the Committee found that the organization violated the Code's rules on solicitation and recommendation of professional employment. Noting that a lawyer "shall not solicit employment as a private practitioner . . . (DR 2-103(A)), or give anything of value to any person for recommending his services (DR 2-103(B)), or with certain specified exceptions . . . request any person to recommend or promote the use of the lawyer's services (DR 2-103(C))," it pointed to the criteria of DR 2-103(D) as the permissible circumstances for a legal referral service. Since the proposed program did not conform to those requirements, the plan did not meet the appropriate ethical standards.

A third New York opinion, by the Ethics Committee of the Nassau County Bar Association (1984), reviewed a plan to establish a divorce resource center that offered various professional services of mental health professionals and financial counselors and purported to provide a legal referral service. While observing that the center did not fit any of the organization types, enumerated in DR 2-103(D) (1) through (4), that may refer clients and promote the use of a particular lawyer's services, the opinion called attention to the fact that DR 2-103(C) (1) permits lawyers to accept referrals from services sponsored or approved by bar associations and urged the center to seek the approval of the appropriate local bar associations for its referral system. Under the existing circumstances, however, the Committee found that any lawyer who accepted the center's invitation to be listed in its referral system would be improperly requesting an organization to recommend or promote the use of his or her services in violation of DR 2-103(C).

To some degree, the 1983 *Model Rules* may have eased some of the formal problems presented by the traditional code provisions on referrals, by collapsing those elaborate rules into a single prohibition in Model Rule 7.2 against giving "anything of value to a person for recommending the lawyer's services." The comment specifically permits an organization or person other than the lawyer to advertise or recommend the lawyer's services. The general concern of DR 2-103 is that there be no interference with the exercise of the attorney's independent professional judgment on behalf of the client. This concern is expressly dealt with by DR 5-107(B), which prohibits a lawyer from permitting a person who recommends, employs, or pays the lawyer to render legal services for another, to direct or regulate the lawyer's professional judgment in rendering such legal services. Similar language now appears in Model Rule 5.4 (c).

At least one bar ethics opinion has emphasized the importance of the attorney's retaining independent judgment and not just rubber-stamping an agreement arrived at by nonlawyer mediators: "The lawyer cannot be influenced by the desire of the institute or center to see that the mediation process is prosecuted to fulfillment if he believes that the mediation process is working against the interests of one, or both of the clients" (Maryland State Bar Association, 1980, p. 4).

A similar concern about referrals was reflected in the *Standards of Practice for Family Mediators* (1984), adopted by the Family Law Section of the ABA. In order to avoid creating "cozy relationships" between mediators and lawyers, thereby reducing the likelihood of truly independent legal scrutiny and advice for the participants, the Standards state that the mediator shall not refer either of the participants to any particular lawyers. If requested by a party, the referral should be to a Bar Association list if available, and alternatively, the mediator may provide only a list of qualified family attorneys in the community (Specific Consideration VIA; see Chapter 20 for further discussion).

Specific attention to the issue of ensuring the independence of a referral lawyer's advice in a mediation setting would appear to be more fruitful than measuring mediation programs against a set of formalized antireferral rules. In light of the Supreme Court's dismantling of other types of antisolicitation rules in *Bates v. United States* (1977) and *In re Primus* (1978), DR 2-103 ought to be construed as inappropriate to the mediation situation, and if guidelines for mediation programs are in order, specific rules should be adopted by the state codes of professional responsibility.

ISSUES OF ADVERTISING

Several issues involving the advertising of divorce mediation services have been the subject of various ethics opinions. The general regulations of lawyer advertising are explicitly set out in DR 2-101, which provides in part that a lawyer shall not use "any form of public communication containing a false, fraudulent, misleading, deceptive, self-laudatory or unfair statement or claim" (ABA, 1969). The aim of this rule seems to be to avoid any statement or claim that is unfair or that might be misleading. As the Supreme Court of New Jersey (1981) has pointed out, there is a significant difference between general advertising of the type and cost of available legal services and advertising that "purports to signify particular legal qualities, areas of specialization or levels of competence" (86 N.J. 473 at 478, 432.A. 2d 39 at 61, 1981). In two opinions issued by the Committee on Professional Ethics of the Nassau County Bar Association (1982, 1984), lawyers are admonished against advertising divorce mediation as easier, less expensive, or in any way superior to traditional adversarial divorce proceedings where the husband and wife are represented by separate counsel.

In order to further reduce the possibility of misleading the public, DR 2-102(B) states in part, "A lawyer in private practice shall not practice under a trade name, a name that is misleading as to the identity of the lawyer or lawyers practicing under such name, or a firm name containing names other than those of one or more of the lawyers in the firm" (ABA, 1969). DR 2-102(C) states, "A lawyer shall not hold himself out as having a partnership with one or more other lawyers or professional corporations unless they are in fact partners." A lawyer in Nassau County, New York, proposed the organization of a divorce mediation service under the name "Law Center for Divorce Mediation," but the bar committee ruled that the use of a trade name by a lawyer in private practice is misleading (Nassau County Bar Association, 1982). In a similar opinion the Oregon Bar (1983) rejected an interdisciplinary group's attempt to use the name "Family Mediation Center" because it did not properly inform the public of the identity, responsibility, and status of the lawyers involved in the organization. Furthermore, the North Carolina Bar (1981b) held that although lawyers may provide mediation services as a part of their regular law practice, they cannot operate a limited practice of marital mediation under a trade name.

A few bar associations have gone a step further in separating the practice of mediation from the practice of law and have held that a lawyer may participate in mediation only if he or she is not identifiable as a lawyer. The Ohio Bar ruled that a lawyer should not list his or her law degree in publicizing mediation services (Ohio State Bar Association, 1982). In a comparable opinion, the Illinois State Bar Association (1982) held that an attorney may not engage in a separate marriage counseling, arbitration, and mediation business in connection with and operated out of his or her law office or advertise as a lawyer in connection with such a service.

CONCLUSION

This survey of the impact of formal legal ethical rules on divorce mediation suggests that serious rethinking is in order. More flexible rules designed to deal with the specific practice of mediation and its proliferation of models are needed. The present rules did not envision mediation, and attempts to interpret and mold these canons to fit a new form of professional practice do not work.

Although the compelling interest of the states in regulating the legal profession through adoption of an ethics code has continued to be recognized, inroads have been made on any claim of unbridled power. The past two decades have seen provisions of such ethics codes challenged on constitutional (*In re Primus*, 1978) and antitrust grounds (*Goldfarb v. Virginia State Bar*, 1975). Antisolicitation rules have been struck down in the name of First Amendment values, and minimum fee schedules have been found to violate the antitrust laws (Huber, 1979). Similar questions are raised by ethical restraints on mediative modes of divorce resolution. Wooden or overdefensive responses by bar committees or state courts to the novel ethical issues raised by divorce mediation will not serve the value of free choice, which has been recognized in those recent decisions.

REFERENCES

Alaska Bar Association v. Foster, No. 73-161 (Alaska Super. Ct. 1973). 38 Unauth. Prac. News 75 (1974).
American Bar Association. *Model code of professional responsibility.* Chicago: Author, 1969.
American Bar Association. *Model rules of professional conduct.* Chicago: 1983.
American Bar Association. *Standards of practice for family mediators.* Chicago: Author.
American Bar Association Commission on Evaluation of Professional Standards. Discussion draft on Rule 5.1 (1980).

American Bar Association Special Committee on Legal Assistants. Proposed curriculum for training of law office personnel (9-19). (1971).

American Bar Association Standards of Practice for Lawyer Mediators in Family Disputes, 18 Fam. L.Q. 363 (1984).

Arizona State Bar Association Committee on Legal Ethics. Opinion 76-25 (1976).

Bates v. United States, 433 U.S. 350 (1977).

Bedford, R. Possible effect on conflict of interests in a divorce action arising from one attorney framing the decree. *Alabama Law Review*, 1963, *15*, 502–516.

Boston Bar Association Committee on Ethics. Opinion 78-1 (1978).

Brotherhood of Railroad Trainmen v. Virginia, 377 U.S. 1 (1964).

California State Bar Association Committee on Professional Responsibility. Opinion 1969-18 (1969).

Connecticut State Bar Association Committee on Ethics. Formal opinion 35 (1982).

Connecticut State Bar Association, Committee on Ethics, Formal Opinion 33 (1982).

Coogler, O. J. Changing the lawyer's role in matrimonial practice. *Conciliation Courts Review*, 1977, *15* 1–8.

Coogler, O. J. *Structured mediation in divorce settlement: A handbook for marital mediators.* Lexington, MA: Heath, 1978.

Crouch, R. Divorce mediation and legal ethics. *Family Law Quarterly*, 1982a, *16(3)*, 219–250.

Crouch, R. Mediation and divorce: The dark side is still unexplored. *Family Advocate*, 1982b, *4(3)*, 27–35.

Fisher, J., & Lachman, D. *The unauthorized practice handbook 2.* Chicago: American Bar Foundation, 1972.

Florida Bar v. Stupeca, 300 S. 2d 683 (Fla. 1974).

Goldfarb v. Virginia State Bar, 421 U.S. 773 (1975).

Huber, S. Competition at the bar and the proposed code of professional standards. *North Carolina Law Review*, 1979, *57*, 559–596.

Illinois State Bar Association Committee on Professional Ethics. Opinion 745 (1982).

In re Primus, 436 U.S. 412 (1978).

In re Proposed Ethics Opinion 447, 86 N.J. 473, 432A. 2d 59 (1981).

Isaacs, S. Mediation and lawyers as witnesses under the new code. *Oregon State Bar Bulletin*, November 1986, 21.

Kansas Bar Association Committee on Professional Ethics. Advisory opinion (1984).

Klemm v. Superior Court of Fresno County, 142 Cal. Rptr. 509 (1977).

Lande, J. Mediation paradigms and professional identities. *Mediation Quarterly*, 1984, *4*, 19–48.

Lay divorce firms and the unauthorized practice of law. *University of Michigan Journal of Law Reform*, 1973.

Levine v. Levine, 45 N.Y. 2d 42 (1982).

Los Angeles County Bar Association Committee on Legal Ethics. Opinion 270 (1962).

Los Angeles County Bar Association Committee on Legal Ethics. Opinion 372 (1978).

Maryland State Bar Association Committee on Ethics. Opinion 80-55A (1980).

Massachusetts State Bar Committee on Professional Ethics, Opinion 85-3 (June 27, 1983).

Minnesota State Bar Association v. Divorce Reform, Inc., No. 396448 (Minn. Dist. Ct. 1975) 39 Unauth. Prac. News 187 (1975).

Mnookin, R., & Kornhauser, L. Bargaining in the shadow of the law: The case of divorce. *Yale Law Journal*, 1979, *88*, 950–977.

NAACP v. Button, 371 U.S. 415 (1963).

Nassau County Bar Association Committee on Professional Ethics. Formal Opinion 82-8 (1982).

Nassau County Bar Association Committee on Professional Ethics. Formal opinion 84-1 (1984).

New Hampshire State Bar Association Ethics Committee. Proposed opinion (April 21, 1981).

New Hampshire State Bar Association Ethics Committee. Formal Opinion, March 16, 1982.

New York City Bar Association Committee on Professional and Judicial Ethics. Opinion 80-23 (1981).

New York City Bar Association Committee on Professional and Judicial Ethics, 82-30 (1982).

New York County Lawyer's Association v. Darcy, 21 N.Y. 2d 694, *rev'd*, 28 A. D. 2d 161 (1967).

New York State Bar Association Committee on Professional Ethics. Opinion 258 (1972).
New York State Bar Association Committee on Professional Ethics, No. 43-83 (1983).
North Carolina State Bar Association Ethics Committee. Opinion 286 (1981a).
North Carolina State Bar Association Ethics Committee. Opinion 316 (1981b).
North Carolina State Bar Association Unauthorized Practice of Law Committee. (1980).
Ohio State Bar Association Ethics Committee, O.S.B.A. Report 780, 783-84 (Opinion 30, May 1975).
Ohio State Bar Association Committee on Legal Ethics. Informal opinion 82-2 (1982).
Oregon Bar Association Committee on Legal Ethics. Opinion 83-488 (1983).
Oregon Bar v. Gilchrist, 272 Or. 551, 538 P. 2d 913 (Or. Ct. App. 1975).
Rhode Island Bar Association Committee on Unauthorized Practice. (1981).
Riskin, L. Toward new standards for the neutral lawyer in mediation. *Arizona Law Review*, 1984, *26*, 329-362.
Silberman, L. Professional responsibility problems of divorce mediation. *Family Law Quarterly*, 1982, *16*, 107-145.
State Bar Association v. Connecticut Bank & Trust, 145 Conn. 222 140A. 2d 863 (1958).
State Bar of Arizona v. Arizona Lamp Title & Trust Co., 90 Ariz. 76 366P. 2d (1961).
State Bar v. Brandon, (Nev. Dist. Ct. 1972), 37 Anauth. Prac. News 32 (1973).
Tennessee Board of Professional Responsibility of Supreme Court. Formal opinion 83-F-39 (1983).
Unauthorized practice of law and pro se divorce: An empirical analysis. *Yale Law Journal*, 1976, *86*, 103-184.
United Mine Workers v. Illinois State Bar Association, 389 U.S. 217 (1967).
Vermont Bar Association Committee on Professional Responsibility. Opinion 80-12 (1980).
Virginia State Bar Association Committee on Legal Ethics. Informal opinion 296 (1977).
Virginia State Bar Association Committee on Legal Ethics. Informal opinion 400 (1979).
Washington State Bar Association Code of Professional Responsibility Committee. Informal opinion 385 (1980).
Washington State Bar Association Code of Professional Responsibility Committee. Informal opinion 680 (1983).
West Virginia State Bar Association Committee on Ethics. Opinion 77-7 (1977).
Wisconsin State Bar Association Committee on Professional Ethics. Opinion E-79-2 (1980).

19

Ethical Constraints: A Mental Health Perspective

ANN MILNE
Private Practice, Madison, Wisconsin

Mental health professionals have generally supported the use of divorce media-
tion as a more therapeutic way of ending a marriage and resolving conflict.
Many therapists now offer mediation services. The ethics of the mental health
field have influenced and helped shape the development of ethics and stan-
dards of practice for divorce mediators. This chapter addresses the similarities
between the values and ethics of the mental health professional and those of
the divorce mediator with a mental health background, and the sometimes
subtle but important differences between the two fields.

Divorce mediation has attracted a significant number of mental health professionals. These individuals have come to be called mental health mediators to
distinguish them from mediators from other disciplines. The ethics of divorce
mediation have been greatly influenced by these professionals. Many of the
ethical demands of the mental health field are similar to those of mediation.
However, some of the ethical demands placed upon the divorce mediator are
distinct from, if not counter to, the ethical demands of the mental health
professional. This chapter explores these influences, similarities, and differences and their impact on the practice of the mental health mediator.

Divorce mediation began without benefit of separate standards or ethical
guidelines that exist for other professional practices. In an effort to fill this void,
the Association of Family and Conciliation Courts (AFCC) served as the con-
venor of three symposiums on Divorce Mediation Standards and Ethics (December 1982, May 1983, May 1984). Over 40 professional organizations, including representatives from various mental health disciplines, participated in these
symposiums (Milne, 1984, 1985b). The "Model Standards of Practice for Family
and Divorce Mediation" (1984) was developed by the symposium participants
(see appendix 20-2). In developing the model standards, symposium delegates
drew heavily upon the ethical codes of various mental health organizations.

THE VALUE SYSTEM OF THE MENTAL HEALTH MEDIATOR

In order to understand the unique ethical issues that confront the mental
health mediator, it is first necessary to understand the value systems that
support the fields of mediation and mental health. A value system is the

foundation for the ethics of a professional practice. There are many similarities between the value system of divorce mediation and mental health; however, there are some critical differences. This section speaks to both.

Several authors have commented on the similarity of values between the fields of divorce mediation and mental health. Gold (1985) notes the similar sociocultural traditions between mediation and therapy. Both provide an opportunity for change and growth; both support the values of autonomy, self-determination, and empowerment. Weaver (1986) compares the goals of divorce mediation to the goals of divorce therapy and notes the following list of shared values: self-determination and self-responsibility leading to full autonomy, continuance of parental role and preservation of family as a unity (though reorganized), and protection of children and facilitation of negotiations espousing best interests.

A task group at the second AFCC symposium on standards and practices (AFCC Toronto, May 1983) developed a list of basic values that underlie the practice of divorce mediation. They include promotion of family relationships, minimization of state intervention, management of conflict, and protection of best interests of children (Milne, 1984).

The similarity of these underlying values with those of the mental health field explain why mediation has attracted the support and participation of mental health professionals. It is, however, the application of these values that accounts for the finely tuned differences between counseling and mediation and makes ethical demands on mediators, notably mental health mediators, that reflect both the overlap of values and the distinguishing differences.

The preamble of the "Model Standards" notes that "mediation is a *family centered conflict resolution process*" (emphasis added). The preamble further states that "mediation is based on principles of problem solving which focus on the needs and interests of the participants, fairness, privacy, self determination and *the best interests of all family members*" (p. 2; emphasis added).

The principle of a family-centered process that addresses "the best interests of all family members" may be troublesome for some mental health professionals who focus on individual well-being and do not practice from a family systems ideology. The desire to support, protect, and advocate for an individual is a recognizable value for a mental health professional but may be in conflict with the value of best interests of all family members, as practiced by the mediator. Although many mental health practitioners subscribe to a family system or family-centered approach, the divorce mediator must espouse the value of the family unit whether united by the legal ties of marriage or continuing parental ties following divorce. Similarly, therapists who are wedded to long-term therapeutic interests and focus on the underlying psychological process may feel uncomfortable with the short-term, more superficial interventions and settlements of mediation (Moore, 1983).

Self-determination is a value shared by the mental health practitioner and the mental health mediator (Reamer, 1983). Client autonomy is promoted by the "Model Standards." "The primary responsibility for the resolution of a dispute rests with the participants. . . . At no time shall a mediator coerce a participant into agreement or make a substantive decision for any participant" ("Model Standards," 1984, p. 4). Self-determination and client autonomy are not, however, in practice universally accepted as terminal values by all mediators, especially those from a mental health background. A more pervasive value of best interests of children seems to ride shotgun over self-determination (Saposnek, 1983). Folger and Bernard (1985) found that mental health mediators tend to score higher on an interventionist scale than mediators from other fields, taking a more active and influential role when mediating issues related to children. Indeed Gold (1985), in distinguishing the difference between a therapist and a mediator, states, "The therapist usually follows the client's lead. The mediator leads the client" (p. 19). Client autonomy may also be affected in those settings where mediation is mandatory and where the mediator provides evaluative information or a custody recommendation to the court. Reflective of their mental health backgrounds, some mental health mediators may place a greater value on protecting the interests of children than on the traditional mediation values of self-determination and autonomy.

Confidentiality, privacy, and privilege are values espoused by those in both mental health and mediation. The codes of ethical conduct for the American Association for Marriage and Family Therapy (1985), the American Personnel and Guidance Association (1974), and the American Psychological Association (1981) establish standards of confidentiality, privacy, and privilege (Folberg & Taylor, 1984; Van Hoose & Kottler, 1985). The "Model Standards" provide that "a mediator shall foster the confidentiality of the process" (1984, p. 3). Mental health mediators tend to support the concept of mediation as a confidential and private process (McIsaac, 1985). Exceptions to this are based upon supraordinate mental health values that, as above, relate to the protection of others, such as the requirement to report child abuse and the duty to warn a potential victim of behavior that is likely to result in imminent death or substantial bodily harm (*McIntosh v. Milano*, 1979; *Tarasoff v. Regents of the University of California*, 1976).

The mental health professional and the mental health mediator support the value of full and open disclosure of information between the participants as well as between the mediator and the participants. Informed consent in therapy includes providing clients with an explanation of the procedures to be used and their purposes, the role of the therapist and his or her professional qualifications, the risks involved, the benefits reasonably to be expected, and alternatives to treatment (Margolin, 1986). Full and open disclosure in mediation supports the mental health value of informed choice and the legal standard of truthfulness. A mediation practice would reasonably follow these principles by requiring "disclosure of all relevant information in the mediation process as would reasonably occur in the judicial discovery process" ("Model Standards," 1984, p. 3). Additionally, the "Model Standards" provide that "the mediator shall disclose to the participants any biases or strong views relating to the issues to be mediated" (p. 2). This would include any custody preferences held by the mediator, such as joint custody, and any sexual biases favoring a particular parent or method of property division or financial support (Cramer & Schoeneman, 1985).

This brief discussion illustrates the similarities and differences between the underlying values of the mental health professional and the mental health mediator. Cooperative dispute resolution is a fundamental value of the mediation process. Cooperative dispute resolution promotes stable family relationships, a fundamental goal of the mental health field. The values of each field help to define the ethics of the practice. We turn now to an in-depth analysis of the role of the mediator, which will further illustrate the influence of the mental health field on the development of standards of practice for divorce mediators and the unique ethical issues that confront mental health mediators.

THE ROLE OF THE MENTAL HEALTH MEDIATOR

Relationship with Clients

Although both the mediator and the mental health professional deal with emotionally charged psychological issues, the relationship between the mental health professional and clients is different from the relationship between the mediator and clients (Kelly, 1983; Milne, 1985a; Sander, 1983; Saposnek, 1985). The mediator addresses psychological conflicts only as they present an impediment to the resolution of the topical issues, such as property division, plans for the children, and financial support. Although an argument may be made that mediation is therapeutic, it is not therapy (Kelly, 1983; Rosanova, 1983; Sander, 1983).

Mental health mediators bring to the mediation process an understanding of families and the dynamics of family conflict. They are experienced in helping individuals communicate more effectively, resolve psychological impediments, and understand the needs of children in divorce. Flushing out disputants' needs and interests is standard procedure in mediation. Parties do not mediate in the vacuum of dollars and cents but deal also with issues of self-esteem, fairness, and trust. But the mental health mediator is often faced with a dilemma when working with divorcing clients, as conflicts take on a psychological base and reflect troubled relationships and behavioral patterns. To address these issues and work for their resolution mixes mediation with counseling; to allow them to continue unaddressed ignores the principles of one's prior training and discipline and may result in an impasse in mediation. Addressing these needs and interests as they relate to a final resolution of the issues may be necessary to facilitate an agreement. This is not therapy but rather a part of the mediation process. The ethics of this become problematic, however, when the psychological issues addressed in mediation are beyond those immediately necessary to reach an agreement. At that point the mental health mediator crosses the professional boundary and begins to provide counseling and therapy services. Although the mediator may possess the requisite skill to provide these services, a referral to a therapist is more appropriate.

When a client contacts a mediator to inquire about mediation services and to initiate the process, it is the obligation of the mediator to clearly define mediation in order to "delineate it from therapy, counseling, custody evaluation, arbitration, and advocacy" ("Model Standards," 1984, p. 2; see also Baker-Jackson et al., 1985; *Colorado Code*, 1982; Lande, 1984). Clients of the mental health practitioner may be unfamiliar with the differences between therapy and mediation. One party may have hopes of resolving marital issues and effecting a reconciliation by choosing a professional who practices both counseling and mediation. Others are attracted to mediation solely as a method that sidesteps the often complex and painful psychological issues. The right to define the issues in mediation must belong to the clients. Mental health mediators may be easily seduced into resolving an emotional conflict, only to find that they have abdicated their effectiveness as a neutral facilitator. Issues of power, control, anger, and unresolved emotional conflicts may be evident to the mental health mediator, but the parties may have chosen mediation in an effort to step aside from these conflicts. The mediator's penchant to resolve relationships must yield to the parties' desires to resolve the issues of property, assets, and children. The mental health mediator can measure the attention paid to the emotional and relationship issues by evaluating how likely they are to prohibit the resolution of the other issues. Mental health mediators can use their expertise in resolving relationship issues by reframing issues so they can be addressed from a less emotional perspective. To flush out and resolve emotional impasse is the forte of the mental health mediator. To become a therapist may be to abandon one's role as mediator and neutral facilitator.

Similarly, a prior counseling or therapeutic relationship with an individual or a couple ought to preclude mediation. A relationship of trust and confidence may have been established between the counselor and the clients, but the move from therapist to mediator is problematic. A counseling relationship is predicated on support, identification, and emotional well-being. The trust and rapport developed during the counseling process may assist in the initial stages of mediation, but these therapeutic alliances can become problematic as the parties proceed to more advanced negotiations. Gold (1985) defines the problem of mediating with prior therapy clients as one of clients' expectations of loyalty, alliance, and support. Former therapy clients are likely to feel betrayed by the mediator's detachment and neutrality. Further, it is difficult for the therapist-now-mediator to disregard information obtained and conclusions reached during the therapy process and to prevent that from influencing the impartiality of the mediation process. Gold (1985) notes that she will provide mediation for former therapy clients in rare circumstances and only when all parties agree, when there has been a trusting, cooperative relationship between the parties, when a period of time has elapsed, and when it is understood that once a new service is provided, that will be the only service provided in the future. Although this policy offers some assistance, it does not address the practical problem created, that when mediation clients need counseling the mediator is preempted from returning to the former role of therapist. The parties are then forced to begin anew with another professional. When possible, it seems to be less problematic for a therapist to remain a therapist and a mediator to remain a mediator.

The *Colorado Code of Professional Conduct for Mediators* (1982) states,

> The mediator must not consider himself or herself limited to keeping the peace or regulating conflict at the bargaining table. His or her role should be one of an active resource person upon whom the parties may draw and, when appropriate, he or she should be prepared to provide both *procedural and substantive suggestions and alternatives* which will assist the parties in successful negotiation. (p. 2; emphasis added)

Many mental health mediators see their role as that of an advocate for the needs and interests of children, often unrepresented parties in mediation. Providing "procedural and substantive suggestions and alternatives" raises several questions. Is it ethical for the mediator to direct the parties toward agreements that reflect the needs of the children? Does providing substantive and evaluative information conflict with the role of the mediator? Should the mediator meet with the children for the purpose of assessing their needs and wishes? How much information and advice does the mental health mediator provide the parties before crossing the lines between mediator, consultant, and evaluator? Is the role of the mediator strictly that of a facilitator of the settlement process, or is the mediator also a conduit of information?

Providing the parents with information gathered from the children may assist in reaching agreements reflective of the needs and interests of the children, but this places the mediator in a position of gatekeeper of this information. How much and what information the mediator reports back to the parents, following an interview with the children, can significantly influence the planning and agreement-making process. Not providing such information may result in an unsatisfactory resolution for the children, even though it is a self-determined agreement for the parents. The mental health mediator may be an expert in child development but is not an expert in the traditions and relationships of a particular family. Mental health mediators should attempt to protect the objectivity of their role and strive to provide information in a way that allows the parties to make informed agreements but does not bias the decision-making process or negate the autonomy and traditions of the family.

Impartiality and neutrality are fundamental to the mediation process. The *Standards of Practice for Lawyer Mediators* approved by the House of Delegates of the American Bar Association (1984) declare that impartiality is "a mediator attribute which may not be compromised" (Bishop, 1984). Impartiality means that the mediator will not favor a particular outcome or party ("Model Standards," 1984). This may be difficult for mental health mediators when resolving issues of custody and visitation or when challenged to become an advocate for a particular party, either because of gender identification or because a party lacks an ability to negotiate effectively in his or her own best interests. Mental health mediators must avoid advocating or supporting an individual or a position. This does not, however, mean that a mediator is silent about unbridled concession making or unfair negotiation tactics. Bishop (1984) states,

> In one view, the mediator should have no duty with respect to the outcome, except to ensure that the husband and wife exchange and understand relevant information and documentation. However, the mediator has a greater duty. If, for example, the mediator believes that a participant is making concessions outside the mediator's sense of what is reasonable, it is appropriate for the mediator to raise that issue for discussion. (p. 10)

This raises the issue of the mediator judging fairness. Labor mediators have been referred to as catalysts (Kressel, 1972). Their role is limited to offering assistance in seeking out possible solutions, and they do not judge the merits of the parties' positions or the final agreement. Saposnek (1985), however, notes that a child-custody mediator has an added ethical and moral responsibility to ensure that settlements are reached that adequately meet the best interests of children. Some authors differentiate divorce mediation from labor mediation and support the mediator's duty to protect the interests of the parties, by arguing that divorce mediation clients are not professional negotiators and children are often unrepresented parties in mediation (Engram & Markowitz, 1985). A possible solution to the dilemma of who shall serve as the conscience of the process is offered by Bernard, Folger, Weingarten, and Zumeta (1984):

> The mediator can identify and share with the parties the mediator's value preferences. In that way the parties retain some control over the influence exerted by the mediator. . . . Deviating from this stance should be explicitly and deliberately chosen and justified. We are impressed with the difficulty of making such powerful value decisions for others. Should mediators attempt to do so, they should act openly and with the obligation to explain their judgment to the parties. (p. 73)

Providing substantive suggestions and value preferences must be weighed carefully against the role of procedural facilitator. Divorcing clients are easily influenced by the suggestions of a professional. Further, they are easily influenced by the slightest appearance of favoritism or a lack of neutrality on the part of the mediator. Providing substantive suggestions and value preferences must be done in a way that avoids undue influence and the appearance of bias. Providing information in an advisory rather than a directive fashion may allow the parties to receive the information and still retain responsibility for how to use the information.

The mental health mediator must also guard against gender or personality identification with a client. Identification between a therapist and client and the dependent relationship that evolves may be appropriate and necessary in therapy but not in mediation. Triangulation between a therapist and clients may signal dysfunctional family constellations and be used effectively in therapy, to resolve issues of power and control. Triangulation in mediation may result in a coercive agreement or may alienate a party from participating fully in the process. Co-mediation may help the mental health mediator avoid this problem (Gold, 1982).

Haynes (1981) argues that neutrality is impossible in the divorce context; the parties "own the agreement" and the mediators "own the process." Haynes views the mediator's role as one of balancing power between the parties, so that interventions are made for the purpose of increasing the power of the disadvantaged spouse, typically the one who is left (see Chapter 14).

Bernard et al. (1984) have offered guidance in this area by differentiating "neutralist" mediators from "interventionist" mediators.

> A neutralist strategy involves seeking to avoid influencing the outcome of the negotiations between the parties. Any decision the parties freely agree on is seen as acceptable in the extreme neutralist position. An interventionist position, in constrast, finds the mediator actively challenging and possibly even refusing to accept an agreement both parties have accepted. The interventionist mediator who believes an agreement is unfair or unjust is likely to present alternatives designed to achieve the mediator's vision of the parties' best interests.
>
> Although both neutralist and interventionist mediators may offer the same information, the interventionist will offer it in order to enhance the bargaining position of the party the mediator considers disadvantaged. . . . It is important to recognize the ethical danger in the ever-present temptation of the mediator to slant the presentation. In reality, mediators can never fully determine the impact of their interventions. . . . Neutrality or intervention must be distinguised by the mediator's motives rather than by the impact. (pp. 62–67)

In practice, the mediator's probative questioning of the parties may lessen the tendency to judge, serve an educational function, and assure that all options have been explored and that agreements and their consequences are fully understood. The raising of issues through questions, such as "Have you considered the consequences of. . . ?" may result in a more meaningful agreement for the parties and one that will stand the test of time as well as legal and judicial review.

Mental health professionals are familiar with confidentiality issues. The *Code of Ethics* of the National Association of Social Workers (NASW, 1980) states, "The social worker should respect the privacy of clients and hold in confidence all information obtained in the course of professional service." The "Ethical Principles of Psychologists" (1981) provide that "psychologists have a primary obligation to respect the confidentiality of information obtained from persons in the course of their work as psychologists" (p. 635).

The freedom to confidentially negotiate and explore alternatives without prejudice is a fundamental principle of the mediation process ("Protecting Confidentiality," 1984).

> If the participants do not trust that the mediation is private and that revelations will be held in confidence by the mediator, they may be reserved in revealing relevant information and hesitate to disclose potential accommodations that may appear to compromise earlier positions. (Folberg & Taylor, 1984, p. 264)

Confidentiality must be upheld by the mediator and broken only in instances where reporting of harmful or potentially harmful behavior is required. Reporting any other information to an agency, court, or individual will severely hamper the development of mediation as a voluntary and cooperative process (see Chapter 16). Making a custody recommendation or providing evidence and testimony to the court regarding matters discussed during mediation belies the principle of the mediator as a neutral facilitator, vests extraordinary power in the mediator, and is contrary to the principles of confidentiality and self-determination. Furthermore, a mediation process can not substitute for a full custody-evaluation process and does not provide a complete investigation into the facts necessary for an adjudicated custody determination (McIsaac, 1985). The intent to resolve issues privately ought not to be undermined by the covert practice of the mediator facilitating the mediation process and at the same time evaluating the parties. This results in a flawed mediation process and a flawed evaluation process (McIsaac, 1985).

The issue of confidentiality is also raised in the use of the caucus. Mental health professionals must address this issue when seeing parties individually during the course of therapy. One procedure is for the therapist to maintain confidentiality and to treat each spouse's confidences as though that person were an individual client. The decision to maintain confidentiality may elicit "rich clinical data" that helps the therapist better understand a particular spouse. However, if the material cannot be discussed openly, as is true for therapy, there may be no advantage to having obtained the information.

> The secret holder has acquired more power by virtue of his or her special relationship with the therapist. The therapist, in turn, has lost power, since he or she no longer is controlling the flow of information or even maintaining the type of relationship he or she desires with the uninformed spouse. (Margolin, 1986, p. 627)

A second strategy in therapy is to explicitly discourage the sharing of any information that is not available for use in the conjoint session. This stance is adopted to block the formation of a special alliance with one person to the exclusion of the mate. Mediators who maintain the confidentiality of a caucus may acquire information that would affect the final settlement. This places the mediator in the position of a gatekeeper of information and jeopardizes the principle of a full and open disclosure of information. Agreeing to keep a secret from one party may compromise neutrality, while disclosing the content of the caucus will breach the assumption of privacy between the mediator and the client. As with therapy, a more reasoned approach to caucusing may be to define at the outset of the process the objective of a caucus and to agree that information discussed during a caucus will ultimately be brought back to the joint session (Margolin, 1986).

Caucuses can be purposeful when used to educate a party regarding his or her negotiation style, to surface suspected secrets that may lead to impasse, or as a last-ditch attempt to explore a possible compromise. As Margolin (1986) states, "There is an important distinction between refusing to guarantee condientiality and refusing to meet separately with the spouses" (p. 628). A spouse's request for a caucus may signal that he or she is looking for guidance in how to broach a difficult topic or how to explore a particular settlement option. A potential conflict of interest can be avoided when the mediator makes it clear to the parties that he or she is not serving as a confidante of either party but as a facilitator of the process. (For an exploration of the legal basis of confidentiality, see Chapter 16.)

The increasing use of mediation in divorce matters will bring challenges to the confidentiality of the process. Legal challenges, including subpoenaing a mediator to testify in court and to produce records, will occur. The *Colorado Code of Professional Conduct for Mediators* (1982) states that a "mediator is obliged to resist disclosure of confidential information in an adversarial process" (p. 3). However, confidentiality should not extend protection to a mediator who has acted in an unethical manner and whose behavior is under question or legal investigation (Kirkpatrick, 1985). Confidentiality provides a shelter to the process, not a cover-up.

The enthusiasm for mediation must be tempered by the knowledge that not all clients are appropriate for mediation. To suspend or terminate mediation where a party is "unable or unwilling to meaningfully participate in the process or when a reasonable agreement is unlikely" ("Model Standards," 1984, p. 4) is not only good practice but affords the necessary protections for the individual and for the mediator. The mental health mediator may be particularly adept at recognizing "manipulative or intimidating negotiation techniques" and can "explore whether the participants are capable of participating in informed negotiations" ("Model Standards," 1984, p. 4).

The mental health standard of informed consent may be particularly useful to the mediator. The Committee on Privacy and Confidentiality of the California State Psychological Association addressed the issue of informed consent as a primary issue for treatment (Everstine et al., 1980). According to these standards, informed consent for treatment must consider the elements of competence, information, and voluntariness. These same considerations can assist the parties and the mediator in the decision to suspend or terminate mediation. The element of "competence" refers to whether the client can "engage in rational thought to a sufficient degree to make competent decisions about his or her life" (Everstine et al., 1980, p. 831). This includes competency to understand the issues to be addressed in mediation and competency to understand the implications of any proposed agreement. In order for this to occur, parties must possess relevant information. This includes specific information about the mediation process, the procedures involved, and alternative methods of resolving disputes, and substantive information about possible solutions and their effects. This information must be presented in a language and manner such that it can be understood by the clients. The decision to suspend or terminate mediation must also be guided by the element of voluntariness. This includes voluntary participation in the mediation process and voluntary assent to proposed agreements. Coercion, force, and manipulation have no place in mediation.

The *Colorado Code of Professional Conduct for Mediators* (1982) provides further guidance for when to suspend or terminate mediation.

In the event that an agreement is reached which a mediator feels (1) is illegal, (2) is grossly inequitable to one or more parties, (3) is the result of false information, (4) is the result of bad faith bargaining, (5) is impossible to enforce, or (6) does not look like it will hold over time, the mediator may pursue any or all of the following alternatives:

1. Inform the parties of the difficulties which the mediator sees in the agreement.
2. Inform the parties of the difficulties and make suggestions which would remedy the problems.
3. Withdraw as mediator without disclosing to either party the particular reasons for his or her withdrawal. (p. 4)

From the initial contact with clients to the completion or termination of mediation, the mental health mediator must be cognizant of the relationship between the mediator and clients. The mediator's role may include familiar mental health practices and procedures that have been adapted to accommodate the distinctive differences of the mediation process. As long as mediation continues to attract professionals from the mental health field, the process will be influenced by these practitioners. Similarly, as the mediation field develops, the role of the mental health mediator will be influenced by the distinct practices of mediation.

Relationship with Other Professionals

The provision of professional services and the promotion of mediation as a community resource is dependent upon a knowledge of related community services and a cooperative relationship with other professionals. Principle 7a of the "Ethical Principles of Psychologists" (American Psychological Association, 1981) states that psychologists shall "make full use of all the professional, technical and administrative resources that serve the best interests of consumers" (p. 636). The mental health mediator must develop a number of professional contacts in the community. This includes relationships with accountants, actuaries, attorneys, financial planners, real estate and property appraisers, therapists, and other mediators.

Referring clients to other professionals for collateral advice allows the mediator to concentrate on the mediation process rather than the substantive issues. The division of property and financial assets can be facilitated through the expertise of an accountant or financial planner who can provide advice about various settlement alternatives. A referral to a counselor may be necessary when clients are stuck on emotional or psychological issues in mediation or wish some independent information regarding their children. The slightest hint of a financial or referral kickback between professionals, however, will tarnish the reputation of the mediator and will undermine clients' rights to independent consultation. Mediation clients ought to have the most expert advice that they can afford, irrespective of that expert's familiarity with and support of mediation.

A mediator's contacts with other professionals who are serving as outside sources of information can be problematic. The sharing of information between a mediator and accountants, physicians, therapists, school teachers, guardians ad litem, custody evaluators, and others may expedite the process (Blades, 1984) but can both infringe on the confidentiality of mediation and unintentionally expose the mediator to information that may influence the process. Contacts with other professionals should not be made for the purpose of divulging information derived from the mediation process and should be limited to reporting agreements reached in mediation, and only with the parties' consents. Mental health mediators must also guard against the unintended breach of privacy. Case consultations with agency colleagues may lead to problems should mediation reach an impasse and a consulting staff member be called upon to conduct a custody evaluation. Similarly, receiving information from others may jeopardize the mediator's role as a neutral facilitator of the process and unduly influence the course of mediation and the parties' agreement making. In most cases, clients ought to be encouraged to make direct contact with outside consultants and be held responsible for making this information available during the mediation process.

The mediator's relationship with local attorneys is essential to the ethical practice of mediation. Optimally, clients entering mediation will have selected independent legal counsel. In practice, this is not always the case. Clients needing legal assistance may ask the mediator to provide a referral to an attorney. Most mediation clients have not been previously divorced and are not familiar with the legal process or with attorneys who practice in this area. Some mediators will establish a list of attorneys to whom they routinely refer clients for legal advice (Coogler, 1978). These attorneys tend to be familiar with the mediation process and support the principle of cooperative conflict resolution. The mental health mediator must be aware of the ethical dilemma of referring clients to attorneys merely because they support mediation as opposed to being advocates for the legal interests of the client. Mental health mediators who discourage legal consultation during mediation are not serving the interests of clients and may alienate the support of the bar. Clients ought to be encouraged to consult with independent legal counsel of their choice at any point in the mediation process. To preclude this consultation does not afford clients a complete understanding of the issues and possible solutions, and subjects mediation to being a lesser process than the adversarial system. Educating attorneys, participating in and promoting continuing legal education programs on mediation, and inviting attorneys to join mediation organizations will further the institutionalization of divorce mediation and the provision of an ethical practice.

A cooperative and noncompetitive relationship with other mediators will serve to promote the practice of mediation. The NASW *Code of Ethics* (1980) provides that "the social worker should cooperate with colleagues to promote professional interests and concerns" (p. 6). Networking can provide the opportunity for case consultation, continuing education, and peer supervision. A local tutorial group that draws upon the experiences of group members can serve as a means of providing in-service training and consultation. The public acceptance of mediation can best be accomplished by mediators who are willing to work together for the furtherance of the practice. It is too tempting to try to exclude mediators who have limited credentials or who practice in a fashion dissimilar to one's own. Professional ethics dictate working with such individuals to enhance their practice rather than shunning them and allowing them to continue to practice in a vacuum. Local mediation associations or chapters of mediation organizations can serve as clearinghouses for information about mediation, act as speakers' bureaus, and be sources of referrals. Speaking engagements and media features, when sponsored by a network of mediators, add to the credibility of mediation rather than the enhancement of a single practitioner.

In order for the field of divorce mediation to grow, mediators must be dedicated to high standards of professional competence and integrity. Sound relationships with other professionals, including sources of referral, outside experts, and other mediators, will further the provision of an ethical and professional practice.

FURTHER ETHICAL CONSIDERATIONS

Mental health mediators are not, by training, experts in legal and financial matters. To mediate in these areas without benefit of substantive information, experience, or recourse to professional consultation places the parties in jeopardy and compromises the practice of mediation. Divorce is a legal entity involving rights of property and financial entitlement for spouses and children. The "Model Standards" (1984) provide that "a mediator shall give information only in those areas where qualified by training or experience" (p. 4). Perhaps the "Model Standards" do not go far enough in this area and ought to reflect not only caution about the giving of information but should limit the practice of mediation to those with experience and training in the substantive areas. The potential for the mental health mediator to be charged with the unauthorized practice of law and subject to local bar sanction or to be the defendant in a malpractice suit brought by a disgruntled client may only be a matter of speculation today, but could result in restrictive limits being applied to mental health mediators in the future. Advising parties of their legal rights, interpreting the intent of the law, and drafting a formal marital settlement agreement may be viewed as the practice of law. Mental health mediators can minimize these dangers by making it clear that they expect clients to consult with independent legal counsel. An introductory letter confirming the nature of the mediation relationship and advising parties that the mediator will not be providing legal advice will offer further protection. Drafting a memorandum of agreement at the conclusion of the process or simply a letter which summarizes the agreements avoids some of the problems inherent in the drafting of formal agreements. It behooves the mental health practitioner to act in a manner that protects the legal interests of clients and that will allow the practice of mediation to continue unfettered by reactionary sanctions resulting from unprofessional practices.

Mental health mediators should not rely on malpractice insurance issued for activities performed during the course of one's counseling or therapy practice without confirming with the insurance company that the policy covers mediation. The delineation between therapy and mediation has been noted in the literature and in the "Model Standards" (1984; Folberg & Taylor, 1984; Kelly, 1983; Moore, 1983; Rosanova, 1983; Sander, 1983). Liability and malpractice coverage for mediators is available through membership in the Association of Family and Conciliation Courts and the Academy of Family Mediators. The exposure is too great to risk practicing without adequate liability protection in a field susceptible to so many unresolved questions. (For a full discussion of professional issues see Chapter 17.) Advertisements that inform colleagues and clients of the availability of mediation services ought to reflect the principles of cooperative conflict resolution and not the hucksterism of a cheap and quick divorce. Exaggerated promises of savings in costs, time, and satisfaction with the ultimate settlement may offend other professionals and result in legal suits for false claims. The American Psychological Association's "Ethical Principles of Psychologists" (1981) states, "Announcements of services, advertising and promotional activities serve the purpose of helping the public make informed judgments and choices" (p. 634). Advertisements and promotional materials should support truth in advertising. The public needs to be accurately informed about the service so that they can distinguish mediation from other related services and can choose a mediator based upon an accurate representation of his or her education and experience.

The use of health insurance for the reimbursement of fees for psychotherapy is an accepted practice by most mental health professionals. An individual psychiatric diagnosis is made and payment is received. In many cases therapists strive to make the most innocuous diagnosis possible, knowing that the presenting issues are not those of psychopathology but rather those of problematic relationship styles and communication patterns. To use health insurance coverage for mediation services would require a psychiatric diagnosis of one or both parties and implies that mediation is a health service. Mental health mediators diagnose impediments to communication rather than the etiology of psychological dysfunction. Requiring a psychiatric diagnosis redefines mediation as a psychiatric intervention rather than a dispute settlement service. Clients in mediation have a right to be treated only as disputants and not as patients (Milne, 1983).

In some instances, mediation is attracting couples who have no identifiable divorce disputes, do not want to participate in the adversarial process, and see a mediation office as a more comfortable forum for planning and making decisions about their divorce. A divorce "expediter" may facilitate the cooperative processing of a divorce, but some observers may question whether it is appropriate to call this mediation, as there are ostensibly no disputes to mediate. Others would say that providing a forum for parties to discuss common issues and make decisions is a legitimate function of mediation.

Going beyond that, however, and serving as a legal technician may facilitate the divorce process but may constitute the unauthorized practice of law, a matter to be avoided by mental health mediators.

Education and training programs for divorce mediators have yet to fill the need for "substantive knowledge and procedural skill in the specialized area of practice" ("Model Standards," 1984, p. 5). The "Model Standards" recommend training to include "family and human development, family law, divorce procedures, family finances, community resources, the mediation process and professional ethics" (p. 5). Whether mediators will continue to be drawn primarily from the mental health and legal fields is debatable. Moore (1983) suggests that specialized training in mediation ought not to be limited to a previous professional vocation and advocates that training should include four categories of information and skill building: (1) substantive information (data about divorce and custody law, budgeting and accounting, custody and visitation models, child-support models, property division models, spousal support, and family psychodynamics); (2) negotiation and mediation procedures and skills (general problem-solving steps initiated by mediators or negotiators in all family disputes, specific techniques that assist parties to handle special situations); (3) conciliatory procedures ("applied psychological tactics aimed at correcting perceptions, reducing unreasonable fears and improving communications to an extent that permits reasonable discussion to take place" (Curle, 1971, p. 177); and (4) ethics; (normative standards that describe not only the professional's behavior toward clients but also the behaviors required in relation to other professionals and the public at large).

It is hard to imagine that the current vogue of 1- to 5-day training workshops can provide the training and experience necessary for proficient practice. Such programs may provide an adequate orientation to the field of family and divorce mediation and serve as vehicles for continuing education, but are limited by time and focus. Academic programs that offer degrees and credentials in family and divorce mediation can be improved when augmented by a supervised clinical or work–study experience, an accepted practice in the mental health field, and when further research on effective mediation interventions has been concluded. The development of model guidelines for training programs will further the acceptance of family and divorce mediation and the ethics of the practice.

FUTURE CONSIDERATIONS

Many questions exist regarding the place of mediation within the mental health community. For some mental health professionals, mediation is nothing more than a familiar counseling technique. Some court-employed custody investigators may believe that mediation interferes with the *parens patriae* responsibility of the court and may question whether mediation protects the best interests of children (Duryee, 1985). Few mental health mediators have given up a counseling practice in favor of a full-time mediation practice. Most offer mediation as a complimentary service to their traditional counseling practices (Milne, 1983; Pearson, Ring, & Milne, 1983). Commingling divorce mediation services with a counseling practice may be necessary for the foreseeable future until the market is more developed. The professionalization of mediation and the development of specialized training and academic programs will eventually produce mediators who come to the practice via a more direct route, as opposed to coming from another field of practice. This is likely to result in the eventual decline of the term "mental health mediator." At that point, divorce mediation will have established a body of knowledge and an identity of its own, apart from the fields of practice that have influenced its development.

The ethics of divorce mediation are shaped by personal, social, and professional values. Ethics develop as a practice develops (Schneider, 1985). The dissolution of a marriage spans legal and psychological parameters. Divorce conflicts are a meld of the two. The standards and ethics of divorce mediation have been shaped by the parent professions of mental health and law. As the field of divorce mediation continues to evolve into a separate and distinct practice, with separate and distinct issues, standards of practice will evolve that recognize the need to strike a balance between the unique character of mediation and the benefits of the professions and practices that have influenced its development.

REFERENCES

American Association for Marriage and Family Therapy. *Code of ethical principles for marriage and family therapists.* Washington DC: Author, 1985.

American Bar Association. *Standards of practice for lawyer mediators.* Chicago: Author, 1984.

American Personnel and Guidance Association. *Code of ethics.* Alexandria, VA: Author, 1974.

American Psychological Association, Ethical principles of psychologists. *American Psychologist,* 1981, *36*(6), 633–638.

Baker-Jackson, M., Bergman, K., Ferrick, G., Hovsepian, V., Garcia, J., & Hulbert, R. Ethical standards for court-connected mediators. *Mediation Quarterly,* 1985, *8,* 67–72.

Bernard, S., Folger, J., Weingarten, H., & Zumeta, Z. The neutral mediator: Value dilemmas in divorce mediation. *Mediation Quarterly,* 1984, *4,* 61–74.

Bishop, T. Mediation standards: An ethical safety net. *Mediation Quarterly,* 1984, *4,* 5–17.

Blades, J. Mediation: An old art revitalized. *Mediation Quarterly,* 1984, *3,* 59–98.

Colorado code of professional conduct for mediators. Denver, CO: Center for Dispute Resolution, 1982.

Coogler, O. J. *Structured mediation in divorce settlement: A handbook for marital mediators.* Lexington, MA: Heath, 1978.

Cramer, C., & Schoeneman, R. A court mediation model with an eye toward standards. *Mediation Quarterly,* 1985, *8,* 33–46.

Curle, A. *Making peace.* London: Tavistock, 1971.

Duryee, M. Public-sector mediation: A report from the courts. *Mediation Quarterly,* 1985, *8,* 47–56.

Engram, P., & Markowitz, J. Ethical issues in mediation: Divorce and labor compared. *Mediation Quarterly,* 1985, *8,* 19–32.

Everstine, L., Everstine, D., Heymann, G., True, R., Frey, D., Johnson, H., & Seiden, R. Privacy and confidentiality in psychotherapy. *American Psychologist,* 1980, *35*(9), 828–840.

Folberg, J., & Taylor, A. *Mediation—A comprehensive guide to resolving conflicts without litigation.* San Francisco: Jossey-Bass, 1984.

Folger, J., & Bernard, S. Divorce mediation: When mediators challenge the divorcing parties. *Mediation Quarterly*, 1985, *10*, 5-23.

Gold, L. The psychological context of the interdisciplinary co-mediation team model in marital dissolution. *Conciliation Courts Review*, 1982, *20(2)*, 45-53.

Gold, L. Reflections on the transition from therapist to mediator. *Mediation Quarterly*, 1985, *9*, 15-26.

Haynes, J. *Divorce mediation—A practical guide for therapists and counselors.* New York: Springer, 1981.

Kelly, J. Mediation and psychotherapy: Distinguishing the difference. *Mediation Quarterly*, 1983, *1*, 33-44.

Kirkpatrick, G. Should mediators have a confidentiality privilege? *Mediation Quarterly*, 1985, *9*, 85-108.

Kressel, K., *Labor mediation: An exploratory survey.* New York: American Association of Labor Mediation Agencies, 1972.

Lande, J. Mediation paradigms and professional identities. *Mediation Quarterly*, 1984, 4, 19-47.

Margolin, G. Ethical issues in marital therapy. In N. Jacobson & A. Gurman (Eds.), *Clinical handbook of marital therapy* (pp. 621-636). New York: Guilford Press, 1986.

McIntosh v. Milano, 403 A. 2d 500 (N.J. 1979).

McIsaac, H. Confidentiality: An exploration of issues. *Mediation Quarterly*, 1985, *8*, 57-66.

Milne, A. Divorce mediation: The state of the art. *Mediation Quarterly*, 1983, *1*, 15-31.

Milne, A. The development of parameters of practice for divorce mediators. *Mediation Quarterly*, 1984, *4*, 49-59.

Milne, A. Mediation or therapy—Which is it? In S. C. Grebe (Ed.), *Divorce and family mediation* (pp. 1-15). Rockville, MD: Aspen Systems, 1985a.

Milne, A. Model standards of practice for family and divorce mediation. *Mediation Quarterly*, 1985b, *8*, 73-81.

Model Standards of Practice for Family and Divorce Mediation. *Conciliation Courts Review*, 1984, *22(2)*, 1-6.

Moore, C. Training mediators for family dispute resolution. *Mediation Quarterly*, 1983, *2*, 79-89.

National Association of Social Workers. *Code of ethics.* Washington, DC: Author, 1980.

Pearson, J., Ring, M., & Milne, A. A portrait of divorce mediation services in the public and private sector. *Conciliation Courts Review*, 1983, *21(1)*, 1-24.

Protecting confidentiality in mediation. Comment in *Harvard Law Review*, 1984, *98*, 441-459.

Reamer, F. Ethical dilemmas in social work practice. *Social Work*, 1983, *1*, 31-35.

Rosanova, M. Mediation: Professional dynamics. *Mediation Quarterly*, 1983, *1*, 63-73.

Sander, F. Family mediation: Problems and prospects. *Mediation Quarterly*, 1983, *2*, 3-12.

Saposnek, D. *Mediating child custody disputes.* San Francisco: Jossey-Bass, 1983.

Saposnek, D. What is fair in child custody mediation? *Mediation Quarterly*, 1985, *8*, 9-18.

Schneider, D. A commentary on the activity of writing codes of ethics. *Mediation Quarterly*, 1985, *8*, 83-97.

Tarasoff v. Regents of the University of California, 131 Cal. Rptr. 14, (1976).

Van Hoose, W., & Kottler, J. *Ethical and legal issues in counseling and psychotherapy* (2nd ed.). San Francisco: Jossey-Bass, 1985.

Weaver, J. Therapeutic implications of divorce mediation. *Mediation Quarterly*, 1986, *12*, 75-90.

20

Standards of Practice for Divorce Mediators

THOMAS A. BISHOP
Private Practice, New London, Connecticut

Standards of practice serve as a basis for the formulation of client expectations and the evaluation of professional performance. They help clarify the goals of a service, enhance quality, and assure the integrity of the process. The emergence of a new area of practice provides an opportunity to shape standards from scratch and, in the process, develop expected norms for those launching an uncharted profession. The author has been central to the creation of divorce mediation standards, having chaired or served on the committees drafting standards for the American Bar Association; the Academy of Family Mediators, and the Association of Family and Conciliation Courts. Not surprisingly, the standards developed by those organizations are very similar. Here the author explains the standards and the rationale for them. The standards themselves are reproduced as appendices at the end of this chapter.

THE DRAFTING OF STANDARDS

In the spring of 1982, I and Lois Gold were assigned as members of the Board of Directors of the Academy of Family Mediators to develop proposals for membership standards as well as standards of practice for Academy members. Ms. Gold took primary responsibility for developing membership standards; I prepared an initial draft of practice standards. That early draft of practice standards was presented in May 1982 at a meeting of the American Bar Association's (ABA's) Committee on Alternate Means of Dispute Resolution in Washington, D.C. In June 1982, the same proposed standards were adopted as a working draft by the Mediation and Arbitration Committee of the ABA's Family Law Section, then chaired by Jay Folberg. Following a debate on the general topic of divorce mediation in January 1983, the Family Law Section created a mediation task force, chaired by Leonard Loeb. Numerous concerns motivated the creation of the task force.

1. With apparent growing popular interest in divorce mediation, family lawyers felt, from a policy viewpoint, that the parameters of divorce mediation should be more carefully described, so that both its practitioners and its users would have a better understanding of its purpose and scope.

2. Family Law Section members were interested in the relationship between divorce mediation and the law, the question of the state's interest in the ingredients of privately ordered divorce agreements, and whether community norms for fairness in divorce should have any relevance to decision making in divorce mediation.

3. Flowing from the question of the relationship between private decision making and community norms were a number of questions involving the roles of lawyers and nonlawyers in the divorce mediation process. In the first instance, the task force members were concerned with whether the activity of divorce mediation constituted the practice of law for the mediator. If so, there was the further question of whether this should be permissible activity for a lawyer. Reciprocally, if divorce mediation was believed to constitute the practice of law, there was the issue of whether its practice by nonlawyers constituted the unauthorized practice of law.

While the task force did not publish explicit conclusions on each of its concerns, the document that resulted from its proceedings reflects a belief that divorce mediation has emerged in both a legal and a social context. One of the principal aims of the task force was to develop standards that would emphasize the right of the participants to fashion their own agreements but that would also encourage the mediator to make the participants aware that there are community standards for fairness as reflected in the statutory and decisional law of the various states. While the task force did not conclude that the practice of mediation constitutes legal practice, the relationship between law, fairness, and the mediation process is treated in the standards formulated. During the winter and spring of 1983, the task force members revised the working draft and developed a document, *Standards of Practice for Divorce Mediators.* This document was adopted in principle by the Family Law Section of the ABA at its annual meeting in August 1983 and returned to the task force for further development and refinement. The task force met in the winter and spring of 1984 to review and further refine its draft document. In this effort, the task force collaborated with the Special Committee on Alternate Dispute Resolution of the ABA. In August 1984, the document, as revised from the previous year, was adopted by the House of Delegates of the ABA. The ABA standards are reprinted in Appendix 20-1.

While this activity of standard development was taking place within the ABA, another organization, the Association of Family and Conciliation Courts (AFCC), was working on a parallel track. The AFCC is an international organization of judges, lawyers, and mental health professionals both in and out of the court system, all of whom share a common interest in a rational and efficient judicial process for divorcing couples. The AFCC, through its Mediation Committee, chaired by Ann Milne, sponsored three symposia on the topic of divorce mediation practice and standards. The initial meeting was conducted in San Diego in December 1982. To this meeting were invited delegates from several organizations, including the American Psychological Association, the American Association of Marriage and Family Therapists, the Family Mediation Association, the Academy of Family Mediators, the American Arbitration Association, the ABA, the American Academy of Matrimonial Lawyers, and several state and regional mediation organizations whose members were working on standards. Additionally, there were a number of participants from universities with an interest in curriculum development for mediation. At the San Diego meeting the participants developed a list of concerns for the emerging practice of divorce and family mediation, including ethical issues regarding the client, mediator qualifications, the practice of mediation, and the relationship between mediation and the community.

During May 1983, the second AFCC-sponsored symposium was held in Toronto, Ontario. As a result of that meeting, a tentative report was prepared that encompassed mediation practice, the suggested educational background, continuing education appropriate for divorce mediators, and the relationship between mediators, mediation, and other professionals and processes. The third and last symposium was conducted in Denver, Colorado, in May 1984. Those attending the Denver meeting discussed and debated a working draft which dealt with the areas of concern developed at the earlier symposia. At the conclusion of the Denver meeting, the symposium delegates approved a draft document, *Model Standards of Practice for Divorce and Family Mediators*, and agreed to recommend the adoption or ratification of this document in the councils of the various organizations they represented. The AFCC standards follow this chapter as Appendix 20-2.

During August 1984 the National Institute for Dispute Resolution held a working session in Washington, D.C., to discuss the status of standards in divorce mediation. Representatives from the ABA Family Law Section task force and from the AFCC Mediation Committee participated with other leaders in the divorce mediation field in a discussion of the status and the appropriateness of standards in this area. The participants reviewed the ABA- and the AFCC-sponsored standards and concurred, in general, that although they were different in tone, emphasis, and scope, the documents were complementary to one another and parallel with respect to the mediator behaviors they posed as ethically significant. Additionally, the participants concurred that the preparation and dissemination of standards represented a worthwhile effort in the growth of mediation as an activity for practitioners as well as a dispute-resolution option for divorcing couples.

THE RATIONALE FOR STANDARDS

The development of practice standards accepted by the national organizations whose members comprise most of the family and divorce mediators may be seen as an indication that mediation as a practice and as a profession is maturing. Some argue that standards represent a premature and inappropriate formalization of the process, a restriction that might stifle creative development and experimentation with the process of mediation. Those who support the standard-making effort believe that development of standards benefits the public by making the purpose and scope of mediation more clearly known. Similarly, it is argued, the dissemination and acceptance of standards should meet the desire of mediators for mediation to take hold as an accepted and discrete decision-making process for divorcing couples.

The essential purpose of standards in this field should be educational. Whether to adopt any standards as formal rules of behavior remains a decision for mediator organizations, for state and local bar associations, for rule makers, and for legislators. The standards developed by the ABA and by the AFCC symposia merely express the thinking of those who participated in these drafting processes. To the extent that these standards may contain infirmities, those deficiencies will be brought to public and professional attention by critics in the professional and popular literature as well as in the councils of those organizations that are asked to adopt the standards.

The formation and publication of standards is a continuing activity. The ABA and other national organizations that are in the process of adopting standards generally agree that the language of their standards may be amended over time, as experience and research findings lend more wisdom to current beliefs. At this juncture, the dissemination of standards should meet a public need. Mediation is in the public eye; it is a novelty that enjoys favorable media attention. Divorce and family mediation have come to the fore amidst public criticism of the traditional adversary process of divorce; many people believe that the courts are neither capable of nor suitable for the resolution of family disputes. These factors tend to inflate mediation and to create the illusion that it is more of a solution than it really is. There is an attendant risk that couples may turn to mediation with unrealistic expectations and that they may be harmed because the process is not what they expect it to be.

The publication of standards should assist potential mediation participants to have a better understanding of the purpose of the process and its characteristics, before they commit themselves to participate. The language of the standards is intended to assist the public in understanding that mediation is neither easy nor inexpensive. Read by potential mediation consumers, the standards are, in a sense, a label for the practice. A reading of the standards permits would-be participants to make a preliminary assessment of whether the process makes sense for them.

The existence of standards also aids in the institutionalization of family and divorce mediation as a discrete decision-making process. If mediation has characteristics that are commonly known and accepted by its practitioners, the public acceptance of the process should be enhanced. For example, for those who may be initially concerned that mediation is antilawyer, or anti-justice system, the standards make it clear that the process of mediation is not a substitute for the benefit of the advice of separate legal counsel, but that the process should be used in conjunction with a clear understanding of one's legal rights and obligations. Similarly, the standards propose that divorcing couples should reach agreement only after acquiring and understanding sufficient information to make decisions, and that information includes an understanding of one's legal entitlements as well as other kinds of necessary information.

The mediator must understand that the ultimate responsibility for decision making rests with the disputants. That is why, for example, the standards impose an ethical responsibility on the mediator to be impartial and to make sure that the participants have all the information they need as well as an understanding of it. The standards suggest that the mediator should take certain actions and refrain from others, so that the participants may come to the fore in their decision making. It is said that in mediation the mediator is an advocate for the process. The mediator's duty is to avoid intervention except when it may become necessary to protect the process. For participants as well as their mediators, these may be new ground rules.

Unlike the justice system in which the process is controlled by rules and statutes created by third parties, in mediation the course of decision making, as well as specific terms of any alternate agreements, must be mutually decided. In the interplay between community standards for fairness and the value system of the divorcing couple, it is, in the main, the latter which primarily guides the decision-making process. If the existence of community rules of fairness for outcomes in divorce may be viewed as paternalistic, then the mediation process should be seen as liberating. This is the idea of empowerment. Dissemination of the standards is intended, in part, to bring to the attention of would-be participants that they are less protected in mediation and more exposed to the result of their own decision making than they would be in the more traditional divorce process.

PROFESSIONALIZATION AND ACCESS

Even though standards developed on a national level have no direct impact on local practice, there are some who claim that the practice of divorce and family mediation is too unformed to attempt a definition necessary for the promulgation of standards. These critics believe that the promulgation of standards will unnecessarily restrict the growth of mediation. There is also concern that the implementation of standards may result in the professionalization of mediation practice and that professionalization may restrict access. On one hand, it is argued that since divorce mediation involves decisions that relate not only to the law but also to child development, asset valuation, taxation, and all the subject matters that normally are encompassed in the divorce process, those who offer mediation should have a knowledge not only of conflict resolution, but also of all the substantive subject areas that are involved in divorce. To be able to conduct divorce mediation, it is felt that the mediator must have certain fundamental skills and knowledge not generally acquired by the community-based mediator. On the other hand, mediation is intended to be a process controlled by the disputants. In the jargon of the profession, it is intended to be an "empowering" process. But can it really be so if the mediator is merely another professional imposed on the couple to lead them through the divorce-process thicket?

For those who support standards that require both formal education and training as preparation to mediate divorces, it must be understood that divorce mediation should not be promoted as a process that enhances the access of lower- and middle-income individuals to the justice system. The issue of access to the process is not met by limiting the numbers of those who may provide mediation services. Therefore, in supporting the development of mediation, policy makers need to understand the limitations as well as the benefits that result from the promulgation and implementation of standards.

However, access to the process and participation in the process are issues with a different value base. The adoption of standards that suggest that a mediator have certain educational qualifications may limit access to the mediation process. Without public funding and *pro bono* services, this limitation may cause divorce mediation to be beyond the reach of the economically disadvantaged. This is a serious social concern, which should be viewed in the broader context of access to the justice system. While the adoption of a standard that suggests prior and continuing education for the mediator may limit the field of mediators, the purpose for such a requirement is to enhance the possibility that mediators will have the skills necessary to facilitate self-determination by the participants.

It may seem ironic that a standard that limits the availability of mediation services is intended to enhance the use of the process by its participants. For social planners, this is a dilemma that calls for creative solutions. Perhaps those who have helped shape the community dispute-resolution centers have information and experience that might guide good thinking in this area.

For those who are promoting the development of private mediator organizations with membership standards, this should also be a concern. The Academy of Family Mediators has adopted membership standards which one must meet to join the academy. While there are different membership categories, in general the membership standards require that an applicant have a college-level degree, a certain base of experience in his or her chosen profession, specific training in a number of divorce mediator skill areas, and participation in some form of continuing education. While these standards directly pertain to membership in only one organization, they are educational: they reflect the belief of at least one major mediator organization that there may be certain minimal educational and experiential qualifications appropriate to the title of divorce mediator.

While it is instructive for private organizations to publish their own threshold requirements, no mediator is compelled to join any organization. Certainly no private organization is endowed with the authority to certify publicly the competence of divorce mediators. As professional organizations develop, publicize, and enforce membership standards to the extent that they are consistent with one another, those qualifications may become the norms. Though expressed as standards for organizational membership, the preparation and training they require may become generally accepted standards for mediator qualifications. In the absence of state legislative action, the public may be served by the publication of organizational membership standards. Knowledge of these yardsticks may enable the potential mediation participants to evaluate would-be mediators.

One must weigh the benefit of even informally accepted qualification standards for mediators against the resulting implication that those without such education or experience may not be qualified to mediate. The area shoemaker may be the locale's best intermediary because of his intuitive good sense and personal character, but he probably won't have the standard educational or training qualifications. Unless private mediation is to be exclusively a service for the upper income population, consideration must be given to either subsidized services for people less economically well-off or to the training of mediators who may not have the requisite educational background. If mediation serves a public need, it should be accessible to all the public. Safe but innovative programs should be developed to encourage the delivery of mediation services to lower-income families.

SUBSTANCE OF THE STANDARDS

The following discussion is not intended to be an analysis of any particular standard but is rather a general discussion of the areas that are encompassed in both the ABA and the AFCC symposia standards. With respect to the practice standards, the general areas of concern may be divided into two categories:

1. What activity between the couple and the mediator should take place before the couple and the mediator begin the process of mediation?
2. What are the ethical behaviors of the mediator during the process itself?

Preliminary Information Sharing

The standards suggest that there must be some information sharing prior to the beginning of mediation. The general purpose of sharing information is for the mediator to be sure that the couple understand what they are about to do. Because the process is relatively new and not well defined, the mediator may have a heightened responsibility to the couple to make sure they understand what mediation is and what the mediation experience will require of them. The mediator should also be certain that the couple understand the limitations of mediation and what it is not intended to be. This standard reflects a concern for the couple who may choose mediation but in reality wish marriage counseling or therapy. Sharing such information clarifies expectations and makes sure there is a common purpose established before the process commences.

A second reason for sharing information prior to actually beginning the process is to enable the mediator to assess the appropriateness of the couple for mediation. This relates to cognitive as well as emotional factors. Do the parties have a shared perception of their status? Although it may be that in practically every divorce one spouse wants the marriage to end more than the other does, it is generally thought that for mediation to work there must at least be a mutual perception by the couple that the marriage is over and a shared view of the specific task at hand. Additionally, it is felt that there must be an acceptance by the couple of the reality of the situation.

This standard also suggests that the mediator should assess the cognitive ability of the couple to deal with one another. This relates to their fund of information. Is their knowledge so disparate that balanced bargaining would be impossible or unlikely? How have they argued with one another in their marriage? The mediator, at this initial stage, should also be involved in self-assessment. Implied in this consideration is a suggestion that the mediator ask himself or herself if he or she can deal with the couple on the issues they present, whether the mediator has biases that might lead to inappropriate interventions in the couple's decision making, whether the mediator is qualified by education and experience to deal with the subject matters of the dispute, and whether the mediator by personality or inclination wishes to deal with the individuals and their issues.

It is suggested, therefore, as standard practice, that there be an initial orientation session that serves the dual purpose of assessment and information sharing. These purposes are interrelated. As the mediator and the couple share information with one another, they are engaged in an assessment of whether or not to proceed.

The standards also suggest that there is certain specific information that should be shared at the orientation session.

1. In defining the process of mediation, it should be delineated from other processes of conflict resolution.

2. Mediation should be distinguished from marriage counseling and from therapy.

3. The cost of mediation should be discussed as well as the manner of payment and the relative payment obligation of the husband and the wife.

4. The responsibility for the flow of the process should be discussed, and in this conversation the mediator should acknowledge that the couple, and not the mediator, carry both the burden and the right to conduct their own negotiations.

5. The process should be discussed by the couple and the mediator, and agreements should be reached with respect to the quantity and character of information that will be shared, whether or not it would be appropriate for the mediator to work with either the husband or the wife alone or with any third parties, and the right of anyone to quit the process at any time, including the reasons for which it would be fair for the mediator to terminate or suspend the process.

In addition to suggesting that there be a dialogue to cover specific topics, the standards suggest some criteria that are appropriate concerning the areas to be covered. With respect to fees for mediation, the standards suggest that there should be no rewards to the mediator for a successful mediation agreement. Therefore, contingency-fee arrangements which might reward the mediator only if an agreement is reached would be viewed as inappropriate. Since the couple, not the mediator, take the full responsibility for their negotiation, they should be entitled to foreseeability with respect to their fees, regardless of the mediation outcome. Most of the drafters believed that an hourly rate would be the most appropriate method to charge for mediation services.

Third-Party Roles

Other parties may have a role in mediation; the standards suggest that the mediator and the couple need to develop an understanding with respect to the appropriateness of the mediator's communications with therapists, relatives, children, and attorneys. While the standards do not suggest that there should be any fixed rule with respect to third parties and mediation, they do require that the mediator reach an agreement with the couple in this area of outside communication. In arriving at this agreement, the mediator must be guided by a duty to remain impartial. Similarly, none of the standards restrict the right of the mediator to caucus with either the husband or the wife alone. But while there is no absolute prohibition, the standards suggest that in deciding whether or not to caucus separately, the mediator must view the question in a context of impartiality and fairness as well as power balancing.

The standards deal with the relationship between mediation and the law and, in that context, the relationship between the couple and lawyers. In both documents, the standards reflect the belief that law does have relevance to mediation and that the participants to mediation should understand their legal rights and jeopardies. Neither the ABA or the AFCC symposia standard suggests that only lawyers should mediate, but both impose the duty on the mediator to recommend that the participants obtain separate legal advice and counsel during the bargaining process of mediation. Additionally, the standards suggest that if the mediator is a lawyer by training, the lawyer–mediator should understand that his or her role in mediation is to mediate, and that the mediator who is a lawyer should not permit himself or herself to become a substitute lawyer for the couple in their divorce process.

Confidentiality

The standards suggest that among the areas that should be covered in the orientation session is confidentiality. Most people are attracted to mediation for its quality of privacy. It is the belief of most mediating couples that they are entitled to determine the ingredients of their agreement without public note. They generally wish to avoid a public airing of their private woes. It is natural then, that the mediator should promise to keep secret what is said in the mediation sessions and to ask the husbands and the wives similarly to keep private what is said to one another during the process.

The standards make it clear, however, that having asked for a commitment of confidentiality and having made that promise, the mediator has the duty to inform the couple that these commitments may be based upon unenforceable trust and not supported by a court order. The husband and the wife should each understand that their promise not to use in court what they learn in mediation may not be binding upon them. Similarly, the couple should understand that the agreement they make not to require the mediator to testify in court may not be enforceable if either of them decides to renege and to seek testimony from the mediator in court. This protection of the mediator is not intended to be primarily for the mediator's benefit. In order to promote the integrity of the mediation process, it is desirable to obtain a commitment from the couple that neither will attempt to require the mediator to testify. The mediator who may be called to court is an easy target for manipulation. If either the husband or the wife believes that he or she is speaking to a conduit, the message may be skewed. Additionally, the mediator, if seen as a conduit, will also be viewed as an authority figure. This contradicts the notion that it is the couple, not the mediator, with whom the power should rest in the mediation process.

Impartiality

The standards deal with the need of the mediator to be impartial. In this regard, impartiality implies an even state of mind, as well as impartial conduct. Additionally, it suggests the importance of the appearance of impartiality as well as impartial conduct. If either the husband or the wife perceives the mediator to be partial, the ability of the mediator to aid that couple will be compromised. The ABA standards require that the mediator who is a lawyer must not have represented one of the parties in the past, must not represent them in the divorce, and must not represent either of them in the future. Similarly, the AFCC symposia standards prohibit a therapist from serving as a mediator if he or she has provided separate therapy to either of them in the past. The therapist–mediator is also prohibited from providing separate therapy in the future.

The AFCC symposia standards suggest that the mediator who is a marriage counselor and has conducted marriage counseling for the couple may mediate with the couple if they fully understand the implications of an agreement for that counselor now to mediate, and if each of them equally desires that the marriage counselor now proceed with the mediation. This difficult area inspired considerable debate by the standard drafters. The therapist or counselor who wishes to mediate needs to proceed with extreme caution and to be aware that a role change from counselor to mediator may have significant impact on the issue of impartiality as well as empowerment. The ABA standards do not specifically address prior joint representation but imply a standard in such event, similar to that expressed for counselor–mediators in the AFCC symposia standards.

In the field of divorce mediation, there is a distinction between impartiality and neutrality. In some settings, perhaps most notably in labor negotiations, the mediator may be neutral as to outcome. So long as each side understands the terms of the agreement and adopts them, the mediator may have little interest in its ingredients. In divorce mediation, while the mediator stands in the middle between the participants, the mediator also has some commitment to reasonableness. Although recognizing that in any divorce there may be a broad range of reasonable agreements, the standards suggest that a mediator should become disassociated from an agreement with unreasonable terms. Implicitly, the mediator has a duty to promote fairness. This duty is invoked by standards that exhort the mediator to refer mediation participants to outside sources of information and assistance and that suggest the mediator should suspend any mediation that has become counterproductive.

The specific ingredients of reasonableness vary from couple to couple and from state to state. A standard requirement that the mediator promote reasonableness highlights the distinction between impartiality and neutrality and illuminates objective reasonableness as a goal of mediation. Such a requirement, however, should be read in the broad mediation context, which values the right of the couple for self-determination. Whether the mediator intervenes by suspending, by suggesting outside consultation, or by artful teaching, the mediator should understand that a standard that suggests adherence to reasonableness is not permission for the mediator to impose his or her views of what is best for the couple upon them in the mediation process. The standard that suggests adherence to reasonableness presumes an awareness that the parameters of reasonableness are broad and that substantive intervention by the mediator in this area should only be as necessary.

Most divorce mediators, and the standards that have been adopted, concur that the mediator has a duty to promote the best interests of children in the mediation process. In the interest of standard setting, this loyalty to children may be seen as an exception to the duty to be impartial. The mediator must be partial to the children. The standards state that not only should the mediator promote the children's interests, but the mediator must warn the couple at the outset that the children's needs should be protected in the process. As part of this warning, the standards suggest that the mediator must indicate that the children's needs may be in conflict with the participants' desire to make easily digestible compromises with one another. No standards can describe all the ways in which a mediator may meet this responsibility. That is a matter of mediator proficiency.

Full Disclosure of Information

The standards suggest that mediation participants should make their decisions based upon full and complete disclosure of relevant information to one another and an understanding of that information. This involves considerably more than legal information. It encompasses all of the financial and factual information each must have in order to make reasoned decisions. The supporters of mediation claim that mediation agreements are durable. Once the agreement is reached, it tends to become the basis for a divorce judgment. There is some indication from research that mediation agreements are more long lasting than litigated ones. Those couples who successfully mediate are less likely to seek alterations in their agreements through subsequent litigation. If an agreement is to be durable, the couple who make it must be attached to it. They are more committed to it. The bias of those who drafted the standards is that this durability is enhanced if mediation agreements are made following the objective evaluation of relevant data. What feels good today may not be adequate tomorrow. It is not enough that mediation be a process in which the participants voluntarily reach consensus; it is the reflected belief of the standard drafters that it is essential to the mediation process for the concurrence of its participants to flow from an intelligent analysis and assimilation of information. Therefore, the standards require the mediator to inform the participants from the outset that they must be candid with one another in developing and exchanging all the information necessary for intelligent decision making.

Additionally, the standards impose a duty upon the mediator to assure that, during the process of mediation, the couple do in fact provide sufficient information to one another and that each partner understands the information before agreements are reached. The mere recitation of such a standard does not, of course, assure its fulfillment. It is relatively simple for the mediator to inform the participants that each must bring certain financial and other factual data to the process and even to suggest the evaluation of certain assets. In the absence of court sanctions, the mediator must use his or her experience to determine whether or not full disclosure has taken place. As a safety net, the standards suggest to the mediator that the process should proceed only if there has been an open exchange and a complete understanding of information.

CONCLUSION

In the last part of this chapter, certain mediator behaviors have been highlighted as suggested norms of ethical behavior. This enumeration of behaviors is not all-inclusive, and the adoption of any particular set of mediator behaviors will not guarantee an ethical process.

While the publication of standards should aid the public to assess more intelligently the appropriateness of divorce mediation, those in positions of public authority may wish to be cautious in adopting any standards as coercive rules. At this juncture, it may be a wise course to restrict legislation and rule making to the necessary and immediate while nurturing the development of the normative mediator through thoughtful articles, symposia, and exchange of information based upon the practical experience of divorce mediators.

APPENDIX 20-1: STANDARDS OF PRACTICE FOR LAWYER MEDIATORS IN FAMILY DISPUTES, AMERICAN BAR ASSOCIATION

PREAMBLE

For the purpose of these standards, family mediation is defined as a process in which a lawyer helps family members resolve their disputes in an informative and consensual manner. This process requires that the mediator be qualified by training, experience, and temperament; that the mediator be impartial; that the participants reach decisions voluntarily; that their decisions be based on sufficient factual data; and that each participant understands the information upon which decisions are reached. While family mediation may be viewed as an alternative means of conflict resolution, it is not a substitute for the benefit of independent legal advice.

I. The mediator has a duty to define and describe the process of mediation and its cost before the parties reach an agreement to mediate.

SPECIFIC CONSIDERATIONS

Before the actual mediation sessions begin, the mediator shall conduct an orientation session to give an overview of the process and to assess the appropriateness of mediation for the participants. Among the topics covered, the mediator shall discuss the following:

A. The mediator shall define the process in context so that the participants understand the differences between mediation and other means of conflict resolution available to them. In defining the process, the mediator shall also distinguish it from therapy or marriage counselling.

B. The mediator shall obtain sufficient information from the participants so they can mutually define the issues to be resolved in mediation.

C. It should be emphasized that the mediator may make suggestions for the participants to consider, such as alternative ways of resolving problems, and may draft proposals for the participants' consideration, but that all decisions are to be made voluntarily by the participants themselves, and the mediator's views are to be given no independent weight or credence.

D. The duties and responsibilities that the mediator and the participants accept in the mediation process shall be agreed upon. The mediator shall instruct the participants that either of them or the mediator has the right to suspend or terminate the process at any time.

E. The mediator shall assess the ability and willingness of the participants to mediate. The mediator has a continuing duty to assess his or her own ability and willingness to undertake mediation with the particular participants and the issues to be mediated. The mediator shall not continue and shall terminate the process, if in his or her judgment, one of the parties is not able or willing to participate in good faith.

F. The mediator shall explain the fees for mediation. It is inappropriate for a mediator to charge a contingency fee or to base the fee on the outcome of the mediation process.

G. The mediator shall inform the participants of the need to employ independent legal counsel for advice throughout the mediation process. The mediator shall inform the participants that the mediator cannot represent either or both of them in a marital dissolution or in any legal action.

H. The mediator shall discuss the issue of separate sessions. The mediator shall reach an understanding with the participants as to whether and under what circumstances the mediator may meet alone with either of them or with any third party. *Commentary:* The mediator cannot act as lawyer for either party or for them jointly and should make that clear to both parties.

I. It should be brought to the participants' attention that emotions play a part in the decision-making process. The mediator shall attempt to elicit from each of the participants a confirmation that each understands the connection between one's own emotions and the bargaining process.

II. The mediator shall not voluntarily disclose information obtained through the mediation process without the prior consent of both participants.

SPECIFIC CONSIDERATIONS

A. At the outset of mediation, the parties should agree in writing not to require the mediator to disclose to any third party any statements made in the course of mediation. The mediator shall inform the participants that the mediator will not voluntarily disclose to any third party any of the information obtained through the mediation process, unless such disclosure is required by law, without the prior consent of the participants. The mediator also shall inform the parties of the limitations of confidentiality such as statutory or judicially mandated reporting.

B. If subpoenaed or otherwise noticed to testify, the mediator shall inform the participants immediately so as to afford them an opportunity to quash the process.

C. The mediator shall inform the participants of the mediator's inability to bind third parties to an agreement not to disclose information furnished during the mediation in the absence of any absolute privilege.

III. The mediator has a duty to be impartial.

SPECIFIC CONSIDERATIONS

A. The mediator shall not represent either party during or after the mediation process in any legal matters. In the event the mediator has represented one of the parties beforehand, the mediator shall not undertake the mediation.

B. The mediator shall disclose to the participants any biases or strong views relating to the issues to be mediated, both in the orientation session, and also before these issues are discussed in mediation.

C. The mediator must be impartial as between the mediation participants. The mediator's task is to facilitate the ability of the participants to negotiate their own agreement, while raising questions as to the fairness, equity and feasibility of proposed options for settlement.

D. The mediator has a duty to ensure that the participants consider fully the best interests of the children, that they understand the consequences of any decision they reach concerning the children. The mediator also has a duty to assist parents to examine the separate and individual needs of their children and to consider those needs apart from their own desires for any particular parenting formula. If the mediator believes that any proposed agreement of the parents does not protect the best interests of the children, the mediator has a duty to inform them of this belief and its basis.

E. The mediator shall not communicate with either party alone or with any third party to discuss mediation issues without the prior consent of the mediation participants. The mediator shall obtain an agreement from the participants during the orientation session as to whether and under what circumstances the mediator may speak directly and separately with each of their lawyers during the mediation process.

IV. The mediator has a duty to assure that the mediation participants make decisions based upon sufficient information and knowledge.

SPECIFIC CONSIDERATIONS

A. The mediator shall assure that there is full financial disclosure, evaluation and development of relevant factual information in the mediation process, such as each would reasonably receive in the discovery process, or that the parties have sufficient information to intelligently waive the right to such disclosure.

B. In addition to requiring this disclosure, evaluation and development of information, the mediator shall promote the equal understanding of such information before any agreement is reached. This consideration may require the mediator to recommend that either or both obtain expert consultation in the event that it appears that additional knowledge or understanding is necessary for balanced negotiations.

C. The mediator may define the legal issues, but shall not direct the decision of the mediation participants based upon the mediator's interpretation of the law as applied to the facts of the situation. The mediator shall endeavor to assure that the participants have a sufficient understanding of appropriate statutory and case law as well as local judicial tradition, before reaching an agreement by recommending to the participants that they obtain independent legal representation during the process.

V. The mediator has a duty to suspend or terminate mediation whenever continuation of the process would harm one or more of the participants.

SPECIFIC CONSIDERATIONS

A. If the mediator believes that the participants are unable or unwilling to meaningfully participate in the process or that reasonable agreement is unlikely, the mediator may suspend or terminate mediation and should encourage the parties to seek appropriate professional help. The mediator shall recognize that the decisions are to be made by the parties on the basis of adequate information. The mediator shall not, however, participate in a process that the mediator believes will result in harm to a participant.

B. The mediator shall assure that each person has had the opportunity to understand fully the implications and ramifications of all options available.

C. The mediator has a duty to assure a balanced dialogue and must attempt to diffuse any manipulative or intimidating negotiation techniques utilized by either of the participants.

D. If the mediator has suspended or terminated the process, the mediator should suggest that the participants obtain additional professional services as may be appropriate.

VI. The mediator has a continuing duty to advise each of the mediation participants to obtain legal review prior to reaching any agreement.

SPECIFIC CONSIDERATIONS

A. Each of the mediation participants should have independent legal counsel before reaching final agreement. At the beginning of the mediation process, the mediator should inform the participants that each should employ independent legal counsel for advice at the beginning of the process and that the independent legal counsel should be utilized throughout the process and before the participants have reached any accord to which they have made an emotional commitment. In order to promote the integrity of the process, the mediator shall not refer either of the participants to any particular lawyers. When an attorney referral is requested, the parties should be referred to a Bar Association list if available. In the absence of such a list, the mediator may only provide a list of qualified family law attorneys in the community.

B. The mediator shall inform the participants that the mediator cannot represent either or both of them in a marital dissolution.

C. The mediator shall obtain an agreement from the husband and the wife that each lawyer, upon request, shall be entitled to review all the factual documentation provided by the participants in the mediation process.

D. Any memo of understanding or proposed agreement which is prepared in the mediation process should be separately reviewed by independent counsel for each participant before it is signed. While a mediator cannot insist that each participant have separate counsel, they should be discouraged from signing any agreement which has not been so reviewed. If the participants, or either of them, choose to proceed without independent counsel, the mediator shall warn them of any risk involved in not being represented, including where appropriate, the possibility that the agreement they submit to a court may be rejected as unreasonable in light of both parties' legal rights or may not be binding on them.

APPENDIX 20-2: MODEL STANDARDS OF PRACTICE FOR FAMILY AND DIVORCE MEDIATION, ASSOCIATION OF FAMILY AND CONCILIATION COURTS

PREAMBLE

Mediation is a family-centered conflict resolution process in which an impartial third party assists the participants to negotiate a consensual and informed settlement. In mediation, whether private or public, decision-making authority rests with the parties. The role of the mediator includes reducing the obstacles to communication, maximizing the exploration of alternatives, and addressing the needs of those it is agreed are involved or affected.

Mediation is based on principles of problem solving which focus on the needs and interests of the participants, fairness, privacy, self-determination, and the best interests of all family members.

These standards are intended to assist and guide public and private, voluntary and mandatory mediation. It is understood that the manner of implementation and mediator adherence to these standards may be influenced by local law or court rule.

I. INITIATING THE PROCESS

A. Definition and Description of Mediation

The mediator shall define mediation and describe the differences and similarities between mediation and other procedures for dispute resolution. In defining the process, the mediator shall delineate it from therapy, counseling, custody evaluation, arbitration, and advocacy.

B. Identification of Issues

The mediator shall elicit sufficient information from the participants so that they can mutually define and agree on the issues to be resolved in mediation.

C. *Appropriateness of Mediation*

The mediator shall help the participants evaluate the benefits, risks, and costs of mediation and the alternatives available to them.

D. *Mediator's Duty of Disclosure*

1. BIASES

The mediator shall disclose to the participants any biases or strong views relating to the issues to be mediated.

2. TRAINING AND EXPERIENCE

The mediator's education, training, and experience to mediate the issues should be accurately described to the participants.

E. *Procedures*

The mediator shall reach an understanding with the participants regarding the procedures to be followed in mediation. This includes but is not limited to the practice as to separate meetings between a participant and the mediator, confidentiality, use of legal services, the involvement of additional parties, and conditions under which mediation may be terminated.

F. *Mutual Duties and Responsibilities*

The mediator and the participants shall agree upon the duties and responsibilities that each is accepting in the mediation process. This may be a written or verbal agreement.

II. *IMPARTIALITY AND NEUTRALITY*

A. *Impartiality*

The mediator is obligated to maintain impartiality toward all participants. Impartiality means freedom from favoritism or bias either in word or action. Impartiality implies a commitment to aid all participants, as opposed to a single individual, in reaching a mutually satisfactory agreement. Impartiality means that a mediator will not play an adversarial role.

The mediator has a responsibility to maintain impartiality while raising questions for the parties to consider as to the fairness, equity, and feasibility of proposed options for settlement.

B. *Neutrality*

Neutrality refers to the relationship that the mediator has with the disputing parties. If the mediator feels or any one of the participants states that the mediator's background or personal experiences would prejudice the mediator's performance, the mediator should withdraw from mediation unless all agree to proceed.

1. PRIOR RELATIONSHIP
A mediator's actual or perceived impartiality may be compromised by social or professional relationships with one of the participants at any point in time. The mediator shall not proceed if previous legal or counseling services have been provided to one of the participants. If such services have been provided to both participants, mediation shall not proceed unless the prior relationship has been discussed, the role of the mediator made distinct from the earlier relationship and the participants have been given the opportunity to freely choose to proceed.

2. RELATIONSHIP TO PARTICIPANTS
The mediator should be aware that post-mediation professional or social relationships may compromise the mediator's continued availability as a neutral third party.

3. CONFLICTS OF INTEREST
A mediator should disclose any circumstance to the participants which might cause a conflict of interest.

III. *COSTS AND FEES*

A. *Explanation of Fees*

The mediator shall explain the fees to be charged for mediation and any related costs and shall agree with the participants on how the fees will be shared and the manner of payment.

B. *Reasonable*

When setting fees, the mediator shall ensure they are explicit, fair, reasonable, and commensurate with the service to be performed. Unearned fees should be promptly returned to the clients.

C. *Contingent Fees*

It is inappropriate for a mediator to charge contingent fees or to base fees on the outcome of mediation.

D. Referrals and Commissions

No commissions, rebates, or similar forms of remuneration shall be given or received for referral of clients for mediation services.

IV. CONFIDENTIALITY AND EXCHANGE OF INFORMATION

A. Confidentiality

Confidentiality relates to the full and open disclosure necessary for the mediation process. A mediator shall foster the confidentiality of the process.

1. LIMITS OF CONFIDENTIALITY
   The mediator shall inform the parties at the initial meeting of limitations on confidentiality such as statutorily or judicially mandated reporting.

2. APPEARING IN COURT
   The mediator shall inform the parties of circumstances under which mediators may be compelled to testify in court.

3. CONSEQUENCES OF DISCLOSURE OF FACTS BETWEEN PARTIES
   The mediator shall discuss with the participants the potential consequences of their disclosure of facts to each other during the mediation process.

B. Release of Information

1. The mediator shall obtain the consent of the participants prior to releasing information to others.
2. The mediator shall maintain confidentiality and render anonymous all identifying information when materials are used for research or training purposes.

C. Caucus

The mediator shall discuss policy regarding confidentiality for individual caucuses. In the event that a mediator, upon the consent of the participants, speaks privately with any person not represented in mediation, including children, the mediator shall define how information received will be used.

D. Storage and Disposal of Records

The mediator shall maintain confidentiality in the storage and disposal of records.

V. FULL DISCLOSURE

The mediator shall require that there is disclosure of all relevant information in the mediation process as would reasonably occur in the judicial discovery process.

VI. SELF-DETERMINATION

A. Responsibilities of the Participants and the Mediator

The primary responsibility for the resolution of a dispute rests with the participants. The mediator's obligation is to assist the disputants in reaching an informed and voluntary settlement. At no time shall a mediator coerce a participant into agreement or make a substantive decision for any participant.

B. Responsibility to Third Parties

The mediator has a responsibility to promote the participants' consideration of the interests of children and other persons affected by the agreement. The mediator also has a duty to assist parents to examine, apart from their own desires, the separate and individual needs of such people. The participants shall be encouraged to seek outside professional consultation when appropriate or when they are otherwise unable to agree on the needs of any individual affected by the agreement.

VII. PROFESSIONAL ADVICE

A. Independent Advice and Information

The mediator shall encourage and assist the participants to obtain independent expert information and advice when such information is needed to reach an informed agreement or to protect the rights of a participant.

B. *Providing Information*

A mediator shall give information only in those areas where qualified by training or experience.

C. *Independent Legal Counsel*

When the mediation may affect legal rights or obligations, the mediator shall advise the participants to seek independent legal counsel prior to resolving the issues and in conjunction with formalizing an agreement.

VIII. *PARTIES' ABILITY TO NEGOTIATE*

The mediator shall assure that each participant has had an opportunity to understand the implications and ramifications of available options. In the event a participant needs either additional information or assistance in order for the negotiations to proceed in a fair and orderly manner or for an agreement to be reached, the mediator shall refer the individual to appropriate resources.

A. *Procedural*

The mediator has a duty to assure balanced negotiations and should not permit manipulative or intimidating negotiation techniques.

B. *Psychological*

The mediator shall explore whether the participants are capable of participating in informed negotiations. The mediator may postpone mediation and refer the parties to appropriate resources if necessary.

IX. *CONCLUDING MEDIATION*

A. *With Agreement*

1. FULL AGREEMENT
The mediator shall discuss with the participants the process for formalization and implementation of the agreement.

2. PARTIAL AGREEMENT

When the participants reach a partial agreement, the mediator shall discuss with them procedures available to resolve the remaining issues.

B. *Without Agreement*

1. TERMINATION BY PARTICIPANTS

The mediator shall inform the participants of their right to withdraw from mediation at any time and for any reason.

2. TERMINATION BY MEDIATOR

If the mediator believes that participants are unable or unwilling to meaningfully participate in the process or that a reasonable agreement is unlikely, the mediator may suspend or terminate mediation and should encourage the parties to seek appropriate professional help.

3. IMPASSE

If the participants reach a final impasse, the mediator should not prolong unproductive discussions that would result in emotional and monetary costs to the participants.

X. *TRAINING AND EDUCATION*

A. *Training*

A mediator shall acquire substantive knowledge and procedural skill in the specialized area of practice. This may include but is not limited to family and human development, family law, divorce procedures, family finances, community resources, the mediation process, and professional ethics.

B. *Continuing Education*

A mediator shall participate in continuing education and be personally responsible for ongoing professional growth. A mediator is encouraged to join with other mediators and members of related professions to promote mutual professional development.

XI. *ADVERTISING*

A mediator shall make only accurate statements about the mediation process, its costs and benefits, and about the mediator's qualifications.

XII. RELATIONSHIPS WITH OTHER PROFESSIONALS

A. The Responsibility of the Mediator Toward Other Mediators

1. RELATIONSHIP WITH OTHER MEDIATORS
    A mediator should not mediate any dispute which is being mediated by another mediator without first endeavoring to consult with the person or persons conducting such mediation.

2. CO-MEDIATION
    In those situations where more than one mediator is participating in a particular case, each mediator has a responsibility to keep the others informed of developments essential to a cooperative effort.

B. Relationship with Other Professionals

A mediator should respect the complementary relationship between mediation and legal, mental health, and other social services and should promote cooperation with other professionals.

XIII. ADVANCEMENT OF MEDIATION

A. Mediation Service

A mediator is encouraged to provide some mediation service in the community for nominal or no fee.

B. Promotion of Mediation

A mediator shall promote the advancement of mediation by encouraging and participating in research, publishing, or other forms of professional and public education.

PART SIX

DIVORCE MEDIATION
RESEARCH AND ANALYSIS

21

Divorce Mediation Research Results

JESSICA PEARSON
NANCY THOENNES
Center for Policy Research, Denver, Colorado

Does the use of mediation to resolve divorce disputes make a difference? What percentage of disputants reach an agreement? How do parties feel about the mediation process and the agreements they have reached? Does mediation save time and money and ease the workload of our justice system? Do children benefit from mediated agreements? Reliable answers to these questions can only be found through careful research and analysis. This chapter reviews the findings of two major research projects and discusses the data as they relate to some of these important questions. The chapter concludes with a summary of the areas requiring further empirical study and the questions that must still be addressed in shaping mediation policy.

During the past 10 years, we have conducted two major research projects dealing with the mediation of divorce disputes, particularly those involving contested child custody and visitation. One study, the Denver Custody Mediation Project (CMP), employed a quasi-experimental design in which comparable cases involving contested child custody were assigned to mediation and control-group categories on a random basis, although ultimate participation in mediation was voluntary. The second study, the Divorce Mediation Research Project (DMRP), involved user surveys, observations, interviews, and an analysis of mediation tapes generated at public mediation programs at the Los Angeles Conciliation Court, the Family Relations Division of the Connecticut Superior Court, and the Domestic Relations Division of the Hennepin County Family Court; surveys with divorcing parties who were litigating custody-visitation; and surveys of another group not contesting the issues in one state where court-based mediation was not available.

In both studies, mediation clients and their nonmediating counterparts were interviewed either face-to-face or by telephone at three time points.

In the CMP (1979–1981), we conducted interviews with approximately 470 mediation clients, individuals who rejected the mediation offer, and control-group respondents on three occasions: upon identification by the court as involving contested child custody and visitation; after the promulgation of final orders; and approximately 6 months after the second contact. We also reviewed court files for respondents in all three groups approximately 17 months after the promulgation of final orders, in order to gather reliable information on relitigation and punitive legal activity.

In the DMRP (1981–1983), we identified a sample of 530 clients who used the courts' mediation services and administered a questionnaire prior to the initiation of mediation and again approximately 15 weeks after our first contact. A third questionnaire was administered to all respondents approximately 13–15 months after the initial interview. To gain a picture of the more lasting effects of mediation we conducted interviews with a sample of individuals at each site who litigated or mediated child custody approximately 5 years earlier, in 1978 or 1979. Finally, to compare the experiences of divorcing litigants who utilize mediation services with those who have no access to public sector mediation, as well as those who divorce without disputing custody or visitation, we developed a sample of contesting and noncontesting couples in Colorado and administered questionnaires to them at the same time points used at the mediation research sites.

The CMP and the DMRP offer a relatively reliable assessment of the effectiveness of mediation in achieving a broad range of goals. This chapter reviews our major findings to date. Specifically, we discuss the major research questions we have posed and the answers we have generated. Our review concludes with a discussion of questions that remain to be answered and the future research strategies that might be most promising to pursue.

MAJOR RESEARCH QUESTIONS

Many goals have been posited for mediation by its proponents. For some, the objective is simply to reduce court congestion and costs. Others stress goals such as increasing access to justice, improving perceptions of fairness, and enhancing client satisfaction with the process and outcome of dissolution proceedings. Still others emphasize the potential benefits mediation holds for children, as a result of improved parental communication, reduced hostility, and continued contact with both parents. Finally, proponents contend that mediation is more effective than adversarial interventions in generating appropriate resolutions and improving compliance and reducing relitigation. (See Pearson, 1982, and McEwen & Maiman, 1982, for a more general comparison of the effectiveness of mediation and adjudication.)

In this chapter we explore, within the constraints of the data generated in the CMP and the DMRP, a variety of key questions about divorce mediation patterns, outcomes, and impact. Specifically, we consider the characteristics of litigants who opt to mediate custody and visitation issues as compared with those who adjudicate; the format and duration of the mediation process; dispute outcomes and the extent with which cases are successfully resolved in mediation; the types of disputes and disputants associated with successful mediation interventions; user reactions to mediation and the adversarial process, including sources of satisfaction and dissatisfaction; the reactions of men and women to the mediation intervention and areas of systematic differences; the impact of mediation and adversarial interventions on children; the effect of mediation on compliance and relitigation patterns; and the savings in time and money.

SUMMARY OF RESEARCH FINDINGS

The Use of Mediation Services by Divorcing Couples

With few exceptions, the divorce mediation programs with the highest participation rates are compulsory services housed in courts. Mediation in California's courts exemplify this fact. Custody–visitation mediation is mandated by statute in all cases of contested child custody and visitation in California (McIsaac, 1981). In 1982, the Conciliation Court of Los Angeles handled 4,458 custody and visitation mediations. Voluntary mediation programs, however, typically fail to attract a substantial number of participants. Of the disputants in the CMP offered free mediation services to resolve contested child-custody and visitation matters, fully half rejected the offer (Pearson & Thoennes, 1982b). A 1981 survey of divorce mediation services in the public and private sector revealed that 93% of the private mediation services conducted fewer than 50 mediations and 51.3% handled fewer than 10 cases (Pearson, Ring, & Milne, 1983). Since mediation outcomes have been shown to track with the experience level of the mediator (Kochan & Jick, 1978; Pearson, Thoennes, & VanderKooi, 1982), these participation patterns are of concern.

An analysis of the characteristics of individuals who agree to mediate custody issues indicates that, compared with their rejecting counterparts, mediation candidates tend to score higher on traditional socioeconomic indicators and exhibit better spousal communication patterns. Women who prefer mediation view it as less remote and impersonal than the court system; men choose to mediate largely because they perceive their chances of winning in the adversarial process to be relatively low. In addition, men who are ambivalent about the divorce or interested in reconciliation are also eager to try mediation. Lastly, men and women choose to mediate because their attorneys encourage them to try. While 69% of the mediating men and 72% of the mediating women said their lawyers encouraged them to try, only 32% of the rejecting men and 18% of the rejecting women had attorneys who were perceived as enthusiastic about mediation (Pearson, Thoennes, & VanderKooi, 1982).

These findings suggest that low participation is tied to the attitudes of the legal community and public ignorance about the mediation alternative. As long as mediation remains an alien concept to the general population, it may be attractive only to better educated and higher income individuals who traditionally adopt innovations and new technologies. To the extent that the legal community is ambivalent about mediation, disputants may be reluctant to try, and program use will remain low.

Does compulsory mediation affect outcomes or reactions by users? While some argue that compulsory mediation contradicts the emphasis placed on voluntariness in mediation ideology (Danzig, 1973), there is little evidence that it produces harmful effects. For example, the concept of mandatory mediation of custody and visitation disputes enjoys strong public support. In our sample 60%–70% of respondents who used court-based mediation services in Los Angeles, Minnesota, and Connecticut in 1978/1979 favored this approach. Among those who reached agreements in mediation in 1982, the proportion favoring a mandatory attempt stood at 85%–91%. And even 62%–68% of those who failed to produce a mediation agreement would "definitely" or "probably" favor a mandatory attempt.

   Nor does voluntariness appear to be a key to a successful mediation outcome. Comparable proportions of users of mediation services in a mandatory program in California (41%) and voluntary ones in Connecticut (35%) and Minneapolis (41%) report reaching a final agreement in mediation. Comparable numbers also indicate that they definitely would recommend mediation to a friend (64% in California, 43% in Connecticut, 53% in Minneapolis) and are very glad that they tried mediation (59% in California, 42% in Connecticut, 54% in Minneapolis). Lastly, roughly comparable proportions of respondents in California (23%), Connecticut (20%) and Minnesota (12%) agree with the statement, "The mediator pressured me or my (ex-) spouse into an agreement." Thus, a mandated attempt to mediate does not necessarily affect the participatory nature of the mediation process, the voluntariness of mediated outcomes, or satisfaction with the process. Methods of implementing divorce mediation services in the public sector, including basis of legal authority, structure, and substantive provisions, are chronicled in an article by Comeaux (1983). The analysis reveals a wide range of mechanisms for program creation, including statutes, court rules, and administrative orders, as well as procedures for program funding, organization, and implementation.

The Mediation Process

The mediation process varies in scope and duration in the public and private sectors. As a rule, cases are mediated more rapidly in the public sector and involve fewer sessions. For example, a 1981 survey of public and private sector services offering divorce mediation revealed that the average case in the private sector takes 8.7 hours. About half the cases require 9 hours or more. In the public sector, the average case requires 6.3 hours and nearly half are handled in 4 hours or less. Cases in the private sector require an average of 6.2 sessions of mediation, with 66% lasting 5 sessions or more. In the public sector, cases require 3.4 sessions, with one third completed in 1 or 2 sessions (Pearson, Ring, & Milne, 1983).

   Public and private services also differ in the scope of the issues mediated, with most private sector programs mediating all child and financial issues of divorce and most public programs concentrating on custody and visitation mediation. There are exceptions to this rule, such as the Family Court of Delaware, which requires the mediation of child-support petitions including arrears and modifications (Delaware Family Court, 1983). At all three court programs we explored, the scope of mediation was restricted to custody and visitation issues, with only 4%–6% of the respondents reporting that they resolved financial issues in mediation. More typically, mediation clients resolve spousal and child-support issues in court and divide marital property on their own.

In addition to these distinctions between the public and private sector, we find differences in the scope and format of mediation at individual courts. For example, there is some variation in the average amount of time devoted to a case at each court site in the DMRP. In Minnesota, the process takes an average of 3.3 sessions and 4.3 hours. Viewed somewhat differently, only 21% of the respondents in Minnesota report attending only a single mediation session, and only 15% say their mediation lasted 1 hour or less. At the Los Angeles Conciliation Court, cases average 1.7 sessions and 3.0 hours; 57% of the respondents report attending only a single session. In Connecticut, the average number of mediation sessions is 1.5, and 65% of the respondents report attending only one session. The average number of hours per case stands at 2.3. Although all of the courts officially permit a larger number of hours and/or sessions to be expended per case, cases are usually terminated, with or without a resolution, before the upper limit is reached.

The mediation sites also differ with respect to the participation of children and attorneys. While 75% of the Los Angeles respondents report that their lawyers were seen by the mediators, this is noted by only 16% of the Minneapolis and 11% of the Connecticut respondents. Children are most likely to have been seen by mediators in Minneapolis (66%) and were seen in only 28% and 15% of the Los Angeles and Connecticut cases. In addition, mediations in Connecticut are routinely conducted by teams comprised of a male and a female, while in California and Minnesota sessions are most commonly conducted by single mediators of either sex. And in Connecticut and Minneapolis mediation sessions are scheduled in advance using an appointment system, while in California families typically move directly to mediation from a preliminary court appearance.

Despite differences in format and duration, there are few differences in agreement rates for court mediation programs. Approximately 40% of disputants who use court-based mediation services in Los Angeles, Minneapolis, and Connecticut reach full agreements on custody and visitation, and another 20%–30% report reaching partial or temporary agreements (Pearson & Thoennes, 1984b).

Of course, most civil and criminal complaints end in dismissal, default, or negotiated settlement rather than trial (Cook, 1980; Davis, 1979; Felstiner & Williams, 1979–1980). This raises the question whether mediation is as effective as pending litigation in generating out-of-court agreements and interparty stipulations.

To address this question in the CMP, we compared the incidence of stipulation making among disputants exposed to mediation and those with comparable disputes who were randomly assigned to a control group and pursued their disagreements through the court with no opportunity for free mediation. Since half of the experimental group refused mediation, the conclusions are only generalizable to those who opt to mediate. Nevertheless, fully 60% of couples who mediated reached an agreement, and a majority of those who tried, but failed, to produce an agreement in mediation generated stipulations prior to their court hearings. By contrast, only half of the individuals in the adversarial samples stipulated before reaching court, and half relied upon judicial determinations. Viewed from another angle, over 80% of those exposed to mediation produced their own custody and visitation agreements, either during or after the process. Less than 20% turned to the court for a solution. However, almost half of those never exposed to mediation relied on the court for a decision (Pearson & Thoennes, 1982b, 1984a).

Client, Case, and Mediator Characteristics Associated with Successful Mediations

Logically, successful mediation outcomes are a result of dispute and disputant traits as well as mediator characteristics. To date, these variables have not been examined simultaneously. One body of literature deals with mediator styles or roles (Kressel, 1971) or the principal events or stages of the mediation process (Black & Joffee, 1978). The underlying assumption is that mediator behaviors have a significant impact on the success of the session.

The second set of literature suggests that the outcome of mediation is largely dictated by preexisting characteristics of the dispute and disputants. For example, according to some researchers, suitability for mediation is tied to the degree of ambivalence about the divorce, the level of anger, and the couple's ability to communicate (Kressel, 1985). Others have discovered that the intensity of the dispute (Kochan & Jick, 1978) and the relative attractiveness of the alternatives to settling in mediation (Felstiner & Wiliams, 1979–1980) are relevant in determining the outcome of mediation.

To determine how well background factors and the mediator behavior factors are able to predict the actual outcome in mediation in the DMRP, we conducted a discriminant analysis. The analysis enabled us to predict settlements in 67% of the cases that resulted in full agreements. Of the various factors used in the analysis, the index that aided most in outcome predictions was the user's perception of the mediator's ability to facilitate communication. This was followed by measures related to

    providing clarification and insight
    evaluation of chances of success in alternative forum
    magnitude of the dispute
    duration of the dispute
    relationship with an ex-spouse
    balance of power

diffusion of anger
acceptance of the divorce
setting the stage

In a second discriminant analysis, we used the factors to predict respondents' willingness to recommend mediation. We correctly predicted (93%) willingness to recommend the process but were less successful (75%) in predicting unwillingness to recommend mediation. The following list indicates the order in which the factors contributed to predicting respondents' willingness to recommend mediation:

facilitating communication
providing clarification and insight
diffusion of anger
magnitude of the dispute
duration of the dispute
relationship with an ex-spouse
evaluation of chances of gaining custody
balance of power
acceptance of divorce
setting the stage

Thus, to the extent we are able to predict outcomes, we find the two indexes that appear to be best able to predict both settlement and willingness to recommend the process are the user's perceptions of the mediator's ability to (1) facilitate communication and (2) provide users with a better understanding of their feelings as well as those of their children and ex-spouse. This underscores the importance of open communication and insights into oneself and others and is consistent with findings reached by other researchers. For example, Hochberg and Kressel (1983) conclude that couples who were apprehensive about communicating during the divorce and whose attorneys did not adopt a counseling orientation were subsequently more dissatisfied with the divorce experience and less cooperative with one another.

The preexisting characteristics that appear to be best able to differentiate between those who settled and those who did not, and between those who would recommend the process and those who would not, are the duration of the custody dispute, the intensity of the dispute, and the quality of the relationship with the ex-spouse. Postdivorce cooperation is associated, in part, with limited differences over the terms of the divorce agreement and a cooperative orientation during the divorce process.

Our findings suggest that mediator's actions play a key role in determining the success of the process and underscore the need for mediator training and experience as much as case screening, although it is possible that the screening currently conducted by the courts has resulted in the elimination of cases least suited to mediation. While a somewhat similar multivariate analysis of preexisting and process variables conducted by Kochan and Jick (1978) resulted in the conclusion that the parties, not the mediators, are instrumental, it is relevant to note that our sample of disputants who are unfamiliar with the bargaining process differ substantially from Kochan's and Jick's sample of experienced union and management negotiators. And Kochan and Jick note that "the personal qualities and strategies of the mediator have the greatest impact on cases where the parties are somewhat less sophisticated regarding the bargaining process" (1978, p. 236).

Our results are also consistent with the analysis of audio tapes of successful and unsuccessful divorce mediations. Using tape recordings of 10 successful and 10 unsuccessful mediations, generated in the DMRP, Donohue, Diez, and Weider-Hatfield (1984) conclude that more successful mediators use more intense *structuring* and *reframing* interventions in response to attacks than unsuccessful mediators.

Finally, our results reflect the importance of behaviors that mediators themselves value most highly. Asked how they approach the process, most mediators in the CMP stress making suggestions, giving opinions, and other active roles (VanderKooi & Pearson, 1983), and an analysis of case experience and mediation outcomes in the CMP revealed that the experience level of the mediator was the key, with major improvements in outcomes for mediators (lawyers and mental health professionals) who handled six or more cases. While 30% of all cases handled by new mediators, with only one or two prior cases, resulted in agreement, the percentage of successful cases among those who had mediated 6-10 cases averaged 64%.

Types of Mediated and Adjudicated Agreements

Theory alone would lead us to predict that mediation would be more accommodative and conducive to compromise than the adversarial process. Not surprisingly, this appears to be the case. In the CMP, most couples who produce mediated agreements in custody disputes opt for joint legal custody, an arrangement rarely selected by those who are exposed only to the adversarial process. Among mediation couples who select sole custody, noncustodians receive more visitation than is commonly found in nonmediated agreements (Pearson & Thoennes, 1984a). Joint custody is also the most common arrangement reported by couples who reach agreements in mediation programs in Los Angeles and Minneapolis, but not in Connecticut (Lyon, Thoennes, Pearson, & Appleford, 1983). Thus, it appears that, although it is not uniformly the case, there is usually more give and take in custody mediation than in adjudication.

Because financial issues are not routinely mediated in public sector divorce mediation programs, it is impossible to compare reliably the financial effects of mediation and adjudication for adults and children. Based on the information we have assembled, however, we find that there are few differences in child-support arrangements among individuals exposed to mediation versus those relying on lawyer negotiations or court decree. For example, in the

CMP, respondents who reached custody agreements in mediation were somewhat more likely to have no child-support arrangement in effect—largely due to the greater incidence of joint custody. Those fathers who are to pay child support, however, tend to have agreements requiring them to pay a higher proportion of their income for child support; 34% are to pay at least one quarter of their net monthly income for child support versus 22% in the adjudication category. Joint custody and mediation fathers are also more apt to make other financial contributions to the care and upbringing of their children, including payments for medical and dental expenses, entertainment costs, and child-care expenses.

Finally, the results of the DMRP indicate considerable public support for the mediation of financial issues. Approximately 50% of respondents with custody or visitation disputes also report conflicts over child support and/or the division of marital property. When interviewed, approximately 50% of the respondents in California, Minneapolis, and Connecticut who used court mediation services several years earlier, as well as half of the sample currently mediating or litigating custody–visitation disputes said they would "definitely" or "probably" favor the mediation of financial issues. While a number of courts are currently experimenting with the mediation of child-support and property division issues (e.g.; the Family Court of Delaware) and such issues are routinely mediated in the private sector, conclusions about the advisability of financial mediation must await a more systematic evaluation.

User Satisfaction

Looking across our program evaluations, we consistently find that individuals who mediate are extremely pleased with the process, whether or not they reach an agreement. For example, in the CMP, 77% of all those interviewed expressed extreme satisfaction with mediation. No more than 40% of respondents in any of the mediation or adversarial samples reported being satisfied with the court process (Pearson & Thoennes, 1982b). In a similar vein, regardless of outcome, most respondents in the DMRP say they are glad they tried mediation, would recommend it to a friend, and believe that it should be mandatory for couples with custody disputes.

Evaluations of the legal system, however, are not nearly as favorable. Of those who had a custody investigation conducted, 40%–60% felt dissatisfied with the service and perceived it to be unfair. Between 50%–70% of the respondents at all sites also expressed general dissatisfaction with the legal system.

These percentages are fairly comparable to those reported by the National Center for State Courts (1978) in their evaluation of the public image of the courts. They note that 40%–50% of their respondents who had been to any court as a defendant, plaintiff, or witness, held an unfavorable view of their court experience.

While the reasons behind the dissatisfaction with the legal system are numerous and complex, many respondents basically seemed to object to private issues being treated in a public forum. The perceived contrast between the nature of the dispute and the nature of the legal process was evident by the number of respondents voluntarily mentioning that a court appearance seemed to suggest criminal behavior. The impersonality of the experience and the degree of control exercised by the legal actors seemed shocking to many: "It was impersonal and slipshod, all the deals were made in the halls, and there was no concern about anyone's best interest;" "I felt low and common to be there. I expected a normal, dignified experience;" "Cold, very cold. I understand that the law is in black and white and not in color . . . I knew it was going to be in black and white."

Respondents in both CMP and DMRP mention very similar factors when they praise mediation. First, 60%–90% agree that mediation helped them to focus on the needs of the children and that the child-oriented focus was beneficial. In the words of one Connecticut mother, "It made me feel more considerate towards the kids and their feelings."

A second benefit attributed to mediation by 70%–90% of the respondents at each of the sites is the opportunity to air grievances. These respondents agree with the statement, "Mediation gave me a chance to express my own point of view."

Other features of mediation endorsed by many respondents at each site include its ability to identify the real, sometimes underlying, issues in a dispute; the process is less rushed and superficial; and it affords a less tense and defensive atmosphere. As one father put it, "The mediators brought up things, . . . options regarding . . . [visitation] that I hadn't even considered. We ended up compromising. . . . I got a chance to present everything that I wanted to present. It helped us understand each other."

Satisfaction with the mediation alternative was greatest in the 1981 sample. Respondents in the 1978 sample were less uniformly complimentary. There are several possible reasons for this finding. One possibility is that, with greater distance, mediation is viewed with less enthusiasm. Conceivably those closer to the event are more impressed by the fact that they dealt rationally with an ex-spouse and felt listened to by the mediator. Second, quite possibly mediation has enjoyed more popularity and acceptance over time and has met with a more receptive client base in recent years. Certainly the profile of court clients has changed somewhat over the years, and this may have some bearing on the perceived quality of the service. Most notably the respondents from the 1981 sample, compared to the 1978 sample, were younger couples with shorter marriages and younger children.

Still a third, and compelling, possibility is that the mediation services provided by the courts have improved over time. In 1978, the programs were new. Connecticut's had been in operation less than 1 year, the Hennepin County program was about 3 years old, and in Los Angeles, the oldest conciliation court in the country, custody–visitation mediation was only 5 years old. It is possible that the quality of mediation offered by these courts improved over time. Some evidence for this explanation comes from the fact that there was a 15% increase in the number of respondents from 1978 to 1981 who expressed the belief that the mediator understood the underlying problems and issues.

User Dissatisfaction

Despite generally high levels of satisfaction, about half the respondents at each site in the DMRP agree "somewhat" or "strongly" with the statement, "The sessions were tension-filled and unpleasant" and "I felt angry during much of the session." About 45% of respondents at each location report feelings of defensiveness. Although a slightly different set of questions was used in the CMP, we do find approximately 15% of the sample agreeing that the mediator failed to control arguing or put them on the defensive. There are several possible reasons for these reactions. For example, custody and visitation disputes may be so emotionally taxing that any method of dispute resolution will necessarily be unpleasant and evoke defensive reactions. For other individuals, the sense of defensiveness may result from apprehensions about dealing with an untrustworthy but persuasive ex-spouse. As one Connecticut woman put it, "He's smart . . . he can do anything . . . I was afraid that they (the mediators) would believe him."

Still other respondents may well have felt tense, angry, and displeased as a result of faulty preconceptions about the mediation process. We do not know how prevalent misconceptions were in the CMP; however, DMRP data indicate that at each site 20%–30% of the respondents agreed with the statement, "Mediation was confusing," and in-depth interviews with respondents often revealed profound misconceptions about the goals of mediation. For example, a number of respondents were under the impression that the process was designed to save the marriage and as a result began the session feeling annoyed. Others who were interested in reconciling were upset by the fact that the mediators did not urge the partner to give the marriage another chance, and still others had the false impression that the mediators would make the final custody decision or that mediation was merely another variety of counseling.

Between a quarter and a third of the respondents in each location felt that the process was rushed and should be given more time. For some, the short duration of mediation created anger and feelings of assembly-line treatment. In the words of one respondent, "They should not take people and grind them through." However, it is not exactly clear how much time respondents feel they need. One woman anticipated weekly meetings. Another respondent who felt pressured to resolve matters had attended four sessions before mediation was terminated. Still another woman felt more time should have been devoted so there could be "more counseling, and maybe more investigations." Both are activities that are generally considered to be inappropriate in the mediation process.

Reactions of Men and Women

Although mediation receives the support of many advocates as a means to circumvent the court system, which is frequently accused of discriminating against both men and women, there is growing skepticism among feminists on the appropriate use of mediation. While the resistance is strongest in domestic abuse cases, which are the subject of numerous mediation projects based in prosecutors' offices and courts, similar arguments are made against the use of mediation in divorce, custody, and property disputes.

One chief criticism made by feminists is that mediation is most effective when both parties hold relatively equal bargaining positions. Such equality, they argue, is too often missing in cases of divorce and/or custody–visitation disputes. In such situations, many feminists feel that adversary proceedings are the best way to protect the rights of a "weaker" party and/or to punish or deter criminal conduct.

Feminists also part ways with mediation advocates regarding state intervention in family problems. While mediation enthusiasts regard the family as a private ordering system with a capacity for solving its own disputes (Mnookin & Kornhauser, 1979), feminists maintain that many family problems and divorce disputes cannot be addressed by approaches stressing communication, love, and trust and require behavior-oriented rules and sanctions to protect women. They cite research conducted by the Police Foundation, which concluded that arrest was most effective in deterring subsequent assault. In an analogous fashion, they point to research revealing that strong enforcement techniques, including the use of jail sentences, are most effective in producing compliance with child-support orders.

Finally, feminists question the viability of the mediation process because of the joint custody agreements it frequently inspires. Joint custody, it is argued, expands the rights of the parent who is not responsible for the child's day-to-day care and simply interferes with the mother's ability to make needed and timely decisions regarding the child's welfare. In cases of spouse abuse, joint custody may actually present a life-threatening situation. And rather than reducing the trauma of divorce to children, joint custody may prolong the battle between parting spouses. Indeed, mediation and joint custody are viewed by some feminists as evidence of a trend toward sex-discriminatory judicial reasoning in which mothers are losing custody of their children.

To assess whether men and women who participate in court-based divorce mediation evaluate their experiences differently, we analyzed the responses of male and female interviewees separately and compared the results. The analysis revealed many significant differences. On the positive side, women were more likely to report that mediation helped them understand their ex-spouse's point of view, focus on the children, keep the discussion on track, bring issues and problems out into the open, identify problems, and understand their own feelings. At the same time, compared with their male counterparts, women were more likely to report that in mediation their ex-spouse pressured them into an agreement, they never really felt comfortable expressing their feelings, mediation was tense and unpleasant, they felt angry during much of the session(s), and that the mediator was very directive and essentially gave them the terms of the agreement. The items that male respondents were more apt to note about the mediation experience were waiting too long to get into mediation, spending too much time in mediation on the past, feeling comfortable and relaxed, and feeling mediation was rushed. Thus, although women appreciate many positive aspects of mediation, they are clearly most apt to report unfavorable reactions, including feeling pressured by an ex-spouse.

To distinguish women who felt pressured by an ex-spouse in mediation from their unpressured counterparts, we conducted a discriminant analysis using a variety of attitudinal and background variables as possible predictors. The best predictor of a sense of pressure by one's ex-spouse was an item measuring ease of communication during the marriage. Women who said they had problems clearly and calmly expressing themselves during the marriage were likely to feel pressured. Except as they relate to this measure, other factors, such as reported level of violence of winning arguments during the marriage, did not significantly predict a sense of pressure during mediation.

Regardless of their income patterns during marriage, many women reported having problems expressing themselves during marital discussions. Indeed, the only subgroups not reporting this problem were women with graduate-school educations and/or women over the age of 45.

Do women differ from men in their postmediation ratings of the experience? Despite the mixed reactions that they report, women are not statistically different from men in their satisfaction with the division of property, the child-support arrangement, their willingness to recommend mediation, and their belief that mediation should be a mandatory intervention. Indeed, compared with men, they are more apt to express the view that mediation should be offered to resolve financial disputes.

This suggests that while the intervention is perceived by many women to involve elements of coercion and pressure by an ex-spouse, the benefits outweigh the unpleasantness and their overall assessments are favorable, not unlike those reported by men.

Compliance and Relitigation

There is mixed evidence regarding the compliance patterns associated with mediated and ajudicated agreements. A long-term follow-up interview in the CMP revealed that 79% of those clients who reached agreements in mediation reported their spouse to be in compliance with all the terms of the agreement, and this was reported by 67% of adversarial respondents. While 33% of the latter group reported that serious disagreements had arisen over the settlement, this was noted by only 6% of successful mediation clients (Pearson & Thoennes, 1982b). Once we control for preexisting factors, most notably the initial cooperation level between spouses, we see smaller differences between successful and unsuccessful clients. However, the overall patterns do persist.

In a similar vein, an analysis of compliance with child-support and visitation orders in the 1981 sample of the DMRP reveals that over a 12-month period, noncompliance was a significant problem for all dispute categories, regardless of whether or not custody was initially disputed or mediation tried. Nevertheless, the patterns do favor the mediation group. Based upon reports from those who are supposed to receive support, it appears that about a third of those who mediated or stipulated custody reported irregular or absent child-support payments, while this was the case in over half of those who litigated custody. A comparison of accounts by those who are supposed to be exercising visitation rights reveals that none of those who resolved their custody dispute in mediation report visitation to be infrequent while this is reported to be the case by 30% of noncustodians in every other dispute category.

These patterns of poorer payment and visitation in the adversarial group, however, do not hold with DMRP samples of people who mediated and adjudicated in 1978. Inerviews with the respondents who utilized mediation services 4–5 years earlier reveal few differences in compliance. Approximately 60% of all mediating and adjudicating respondents report satisfaction with custody arrangements today. The highest proportion of respondents reporting very regular visitation and child-support payment patterns are those who adjudicated custody 4–5 years ago and were never even exposed to mediation. Comparable proportions of respondents in each mediation and adjudication category report frequent disagreements over visitation (8%–13%).

There is even more debate about the capacity of mediation to reduce relitigation. In the CMP, there is evidence of lower recidivism among mediation clients. At a 2-year follow-up, only 13% of successful mediation clients had filed court modifications, as opposed to 35% of their adversarial counterparts. Moreover, successful mediation clients appear to be more confident about their ability to work out future disagreements autonomously or with the assistance of a mediator and do not intend to return to court. Disputants who do not develop mediation agreements are more likely to believe that a future disagreement or modification will necessitate litigation (Pearson & Thoennes, 1984a).

Based on reports from the 1981 sample of the DMRP at the final interview, we also observe statistically lower levels of relitigation by those who produce final arrangements in mediation versus all others. Thus, between the first and final interview, 21% of those who resolved the custody dispute in mediation had been back to court to file contempt citations, take out temporary restraining orders, or to change custody, visitation, or child support. Among those who reached no agreement in mediation, 31% had returned to court. Among the adversarial group, 36% had returned, and 13% had been back at least twice. Only 6% of those settling in mediation had returned to court that often.

Our survey of individuals who disputed custody–visitation in 1978, however, reveals that families who mediate and those who use the adversarial process are equally apt to return to court to modify. Based on self-reports, a quarter of those who reached agreements, a quarter of those who did not reach agreements in mediation, and about a quarter of the adversarial group had returned to court on custody–visitation matters within the last 4–5 years.

Given the inconsistent patterns across the different samples, it may be safest to conclude that while mediation may not always be more effective than court adjudication in preventing recidivism, it certainly does not produce a rash of relitigation activity. Mediated agreements are no less stable than those originating in lawyer negotiations or court orders. Moreover, in many respects these findings are consistent with previous research comparing mediation and adjudication in a variety of substantive settings (McEwen & Maiman, 1982; Pearson, 1982), with evidence of strong user satisfaction with the mediation process and more ambivalent patterns regarding compliance and relitigation.

Effects on Relationships with Ex-Spouses

To assess whether exposure to mediation promotes subsequent cooperative interaction between spouses, we asked respondents in the 1981 sample of the DMRP to assess whether or not mediation had made a difference in the way they interacted with their former spouse. They were also asked whether or not the involvement of judges, lawyers, and other legal actors had had an effect on patterns of interspousal interaction.

The responses suggest that, while mediation cannot produce cooperative couples, it is a less damaging intervention than court. For example, at the interview conducted 3 months following the initial contact, a small proportion (15%) of the 1981 sample credited the court system with improving their relationship with an ex-spouse. About 40% indicated that court had had a detrimental effect on the relationship, and the remainder felt it had no impact on their relationship. At this 3-month follow-up interview, mediation was credited with improving spousal relations by very few (7%) of those who produced no agreement in mediation. However, 30% of those producing an agreement felt it improved the relationship. Further, regardless of the outcome, less than 15% indicated that mediation hurt the relationship. Thus, compared to court, mediation is credited to be a less damaging intervention.

A second indicator of spousal cooperation comes from DMRP respondents' responses regarding the degree to which they were able to cooperate and get along with their ex-spouse. Between the time of the second and third interviews, the mediation groups experienced some gains in the number of respondents reporting that some cooperation was possible, while there was some decline in the proportion of the adversarial group reporting cooperation. Thus, by the time of the last interview, over 60% of those who successfully mediated and those who did not contest the divorce reported that some cooperation with an ex-spouse was possible. But only 10% of those who did not settle in mediation and 30% of the adversarial group reported cooperation to be possible.

Still another measure of the quality of the relationship with an ex-spouse is the number of problems surrounding visitation. An analysis of responses to questions about the incidence of problems with visitation reveals similar patterns for all respondents and shows no particular benefits for those in the mediation group. At each interview we asked respondents about the frequency of problems with the children's safety and well-being, the amount of time spent with an ex-spouse's family, lack of discipline and overindulgence, late return following visitation, a lack of activities during the visit, or one parent criticizing the other in the presence of the children. At the initial interview, prior to any intervention of an adversarial or nonadversarial nature, about 45%–50% of all respondents who were contesting custody–visitation reported that three or more of these issues were sometimes or often a problem. Among respondents in the noncontesting category where custody–visitation was not in dispute, only about half this many (25%) reported problems with three or more of these issues. By the final interview, the number of respondents reporting three or more problems had declined to 30%–40% for all mediation and adversarial group respondents and remained at about 25% in the noncontesting group.

There are several reasons why mediation appears to have only a modest ability to alter basic relationship patterns or promote cooperation between disputants with this sample of respondents.

First, mediation in court settings is a brief intervention, typically taking an average of 1.6 sessions and 2–3 hours. There are clearly limits to the relationship changes that would be expected to ensue from a short-term intervention; mediation is clearly not a substitute for counseling and more sustained support services.

Second, unlike mediations between nonstrangers in other civil settings, divorce mediation involves parties with lengthy, intimate, and problem-ridden histories and deeply established behavioral patterns including spousal abuse and noncommunication. Statements such as the following are typical: "We never talk. The last time I called him up was when I was having problems with my older son. The first thing he said after I explained the situation was, 'What did you do to provoke him? You provoked me for 15 years.'" In addition, future interactions between divorcing parties are likely to be more frequent and involve complex and emotion-laden issues such as child support, visitation, and child care. They are likely to afford many opportunities for noncompliance. By comparison, mediations between nonstrangers with continuing relationships, such as landlords and tenants, employers and employees, and neighbors, are simpler; the emotional and financial stakes are usually lower and the opportunities for continued contact and interaction are typically more limited.

In light of all these facts, it seems noteworthy that over the span of 12–15 months with the 1981 sample and even 4–5 years with the 1978 sample, we continue to observe differences between those who mediate and those who adjudicate. Further, like our previous research comparing who mediate and adjudicate child custody (Pearson & Thoennes, 1984a), the differences noted herein continue to hold after statistically controlling for the initial level of cooperation reported by the respondents. Thus, the differences that do exist between successful mediation clients and other respondents in our survey are not merely the result of the fact that cooperative individuals are likely both to succeed in mediation and later to cooperate and comply. Indeed, these patterns indicate that even brief mediation interventions with a troubled population have a salubrious effect that holds up over time.

Effects on Children

According to mediation proponents, the process should enhance a child's adjustment to divorce by reducing levels of parental conflict, increasing the quality of consistency of visitation, and reducing abandonment by the noncustodial parent.

Our two research projects led to two different conclusions regarding the custody–visitation arrangements produced in mediation. In the CMP, mediation definitely translated into more joint custody and visitation. While 70% of those who reached agreements in mediation opt for joint custody and 20% select traditional, mother-only custody awards, joint custody characterizes fewer than 30% of nonmediated outcomes. As to visitation, we find that plans developed in mediation allow fathers, on the average, 6.5 days per month of contact. Where parents do not resolve visitation issues in mediation, fathers have the children on the average of 5 days per month. At a subsequent follow-up interview, these visitation patterns persist.

Data from the DMRP, on the other hand, reveal few measurable differences in visitation according to the mediation and adjudication status of parents. Although parents who successfully mediate are more likely to opt for joint custody than their less successful mediation or adversarial counterparts, visitation patterns are very comparable for all clients in the DMRP at comparable time points. For example, at 3 months postmediation, visitation at each site and for all clients ranges from 6–8 days per month, with unsuccessful mediation clients in Minneapolis and Connecticut reporting even more visitation than their successful counterparts. By 12 months, approximately 60% of respondents were "fairly" or "very" satisfied with the time they spent with their children, while 40% were dissatisfied, regardless of where custody–visitation arrangements were produced.

An analysis of the reports of parents of 6- to 11-year-olds who completed the Achenbach–Edelbrock Behavior Checklist, a 112-item, three-point behavior rating scale (Achenbach & Edelbrock, 1981), revealed no statistical differences in child adjustment by mediation or adversarial category. Nevertheless, there were some encouraging patterns. Although it only approached statistical significance, children whose parents successfully mediated had the best rating on all the Achenbach scales, with the exception of the somatic complaints subscale.

In an effort to determine what factors aid or hinder child adjustment to divorce, we performed multiple regression analyses, using as dependent measures the Achenbach-Edelbrock child-behavior checklist scales, and created indexes dealing with the child's relationship with the custodial parent, acceptance of the divorce, and problems with the custody arrangement. Our independent variables were the ones typically mentioned in the literature as influential in children's adjustment. These independent variables fall into the general categories: background of the family, such as number of children; dispute/ divorce-specific factors, such as stage in the divorce; child-specific variables, including age and sex; custody–visitation variables, such as the regularity and frequency of visitation; and characteristics of the parental relationship, such as cooperation, violence during the marriage, and differences in childrearing philosophies.

Explaining the variance in the Achenbach measures proved to be exceedingly difficult. In part this was no doubt due to the small amount of variance present: all but one child rated in the lowest third of the scale prior to and following their parents' mediation and/or adjudication experiences. Predicting the variance in the indexes of adjustment and acceptance of the divorce, problems with the divorce, and quality of the relationship with the custodian was somewhat better. The adjusted r^2 ranged from 11%–23%.

Looking across the regressions, we found eight variables that made a significant contribution to at least half of the regression analyses. These variables are (1) child's age; (2) level of physical violence during the marriage; (3) parental cooperation at the final interview; (4) changes in the child's life, for example, moves, changing schools, held back a grade; (5) basic differences between parents in childrearing; (6) child's awareness of the anger between parents; (7) distance separating the child and the noncustodian; and (8) frequency of visitation at the time of the first interview. These factors clearly deal with family dynamics, child characteristics, and parent–child relationships. This suggests that these elements are more helpful in understanding children's adjustment than is the formal dispute status of the case or the parents' dispute-resolution experience, including whether the case is noncontested, adversarial, or mediated.

There are a number of reasons why mediation fails to produce consistent, measurable effects in children. First, we have not been able to precisely recreate the Achenbach-Edelbrock measures; to do so would require larger sample sizes so that subscales could be developed separately for three age groups and both sexes. In addition, 12–15 months may not be a long enough span of time in which to see differences emerge. Another possibility is that the measures are simply not sensitive to divorce adjustment patterns and that children experience indirect or "trickle down" effects that are not detected by conventional measures of adjustment. Parents who use mediation report that the sessions focus on the children and aim at educating parents about children's needs in divorce. These are not comments typically proffered about court hearings or other adversarial interventions. Nevertheless, our findings suggest that the child's adjustment is more a factor of family dynamics and overall environment than a result of having parents who do not contest custody, mediate custody, or pursue the issue through the courts.

Savings in Time and Money

Mediation procedures tend to translate into time savings for disputing parties, although savings vary with program format and outcome. In the CMP, mediation translated into time savings only if it was successful. The average number of months between the initiation of proceedings and the promulgation of final orders was lowest for successful mediation respondents, 8.5 months. In the purely adversarial samples, the average number of months between filing and final orders was between 10 and 11 months. For unsuccessful mediation respondents, however, the average was 14.2 months. Since custody mediation often requires the postponement of an investigation and the continuation of a hearing, it is not surprising that cases move faster for those who either mediate or litigate than for those who must try both (Pearson & Thoennes, 1982b).

Similarly, mediation appears to translate into savings in attorney fees, although such savings are neither consistent nor great. For example, where legal fees were incurred, successful mediation-group respondents paid $1,660, on the average, in the CMP. For unsuccessful mediation-group respondents, it was $2,010. And for the purely adversarial respondents, it was approximately $2,360.

In order for mediation to produce substantial savings, the parties must be diverted to it early in the dispute and must succeed in resolving the dispute. For example, individuals who successfully mediated before receiving a final divorce decree paid an average of $1,650 in legal fees—about $680 less than the average $2,330 paid by predecree members of the control group.

Reports from the 1978 and 1981 samples of the DMRP also suggest that mediation may produce financial savings for users. For cases involving a custody dispute in 1978, whether prior to or following the promulgation of a divorce decree, only about 20% of the respondents who successfully mediated a final agreement reported attorney fees in excess of $3,000. For the adversarial group, the percentage was approximately 45%. About 30% of those who did not produce a final agreement in mediation incurred attorney fees over $3,000. Among those contesting custody, both prior to and following the divorce decree in 1981, about 35% of those who were unsuccessful in mediation and 35% of the adversarial group had legal fees in excess of $3,000. By contrast, only 20% of those who successfully mediated final custody–visitation arrangements paid this much.

Based upon these figures, we can conclude that mediation translates into modest financial savings when it results in an agreement. Moreover, although mediation does not produce savings in attorney fees when it is unsuccessful, it does not appear to result in higher legal fees either.

Public cost savings are even more difficult to calculate for mediation programs. Because they lack large volume and perhaps attract cases that would not otherwise be adjudicated, some researchers conclude that mediation programs are more expensive than per case costs in courts. For example, an evaluation of a court-connected family counseling service that offers custody mediation to divorcing couples in Clackamas County, Oregon, concludes that the service cannot be justified on economic grounds. The average cost of providing service to divorcing couples at the Family Counseling Service comes to $307 to $338 per case; trial costs for comparable cases range from $96 to $247. Moreover, since the counseling service only handles child-related disputes, a sizeable proportion of couples must use the court to resolve money and property disputes and are consequently involved in both a court trial and mediation (Cohen, 1982).

The director of the Domestic Relations Division of Hennepin County (Minneapolis), however, finds evidence of savings while noting that any conclusions require reliance on numerous estimates. In 1982, estimated per case costs for those needing only mediation treatment was $238. Per case costs for those requiring a custody evaluation was $1,530. Cases requiring both treatments cost the county $1,645, although only 16% of 1982 cases fell into this category. According to the director, the use of mediation in 1982 rather than the automatic assignment of contested cases for an evaluation saved the country approximately $139,000 (Cauble, 1983).

Lastly, mandatory mediation programs appear to be decidedly cost effective. For example, in 1978, the Los Angeles Conciliation Court, the largest jurisdiction offering public sector mediation services, handled 747 cases with an estimated net savings to the County of Los Angeles of $175,004. The procedure was found to be so satisfactory and cost effective that it was made mandatory in 1981 with the enactment of S.B. 961. It is paid for by an earmarked increase of $15 for the divorce filing fee, $5 for the marriage license fee, and an assessment of a $15 fee for any motion to modify or enforce a custody and visitation order (McIsaac, 1981).

CONCLUSIONS

This research summary acknowledges the limitations as well as the strengths of the divorce mediation alternative. Regarding limitations, we find that, despite professional enthusiasm for divorce mediation and the rapid, recent proliferation of public and private mediation services, voluntary programs typically fail to attract large numbers of clients. Although divorce mediation is somewhat more attractive to better educated individuals, who are traditionally receptive to new ideas and technologies, the use of divorce mediation programs remains tied to the attitudes of the legal community. Individuals whose attorneys are ambivalent or opposed to mediation are very reluctant to try it. This underscores the importance of obtaining the support and cooperation of attorneys in the development and spread of the mediation alternative.

The low level of use of mediation by divorcing couples has serious consequences for courts, the general public, and the private sector mediation profession. Specifically, low usage affects the ability of such programs to be cost effective, to reduce the burden of caseload on courts, and to promote the development of a cohort of experienced mediators.

Compulsory mediation programs appear to handle a much larger volume of cases than voluntary programs and in some settings have been found to be highly cost effective and helpful to courts. In point is the adoption of a statute in California and local court rules in Reno, Nevada; Pima County, Arizona; Honolulu, Hawaii; and elsewhere, making mediation mandatory in all cases of contested child custody and visitation.

Looking beyond user participation, savings in time and money, and impact on courts, however, divorce mediation programs rate more favorably. Obviously, our research is somewhat affected by the selective, preexisting characteristics and attitudes of mediation clients, because, with the exception of data on respondents in California where mediation is mandatory, our research documents the experiences of those who voluntarily agree to mediate or those who are believed to be acceptable candidates in the eyes of the court official referring couples to mediation. Nevertheless, in controlled research settings, mediation appears to be more effective than adjudication in generating stipulation making.

Mediation clients also experience more user satisfaction than their adversarial counterparts. Disputants who successfully mediate generate compromise agreements that are perceived to be fair, equitable, and in some instances better complied with over time. Although the evidence on relitigation is mixed, with more recent samples revealing evidence of lower relitigation and enhanced compliance and older mediation and adversarial samples exhibiting no differences in compliance and relitigation, mediation certainly does not generate excessive relitigation or simply defer inevitable litigation. Similarly, while mediation cannot address the deep-rooted emotional and social causes of many divorce disputes and alter relationships between ex-spouses, it does permit a more complete airing of grievances, which is widely appreciated by litigants and is perceived to be a less damaging intervention. Although analysis to date fails to reveal that mediation has measurable effect on child adjustment, children whose parents mediate are more likely to wind up with joint custody arrangements following parental divorce, and in the CMP, such children also experience more frequent visitation.

Lastly, while a separate analysis of responses given by men and women reveals that women have more concerns about the mediation process than do men and are more apt to report feeling pressured by an ex-spouse, they are identical to men in their overall ratings regarding user satisfaction, willingness to recommend the process to others, and support for mandatory mediation.

On one hand, mediation is not a panacea for divorcing families and their children. On the other hand, it is at least as effective as adjudication; litigants are far more satisfied with the mediation procedure and rate it more favorably than they do adjudication. The research results to date definitely justify the provision of mediation services to divorcing couples and the schooling of attorneys, mental health professionals, judges, court personnel, and others who serve the divorcing population in mediation techniques. Moreover, since an analysis of disputes, disputant, and mediator factors in successful mediation outcomes underscores the importance of mediator variables, emphasis should be placed on mediator training in addition to appropriate case screening.

REMAINING RESEARCH QUESTIONS

Our research raises several policy issues that warrant additional research and attention. One such issue deals with the pros and cons of mediating the financial aspects of divorce. As we have noted, most court programs restrict mediation to the child-related issues of custody and visitation. Our research confirms that at least 50% of individuals with custody–visitation disputes also have disagreements about financial issues and that the same proportion of divorcing litigants favor the mediation of these matters. While some mediators contend that the mediation of financial issues will result in more generous financial settlements and that this will enhance the financial status of women and children following divorce, others maintain that mediation is often harmful to women, since husbands frequently possess greater financial acumen. Empirical research is clearly needed to assess and compare the quality of mediated and adjudicated financial settlements and resolve the largely hortatory debate surrounding this issue.

A second policy consideration deals with the setting, duration, and format of mediation sessions. Without a doubt, the greatest volume of divorce mediation activity occurs in public, court-based programs, some of which are compulsory, that are typically available to litigants at no charge and supported by earmarked filing and/or marriage license fees. Qualifications for court mediators vary from jurisdiction to jurisdiction, with some jurisdictions assigning mediation duties to probation officers, custody evaluators, special masters, and referees. The number of hours expended on each case also varies by jurisdiction, with cases usually terminated, with or without a resolution, well before the upper limit of permissible hours is reached and well in advance of the time typically devoted to a case in the private sector.

Naturally, these patterns raise legitimate questions about the compatibility of program efficiency and program outcome. For example, many feel that mandatory mediation contradicts the ideology of mediation and requires disputants to submit to resolution procedures that lack adequate procedural and constitutional protections. Still others maintain that programs that achieve large case volumes must devote less time to each case and that this undermines the qualitative program objectives of favorable and durable outcomes, user satisfaction, and perceptions of equity. It will take additional experimentation and evaluation to identify the ideal format for implementing mediation programs so that they are effective in attracting litigants and achieving a broad array of qualitative goals.

A third issue is public and professional education about the mediation process. Such education may promote client usage of mediation, eliminate erroneous client expectations of lengthy counseling or evaluations, and enhance satisfaction. Goal clarification may also enhance client cooperation and eliminate the resistance shown by those who come to mediation believing that they are being asked to reconcile or are being judged. Finally, professional education may reduce skepticism about mediation and encourage the view that mediation is complementary to legal interventions and not a source of competition. A future area of needed experimentation and evaluation will attempt to discern the most effective methods of public and professional education.

Finally, additional research is needed to document the differential impact of various types of mediators. Mediation is currently a nonregulated profession. With the exception of a 2-year postgraduate program just begun at Catholic University of America, mediation courses typically run about a week. Although some mediation training programs require that trainees hold an advanced degree in law and/or a behavioral science and possess a certain amount of working experience with families, other training programs are open to people of all ages and all backgrounds. Indeed, divorce mediators may be lawyers, mental health professionals, clergy, and laypersons.

In the public sector, there are few statutory and administrative provisions dealing with the qualifications of divorce mediators who work in courts. While these provisions usually call for a master's degree in family counseling, social work, or a related field and a substantial amount of working experience, this is not always the case. Some courts utilize clergy, marriage counselors, mental health professionals, or trained volunteers to perform mediation services. Others hire employees exclusively to do mediation. Still others retain employees who perform other agency duties such as probation supervision, custody investigation, and domestic relations counseling. In the private sector there are no regulations governing training or education of mediators.

There is only sparse research on the qualities and training of effective mediators working in any substantive setting. In light of this fact, there has been a reluctance to impose requirements or even to endorse guidelines in mediation training and certification. Hopefully, future research will identify the type of professional orientation, personality characteristics, and training associated with effective mediation interventions dealing with divorce disputes.

REFERENCES

Achenbach, T. M., & Edelbrock, C. S. Behavioral problems and competencies reported by parents of normal and disturbed children aged 4 through 16. *Monograph of Social Research in Child Development*, 1981, *46*, 188.

Black, M., & Joffe, W. A. Lawyer/therapist team approach to divorce. *Conciliation Courts Review*, 1978, *16*, 1–5.

Cauble, E. A., Thoennes, N., Pearson, J., & Appleford, R. A case study: Custody resolution counseling in Hennepin County, Minnesota. *Conciliation Courts Review*, 1985, *23*, 2.

Cohen, S. *The diversion study: A preliminary report.* Unpublished report of Clackamas Circuit Court, Oregon City, OR, 1982.

Comeaux, E. A guide to implementing divorce mediation in the public sector. *Conciliation Courts Review*, 1983, *21*(2), 1–25.

Cook, R. F. *Neighborhood Justice Centers field test: Final evaluation report.* Washington, DC: Institute for Social Analysis, 1980.

Danzig, R. Toward the creation of a complementary decentralized system of criminal justice. *Stanford Law Review*, 1973, *26*, 1–54.

Davis, R., Tichane, M., & Grayson, D. *Mediation and arbitration as alternatives to prosecution in felony arrest cases—An evaluation of the Brooklyn Dispute Resolution Center.* New York: Vera Institute of Justice, 1979.

Delaware Family Court. Revised Court Rule 151 (1983).

Donohue, W. A., Diez, M. E., & Weider-Hatfield, D. Skills for successful bargainers: A valence theory of competent mediation. In R. N. Bostrom (Ed.), *Competence in communication: A multi-disciplinary approach* (pp. 1–40). Beverly Hills, CA: Sage, 1984.

Felstiner, W., & Williams, L. *Community mediation in Dorchester, MA: Final report.* Los Angeles: University of Southern California, Research Institute, 1979–1980.

Hochberg, A., & Kressel, K. *Determinants of successful and unsuccessful divorce settlement negotiation.* Paper presented at the annual meeting of the American Psychological Association, August 1983.

Kochan, T., & Jick, T. The public sector mediation process: A theory and empirical examination. *Journal of Conflict Resolution.* 1978, *22*, 209–240.

Kressel, K. 1971. *Labor mediation: An exploratory survey.* Albany, NY: Association of Labor Mediation Agencies, 1971.

Kressel, K. *The process of divorce: How professionals and couples negotiate settlements.* New York: Basic Books, 1985.

Lyon, E., et al. A case study: The custody mediation services of the Family Division, Connecticut Superior Court. *Conciliation Courts Review,* December 1985, *23*, 2.

McEwen, C., & Maiman, R. *Mediation and judicial legitimacy: Achieving compliance through consent.* Paper presented at the meetings of the Law and Society Association, Toronto, 1982.

McIsaac, H. Mandatory conciliation custody/visitation matters: California's bold stroke. *Conciliation Courts Review,* 1981, *19(2)*, 73–77.

Mnookin, R., & Kornhauser, L. Bargaining in the shadow of the law: The case of divorce. *Yale Law Journal,* 1979, *88*, 950–977.

Pearson, J. An evaluation of alternatives to court adjudication. *Justice System Journal,* 1982, *73*, 420–444.

Pearson, J., Ring, M., & Milne, A. A portrait of divorce mediation services in the public and private sector. *Conciliation Courts Review,* 1983, *21(1)*, 1–34.

Pearson, J., & Thoennes, N. The mediation and adjudication of divorce disputes: Some costs and benefits. *Family Advocate,* 1982a, *4(3)*, 26–32.

Pearson, J., & Thoennes, N. Mediation of contested child custody disputes. *Colorado Lawyer,* 1982b, *11(2)*, 337–355.

Pearson, J., & Thoennes, N. Mediating and litigating custody disputes: A longitudinal evaluation. *Family Law Quarterly,* 1984a, *17*, 197–524.

Pearson, J., & Thoennes, N. A preliminary portrait of client reactions to three court mediation programs. *Mediation Quarterly,* 1984b, *3*, 21–40.

Pearson, J., Thoennes, N., & VanderKooi, L. The decision to mediate: Profiles of individuals who accept and reject the opportunity to mediate contested child custody and visitation issues. *Journal of Divorce,* 1982, *6(1)*, 112–130.

Simkin, W. E. *Mediation and the dynamics of collective bargaining.* Washington, DC: Bureau of National Affairs, 1971.

VanderKooi, L., & Pearson, J. Mediating divorce disputes: Mediator behaviors, styles and roles. *Family Relations,* 1983, *32*, 557–565.

22

Mediated and Adversarial Divorce: Initial Findings from a Longitudinal Study

JOAN B. KELLY
LYNN GIGY
SHERYL HAUSMAN
Northern California Mediation Center, Corte Madera, California

This chapter presents initial findings from a longitudinal study of divorce investigating the effectiveness of mediation as a method for reaching final divorce agreements, as compared to the more traditional two-attorney adversarial process. Three questions are addressed and answered. First, are couples who choose mediation different from those who follow the more traditional adversarial route to final divorce? Second, is comprehensive mediation more effective than the adversarial process in reducing the acute psychological distress and dysfunction experienced by many men and women during the divorce experience? Third, what factors distinguish those clients who complete the mediation process from those who terminate mediation prior to reaching agreement? Some surprising results emerge from the initial data of this important and unique research study.

Enthusiastic claims have been made on behalf of the divorce mediation process by its practitioners and supporters. In particular, mediation is thought by many to reduce hostility and stress, improve the communication and cooperation of the participants, accelerate the psychological adjustment to divorce, result in higher levels of satisfaction with the result, lead to greater compliance with the agreements after divorce, and reduce the cost and time necessary to obtain final divorce. Few research studies had addressed these claims. The major studies thus far have been two sociological investigations, conducted by Pearson and her colleagues, of the effectiveness of court-connected mediation for custody and visiting disputes. Mediation clients reported better postdivorce relationships with ex-spouses than did adversarial respondents not choosing mediation, and high levels of satisfaction with the process and result (Pearson & Thoennes, 1982, 1984a, 1984b). Mediation has been found to result in more joint legal custody agreements and a lower rate of relitigation of child-related issues

Research reported in this chapter was supported by the San Francisco Foundation. We gratefully acknowledge the ratings of mediation clients completed by Joel Shawn and Carl Zlatchin and are indebted to Carol Ramos for her insightful review of the mediators' notes.

(Pearson & Thoennes, 1984a, 1984b). Modest cost savings have been demonstrated (Bahr, 1981; Pearson & Thoennes, 1982). None of the studies measured, prior to the mediation intervention, levels of anger, conflict, communication, and cooperation to determine the impact of the intervention itself, and the Pearson studies focused on the mediation of custody and visiting disputes only, rather than on comprehensive divorce mediation encompassing all issues.

OVERVIEW OF THE STUDY

Begun in 1983, the longitudinal Divorce and Mediation Project being conducted at the Northern California Mediation Center (NCMC) has been designed to assess the effectiveness of comprehensive divorce mediation and to investigate other selected aspects of the mediated and adversarial divorce experience. The major variables of the study cluster into eight main categories: (1) demographic; (2) individual psychological (e.g., anger, depression, and stress); (3) interpersonal (spousal and ex-spousal) relationship (e.g., cooperation, conflict, communication, and view of spouse); (4) coparental relationships and parental functioning (e.g., child-specific conflict, cooperation and support, role responsibilities, abilities, and attitudes); (5) parent–child relationships (custody and visiting agreements); (6) satisfaction with process and result; (7) postdivorce compliance with all agreements; and (8) situational, legal, cost, and divorce settlement variables. These variables were selected for their relevance to the legal and psychological divorce process itself, to the adjustment and interaction of adults and children during and after divorce, to the various economic and parent–child outcomes of the divorce, and to postdivorce issues of compliance, conflict, and legal action. Divorce-specific and standardized scale data were collected from the respondents, the respondents' spouses (when available), and the mediators after specified sessions with the mediation clients.

DESIGN OF THE LONGITUDINAL STUDY

Two samples of divorcing people are studied at five points in time, beginning with entry into mediation or the adversarial process, and ending 2 years postdivorce. The overall schematic representation of the longitudinal design can be seen in Figure 22-1. At Time 1, a baseline assessment of all individuals entering the study was made, using standardized and divorce-specific questionnaires, measures, and interviews. Time 2 questionnaires are collected for the mediation respondents at the completion or termination of the mediation process. Adversarial respondents receive an abbreviated version of the Time 2 questionnaire 6 months after their initial interview. This timeframe corresponds to the average length of time needed for couples to complete the mediation process, including a signed agreement. The Time 3 data collection occurs at final divorce for all respondents. Time 3 questionnaires are sent 6

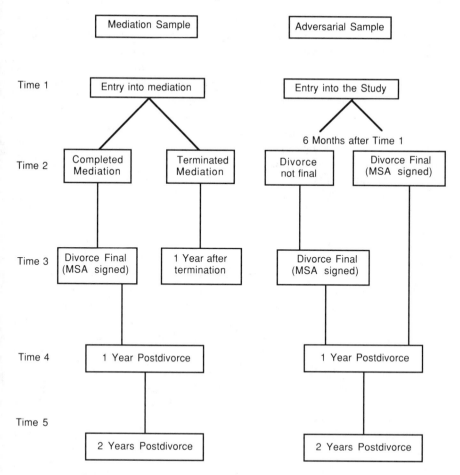

Figure 22-1. Mediated and adversarial divorce study design.

months after Time 2, or when the respondent indicates that the divorce is final.Both samples are monitored in order to obtain Time 3 data as close to final divorce as possible. Couples who terminated mediation are sent questionnaires after termination (Time 2) and again 1 year later. Time 4 and 5 data collection occurs at 1 and 2 years postdivorce for the adversarial sample and all respondents completing mediation.

THE MEDIATION INTERVENTION

The mediation intervention was a comprehensive, task-focused, problem-solving process that had the explicit goal of reaching agreement on all relevant issues to the divorce. As a model of intervention, mediation was distinguished from psychotherapy, arbitration, and lawyering. Ultimate responsibility for decision making remained with the couple. The mediator's responsibilities included identifying client interests, needs, and goals; facilitating discussion; managing conflict; structuring appropriate data collection; educating clients regarding the data and the options available; empowering clients to participate fully in the process; conducting negotiations; recording agreements; and writing a comprehensive Memorandum of Understanding. The average number of sessions required to complete a comprehensive mediation was 10, lasting on average 5–6 months from entry into mediation to approving or signing the Memorandum. The number of sessions varied depending upon the complexity of issues, amount of conflict, motivation of clients, and amount of work completed by the clients between sessions. The complexity of California family law and the precision it requires in the division of property also influenced the number of sessions.

SAMPLE SELECTION

The two subsamples were generated through different selection procedures. The mediation sample consisted of divorcing couples who came voluntarily to the Northern California Mediation Center for the comprehensive mediation of all issues pertaining to their divorce. Couples were referred by attorneys, mental health professionals, or friends or learned of the services on their own. Mediation respondents were invited to participate in the research after signing an agreement, during the course of an initial consultation, to mediate their divorce. Ninety-eight percent of clients entering mediation agreed to participate and were then given Time 1 questionnaires to be returned prior to the first regular mediation session.

Adversarial respondents were identified through Marin County records of divorce petitions filed. Those for whom addresses could be established were invited by letter to participate in the study 1 month after their divorce petition was filed. Couples who had been married less than 1 year were excluded. Because this study was intended to compare mediated divorce with two-attorney adversarial divorce, individuals filing *in pro per*, without attorney assistance, were also excluded from the sampling procedure. This may have eliminated divorcing individuals with shorter marriages, little or no property to distribute, and/or lower incomes. Respondents who agreed to participate in the study came to the Mediation Center for 1-hour interviews, completed demographic data forms, and were given Time 1 questionnaires to complete and return by mail.

SAMPLE DESCRIPTION

The Divorce and Mediation Project sample consists of 437 individuals; 212 men and women (106 couples) who chose comprehensive mediation and 225 men and women (including 47 couples) who used the two-attorney adversarial process for their divorces. The mediation clients were significantly younger than adversarial respondents (mean age of mediation men = 40.5, women = 37.8 years; mean age of adversarial men = 44.3, women = 40.7 years). The mean age of both samples was higher than that of all divorcing men and women (mean = 36.1 and 33.5 years, respectively) in the United States. Respondents in both groups had been married 12–13 years prior to separation, which again contrasts to the national mean length of marriage of 9.6 years (National Center for Health Statistics, 1985). These differences from national norms can in part be accounted for by the exclusion of individuals married less than 1 year, in the current study.

Two thirds of the mediation sample were separated at entry into mediation. Although only 28% had filed a petition for divorce, more than half had consulted an attorney at least once. This is in contrast to 92% of the adversarial respondents separated (and 100% having filed a petition with an attorney's assistance). Somewhat surprising is the finding that, of those separated, both adversarial and mediation respondents delay for a prolonged period of time (on average, 8 months) before taking some formal action to resolve their divorce.

Approximately one third of the respondents had a definite or possible interest in reconciliation, with the exception of the adversarial women, who were significantly less likely to be interested in reconciling ($\chi^2[3, N = 403] = 15.37, p < .01$). The nonmutuality of a high number of divorce decisions is true for both mediation and adversarial respondents. One third of the adversarial group had been previously married, compared to 20% of the mediation clients. Several in both groups had been married twice before. There were no differences between the two groups with respect to obtaining marital or individual psychotherapy prior to separation.

There was a significant difference between the educational level attained by the mediation and adversarial respondents: Mediation men and women were more likely to have completed college or graduate studies. As would be expected, there was also a sex difference: 74% of the men and 56% of the women had attained at least a college degree. The average income of the total sample ($37,349) was higher than the Marin County mean of $32,000. As expected, men's income (mean = $56,100, median = $44,550) was significantly higher than women's (mean = $17,800, median = $13,600). There were no overall group differences in mean income. Less than one half of the women in both samples were employed full-time, and approximately one quarter were not employed.

Mediation draws a higher number of couples with children under age 18. Eighty-three percent of the mediation respondents had children, compared with 52% of the adversarial men and women. As will be discussed later, a potential motivating factor in choosing mediation may be related to having children, but the differences may also be accounted for by the greater age of the adversarial respondents. It should be noted that clients without children, or with adult children, were not excluded from this study, because of the wish to study the effect of the mediation intervention across a broad range of couples.

DO COUPLES CHOOSING MEDIATION DIFFER FROM THOSE IN THE ADVERSARIAL GROUP?

Perspectives on the Marriages

Mediation and adversarial respondents did not differ significantly in the amount of open marital conflict reported in the last few years of the marriage. On a 5-point scale of frequency of conflict, the median for both groups was 4 (often). Over 50% of all respondents reported conflict at the two highest indicators on the scale (often and always). Thus the belief, most often advanced by the legal profession, that the people who come to mediation have "friendlier" marriages, or are the less angry, more civilized, and "easy" clients, is not the case. It should also be noted that 27% of these divorcing men and women report little or no conflict, a finding that suggests that the stereotype of the angry and conflicted marriage should be replaced by a more discriminating view of marriages that end in divorce. The amount of marital tension reported was considerably higher than open conflict in both samples. Conflict and tension were combined into a scale, Marital Conflict–Tension (Cronbach's $\alpha = .78$), and on this scale there were no group or sex differences.

Seven aspects of marital communication were measured for quality of communication on 5-point scales ranging from very poor to very well. The intent was to determine if some arenas of marital communication were more successful than others. Mediation and adversarial respondents did not significantly differ on any of these seven variables. In general, communication ranged from very poor to adequate. Of considerable interest was the finding that men and women in both groups reported the quality of communication about their children to be significantly better than any other aspect of communication measured. Men perceived the quality of communication about their children to be significantly better than women did ($t(332) = 4.23, p < .001$). A scale was created combining all seven measures, Marital Communication (Cronbach's $\alpha = .75$), which was used in subsequent analyses.

The Decision to Divorce

In light of both clinical and research observations that the spouse who initiates the decision to divorce often has different and less acute psychological reactions to divorce than the spouse without that control, several questions assessed the extent to which each spouse initiated the divorce and his or her attitudes toward the divorce. A Divorce Control scale (Cronbach's $\alpha = .86$) was created, which included the respondents' positive or negative feelings about the divorce, which spouse made the decision to divorce, and the respondent's perception of his or her spouse's feelings about the divorce. There were no group differences on this scale. However, consistent with several other studies, women were significantly more likely to have initiated the divorce, that is, were more in control of the decision to divorce ($F[1,397] = 21.11$,

$p < .001$). The men confirm that their wives had more positive feelings about the divorce. An age and sex interaction is present, however, with women less than 45 years of age significantly more likely to have initiated divorce than older women or all men. Thus, while attitudes toward divorce are negatively correlated with age for women ($r = -.15$, $p < .05$), such an association between age and Divorce Control does not appear for men.

Respondents with high Divorce Control scores reported higher levels of marital conflict and tension ($r = .24$, $p < .001$) and lower levels of depression ($r = -.36$, $p < .001$), stress ($r = -.14$, $p < .05$), and anger ($r = -.14$, $p < .05$). Thus, men and women who initiated and had positive attitudes toward the divorce were more likely to have acknowledged high levels of marital conflict and were less depressed, angry, and stressed about the divorce itself. Feeling less in control of the divorce was more likely to be associated with high anger in men ($r = -.24$, $p < .001$).

Women were generally dissatisfied with more aspects of their marriage than men, a finding consistent with their more frequent decision to end the marriage. Respondents were asked to indicate, from a checklist of 27 items, which reasons were important to them in the breakdown of the marriage and the decision to divorce. Women checked significantly more items than men ($t[410.1] = 3.53$, $p < .001$). There were no differences between the adversarial and mediation groups. A "gradual growing apart, losing sense of closeness" was checked most often, followed closely by sexual intimacy problems, and not feeling loved or appreciated by spouse.

Spousal Interactions and Assessments

In order to determine whether men and women who chose mediation differed from adversarial respondents in some critical personality and interactive ways during marriage, a number of variables were included that assessed dimensions of spousal interactions as well as spouses' perceptions of character traits in each other. We hypothesized that variables such as ability to win arguments, power, fairness, and honesty might differentiate mediation and adversarial respondents.

Mediation and adversarial respondents did not differ in ability to argue for their position during marriage, but women perceived themselves as less able in this regard ($F[1,404] = 17.58$, $p < .001$). However, in rating who more often *won* arguments, there was no significant difference with over 80% of both the men and women reporting that things were resolved in their favor only half the time or less. Even though women were more likely to report that their spouses took advantage of them ($F[1,399] = 40.65$, $p < .001$), they did not perceive their spouses as particularly powerful, and women were no less confident of reaching a fair settlement in their divorces than the men in both the mediation and adversarial groups.

Group differences emerged on several of the measures of personality or character traits. Mediation respondents held a view of their spouses as being somewhat more powerful than did the adversarial respondents

($F(1,403) = 6.93, p < .01$), but the mediation respondents were less likely to report that their spouses took advantage of them during the marriage ($F(1,399) = 4.12, p < .05$). However, mediation respondents rated their spouses as more honest than did the adversarial men and women ($F[1,401] = 20.90, p < .001$). Further, they perceived their spouses to be more fair ($F[1,403] = 5.45, p < .02$) and flexible ($F[1,402] = 9.34, p < .01$) than did adversarial men and women, who were more likely to see their spouses as rigid and/or unfair. Despite these group differences, mediation and adversarial respondents did not differ significantly in their ratings of their spouses' ability to compromise. These latter three variables combined to create a reliable scale, Fair-Mindedness (Cronbach's $\alpha = .83$), on which mediation respondents scored significantly higher ($F[1,402] = 8.12, p < .01$). There was no significant sex difference on this scale. These findings suggest a view of the spouse as having greater integrity and some greater potential for negotiating a satisfactory result for each spouse in the mediation. Conversely, the view of the adversarial spouse as having less integrity and ability to negotiate fair agreements might lead the adversarial group to feel they would be better off with attorneys in charge of their divorce process.

Respondents rated their general level of cooperation with their spouses at entry into the study. Mediation and adversarial respondents did not differ in self-ratings of cooperation, nor were there sex differences. Looking at the sample as a whole, 26% reported that cooperation was nonexistent or very difficult, while at the other end of the scale, an equal number viewed their current cooperation as "quite good."

Coparental Relationships and Functioning

Parent–child information was obtained from a total of 179 families, consisting of 284 adults with 317 children under the age of 18. The mediation subsample with children consisted of 172 respondents (86 couples) with a total of 158 children. The adversarial subsample consisted of 113 respondents (49 men and 64 women) with a total of 159 children. These families averaged 1.8 children per family, with the children well distributed across all age groups. There were no differences between the adults with and without children in household income or education.

As reported earlier, 83% of the mediation respondents had children, compared to 52% of the adversarial respondents. The adversarial respondents are consistent with the national statistic that 54% of divorcing couples have children (National Center for Health Statistics, 1983). Why is mediation drawing significantly more couples with children under 18? For the majority of men and women with children under 18, the desire to work out custody and visitation arrangements was not the *primary* or even the *secondary* reason or motivation indicated for entering mediation. However, approximately one-half of the men and women did cite custody and visitation arrangements as *one* of several reasons for entering mediation. There was a low but significant correlation between coming for custody reasons and the desire to reduce hostility (r[155] = .29, $p < .01$) as well as the desire to improve communication with their spouse (r[155] = .17, $p < .02$). Thus it appears that divorcing couples with children came into mediation in search of a more amicable forum to resolve their disputes, because they recognized a need for a continued long-term partnership in their parental functioning and roles. Mediation may have been viewed by these individuals as a less hostile process than litigation, a process that would allow for the continuation of shared parenting responsibilities and perhaps some longer-term cooperation, despite the termination of the marital relationship.

Temporary custody arrangements were often already in place at the time of entry into the study for both the mediation and adversarial groups. Maternal custody was predominant, followed by a smaller percentage of joint custody arrangements. In the mediation group, 29% of the families had a still unsettled or fluid situation, which became an early focus of the mediation, as compared to 6% of the adversarial sample.

The adversarial group was significantly more likely to require court involvement in resolving initial and more permanent custody and visiting decisions. Twenty-four percent of the men and women in the adversarial group already had some contact with the courts, either through mandatory court mediation or a settlement conference with the judge, compared to 6% of the mediation sample. Before mediation was mandated, it was estimated that 10%–15% of the divorcing population with children took their dispute regarding the children to the courts. In California, however, the meaning of court involvement has changed dramatically since the institution of mandatory court mediation in 1981. This mandate requires that when a divorcing party indicates on their divorce petition or subsequent filing a dispute regarding custody or visitation, they must initiate contact with court mediation services within several days. With a mandatory mediation system in place, it appears that a higher percentage of families may be using the court system, particularly at the level of the court-connected mediation intervention.

Parental Communication

Mediation and adversarial respondents did not differ in the quality or adequacy of child-related communications prior to divorce. As described earlier, child-focused communications in the marriage were reported by all respondents to be significantly better than communications in other marital arenas. Approximately two thirds of the women reported adequate or good child-oriented communication with their husbands, and approximately four fifths of the men reported similarly acceptable levels of communication. When better levels of communication between spouses about their children were reported, men and women also reported the presence of significantly less conflict about their children during the marriage (r[262] = −.49, $p < .001$). Further, they were more likely to expect that they could cooperate about the children (r[258] = .30, $p < .001$). Not surprisingly, parents who rated their parental communication more highly also perceived each other to be more capable as parents (r[262] = .54, p < .001) and more highly involved in the child's life prior to separation (r[256] = .46, p < .001).

Parental Conflict

For both mediation and adversarial respondents, the frequency of child-specific conflict during the marriage was quite low and there was no group difference. Of considerable interest is the finding that all respondents reported significantly more general marital conflict than conflict focused on the children during the marriage (t[262] = 9.50, p < .001). With the exception of the adversarial women, only 12% of the respondents reported a high frequency of conflict around their children during the marriage. Twenty-seven percent of the women in the adversarial group reported high levels of conflict. The frequency of child-specific conflict is not associated with the amount of time a parent wants to have the child live with him or her after the divorce. It is, however, significantly related to the view of the other spouse's parenting ability (r[263] = −.29, p < .001). That is, when there are low levels of child conflict in the marriage, spouses feel more positive about each other's parenting ability.

Parental Cooperation

Even though mediation and adversarial groups did not significantly differ in their parental communications or the frequency of child-related conflict, adversarial respondents did perceive themselves as being less able to cooperate regarding the children after the divorce (F[1,258] = 26.35, p < .001). Further, adversarial respondents were much less likely to have spoken with each other about how they were going to continue their respective parenting roles after the divorce (F[1,261] = 12.34, p < .001). This absence of communication about postdivorce parenting was associated with anticipated poor parental cooperation after divorce (r[259] = .37, p < .001). Nearly one quarter of the adversarial parents anticipated very minimal cooperation about the children, whereas only 5% of the mediation parents anticipated poor cooperation. Parents perceived that they could cooperate significantly better about their children as compared to their adult-to-adult or overall interspousal level of cooperation (t[257] = 6.25, p < .001). This difference parallels the findings regarding communication and conflict. Thus, while it is commonly believed that parents are unable to cooperate about their children if they are divorcing, a clear majority of the respondents in both groups expected at least some, if not high levels of, parental cooperation postdivorce.

The findings that parents communicate and cooperate better and have less conflict regarding the children than in other marital areas suggests that the majority of divorcing couples can separate their observations about the parental function in the marriage from their attitudes towards their spouse and marital relationship. This implies that, although not initially easy, a restructured parental relationship in the face of the termination of the marital relationship is indeed possible. This is an important concept in helping divorcing couples work towards resolution of custody and visitation disputes at the time of divorce. Certainly mediation provides a forum for discussing and working toward the postdivorce parental partnership; that forum is not generally available in the adversarial process.

INITIAL (TIME 1) PSYCHOLOGICAL REACTIONS TO DIVORCE

Various measures and scales were used to assess the respondents' psychological reactions to the divorce at Time 1 and thereafter. One standardized inventory used, the SCL-90 (Derogatis, 1977), is a 90-item, self-report, psychological symptom inventory, designed to be a measure of current psychological status and to be repeated over time. The SCL-90 yields nine symptom dimensions, such as hostility, depression, anxiety, paranoia, and somaticism, and a global index of symptomatic distress. Alpha and test–retest reliabilities are high. Divorce-specific measures of anger, depression, guilt, stress, and anxiety about the future were developed for the Divorce and Mediation Project as well.

Overall, on the SCL-90 the divorcing men and women in this study scored significantly *higher* than the adult nonpatient normative sample for the scale on all nine subscales as well as on the general symptom index. They also scored significantly *lower* than psychiatric outpatient norms. They were, in a sense, at midpoint between the two groups, providing confirmation that divorce creates a heightened level of psychological distress and symptomotology.

Anger

General hostility was measured by the SCL-90 Hostility subscale, and more specific anger at one's spouse was measured on an NCMC 5-point scale. The correlation between these two measures was .32 at Time 1, $p < .001$, suggesting that the NCMC measure was valid and measuring some overlapping psychological response, but also tapping into some psychological reaction that may be specific to divorce. Adversarial respondents were neither more hostile on the SCL-90 nor more angry at their spouses than mediation men and women. The common assumption that clients seeking mediation are a less angry group was not supported in this study. Women, however, were significantly more angry than men at their spouses ($F[1,399] = 13.47$, $p < .001$) regardless of group. Twenty-eight percent of the total sample reported very high or extreme levels of anger at their spouse, 30% moderate anger, and 40% only mild or no anger. High levels of anger were associated with the perception that one's spouse was also very angry, suggesting that there may be a certain circularity or reciprocity in angry feelings after separation in addition to whatever angers were engendered by the marriage. Anger was also highly correlated with depression about the divorce (whole sample, $(r = .36$, $p < .001$) and with the amount of stress that the respondent reported experiencing ($r = .46$, $p < .001$). As might be expected, angry respondents more often reported poor cooperation ($r = -.45$, $p < .001$) higher marital conflict/tension ($r = .21$, $p < .001$) and they rated their spouses lower on the Fair-Mindedness scale (whole sample, $r = -.40$, $p < .001$).

Depression, Stress, and Guilt

SCL-90 scores on the Depression subscale were highly correlated with the NCMC measure of depression engendered by the divorce ($r = .61$, $p < .001$). On the divorce-specific measure of depression, 69% of all men and women reported they were experiencing moderate to very high levels of depression. Depression and stress were highly correlated ($r = .63$, $p < .001$), and 80% reported similar high levels of stress. Stress also affects the cooperation between couples, with the more stressed respondents reporting lower levels of cooperation ($r = -.31$, $p < .001$). Guilt about the marriage ending was also found to be significantly linked to depression or sadness engendered by the divorce ($r = .46$, $p < .001$).

Of considerable interest was the finding that mediation respondents reported significantly higher levels of depression ($F[1,402] = 7.00$, $p < .01$), stress ($F[1,401] = 10.06$, $p < .01$), and guilt ($F[1,402] = 10.21$, $p < .001$) than adversarial respondents. They also perceived their spouses as more depressed ($F[1,400] = 9.43$, $p < .01$) and stressed ($F[1,398] = 15.10$, $p < .001$) than did the adversarial respondents. It would appear that these men and women, who we described earlier as viewing their spouses as having more integrity or at least as possessing some redeeming character features, may pay a higher price for their divorce. Their greater depression and stress may reflect their inability to be totally rejecting and hostile toward their spouses, even though they are committed to divorce. Guilt and depression engendered by the divorce, and a greater sensitivity to their spouses' feelings, may in fact lead such men and women to choose mediation as a more humane way of divorcing, a process that also allows them to retain some respect for each other. Further, in the face of reported high levels of depression and stress, mediation respondents may seek mediation because it is perceived as a more protective environment, less likely to intensify or exacerbate feelings than the adversarial process.

PSYCHOLOGICAL DISTRESS AT TIME 2 AND THE EFFECTIVENESS OF MEDIATION

In order to determine whether the mediation intervention was more effective in reducing psychological dysfunction or distress, when contrasted to a comparable period within the adversarial proceeding, repeated measures analyses (MANOVA) were conducted using the Time 1 and Time 2 scores on the SCL-90 and NCMC psychological measures. For the mediation sample, the Time 2 scores reported include, except where noted, only those respondents who completed the mediation, so that the effect of the intervention can be assessed.

On the SCL-90, mediation and adversarial respondents' scores decreased between Time 1 and Time 2 in the direction of fewer symptoms on each of the nine subscales. The change was significant on eight of the nine subscales: Depression, Hostility, Anxiety, Somatization, Obsessive-compulsive, Phobic Anxiety, Paranoid Ideation, and Psychoticism. The MANOVA indicated that the passage of time was the important factor reducing the scores, not the intervention.

As before, the SCL-90 scores for both mediation and adversarial respondents were significantly lower than those of the SCL-90 outpatient normative sample. Although there were significant reductions in symptoms on 8 of the 9 subscales, divorce respondents remained significantly more symptomatic at Time 2 than the SCL-90 normative sample of nonpatients on all but two subscales, somaticism and phobic anxiety.

With respect to the NCMC divorce-specific psychological measures at Time 2, the amount of reported anger at one's spouse had diminished significantly ($F[1,254] = 16.61, p < .001$) for both groups by Time 2. However, this decrease can be accounted for primarily by the significant diminution in women's anger at their spouses over time ($F[2,254] = 13.40, p < .001$). There was very little change over time in the men's anger at their spouse. The mediation intervention was slightly more effective in reducing anger at spouse than the adversarial process, but not significantly so. Not only were respondents reporting less anger at their spouses at Time 2, but also they perceived that their spouses were less angry as well ($F[1,247] = 14.26, p < .001$). However, here the intervention was a factor with the mediation group perceiving a significantly larger reduction in their spouse's anger ($F[1,247] = 6.68, p < .01$). Depression, stress, and guilt also decrease significantly for each group from Time 1 to Time 2 as a result of the passage of time but not of the intervention ($p < .001$).

The mediation intervention was significantly more effective than the adversarial process in increasing cooperation between spouses. Cooperation between spouses improved in both groups as a result of the passage of time ($F[1,255] = 3.91, p < .05$) but the change was significantly greater in the mediation group ($F[1,255] = 3.86, p < .05$).

One unexpected finding is a change in how the respondents felt at Time 2 about their divorces. The initial finding that women were more positive than men about seeking the divorce continued to exist at Time 2. However, the mediation respondents reported being significantly less positive about their divorces ($F[1,253] = 19.24, p < .001$) over time. It may well be that, as a result of communicating directly and effectively enough with each other to be able to reach a series of agreements, the mediation respondents became more ambivalent about their pending divorces. It seems reasonable to speculate that the ability to resolve these issues together in a cooperative, problem-solving context may create more doubts, particularly if the mediators effectively contained the clients' conflict.

The findings of this study did not support the hypothesis that mediation is significantly more effective in reducing psychological distress and dysfunction.

The mediation intervention was not powerful enough to selectively reduce major psychological distress beyond the effects of the passage of time. This finding calls for a more detailed consideration of the variations in both mediation and adversarial clients as they begin the divorce process. A substantial number of clients, for example, enter the mediation process without much anger and have little if any anger to be reduced by the process. And while the majority of clients become less angry overall at their spouses, there are also a number who become more angry at their spouses during the process. Some angry clients reach agreements and do not experience a decrease in their anger. Thus, the expectation that mediation clients would, as a group, be universally affected by the process more beneficially than a group of adversarial respondents was a somewhat oversimplified one. Where mediation *was* found to be more effective was in the impact on the interspousal relationship. The finding that cooperation was enhanced is a more fitting outcome of a process that specifically encourages direct communication and cooperation in reaching mutually satisfactory agreements. Further, the mediation process enabled clients to observe directly the reduction in each other's anger that occurred during this period, as evidenced by the finding that mediation respondents, by Time 2, perceived greater reduction in their spouses' anger than did the adversarial respondents.

FACTORS ASSOCIATED WITH NOT REACHING AGREEMENT IN MEDIATION

Mediation may not be an appropriate alternative for as many as 60% of the couples who attempt to reach agreements through the mediation process. In his 1985 review, Kressel indicated that the range of settlement rates reported across studies is 22%–97%, with most falling between 40% and 70%. Forty-three percent of the couples who initiated mediation at NCMC terminated the process before they reached agreement on all the issues or signed a Memorandum of Understanding. It is important to understand why some people who choose mediation do not complete the process.

The following section presents data comparing the 43%, or 92, terminators at NCMC with 120 individuals who completed mediation, that is, who actually approved and/or signed a Memorandum of Understanding containing all their agreements. A note of caution is in order: the distinction between completers and terminators is not as clean as it might appear. For research purposes, we have operationally defined completion as actually reaching final divorce agreements and signing a Memorandum. This does not allow for the very real possibility that considerable work and agreement may take place among the termination group without reaching complete agreement and, conversely, for the possiblity that a couple can sign an agreement but still have disagreement in other areas (see Kelly & Gigy, in press). There is considerable overlap in the number of mediation sessions the groups participated in, with the completers ranging from 3 to 27 with an average and median of 10 sessions, and the terminators ranging from 1 to 11 sessions with an average of 4.5 and a median of 4 sessions.

Comparison of Terminators and Completers on Time 1 Variables

First, it is notable that basic demographic characteristics did not distinguish couples who terminated mediation before completing an agreement from those who successfully reached comprehensive agreements. We found no statistically significant differences between the groups in age, education, work status, length of marriage, or whether they had previous marriages.

Several studies have found couples with low income or financial strain to be poor candidates for mediation (Doyle & Caron, 1979; Kressel, Jaffee, Tuchman, Watson, & Deutsch, 1980; Pearson, Thoennes, & VanderKooi, 1982). However, in the Divorce and Mediation Project study samples, neither the mean nor the median split differences were significant for self-reported household income. To see if the terminators were disproportionately low-income families, we divided the sample into quartiles and again found no statistically significant difference between the samples. Further, there were no significant differences between the groups for individual salaries for men and women. Thus, within the income range of $20,000 to well over $100,000, a relatively lower income was not associated with failure to complete mediation.

Another distinguishing characteristic suggested in the literature (Doyle & Caron, 1979; Pearson & Thoennes, 1982) is that of having a wide range of highly disputed issues. At entry into the study, the respondents were asked to rate each of 14 areas of anticipated possible disagreement. No statistically significant difference between the groups was found in the mean number of items checked or in the average amount of anticipated disagreement. However, these data are based on *anticipated* disagreements and may not parallel the number or degree of the *actual* disagreements that emerge during the mediation process. Some of the anticipated disagreements may evaporate, and other disagreements can unexpectedly emerge with more information and disclosure.

The work of Kressel et al. (1980) suggests that couples who have a high level of conflict may be poor candidates for mediation. However, no statistically significant differences between the terminating and completing groups were found on measures of the amount of marital conflict and tension the respondent perceived to exist in the 2 years prior to separation. Further, significant differences were not found on measures of the respondents' anger toward their spouse or on their perception of their spouse's anger toward them. Thus, marital conflict and anger toward a spouse at time of entry into mediation does not seem to play a role in hindering a couple's reaching final written agreement.

It has been suggested that an ability to communicate and cooperate may be critical in reaching an agreement in mediation (Kressel et al., 1980). On a

5-point scale measuring level of cooperation with one's spouse, both groups averaged between "strained" and "some" cooperation, and there was no significant difference between them. On the Marital Communication scale, described earlier, self-perceived ability to communicate during the marriage did not influence the couple's ability to reach a mediated agreement.

Self-perceived lack of ability for self-representation, in one or both of the parties, has been seen as associated with not being able to complete mediation (Kressel et al., 1980). Again the Divorce and Mediation Project Time 1 data do not support a hypothesis suggested in the literature. No statistically significant differences between the groups were found on Time 1 measures of self-confidence in the ability for self-representation. Both groups reported equal abilities to negotiate and win in disputes, and felt similarly about whether their spouses had taken advantage of them.

Based on the experience of various mediators, it was hypothesized that psychopathology or psychiatric disturbance in one or both spouses could interfere with the mediation process and its successful completion. To address the issue of pathology, the Time 1 SCL-90 scores from both groups were compared, as were the respondents' scores on the NCMC measures of psychological adjustment. There were no statistically significant differences found between the groups for any of the nine SCL-90 factors nor for the more divorce-specific NCMC measures of anger, stress, and depression. Therefore, overall pathology does not seem to be a significant determinant of the mediation outcome. To test the possibility that it may be the presence of pathology in only *one* member of the couple that impairs the couple's ability to mediate, we compared the groups on whether at least one of the two of the parties had a score higher than one standard deviation away from the mean on any of the nine symptom factors. Again, no significant relationships between psychopathology indexes and the ability to mediate were found.

Another distinguishing characteristic suggested in the literature is that of a continuing psychic attachment (Irving, Benjamin, Bohm, & MacDonald, 1981; Kressel et al., 1980). Kressel et al. suggested that "psychic attachment" implies a high degree of nonmutuality in the divorce decision, which results in high enmeshment characterized by high conflict. As discussed earlier, no statistically significant differences between the completers and terminators were found on measures of conflict at entry into the study. To address the nonmutuality aspect of the psychic attachment hypothesis, scores of Divorce Control scale difference within terminating and completing couples were compared. There was no statistically significant difference in the disparity in control within couples from the two groups. Nonmutuality of the divorce decision was not more characteristic of the terminators than of the completers in the Divorce and Mediation Project sample.

In pursuing the attachment hypothesis, concrete evidence of current ties were investigated: whether the couple have actually separated, whether they have actually filed for divorce, and whether they report being interested in reconciliation.

As can be seen in Table 22-1, the presence of current ties or connections at entry into the study is related to terminating mediation in the Divorce and Mediation Project sample. Not being separated, not having filed for divorce, and maintaining an interest in reconciliation related to terminating mediation without reaching a signed agreement. These terminating couples may be less willing to let go of their relationship or, at the very least, clearly have taken fewer concrete steps toward divorce. If mediation is perceived of as a sure and clear path to divorce, perhaps the parties feel a need to withdraw from mediation, as a means of holding on to the marital relationship. Thus, in the Divorce and Mediation Project, it was current ties, rather than communication, cooperation, conflict, psychopathology, or the range of issues at entry into the study, which differentiated between couples who completed and terminated mediation.

Factors Distinguishing Terminators and Completers during Mediation

What reasons do the terminators themselves give for stopping mediation? What are the mediators' impressions of the sessions and the eventual outcome? Terminators were given a 21-item checklist of possible reasons for quitting mediation. Multiple responses by one individual were possible. The first of the most frequently checked reasons (39%) was "mediation is too expensive." It is interesting to note that this response was not related to income. The other most frequently checked item (37%) was that terminating was actually a unilateral decision on the part of the spouse; that is, the respondent was not the one who chose to quit.

Most of the remaining items fell into two distinct correlational clusters. The first of these was comprised of nine items reflecting feelings of being overwhelmed or lacking empowerment within the process. The items include such things as seeing the issues as too complex, a feeling of not having enough power, lacking financial knowledge, feeling emotionally drained, feeling unprotected, and feeling unable to have one's say. This Lack of Empowerment scale ($\alpha = .88$) clearly relates to the distinguishing characteristic described by

Table 22-1. Indications of Current Ties

	Terminators (%)	Completers (%)
Separated[a]	44	78
Has *not* filed for divorce[b]	80	67
Interested in reconcilation[c]		
no	58	76
some	33	15
very	9	9

[a]$\chi^2(1) = 11.09, p < .001.$ [b]$\chi^2(1) = 3.59, p < .06.$ [c]$\chi^2(1) = 8.84, p < .01.$

Kressel et al. (1980), in which one or both parties do not believe they have the resources or strengths for self-representation.

The issue of empowerment and the ability for self-representation is an important one in mediation, especially as it relates to women. Here a sex difference was found that did not appear in the Time 1 overall group findings for self-representation. There was a significant difference between the terminating men and women on the Lack of Empowerment scale, with the women's mean being significantly higher ($T[39] = 3.64, p = .001$). Another finding is of interest here. A scale of Self-Efficacy indicated that, after mediation, women report more increased self-efficacy than men ($F[1,104] = 4.68, p = .05$), with the greatest effect being contributed by the women who complete mediation agreements. Thus it appears that many women do feel empowered by the mediation, but that those who feel overwhelmed and lacking a sense of empowerment tend to terminate mediation before an agreement is reached.

The second cluster of reasons given for terminating focuses on the spouse, with the spouse seen as unreasonable, untrustworthy, and angry, and the respondent reporting not being able to tolerate being with the spouse. No significant sex difference was found for this "I Can't Stand My Spouse" scale ($\alpha = .78$), and there was no correlation between the Lack of Empowerment and the "I Can't Stand My Spouse scales ($R[41] = .002$). Thus, clients terminated for one or the other cluster of reasons, not for both.

It is of interest that no statistically significant differences in logically relevant Time 1 variables were found for terminators who gave either Lack of Empowerment or "I Can't Stand My Spouse" reasons. That is, terminators who gave "I Can't Stand My Spouse" reasons for terminating were not distinguishable from other terminators on Time 1 variables of Marital Conflict–Tension or anger with spouse. Similarly, terminators who gave Lack of Empowerment reasons for terminating were not statistically distinguishable from other terminators on logically relevant Time 1 variables including self-rated ability to argue, how often they were able to win in a disagreement, their view of their own powerfulness, and their degree of financial knowledge.

Along with interest in the reasons the terminators gave for quitting, was interest in the comparative satisfaction the terminators and the completers had with the mediation process. Not surprisingly, a significant difference between the completers and the terminators was found in their overall satisfaction with the mediation experience in general, with the completers indicating higher satisfaction ($t[101] = 3.20, p = .002$). However, it is important to note that over half of the terminators were either neutral or satisfied with mediation.

The remaining data regarding termination from mediation are the perceptions of the mediators themselves. The mediators completed Mediator Rating scales and recorded notes after mediation sessions. The data reported here are ratings made by the mediator after the first and third mediation sessions. What is striking about the analysis is that not one of the 21 *first-session* ratings distinguished between the eventual completers and terminators. The mediators did not perceive any difference between the groups at entry into mediation and, therefore, presumably could not predict on the basis of the initial session which couples will complete the mediation process.

However, by the third session there were statistically significant differences between the groups on 8 of the 21 ratings (see Table 22-2). After session three, the mediators rated individuals who eventually completed mediation as more willing to mediate, more involved and active in the sessions, less angry, and having higher self-esteem. Based on their appraisal of the interaction between the couple, the mediators reflected more confidence that the completers would mediate successfully. By session three, the mediators also detected that anger toward the spouse, depression, and emotional reactions were interfering with the mediation process. It was not the presence per se of the respondents' depression or emotional responses, but rather their continued or unabated intrusion into the process, which predicted termination.

One possible explanation for the clarity with which mediators saw differences by session three, in addition to just having had more contact with the couple, is that session three is often when the real process of negotiation gets well under way. Sessions one and two focus more on information gathering, delineating budgets, and exploring options. Thus the first two sessions may be less demanding cognitively and emotionally and may not appear to be moving quite so inexorably to divorce. The terminators' ambivalence or feelings of being overwhelmed may not crystallize until the third session.

A clinical review of the mediators' case notes revealed that couples also terminated for reasons other than those described so far. Some seemed to have terminated for reasons having little if anything to do with mediation. One couple went bankrupt, and the courts took over their settlement issues. Others had problems with full disclosure of information, or were resistant to organizing and bringing necessary materials to the mediation. The review also indicated evidence of personal pathology interfering with the mediation process in certain cases, particularly those involving severe depression, extreme passive-aggressive behavior, or a characterological fear of confrontation, conflict, and/or anger.

Table 22-2. Mediators' Session Ratings (5-Point Scale)

	Terminators mean	Completers mean
Willingness to mediate[a]	3.71	4.14
Anger toward spouse[b]	3.00	2.42
Self-esteem[c]	2.82	3.28
Anger interferes with mediation[d]	1.71	1.34
Depression interferes with mediation[e]	1.45	1.17
Emotions interfere with mediation[f]	1.92	1.56
Involvement in session[g]	3.39	3.76
Prediction of mediation success based on interaction[h]	3.31	3.92

[a]$t(100) = 2.82, p < .01.$ [b]$t(101) = 2.67, p < .01.$ [c]$t(99) = 2.33, p < .05.$ [d]$t(62) = 2.26, p < .05.$ [e]$t(52) = 1.95, p < .05.$ [f]$t(102) = 2.06, p < .05.$ [g]$t(102) = 2.20, p < .05.$ [h]$t(102) = 3.59, p < .001.$

These data indicate that the presence of current ties and a lack of concrete steps toward divorce may be the best Time 1 predictor of which couples will terminate mediation before reaching a signed agreement. Contributing factors may include one or both of the parties not believing that they have the personal resources for adequate self-representation. The presence of certain psychopathologies, such as depression or passive–aggressive behavior, in one or both of the parties may also hinder or distort the mediation process. Lastly, such characteristics as willingness to mediate, anger, hostility, and self-esteem do not surface as predictors until the mediation process is well under way.

SUMMARY

This chapter has presented some initial findings from the first two stages of a five-stage longitudinal project investigating the effectiveness of mediation as a method for reaching final divorce agreements. It is remarkable just how few differences exist between individuals choosing to come to mediation, as contrasted to a sample of individuals using the more traditional adversarial process for divorce. The marital history, particularly in terms of amount of conflict, adequacy of communication, and reasons for divorce, as well as many aspects of the spousal interaction, do not distinguish between the two groups. Surprisingly, neither does the level of anger at one's spouse nor the degree of cooperation. Differences between the adversarial and mediation respondents were concentrated in their perceptions of the spouse's character or personality, and in their own psychological reactions to the divorce. Mediation respondents held a more positive view of their spouses as individuals. Their recognition of each other as more honest and fair-minded, in association with their higher levels of depression, stress, and guilt about the divorce, may have led them to choose mediation as a more humane process which might allow them to preserve some regard for each other. Another finding of importance is the ability of the majority of divorcing parents to distinguish the conflicts and poor communications of the marital relationship from the generally less conflicted parental interactions and responsibilities.

Mediation was not found to be significantly more effective overall in reducing divorce related psychological distress than the adversarial divorce process. The reductions in anger, depression, stress, and guilt were a function of the passage of time for both groups. Thus, mediation, as a short-term focused intervention, should not be expected to have a substantial effect individual psychological functioning. Instead, these findings indicate that the value of mediation lies in its ability to affect the quality and future direction of the spousal relationship, particularly with regard to the ability to cooperate after divorce and the more realistic perception of each other's anger. In addition to enhanced cooperation, preliminary analyses indicated greater satisfaction with the divorce process and outcomes among mediation clients (Kelly, 1987).

REFERENCES

Bahr, S. Mediation is the answer: Why couples are so positive about this route to divorce. *Family Advocate*, *3*, 32–35.

Derogatis, L. *SCL-90 administration, scoring and procedures manual* (rev. version). Unpublished manuscript, 1977.

Doyle, P., & Caron, W. Contested custody intervention: An empirical assessment. In D. H. Olson (Ed.), *Child custody: Literature review and alternative approaches*, University of Minnesota, Department of Family Social Sciences, 1979.

Irving, H. H., Benjamin, M., Bohm, P. E., & MacDonald, G. A study of conciliation counseling in the Family Court of Toronto: Implications for socio-legal practice. In H. H. Irving (Ed.), *Family law: An interdisciplinary perspective* (pp. 41–70). Toronto: Carswell, 1981.

Kelly, J. B. *Mediated and adversarial divorce: Comparisons of client perceptions and satisfaction.* Paper presented at the American Psychological Association annual meeting, New York, August, 1987.

Kelly, J. B., & Gigy, L. Divorce mediation: Characteristics of clients and the process. In K. Kressel & D. Pruitt (Eds.), *The mediation of disputes: Empirical studies in the resolution of conflict.* San Francisco: Jossey-Bass, in press.

Kressel, K., Jaffee, N., Tuchman, B., Watson, C., & Deutsch, M. A typology of divorcing couples: Implications for mediation and the divorce process. *Family Process*, *19*, 101–116.

Kressel, K. *The process of divorce: How professionals and couples negotiate settlements.* New York: Basic Books, 1985.

National Center for Health Statistics. Advance report of final divorce statistics, 1983. *Monthly vital statistics report* (Supp. DHHS Publication No. PHS 86-1120). Hyattsville, MD: Public Health Service, 1985.

Pearson, J., & Thoennes, N. The benefits outweigh the costs. *Family Advocate*, 1982, *4*, 26–32.

Pearson, J., & Thoennes, N. Mediating and litigating custody disputes: A longitudinal evaluation. *Family Law Quarterly*, 1984a, *17*, 497–524.

Pearson, J., & Thoennes, N. A preliminary portrait of client reactions to three court mediation programs. *Mediation Quarterly*, 1984b, *3*, 21–40.

Pearson, J., Thoennes, N., & VanderKooi, L. The mediation of contested child custody disputes. *Colorado Lawyer*, 1982, *2*, 337–335.

23

Divorce Mediation Behaviors: A Descriptive System and Analysis

KARL A. SLAIKEU
The Center for Conflict Management, Inc., Austin, Texas
JESSICA PEARSON
NANCY THOENNES
Center for Policy Research, Denver, Colorado

This chapter describes mediator and spousal behaviors during mediation through a systematic analysis of taped custody and visitation mediations conducted at several court-based programs in the United States. The authors describe mediator and spousal behaviors during mediation, identify how these behaviors are related to one another, and test whether any of these behaviors or clusters of behaviors are related to settlements in mediation. This chapter is the needed first step in a systematic analysis of communicative tactics and strategies associated with successful mediation outcomes.

ROLES AND BEHAVIORS IN THE MEDIATION LITERATURE

To date the literature on mediation has been largely anecdotal, descriptive, and prescriptive (Haman, Brief, & Pegnetter, 1978), or it has focused on social psychological and anthropological investigation aimed at distinguishing mediation from other third-party interventions (Druckman, 1977; Gulliver, 1979; Rubin, 1981; Witty, 1980) and the litigation process (Bohannon, 1970; Coogler, Weber, & McKenry, 1979; Gold, 1981). The more limited literature on mediation behaviors has largely consisted of attempts by practitioners to identify and categorize the steps involved in the process. For example, Kessler (1978) identifies a four-phase approach to mediation, involving introductory

This chapter was prepared with the support of the Children's Bureau, Grant 90-CW-634, Administration of Children, Youth, and Families of the United States Department of Health and Human Services. The grant was administered by the Research Unit of the Association of Family and Conciliation Courts. Any opinions, findings, conclusions, or recommendations expressed in this publication are those of the authors and do not necessarily reflect the view of the Children's Bureau or the Association of Family and Conciliation Courts.

Extracted versions of this chapter appeared in *Mediation Quarterly, 10,* under the titles, "Process and Outcome in Divorce Mediation" and "Mediation Process Analysis: A Descriptive Coding System."

behaviors of establishing ground rules and rapport, followed by the steps of defining, processing, and resolving issues. Haynes (1978, 1982) argues that the process of divorce mediation includes referral, intake and orientation, budget development, reconciliation of budgetary needs, identification of assets, identification of potential goals, clarification of issues, rank order of issues, identification of options, bargaining, drafting the memorandum of understanding, and consultation with attorneys.

Moore in Chapter 13 of this book identifies 10 task-specific stages of negotiation. They are (1) searching for an approach and arena; (2) conciliation; (3) determining negotiation strategy; (4) defining dispute parameters; (5) defining issues and establishing an agenda; (6) identifying interests; (7) generating settlement alternatives; (8) assessing options; (9) final bargaining; and (10) implementing, monitoring, and formalizing the settlement.

Each of the authors cited above suggests that specific mediator behaviors or techniques are associated with the stages they outline. A slightly different approach to the study of mediator and disputant behaviors is Wall's mediation negotiation paradigm (1981). Focusing on interactions of the actors, he generates a list of more than 100 mediation techniques that facilitate the relationships necessary for effective conflict resolution, that is, the internegotiator, mediator–negotiator, negotiator–constituency, and mediator–constituency relationships.

Based on labor–management situations, Kochan and Jick (1978) developed a model of the mediation situation which considers the effects of four determinants of mediation outcomes: sources of impasse, situational factors, mediator strategies, and mediator characteristics. Using data generated in interviews with union and management negotiators and mediators, Kochan and Jick maintain that successful outcomes track with certain dispute and disputant characteristics as well as with mediator qualities such as experience level and the use of aggressive tactics. Ultimately they conclude that characteristics of the dispute, not the mediators, are instrumental in explaining outcomes, although they also note that the qualities and strategies of the mediator have a great impact in cases where the parties are somewhat less sophisticated regarding the bargaining process.

Thoennes and Pearson (1985) explored the relative importance of disputants' perceptions of mediator behaviors and the characteristics of disputes and disputants, to explain outcomes in cases involving contested child custody. Based upon interviews with clients, the authors found that the users' perceptions of a mediator's skill was closely tied to satisfaction with and settlement in mediation. Most important was the user's perception of the mediator's ability to facilitate communication and provide parties with a better understanding of their own feelings as well as those of their children and their ex-spouse. There was less evidence of the importance of dispute and disputant characteristics in explaining mediation outcomes, although the intensity and duration of the dispute and the quality of the relationship between ex-spouses were relevant.

All the above cited literature on the behaviors of mediators and disputants relies on self-reports by mediators or disputants, or observations and qualitative analysis by another party. The units of behavior studies have not been uniform, and frequently the investigator is forced to make assumptions about the intent underlying observable behaviors. This chapter represents a first attempt to explore quantitatively the verbal behavior of mediators and disputants, using audiotapes generated in actual mediation sessions, to determine if and how these behaviors are related to the production of settlements in mediation.

SAMPLE OF MEDIATION CASES

Audiotapes of a sample of mediation cases were generated at three courts that offer divorce mediation services to litigants with custody or visitation disputes: the Los Angeles Conciliation Court, the Family Division of the Connecticut Superior Court (Hartford), and the Domestic Relations Division of Hennepin County (Minneapolis). In other papers we have described the format of the mediation service at each court and the initial reactions of users (Pearson & Thoennes, 1984b) as well as the more lasting effects of the mediation intervention (Pearson & Thoennes, 1984a).

Our sample of taped mediation sessions was made from May through July, 1982. Mediators at each court were asked to tape all mediation cases in their entirety. Confidentiality and anonymity were assured to both clients and mediators. Of the pool of 15 mediators in California, 17 in Minneapolis, and 37 in Connecticut, 36 (52%) ultimately took part in the taping. Of those participating, 10 mediators were from California, 4 from Minneapolis, and 22 from Connecticut. A comparison of the mediators included in the study with general characteristics of all the mediators at each site yielded no evidence of significant differences in age, sex, and experience levels.

In the data-collection process, tapes were generated for 149 mediation cases. Fifty-one cases were subsequently found to be inaudible or otherwise unusable for coding purposes, 6 were used only to pretest the coding scheme and establish interrater reliabilities, and 12 were completed too late to be included in this analysis. The final sample of taped mediation sessions that were coded and analyzed included 80 cases distributed across the sites as follows: 2 from Minneapolis; 23 from Connecticut; and 55 from California, where the annual volume of cases is greatest.

Of the cases taped and coded for analysis, 51 (64%) achieved some level of success through the mediation process. This success rate mirrors the settlement rate (approximately 60%) that was found in a survey of users at these three courts, conducted during the same time period (Pearson & Thoennes, 1984b). Operationally, success in mediation was defined as reaching agreement on either child-custody or visitation issues (or both). Twenty-two couples did not reach a mediated agreement on either custody or visitation issues. The majority of these (18) chose litigation to resolve their differences, while four chose or were ordered into a custody study. Because a custody study is often the first step in the litigation process, these two subgroups were combined and represent the "no settlement" condition for subsequent analyses. Cases that resulted in a decision to seek various additional forms of counseling as well as those for which a clear determination of success or failure could not be made ($N = 7$) were excluded from the study.

The mediation sessions were of varying length, ranging from 18 minutes to over 3 hours (the longest was 196 minutes). The mean session length was 93 minutes or about 1½ hours. Table 23-1 shows the length of the sessions cross-tabulated by successful versus unsuccessful outcomes. There was no significant difference between the means of the two success groups on this variable.

CODING SYSTEM

As tapes were collected from the three mediation sites, they were assigned identification numbers and coded by two graduate assistants who were unaware of the settlement status of each case. The coding system utilized is an original one (Slaikeu, Pearson, Luckett, & Costin-Myers, 1984), the mediation process analysis (MPA). The MPA builds on Gottman's couple communication system (1979), although the MPA adds or revises categories as a result of a review of mediation literature and an analysis of a pilot sample of taped mediations. The MPA requires that at 2-minute intervals during a mediation session, eight units of speech be coded along five different dimensions. These dimensions are (1) who is speaking (mediator, husband, wife); (2) target of the message (mediator, husband, wife); (3) whether this unit is a statement or a question; (4) the tone of the message (positive, negative, neutral); (5) and the content of the statement.

The content codes consist of 32 specific behaviors that are believed to capture the full range of statements made during mediation sessions (Table 23-2). To aid coders in identifying the appropriate category, the behaviors were grouped under seven major headings that were developed a priori. The main headings and specific content codes are described below.

Process

The overall goal of the process category is to capture discussions of what and how to negotiate. It is similar to Gottman's metacommunication category, although the specific behaviors that are coded are slightly different.

Table 23-1. Frequencies of Session Length, by Mediation Outcome

	No settlement (%)	Settlement (%)
Less than 1 hour	37	21
1 to 1½ hours	18	20
1½ to 2 hours	27	35
Over 2 hours	18	24

Table 23-2. Content Codes of Statements Made during Mediation

Behavior category	Content codes
Process	Agenda
	Suggestions regarding negotiating behavior
	Correction of negotiation behavior
	Praise of negotiating behavior
Information	About mediation and its alternatives
	About children
	About spouse
	About self
	About other party
Summarize other	
Self-disclosure	Agree
	Disagree
	Feelings
	Empathy
	Other self-disclosure
Attribution	Of spouse's attitudes
	About spouse's behavior
	About both spouses' attitudes
	About both spouses' behavior
	About children's attitudes
	About children's behavior
	About others' attitudes
	About others' behaviors
Proposed solution	Regarding husband
	Regarding wife
	Regarding both spouses
	Nonspecific
	Problem with a solution
Agreement	Before mediation
	Here and now
	Final settlement
	Future dispute
Interruption	

The *agenda* code includes comments that directly relate to the issues to be mediated. Thus the agenda category includes statements or questions regarding what issues the mediation will cover, observations that the discussion is straying from these issues, and remarks aimed at redirecting the conversation to the relevant topics. We would expect to find mediators using agenda comments to identify items for discussion and to help the parties return to the topic if conversation drifts away. Controlling the mediation session is frequently mentioned in the mediation literature as a key mediator job. It is offered as a means of establishing trust (American Arbitration Association [AAA], 1980) and facilitating cooperation (Coogler, 1978). In the following exchange the mediator asserts control over the situation and refocuses the angry spouses with an agenda question.

Wife: I was at the store that day and I came home and you people [husband and friends] were in the den and you allowed them to smoke it [marijuana] in my home.

Husband: Yes, okay. Twist it around any way you want. It doesn't matter anymore.

Mediator: Can we return to the issue of the kids?

Another element of process communications is coded under *suggestions regarding negotiating behavior.* A number of authors have noted the need to teach parties negotiating skills during mediation. This need is important when, as in divorce cases, the disputants enter the process with little previous exposure to formal bargaining. Suggestions regarding negotiating behavior can also help establish the mediator's neutrality and concern and set ground rules for the discussion.

Mediator: What I would like to see you do here is to listen carefully to each other. Listening doesn't mean that you are agreeing with what the other person says. You can still maintain your own position, but if you find that there are some good points . . . it might even make it better.

The suggestions may include many of the techniques Kessler (1978) offers as a means of breaking an impasse, for example, recommendations for a time-out or period of silence. Other suggestions might call for role playing in which disputants exchange roles or rephrase what the other party has been saying, for asking the spouses to address comments directly to one another instead of always speaking to the mediator, or for recommending that each party meet separately with the mediator for a short while.

The final subcategories under process include *correction of negotiating behavior* and *praise of negotiating behavior.* Gold (1981) notes that effective mediation eliminates destructive and competitive communication patterns, and other authors (AAA, 1980) caution that mediators may easily lose control of mediation sessions, if the mediators fail to terminate unproductive communication patterns. Conversely, praising offers to make concessions or cooperate, or, more modestly, a willingness to try resolving the problem, has been cited as a valuable means of gaining parties' commitment to the process and fostering further cooperation (Coogler, 1978; VanderKooi & Pearson, 1983).

Information

Unlike Gottman's scheme, the present system separates the behaviors "problem solving and information exchange." Here the information category contains subheadings used to categorize all proffered information and requests for information. The single exception is self-disclosures, which are differentiated from general information and discussed below. The behaviors subsumed under the information heading are varied and serve many functions that have been posited as essential for successful mediations. The first subheading, information about mediation and its alternatives, may be used to code any requests for, or information about, mediation, court hearings, and custody studies. It has been suggested that a clear understanding of the operating procedures and the goals of each process will help mediators to establish rapport with the parties and gain their trust and a commitment to mediation (Felstinger & Williams, 1978; VanderKooi & Pearson, 1983). One mediator prefaced his information giving with the explanation, "I think that the better you understand what it is we are about to do, the better use you can make of this process." Typically, mediators begin the session with comments that fall into this category. "I don't listen to evidence on one side and evidence on the other side and make some decision about who is right or wrong. . . . The purpose is only to work out a plan that can be satisfactory to everyone."

Clearly, more directive mediators may choose the facts they present so as to predispose clients toward a settlement, for example, "I don't have to tell you that legal costs are high, so anytime you can avoid going to court it saves you money." Less directive mediators may make little mention of the alternatives to mediation.

Additional subheadings include information about children, about spouse, about self, and about other party. In each case only clear statements of fact are coded here, not opinions, feelings, or assumptions. Thus, the fact-finding stage of mediation described by some writers would consist largely of statements in these categories. The information provided may give the mediator an idea of how power is balanced in the relationship, the resources for a settlement, and the potential obstacles. "He travels. He's out of town 8 days a month" is coded as information about spouse. A request for information about self might be, "How far do you live from the school where he attends?" And a simple statement of the ages of the children would be coded as information about children.

Summarize Other

One of the most frequently cited goals of mediation is the fostering of communication between the disputants. In order for this communication to be effective, it is imperative that the intent of each statement be apparent. Not surprisingly, one of the most frequently mentioned techniques in mediation involves rephrasing statements made by another speaker in order to clarify what is being conveyed and check the accuracy of interpretation (Bartunek, Benton, & Keys, 1975; Burton, 1969; Jackson, 1952). While requests for either party to try restating what has just been said would fall into the category *suggestions regarding negotiating behavior*, the actual paraphrase would be coded here.

Mediator: Excuse me, excuse me. You seem to be saying that if you were to follow the existing plan then that would be your weekend.
Wife: That's right.

Rephrasing may offer the added benefit of forcing a party to look carefully at statements he or she has made. Similarly, when the poorly expressed ideas offered by one party are rephrased by the mediator, there may be the benefit of, at least partially, balancing the power between the parties.

Self-Disclosure

Unlike the information category, the self-disclosure category includes subheadings that allow for the coding of statements regarding one's opinions or feelings, which are not properly considered observable facts. Two subheadings, *agree* and *disagree*, are used to indicate simple assent or dissent to previous statements.

> *Wife:* She was upset because you didn't come in the house with her [daughter].
> *Husband:* That isn't true. [Disagree]

The *feelings* subcategory is used to code statements or questions that provide or request disclosures not about ideas but about emotions. Many mediators feel it is necessary to bring feelings out into the open and to validate the person's right to such emotions in order that undisclosed anger and fear not create obstacles to a resolution (Felstinger & Williams, 1978). In the following examples the mediator, first directly and then indirectly, asks for a self-disclosure of feelings:

> *Mediator:* How do you feel about Lynn now?
> *Husband:* I love her, and it's been very hard not having the feelings there from her. It's just very sad.
> *Mediator:* I don't know if you're talking about working out something in regard to custody or something regarding your marriage.
> *Wife:* Both.

The amount of time the mediators allow the parties to spend expressing such feelings is one indicator of the mediators' orientation or preferred role. Those with counseling approaches may devote an entire session to an exploration of the feelings surrounding the divorce, while more directive, task-oriented mediators typically spend only moments discussing such issues (VanderKooi & Pearson, 1983).

The *empathy* subcategory is used to code statements or questions that indicate that the speaker understands and cares about another's feelings or needs. Empathy moves a step beyond summarizing the other. The speaker does not merely restate what has been said in order to indicate a clear understanding of the literal meaning but rather indicates that he or she appreciates how the other party feels.

Empathy statements made by mediators may be used to establish and maintain rapport with the parties: "I can hear the emotional turmoil that you and Pat are experiencing; this really must be a rough time for both of you."

Other self-disclosures might include statements of intent, such as when a mediator reassures a defensive party about the mediator's neutrality and concern: "What I'm trying to do is this—take the plan he's proposed, and which you find unacceptable, and modify it."

Empathy statements from one spouse to the other often help to alleviate fears and to create a sense of cooperation.

Attribution

Attribution statements, or "mind reading" in Gottman's schema (1979), assign ideas, emotions, or behaviors to one's spouse or children, to the couple, or to another relevant actor. Subcategories specify whether attitudes or behaviors are being attributed and to whom the attributions are made. Attributions may be in reference to past, present, or future conditions. In the following exchange the wife attributes a variety of negative attitudes to her husband, thus explaining why they cannot cooperate.

Mediator: How are you and Jerry getting along in view of this situation?
Wife: We're not. He's extremely angry, extremely hostile, very intent on controlling and manipulating.

In turn, her husband attributes to the children feelings of distress at the way their mother is taking care of them and is cautioned by the mediator not to mind read.

Husband: The reason they [children] are so upset is that she [mother] is so disorganized—they never get to bed on time; the house is a mess—
Mediator: Excuse me, let me interrupt you; it's very difficult to know why they're upset. It could be a combination of things. It could be the realization, you know, that the two of you are separating.

In a second example, the husband makes an attribution about the causes of the divorce: "The only reason that my wife and I are splitting up is because she wants too much freedom; she's too selfish, and you can't keep a marriage together that way."

Proposed Solution

In the course of mediating disputes, a variety of settlement options are generally broached, discussed, and accepted or rejected. The five subcategories under this heading are used to code proposed solutions that focus on actions to be taken by either one or both parties.

Mediator: What do you think of the idea of her [wife] having custody from September to May and you having Jody [daughter] during the summer? [Solution regarding both spouses]

Husband: I'd just have to plan my vacation during the month I have her [daughter]. [Solution regarding husband]

Wife: We could put into the agreement that I will take her to church for Sunday school when I have her. [Solution regarding wife]

In addition to proposals for resolving issues, this category includes the topic *problem with a solution*, which is used to note objections or potential problems with a proposal.

Mediator: You know, any time that either of you are not able to take the child, even though it's your time, why wouldn't it be better to call the other person and say, "I've got something to do. . . . I will get a babysitter unless you want to take the child."

Wife: Now, something like that would work if it was because I needed to work. Say I had an opportunity to go skiing. . . . If he knew I was going skiing he'd say, "No, get a babysitter." Just out of spite.

Felstinger and Williams (1978) note that mediators frequently provide a check on reality for the couple. Many of the problems with a solution offered by mediators may serve the purpose of helping the couple to recognize when their solutions are unrealistic. For example, when the couple agree to leave the time when the children return from visitation entirely open, the mediator cautions, "That's fine. But where that runs into problems is if you have already made other plans."

The subcategory *non-specific* is used to code problem-solving statements not codable elsewhere.

Agreement

The agreement heading should not be confused with the more narrowly focused subcategory of self-disclosure, labeled agree. Rather than indicating simple assent to prior statements on behalf of one of the parties, the present heading and its subcategories are used to denote substantive points of consensus between the disputants. For example, if the couple noted at the outset of the session that both parties agreed to joint custody and were now in mediation to set specific arrangements, the comment would be coded under agreement before mediation.

Points of agreement noted throughout the session would be coded *here and now*. A number of authors have stressed the importance of mediators noting all points of agreement as they emerge and responding to them immediately. This helps establish a pattern of success and helps put closure on issues (Kessler, 1978, VanderKooi & Pearson, 1983). Felstinger and Williams (1978) suggest that the mediator may even put into words the agreement that is imminent. Hearing a source of agreement pointed out by a neutral party may aid both sides in acknowledging a solution withoui losing face.

The subcategory *final settlement* is used to capture summary statements about the final agreement. For example, a mediator says, "Okay, so every other weekend [of visitation] during the month the other parent has her [daughter]." Or a mediator may restate an agreement while writing it down, "So, you have agreed that either parent can have the child on the parent's own birthday if a notice is given 2 weeks in advance."

A final subcategory of agreements deals with *future disputes* arising from the agreement. The thrust of such statements is to anticipate future areas of conflict and recommend measures to ameliorate the problem.

Mediator: So, we're always here [court mediation service] to help you with any changes. If you have problems and are not able to talk to each other, you're always welcome to come back here.

DESCRIPTION OF MEDIATION BEHAVIORS

The first analysis of the coded audiotapes involved calculations comparing mediator and spouse verbal behavior on several dimensions across the entire sample of taped sessions. Speaker time was fairly evenly divided among the parties in a mediation session. About 40% of coded units originated with the mediator, while husbands and wives each made about 30% of the statements. However, while the mediator typically addressed both parties, husbands and wives generally directed their remarks to the mediator.

Mediators at the court sites under investigation seemed to be aware of this pattern. Observations of sessions and interviews with mediators revealed that they often requested that one party speak directly to the other, rather than talking through the mediator. Another mediator voiced the hope that by speaking rationally and directly to both parties about the issues as well as the emotions, she might act as a role model and teach couples a few communication skills.

As Table 23-3 indicates, mediators also appeared to be responsible for most of the questioning in a mediation session. About a quarter of their speaking time was devoted to questions, while both husbands and wives spent 93% of their time making declarative statements. Further, 80% of the mediators' statements were offered in neutral or positive voice tones while the bulk of the statements made by husbands (55%) and wives (60%) were negative in tone. Future research aimed at determining the causes and consequences of mediators' negative remarks might well prove that they serve constructive as well as destructive purposes. In interviews, some mediators noted that they sometimes use confrontation or anger when parties need to be shocked out of old habits or unproductive interactions. However, as one mediator honestly observed, "Confrontation can be risky. I've almost lost it at times when I reacted to a

Table 23-3. Use of Speaking Time (Percentage)

	Speaker		
	Mediator	Husband	Wife
Percentage of comments that are:			
Questions	26	7	7
Statements	74	93	93
Negative tone	19	55	60
Neutral tone	65	41	35
Positive tone	16	4	5
Process	13	3	2
Information	25	23	26
Summarizing other	8	3	2
Self-disclosure	26	37	36
Attribution	7	18	21
Proposed solution	15	10	8
Agreement	4	2	2
Interruption	2	4	3

client too personally." Another mediator observed that the advantage of mediating in a team is that it allows the team to use both negative and positive approaches: while one mediator "plays the tough-guy role," the partner is supportive and patient.

Total interruptions during which speakers are not allowed to finish their thoughts were relatively rare: fewer than 3% of the coded utterances fall into this category. More typically, a speaker's statements were interrupted by another's comments but were completed as soon as the interruption ended. Further, husbands and wives were equally likely to be interrupted, while this was somewhat less true of mediators.

A comparison of percentages of each speaker's statements devoted to the 32 behaviors coded revealed several patterns. First, almost 13% of the statements made by mediators served the purpose of informing spouses about what mediation is and is not, and another 13% of the statements were devoted to process communications—establishing the agenda, returning the conversation to relevant topics, suggesting ways for the parties to negotiate, and positively or negatively reinforcing the negotiating behavior of one or both spouses. Looked at from a different angle, slightly more than a quarter of the mediator's time was devoted to these procedural issues, while procedural issues consumed less than 5% of the spouses' speaking time. Mediators were also more likely to spend time stopping or correcting negative negotiating behavior than to devote time to praising cooperative attempts. These patterns underscore the active role of the mediator in the process and distinguish it from less directive therapy interventions.

Requests for information about oneself, children, spouse, or other parties and the provision of such information were about the same for wives (26%), husbands (23%), and mediators (25%). Compared to their husbands, wives offered more statements of fact regarding the children, a finding that may be explained by the greater likelihood that the children resided with the mother at the time of the mediation. Mediators, on the other hand, were more likely to offer statements summarizing what another party had said. This indicates that mediators may attempt to facilitate communication by paraphrasing the remarks of disputants and clarifying the issues in dispute.

In contrast to the neutral, facilitative remarks of the mediators, husbands and wives were more likely to offer statements revealing their opinions or attitudes. Indeed, slightly over 35% of the statements made by both husbands and wives were such self-disclosures. Mediators also differed from spouses in the proportion of empathic statements they made. This suggests that mediators use such statements as a means of establishing rapport and encouraging the spouses to share their feelings. Indeed, interviews with mediators revealed that they recognize the importance of their ability to empathize with the parties, although few mediators phrase their role in this manner. One mediator noted at the outset of each session that he gives himself the task of finding something about each party that he likes. Another mediator says that she routinely reminds herself that while she does not "have to like the parties, have all the answers, or solve everything, she does have to be kind."

About 20% of the statements made by both husbands and wives involved mind reading or making attributions about the attitudes, motives, and behaviors of others—typically the other spouse. Mediators engaged in only about half as many of these attribution statements.

Finally, mediators were responsible for making most of the proposed solutions. This conforms to previous research findings, which stress the active role of mediators in generating options and proposing solutions (VanderKooi & Pearson, 1983). Typically, proposals made by mediators included suggestions for action that involved both husbands and wives. In other words, mediators were likely to balance their suggestions by specifying how both parties would be involved in a solution to a dispute. By contrast, husbands' proposals usually specified what husbands would do and wives' proposals focused on what wives might do.

Overall, it appears that mediators in this sample attempted to be neutral. They offered suggestions that involved both spouses and addressed both parties in neutral or encouraging tones. However, mediators were far from passive actors. They engaged in fact-finding and were responsible for generating the bulk of the proposed solutions. On one hand, this raises some questions about ownership of the mediated solution, since one of the tenets of mediation is that the disputants generate solutions to their problems. On the other hand, it is clear that mediators worked to achieve joint outcomes, while spouses tended to operate as individual advocates. Spouses clearly proposed solutions that related to their own behaviors, offered their own attitudes and opinions, requested little information from others, and addressed their remarks to the neutral party rather than to one another. The mediator focused on outcomes that transcended an individual perspective.

FACTOR ANALYSIS OF BEHAVIOR CATEGORIES

The seven headings under which the 32 individual behaviors were grouped proved to be effective in helping coders to categorize statements. However, given that these categories were developed a priori, an empirical examination of how the specific behaviors were related was needed for subsequent analysis of mediation outcomes and for a more complete understanding of what takes place during mediations. The data generated in the course of coding the 80 tapes were factor analyzed; spouses and mediators were analyzed separately. The factor analysis was based on the frequency of occurrence of each of the 32 behaviors noted in the content codes. The analysis yielded eight mediator and seven spouse behavior factors. As Tables 23-4 and 23-5 indicate, each of these factors is made up of two to five of the behaviors.

The descriptive labels given to each of the factors represent an attempt to summarize the main theme emerging from each grouping of behaviors. The headings and component behaviors differ for spouses and mediators. They also differ from the headings and content items generated in an a priori fashion, based on themes described in the mediation literature. Factor heading and component behaviors for mediator behavior factors are presented in Table 23-4.

Fact-Finding consists of statements requesting information about each of the spouses or about other matters relevant to mediation (e.g., property), and includes "playing back" the information (summarize other) to check its accuracy.

Table 23-4. Mediator Factors—Factor Loadings

Factor	Factor item	Loading
Fact-finding	Information: self	.69
	Information: other party	.60
	Information: spouse	.59
	Summarize other	.57
Coaching re: Behavior	Process: suggestions	.78
	Process: correction	.49
	Information: mediation	.40
Child Advocacy	Attribution: child attitudes	.70
	Attribution: child behavior	.67
Attribution-Attitude	Attribution: spouses' attitudes	.66
	Attribution: others' attitudes	.59
	Attribution: spouse's attitudes	.38
Attribution-Behavior	Attribution: spouse's behavior	.82
	Attribution: spouses' behavior	.48
Directing Process toward Solution	Proposed solution: both spouses	.74
	Proposed solution: wife	.65
	Process: agenda	.65
	Proposed solution: husband	.51
Reacting to Solution	Proposed solution: problem	.84
	Self-disclosure: agree	.58
Consolidating Agreement	Agreement: final settlement	.73
	Process: praise	.61
	Agreement: here and now	.59

Table 23-5. Spouse Factors—Factor Loadings

Factor	Factor item	Loading
Mediation Process: Now and Later	Agreement: future disputes	.83
	Information: mediation	.47
Attributing—Disagreeing	Attribution: others' attitudes	.60
	Self-disclosure: disagree	.54
	Attribution: spouse's attitudes	.54
	Attribution: spouse's behavior	.36
Directing the Negotiation Process	Process: correction	.82
	Process: agenda	.45
	Process: suggestions	.37
Self-Disclosure: Me/Us	Self-disclosure: feelings	.74
	Attribution: spouse's attitudes	.49
Cooperative Talk	Information: other party	.77
	Self-disclosure: agree	.71
	Information: self	.62
	Process: praise	.59
	Summarize other	.53
Children Talk	Attribution: children's attitudes	.89
	Attribution: children's behaviors	.89
	Information: children	.54
Solution Talk	Proposed solution: both spouses	.76
	Proposed solution: wife	.70
	Proposed solution: problem	.50
	Proposed solution: husband	.46

Coaching re: behavior consists of mediator behaviors that suggest how to negotiate, as well as correcting negotiating behavior. It also includes descriptive information about the mediation process and its rules.

The *Child Advocacy* factor consists of attribution statements about the behaviors and attitudes or feelings of children.

The *Attribution-Attitude* factor includes an array of mediator comments that have to do with what one spouse (husband or wife), both spouses, or some other party thinks or feels.

The *Attribution-Behavior* factor includes mediator attributions about either one or both spouses' past, present, or future behavior.

Directing the Process toward Solution includes a variety of relatively directive behaviors by the mediator. Specifically it includes statements regarding what items will be mediated and comments that move the discussion back to these items. It also includes suggestions regarding possible solutions directed at either one or both parties. In many ways this factor appears to relate closely to Fisher and Ury's "inventing options" during negotiation sessions (1981), and includes solutions oriented toward husbands, wives, or both parties.

The *Reacting to Solutions* factor consists of statements agreeing with solutions on the table and identifying problems with solutions.

Consolidating Agreement includes statements by mediators regarding points of agreement in the discussion; items to be included in the final agreement; and positive reinforcement offered by the mediator to one or both spouses for cooperative, constructive bargaining.

The seven spouse factors are also comprised of items from the list of 32 mediation behaviors.

Mediation Process: Now and Later deals primarily with statements and questions about mediation as a way to resolve disputes, both now (discussing information about what mediation involves) and in the future (what spouses will do should they have a disagreement in the months and years after the settlement has been reached).

The *Attributing–Disagreeing* heading involves four items, three of which involve attributions of what the other spouse thinks, attributions or perceptions of the other spouse's behavior, attributions regarding what a third party thinks and feels, and one behavior that consists of a straightforward disagreement with another's statements.

Directing the Negotiation Process includes three behaviors: correcting or criticizing a negotiating behavior, dealing with the items to be mediated during the session, and suggesting how to negotiate. Together these behaviors suggest that the spouse is taking an active role in directing how the negotiation process will proceed.

The *Self-Disclosure: Me/Us* factor includes two sets of behaviors: self-disclosure of one's feelings, and attributions made by one spouse regarding what the couple think or feel.

Cooperative Talk includes five behaviors that are involved in the cooperative discussion of issues by spouses. These include rewarding one another for contributions to the process, providing information about oneself or about another party, making summarizing or reflective statements about what another person has said, and agreeing with what another party has said.

Children Talk includes three behaviors that involve attribution about the behavior or attitudes and feelings of children, and offers of or requests for information about children.

Solution Talk involves four different kinds of solutions: those oriented toward wives, husbands, both spouses, or particular problems.

Overall, the analysis of mediator statements yields more task-oriented and directive factors. The analysis of spousal statements produces more factors that deal with the expression of opinions and feelings. This is consistent with patterns noted in the preceding description of the sessions and the frequencies of individual mediator and spouse behaviors.

PATTERNS IN SUCCESSFUL VERSUS UNSUCCESSFUL MEDIATIONS

As Table 23-6 indicates, analysis of variance reveals several differences in the behavior of mediators and spouses in cases that do and do not settle. One difference is obvious: in cases that settle, mediators spend significantly more time discussing the terms to include in a final settlement. However, in success-

Table 23-6. ANOVA Results on Content Items, for Failed and Successful Mediations

Variable	Failure	Success	F	p
Mediator Items				
Information: mediation	16.0	11.3	4.7	.034
Self-disclosure: feeling	3.1	1.8	4.7	.033
Attribution: others' attitudes	1.2	0.3	15.9	.0002
Proposed solution: nonspecific	2.1	4.0	4.6	.035
Agreement: final settlement	0.5	2.6	6.0	.017
Spouse Items				
Information: spouse and self	6.2	3.7	11.4	.001
Self-disclosure: agree	7.2	11.2	8.0	.006
Self-disclosure: empathy	0.0	0.6	8.6	.005
Attribution: spouse's behavior	9.7	6.7	4.6	.036
Proposed solution: husband and wife	0.5	1.4	4.5	.038
Proposed solution: nonspecific	0.5	1.4	6.6	.012
Interruption	1.3	2.7	6.5	.013

ful cases mediators also spend more time discussing possible solutions in general terms as opposed to the more specific behavioral prescriptions required of one or both spouses. In successful cases, mediators also spend less time explaining the mediation process to clients and comparing and contrasting it to other settlement forums. They spend less time making or requesting disclosures of feelings and make fewer attributions about the attitudes of parties other than spouses or children.

In unsuccessful cases, spouses offer more statements of fact about their spouses or about themselves as a couple and do more attributing about past, present, or future behaviors and the motives behind them. In successful cases, there are more empathetic statements between spouses, more statements of simple assent, and more solution proposals.

As Table 23-7 indicates, none of the composite measures of spousal behaviors derived from the factor analysis distinguishes between cases that settle and those that do not. However, among mediator behaviors, three of the eight composite measures derived from the factor analysis show significant differences. In successful cases, mediators engage in more behaviors to consolidate agreement, spend less time coaching spouses on how to negotiate, and make fewer attributions about what others think or how they feel.

Interpreting these differences is difficult; cause and effect relationships cannot be reliably inferred. One plausible interpretation is that unsuccessful cases involve spouses with poor communications skills. It is possible that parties who communicate inefficiently, perhaps angrily, require more help in negotiating. If the parties present themselves in a verbal fashion very poorly, mediators may begin assuming or attributing behaviors. Given the limited time

Table 23-7. ANOVA Results on Mediator and Spouse Factors, for Failed and Successful Mediations

Variable	Failure	Success	F	p
Mediator Items				
Consolidating Agreement[a]	1.2	4.7	4.8	.031
Directing Process toward Solution	11.4	13.11	0.4	.523
Fact-Finding	15.8	14.3	0.4	.551
Child Advocacy	1.7	1.4	0.3	.597
Coaching re: Behavior[a]	17.7	10.8	8.3	.005
Attribution-Attitude[a]	3.1	1.8	4.0	.048
Reacting to Solution	7.5	9.4	0.9	.353
Attribution-Behavior	1.9	1.4	1.1	.302
Spouse Factors				
Cooperative Talk	35.7	39.2	0.4	.528
Children Talk	12.8	16.1	0.8	.360
Solution Talk	6.7	9.8	2.2	.145
Self-Disclosure: Me/Us	11.3	10.8	0.0	.826
Directing the Negotiation Process	2.8	3.2	0.2	.694
Mediation Process: Now and Later	0.9	1.0	0.2	.657
Attributing–Disagreeing	15.8	15.4	0.0	.884

[a]Statistically significant.

allotted for mediation, the fact that a disproportionate amount of time is spent on basic communication skills may mean that the session cannot progress to real problem solving and agreement making.

This scenario receives some tentative support from the differences in the individual behaviors noted for successful versus unsuccessful spouses. That is, in cases which do not result in settlement, spouses spend more time attributing ideas, feelings, and behaviors to others, and offering facts about the other party or the couple rather than information that pertains to themselves. Nonsettlement spouses also offer fewer statements indicating an ability to empathize with the other party, and generally offer fewer statements of agreement or assent and fewer possible solutions. Thus, their communication behavior seems decidedly less than direct and indicates little ability to work cooperatively.

These patterns are also congruent with results obtained in a survey of clients at these same three court-based programs at approximately the same time period (Thoennes & Pearson, 1985). The best predictors of success in mediation were the clients' perceptions of the mediator's ability to facilitate communication by bringing out relevant issues, allowing each side to be heard, and identifying solution options; and the clients' perceptions of the mediator's ability to aid parties in better understanding their own feelings as well as the feelings of the spouse and children (i.e., promoting empathy). In addition, successful cases were those where spouses evidenced some prior ability to cooperate and where disputes were newer and less intense.

DISCUSSION

A theme supported by the present investigation is that it is important for spouses not only to understand the other parties' point of view, but also to have some appreciation for its reasonableness, or according to the definition in our coding manual, to have some concern or caring about the other individual's situation and point of view. This element of caring or concern was the primary difference between simply reflective statements (summarizing other) and empathy statements in our coding system.

The implication of this finding is that spouses who bring a capacity to empathize to the mediation session will be more successful at the process. If couples lack this capacity, the job of the mediator is to do whatever he or she can to foster understanding and empathy. The bilateral focus technique of Rapoport (1964) is one such technique. This is actually a step beyond the active listening taught by Gordon (1970) and suggested by Fisher and Ury (1981). Since it is to be expected that many couples may well begin divorce mediation with a preoccupation with their own positions—a preoccupation imbedded in a range of emotional hurts, anger, or bitterness—this means that the mediator will need to take a proactive, even aggressive, stance in fostering understanding of the opposing parties' situation. For example, instead of simply playing back or reflecting spouse statements to see that they are being understood, the mediator might look for ways to draw each spouse into the other spouse's world, so to speak, in order to understand the dilemmas faced by each spouse, all with a view to maximizing empathy.

FUTURE RESEARCH

Future research on communication strategies in mediation should go beyond the sampling and analysis limitations contained in this effort. As to sampling, it should be noted that this study relies on a sample of tapes for which the chief criterion for inclusion is simply that the mediation session was completely taped and audible. This meant that mediators at the three sites whose taping behavior was better than their colleagues' stood a greater chance of being included in the study. Since taping of sessions was a new procedure for all mediators, it was necessary to motivate mediators to tape completely, by stressing that the research was important, that the findings would be beneficial to everyone, and that there was no attempt to evaluate the performance of any particular mediator. Some mediators responded more cooperatively than others to this proposal. It is probable that mediators who were more defensive about their work were reluctant to tape completely (i.e., make sure that the tape recorder was set up and ready to go, turned on at the beginning of the session, and placed in the room in such a way that the verbal comments of all parties could be recorded). It is, therefore, possible that the present study draws not only the more cooperative, but also the more confident and possibly more capable mediators, even though the mediators included in the sample were not significantly more or less experienced than those who were not included. In future research, a better approach might be to sample cases conducted by mediators who have a low record of success and compare them with those who have a high record of success (matched on other variables such as age, sex, and experience). It is possible that such a procedure might not only yield stronger, distinct patterns associated with successful versus unsuccessful outcomes but also increase the strength of the differences found in the present study.

As to the limitations of the present analysis, we note the absence of any time-sensitive techniques that are attuned to the sequencing of behaviors in interactions. Many writers have noted that there are distinct phases in the mediation process. Earlier mediator and spouse behaviors may give rise to distinct types of subsequent disputant behaviors. Certain clusters of behavior may occur in early, middle, and late phases of the process, and the phases of mediator interaction may differ in successful versus unsuccessful cases. To the extent that phase patterns are dominant and that they differ in successful and unsuccessful cases, analysis techniques that are sensitive to these patterns may increase the strength of the differences found in the audiotapes assembled for this study.

To some extent, these limitations are being addressed in several research efforts currently in progress. One such effort is a reanalysis of the sample of audiotapes to determine the language patterns used by mediators to create positive momentum in support of a proposition that produces a solution (Donohue, Diez, & Weider-Hatfield, 1984). According to this approach, the mediator decides on a viable solution and uses language that influences disputants to adopt this perception in order to achieve resolution of the conflict. Twenty of the audiotapes from the three courts are currently being reanalyzed to detect subtle linguistic patterns that are indicative of development.

A second analysis (Jones, 1984) is being conducted with 18 successful and 18 unsuccessful mediation interactions, utilizing a slightly modified version of the coding scheme used in the present analysis. In addition to coding all verbal statements made by all participants, rather than a sample of utterances, Jones intends to analyze the data using several techniques sensitive to changes in patterns of interaction that occur over time. This includes log linear analyses to determine the effects of mediator and disputant behaviors on mediation outcomes, lag sequential analyses to determine the effects of specific mediation and disputant behaviors on subsequent disputant behaviors, and phase analyses to compare clusters of behaviors with phase structures suggested in the literature. Hopefully, these studies will make the use of strategy and tactics in mediation less dependent upon intuition and more rooted in empirical evidence.

REFERENCES

American Arbitration Association. *An overview of mediation.* Unpublished manuscript, 1980.
Bartunek, J. M., Benton, A. A., & Keys, C. B. "Third party intervention and the bargaining behavior of group representatives. *Journal of Conflict Resolution,* 1975, *19,* 532–557.

Bohannon, P. *Divorce and after: An analysis of the emotional and social problems of divorce.* Garden City, NJ: Doubleday, 1970.

Burton, J. W. *Conflict and communication: The use of international relations.* New York: Macmillan, 1969.

Coogler, O. J. *Structured mediation in divorce settlement: A handbook for marital mediators.* Lexington, MA: Heath, 1978.

Coogler, O. J., Weber, R., & McKenry, P. "Divorce mediation: A means of facilitating divorce and adjustment." *The Family Coordinator,* 1979, *28,* 225–259.

Donohue, W. A., Diez, M. E., & Weider-Hatfield, D. Skills for successful bargainers: A valence theory of mediator competence. In R. N. Bostrom (Ed.), *Competence in communication* (pp. 219–258). Beverly Hills, CA: Sage, 1984.

Druckman, D. *Negotiations.* Beverly Hills, CA: Sage, 1977.

Felstinger, W., & Williams, L. Mediation as an alternative to criminal prosecution: Ideology and limitations. *Law and Human Behavior,* 1978, *2,* 223–244.

Fisher, R., & Ury, W. *Getting to yes: Negotiating agreement without giving in.* Boston: Houghton Mifflin, 1981.

Gold, L. Mediation in the dissolution of marriage. *Arbitration Journal,* 1981, *36,* 9–13.

Gordon, T. *Parent effectiveness training.* New York: Wyden, 1970.

Gottman, J. M. *Marital interaction: Experimental investigations.* New York: Academic Press, 1979.

Gulliver, P. H. *Disputes and negotiations: A cross-cultural perspective.* New York: Academic Press, 1979.

Haman, D. C., Brief, A. P., & Pegnetter, R. Studies in mediation and the training of public sector mediators. *Journal of Collective Negotiations in the Public Sector,* 1978, *7,* 347–361.

Haynes, J. M. *Divorce mediation: Theory and practice of a new social work role.* Unpublished doctoral dissertation, Union Graduate School, 1978.

Haynes, J. M. A conceptual model of the process of family mediations—implications for training. *American Journal of Family Therapy,* 1982, *10,* 5–16.

Jackson, E. *Meeting of minds: A way to peace through mediation.* New York: McGraw-Hill, 1952.

Jones, T. *An investigation of communication behaviors and phases in divorce mediation interaction.* Prospectus for doctoral dissertation, Ohio State University, 1984.

Kessler, S. *Creative conflict resolution: Mediation.* Atlanta: National Institute for Professional Training, 1978.

Kochan, T., & Jick, T. The public sector mediation process: A theory and empirical investigation. Journal of Conflict Resolution, 1978, *22,* 209–240.

Pearson, J., & Thoennes, N. Mediating and litigating custody disputes: A longitudinal evaluation. *Family Law Quarterly,* 1984a, *17,* 497–524.

Pearson, J., & Thoennes, N. A preliminary portrait of client reactions to three court-based mediation programs. *Mediation Quarterly,* 1984b, *3,* 21–40.

Rapoport, A. *Strategy and conscience.* New York: Harper & Row, 1964.

Rubin, J. Z. *Dynamics of third party intervention: Kissinger in the Middle East.* New York: Praeger, 1981.

Slaikeu, K., Pearson, J., Luckett, J., & Costin-Myers, F. Mediation process analysis: A descriptive coding system. Unpublished manuscript, 1984.

Slaikeu, K. A., Pearson, J., Luckett, J., & Costin-Myers, F. C. Mediation process analysis: A descriptive coding system. *Mediation Quarterly,* 1985, *10,* 25–53.

Slaikeu, K. A., Culler, R., Pearson, J., & Thoennes, N. Process and outcome in divorce mediation. *Mediation Quarterly,* 1985, *10,* 55–74.

Thoennes, N., & Pearson, J. Predicting outcomes in mediation: Pre-existing factors and the assessment of the process. 1985.

VanderKooi, L., & Pearson, J. Mediating divorce disputes: Mediator behaviors, styles and roles. *Family Relations,* 1983, *32,* 557–566.

Wall, J. A., Jr. Mediation: An analysis, review and proposed research. *Journal of Conflict Resolution,* 1981, *25,* 157–180.

Witty, C. *Mediation and society: Conflict management in Lebanon.* New York: Academic Press, 1980.

Index

DIVORCE MEDIATION

DIVORCE MEDIATION
Theory and Practice

Edited by

JAY FOLBERG
Northwestern School of Law,
Lewis and Clark College

ANN MILNE
Private Practice, Madison, Wisconsin

THE GUILFORD PRESS
New York   London

© 1988 The Guilford Press
A Division of Guilford Publications, Inc.
72 Spring Street, New York, N.Y. 10012

Printed in the United States of America

Last digit is print number: 9 8 7 6 5 4 3 2

LIBRARY OF CONGRESS CATALOGING-IN-PUBLICATION DATA

Divorce mediation: Theory and practice.

  Bibliography: p.
  Includes index.
  1. Divorce mediation—United States. I. Folberg,
Jay, 1941- . II. Milne, Ann.
KF535.D584   1988   346.7301′66   87-19656
ISBN 0-89862-708-7   347.306166

An invasion of armies can be resisted, but not an idea whose time has come.

—VICTOR HUGO